The Venture of Islam

The Venture of Islam

Conscience and History in a World Civilization

MARSHALL G. S. HODGSON

VOLUME TWO

THE EXPANSION OF ISLAM IN THE MIDDLE PERIODS

THE UNIVERSITY OF CHICAGO PRESS
CHICAGO AND LONDON

Some of the material in these volumes has been issued in a different form in *Introduction to Islamic Civilization* (volumes 1, 2, 3, Copyright © 1958, 1959 by The University of Chicago), in *A History of Islamic Civilization* (Copyrght © 1958 by Marshall G. S. Hodgson), and in an earlier version of *The Venture of Islam* (volumes 1, 2, Copyright © 1961 by Marshall G. S. Hodgson).

The University of Chicago Press, Chicago 60637
The University of Chicago Press, Ltd., London

Printed in the United States of America

International Standard Book Numbers: 0-226-34677-3 (3-vol. set); 0-226-34678-1 (vol. 1); 0-226-34680-3 (vol. 2); 0-226-34681-1 (vol. 3)

Library of Congress Catalog Card Number: 73-87243

87 86 85 84 83 82 81 80 6 5 4 3 2

CONTENTS

VOLUME II

CHARTS

VOLUME II

Book Three

Book Four

MAPS

VOLUME II

BOOK THREE

The Establishment of an International Civilization

All truth is a shadow except the last, except the utmost; yet every truth is true in its own kind. It is substance in its own place, though it be but shadow in another place. . . .

—Isaac Pennington

PROLOGUE TO BOOK THREE

The Middle Periods of Islamicate history

After 945 CE, the most characteristic traits of the classical 'Abbâsî world, with its magnificent caliphal empire and its Arabic-language culture, were gradually altered so greatly that we must set off a major new era. The world of al-Manṣûr, of Hârûn al-Rashîd, of al-Ma'mûn, still readily discernible in its outlines in the time of al-Muqtadir (908–932), was scarcely recognizable five or six generations later. Baghdad gradually became a provincial town and the very name of the caliphate eventually disappeared. During the five centuries after 945, the former society of the caliphate was replaced by a constantly expanding, linguistically and culturally international society ruled by numerous independent governments. This society was not held together by a single political order or a single language of culture. Yet it did remain, consciously and effectively, a single historical whole. In its time, this international Islamicate society was certainly the most widely spread and influential society on the globe. (We shall refer to the period before about 1250 as the Earlier Middle Period; to the period from then to about 1500 as the Later Middle Period.)

So far as there has been any common image of Islamicate culture, it has tended to be that of the Middle Periods—the periods after the pre-Islamic traditions in the Nile-to-Oxus region had died out (with the decline of the dhimmî population to markedly minority status), but before the Oikoumenic context (in terms of which the Islamicate culture was formed) began to be disrupted by the basic social transformation of one of its regions, the Occident. Taken narrowly, this means the time between the mid-tenth century at the collapse of the classical caliphate, under whose auspices the culture had been taking form, and the end of the fifteenth century, when a new world geographical balance gave its first intimations with the opening up of the wider oceans by Occidentals. The period of the High Caliphate tends to be seen through the image formed of it in the Middle Periods; those elements of its culture are regarded as normative that were warranted sound by later writers. More important, the problems that we have seen as distinctive of the Islamicate culture as such—the problems of political legitimation, of aesthetic creativity, of transcendence and immanence in religious understanding, of the social role of natural science and philosophy—these become fully focused only in the Middle Periods.

This way of seeing Islamicate culture is partly legitimate. To the end of the High Caliphal Period, the Islamicate culture was still in process of formation; it was still winning the population to Islam and transforming the Irano-Semitic traditions into the new form which only after 945 was ready to be carried through large parts of the hemisphere. And by the sixteenth century, quite apart from the first glimmerings of the Occidental transformation yet to come, new tendencies within Islamdom had reached a point where—at least in the three main empires then formed—in many ways, the problems we see at the start of the Middle Periods were at least transposed; even before being superseded by the radically new situation in the Oikoumene that supervened by the eighteenth century. The Middle Periods form a unity which encompasses the bulk of the time of fully Islamicate life. But it must be recognized that the Earlier Middle Period, up to the mid-thirteenth century, differed in its historical conditions rather importantly from the Later Middle Period, the period after the Mongol conquest had introduced new political resources, and the rather sudden collapse of the previously expanding Chinese economy produced—or reflected—a deterioration in the mercantile prosperity of the mid-Arid Zone. What was to be so different in the sixteenth century was well launched in the Later Middle Period.

The Earlier Middle Period was relatively prosperous. By Sung times (which began about the end of the High Caliphal Period), the Chinese economy was moving from a primarily commercial expansiveness into the early stage of a major industrial revolution, in which industrial investment was increasing at a fast and accelerating rate in certain areas, especially in the north, while in the south new methods were multiplying the agricultural productivity. The Chinese gold supply multiplied enormously with new mines opened up, and its trade to the Southern Seas (the Indian Ocean and the adjoining seas eastward) naturally increased in quantity and quality as well. Conceivably in part in response to the increased supply of gold, traceable to China, the pace of commerce and of urban activity was speeded up elsewhere also, most notably in the Occident of Europe, itself newly intensifying agricultural exploitation of its cold and boggy north by use of the mouldboard plough. In such circumstances, the Islamicate lands, still at the crossroads of hemispheric commerce, would find their commercial tendencies, over against the agrarian, still further reinforced; the results were not necessarily the most favourable, in the long run, even for commerce, yet they would allow the Muslims to demonstrate the strength and expansiveness of their social order.

The precariousness of agrarianate prosperity

Opportunities for cultural expression within a society are increased with the diversity and differentiation of social institutions through which individuals can find expression. Institutional differentiation, in turn, depends on a high level of investment, not only in the ordinary economic sense but in the sense of investment of human time—of specialized effort and concern—such as makes possible, for instance, cumulative investigation in science. But high investment presupposes prosperity, in the sense not merely of a well-fed peasantry (though in the long run this may be crucial) but of a substantial surplus available for other classes, allowing them both funds and leisure to meet specialized needs. Hence while prosperity cannot assure cultural creativity, in the long run it is a presupposition for it.

The opportunities for Muslims to take full advantage of the potentialities for prosperity and creativity offered by the Oikoumenic situation were limited by a feature of any society of the agrarianate type: that is, the precariousness of any prosperity, and of the complexity of institutions that tends to come with sustained prosperity, if it rose above a minimum institutional level. Once an urban-rural symbiosis was achieved on a subsistence level, so that agriculture could hardly proceed normally without the intervention of urban products and even urban management, almost no historical vicissitude short of a general natural disaster was likely to reduce the society to a less complex level than that. But many events might ruin any further complexity, beyond this level, that might have arisen in a society, any complexity of institutions either imaginative or especially material; and might force the society (at least locally) down nearer to the basic economic level of urban-rural symbiosis.

Massive assault from less developed areas, whose masters were not prepared to maintain the sophisticated pattern of expectations that complex institutions depend on, could reduce the level of intellectual and economic investment and with it the level of institutional complexity of a more developed area, if that area was not so highly developed as to possess unquestionably stronger force than peoples less developed. Gibbon noted this point in comparing the predicament of the agrarianate-level Roman empire with the Occident of his day, which could not be conquered except by people who had themselves adopted its technical level. As Gibbon also noted, internal pressures also could reduce the level of complexity. Spiritual, social, or political imbalances might cripple a ruling élite and its privileged culture in several ways: they could evoke outright disaffection in less privileged classes —a disaffection that might be expressed in a drive for social and spiritual conformity to populistic standards, as well as in outright rebellion; or they could result in paralysis within the ruling élites themselves, which could hasten political collapse and military devastation. Then could emerge a militarized polity, with despotism at the point of military power and anarchy at the margins, neither of which served to support delicate balances among institutions.

Complex institutions might survive many a conquest and much serious internal tension, and more often than not the ravages of warfare or the damages of political mismanagement could be repaired if they did not recur too continuously for too long. But in the long run, such resiliency depended on a high level of prosperity, which in turn depended on a balance of many favourable circumstances which were not necessarily self-perpetuating. Too much political failure could undermine the very resources with which ordinary political failure could be counteracted. The disturbance of this balance in any way could lower the level of social complexity or even

The Islamic Earlier Middle Period, 950–1250, with Reference to Events in the Oikoumene

	European Region	Nile-to-Oxus Region	Far Eastern Region
900	After 900, towns begin to grow in N.W. Europe; Baltic countries, Hungary converted to Christianity	Shî'î Ḥamdânids in Aleppo; Sâmânids virtually independent in Transoxania	
945		Shî'î Bûyids in Baghdad, to 1055	
960/1		960? Traditional date for conversion of Turks along Syr (Jaxartes) river	Sung dynasty in China; steppe peoples to N.W. and N. remain strong
	Byzantines strong in Anatolia, push into Syria (to 1025)		
969		Shî'î Fâṭimids in Egypt (to 1171); found Cairo	
			Civil service examination system; merit system built around knowledge of literary classics
989	Prince of Kiev converted to Christianity		
997–1030	Normans invade S. Italy	Maḥmûd of Ghaznah; expands into India, Khurâsân, and Transoxania	Sungs encourage sea trade; compass in use; printing of classical texts using movable type
After 1000	Ḥamdânids collapse	Sâmânids collapse and their domains divided between Maḥmûd and Ḳara-khânids; Ḳara-Khiṭays press Turks from E.	Cities proliferate and flourish; merchants more important
1017/18	Italian cities rise to international importance, look to E. Mediterranean and Black Sea trade	Caliphate of Córdova collapses	Paper money used as well as coins Sungs lose control of territories in their N.W. and N.E. to steppe peoples (?)
1055		Sunnî Seljuḳs into Baghdad and lands N. and W.	
1060	Almoravids found Marrâkash		

1066	Normans invade England (and Sicily, 1060)		
	Seljuḳs begin pushing into Anatolia		
1085	Toledo falls to Reconquista Christian forces		Khitay people (related to 'Mongols') rule N. China as Liao dynasty
1090	Saint Mark's Cathedral built at Venice	Nizârî assassins formed	
1099		Crusaders into Syria (to 1291); take Jerusalem (to 1187)	
1122			Juchên, from N.E. enter and rule N.China, displace Khitays, who move toward W., set up 'Ḳara-Khitay' empire
1130		Ḳara-Khiṭays (to 1211) begin rule in E. Turkestan	
1154	Death of Roger II of Sicily, patron of Islamic learning		
1187		Saladin takes Jerusalem from the Crusaders and most of the rest of Syria	
1190?		Khwârazm shâhs expand their power; Ghûrîs take Delhi, 1190	
1204	Latin Crusaders take Constantinople		
1211		Mongol detachment appears N.E. of Transoxania, Ḳara-Khiṭays go down before Khwârazm shâhs and steppe nomads	
1215	Magna Charta		Chingiz Khân takes Yenching (capital) from Juchên
1220's		Mongols devastate Transoxania and Khurâsân	
1244		Crusaders lose Jerusalem for last time	
1249–50	Saint Louis in Egypt		
1258		Mongols sack Baghdad, kill caliph	
1261		Mamlûk forces turn back Mongol forces in Syria, Mamlûks displace Ayyûbid rulers; Hülegü distracted from Syrian venture by troubles with Berke	

occasionally reduce it, at least locally, to the minimum economic base-level of society of the agrarianate order.

To some degree, in some periods and areas in Islamdom in the Middle Periods, this precariousness of agrarianate-level prosperity did make itself felt. On the whole, the prosperity of much of Islamdom evidently declined especially in the later part of the Middle Periods, and a limit was presumably put to further development of institutional complexity. In some cases, there was a retrogression; though the impression that has been prevalent among historians, that there was a general retrogression proceeding through the Middle Periods, is probably incorrect. We have far too little evidence, as yet, to define precisely what happened. In any case, there was clearly no economic expansion within most Muslim lands comparable to what took place in western Europe or in China during the first part of the Middle Periods. This fact forces the student of the society to confront two questions. First, the great political question, in many cases, must be: how was the inherent threat of political disintegration to be met? Second, if any general consequences of hemispheric economic activity are to be looked for, we must often inquire what sorts of social orientation were encouraged as a result in the mid-Arid Zone, rather than expecting an overall higher level of investment and of institutional differentiation.

But though such questions must repeatedly be posed, economic precariousness is not yet the same as general economic decadence. Documentable decline in prosperity often turns out to have been local rather than general. Moreover, the effect of any economic decline on cultural activity and institutional complexity may be temporary; if a new (lower) level of resources is stabilized, prosperity on that base can again be a very effective foundation for cultural activity. It must be recognized that, at least in some fields, effectively high levels of prosperity were often reached in Islamdom. An agrarianate economic base-level was almost never fully reverted to, and even in the most unprosperous periods and regions a certain amount even of economic development was taking place. Meanwhile, in many parts of Islamdom some portions of the Middle Periods were very prosperous indeed, even if sometimes on a quantitatively narrower base than once. Such prosperity led to high creativity; probably at least as high as in most periods and most areas of the Oikoumene before the Modern Technical Age.

On cultural unity

Between 950 and 1100 the new society of the Middle Periods was taking form. A time of disintegration for the classical 'Abbâsî patterns was thus a time of institutional creativity from the perspective of the Middle Periods themselves. By the beginning of the twelfth century, the main foundations of the new order had been laid; between 1100 and 1250 it flowered, coming to its best in those fields of action most distinctive of it.

This society was at the same time one and many. After the decline of the caliphal power, and with the subsequent rapid enlargement of the Dâr al-Islâm, not only Baghdad but no other one city could maintain a central cultural role. It was in this period that Islam began to expand over the hemisphere: into India and Europe, along the coasts of the Southern Seas and around the northern steppes. There came to be considerable differentiation from one Muslim region to another, each area having its own local schools of Islamicate thought, art, and so forth. In the far west, Spain and the Maghrib were often more or less united under dynasties sprung from the Berber tribes of the Maghrib hinterland; these countries had a common history, developing the art which is known from the Alhambra palace at Granada, and the philosophical school of Ibn-Ṭufayl and Ibn-Rushd (Averroës). Egypt and Syria, with other east Arab lands, were commonly united under splendid courts at Cairo; they eventually became the centre of specifically Arabic letters after the decline of the Iraq with the Mongol conquests (mid-thirteenth century). The Iranian countries developed Persian as the prime medium of culture, breaking away seriously from the standards of the High Caliphal Period, for instance in their magnificent poetry. Muslims in India, opened up to Islamicate culture soon after 1000, also used Persian, but rapidly developed their own traditions of government and of religious and social stratification, and their own centres of pilgrimage and of letters. Far northern Muslims, ranged around the Eurasian steppes, likewise formed almost a world of their own, as did the vigorous mercantile states of the southern Muslims ranged around the Indian Ocean.

Yet it cannot be said that the civilization broke up into so many separate cultures. It was held together in virtue of a common Islamicate social pattern which, by enabling members of any part of the society to be accepted as members of it anywhere else, assured the circulation of ideas and manners throughout its area. Muslims always felt themselves to be citizens of the whole Dâr al-Islâm. Representatives of the various arts and sciences moved freely, as a munificent ruler or an unkind one beckoned or pressed, from one Muslim land to another; and any man of great stature in one area was likely to be soon recognized everywhere else. Hence local cultural tendencies were continually limited and stimulated by events and ideas of an all-Muslim scope. There continued to exist a single body of interrelated traditions, developed in mutual interaction throughout Islamdom. Not only the cultural dialogue that was Islam as such, but most of the dialogues that had been refocused under its auspices in the Arabic language, continued effective even when more than one language came to be used and Arabic was restricted, in the greater part of Islamdom, to specialized scholarly purposes.

But the unity of the expanded Islamdom of the Middle Periods did not hold in so many dimensions of culture as it had, in the greater part of Islamdom, under the High Caliphate. The Islamicate society as a whole had initially been a phase of the Irano-Semitic society between Nile and Oxus, building on the everyday cultural patterns of its underlying village and town life. In the Islamicate lettered and other high-cultural traditions we find a greater break with the past than in most traditions of everyday life in the region; yet the Irano-Semitic high-cultural traditions, of which the Islamicate formed a continuation, had always been nurtured by the humbler regional traditions of everyday life. But as Islamdom expanded extensively beyond the Nile-to-Oxus region, the cultural break became more total. The everyday culture of the newer Muslim areas had less and less in common with that in the original Irano-Semitic lands. Not only language differed, and many patterns of home life, such as cuisine or house building, but also formative features like agricultural technique, and even much of administrative and legal practice.

What was carried throughout Islamdom, then, was not the whole Irano-Semitic social complex but the Islamicized Irano-Semitic high cultural traditions; what may be called the 'Perso-Arabic' traditions, after the two chief languages in which they were carried, at least one of which every man of serious Islamicate culture was expected to use freely. The cosmopolitan unity into which peoples entered in so many regions was maintained independently of the everyday culture, and on the level of the Perso-Arabic high culture; its standards affected and even increasingly modified the culture of everyday life, but that culture remained essentially Indic or European or southern or northern, according to the region.

Indeed, even between Nile and Oxus local cultural patterns had varied greatly and the Islamicate unity prevailed only limitedly on the local, everyday level. Customary law could be as distant in Arabia itself from the Shari'ah law of the books as in the remotest corner of the hemisphere. Yet the Irano-Semitic core region continued to be distinguishable within the wider Islamdom. There the Islamicate society and its specifically high culture, because of its original relation to local conditions and patterns, had deep local roots as compared to the areas in which the Perso-Arabic tradition meant a sharp break especially with the high culture of the past and had little genetic connection with the everyday levels of culture. We may call this central region the 'lands of Old Islam', though the point is not the priority of Islam there but its continuity with earlier traditions; Islam in the Maghrib was almost as old as between Nile and Oxus, yet the Islamicate culture was not much founded in the Latin culture which had preceded it there and the Maghrib cannot be regarded as part of its core area. Throughout the Middle Periods, the lands from Nile to Oxus maintained a cultural primacy in Islamdom which was generally recognized. Muslims from more outlying areas were proud to have studied there and, above all, emigrants from those lands, men whose mother tongue was at least a dialect of Persian or Arabic, had high prestige elsewhere. The social patterns and cultural initiatives of the core area were accorded a certain eminence even when not followed.

The Middle Periods, then, which pre-eminently represent Islamicate culture to us, suffered two pervasive cultural limitations: despite considerable prosperity, their high culture was repeatedly threatened with a reduction of economic and social investment toward minimal agrarianate levels; and in the increasingly wider areas of Islamdom outside the region from Nile to Oxus, the Islamicate high culture was always tinged with alienness. These facts pose underlying problems, which may not be the most important historical problems for the student of the Middle Periods, but which are never quite to be escaped. Why should such weaknesses have appeared in the civilization at all? But then why, despite them, the tremendous cultural vigour, power, and expansiveness of Islam and the Islamicate civilization throughout these periods, when in the name of Islam a richly creative culture spread across the whole Eastern Hemisphere?

I

The Formation of the International Political Order, 945–1118

The Earlier Middle Period faced problems of totally reconstructing political life in Islamdom. The time saw great political inventiveness, making use, in state building, of a variety of elements of Muslim idealism. The results proved sound in some cases, but provided no common political pattern for the Islamicate society as a whole; but that society nonetheless retained its unity. This was provided rather by the working out of political patterns on relatively local levels, both military and social, which tied the world of Islamdom together regardless of particular states. The Jamâʻî-Sunnî caliphate assumed a new role as a symbolic rallying point for all the local units. The resulting political order turned out to have remarkable toughness and resiliency and expansive power.

Development of political and cultural multiplicity

From the point of view of what had preceded, the political developments of the tenth century can be looked at as the disintegration of the caliphal empire. Where opposition Shîʻî movements did not gain a province outright, the provincial governors became autonomous and founded hereditary dynasties, or local herdsmen-soldiers seized power and gave the caliph only a nominal allegiance. In any case, this one generally acknowledged authority was rendered impotent and, after 945, the government he headed, already internally disrupted by its mercenary soldiers, lost control even of its home provinces. The caliph became a mere cipher in an empire parcelled out among usurpers.

What broke down, of course, was the political idea that had supported the caliphal power. It is what may be called a 'political idea' which gives individuals and groups a historical basis for expecting that the state will endure as a power to be reckoned with despite any given current crisis. This implies not merely the subjective prestige of legitimacy (important though that is) but also concrete geographical, economic, military, and socio-cultural components which gather together standing group interests effectively enough to give most groups concerned a practical reason for hoping the state will survive, or at least for expecting others will so hope. On this basis they will, willingly or by way of precaution, forgo short-term interests if they conflict with the long-term interests of the state power.

It was a conception of the advantages of the unity of the Muslims that had held the caliphal state together through a series of major crises—the first fitnah at the time of 'Alî, the second at that of 'Abd-al-Malik, then the revolution which overthrew Marwânî power, and finally the division of the empire between al-Ma'mûn and al-Amîn. All parts of the arid region from Nile to Oxus had relatively close ties with the rest; men in any part of the region were likely to travel to other parts or at least have connections there, and were concerned to see a common political stability. Sustained by the concentrated resources of the Sawâd, the central bureaucracy was able, on the whole, to command peace within the region as a whole and to suppress local inequities, and to assure the free flow of trade and the existence of large concentrated markets. Throughout the empire, the idea prevailed among the politically active that not only the greatest moral prestige but also the greatest material advantage was to be had through unity—in practice, that is, through accepting whichever claimant to central power could command strongest support. In the last resort, if secondary interests proved inconsistent with unity there were usually enough who chose to bet on the side of unity to ensure its victory. Consequently in any crisis, when some section of the body politic defected, the central power was able to command the support of other sections in sufficient strength to break up the points of resistance.

But by the time of al-Mutawakkil, the central civil authority was becoming discredited. However much ideally the notion of Muslim unity was still cherished, in practice the idea had ceased to work. The court was financially mismanaged and unable to give effective leadership; under these circumstances, the soldiery, which as a body of mercenaries did not identify itself with the Muslim community at large so much as with their individual commanders, ceased to respect the court; their commanders were therefore in a position to override the civil authority; and—the crucial point—there was no other section of the population which identified its interests with the central caliphal power and possessed enough solidarity to counterbalance the soldiery if the soldiers ever united on anything. With the central power thus paralyzed at home, respect for it failed in the provinces; those who counted there politically found it profitable and feasible in the immediate circumstances to support a governor who retained the revenues at home rather than send them to Baghdad. As the court's revenues diminished, its power of attraction dwindled and defection snowballed.

In the tenth century it was still locally established powers, or the armies they had originally raised, that took up the leadership that the Baghdad court no longer provided. But the separate governors and generals stood, in themselves, for no serious political ideas; they presented mere fragments of the old caliphal state. By the eleventh century political disintegration had proceeded so far that alien wandering Turkic nomads, possessed of the single unpurchasable virtue of military loyalty to their tribe, had solidarity

Comparative Chronology: The Transition into the Middle Periods, 945–1118

Maghrib and Spain
Sudan
Egypt and Syria
Arabia and East Africa
Anatolia and the Balkans
Iraq, Caucasus, West Iran
East Iran and Transoxania
Central Eurasia
North India
South India and Malaysia

945–1055 Predominance of Shî‘î powers, failure to establish a Shî‘î caliphate

961–976 al-Ḥakam II of Spain (and Morocco), fosters science and letters at Córdova; improves Córdova mosque

978–1008 al-Manṣûr (and son, 1002–8) effective rulers in Spain; peak of Muslim power there

***969–1171** Fâṭimid dynasty in Egypt on basis of Ismâ‘îlî Shî‘ism (not recognized by other Shî‘îs); builds naval empire

952–975 al-Mu‘izz: Cairo founded and becomes Fâṭimid capital, 972

996–1021 al-Ḥâkim: his eccentric life is occasion for founding of Druze sect; patron of optician Ibn-al-Haytham (965–1039)

944–967 The Ḥamdânid Sayf-al-dawlah tries to head off Byzantine aggression at Aleppo, where Ḥamdânids hold till about 1015 in some form; patronized al-Mutanabbi' (915–965), poet; also the pioneering Faylasûf, al-Fârâbî (d. 950)

968 Antioch lost to Byzantines

949–82 ‘Aḍud-al-dawlah, maintains Bûyid centre in Iran and Iraq; caliph, since 945, figurehead under Bûyids

976–997 Nûḥ II, last strong Sâmânid ruler maintaining caliphal administrative traditions; his libraries educate Ibn-Sînâ (980–1037), physician reckoned the greatest Faylasûf

1010 A king at Gao on the Niger converted to Islam

*See the following chart, on the chronology of the individual states, for further details.

Maghrib and Spain | Sudan | Egypt and Syria | Arabia and East Africa | Anatolia and the Balkans | Iraq, Caucasus, West Iran | East Iran and Transoxania | Central Eurasia | North India | South India and Malaysia

1031–90 Numerous small dynasties rule various parts of southern Spain (called Reyes de Taifas); peak of Spanish Arabic poetry

1034–67 'Alî al-Dâ'î, first Ṣulayḥid, rules much of Yemen and the Ḥijâz; high point of Fâṭimid Ismâ'îlism in Arabia

999–1165 Ileg-khâns, heads of a Turkish tribe since 932, small Muslim power at Kâshghar, take Transoxania from Sâmânids

***998**–(**1161**) Khurâsân goes to the Ghaznavids in the Afghan mountains (from 976 the area had been newly Islamized under Sâmânid aegis); after 1001 the Ghaznavids also control the Panjâb

998–1030 Maḥmûd of Ghaznah devastates N. W. India and attracts scholars from former Sâmânid territories

1010 *Shâh-Nâmah* written by Firdawsî, epic of pre-Islamic Iranian kings

973–1048 al-Bîrûnî, historian and mathematician, makes a sophisticated study of Indian culture

1050 The Fâṭimids send the Arab Bedouin Banû Hilâl into N. Africa to punish defection from Ismâ'îlî cause; they devastate large areas

973–1058 Abû-l-'Alâ'al-Ma'arrî, sophisticated ascetic poet of Syria, last great figure of classical Arabic tradition

1055–1220 Restoration of Sunnism on an international basis (with caliph acting as a political accreditor. Military leaders as amîrs: madrasah-trained 'ulamâ' setting the intellectual tone and that of civil administration, Ṣûfî shaykhs leading in spiritual life, all—amîrs, 'ulamâ', and shaykhs—tending to hold position as much by personal prestige as by hereditary position or by subordination to authority, and to be relatively free to move from one Islamic land to another with role unchanged

Comparative Chronology—*continued.*

Maghrib and Spain
Sudan
Egypt and Syria
Arabia and East Africa
Anatolia and the Balkans
Iraq, Caucasus, West Iran
East Iran and Transoxania
Central Urasia
North India
South India and Malaysia

***1055–92** Ṭoghrîl-beg, Alp-Arslân, and Malikshâh, the three great Seljuḳ sultans (having first, as Turkish tribal leaders, seized power in Khurâsân, 1037) rule in succession as Sunnîs throughout Transoxania, Iran, Fertile Crescent, and much of Arabia, displacing Bûyids as masters of the caliphs

1063–92 Rule of Niẓâmulmulk, vizier who tried to organize the empire on the basis of compromise between the military Turkish régime of the Seljuḳs and the civil Sâsânî-caliphal administrative tradition, staffed by Sunnî 'ulamâ'

1065 Niẓâmiyyah madrasah in Baghdad, most important of his schools for 'ulamâ'

1071 Battle of Malazgirt, Seljuḳs defeat Byzantines; Anatolia open to Turkish immigration (1072–1107, Sülaymân rules in Anatolia)

***1036–94** al-Mustanṣir in Egypt (1062–74, crisis in Cairo; 1074–94, Badr al-Jamâlî military vizier; to 1121, his son Afḍal; end of Egyptian expansiveness)

1074 Death of al-Qushayrî, who led in reconciling the Sunnî 'ulamâ' with Ṣûfism

1077–1166 'Abdulqâdir Gîlânî, Sunnî Ṣûfî teacher in Baghdad, around whose followers was built the Qâdiriyyah ṭarîqah

***1056–1147** Almoravid dynasty in Senegal, Morocco, and after 1090 in Spain, insists on strict Sunnî orthodoxy, discouraging other study than the fiqh; halts a Christian advance in Spain

1059–1106 Yûsuf b. Tâshfîn, chief Almoravid leader; 1062 founds Marrâkash; 1068 takes Fâs

1085 Christians take Toledo; 1086 defeated by Almoravids at Sagrajas

Maghrib and Spain	Sudan	Egypt and Syria	Arabia and East Africa	Anatolia and the Balkans	Iraq, Caucasus, West Iran	East Iran and Transoxania	Central Eurasia	North India	South India and Malaysia

***1092–1117** Seljuḳ empire in dissolution (after 1104, Sultan Muḥammad restores partial unity); separate rulers of the Seljuḳ family, or their generals, in each area

1111 Death of al-Ghazâlî

1054–1122 al-Ḥarîrî, perfected intricate prose and verse form of the maqâmât

1132 (?) Death of ʻUmar Khayyâm, mathematician and sceptical poet

1090–1118 The Nizârî Ismâʻîlî uprising, centered at Alamût, which continues the center of Ismâʻîlî state till 1256

1096–1187 Crusaders in Syria (and Byzantines in Anatolia) put local rulers on defensive (1099, take Jerusalem; Crusader states last on coast till 1291)

sufficiently greater than that of any other body, to enable them to seize power in the heart of Iran and to lord it over the caliphs.

Looked at from the point of view of the caliphal state, this was a process of almost unrelieved political disintegration. But the same process can be looked at from the point of view of the international society which followed. From this viewpoint we can see it as the beginnings of an articulation of the society of Islamdom on a new and more flexible basis. As the great political idea of the caliphate proved unworkable, there were gradually worked out new political ideas. This was usually by accident; some of those who created them intended simply to renew the Muslim unity on a different basis, for instance, and their success in creating an actual state meant a failure in their wider intentions. Whatever the conscious motives, in fact a series of new state structures, based on new political ideas, ensued. And one of the greatest of these was the work of those wandering Turkic tribesmen.

Chronology of the Individual States, 945–1118

IN EGYPT AND SYRIA

	Ikhshîdids (935–969), independent dynasty founded by the Turk Muḥammad b. Ṭugh (935–946) nominally acknowledging the ʻAbbâsid caliphs; they control also Syria and the Ḥijâz
	Ḥamadânids (Shîʻî Arab tribesmen) of Mosul (929–991) and Aleppo (944–1003); Sayf al-dawlah (944–967) of Aleppo takes that city and Ḥimṣ from Ikhshîdids, fights Byzantines; his successors carry on war with Byzantines and Aleppo; court patronage of the poet al-Mutanabbiʼ (d. 965), of the literary historian al-Iṣfahânî (d. 967) and the Faylasûf al-Fârâbî (d. 950)
	Fâṭimids (969–1171), established in Tunis in 909 (overthrowing the Aghlabids) by a purported ʻAlid descendant of Ismâʻîl b. Jaʻfar al-Ṣâdiq; already in the earliest years had organized missionary efforts carried out by dâʻîs (propagandists, missionaries); in the decades following 909, Fâṭimids extend their power over the Maghrib and on the sea; 969, capture of Egypt; foundation of Cairo and of al-Azhar mosque, which shortly thereafter becomes Shîʻî centre of learning and with Dâr al-Ḥikmah, of missionary efforts; Fâṭimid military power built on slave troops and Berber mercenaries
996–1021	Reign of al-Ḥâkim, rise of Druzes in Syria
1036–1094	Reign of al-Mustanṣir, weakening of Ismâʻîlî impetus
1039	Death of the astronomer Ibn-al-Haytham, who worked in al-Ḥâkim's observatory
1043	Syria slips away from Fâṭimid control
1046–49	Visit to Egypt of the Shîʻî writer Nâṣir-e Khusraw
1050	Arab Banû Hilâl and Sulaym tribes sent west across N. Africa from Upper Egypt; they raid and devastate, ruining parts of the Maghrib
1062	Central political control weakens
c. 1060–91	Normans conquer Sicily, take Palermo, 1071
c. 1070	Seljuḳs in Syria
1090	Ḥasan-e Ṣabbâh takes Alamût stronghold in Iran; beginning of Ismâʻîlî assassins
1094	Central Fâṭimid political control weakens further, court intrigues and factions almost continuous
1101–30	Reign of al-Amîr, last strong Fâṭimid caliph

IN SPAIN AND THE MAGHRIB

912–961	Reign of ʻAbd-al-Raḥmân III, absolutist ruler, declared himself caliph in 929; exercised strong central control in Spain and warred in the Maghrib against Fâṭimids and Berber forces
969–1027	ʻ(Umayyad) caliphate of Córdova'; city is a center of learning

1010	Central power weakens, beginning of century of petty amirates (Mulûk al-ṭawâ'if = reyes de taifas) First half of eleventh century: Christian powers in northern Spain ally together, begin pushing south
1062	Marrâkash founded by rising puritan literalist Berber al-Murâbiṭs (Almoravids)
1064	Death of Ibn-Ḥazm, poet, vizier, theologian
1085	Toledo falls to Christian Reconquista forces
1090–1147	Murâbiṭs rule in Spain, push back Christians
1099	Death of the Cid, soldier of fortune
1130	Death of Muḥammad b. Tûmart, proclaimed Mahdî, preacher to Berbers who become al-Muwaḥḥids (Almohads)
1138	Death of Ibn-Bajjah, Faylasûf

IN THE IRANIAN LANDS

	The Sâmânids (874–999): Sunnî 'Transoxanian Iranian' dynasty
913–942	Naṣr II, sympathetic to Shî'î and Ismâ'îlî learning; maximum extent of Sâmânid rule centered on Khurâsân and Transoxania but including W. to Rayy and Kirmân; capital Bukhârâ; Samarqand important center; Sâmânids patrons of learning and of Persian literary renaissance (al-Râzî, d. 925; Ibn Sînâ, d. 1037; Rûdaqî, fl. 930s; Firdawsî, d. 1020); dynasty maintained centralized bureaucracy supported by landed nobles (dihqans) and paid Turkish slave troops; also important were ghâzî warriors for the faith on the frontier to N. and E.
940s	Loss of W. holdings to Shî'î (generally Twelver [=imâmî]) Bûyids
942	Weakening of central Sâmânid family and court control; palace intrigues; revolution begins
c. 950s	Conversion of (mainly Ḳarluḳ?) Turks E. of Syr (Jaxartes) river including Ḳara-khânids (called also Ileg-khân), purported ruling house of Ḳarluḳs
962	Alptigîn, Turkish military chief under the Sâmânids, and possibly a Ḳarluḳ, siezes Ghaznah; his slave commander and son-in-law Subuktigîn founds Ghaznavid dynasty (976–1186)
990s	Ḳara-khânids and Ghaznavids take over and divide Sâmânid domains between them, the Ḳara-khânids holding the lands E. of the Oxus river except for Khwârazm, the Ghaznavids the other lands; Turkish groups now in firm political and military control of these lands
	The Bûyids
	Imâmî (Twelver) Shî'î mountaineers from Daylam, the three founding brothers rising to power in the 930s; took over W. Iran, and in 945 Baghdad, S. Iraq, and for a short while 'Umân; war with Ḥamdânids to N.W., Sâmânids to E.; Baghdad begins to lose its singular prominence; Shîrâz begins to rise in importance, also Córdova, Cairo

Chronology of the Individual States—*continued.*

983	Bûyid unity begins to fall apart, local provincial autonomy begins to appear; Ikhwân al-Ṣafâ' flourishes, also the poet al-Ma'arrî
1030	Maḥmûd of Ghaznah takes Rayy; Ghaznavids strong in W. Iranian plateau areas
1031–75	Reign of Caliph al-Qâ'im; he champions a revival of Sunnism and (in Iraq) a limited personal power
	The Ghaznavids
976–997	Sabuktigîn extends his power from Peshawar in N.W. India through Khurâsân
999–1030	Maḥmûd of Ghaznah, enthusiastic Sunnî, conducted campaigns in N.W. India, founded permanently effective Muslim power and expansion there; called *ghâzî* (warrior for the faith); acknowledged suzerainty of the caliph; took over Khwârazm, Rayy, Iṣfahân, Jibâl; benefited from enormous wealth of booty gained in Indian expeditions, maintained splendid court (Firdawsî, *c.* 1010); but maintained also large army and heavy taxes
1040	Seljuḳs defeat Ghaznavids; their power in Khurâsân and W. Iranian lands collapses; they are henceforth confined to Ghaznah area and N.W. India where they continue in power and to expand in N. India
1118	Ghaznavids become tributary to Seljuḳs
	Seljuḳs
990s	Seljuḳ Turkish family become Muslims; located along lower Syr (Jaxartes) river; leaders of Oghuz Türkmen nomads
	Beginning eleventh century: Seljuḳs and followers enter Transoxania and Khwârazm, warring with and against factions of Ḳara-khânids
1030s	Seljuḳs and followers in Khurâsân then into W. Iran, war against Ghaznavids, raid towns; campaigns are destructive, so also the Türkmen pastoralism to settled agriculture; 1040, decisively defeat Ghaznavids there; Türkmen especially little amenable to bureaucratic system depending on settled agriculture; Seljuḳ leaders begin to recognize necessity of imperial control, yet parcel out governing regions to members of family
1040s	Türkmen push into Azerbaijan and the Jazîrah; successes attract more Türkmen from Khurâsân and Transoxania; Ṭoghrïl-beg (1038–63), exercising Seljuḳ authority in W. Iran, tries to control or divert to hinterlands these Türkmen
1055	Ṭoghrïl and Seljuḳs into Baghdad
1063–92	Alp-Arslân rules for 10 years, followed by his son Malikshâh; vizier Niẓâmulmulk; Türkmen sent westward into Syria and Anatolia; attempt at centralizing administration and protection of agriculture and towns; roads and mosques built

1065–67	Niẓâmiyyah madrasah built at Baghdad
1071	Crushing of Byzantines at battle of Malazgirt (Manzikert) assures Anatolia's being open to Türkmen, who within a decade penetrate to Aegean Sea, are involved with Byzantine claimants to the throne
1070s	Seljuḳs war with Fâṭimids and local rulers in Syria
1091	Seljuḳs settle their capital at Baghdad
1094	Byzantine emperor appeals to pope for help
1099	Jerusalem taken by Crusaders; Baghdad and Seljuḳs do nothing Beginning twelfth century: local Türkmen dynasties begin to arise
1111	Death of al-Ghazâlî
1118	With death of Muḥammad, Seljuḳ domains now permanently break up into independent principalities, noteworthy being Seljuḳs in Rûm (Anatolia—traditional dates 1077–1307), in Khurâsân (Sanjar nominal sultan of all—1097–1157); Iraq and Syria under local provincial rulers including Seljuḳ claimants
	Ḳara-khânids (or Ileg [Ilig]-khâns): Muslim Turkish group important in lands E. of Syr (Jaxartes) river including Semirichye and Kâshghar converted to Islam 950s
990s	Take over Sâmânid domains N. and E. of Oxus (Transoxania); later split into a W. line centered on Samarqand and Bukhârâ, and an E. line centered on Balasaghun and Kâshghar; in early eleventh century they received patent of authority from caliph (like Ghaznavids); Seljuḳs and Türkmen tribesmen in their territories become a faction in 1020s Eleventh century: Ḳara-khânid groups war with each other, hold sway in various provincial capitals of lands including Semirichye, Kâshghar, Transoxania
1069	Yûsuf of Balasaghun writes allegorical poem in Turkish; first example of belles-lettrist literature Late eleventh century: Seljuk campaigns against Ḳara-khânids, hold nominal suzerainty in parts of Transoxania

The Fâṭimîs: a Shî'î state based on the Nile and a navy

Before those tribes came on the scene, the most grandiose of the efforts to restore Muslim unity had been worked through. The ideal of the Fâṭimid rulers of Egypt, and of the Ismâ'îlî Shî'î sect which supported them in all the lands of Islam, was to reunite the Muslims under a new 'Alid caliphate and to bring it to final victory in the whole world. In this they failed. They did succeed, however, in making of Egypt, and of their new capital Cairo, a centre of commerce and of the arts and sciences, which rivalled Baghdad in the eleventh century. The Fâṭimî state was one of the most successful in overcoming the threat of reduction to despotism and anarchy. This state was based on a threefold political idea. A primary component in the political synthesis was the agrarian wealth of Egypt. The Fâṭimîs maintained in full the bureaucracy of the Nile valley. A second, and more distinctive, foundation of the Fâṭimî Egyptian prosperity was sea commerce. On the basis of this commerce (combined with the natural productivity of Nile-fertilized Egypt), wealth flowed into Cairo, to be distributed again from there. The government at Cairo was thereby enabled to hold the sort of loyalties that Baghdad had forfeited, and to set the fashions within its sphere. Finally, a third component in the political idea, of more ambivalent effect, was the standing appeal of the Cairo régime to the Ismâʿîlî subjects of its rivals throughout Islamdom.

Egypt has commonly been two societies in one: that of the land and that of maritime commerce. Flooded yearly with silt-rich Nile water, Egypt has for millennia been a fabulously productive agricultural land, apparently not subject to the natural vicissitudes of the Iraq. Though sometimes agriculture was more extensive than at other times, Egypt's rulers have never wanted for agrarian wealth. But the peasants and their gentry have tended to form a closed society, set apart from the constantly changing society of the cosmopolitan commercial classes, which in turn have often had alien origins and sympathies. (This may partially account for the relative sterility of Egypt in bringing forth figures great beyond its own confines.) These commercial classes have sometimes been more dominant and sometimes less, for the use made of Egypt's geographical position for commerce has been less unvarying than its agriculture, and has largely determined its relative prosperity from time to time. It is perhaps especially in Ptolemaic, Fâṭimî, and latterly in Levantine Egypt that the 'alien' commercial classes set the tone of the Egyptian state.

The Egyptian rulers and merchants of Hellenistic and Roman times had much increased their wealth from the trade between India (and all the Southern Seas) and the Mediterranean lands, one of the two best routes for which was the nearly all-water route across the Arabian Sea, up the Red Sea, and across a brief portage (sometimes made into a canal) to the Nile and thence the Mediterranean. India and the Indies produced a variety of luxury goods—spices, perfumes, fine cloths, steel goods, etc.—which found a ready market in Syria, Anatolia, the Ukraine, Greece, and the other Mediterranean lands; they were paid for with fine glassware, cloths, and other works of handicraft or else with unworked products of the northern and southern hinterlands such as furs and gold. Much of this trade passed through Alexandria, and the Egyptian middlemen reaped great profit. But always other routes were at least as advantageous, and especially since about the third century, when the Sâsânian empire had come into being, the Egyptian trade route had been less prominent; for a still larger share of the trade than usual went along the chief rival route (the best route by nature): passing up the Persian Gulf and the Tigris-Euphrates rivers, in Sâsânian territory, and thence overland through Syria to the Mediterranean. With the breakdown of 'Abbâsî authority and the reduction of purchasing power at Baghdad itself, and the advent of a number of petty states in the Fertile Crescent, often at war with each other, the Euphrates trade route apparently became less profitable as compared with the route via the ever-opulent Nile delta.

The Egyptians, under a series of essentially independent governors, took advantage of the situation to lure a larger share of the trade back to the Red Sea and the Egyptian ports. This policy came to full fruition under the Fâṭimid dynasty, which was able to maintain in dependency many distant provinces important for the trade, to the advantage of the Egyptian privileged classes. The Ismâ'îlî Shî'îs who had come forth in rebellion in 909 in North Africa and established their imâm in place of the Aghlabid ruler in what is now Tunisia, had enlarged on the strong Aghlabî position in the west Mediterranean, extending their sway even to Morocco. In 969, after numerous tries, they annexed Egypt with the aid of a few local Shî'î supporters, of many other Egyptian malcontents, and of Berber tribal troops from the Maghrib. In Egypt they continued to be naval-minded. There they built a new city, next to the old capital, Fusṭâṭ; this was Cairo, designed to rival Baghdad; and they ruled as caliphs. But Cairo was not only a strategic centre but also an inland port with busy ship traffic up the Nile; it quickly became a major transshipment point between the Mediterranean and the Southern Seas. The first caliph at Cairo, al-Mu'izz, was glad to foster the prosperity of his new seat of power.[1]

In accordance with the Ismâ'îlî ideal of making Islam triumphant in all the world, it was hoped the strong Fâtimî navy could be used in the conquest of Constantinople and the Christian empire. In the meantime, it was useful in ensuring Egyptian prosperity. Already Ibn-Killis (d. 991), the vizier of al-Mu'izz, took pains toward the end of the tenth century to foster trade. The Fâṭimids had strong religious reasons for controlling Mecca and Medina, where their caliphate could be proclaimed to all the Muslim world. This coincided with a need to maintain political oversight of the coasts of the Red Sea as far south as the Yemen, so that there could be no excessive interference with trade by local middlemen there. The Fâṭimî navy controlled both the Red Sea and the eastern Mediterranean seaways; Fâṭimî power was respected from Sicily, which owned Fâṭimî overlordship, to Sind, where an Ismâ'îlî dâ'î was established. Though the Ismâ'îlî party was very strong in the inland areas of the Iraq and Iran, the Fâṭimîs had little fortune there;

[1] S. D. Goitein, 'From the Mediterranean to India: Documents on the Trade to India, South Arabia, and East Africa from the Eleventh and Twelfth Centuries', *Speculum*, 29 (1954), 181–297, on the trade patterns of the time must be corrected by his later books. His experience is revealing: at first he thought that India exported chiefly raw materials and saw the Mediterranean as a more active economic centre; only later he came to realize that this was untrue and moreover that it led to a serious misconception of the trade as a whole (and of the relations to societies)—in fact, Indian export of manufactured goods was a major determinant of the trade.

to the end, it was the reach of the Fâṭimî navy that determined the extent of the dynasty's control outside Egypt.

Nevertheless, Ismâ'îlî loyalties helped mould both the internal and the foreign policy of the state. By the time the Fâṭimîs took over Egypt, they had little of the revolutionary left in their practical programme. But they intensified their radical theoretical appeals to the underground Ismâ'îlî movement that still was proving popular with malcontents in the central Muslim lands. The Qarmaṭians of Baḥrayn, independent in east Arabia, were not disposed to recognize the enthroned imâm. But the ordinary Ismâ'îlî dâ'îs in the Iraq and Iran mostly decided to recognize the new power, which was quick to honour them and their ideas; with fresh vigour, they renewed their efforts and hopes for completing the goals of the Ismâ'îlî movement throughout Islamdom.

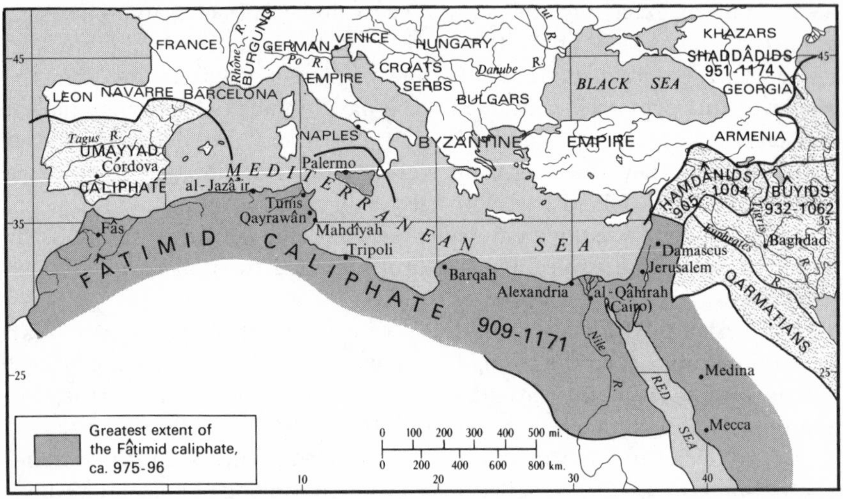

The age of the Fâṭimid Dynasty

These Ismâ'îlîs living outside the Fâṭimî state supplied both a ready-made foreign policy and a source of internal leadership. Unless it disowned them altogether, the Egyptian government had to serve as an eccentric focus for revolutionary forces from Nile to Oxus, and necessarily stood opposed to the entire series of Iranian régimes that were occupying the former 'Abbâsî territories, whatever their relations among themselves. But these foreigners also contributed a certain number of disciplined and intelligent administrative leaders to Egypt itself. Parallel to the regular state organization was a religious hierarchy, charged with teaching the Ismâ'îlî doctrine to those who chose to be initiated, and also with organizing and disciplining the movement both beyond the Fâṭimî frontiers and within them. This Ismâ'îlî hierarchy had almost as much prestige as the governmental hierarchy; the chief dâ'î at its head ranked alongside the vizier; indeed, the same man sometimes served in both posts at once.

The consequences of this Ismâ'îlî presence may have been felt chiefly in the continuity and dependability of the Fâṭimî policies, which gave the dynasty a prestige and longevity unparalleled in Islamdom in that period. Indeed, the social structure within Egypt continued little changed—unless, perhaps, so far as it was marked by a systematic concern for the needs of the commercial and tradesman classes. But the intellectual atmosphere was one of notable ferment (though much of its more distinctive activity, being restricted to an Ismâ'îlî context, had little overt effect on later periods in Islamdom). The old Ismâ'îlî interest in Falsafah was now given free rein among the intellectuals; it was, in effect, just another sort of luxury indulged in by those who could afford it. Ismâ'îlî thinkers had only their hierarchical superiors to answer to for their inner beliefs, and delighted in a wide range of speculation. Much of this was a matter of strictly Ismâ'îlî allegorism and symbolism: beautiful systems were built up in which the figures mentioned in the Qur'ân and in Shî'î lore shadowed forth the spiritual structure of the universe. But an interest was also taken in every aspect of natural and philosophic inquiry. The Ismâ'îlîs made Cairo a centre of learning. The Azhar mosque, the chief mosque of the city, was (as it is even now, under Jamâ'î-Sunnî auspices) above all a centre of study, endowed for this purpose by several Fâṭimid caliphs, notably al-'Azîz (976–996) and al-Ḥâkim (996–1021), the successors of al-Mu'izz. It had a library, and stipends for teachers and students.

The brilliance of Fâṭimî high society shows most readily in its fine arts. Egyptian commercial prosperity was not based only on the transit trade. Egyptian handicraft industry was itself an important element in the trade. Among other things, fine fabrics were made, especially in certain towns near the coastline or actually on it, where the air was conducively humid. These industrial arts were inherited from the pre-Islamic Coptic times. They were controlled by the government, which absorbed a large part of the product. The rest went to the luxury markets everywhere between Nile and Oxus, and far beyond.

These luxury crafts were significant both from an economic and from an artistic point of view. By way of productive activity they contributed to the opulence of the Egyptian ruling classes both directly and by providing articles of trade. Thereby they assured several flourishing town populations of a share in Egypt's agricultural produce. At the same time the craft work had aesthetic merit. This appeared in the colour designs in the cloth, and in the form and decoration of pottery and of crystal ware as well as of bronze pieces, of all kinds of jewellery, and generally of all articles of use which were susceptible of being made beautiful. The lovely treasures of our museums labelled 'Fâṭimid' allow us to share remotely in the luxury those craftsmen made possible.

The Fâṭimî period is famous for solidly beautiful pieces of glaze or crystal ware. Some older Coptic traditions were used in its design; Iranian themes are more evident; but all were reworked for Fâṭimî taste. The growing independence of Egypt as an artistic centre is especially clear in architecture. Under the Fâṭimids, forms continued to be borrowed from Iran—for instance, the domed tomb—but in the course of this there was established the distinctive tradition that was to culminate in the Mamlûk mosques: for instance, the early experimentation with 'stalactite' forms at the corners where a square base meets a domed roof, and the grooved treatment of the miḥrâb, the niche indicating the qiblah toward Mecca, which at times could produce an effect of wonderful concentration. In such ways, the Fâṭimî aesthetic life was endowed with a notable continuity of style which set off this side of the state, complementing its political and social life.

The decline of Fâṭimî power

Once it had been well established, the independent cultural and economic prosperity of Egypt long outlasted the specifically Ismâ'îlî forms with which it was tied up in early Fâṭimî times. So long as the Red Sea trade route flourished, the main lines of the Egyptian state remained sound. On the other hand, Ismâ'îlism began to weaken even before the end of the Fâṭimid dynasty. Ismâ'îlism, however, had been a key element in the Fâṭimî élan within the limits imposed by naval possibilities. It had brought with it special cultural and political opportunities and also special paradoxes and weaknesses. With the slowing down of the Ismâ'îlî impulse, the Egyptian power became more localized, never bearing quite so wide a sway; and the peculiar Ismâ'îlî intellectual and political experiments did not outlast it.

The decline of the Fâṭimid dynasty was tied in with the special paradoxes of Ismâ'îlism itself. It had begun already before the end of the tenth century, when the Fâṭimids' lieutenant on the North African mainland, Ibn-Zîrî, relying on his Berber tribal connections, refused to acknowledge the imâm any further but set up an independent dynasty. Nevertheless Fâṭimî authority completely disappeared in the Maghrib and Sicily only gradually in the first half of the eleventh century. More serious from an Ismâ'îlî point of view—and hence from the point of view of the stability of the dynastic appeal—were internal schisms.

The first of these occurred under the eccentric al-Ḥâkim (996–1021). Al-Ḥâkim seems to have been an effective ruler. Defying dynastic precedent, he appointed a Sunnî chief qâḍî on the ground that he was both the justest and the shrewdest man available (on points of law the qâḍî was guided by Ismâ'îlî muftîs). In his time, the Ismâ'îlî power reached its greatest extent in Syria and remained generally at the summit of its prestige. But al-Ḥâkim was personally subject to bizarre moods and fits of cruelty. Thus he insisted at one time that the shops of Cairo be lit all night, as he preferred to be active then; men had to take their sleep in a prolonged daytime siesta. He is said to have offered a sort of lottery, in which some prizes were unexpected fabulous rewards, but others provided for sudden death—so emulating the hand of Providence. Tales are told of his gross personal brutality.

But even the most bizarre of his whims seems to have been touched with a serious religious purpose. Thus it would seem that his decree about night-time business was partly designed to demonstrate that his police were so efficient and his justice so rigorous that night was as safe as day; and indeed he seems to have been vindicated. Al-Ḥâkim took an intense personal interest in religion, which as imâm he had a right to do; but he did not always remain within the scope laid down by general Ismâʿîlî principles, which his position as imâm presupposed. Some of his actions expressed chiefly a puritan rigour. He wished, above all, to be the perfect ruler; widely generous, enforcing strict good order, and absolutely just to all the people. Personally, he avoided all luxury and mounted a simple donkey for his excursions. He was merciless to any of the great who, he thought, took advantage of their position. (It was on such that he commonly vented his cruelty.) His puritanism led him to decree the destruction of Egypt's vineyards so as to eliminate wine at its source, to impose heavy disabilities on dhimmîs, and to forbid the women of Cairo to stir from their homes.

But increasingly his measures expressed an interest in religious doctrine. Greatly interested in learning, he early set up a well-equipped library and school for Ismâʿîlîs in a mosque of his erection, where not only Ismâʿîlî dogmatics but various sciences were studied. But then he turned gradually to favour the Jamâʿî-Sunnism of the masses of his subjects and even made difficulties for the Ismâʿîlî hierarchy. Finally, however, he came to favour the idea of a new revelation altogether. He allowed violence to flare up between his troops and the Cairo bourgeoisie (through all the disorder he, personally, wandered unguarded and untouched) and encouraged enthusiasts who looked for a millennial culmination of the troubles. Then one night he rode out quite unattended onto the desert, and no unquestionable trace of him was ever found.

After his disappearance, the status quo ante was restored; the wealthy returned to their luxury and gaiety, and such property as he had confiscated and given out was restored to the legitimate owners. But the spectacle of the royal experimenter had given an unusual impetus and consistency to that side of the Ismâʿîlî vision which concerned rather equal social justice for common people than the universal establishment of a conventional Sharîʿah which still allowed gross inequalities. The remarkable personality of al-Ḥâkim persuaded certain Ismâʿîlî enthusiasts to look on the shifting phases of his life as an allegory of all human history, and to regard al-Ḥâkim himself as a manifestation of Deity. Making use of the allegorical tendencies of Ismâʿîlî doctrine, they worked out a new 'inward' truth to supersede the conventional Ismâʿîlism. Though they won a certain hearing among Ismâʿîlîs everywhere, they could not persuade the official Ismâʿîlî hierarchy, who reacted by defining orthodoxy all the more closely. But they did win the allegiance of a peasant revolt which then broke out in Syria, and which became unusually widespread and persistent under sophisticated Ismâʿîlî leaders. The remnants of the rebels were eventually gathered in independent mountainous refuges, where they became the enduring sect of the Druzes, ever looking to the return of al-Ḥâkim to bring justice to the whole world.[2]

In the long reign of al-Ḥâkim's grandson al-Mustanṣir (1036–1094), the weakening of the Ismâʿîlî impetus took a decisive turn. In the first part of the reign the state, which had easily survived the antics and even the divisive incitements of al-Ḥâkim, seemed to be still sound. In 1058 Baghdad and part of the Iraq were temporarily brought to Fâṭimid allegiance—not, however, so much through the strength of either Egyptian or Iraqi Ismâʿîlî forces, as through the policy of a single powerful general who wanted Egyptian help against his enemies. But by 1062 the Egyptian government itself was engulfed in an internal crisis. The mercenary soldiery—as in the days of ʿAbbâsî decline—got out of hand, and for about a decade there was mounting chaos in Cairo as different factions of troops disputed for the spoils of the upper classes. When Badr al-Jamâlî, a competent general from the Syrian province, was called in to clean up the mess, in 1074, he reconstituted the Fâṭimî state on a less ambitious basis.

In 1071 Sicily had been lost to the Franks while the Fâṭimîs were helpless, and a few years later, while Badr was in Egypt much of Syria was taken by the Saljuks, then ruling in Iran in the name of the ʿAbbâsid caliphs. Though the Ismâʿîlî dâʿîs still held parts of the Yemen, concern with other outlying areas was abandoned. Badr and his son, who succeeded him as vizier, made little effort to control more than Egypt itself and southern Syria. On al-Mustanṣir's death (1094), most of the non-Egyptian Ismâʿîlîs, especially those in Iran, repudiated the leadership of the Fâṭimid dynasty (they became the Nizârî Ismâʿîlîs, most of whom now adhere to the Âghâ Khân, leader of the Khojas of India). On the death of the last strong Fâṭimid caliph, al-Âmir (1101–1130), the Ismâʿîlîs of Arabia and the Indian Ocean coasts repudiated them likewise (they became the Ṭayyibîs, now chiefly represented by the Indian merchant community of the Bohras). The fractional Ismâʿîlî sect that remained loyal to the Egyptian dynasty ceased to play much of a role in the state, and disappeared some time after the dynasty was extinguished by the Sunnî Saladin in 1171. The state was then reconstituted on a Jamâʿî-Sunnî foundation, but continued, when strong, to control Syria and the Ḥijâz with its navy and to foster Indian Ocean–Mediterranean trade through its ports, down to the end of the fifteenth century.

[2] Silvestre de Sacy's *Exposé de la religion des Druzes*, 2 vols. (Paris, 1838), drawn up in a spirit of horror at heresy, but very painstaking and full, is still the only serious discussion; it deals only with the beginnings of the sect. It must be corrected by Marshall Hodgson, 'Al-Darazî and Ḥamza in the Origin of the Druze Religion', *Journal of the American Oriental Society*, 82 (1962), 5–20. The study by Philip Hitti, *The Origins of the Druze People and Religion* (New York, 1928), adds nothing of value and contains pervasive misleading errors; it is to be avoided.

Party kingdoms in Spain: the collapse of Spanish independence

Egypt could develop an independent state and cultural autonomy on the basis of a peculiar commercial position. Spain, perhaps, developed its autonomy on the basis of sheer geographical isolation. For a long time, Islamicate high culture was relatively weak in Spain (which had had a Latin high-cultural life rather different from the Irano-Semitic, and distinctly less active); Spain remained dependent upon impulses from more central areas. In the ninth century one Ziryâb, coming from Baghdad, set the tone of musical and courtly fashion, and a disciple of the legist Mâlik b. Anas loyally introduced the latest fiqh from its homelands. But already in the tenth century, Spanish Muslims began to show their independence when, in 929 at the end of al-Muqtadir's reign, the Spanish Umayyad amîr took the title of caliph and Spanish power spread over much of the Maghrib. The title represented a real access of central power in the Muslim state there. He established his control both in the Muslim cities of the south, often almost autonomous, and in the Muslim marches north of Toledo. This was the more feasible because, by the tenth century, the Muslim population had grown in Spain as it had from Nile to Oxus, and the inherited feuding of Arab and Berber tribes was politically less decisive than the common needs of an increasingly flourishing society.

'Abd-al-Raḥmân III (912–961), the new caliph, was successful in fighting for more than a nominal rule; he set up a Spanish version of the 'Abbâsî absolutism. His court fostered the same sorts of learning, literary and philosophical, that had graced the High Caliphal court. His absolutism was even completed likewise with alien troops; Berbers from the south, and western and eastern European slaves from the north (the latter being called 'Slavs') who eventually, in turn, quarrelled and asserted their power. 'Abd-al-Raḥmân's authority was resumed by Ibn-abî-'Âmir al-Manṣûr, a potent minister (under an Umayyad figurehead) who became, in effect, sovereign (976–1002). He abandoned anything but titular power in the Maghrib, where the Fâṭimîs, even when they moved to Egypt, retained more power, and Berber tribal blocs proved most powerful of all. But he concerted all Muslim resources in campaigns to subdue the independent Spanish Christians of the northern fringes of the peninsula. His greatest achievement was to destroy the great shrine of St. James (Santiago) at the furthest northwest extreme of Spain, a shrine dear to all the Occident.

But this interim of Spanish political power was short-lived. After 1010, when the power of al-Manṣûr's sons was broken amidst quarrels among the alien soldiery, no one military party inherited Spain as a whole. Rather, independent courts sprang up in almost every Spanish city. Their rulers were called *mulûk al-ṭawâ'if*, 'party kings' (in Spanish, *reyes de taifas*); for, depending as they did on the support of local partisans, they were generally not absolute rulers but more or less heads of factions. Within a decade or so,

Spain was covered with such courts and the Umayyad caliphate had disappeared. Some of these courts represented a Slav factional power and some a Berber, but some represented local civic loyalties, and carried on a vigorous political life within the limits of local resources. In particular, in Seville a family of qâḍîs (the 'Abbâdids) led the local notables so effectively that gradually Seville gained control over much of southwest Spain. But whereas the Spanish Umayyad caliphate had been able to maintain internal peace, the lack of political integration that had forced (and allowed) the strongest Umayyads to depend on alien troops showed up even more directly in constant warfare among the party kings, which Spanish Muslims had to put up with. Like Muslims elsewhere, the Muslims of Spain never succeeded in creating a national political structure rooted in the land; nor did they discover a political idea that would make up for this by way of special combinations of interests.

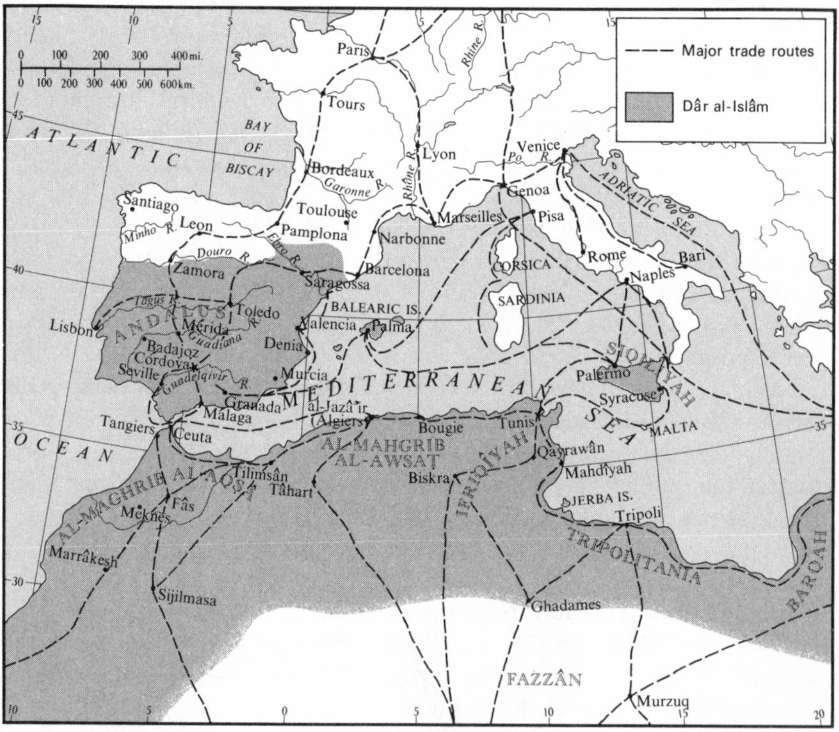

The western Mediterranean

Nevertheless, it was in these petty states that the high culture introduced by the Spanish caliphs had its fruition. These courts are particularly famous for the distinctive poetry cultivated at them. Even within the standard verse forms, a fresh love of nature appeared; eventually, new verse patterns were developed—stanza forms, till then alien to Arabic poetry; and even a controlled interspersing of vernacular speech, popular Arabic and Romance. Whereas in the central regions, the Pahlavî and Aramaic heritages, to the extent that they survived, were incorporated into the new Arabic literature in the course of its very formation, the Romance heritage of Spain was introduced late into an Arabic literary tradition already well formed. It gave it a special provincial flavour, attractive for its relative freedom from established restraints; the Spanish experiments even influenced Arabic literature further east.

The poet-theologian Ibn-Ḥazm (994–1064) typifies the peculiar Spanish setting. As a poet, he illustrated with his own poems in his 'Dove's Neck Ring' (translated into most Western languages), the various phases and moments of the sort of chivalric love subsequently elaborated by the Provençal troubadours. This love posture, inherited in part from earlier Arabic writers, was highly cultivated in Spain then; Ibn-Ḥazm endowed it with rigorous, if not profound, system.

As a thinker, he found himself in opposition to the rigid Mâlikî faqîhs, as was the case with nearly every independent Spanish mind. He adopted a theological position assumed by some other Spaniards also: that of the Baghdad jurist Dâ'ûd al-Ẓâhirî, the 'externalist'. This position, developed at a late period when the number of available ḥadîth reports had greatly multiplied, insisted on restricting legal speculation to the minimum by depending exclusively on ḥadîth, even relatively poorly attested ones; it had the advantage of by-passing the mass of learnèd doctrine of the Mâlikîs in favour of a body of reports in principle more available to everyone equally. It has been suggested that part of the appeal of the Ẓâhirî position for Ibn-Ḥazm lay in its allowing wide scope to individual choice, placing actions on which no sound ḥadîth report could be found into the neutral 'permissible' category; thus its late development would coincide with a relative freedom from Marwânî Arab tradition and a deep involvement in the requirement of urban culture for maximum flexibility consistent with essential discipline.[3]

Ibn-Ḥazm also developed an elaborate critique of Muslim and non-Muslim theological positions from an essentially common-sense standpoint which rejected all spiritual or metaphysical subtleties in favour of monotheistic propriety and morality. He rejected kalâm disputation as such, though he argued closely in rejecting it. He always cut through to an incisive point, even when he was overly schematic in describing sects of less interest to him. (Thus in discussing the Shîʿîs, rare in Spain, he systematically made every group regard its imâm as prophet or as god, in a standardized formula remote from the actual sect's human position; yet he did bring out, in his thirst for system, unlike most writers, the most decisive difference between the Zaydî Shîʿîs and those more radical—their attitude toward a naṣṣ

[3] Ignaz Goldziher, *Die Ẓâhiriten* (Leipzig, 1884), the great study of the school, is incidentally very useful in its early part on clarifying also the history of the Ahl al-Ḥadîth and the schools of fiqh.

imâmate.) He even took the trouble to analyze the Bible text itself when pointing out the self-contradictions of Jews and Christians.

Full of vigorous life, Ibn-Ḥazm survived in sorrow the last of the Spanish Umayyad caliphs, whom he had served as vizier as a young man, to retire from politics into a varied and always polemical scholarly life. The poets and scholars of Spain were, like him, by turns lyrical and polemical—and often rather prosaic or even rigid in matters of ultimate allegiance.

The Spanish courts for almost a century carried on a brilliant cultural life without fear of the equally disunited Christians to the north or of the Berber tribes that ruled loosely in the Moroccan cities across the straits. Their Mediterranean seaports grew rich with the reviving west Mediterranean trade, as Italy, Gaul, and Germany went into a rapid economic development at this time. In the 1050s, the ʻAbbâdid dynasty of Seville, having displaced a number of the lesser city dynasties, became peculiarly famous for the same gay life of poetry and music; a life for which this age in Spain was long remembered. These little courts were not able to maintain themselves, however. The Christians of northern Spain eventually concentrated their forces and threatened the Muslims with conquest. Toledo fell in 1085.

The Muslim Spaniards had to call in a newly arisen Berber power—the Murâbiṭs (Almoravids), whom we shall discuss in more detail subsequently; on the basis of the enthusiasm aroused in Islamizing frontier populations, certain Berber tribes were able to support a stronger government than usual, which had taken over in Morocco. The Murâbiṭs now crossed into Spain to defend it against the Christians. The Murâbiṭs beat back the Christians, but imposed their own rule, in which the most puritanical faqîhs had their way. The cultivated Spanish life continued, but in the sombre atmosphere imposed by Berber military masters. Ultimately, the Berbers could not maintain themselves in an unsympathetic Spain; the long-run effect of the failure of the party kingdoms was to abandon Spain to the less luxurious northern Christians, who proved able to maintain themselves without dependence on foreign intervention.[4]

The Persian provincial successor states

In the central areas, the Fertile Crescent and the Iranian plateau—and in the Oxus basin—the tradition of the caliphal state was not readily replaced by an essentially local continuity, as in Egypt, or overthrown by locally successful alternative political ideas as in remoter areas like the Maghrib, Arabia, and Sind. At first the new powers merely continued, more or less

[4] W. Montgomery Watt, *A History of Islamic Spain* (University of Edinburgh Press, 1965), is a very useful summary of cultural as well as political history, and incidentally carries the story beyond the period focused on by E. Lévi-Provençal, *Histoire de l'Espagne musulmane*, 3 vols. (Paris, 1950–53). It contains both bibliography and numerous questions for further research.

skilfully, the administrative and social patterns bequeathed them by the caliphal government.

The Sâmânid governors in the east, who had inherited the position of the Ṭâhirids, had been well established in their autonomy since before the caliphal collapse. They maintained at Bukhârâ an efficient bureaucratic administration in the Oxus basin and Khurâsân throughout the tenth century; they remained loyal to the caliphs so far as such loyalty had any meaning, and the disappearance of an independent power at Baghdad made little difference in their status or activity.

Nevertheless, after the reign of Naṣr II (913–942), the Sâmânî power was weakened. Territorially, it had to yield its western Iranian lands to the Bûyids. More important, internally it was unable to find a lasting basis for the central bureaucracy. Sâmânîs faced again problems that Sâsânîs and 'Abbâsîs had faced, but on a reduced scale and hence with a less cosmopolitan base, and without the full equivalent of the Sawâd of the Iraq (despite some very highly developed irrigation engineering in some parts) to provide central funds. In the attempt to maintain an adequate independence for the central authority, the Sâmânids turned, as had the 'Abbâsids, to Turkic slave soldiery. But these allied themselves with other elements opposed to the dihqân gentry and succeeded in undermining the synthesis on which the state had depended—the equation of defence of the state with defence both of Iranianism (as represented in the dihqân gentry) and of Islam and its cities.

Some of the Turkic soldiery of the Sâmânîs seem to have preferred the ways of a new Muslim Turkic dynasty, rising eastwards, to the ways of the Sâmânîs. In the mountains of the upper Oxus and Syr rivers, at the fringes of what had been the caliphal empire, arose in the tenth century among the Ḳarluḳ tribes of Turkic nomads a new dynasty, controlling the cities that lay among them and eventually adopting Islam, but making use of an elaborate tribal-based structure of power which owed little, at least directly, to the caliphal administration. It was frankly based on pastoral military power and did not even attempt a close centralization; various members of the ruling dynasty, the Ḳara-khânids (or Ileg-khâns), ruled in different areas in considerable autonomy from the prime ruler. In the later reigns of the Sâmânids, their own Turkic frontier governors had increasingly to intervene at the capital to help the Sâmânids in their disputes with their gentry. At the end of the tenth century, the Ḳarluḳ Turks, allied in sentiment with the Sâmânî Turks, were ready to take over the Sâmânî domains with the support of many elements within those domains. In 999 they occupied most of the Sâmânî territories of the Oxus and Syr basins (but not Khwârazm), while the most powerful Turkic frontier governor of the Sâmânîs, ruling almost independent at Ghaznah, intervened to hold Khurâsân—in his own name. The Ḳarluḳs never developed a brilliant central court as a focus for Islamicate letters, but they ruled the Syr and Oxus basins in independent power for

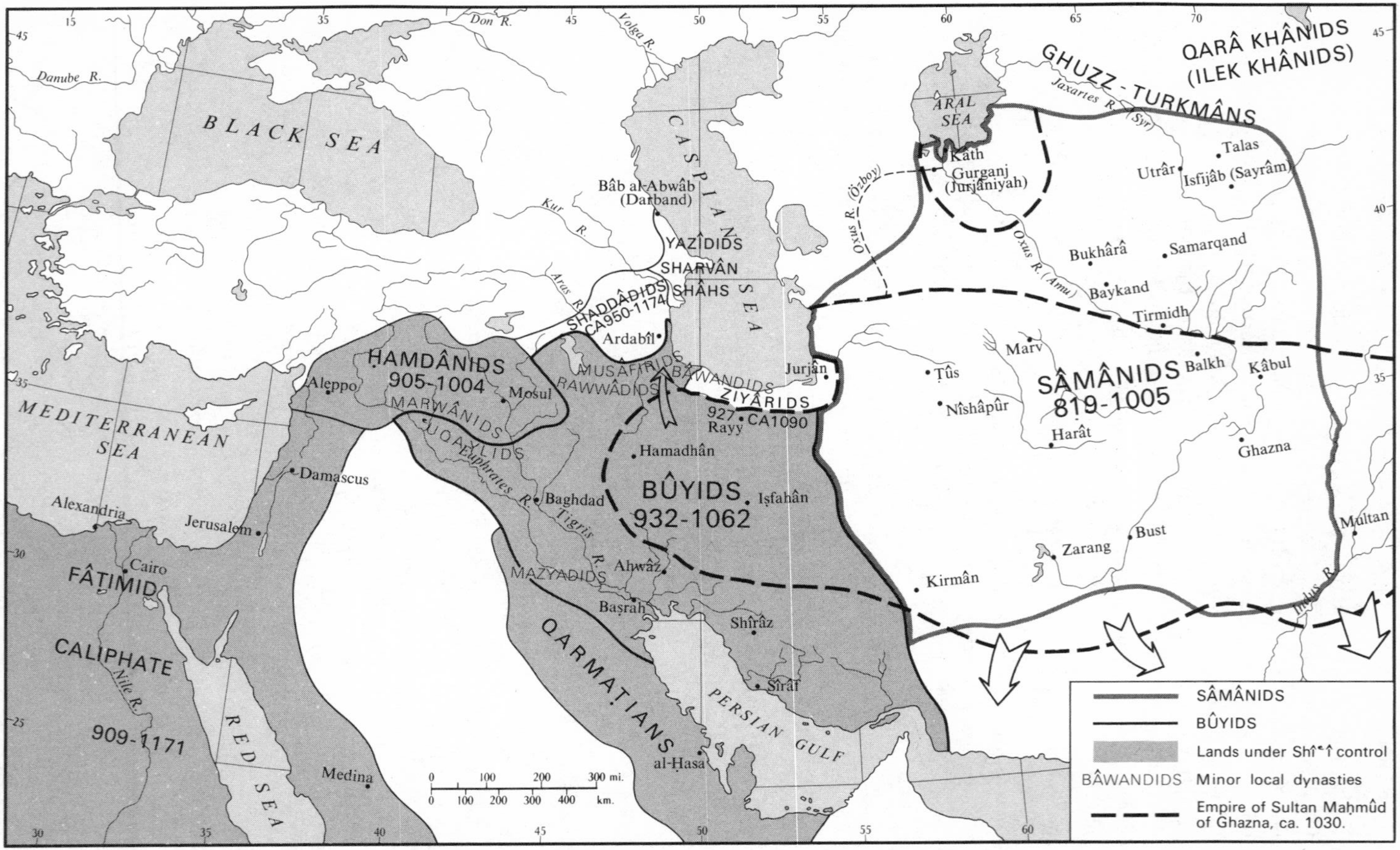

Sâmânids, Bûyids, and Ḳara-khanids

two centuries, from their various centres, except when later the Seljuḳs were able to force some of them, for a time, into subordination.

Meanwhile, the Iranian rivals of the Sâmânids in western Iran, the Bûyids (Buwayhids), with their Daylamî soldiery, made a less consistent effort than had the Sâmânîs to maintain the caliphal administrative patterns, for they were much more dependent than the Sâmânîs on directly military resources for power. By 945 the three Bûyid brothers, with courts at Shîrâz, Iṣfahân, and Baghdad, shared among themselves the most important of the territories that had remained to the last under the caliphs' government. They left the caliph at Baghdad as a figurehead with little authority outside his own household; much of the same vizieral administration continued, but it was responsible to the Bûyids as military lords, and acted separately in their several provinces. The three brothers co-operated effectively so long as they lived, from 932 when they seized power till 977, when the last of them died; then 'Aḍud-al-dawlah, the strongest of the next generation, kept the family in order and united much of the area under his personal rule till 983. The Bûyids controlled for a time the 'Umân coast, whence Persian Gulf trade might be threatened, and even expanded somewhat the effective limits of Islamization in southeast Iran. During this period, prosperity remained high and irrigation works were to some degree restored after the disruptions of the last years of the caliphal state.

The Bûyids and their viziers took over likewise the task of cultural patronage from the caliphs, though such patronage was now distributed not only among the three Bûyid capitals but, of course, among the other capitals of Islamdom. The Bûyids, as Shî'îs, encouraged public Shî'î festivals and Shî'î theological writers, so that under them the Twelver Shî'ah laid its firmest intellectual foundations; they endowed a special Shî'î school, evidently the first independent Muslim college in Baghdad. Their attitude benefited especially the Twelvers, but they encouraged every sort of Shî'î on occasion. They separated the organization of the Ṭâlibids (including the 'Alids) from that of the 'Abbâsids for purposes of settling disputes on property and genealogy and gave the first official recognition of their special status. Their policy seems to have been to encourage Shî'î learning and to allow the caliphs, who still were granted substantial income, to encourage Jamâ'î-Sunnî learning (which the court of the caliphs soon proceeded to do in a dogmatically narrow way). But along with Shî'ism the Bûyids encouraged speculation generally: kalâm, in Mu'tazilî form, and Falsafah; though they did not patronize the Ḥadîthî persecutors of Shî'ism.

Nevertheless, the Bûyid régime did not maintain the full bureaucratic tradition even in a decentralized form. Even some early caliphs had made a practice, at moments of irresponsibility, of allowing private grants of state land; and at moments of fiscal urgency, the later caliphs had even assigned to private persons the taxes of districts, in lieu of direct payment of soldiers' salaries. Such assignments were known as *iqṭâ'*, The Bûyids developed a looser form of such assignments: like the Ḥamdânids, their contemporaries in the northern parts of the Fertile Crescent, they assigned even whole districts without even the obligation to pay the Muslim tenth out of the kharâj, which the 'Abbasîs had required; the public fisc lost control of such lands altogether. (These land assignments were not, of course, fiefs; they were regarded as means of paying salary, and if the assignment failed to yield the proper amount it was exchanged for another; in principle, the inhabitants were not subject to other than the fiscal jurisdiction of the assignee.) Such a practice was devastating to the fiscal bureaucratic system and too often to the lands involved, which were milked dry before being 'exchanged'; ordinary soldiers, however, were still paid from the central treasury, which did not abdicate all its resources.

Simultaneously with this economic threat, in the latter part of the tenth century, much of the trade between the Indian Ocean and the Mediterranean was diverted from the Persian Gulf and the Fertile Crescent to the Red Sea and Egypt. Prolonged political and military confusion in the Fertile Crescent, especially the Jazîrah under the Ḥamdânids and then under still pettier dynasties, contributed to this, as did the deliberate policies of the Fâṭimids in Egypt. After 983, the Bûyids' territories were split among four or five states which were frequently at feud with each other. At the same time, in the Daylamî and the Kurdish mountains and in the Jazîrah several petty dynasties of mountaineer or of Bedouin tribal origin established themselves locally, some extending their control fairly widely for a moment. The Bûyids themselves meanwhile became increasingly dependent on Turkic slave soldiery, quite as the Sâmânids were. The Bûyid states outlasted the Sâmânid by half a century, but meanwhile they helped establish the tradition of a Turkic military dominance in central Islamdom. Their control of 'Irâq 'Ajamî was limited by the expanding power of the Sâmânids' former Turkic frontier governors of Ghaznah after these had taken over Khurâsân; the remainder of the Bûyid dynasties succumbed by 1055 to the Seljuḳ power.

The Shî'î century

The age of Fâṭimid and Bûyid pre-eminence in some of the central lands of Islamdom has been called 'the Shî'î century' because of the prominence of Shî'îs then in various capacities. It was not a Shî'î century in the sense that Shî'ism as such dominated either political or social and intellectual life. Yet the designation does point up a reasonably striking phenomenon—especially in its contrast to the immediately following period, when Shî'îs are much less heard from.

In Shî'î history, the century stands out as a time of creative religious writing which laid a foundation for all that followed. In the time of the Twelvers' lesser Ghaybah (873–940, the period when the Hidden Imâm was still represented by wakîls in his community), not only the Twelver but also the Ismâ'îlî branch of Ja'farî Shî'îs had taken definitive sectarian form (while the Zaydîs crystallized their sectarian pattern by establishing local states). Between the end of the lesser Ghaybah and the Seljuḳ occupation of Baghdad (940–1055) cluster the great early names in doctrine, both Twelver and Ismâ'îlî. Of the four canonical books of Twelver ḥadîth, for instance, that of al-Kulînî (d. 941) belongs to the lesser Ghaybah, but the other three, written by Ibn-Bâbûyah al-Shaykh al-Ṣadûq al-Qummî (d. 991) and by Shaykh al-Ṭâ'ifah al-Ṭûsî (d. 1067), belong to the 'Shî'î century'; as does the poet, al-Sharîf al-Raḍî (d. 1016), who assembled and edited the poems and sermons ascribed to 'Alî into a beloved devotional collection called *Nahj al-Balâghah*. His contemporary, Ḥamîd-al-dîn al-Kirmânî, chief dâ'î under al-Ḥâkim, was the greatest of the Ismâ'îlî philosophers.

Even in Muslim history generally, there is some reason to mark off this period as one of Shî'î prominence. A disproportionate number of the scholars and littérateurs of the time were Shî'îs, even in fields other than the explicitly religious. But this fact had little connection with politics. Of the dynasties of Shî'î allegiance that ruled then, only the Fâṭimid and the little Zaydî powers ruled in the name of the Shî'ah. And while Fâṭimid patronage does help account for the refinement of Ismâ'îlî thought of the time, Bûyid or Ḥamdânid patronage was probably only of secondary importance in evoking the Twelver Shî'î flowering. The intellectual prominence of Shî'îs at the time probably resulted from developments of the preceding period. The Iraq still played an influential role in the first generations after the end of caliphal power, and in the Iraq many of the old families inherited the Shî'ism of Kûfah. Perhaps it was especially the upper bourgeoisie, inheriting the sympathies of the non-Arab Mawâlî of Kûfah, who were Shî'î, while the more recently converted elements had accepted the dominant Jamâ'î-Sunnism. As we have noted, the Karkh quarter of Baghdad was at once a centre of trade and of Shî'ism. At the moment when all the culture of the region was flowing, without any rival, within the Islamic context, but before Islamicate culture began to be dispersed in many centres, the older mercantile classes of the Iraq would be especially likely to figure as its carriers; to the extent that these were Shî'îs, it is not surprising to find Shî'îs figuring prominently in the cultural scene, apart from any political patronage.

But since the several points of Shî'î prominence which go to make up the impression of a 'Shî'î century' were of disparate origins, we need not be surprised that the Shî'î prominence disappeared fairly quickly in the following generation or so. Not only were the intellectual and the political prominence of essentially unrelated origins. The convergence of political power in Shî'î hands had been itself essentially accidental. One may trace the Ḥamdânid power to the conversion of the Arabs of the Syrian desert to Shî'ism after Khârijism lost its appeal—evidently the Bedouin felt a need to be in opposition somehow to the ruling settled powers. Indirectly, the Ismâ'îlî movement of the Fâṭimids had the same origin, but in practice it proved to be not the Qarmaṭians of the Syrian desert, but the Berbers of the Maghrib, that carried them to power. Bûyid Shî'ism is traceable to the conversion of the Caspian frontier by Shî'îs. If there is something in common among these cases, it is that in the preceding century there was a tendency for those outside the main power structure to become Shî'îs rather than Khârijis; and now, with the breakdown of the central power, it was those outsiders who were seizing power. But with the passing of the central power, there was less reason for outsiders to be Shî'î and, in fact, the newer outsiders proved not to be so. Like the intellectual prominence of the Shî'îs, their political prominence had a small popular base; and the Shî'îs having no success, during their moments of apparent advantage, in converting the masses, their prominence was transitory.

Nevertheless, the Shî'î connection of much of the intellectual and imaginative work of the period helped the Shî'î movement, or (more generally) 'Alid loyalism, to exercise the pervasive influence it had in subsequent centuries within Jamâ'î-Sunnî circles. The chemistry or alchemy of Islamdom was founded on the corpus of Jâbir, which can be largely ascribed to this period and is of a markedly Ismâ'îlî cast. Indeed, Muslim interpretations of the general history of science reflect a notion of the role of ancient prophets as transmitters of secret lore which was congenial especially to Shî'îs. But even within the realm of personal piety, the Shî'î influence appears not merely in the general exaltation of 'Alî, but specifically in the very widespread use of the *Nahj al-Balâghah,* compiled by al-Sharîf al-Raḍî, almost as a secondary scripture after the Qur'ân and ḥadîth even among many Jamâ'î-Sunnîs. After the Shî'îs ceased to be so prominent, their works remained as an enduring heritage.

We may consider, at this point, why the Shî'îs, unlike several other movements of the time—the Ḥanbalîs or the Karrâmîs, for instance—could not be fully assimilated into Jamâ'î-Sunnî Islam at large. As a general stock of sentiments, 'Alid loyalism, indeed, was so assimilated. We must recognize that, unlike some movements, such as the Mu'tazilî (always primarily a school of kalâm, whose members might accept diverse positions in fiqh or the like), the Ḥanbalîs and Karrâmîs, like the Twelvers and Zaydîs, formed many-sided religious movements, potentially complete in themselves: they had their own forms of piety, their own fiqh, and their own viewpoint on kalâm disputation. Yet they did not, finally, separate from the community at large, however much they were rivals for the allegiance of its masses. One point only seems to have been too far-reaching to allow compromise. Those Shî'îs who insisted on allegiance to a special imâm apart from the community at large necessarily did form independent sects, even on the level of the populace; maintaining a complete complement of sectarian religious positions, kept jealously distinct from those of others even when substantively identical with theirs. (Thus the Twelvers adopted, in this period, an essentially Mu'tazilî theological doctrine; but they refused to admit any identification with the Mu'tazilî doctors.) It is only the Khârijîs (Ibâḍîs) and the sectarian Shî'îs (Zaydîs, Ismâ'îlîs, Twelvers) that are thus to be set off from the Jamâ'î-Sunnîs in the sense that a conflict of allegiance would arise if one tried to participate fully in both traditions.

It is, then, not at any point of metaphysical doctrine or even of law, but at a point of historical and political concern that a difference of viewpoint among Muslims became most irreconcilable; a fact consistent with the emphasis of the Qur'ânic message upon the historical responsibility of the community. Efforts were made, it is said, already in Bûyid times to have the Twelvers recognized in Baghdad, as 'Ja'farîs', as a school of fiqh law parallel to the other schools of fiqh recognized there. But such an effort was surely foredoomed: the significant difference between Shî'î and Jamâ'î did not lie in the fiqh. Rather, Shî'ism, however much individual Shî'î writers or doctrines influenced Islam generally, remained the persistent custodian of the latent revolutionary challenge of Islam. Especially at the hands of the wealthier merchants, the oppositional implications of Shî'ism were withdrawn into a subjective personal stance or a hope for a miraculously juster future (just as the oppositional implications of Jamâ'î-Sunnism became very limited at the hands of the established classes). For all that, Shî'ism still was a perennial source of chiliastic hopes, which emerged fatefully in later periods.

The Ghaznavîs: a Turkic successor state

A political structure temporarily more brilliant than even the Sâmânî was built in the Afghân mountains on the far eastern rim of the Iranian highlands. These mountains were only gradually Islamized, and had formed a march of the Sâmânî power in Khurâsân. The Turkic slave garrison that governed there at Ghaznah at the end of the tenth century, under Sebüktegin (976–997), became independent in effect with the decline of Sâmânî strength; Sebüktegin controlled, on the west, Khurâsân, nominally as governor, and on the east, conquered and held the passes into India. His son Maḥmûd (998–1030), who, upon the downfall of the Sâmânids (999), partitioned their territory with the Ḳarluḳ Turks, expanded his empire even into western Iran, eliminating the Bûyids from Rayy and persecuting Shî'îs there. He did his best to limit the expansion of the Ḳarluḳ Turks in the Oxus basin, and garrisoned Khwârazm to the northwest of them. But he derived his wealth from a series of vast plundering expeditions on which he destroyed works of art (as idolatrous) and looted all accessible goods across the whole of northwestern India. In most places there his raids were transitory, but he established a permanent rule in the Panjâb.

Maḥmûd thus built up an empire territorially vast but still insecure. Much of his effort went to remedying this insecurity by building his prestige. And, though he derived wealth and honour from the Indian campaigns,

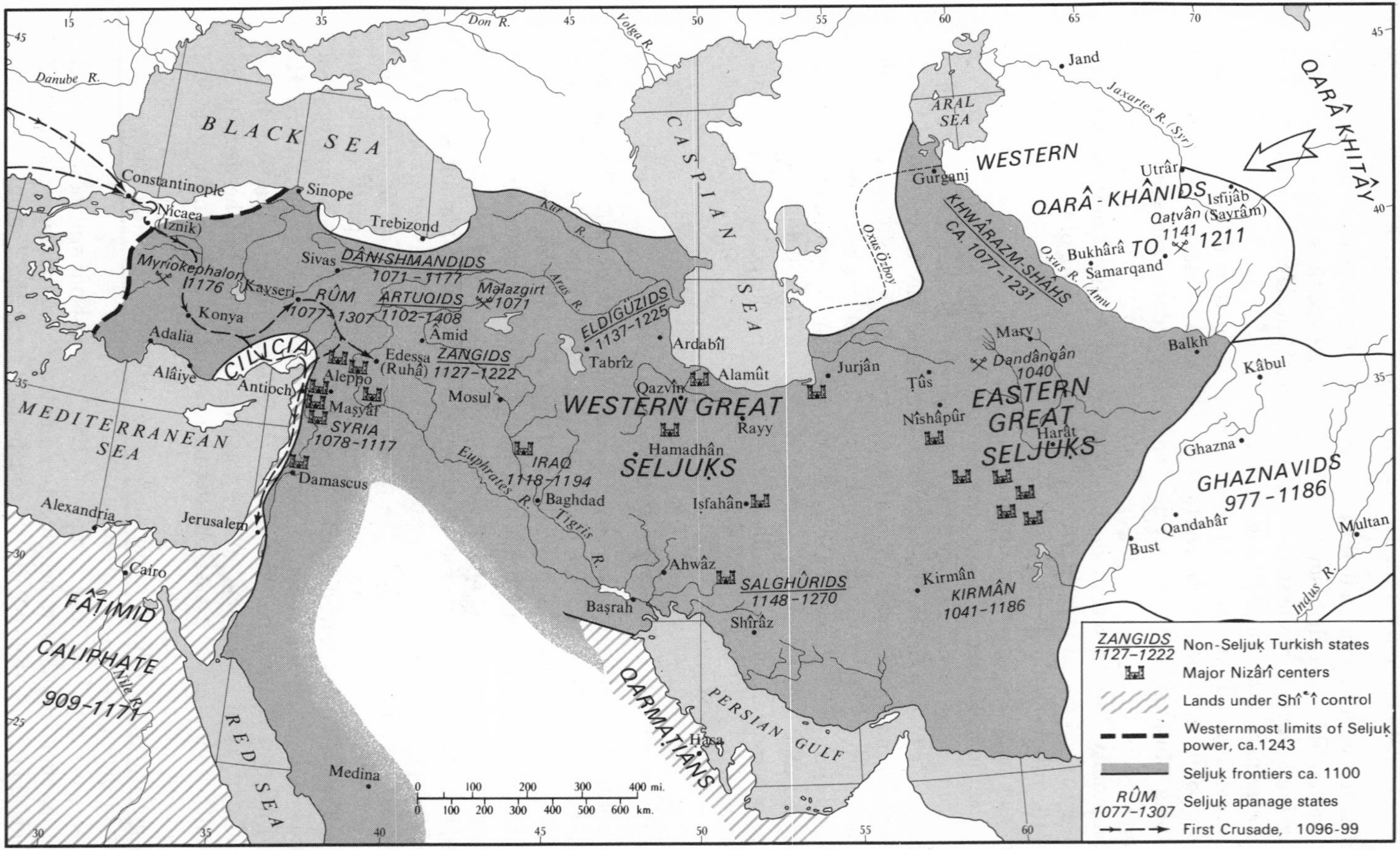

The Ghaznavids and the Seljuk empire

which made him a Muslim legend as a ghâzî against the infidel, it was his power in Iran that gave him his most immediate prestige; for it was within the lands of 'old Islam' that power and especially patronage—of scholars and poets who dedicated their work to the ruler—could meet the standards of the international Muslim community. Maḥmûd was conscious of being rather an upstart (and the son of a slave) and was especially eager to receive an honorific title from the caliph (over the heads of his enemies the Bûyids), whom he hoped to win over with some of the Indian booty. It was part of his success that, as a centre of wealth and power the Ghaznavî state became a centre of culture as well; in particular, Ghaznah became under Maḥmûd (partly by way of forced residence for writers) the centre of the revival of Iranian traditions, and of the memory of Sâsânian glories. It was to Maḥmûd's court that Firdawsî brought the Shâh-Nâmah, an epic recounting the story of the olden monarchs of Iran. Despite the objections of scholars like al-Bîrûnî, who clung to Arabic, Persian came to be a preferred language (even though the rulers themselves used Turkish); it was in keeping with the Ghaznavî tradition that later in India Persian very nearly eclipsed Arabic except in the realm of Shar'î religious scholarship.

But Maḥmûd's construction was largely accidental, the resultant of his personal military genius combined with a fluid political situation in Iran. He seems to have taken a largely personal interest in creating vast power. His administration was often harsh, pressing exactions to a ruinous point, though he continued, with modifications, the Sâmânî tradition so far as he could. He may have seen a zealous religious communalism as more important than a just administration: he persecuted bloodily those whom the ḥadîth-minded Jamâ'î-Sunnîs about him regarded as heretics, especially Shî'îs and even the Karrâmîs, whom his father Sebüktegin had favoured. (On the other hand, he was not squeamish about religion: he used unconverted Hindu troops recruited in India, and even a Hindu general, against Muslims who resisted him.

Already in Maḥmûd's time the nomad Seljuḳ Turks were proving hard to control in Khurâsân. His son Mas'ûd (1030–41) lost all control over them. The notables of the Khurâsân cities, already alienated by severe taxation, could not ignore the depredations of the pastoralists, who were ruining their farm lands. They withdrew their allegiance from Ghaznah and made arrangements with the Seljuḳ leaders. After the long disastrous battle of Dandânqân (1040), Mas'ûd, abandoning Khurâsân decisively, set off for an Indian refuge, in effect acknowledging the destruction of Maḥmûd's empire.

His successors abandoned all provinces west of the Afghân mountains; but under the rule of Ibrâhîm (1059–99), seeming collapse was retrieved, and a viable political idea was found to support what was left to Ghaznah. The Ghaznavî state, after the loss of Khurâsân, depended on combining the Muslim mountaineers as military power with the plainsmen of the Hindu Panjâb as rich taxpayers. By the middle of the twelfth century, Ghaznavî power in the highlands was undermined by nomadic Ghuzz Turks and by the Iranian Sûrids of Ghûr, a backwoods mountain district. Under such pressures, the capital was settled in Lahore, natural centre for tax collection in the Panjâb, in the midst of a Hindu-majority population. But the Ghûrîs took Ghaznah in 1173 and then Lahore in 1187, and thus restored the old Ghaznavî pattern on their own account.

The motive power of the later Ghaznavî state and of its heirs, the Ghûrîs, was of course the idea that the continuing Indian wars of conquest, or even rule over Indian provinces, constituted a jihâd, holy war against the Hindu infidels; and the Muslim soldiers were ghâzîs, religious heroes in such a war. They could recruit volunteers from distant Muslim lands at need. Whereas the Fâṭimîs had built a new state incidentally to an attempt to restore the old unity of the Dâr al-Islâm, the Ghaznavîs built theirs on the basis of expanding the existing Muslim domain. Later, when the greater part of India came under Muslim rule, this particular pattern could not be repeated.[5]

The Seljuḳs: Turkic empire and Muslim unity

The most nearly successful attempt at the restoration of Muslim unity was that made under the Seljuḳid sultans, for the ideal of a single Islamic state was still very powerful in the lands nearest Baghdad, where the Seljuḳs established themselves. The chief effective result of their work, on the contrary, was the emergence of some of the main outlines of the international social order which was to replace the former Muslim unity.

Upon the collapse of Sâmânî authority in Khurâsân, after 999, the Ghaznavîs had not proved able, on the basis of Turkic slave-soldier corps, even with the aid of Indian booty, to restore effectively the Sâmânî empire. The Turks they were confronted with were an insubordinate tribal grouping of nomadic pastoralists of the section broadly called *Oghuz*, a name applied at one time to the Turkic populations north of the Aral Sea, and then (when some of the clans from that area took a leading role further south) to pastoral Turks in the Syr-Oxus basin. The grouping that now crossed south of the Oxus can be called collectively 'Seljuḳ', after their enterprising leading family, the Seljuḳids. These wished to get the maximum profit from the areas in the vicinity of their wanderings, and were held in only temporary submission. From 1037 on, the Seljuḳid leaders, especially Ṭoghrïl-beg and his brother Chaghrï-beg, took possession of the principal cities of Khurâsân, proclaiming themselves the rulers and hence the proper recipients of the taxes. After their defeat of Mas'ûd of Ghaznah (1040), they were accepted throughout Khurâsân as established rulers. It was for them to try to do better than their predecessors.

[5] Clifford E. Bosworth, *The Ghaznavids: Their Empire in Afghanistan and Eastern Iran*, 994–1040 (Edinburgh University Press, 1963), is an extremely industrious study with much data on social conditions, but limited in time, precisely as the title indicates.

The Seljuḳ bands had but recently moved south into Khurâsân from the dry northern steppes, where there had been wider stretches of territory without agricultural cultivation and the cities that depended upon it, and where pastoralists had commonly been freer of the restraints imposed by agrarian civilization. But many of these bands had already served as auxiliaries to Turkic rulers beyond Oxus, notably the Ḳara-khânid Ḳarluḳ amîrs, and unlike some of the Turkic tribes beyond the direct control of Muslim states, these Seljuḳ bands had mostly become Muslim. They seized power as Jamâ'î-Sunnî Muslims and paid a marked deference to Ṣûfî pîrs of any note in the places to which they came. The Seljuḳ leaders seem to have combined an independent spirit with an ability to come to terms with citied society. Within a few years, gathering the tribesmen into regular armies, they were extending their rule over many of the provinces of Iran; members of the Seljuḳid family became lords of provinces.

Ṭoghrîl-beg, who came to be acknowledged as the paramount Seljuḳ ruler, occupied the chief provinces of western Iran and came to an agreement with the caliph, al-Qâ'im (1031–75), whereby he, as a Sunnî, replaced the Bûyid power at Baghdad (1055); almost immediately the rest of the Bûyid territory fell to him. He took as his vizier a learnèd Sunnî, al-Kundurî, formerly the caliph's own man. The Seljuḳid chieftains were given unprecedented honour as the caliphal lieutenants over all the Dâr al-Islâm. In this way the caliphate was asserted to have ultimate authority and dignity, while the military power was at once recognized and, hopefully, put under such obligations as might restrain its arbitrariness. Indeed, the Seljuḳs made a point of their special relation to the caliph and to the Jamâ'î-Sunnî establishment. Al-Qâ'im soon had reason to doubt how much he had effectively gained by the change of masters, for al-Kundurî himself made a point of keeping him in subjection to the new military authorities. But the settlement set the political tone of the new empire. In principle, the new state represented the Muslim pressure for political unity in the central lands, now given new feasibility on the practical basin of pastoral military power.

Like the Ḳarluḳs of the Oxus basin, the Seljuḳs had the advantage, over states based initially on slave-soldier corps, that their Turkic military base had a natural life of its own engendering its own solidarities, that of the horse-nomads living from their sheep. Such troops did not need to be recruited and mastered ever anew by a brilliant general. But they carried with them the disadvantage that they had a will of their own. When the lord of the pastoralists became the supreme ruler and tax-gatherer of the agrarian lands, the pastoralists began moving their herds wherever pasturage seemed most promising; their lords dared not stop them, though they could try to direct them.

Large bands of herdsmen moved westwards and the northwestwards from Khurâsân (and the Oxus basin). They entered especially the relatively well-watered mountainous areas south of the Caucasus and took up any slack land; sometimes they even dispossessed cultivators, when the latter got in their way; especially marginal cultivators were displaced this way. Ṭoghrïl-beg was forced to follow them if he was to retain their allegiance. He attempted to prevent any greater disruption of the agrarian (tax-paying) economy than necessary, and even to encourage the pastoralists (though some of the Turks themselves were hardly Muslims) to attack the non-Muslim peoples of the Caucasian region by preference to the Muslims, who were readily submissive once other established governments were gone. In the Armenian highlands, they began to infiltrate through the inadequately-held Byzantine frontier toward Anatolia. A military eventuality reinforced this movement, confirming the inability of the Byzantine government to control the new wave of pastoralists. As the Seljuḳs (under Alp-Arslân, Ṭoghrïl-beg's successor) turned their attention to occupying Syria, they found their right flank threatened by the Byzantines and had to counter Byzantine power. At Malazgirt north of Lake Van, in 1071, the Byzantine army was wrecked and the frontiers were left wide open. The main Seljuḳ power in the area proceeded to occupy Muslim Syria, eliminating Fâṭimî power and collecting the taxes in its place; meanwhile, Turkic tribal bands happily occupied the defenceless Anatolia, seeking out the best pastures and maintaining themselves by armed solidarity against the hostile population. In several areas, agriculture was seriously disrupted; peasants fled to the towns, working only fields near the walls, or trying to share in a decreasing urban income. The Seljuḳ chief sent a cousin to represent formal Muslim authority, but otherwise could do little; the Islamicate administrative patterns he had adopted would not serve in the alien territory.

The successor of al-Kundurî as Seljuḳ vizier, and ruler of their empire under Ṭoghrïl-beg's martial successors Alp-Arslân (1063–72) and Malikshâh (1072–92), was the great Niẓâmulmulk. He was a pious Jamâ'î-Sunnî Persian trained in the Ghaznavî administration in Khurâsân, where the bureaucratic heritage, through the Sâmânîs, from High Caliphal (and hence Sâsânî) times was more nearly intact than further west. He brought to his administration a spirit which his Turkic masters could admire, though they might not fully understand it: the desire to restore throughout the empire the ancient Iranian political institutions, as he envisaged them, with their stability and agrarianate justice, through the might of these ignorant but well-disposed tribesmen. Since only Persians, sharing to a degree his ideals, were qualified to be administrators, there was no obvious rival Turkic orientation and the Turks had to give him something of his way whether they understood it or not. He focused in himself a number of attempts at social-political reorganization, some of which failed and others of which succeeded in somewhat unexpected ways.

A major aim of Niẓâmulmulk seems to have been to rebuild the full bureaucratic structure of late Sâsânian and High Caliphal times as represented in the Ghaznavî administration. This would have centralized power in the imperial administration at the expense of local grandees. In this he seems largely to have failed. It may be argued that this was unavoidable because the Sawâd irrigation could not be restored. We have seen that it was partly geological and ecological causes that were reducing the yield of the Sawâd. Even if this were not happening, however, the very nature of agrarianate citied life made it difficult to restore so delicate a structure as the Sawâd economy, once it had reached its peak: once the organization of agriculture came to depend so totally on urban arrangements, a disruption of those arrangements could reduce the agriculture even below its original levels—hence even the basis disappeared on which earlier investment had built to the point where empire could thrive. Then the superimposition of an increased pastoral economy upon the existing agriculture of the region made it harder, not easier, to replace the Sawâd as a fiscal resource. But the very attempt to restore a centralized power had its own effects.

One consequence of the lack of a central fiscal resource was a loss in bureaucratic control of the army. A crucial project of Niẓâmulmulk was to restore the barîd, the central information service which allowed the centre to keep tabs on events everywhere independently of the local governors, and so to control affairs on a day-to-day basis. The barîd was instituted; but the too exclusively military character of the new Turkic régime frustrated the plan as a whole; a proper information service was not maintained. Instead, the Seljuḳ sultans depended on their vast power and mobility to crush any rebellion after it had appeared, leaving the central power always with little more than the minimum authority associated with direct conquest. It seems that the subordination of the tribal commanders to civilian oversight (implied in an information service) was an unbearable insult which the Seljuḳ chiefs could not insist on. And there was still no political element beyond the Turkic soldiery strong enough to overrule the sense of tribal honour at stake—a sense of honour which was, in fact, the basis of the Seljuḳ power.

Despite such weaknesses, under Niẓâmulmulk's guidance the empire continued to extend its power and to resemble ever more, in the reach of its sway and even in the relative suppression of revolts and other military disturbances within its region, the inclusive absolute monarchy he dreamed of. Alp-Arslân and Niẓâmulmulk had probably shared the political initiative, but Niẓâmulmulk dominated Alp-Arslân's young son Malikshâh (1072–92) from the start, and found the way to assure much glory and even considerable stability to Malikshâh's throne. In his reign, though the Fâṭimids continued to rule Egypt, the Seljuḳs took from them the overlordship of the Holy Cities in the Ḥijâz and even extended their power as far south as the Yemen. In the other direction, they imposed their overlordship on the Ḳara-khânid Ḳarluḳ Turkic rulers in the Syr and Oxus basins and Malikshâh carried his standards as far as Kâshghar, across the mountains at the western end of the Tarim basin.

But the greater the expanse of the empire, the less it could depend on tribal troops. Very early the Seljuḳs had used also Turkic slave-soldiers like their predecessors. By the time of Malikshâh, despite the misgivings of Niẓâmulmulk, who warned of the importance of retaining the nomads' loyalty, such non-pastoralist soldiery was the main dependence of the empire. By the nature of the monarchy, the old pastoral ties weakened. Niẓâmulmulk himself embodied this fact. Unlike the non-Seljuḳid tribesmen, in the midst of the expanding imperial power Niẓâmulmulk was able to place his many sons and grandsons in responsible positions in the bureaucracy throughout the empire, so that his family formed by its personal ties a certain complement in the administration to the military unity imposed by the Seljuḳid family. Niẓâmulmulk and his family were surrounded by jealousy from Turks and Persians alike and the young king was increasingly restive at his vizier's control; but the vizier held on to power until his death (as an agèd man) by assassination—an act which was laid by some to his enemies at court, but was also claimed by Ismâ'îlî insurgents against the Seljuḳ empire as such. Malikshâh's own death followed within weeks, and the Seljuḳ empire began to break up.

The 'ulamâ' and the amîrs in the international political order

Though Niẓâmulmulk's attempt to ground the Seljuḳ power on the old Iranian political idea of the universal absolute monarchy failed, his policies furthered the evolution of two crucial social classes toward playing their roles in the emerging international order of the Middle Periods. These classes were the religious scholars, the 'ulamâ', and the military, particularly the military captains, the amîrs; 'ulamâ' and amîrs together formed the core of authority in the new society, with its minimal dependence on formal political structures.[6]

A second aim of Niẓâmulmulk, ancillary to his prime aim of restoring the central absolute monarchy, seems to have been the development of a corps of loyal Jamâ'î-Sunnî administrators for his hoped-for centralized bureaucracy. Under the High Caliphate the civil servants, as adîbs, represented a courtly outlook which was often at fundamental variance with that of the 'ulamâ' even when the adîb was of Sunnî allegiance. Often enough he had been a Shî'î—rejecting the established religious settlement quite explicitly. The Jamâ'î and Sharî'ah-minded outlook had commanded popular enthusiasm in some cities, and always commanded respect in ruling circles; but among intellectuals it was by no means sure of decisive attention. The

[6] The term *amîr* means 'commander'; initially, the captain of an armed body or of a garrison; then the ruler of a town or a province by virtue of his garrison. It became the most general term for a Muslim ruler, whether independent or not (a *sulṭân* was expected to be definitely independent, at the least). The term was used to honour many others, including sons of rulers; but the old translation 'prince' is almost always badly misleading in modern English.

'ulamâ' scholars were trained in one specialty among others: their disciples became the qâḍîs, while physicians were drawn from the disciples of Faylasûfs, and writers of elegant state letters had been trained as administrators. In the name of Islam, the 'ulamâ' asserted a claim to intellectual primacy which was hard to enforce. But now arose a new instrument of recruitment and discipline which helped them to establish that primacy, and to enforce their viewpoint on the administrators.

Already in the tenth century, in Khurâsân, Karrâmî 'ulamâ', with their all-inclusive religious system and a propagandist zeal, and then the Shâfi'îs also, had become dissatisfied with arranging instruction in the public mosques and had built special institutions for the lecturing of particularly revered scholars. These were *madrasahs*—schools—and while (as religious institutions) they centred in a prayer hall, and so were a kind of mosque, they were specially arranged to accommodate teachers and students and their books. Often cells for the students to live in were attached, as well as apartments for the teachers. In these madrasahs it was possible to give a systematic range of instruction, centred upon, but not necessarily restricted to, the Jamâ'î-Sunnî legal 'ilm. The madrasahs were probably set up first as a means of furthering the doctrines of one faction or sect against others—the Shâfi'îs, for instance, wanted to provide such training as would enable their school to win out over Karrâmîs, Ḥanafîs, and perhaps Ismâ'îlîs (who had their own effective system of teaching the esoteric *da'wah*). But they had the cumulative effect of affording all the Shar'î 'ulamâ' an enhanced status.

As vizier, Niẓâmulmulk (who was a Shâfi'î and had himself been trained in the Shar'î disciplines before becoming a clerk) was able to help spread the madrasah idea throughout the Seljuḳ domains; the most important madrasah he founded personally (1067) was the Niẓâmiyyah, at Baghdad, where the leading scholars of the next generations taught. As recipients of large endowments, the madrasahs were able to ensure a critical advantage to their students and teachers; Niẓâmulmulk gave fellowships to students as well as stipends to teachers. With state favour, the madrasah graduates were relatively assured of posts at least in the field of the Sharî'ah, as qâḍîs and the like. Each madrasah was appropriated to a particular legal madhhab (eventually, it became customary for all the recognized Jamâ'î-Sunnî madhhabs to teach in a common madrasah); but gradually, in the larger madrasahs, it became possible to introduce all the kinds of training which would enable the 'ulamâ' trained there to man the government bureaux with good Sunnî clerks. Most clerks in most areas probably always received their training on the job; but the madrasah graduates had sufficient prestige to have a large part in setting the intellectual tone far beyond the realm of the details of fiqh.

The madrasahs did not, as it turned out, furnish leadership for a great centralized bureaucracy; yet they did serve the cause of Muslim unity in a different way. As the madrasahs spread throughout Islamdom, their relatively standardized common training allowed them to foster an esprit de corps among Jamâ'î-Sunnî 'ulamâ' independent of local political circumstances. Thus the madrasah became an important medium for perpetuating, in a still more strongly institutionalized form, that homogeneity in the Muslim community which had begun with the pristine community in Medina. In the time of the Marwânids this had been maintained as a spirit of solidarity among the limited numbers of the ruling class, and in classical 'Abbâsî times it had been carried on by the 'ulamâ' in the mosques, with their chains of ḥadîth transmitters from teacher to pupil across the generations. Now, with the loss of the political framework of the caliphal state and of the central role of Baghdad, something further was needed to meet the old threat of disintegration. The relatively formal pattern of the madrasah carried on the task of maintaining essential unity in the community's heritage from Muḥammad, and in the immediate confrontation with God in all aspects of life, which he stood for.

The new endowed institutions had a large stake in the existing social order, and the oppositional role of the 'ulamâ' in political life was perhaps even further diluted. Yet at the same time, the autonomy of the 'ulamâ' and the whole Shar'î system from the military rulers, the amîrs, was given a definitive form. The duty of protest against an unjust ruler had been played down by the Ḥadîth folk, and did not receive an explicit revival by other Jamâ'îs. It was acknowledged that a qâḍî must be appointed by the amîr, if there were one. Yet the qâḍî must be a product of the madrasahs and acknowledged by the madrasah 'ulamâ'; and a generalized notion of the residual social responsibilities of all Muslims (properly formulated in the notion of farḍ kifâyah) was expressed in a tacit disengagement from the amîrs. However much the 'ulamâ' co-operated with the amîrs, it is clear that the distinction between the tradition of Muslim idealism and that of Muslim political responsibility, already adumbrated in the time of the Prophet, articulated under the Marwânids, and confirmed by the 'Abbâsids, was now taken for granted and was reflected in a polarizing of Muslim institutions between those of the Sharî'ah and those of the amîr.

With the madrasahs, and their relatively broad orientation, came ultimately the triumph of that school of 'ulamâ' who were willing to go beyond the bare transmission of ḥadîth reports and fiqh law and to canvass a wider range of intellectual problems. The kalâm disputation, in its Ash'arî and Mâturîdî forms especially (which had been associated with Shâfi'ism and Ḥanafism respectively), eventually became a standard part of the training of 'ulamâ' scholars, despite the objections of the Ḥanbalîs. Once so accepted, the Jamâ'î-Sunnî kalâm was gradually developed into a major segment of a general intellectual life in which elements of Falsafah and Ṣûfism, as well as the varied historical and literary traditions of adab, were to be found together in the same books and the same men. Niẓâmulmulk saw or even anticipated only the barest beginning of all this, which (in some areas) took two centuries to unfold. But he fostered the crucial systematizing of training in 'ilm.

Finally, a third policy of Niẓâmulmulk helped to establish the pattern of government by military amîrs, commanders of districts, who in fact eventually usurped the place of his central administration, and became the patrons of the madrasah 'ulamâ'. This he did by making them more regularly independent of the civil régime, even while he wished the reverse.

An essential feature of the eventual military rule was the assignment of particular land revenues directly to the individual military officers, without the intervention of a civilian administration. This arrangement had become increasingly direct and increasingly prevalent, especially in Bûyid territories and in the Fertile Crescent, as the fisc became increasingly less effective. (The process was in part a vicious circle, in which emergency recourse to payment by land assignments made the emergency harder to overcome.) The use of military land assignment—iqṭâ'—now was regularized under Niẓâmulmulk.

The word *iqṭâ'* (denoting an assignment or a grant of land or sometimes of other sources of revenue) and a variety of other words specifying various sorts of iqṭâ' have often been translated 'fief', and the whole iqṭâ' system has been referred to as 'feudalism'. There were occasional special instances, especially in periods of relative autonomy in some out-of-the-way mountain areas like the Lebanon, for instance, when relations of military landholding somewhat comparable to those found in some kinds of Occidental feudalism did prevail; to these the term 'feudalism' can be applied usefully if proper caution is maintained. In some of these cases, the terminology of the iqṭâ' was used among Muslims in order to bring the anomalous cases under at least a façade of Islamicate propriety. But to apply the iqṭâ' terminology to such semi-feudal instances was an abuse of the terminology. The iqṭâ' system implied in none of its more usual forms a system of mutual obligations of lord and vassal, each of whom had his own indefeasible rights rooted as much in the land as in military service, which is properly called 'feudalism'. Rather, it grew out of an essentially bureaucratic approach, city-oriented and rooted in the conception of monarchical absolutism, from which were derived whatever rights the assignee of an iqṭâ' might have, and it never shook off its urban ties. Terms like 'revenue assignment' or, occasionally, 'land grant' best translate *iqṭâ'* in its several contexts, and help to keep in mind both the proper functioning of the institution and the implications of its various lines of corruption.[7]

[7] Unless 'feudalism' is used in a completely vague way to refer to any social order in which large landholders played a dominant role—a usage found in many writings of a more or less degenerate Marxist inspiration—it should not be misused for the iqṭâ' system just because of some superficial analogies to the Medieval Occidental system. This point has been well brought out by Ann Lambton in *Landlord and Peasant in Persia* (Oxford University Press, 1953), particularly in the chapter on the Seljuḳs, which is important for the study of Niẓâmulmulk's policies. It has been made in an even

Niẓâmulmulk's chief intention seems to have been to keep the military land assignments under bureaucratic control. He had to integrate them into the bureaucratic system so that that system should not wither away, nourished only on the diminishing lands not assigned out, but should again control all the revenues even though on a new basis. But the result of his efforts, it would seem, was to facilitate the use of the iqṭâʿ assignment, thus normalized, on an almost universal basis. A strong bureaucracy could in fact control the iqṭâʿ; in Khurâsân, for instance, the iqṭâʿs were indeed, in the Seljuḳ period, fairly closely under bureaucratic control: they were assessed in terms of the amount of their yield, which was to correspond to fixed salaries assigned for military service. But this ideal was not everywhere so well maintained even under the Seljuḳs. The pattern of depending on land assignments for military pay tended to make building a strong bureaucracy more difficult. It concentrated all local power in a single hand, for the man assigned the land revenues of a given district was incomparably the most powerful figure there, able to dominate or patronize both the simple peasants and the landlords whose overlandlord he readily became.

This concentration was reinforced, presumably, by one of the more important ways through which the iqṭâʿ system seems to have been regularized: the assimilation to each other of the various sorts of iqṭâʿ assignment that had sprung up, so that they could all be handled on a comparable bureaucratic basis. Some assignments made by the government and called 'iqṭâʿ' had been purely personal grants of land, heritable (and, it seems, to be divided according to Sharîʿah law of inheritance) and hardly to be distinguished from personal property. But the chief sorts of iqṭâʿ that we are concerned with were not heritable as such. They were firstly what may be called military assignments—in which the revenues of particular lands were to go to particular officers (whether collected by a central tax service or, as too commonly, by the officer and his men themselves); and secondly what may be called administrative assignments—in which a district, or even a whole province, was assigned to one man, normally a military man, who was to govern and control it and to reimburse himself directly with its revenues (whether he was to maintain troops only for local purposes or also was expected to support troops for central government purposes). The strictly military assignment carried with it no rights to anything but revenue; but he who could collect the taxes easily claimed other jurisdictions by way of abuse. Niẓâmulmulk seems to have handled the two sorts of iqṭâʿ as variants of a single category, presumably trying to make all assignees alike account-

---

more basic way by Claude Cahen in 'L'évolution sociale du monde musulman jusqu'au XIIe siècle face à celle du monde chrétien', *Cahiers de civilisation médiévale: X^{e}–XIIe siècles*, 1 (1958), 451–63, and 2 (1959), 37–51, who points out that the 'usurpation' by private persons of what we would expect to be public functions—another criterion sometimes used for 'feudalism'—has occurred in many diverse social patterns. Cahen's article is of fundamental importance for the whole development of social patterns in Islamdom and in particular for the broader implications of the iqṭâʿ system.

able to the state finance bureaux without depriving them of their independent military dignity, which was so precious to the Turks. His chief measures to this end were to insist on supervision from the centre to prevent arbitrary acts, especially extortions from the peasants; and to shift each assignee frequently from one assignment to another, so as to minimize the degree of local power assignees could build up by way of patronage and custom. But the policy as a whole, if it brought assignees under better central control, also tended doubtless to legitimize the status of iqṭâʿ assignee by giving it an air of regularity; and this will have allowed 'administrative' assignees to assume a more proprietary posture, and 'military' assignees to intervene in local administration in their land assignments despite the rule against it.

The result seems to have been that all but the most clearly private revenue came to be thought of as iqṭâʿ and to be subject to redistribution to private assignees at the will of the king. Even the land revenues reserved for payment of the standing army at large were referred to as 'iqṭâʿ', as if they were 'assigned' to the army office; and Niẓâmulmulk is even said to have claimed one-tenth of the net central income as his iqṭâʿ as vizier, rather than a fixed salary to be paid from the treasury. If terminology is to be trusted, it appears that on occasion, simple private landed property, which was normally still recognized as held more unchallengeably than any iqṭâʿ, was at the royal pleasure.[8] The tenure of old landed families became more uncertain than ever.

It was in the Seljuḳ period that the custom of putting landholdings into the form of *waqf*, pious endowments, inalienable and not subject to government seizure, became common. The dedication of property as waqf, especially city rental property, served to support especially the new madrasahs, though naturally it supported also mosques, hospitals, caravanserais, and all institutions of public service. It also increasingly was used for strictly family purposes—by way of charity to the next of kin, a charity encouraged already in the Qur'ân. (Waqf property was not technically heritable, and so could not be split up; but a member of the family of the founder normally served as its administrator, under the jurisdiction of the qâḍî.) It was chiefly in the guise of waqf that real estate escaped effectively the iqṭâʿ system. As the 'ulamâ' scholars became increasingly dependent on the waqf endowments, they found themselves in a position largely independent of but complemen-

[8] This whole discussion of the development of iqṭâʿ patterns under the 'great Seljuḳs' is even more provisional than most such questions. The most reliable Western writer is Claude Cahen (cf. 'Evolution de l'Iqṭâʿ,' *Annales: Economies, Sociétés, Civilisations*, 8 [1953], 25–52), but still very good are W. Barthold, *Turkestan down to the Mongol Invasion*, 2nd ed. with corrs., E. J. W. Gibb Mem. N.S. vol. 5 (London, 1958), and Lambton, *Landlord and Peasant in Persia*, previously cited. The difficulties are illustrated, for instance, in Lambton's need to deduce attitudes to landownership from passing references in which terms like *mâlik, milkiyyah*—technically implying outright ownership—are used, without clear assurance always that the terms are to be taken in the technical sense (e.g., pp. 60–65); see also her essay in *Cambridge History of Iran*, vol. 5 (Cambridge University Press, 1968), chap. 2.

tary to the amîrs, as the chief alternative beneficiaries of the land revenues, and to that degree they were prepared to sanction the system as a whole.

Probably Niẓâmulmulk's efforts helped prevent the soldiery from plundering unrestrainedly those lands from which the state could hope to get a continued income if they were well maintained, and if the peasantry were kept content enough not to move away. But he did not create a landed gentry, attached to the land and fostering its welfare on the Sâsânian pattern, as he may have wished; still less a feudal system of the west European kind, with fiefs and subfiefs and local manors combining to provide a complexly tenacious system of hereditary rights and obligations. His preoccupation with bureaucratic control would not allow him to endow the iqṭâʿ assignee with the status of gentry. In any case, from Nile to Oxus the cities were strongly entrenched as the centres of all active life, and the officers commonly preferred to congregate there. They merely visited their land assignments—the more so to the degree that they were limited to a term of only a few years—only to collect the revenues: that is, whatever production could be spared by the village beyond its immediate needs. Otherwise the slave-soldiers could have no interest in them any more than would the Turkic pastoral nomads they were replacing.

The break-up of Seljuḳ power

The decentralist implications of Niẓâmulmulk's policies came into their own after his death, when the Seljuḳ empire with its specious appearance of a grand central bureaucratic monarchy broke up. The Seljuḳ empire was held together partly by the hopes stirred in the educated classes by the attempts at renewal of Muslim social vigour as represented by Niẓâmulmulk; but even more, no doubt, by the tribal solidarity of the Seljuḳ clans. If the former could not survive too many of the disappointments which reality brings to the most perspicuous of great hopes, the latter, the Seljuḳ solidarity, could not survive more than a couple of generations of privilege and its luxuries, the accompanying concentration of minds on the individual advantage of powerful factions, and the loss of direct contact with the nomads. The young Malikshâh, at the end of Niẓâmulmulk's life, was already surrounded by intriguing women and the generals whom they favoured; he remained subject to the wisdom of the ageing vizier only by an effort of duty. When Niẓâmulmulk's personality was withdrawn, special pleadings won the day. When the Seljuḳ solidarity disappeared at the centre, there disappeared with it all check on the centrifugal tendencies of the amîrs.

At the end of the eleventh century—after the death of Malikshâh in 1092—the various Seljuḳ armies, with their several leaders (usually scions of the Seljuḳid house), began to fight among themselves for supremacy, or at least for a wider sphere of action within the empire. For a time one or other

Seljuḳid prince achieved an increasingly tenuous supremacy over the others. Out of the often rather sordid struggles among the sons and relatives of Malikshâh to inherit his supreme position among the Seljuḳids, his son Muḥammad Tapar emerged for a time (1104–18) as a herioc figure, unable really to control all the Seljuḳ territories but fighting on the approved side against heretics, and patronizing scholars and poets. In agreement with his brother Sanjar in Khurâsân, in fact, he restored something of the Seljuḳ splendour. On his death, his brother succeeded him as supreme sultan, but did not rule directly outside of Khurâsân; even there he and his military officers finally fell out with the Oghuz Turkic tribesmen who should have been his best source of soldiery, and he had to see his cities devastated by them. West of Khurâsân, a diminishing number of Seljuḳids and a multiplying number of Seljuḳ officers seized power in the various provinces and even in individual cities, fighting endlessly among themselves.

Thus arose, what was to be typical of much of Islamdom for several centuries, a fluid set of purely military governments, most of them founded chiefly on the personal prestige of the amîr or his father; such amîrs commonly held directly from the caliph, as the all-Muslim guarantor of every local authority, unless a neighbour was strong enough to impose his precedence instead. These numerous and shifting governments, which prevailed in most of the more central Muslim lands, were founded on no enduring political ideas and could not form integrated states. Large provinces such as Fârs, ruled from a single bureaucratic centre, did tend to be held in one piece; a certain minimum of political continuity did obtain. But it was Islamdom as a whole that Muslims felt themselves to be citizens of, and the authority of amîrs, whether of a great province or of a little town, could be regarded as being almost as transitory and personal as that of locally prominent 'ulamâ'.

In these conditions, the most important effect of regularizing the assignment of lands to soldiers was to make the soldiery more independent of the ordinary civilian and Shar'î administrations. Thus a split was made down the middle of Muslim political life that remained, in most important Muslim lands, at least till the end of the fifteenth century: a split between the military rule of the amîrs, on the one hand, in whose hands lay the decisive political force, and, on the other, all the other institutions of civil life, economic or legal or religious. This split was foreshadowed in the divisions already present in classical 'Abbâsî life between the 'ulamâ' and the courtiers, with their radically different systems of social order, which to some degree were both realized in actuality side by side. The court society then held a political power which was accommodated to the ideals of the 'ulamâ' only by stretching several points. In a sense, the same tension between the social ideals of Islam and the political actualities was now finding a new and more desperate form. But in many ways this civil-military split in the Middle Periods was a new phenomenon, with its own characteristics.

What took place in many areas was a division between a particular section of society, of crucial importance through its political power, and all the other institutions of civilized society. This was, in the first instance, in the Seljuḳ empire as well as in many other cases, a racial and cultural split: the military rulers were for the most part Turkic (or, for instance, in the corresponding situation in the west Mediterranean, Berber) among populations of Arabs, Persians, Indians, etc., who used Arabic and Persian as the languages of culture. Though the Turks accepted Persian (or Arabic) as cultural language even for governmental purposes, they always stood somewhat apart as military specialists, despising any upstarts of lesser breed. But the more significant aspect of the division was the divorce of military power from full civil responsibility. The soldiery, with its loyalties and mutinies, was scarcely questioned as the arbiter of political power. But such power had a limited relevance. Even in High Caliphal times, the notion that the ruler was primarily the military commander had encouraged limitation of governmental responsibilities to the minimum of external defence, internal security, and dispensing justice. Such limits on any role for the government as such were even more natural now, when its only legitimacy in the eyes of the Sharîʿah was that of sheer necessity; and (unlike the courtly order of High Caliphal Baghdad) it had no other civil tradition to legitimize it. As aliens attached chiefly to the fortunes of war, the Turks might have little involvement in or understanding for local institutions. In effect, their most certain role was commonly that of court of last resort.

Development of integrated states of some durability and predictable stability required, then, special principles that would counteract the tendency to military fragmentation and flux. The transient greatness of the Seljuḳ régime was, in part, an echo of the dying caliphal ideals, the unity of all Islamdom and the absolutism of the great monarch. But the Seljuḳ régime and all its successors through the fifteenth century were incapable of establishing a large stable state in the central regions of Islamdom, the Fertile Crescent and the Iranian plateau. It was in more outlying regions that special circumstances resulted in more durable political creations. Egypt, indeed, formed a centralized state by the nature of the Nile. Elsewhere two special principles intervened. On the one hand, in newly Islamized territories, where the bulk of the population were still dhimmî, the Muslims found it necessary to form a more tight-knit ruling body, composed not only of soldiery but of merchants, scholars, landlords. In Europe and India, therefore, as we shall see, it proved possible to establish relatively integrated states under Turkic rule: for instance, the Ottoman state at the Bosporus, and the kingdom of Gujarât. But even in relatively long-Islamized areas, a second principle allowed the development of powerful, if more transient formations: the cause of religious reform. If joined with the requisite esprit de corps of a tribal group, reform could win material support within the cities, which depended on an appeal to religious spirit for maintaining their internal balance; support enough to moderate somewhat the breach between civil and military populations, and give some consistency to the military government.[9]

The latter-day caliphate and the legitimation of the amîrs

Even before the rise of the Seljuḳs, the caliphs at Baghdad had been becoming bolder as their Bûyid masters declined in strength; often they made direct contact with the Jamâ'î-Sunnî 'ulamâ' and, through them, with the rulers of remoter provinces—not as absolute monarchs but as upholders of the Sharî'ah. The appearance of the Seljuḳs as Sunnî rivals to the Bûyids had been readily accepted by the caliph, alert to exert his authority in new ways; as we have seen, the resultant settlement set the tone of the Seljuḳ empire. When the Seljuḳs too proved less than ideal masters, the caliphs continued to exploit the opportunity they had found for direct relations with the Islamic community as Islamic leaders rather than as monarchs.

Such a role opened new perspectives on the caliphate as a Shar'î institution. From this point on, Shar'î scholars among the Jamâ'î-Sunnîs were no longer content to define an explicit Shar'î sphere and allow a quite general legitimation to a residual political sphere left to the discretion of the caliphs. The caliphate itself was in question, in a world ruled by arbitrary amîrs, and the caliphate had proved willing to turn to Shar'î principles in its crisis. Hence scholars set about developing the theory of a *siyâsah shar'iyyah*, a Shar'î political order, which should be truly comprehensive, making a place (in principle) for all aspects of political organization. The first to do this, already before the advent of the Seljuḳs, was al-Mâwardî (d. 1058), a Shâfi'î; he rethought the operations of the caliphate in the light of 'Abbâsî experience (and tried, so far as possible, to hold to the implications of positions taken by earlier legists—whom, however, he commonly had to cite in only a general way, for want of explicit declarations). He was especially concerned to formulate, in terms of the Sharî'ah, conditions under which caliphal authority could be delegated to subordinates, and tried to bring order and legal legitimacy into such delegation—which seemed likely to prove continuingly necessary. Al-Mâwardî was followed by scholars in other madhhabs (but not among the Shî'îs, who never had occasion for such studies). Such thinking

[9] Abd-al-Raḥmân Ibn-Khaldûn's *Muqaddimah* (the Introduction to his universal history), which is no doubt the best general introduction to Islamicate civilization ever written, stresses the importance of the solidarity of the esprit de corps, under the name '*aṣabiyyah*, in political formations. His argument illuminates very effectively the political state of Islamdom in the Middle Periods, which is the time he knew best (he died in 1406); he was unable to appreciate the role that civil political forces could play in better circumstances, and did play in both earlier and later Islamic times. Unfortunately, both French and English translations are inadequate, but the French is less badly misleading than the English, which radically distorts Ibn-Khaldûn's meaning wherever systematic or philosophical thinking enters in. See the note on the translation, in the chapter Conservation and Courtliness in the Intellectual Traditions in Book Four.

opened the way among the 'ulamâ' for a conception of the caliph that was far removed from the personally responsible leader of the pristine Medina, yet was clearly developed directly out of that ideal.

The hopeful theory of al-Mâwardî was not, in fact, put into practice, though the idea of delegation of powers by the caliph was used to justify the system that did arise. This was the acceptance of a doubling of authority—or a division of it—between the caliph on the one hand the sultan and amîrs on the other. By an easy development from his position vis-à-vis his autonomous governors, the caliph came to be held to be concerned solely with all-Muslim affairs.

Above all, he was regarded as the repository of ultimate Islamic legal legitimacy, each independent local ruler being required to hold a diploma from him as evidence of the legitimacy of the ruler's position in his particular territory. A Jamâ'î-Sunnî ruler normally included the caliph's name on his coins—the emblem of sovereignty—and received formal investiture from the caliph. To begin with, of course, it was the Seljuḳid rulers who were in this position; eventually, however, with the disappearance of a central Seljuḳ rule, the many transitory Muslim rulers, so soon as they found themselves independent of any stronger overlord, marked this fact by arranging to hold power directly under the caliph. In effect, the caliph became an accrediting officer, whose office it was to recognize, on behalf of the Muslim community at large, which of contending local rulers was to be regarded as effectively the master. The caliph rarely used his position to interfere in local struggles; he simply certified their outcome.

In addition, many Muslims expected the caliph to afford leadership in any other matter which concerned the Islamic Ummah as a whole. Most Muslims saw his role as including concerns of the religious establishment; some would extend his duties fairly widely. He should rally the 'ulamâ' to the combatting of subversive heresies, for instance; and should provide moral support, at least, to anyone engaged in defending the frontiers of the Dâr al-Islâm (but not the frontiers of any given ruler's domain, which were a matter of purely local interest). All too often the caliph failed, in fact, to provide this leadership. The weakness of his position in practical terms made it difficult for him to act effectively. After the Seljuḳ state lost its overwhelming power, the caliph emerged as ruler of a local state in the Iraq, and his interests as such may also have preoccupied him from using such wider authority as he did have (thus the caliph of the time, al-Nâṣir, was little help to Saladin against the Crusaders). Yet the caliph's presence afforded a central standard to which the Muslim political conscience could appeal.

Practical government, as against ultimate legitimation from the viewpoint of the Ummah as a whole, was frankly entrusted to the amîr or sultan, who should ideally have sufficient reverence for the caliph to accept his moral leadership, while at the same time possessing the immediate loyalty of troops sufficient to ensure effective power in his territories. Ideally, the sultan also should represent something of the universality of Islam. The first Seljuḳids regarded themselves as, in principle, the sole fount of practical Jamâ'î-Sunnî government, and the term *sulṭân*, with them, came to imply something approaching all-Muslim power (though their domain was limited by that of the equally Sunnî Ghaznavîs in the east and the Shî'î Fâṭimîs in the west). Subsequently any amîr with far-reaching pretensions or who ruled an extensive country might call himself sultan.

The sultanate in its grandest sense was never much more than a personal, fairly transient affair. It was the strictly provincial or local amîr who was of enduring importance in most areas. Already under the first 'great Seljuḳs', the ordinary military commander, the amîr, possessed a certain autonomous importance. With the end of full Seljuḳ unity, after 1092, such amîrs became increasingly independent (as we have seen) in the local territories the chief towns of which they garrisoned; in effect, those that commanded their own garrison might owe no allegiance to any ruler short of the caliph except as one of their number was able from time to time to build an empire of sorts on the basis of the submission of his fellows.

An amîr's rule, even when it extended over a considerable nationality, was essentially a local affair from the viewpoint of Islamdom as a whole, and the boundaries between one amîr's territory and another's were matters of local politics rather than of basic social distinction. A single society, at the head of which stood the caliph, was recognized as prevailing regardless of momentary divisions between the realms of rival amîrs. The various state formations, often of fairly enduring significance—on the order of that of the Ghaznavîs—which arose among them were never given so exclusive an allegiance as to overrule the ultimate ideal unity of the Dâr al-Islâm. A Muslim, whatever his origin, could take his place anywhere in the Dâr al-Islâm on the basis of his established position according to the Sharî'ah, which prevailed irrespective of the local politico-military power and reduced the shifting boundaries of the various states to relative insignificance.

This political order, as it grew out of the Seljuḳ experience, subsequently became the norm almost everywhere, in one form or another, in the Muslim society of the Middle Periods. By about 1100, the broad lines of it had appeared; from this point on, political interference played relatively little role in the cultural blossoming of the autonomous life of local centres, tied together not so much by the amîrs as by their 'ulamâ' scholars and their Ṣûfî pîrs. This culture now entered a period of blossom. In one way these political forms represented an effective international order in a society rapidly growing too large to be held together by a political organism of the usual kind. Nevertheless, the precarious position of any individual government in point of political ideals probably contributed to the lack of stable long-run institutions in the various state formations which did arise, a lack which made for recurrent social destruction on a vast scale in unchecked warfare.

The Ismâ'îlî revolt

Not everyone was willing to accept the Turkic amîrs as a necessary evil for want of a true caliphal government. Various groups of Shî'îs and Khârijîs maintained their alternatives. But one revolt struck at the heart of the system, attempting to overthrow the whole Seljuḳ power. This was the revolt of the Nizârî branch of Ismâ'îlî Shî'îs, known to Crusader history as the 'Order of Assassins'. They attempted to introduce a religious reform precisely in opposition to the whole pattern of Jamâ'î-Sunnî amîrs and 'ulamâ' alike. The heritage of Ismâ'îlî hierarchism gave them an alternative political ideal, which the Jamâ'î-Sunnîs could not provide once the caliphal state broke down.

In the last years of Malikshâh, just before the Seljuḳ empire began to break up, these Ismâ'îlîs began concerted efforts to seize power in Iran. In 1090 they seized the mountain fortress of Alamût, in the Daylamî mountains north of Qazvîn, which later became their headquarters, and various towns in Quhistân, a mountainous area south of Khurâsân. After the death of Malikshâh they broke out into full-scale revolt throughout Iran and the Iraq, and later in Syria as well. The revolt was not carried out (as in the Fâṭimî or 'Abbâsî risings) through a major army aiming at overthrowing the central government but, in a spirit appropriate to the régime of the many amîrs, through a piecemeal seizure of strongholds and through the elimination of individual amîrs (or politically minded 'ulamâ') by assassination when they proved personally dangerous. The conspiratorial resources of the Ismâ'îlî movement, with its secret cells, made it possible to seize any local opportunity that arose to erect an Ismâ'îlî stronghold. Cumulatively, these local efforts should prepare the whole society for the ultimate advent of the Fâṭimid imâm as promised mahdî, to fill the world with justice as it was now filled with injustice.

At first there seems to have been much sentiment against the Turkic rule. The Ismâ'îlîs found partisans, especially among Shî'îs, in some rural areas, in most towns, and even in the lower ranks of the armies. Enthusiasm carried all with it. An occasion was quickly found for the revolting Ismâ'îlîs to free themselves of any control by an Egyptian government grown cautious: the son and successor of the Fâṭimî vizier Badr al-Jamâlî substituted a younger and more compliant son as successor to the Fâṭimid caliph al-Mustanṣir, excluding the designated heir, Nizâr; the Ismâ'îlîs of the Seljuḳ domains insisted on Nizâr's rights as imâm and then (after his death) on the rights of some one—which one was not yet revealed—of his descendants. They thus became independent as 'Nizârîs'. But already they had been an autonomous movement, with their own leadership centred in the dâ'î of Iṣfahân and with their own version of the Ismâ'îlî doctrine, in which they emphasized, with a dialectic that could in that age almost not be gainsaid, the irreplaceable authority of the imâm and hence of the movement that he embodied. (We shall see more of their doctrine when we discuss the work of Ghazâlî.) Their formal independence merely consecrated the spirit of a revolutionary movement.[10]

In the decentralized political mood of the time, in which the central bureaucracy was losing control of the iqṭâʿ assignments anyway, the Ismâʿîlîs were often able to gain a temporary advantage by helping one amîr against another, and the friendly amîr seemed hardly to realize that they were more significant than merely a local popular militia group with their own private religious position; many had little conception of any Seljuḳ state being at stake. On occasion, the Ismâʿîlîs tried to hold a fortress, which in some way they had got control of, as delegates from some Seljuḳ amîr without an immediate clear break, as if they were merely amîrs among the rest.

The most important such fortress was one just outside Iṣfahân, the chief Seljuḳ capital. The man who had seized it was dâʿî, the chief of mission, of Iṣfahân and probably had primacy among all the rebel Ismâʿîlî dâʿîs. He pointed out that he was a Muslim, that his Ismâʿîlîs followed the Sharîʿah, and he claimed he ought to be recognized as a proper Seljuḳ amîr with his own iqṭâʿ, provided he paid tribute to the sultan from the taxes he raised in his area and sent troops at his bidding. The sultan was the ardently Sunnî Muḥammad Tapar; yet even in his camp there were those who were for such an agreement. But certain more intransigent of the Sunnî ʿulamâʾ took the lead against it, denouncing Ismâʿîlism as going outside the pale of Islam because of the high value it assigned to the bâṭin, the inner sense of Qurʾân and ḥadîth and of the Sharîʿah law itself—which made their acceptance of the outer law unmeaning or at least ambivalent (as, indeed, their conspiratorial secrecy made any pledge of allegiance to the sultan likewise ambivalent). Hence, it was argued, the Ismâʿîlîs could not hold an iqṭâʿ assignment but must instead be destroyed as apostates. This position won out. The Ismâʿîlî garrison sold their lives dearly, holding to the last rampart, but were overwhelmed by the Seljuḳ power massed at its very capital (1107).

The ʿulamâʾ carried not only the military decision but the mind of the people. Few might care about the Seljuḳ state, but the unity of the Muslims proved a decisive political value. As the revolt unfolded, most of the popu-

[10] The first Western scholars to write seriously of the Nizârîs, Silvestre de Sacy and Hammer-Purgstall, both were polemicizing against revolution in Europe in their day and deliberately believed the worst accusations against the Nizârî leaders so as to make of them a repulsive example. They conceived the whole movement as a mere manipulation of fools by knaves—superhumanly clever and malignant knaves. Such an evaluation survives even now in those who see all dissent, or at least all 'Oriental' dissent, as the effect of hyprocrisy combined with gullibility. For a recent example of such scholarship by a respected master, see the review of the *Order of Assassins* in the *Wiener Zeitschrift für die Kunde des Morgenlandes*, 1961, where the errors of detail, for instance unevidenced assumptions about Ḥasan-e Sabbâḥ's claims and acts, are less significant than the set of mind, which can dismiss the contest between Nizâr and al-Mustaʿlî as merely a typical 'Oriental' succession dispute—overlooking how untypical it was of either the Fâṭimid or the Nizârî dynasties. Unfortunately such presuppositions, in less blatant forms, can still be pervasively influential.

lation turned against the Ismâʻîlîs. In their piecemeal approach, every town might opt at any time for or against the new hopes, not waiting for a bandwagon victory but simply expressing loyalty to the dream of the imâm. On this basis, the Ismâʻîlîs often demanded, in effect, a decision from everyone for or against, which split the community irrevocably. The presence of secret Ismâʻîlî cells, whose members did not acknowledge their membership, even such tactics as the attempt of an Ismâʻîlî chief to hold his fortress as a Seljuḳ amîr, merely added to the psychological tension: no one could know just who was on which side even though the distinction was becoming all-important.

The Ismâʻîlî use of the technique of assassination probably decided the issue. In a society where everything depended on the prestige of individuals, rather than of bureaucratic office, assassination was already being freely used; but the Ismâʻîlîs made a frank policy of it, even insinuating their men in among a potential enemy's servants in advance, in case he should make trouble. The assassinations were aimed at single prominent enemies who caused them special damage (or at turncoats) and were seemingly calculated to avoid bloodshed among ordinary people, whose champions, in the name of justice, the Ismâʻîlîs felt themselves to be—for the elimination of one man in time could obviate a bloody battle. The Ismâʻîlî assassinations were made as public and dramatic as possible, as warnings, and zealous Ismâʻîlî youths gladly sacrificed their lives in such acts (necessarily without recourse to debilitating *ḥashîsh* as the modern legend would have it!). But in a society where everyone depended on just those single men for immediate stability, the assassinations proved frightening to all. The Ismâʻîlîs' enemies spread wild horror tales, suggesting the Ismâʻîlîs' real aim was to subvert Islam itself and bring ruin to all the Muslims, perhaps in revenge for the Muslim conquest of old Iran; and they were believed. Assassinations were soon countered with massacres of all in a town who might be suspected—or accused by private enemies—of being Ismâʻîlîs; at Iṣfahân, suspects were thrown live on a bonfire in the centre of the town. The massacres in turn provoked assassination of their chief instigators, which evoked further massacres. In the vicious circle, the Ismâʻîlîs lost the popular support that ultimately they would have had to depend on.

Muḥammad Tapar led a general campaign against the Ismâʻîlî strongholds, retaking many for the Seljuḳ power. Some held out in the Elburz range south of the Caspian, and evidently also in the Zagros range. In two provinces the Ismâʻîlîs had succeeded in identifying their cause with the cause of local independence from outside interference: in Daylamân and in Quhistân; large parts of both provinces remained solidly under Ismâʻîlî control. In succeeding years, the Ismâʻîlîs of Syria, who at first had tried to establish themselves as a powerful faction in the towns, especially Aleppo, likewise acquired strongholds in the mountains north of the Lebanon. These several widely scattered and seemingly defenceless little districts, despite almost continuous military pressure from bitterly hostile amîrs, did not come to separate accommodations with Jamâ'î-Sunnî Islamdom; rather, they formed a single state, marked for a century and a half by outstanding solidarity and stability as well as independent local spirit, and loyal under the most various vicissitudes to the dâ'îs of Daylamân, established at Alamût. (Later the dâ'î of Daylamân proclaimed himself imâm.) In contrast to the mercenary army of the Fâṭimids in Egypt, which became the occasion of the state's decay (and in contrast to the Turkic amîrs around it), this Nizârî Ismâ'îlî state was based on the local militias that had established it; and it seems to have retained its vigour to the end.

Perhaps the chief political result of the Ismâ'îlî revolt, apart from their independent state (of a temper so contrasting to most of the states of Islamdom), was to discredit the Shî'î opposition generally, and to assure the allegiance of moderate men, even of Twelver Shî'îs, to the amîrs and the Jamâ'î-Sunnî society they maintained. But the Ismâ'îlî revolt had had both intellectual and imaginative consequences as well. Their doctrine helped to form the intellectual synthesis of the great Jamâ'î-Sunnî, Ghazâlî, who in turn helped Sunnism to find itself in the new age. Imaginatively, they became the stimulus for numerous legends which had in common the fascinating image of devoted men free from the conventional restrictions of society and even of personal caution: they told of men who gathered at night for wild sexual orgies and the next day would hurl themselves from a tower to their death at the word of an all-knowing and inscrutable master. Indeed, the Ismâ'îlîs themselves contributed to the store of legends that were taken up even among the Sunnîs, though the Ismâ'îlîs told, rather, of the invincible generosity, pride, and courage of men wronged by the world and determined to be free.[11]

[11] The standard reference on the Nizârî Ismâ'îlîs is Marshall G. S. Hodgson, *The Order of Assassins: The Struggle of the Nizârî Ismâ'îlîs against the Islamic World* (The Hague, 1955); this is to be corrected in detail by Hodgson's chapter on the Ismâ'îlî state in the *Cambridge History of Iran* (Cambridge University Press, 1968), chap. 5. The most famous legend of Ismâ'îlî origin (but given a Sunnî form) in the West is the tale of the three schoolfellows given in Fitzgerald's preface to his *Rubaiyat of Omar Khayyam*. The most famous anti-Ismâ'îlî legend is the story of the paradisal garden of sweet fruits and fair maidens to which drugged youths were taken, and to which they were told they would return if they died killing for the master.

II

The Social Order: Mercantile Interests, Military Power, Liberty

With the Seljuḳ régime, the Middle Periods were fully launched; for the maturing of the system of military iqṭâʿ assignments, and of autonomous amîrs and their garrisons in the greater cities of central Islamdom, confirmed the ending of the absolutist empire. The society of these Middle Periods, especially in the central lands from Nile to Oxus, was (in the senses we have noted earlier) that to which the term 'Islamicate society' can most typically apply. The bulk of the population now had become Muslim, and such a religious allegiance had not yet ceased to serve to delimit and define the social order as a whole. At this point, then, we need to look more closely at persistent features of that social order, as it came to be structured under Islam; features which the more quickly changing high culture normally presupposed.

Many of these more persistent features of Islamicate social life were not specially distinctive of Islamdom. The everyday life of the less privileged classes—the folk culture—might vary almost as much within Islamdom as among the several agrarianate-level societies. If one looks at the folk-cultural life in its details—at manners of cooking, of house construction, of clothing; at techniques of farming, of handicrafts, of transportation; at ways of child rearing or even at popular festivals—one finds, even within the region from Nile to Oxus, too great a variety to be summarized justly except, perhaps, in broad reference to climatic conditions and to the general poverty, which between them imposed a degree of predictability throughout the mid-Arid Zone. If, on the contrary, one looks at the broadest presuppositions of citied agrarianate life generally, one finds that the most basic traits visible in Islamdom were common to all such societies. If we were considering this level of culture alone, then, there might be little point in distinguishing an 'Islamicate' civilization from ongoing agrarianate-level patterns between Nile and Oxus over the millennia, or even from agrarianate-level patterns throughout the Afro-Eurasian Oikoumene.[1]

Nevertheless, the common problems of agrarianate-level society took a special form in Islamdom in the Middle Periods, which helped to form Islamicate civilization as such. The high culture was persistently remoulded by elements of the local folk cultures, especially those of the central 'lands

[1] Carleton S. Coon, *Caravan, the Story of the Middle East* (New York, 1951), is very naïve historically but invaluable as a survey of the folk culture of much of the area.

of old Islam'. At the same time, especially in the central lands but also wherever Islam was received, the 'high culture' had a steady influence in moulding the everyday culture. The prescriptions of Sharî'ah law, the doctrines of kalâm disputation, or even the canons of poetry and painting commonly suffered strange sea changes when they became adopted as norms by classes less well-to-do than those for whom they were established. And sometimes the new forms were reflected back into the high culture itself. To study the civilization, then, both in its formation and in its consequences, we shall want to discuss several aspects of the everyday level of culture, even though (unfortunately) we cannot discuss it comprehensively. We must limit ourselves here to those features that entered into the formation of what was most persistently distinctive in the Islamicate social order in the Middle Periods. I must add that few adequate studies have yet been made into any of the topics discussed in this chapter. Hence almost all my conclusions are highly tentative or even, sometimes, conjectural.

The liberty of the Muslim and the open structure of his social order

As urbanity and cosmopolitan mingling increased in society on the citied agrarianate level, the reliance was steadily eroded that an individual could place on inherited status or authority to guide his choices in life. It could seem that the individual, with his private interests, might have to face a society in which almost anything might seem as legitimate, or illegitimate, as anything else, and where he must make his way at every moment anew by his wits and by such resources as he could assure himself personally. In the Agrarian Age, such a limiting social condition was not reached, partly because local customs did retain a degree of power despite the mingling of peoples, and partly because each of the great regional societies developed a compensating set of region-wide institutions to assure norms of legitimation and hence some predictability even when people left home. In India, caste was the backbone of such a structure, becoming more elaborately developed as Indian society became more involved in the hemispheric commercial and cultural nexus. In western Europe, the same can be said of the feudal class system.

In the mid-Arid Zone, as we shall see, the pressures toward a cosmopolitan dissolution of local legitimations could be unusually strong. Perhaps on this account, in that region the compensating institutions proved to be the least tightly structured. They were highly flexible, for agrarian times; but they also, more than in either India or the Occident, did tend to leave the individual relatively insecure in status, and face to face with society at large—as his religion left him face to face with the supreme God—with a minimum of buffering intermediaries. The anonymity of the individual was nothing like the anonymity that can emerge in modern society; at most, it was great only relative to other societies on the agrarianate level; but there are suggestive points of comparison between these aspects of pre-Modern Islamdom and Modern world society. In any case, practically all that is distinctive in the Islamicate social order, especially in the Middle Periods but reaching beyond them, can be interpreted in terms of the relative openness of the social structure and the mobility, or insecurity, of the individual within it. The very problem of maintaining a level of social complexity above the agrarianate minimum when the agrarian base was no longer expanding, though in the first instance a problem of the resources of arid lands, was compounded by the open structuring of the social order.

We shall focus particularly on the political aspects of the problem, for these were crucial. In the political realm, a looser structuring meant, pre-eminently, reduced power at the centre, and hence a threat to the specialized institutions that commonly presupposed central power. It was in meeting the difficulty of legitimizing any complex political life that the resources of Islamicate institutions were displayed most comprehensively.

The reduction of central political authority took the form of what was perhaps the most distinctive feature of the Middle Islamic periods in general, as compared with other times and areas in the Agrarian Age: its militarization. This was not the militarization of society as a whole, but that of final governmental power. We may hazard here an oversimplified sketch of how certain aspects of the cosmopolitanism of the mid-Arid Zone could lead to a more open structuring of social forms, which eventuated in militarization. At the same time, the sketch will serve to indicate the main theme that runs through the chapter as a whole. This may be summed up as the emergence and functioning of the *a'yân-amîr* system of social power: where power was normally divided between the *a'yân*, 'notables' of various sorts in the towns and villages, and the amîrs, commanders of relatively local garrisons, with minimal interference from large-scale political organizations.

We may contrast summarily the a'yân-amîr system of the Muslims to corresponding systems among the Chinese, the Hindus, and the Occidentals. The Chinese system of the time functioned by way of such things as: the overall *li* proprieties, with, at the base of the power structure, a civilian gentry dominating the peasants; the prestige of bureaucratic rank; the open examination system; and, at the centre of power, an absolute monarchy; and all these were interdependent. The Hindu system of the time functioned by way of such things as: dharma rules; at the base of power, caste responsibilities; jajmânî obligations among castes; panchâyat councils; and, at the centre, hereditary râjâs. The Occidental system functioned by way of such things as: feudal, canon, and charter law; at the base of power, an enserfed peasantry on manors; municipalities and corporations; succession to office by primogeniture or collegial voting; the chivalric household; and, at the centre, levels of feudal tenure. Correspondingly, the a'yân-amîr system functioned by way of such things as: the Sharî'ah law; at the base of power, a free peasantry under military iqṭâ's; the patronage of the a'yân (notables) of the towns; succession by appointment or by contest; the slave household; and, at the centre of power, the amîrs' garrison courts; and all these presupposed and supported each other. (I shall make a more extensive comparison between Islamdom and Occident in a later chapter.)

We may summarily put the historical development in Islamdom as follows. (I shall try to demonstrate at least the plausibility of this sketch in the rest of this chapter.) The advent of Islam broke the agrarian power from Nile to Oxus; that is, broke the hold of the agrarian gentry as it was expressed primarily through the Sâsânian monarchy (to the extent that that still represented agrarian interests more than any other interests). For a time, Arab interests of an originally mercantile cast were as dominant in the new caliphal state as any; but soon a monarchy was reconstituted in which agrarian interests had the greatest role. But in this reconstituted social structure, as assumptions about legitimacy were remoulded within new Arabic and Islamic forms, a degree of social mobility was encouraged at the expense of the older aristocratic patterns. Egalitarian expectations of relative mobility were then consolidated in the Islamic Sharî'ah law, which maintained its autonomy over against the agrarian empire; the empire was never able to achieve full bureaucratic control—for instance, over tradesmen and their associations. The result, by the tenth century, was the attrition of the pre-Islamic cultural traditions and the reconstitution of not just the empire but the whole society on more openly structured, more egalitarian and contractual, bases, appealing to Islam for legitimation.

This outcome was presumably made possible in part by the central position of the Muslim regions in the geographical configuration of the expanding Afro-Eurasian Oikoumene, and by the effects over time of that expansion. Interregional trade was becoming of increasing importance to many areas, and hence (potentially) was increasingly determinative of the fate of any given region; but its particular effects depended both on the extent of regional participation in it and on the internal balance of social forces in the region.

The agrarian privileged classes in the mid-Arid Zone were at least as insecure as ever in their power (because of the sparseness of concentrated holdings, and because of pastoralist competition). Meanwhile the mercantile classes (whether engaged in distant or in local trade) were strengthened, at least for some time, by the long-distance Oikoumenic commerce, increasing sharply just then. The landed families, accordingly (in contrast to most agrarianate areas) were not able to establish an unchallenged agrarian domination over the cities. But neither were the merchants, in a region open to land-based armies in an agrarian age, able to establish, even locally, a political order entirely under their own control. The result was stalemate between agrarian and mercantile power.

Thus, by the Middle Islamic periods, neither gentry nor bourgeoisie could act in independence. Except for some mercantile republics in desert areas or along remoter seacoasts (which did not set the cultural patterns for Islamdom as a whole, but rather followed the lead of the rest of Islamdom), cities as such were usually unable to establish control of the territories around them. Some sort of agrarian territorial predominance was too thoroughly established in the relatively open stretches between Nile and Oxus for an incipient urban oligarchy to challenge it. The a'yân notables in the cities looked only to what could be assured on the basis of contract and personal arrangements, guaranteed by an autonomous Sharî'ah valid anywhere. But the gentry, far more than in most regions, were drawn to residence in the cities, even while maintaining a strong social identification with their lands. Such a gentry could not escape some conformity to urban expectations that they could not dominate.

When cities and countryside were thus merged under the same authority, it was difficult to create effective legitimacy for common institutions that might either maintain the landed families in power on the land, or support the commercial cities in lasting local autonomy. Such forms of legitimation as were developed—notably the Sharî'ah and administrative precedent—were such as need not presuppose either a strong overall organization or a tight local one. But this stalemate, in turn (once the initial thrust of the caliphal authority was dissipated), carried the penalty of militarized government.

For when, as a result, no internally rooted social body could wield effective power, the solution could only be a military one. Without legitimized tenure, the lands tended to slip away from hereditary families of gentry, whose first base of power had been the land and who then had been soldiers as part of their responsibility as a gentry. The land was again and again distributed to men who were first of all soldiers, and held land only as a consequence of that —and held it only so long as they remained personally the best soldiers locally available. (Of course, these soldiers often tried to found landed families; but the process rarely lasted many generations.) Meanwhile, the cities also could not resist militarization. Without municipal autonomy, the cosmopolitan tendencies of the cities were accentuated. Internally, the city was socially fragmented; yet elements in one city became closely tied to elements in other cities, and came to depend on the common norms of city life throughout Islamdom. This double pull, toward internal plurality and external solidarities, undermined further any local civic power that might be developing; notably, an abortive tendency to rely on urban militias to support the policies of the local a'yân. The military landholders, as much at ease in town life as on the land, then readily seized ultimate power over the cities also.

But such military men were incapable of maintaining a highly complex or centralized governmental structure. The most that the local social structures could do was limit their destructive effects.

However, the quality of Islamicate life was determined at least as much by another dimension of this political situation as by direct militarization. The obverse of weak political power can be, at least if other social institutions intervene to maintain sufficient order, an accession of individual liberty. A relative liberty was encouraged by some of the social conditions of the mid-Arid Zone itself, and then was reinforced by the institutions that arose there; such a tendency, as it grew, contributed to weakening central political power, and then benefited from that weakness to entrench itself further. In Islamdom in the Middle Periods, individual liberty could sometimes go to great lengths, by agrarianate standards. This relative liberty of the individual, unwilling to subordinate his management of his own fate to superior social institutions or to corporate standards other than the minimum imposed by the Sharî'ah law, led to many glorious achievements but also imposed limits on what could be accomplished where sustained corporate effort was required.

This sense of personal liberty on the part of the ordinary Muslim doubtless contributed to the strength of what we shall call the a'yân-amîr system. That system was able to carry the Irano-Semitic culture, in Islamicate form, around the hemisphere; but it was also vulnerable to repeated military conquests, and it rarely allowed for sustained industrial growth alongside the often exceedingly active commercial life. These weaknesses will be a point of departure for our study of later periods. (Thus the problematic of each age was largely determined cumulatively by the problems that had faced earlier ages and the solutions then given them.) After two centuries, the Mongols superimposed on the vulnerable a'yân-amîr system, in its central regions, their conceptions of the patron dynasty—out of which eventually (with the rise of gunpowder techniques) grew new enduring absolutisms under which the a'yân-amîr system was in turn being recast when the whole process was interrupted by fateful transformations in the Occident.[2]

At this point I must add some warnings. An emphasis on consequences of the militarization of government in the Middle Periods can lead to misconceptions. Reduction in central political authority and in institutional complexity may be taken simply to imply social failure. The enormous political power generated under the a'yân-amîr system would belie so simple an evaluation, even apart from the impressive cultural achievement of the times. But we must pinpoint just where reduction in complexity lay. We may say that the a'yân-amîr system in Islamicate society presented a special case of agrarianate-level life: one in which some of the tendencies always

[2] The bad example still set by too many writers, of explaining a given feature of Islamicate culture by one or two independent causes, perhaps makes it wise to recall, after such a summary sketch of complex processes, what serious scholars have always acknowledged: most significant historical developments result from the concurrence of many circumstances, each of which might have had quite different effects in another context. Gunnar Myrdal puts the point very well when speaking of the 'principle of cumulation' in, e.g., 'Appendix 3: A Methodological Note on the Principle of Cumulation', *An American Dilemma* (New York, 1944), pp. 1065–70.

present in such life emerged with special clarity because of the removal of political restraints. But it must be borne in mind that I speak of the 'a'yân-amîr system' as an ideal type, only approximated, at most, in actuality; wherever a major political formation arose, it was superimposed on the system and inhibited its autonomous functioning.

The Middle Periods may be defined as covering that time when no stably bureaucratic empire prevailed in the greater part of Islamdom—that is, between the age of the High Caliphate and that of the great empires of the sixteenth century. In this period, Islamicate political life tended to approximate in certain respects to the minimum complexity of political formations that would be consistent with the continued existence of agrarianate society: that is, it tended to lack any high development of bureaucratic government or any systematic equivalent thereof. Correspondingly, any large-scale specialized, especially industrial, investment was reduced. In such political circumstances, the resources of local institutions, as well as of broader-gauge institutions that were less explicitly political, were called on to play a maximum social role, partially replacing more explicitly political institutions. In this way the latent power of local a'yân and amîrs emerged as decisive.

But even when the a'yân-amîr system was least inhibited, a political minimum was approximated only in certain respects; in terms of other aspects than those unavoidably dependent on centralized power, social and political life could be systematically effective. Open structuring might preclude strong central power and what that power could provide, but significant structuring there was, all the same. Hence the reduction of central political power did not usually result in a reduction of general social complexity to the theoretical economic base-level of agrarianate society. Even in point of centralized power, no real minimum was ever entirely reached, at least not for long. Yet within these limits, such a political minimum did seem continually to be a near possibility after the fall of the High Caliphal state. And as such a minimum was approached, a general simplification of economic relations did tend to set in except so far as it was offset by alternative arrangements.

The Middle Periods have been seen as marking the decadence of the great cultural impulse that came with the Arab conquest and the advent of Islam. But if one looks at Islamicate civilization as the fulfillment of pre-Islamic tendencies in the Irano-Semitic societies, the overall picture changes, quite apart from whether any limitations on economic resources may be ascertained for this period. Already before Islam, between Nile and Oxus, the traditions of prophetic monotheism were coming to favour a cosmopolitan egalitarianism as against an agrarian aristocratic ethos; already the main thrusts of cultural development were making their way within the framework of religious communities dominated by an urban population, at least as much as at the courts of kings or in the temples of a hereditary priesthood; already, the communually organized Irano-Semitic culture was making itself felt ever more widely in the Indo-Mediterranean regions. With the blessing of being integrated within a single comprehensive religious community, it was just such cultural thrusts that made themselves most felt in the expansive Islamicate society of the Middle Periods as it spread across the hemisphere. In a long-run perspective, one may almost regard the High Caliphal state as an interlude, a means of transition from the aristocratic agrarian monarchy of Sâsânian times to a social order at once more urbanized and more decentralized, which was emerging in the region as a result of millennial forces in the hemisphere at large. Such a social order was congenial to the distinctive creativity of the Irano-Semitic society as well as to its expansion. In this long-run cultural development, the Mid-Islamic Periods would not show a breakdown but rather a culmination.

A. THE REGIONAL ECOLOGY

In this chapter we will have to describe the social patterns that emerged as such a political minimum was approached. The tales of the *Thousand and One Nights* form a comprehensive image of that social order, especially on the level of urban private life. The various centralized political formations that did arise in the Middle Periods worked to modify the tendencies described here in one direction or another. But once the minimum political situation was approached, and local resources were called on, it was not easy to reverse the process. The patterns that developed were expressing, in fact, an enduring ecological setting. The efforts of governments to modify the local patterns were effective only so far as they answered to this setting and took its requirements into account.

The cosmopolitanism of the mid-Arid Zone and of its core area

The Irano-Semitic high-cultural traditions had been built upon the life of a particular area, the Fertile Crescent and the Iranian highlands: roughly at a glance, the area represented on current political maps by the states of Syria, Iraq, Iran, and Afghanistan. Even after the great expansion of Islam following the decline of the caliphal state, this area continued to contribute disportionately to the development of Islamicate civilization as a whole. It may be looked on as the core of the Islamicate heartlands.

If one surveys the names of major figures, those exercising an influence on the development of Islamicate culture as a whole (rather than merely some regional form of it), one will find they originated mostly in the Fertile Crescent, the Iranian highlands, and also the Syr-Oxus basin. Few from Arabia after the first generations, fewer still from Egypt; relatively few from Anatolia and the Balkans, perhaps a few more from India; almost none from the steppes of the north or the ocean coasts of the south. A handful of major figures hailed from the Maghrib, generally coming eastward to live, but their number is readily exaggerated if one looks to an influence in the Maghrib alone, failing to take into account the overall Islamicate development. Similarly with basic forms and institutions. It is needless to list those that can be first traced in the Iraq, such as fiqh and grammar and prosody. But how many can be first traced in Khurâsân: the madrasah college, the ṭarîqah form of Ṣûfî organization, the acceptance of kalâm as integral to Islam; perhaps one should add to such practices the social constellations upon which were built initially both the 'Abbâsî and the Seljuḳ empires, each of them influential beyond its borders.

I must add that the greater part of this whole area has been more or less Iranian in ethnic colour—a point that emerges the more strongly if one includes the Syr-Oxus basin along with the Iranian highlands proper. Only the Fertile Crescent has been predominantly Semitic. Scholars used to debate about the extent to which the flowering of Islamicate culture was due to some disproportionate 'Persian' (or even 'Aryan') genius; as if most ordinary Muslims were Semitic, but had yielded to the cultural leadership of a Persian minority. If one is envisaging, in the back of one's mind, a 'Middle East' in which 'Persia' is one out of a dozen countries, most of them Arab, such a misconception can be hard to escape. As so often, the serious student must learn to revisualize his material and deliberately choose sounder categories; recognizing that the majority of the main citied areas from Nile to Oxus used one or another Iranian tongue (among which, Persian was, of course, merely the most prominent).[3]

At the first, the life patterns of the less cultivated classes, the folk traditions of this area, were the immediate source of the learnèd high traditions of the Irano-Semitic culture, which were scarcely to be distinguished from them. But gradually the traditions of specifically citied learning and organization became more complex and independent of village life. In the course of the dialogue of tradition, internal complication inevitably carried many traditions far from their original forms. Moreover, as the Oikoumenic citied zone expanded, high-cultural traditions were carried widely from so nuclear an area, and the area itself was influenced by its wide contacts. Many elements stemming from distant origins, notably from the northern

[3] The unexamined identification of the core area of Islamdom with the Arab lands has persisted despite all contrary experience. Even Noel J. Coulson, for instance, in his excellent history of Shar'î law *Islamic Surveys 2: A History of Islamic Law* (Edinburgh University Press, 1964), refers (p. 135) to Arabs as being able by 'innate temperament' to make Islam 'a way of life' and live the law, while for others it is only a 'religion' and they reject much of the Sharî'ah. Yet (apart from his naïveté about race and about what constitutes 'religion') he knows better. The 'non-Arab' examples he cites of deviation from the Sharî'ah are from lands distant from the whole core area—they are not just non-Arab; whereas he himself knows how great was the contrast between Shar'î and earlier Bedouin patterns, and that many modern Bedouin are still far from observant of the Sharî'ah while such peoples as the Persians have clung to it as closely as any sedentary Arabs. It will require conscious and unremitting attention to eliminate these misleading racialist stereotypes from our mentality.

shores of the Mediterranean, were incorporated in the high traditions; but what is more, these traditions came to be shared among peoples of diverse local conditions—among Egyptians, for instance, and Yemenis, and Khwârazmians from the mouth of the Oxus; all these peoples contributed to the further development of the traditions. Thus the Irano-Semitic high cultural traditions became ever less immediately identifiable with the peasant life patterns of the Crescent and the highlands.

Nevertheless, the lands of the Fertile Crescent and of the Iranian highlands continued to be the most productive centres of high-cultural development even as late as Islamic times. From the beginning, most men who became prominent in the Islamicate tradition were born or lived there. Then, as the 'lands of old Islam', this particular area continued to carry a normative importance for the rest of Islamdom however far it expanded across the hemisphere. It demonstrated a peculiarly seminal cultural vitality in the further development of Islamicate cultural forms, which justified the prestige it had won and kept.

The persistently key role of these areas was surely due in part to their special geographical position within the central region which we may call the 'mid-Arid Zone'. Stretching across the Afro-Eurasian landmass from the Atlantic coast south of the Mediterranean to the steppes and deserts northward from China, the Arid Zone formed a wide central belt separating the two great well-watered parts of the Oikoumene: the European region to the northwest and the Monsoon region to the southeast. The Arid Zone as a whole was thus set inescapably in the midst of Oikoumenic history. But the middle third of this Arid Zone, the region from Nile to Oxus (and southward), was especially central to the Oikoumenic historical configuration. As I suggested in the pre-Islamic chapter, the distinctive traits of the Irano-Semitic cultural tradition generally can be traced, at least in part, to the geographical peculiarities of this mid-Arid Zone, its aridity and its accessibility. These peculiarities were most prominent in the key core lands. Here we must go into their effects more precisely.

There are probably very close limits to how far such an interpretation can be carried. It is not easy to distinguish between the traits of Mediterranean Europe and those of the Nile-to-Oxus region on the level of basic traits such as market orientation and cosmopolitanism. The Mediterranean and the Nile-to-Oxus regions were always more closely linked together than the other core areas of civilization. Even on a high-cultural level, they shared both the monotheistic religious tradition and a common scientific and philosophical heritage. This relationship was not only the direct result of the lack of any major geographical barriers between the two regions. Despite the obvious contrasts between the arid inland realm of the Fertile Crescent and the Iranian highlands, and the sea-girt peninsulas of southern Europe, their peoples have been even racially similar; and even now an unmistakable continuity of folk traits can be traced from Afghanistan through Turkey and Greece to Spain, which the traveller may feel in sharp contrast to some traits in neighbouring India, or northern Europe, or the Sûdânic lands. It is not too much, for some purposes, to refer to an 'Irano-Mediterranean' culture zone.[4] It has been observed, in particular, that the lands from the Iranian highlands to the western Mediterranean long shared, at any given time, a relatively homogeneous pattern of city culture, with many comparable institutions and social expectations; and that this homogeneity lasted till long after the advent of Islam.

Doubtless the Mediterranean region shared with the mid-Arid Zone in a relatively commercialized and even cosmopolitan atmosphere from the time of the ancient Greeks and Phoenicians. And probably this cosmopolitanism made for a mutual assimilation of cultural patterns as long as the most important economic neighbours of the Mediterranean region were the mid-Arid lands. A breach in the Irano-Mediterranean homogeneity has been dated to the twelfth or the thirteenth centuries, to the advent of the commune municipalities in western Europe and of Turkic and especially Mongol military rule between Nile and Oxus. But the discontinuity arose at a point within the Mediterranean region—at the time when the northern parts of Europe, especially in the west, were becoming a major agrarian region, a primary source of economic strength and even, eventually, a source of some cultural attraction to the southerners. Perhaps it was less the Islamicate (and east European) towns than those of the western Mediterranean and their hinterland that introduced, at this time, basic innovations that broke the previous homogeneity; such that thereafter the Occident evolved in differing directions from the rest of the continuum.[5]

But even before any breach in the Irano-Mediterranean continuity, of course, the mid-Arid Zone, and particularly the Irano-Semitic lands, showed distinctive features; and some of these surely reflected, ultimately, the geographical contrasts between the two regions. I shall stress four points: the aridity of the agricultural lands; the convergence of long-distance trade; the accessibility to conquest by land; and the antiquity of agriculture and of empire. All except perhaps the last resulted from the special geography of the mid-Arid Zone and of the lands within it that were most influential; and all, I think, contributed to the market orientation of the society—or at least

[4] The most penetrating analysis of this Irano-Mediterranean homogeneity on the high-cultural level, in early Islamic times, is that by Gustave von Grunebaum in *Mediaeval Islam,* 2nd ed. (University of Chicago Press, 1953); his cultural analysis has been supplemented lately on the economic side by Claude Cahen, S. D. Goitein, and M. Lombard: e.g., Cahen, work cited in note 5 below; Goitein, 'The Unity of the Mediterranean World in the "Middle" Middle Ages', *Studia Islamica,* vol. 12 (1960); Lombard, 'Arsenaux et bris de marine dans la Méditerranée musulmane (VIIe–XIe siècle)', *Le Navire* (1957).

[5] Claude Cahen, 'L'évolution sociale du monde musulman jusqu'au XIIe siècle face à celle du monde chrétien', *Cahiers de civilisation médiévale: X^e^–XIIe siècles,* 1 (1958), 451–63, and 2 (1959), 37–51, a study suggestive not only for this problem but for much else in this chapter, including the futuwwah problem.

to its cosmopolitanism, its relative freedom from agrarian or civic particularism.

The effects of any of these four possible consequences of the mid-Arid Zone's long-range situation might be barely perceptible at any given moment and yet be momentous over the course of centuries and millennia through influencing innumerable marginal decisions in the interplay of developing tradition. For instance, the role of long-distance trade, whatever it may have been, cannot be measured by the importance in a given city in a given century of persons trading in goods from a long distance. Despite the prestige of the long-distance traders in such luxuries as silks and spices in the *qayṣariyyah* covered markets in certain places, probably fortunes were more commonly made in ways less romantic. Yet the variety of choices that proved open in times of local crisis, the diversification of resources possible to families one of whose members was in a distant trade, the influence on the imagination of direct contacts with the remotest parts of the hemisphere, all must have had some cumulative effect on patterns of expectation in the whole mercantile community—and beyond it.[6] Trade passing between distant Oikoumenic regions need not always be basically affected by the agrarian fortunes even of the whole region where the city was located; indeed, the trade of the mid-Arid Zone drew on so many different Oikoumenic regions that the fate of no one major region need be decisive for it. We are quite lacking in the relevant statistics. Even if we had them, we could not readily say what the effect must have been: it might mean openness to varied new techniques and notions, with consequent prosperity; or unsettling of any established legitimations, and even economic paralysis; or many other things, depending on the combination of circumstances. But a unique convergence of long-distance trade cannot be left out of account. And its effect must have been more consequential, the more highly developed was world trade.

The same will hold as to the effect of agricultural sparseness and aridity or of openness to overland armed excursions. Attitudes typical of Muslims, such as that whatever their loyalty to the city they lived in, their first loyalty was to a world-wide Islamic community, cannot simply be ascribed to an arbitrarily given nature of Islam, or even to circumstances that happened to hold at the time and place where Islam was first formulated. They must be accounted for on the basis of persisting circumstances that could continue to colour a tradition over time, even though their effects are very tricky to trace.

I believe it makes sense to suggest that the unusual access to interregional trade in the mid-Arid Zone, combined with its aridity and its openness to overland conquests and to imperial formations, all having increasing effect

[6] Jean Aubin, 'La ruine de Sîrâf et les routes du Golfe Persique aux XIe et XIIe siècles', *Cahiers de civilisation médiévale: X^e–XIIe siècles*, 2 (1959), 295–301, reminds us that a failing prosperity in one place may mean a rising prosperity elsewhere; the trade kept on in the region at large one way or another.

in the course of the millennia, could have resulted, over the whole region rather than just locally, in an unusual degree of legitimation of culture oriented to the market, and this in a form favouring cosmopolitan mobility rather than civic solidarity. Therefore such sorts of cultural legitimation could account for the prevalence of moralistic, populistic tendencies carried in communal traditions not tied locally to the land. And finally, that under the conditions of the Middle Periods they could confirm the relatively open social structuring and the relative individual freedom from either prescriptive custom or hierarchical authority that characterized the a‘yân-amîr system.

Much of this world trade in the three key lands—Fertile Crescent, west Iran, northeast Iran region—was so deeply cut by seas (or effectively traversed by rivers), and it was so centrally placed, that it formed the most active crossroads of hemispheric trade. We may contrast the Maghrib, for instance: it did provide way stations for Mediterranean trade and termini for trans-Saharan routes, but these drew on relatively limited and (till a late period) backward areas. But we can focus even more precisely. Even within this mid-Arid Zone, the several lands varied greatly as to the degree to which they embodied the key traits that gave the region as a whole its distinctiveness. Not all lands of the mid-Arid Zone possessed sufficient resources to maintain a large population; and even among those that did, some had a more dependable mercantile base, in their most influential cities, than others: these were the Fertile Crescent and the Iranian highlands, forming the core of the mid-Arid Zone. As long as the general configuration of Oikoumenic history retained the same overall conformation, the destiny of these exceptional lands was at least partly determined by such traits; and perhaps never more so than in the Middle Islamic periods. (After the sixteenth century, when world trade routes changed, as did indeed world-historical conditions generally, including the historical relevance of such former near-constants as aridity, distance, natural resources, and so on, then the role of these lands changed too.)

We may describe this most active portion of the mid-Arid Zone as formed of three major territories, each of which, though internally diverse, had a degree of geographical and cultural unity. The most important (at least in earlier centuries) was the Fertile Crescent, stretching from the head of the Persian Gulf up the Tigris and Euphrates to the east Mediterranean littoral. The Fertile Crescent contained the most attractive waterway between the Southern Seas and the Mediterranean—given protective political conditions at least: up the Euphrates to an easy portage across Aleppo to a north Syrian port like Antioch. As water carriage was the cheapest for bulky objects, this gave every town between Baṣrah and Antioch enormous commercial potential. The alternative water route, the Red Sea, was dangerous and barren and the portage to the Nile was bleak, save when a canal eliminated it—and in most of the Islamic period the canal was silted up. The twin rivers also formed the terminus of the chief land route eastward to

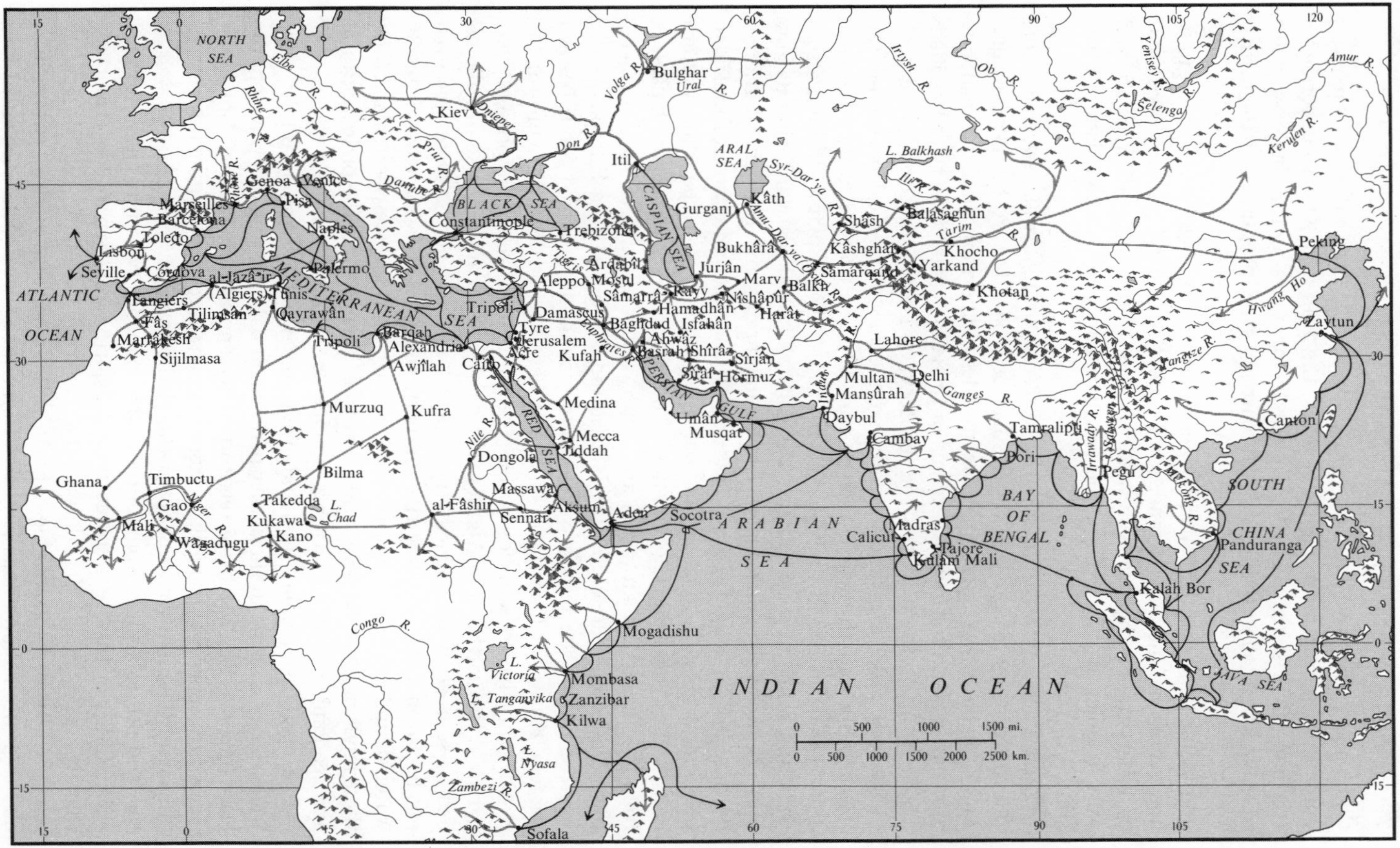

Trade routes through the Afro-Eurasian Arid Zone and the Southern Seas

China and India as well as northward. The Fertile Crescent was, moreoever, potentially rich and diversified in itself: the Iraq and Khûzistân formed a relatively flourishing alluvial plain producing dates and grains even when massive irrigation in the Sawâd had ceased to seem profitable; at the further end of the route, the Syrian coastlands were mountainous in a gentle way and yielded the standard Mediterranean crops, fruits and olives and grain, and even some metals. By land, the Fertile Crescent neighboured, with but easy barriers, on the relatively well-watered Anatolian, sub-Caucasian, and west Iranian highlands; and on the fabulously productive land of the Nile.

The second key territory was the west Iranian highlands, sweeping from the Caucasus mountains and the Caspian Sea south toward the Persian Gulf. The Gulf ports were perhaps inherently less important than the relatively easy passes down to the northern end of the Iraq, to the vicinity of Baghdad. Through the northern part of the territory, and connecting southward both to the Iraq passes and directly to the Gulf, came the readiest route from the Volga basin and the whole eastern part of the European watered zone—around the east end of the Caucasus (or across the Caspian)—to the Persian Gulf, and hence to the Southern Seas generally. And eastward, on a narrow route between the sub-Caspian Elburz mountains and the central Iranian deserts, led for long the only ready land route across central Eurasia to China (and to India so far as land passage was used) from the whole western half of the Afro-Eurasian landmass; and it remained the readiest passage from the Mediterranean region and southwards even after a more northerly route was found (already before Islamic times) from eastern Europe. At the western rim of the territory were rude mountains, reserved for tribesmen (largely Kurds by language) combining herding and local agriculture; the eastern rim shaded into desert; but the plateau between, comprising Azerbaijan in the north, 'Irâq'Ajamî in the centre, and Fârs in the south, abounded in sources of field irrigation. Especially in the north, there was even much seasonal rain. (Along the southern rim of the Caspian was a lushly watered timber and agriculture area.) Cooler than the Mesopotamian plain, these lands produced a population that took advantage of the plain's cultural and economic resources, either as conquerors or as customers.

The northeast Iranian highlands were somewhat less important for their trade routes, at least in the earlier periods; on balance, this was probably the least important of the three territories in Irano-Semitic history. But it too was a hemispheric bottleneck in more than one direction. Through it passed, of course, the great route between the Mediterranean and China, as well as the land routes leading from all the Indic countries (via the Panjâb) toward either China or the Mediterranean or the north—routes only less important than the sea routes. Here it was the eastern edge of the plateau (partly inhabited by Pashtô-speaking 'Afghân' tribesmen) that led to territory high and ruggedly mountainous (and rich in minerals), while the west faded into the central Iranian deserts. Khurâsân and the lands about could depend on irrigation and be richly productive.

The other parts even of the mid-Arid Zone all showed less decisively this combination of long-distance trade in the cities with sparse but substantial agrarian resources. Well-populated Egypt was ever sharply divided between its agricultural sector, rich, dense, and closed in upon itself, and its commercial sector, which only at times could rival the Fertile Crescent in offering a route between the two seas; and it offered only one of several approaches into sub-Saharan Africa. Considering its wealth and political importance, it is remarkable how few men bred in Egypt came into prominence beyond the limits of Egypt except in a strictly political way; until a relatively late period, those who shone culturally the brightest at Cairo tended to be foreigners. The Yemen and western Arabia possessed less considerable trade crossroads and a narrow productive base (mostly agriculture in the Yemen highlands). The Nile Sûdân was even less important; its trade led further west into the Sûdânic lands, but to the south it fronted on a nearly impassable swamp and to the southeast on the Abyssinian mountains. Southeast Arabia and southeast Iran, scarcely populated, offered way stations along the Southern Seas routes, but an unproductive hinterland.

Two other lands were more closely comparable to the three key lands. The Indus basin was populous and relatively important commercially. Sind, indeed, which was to the Indus what Egypt was to the Nile, was not so well developed agriculturally and (being cut off by the Thar desert) offered much less access from the sea to the Indic region as a whole than did Gujarat, eastward along the coast. Through the Panjâb, however, passed all the more important land trade between any Indic country and the rest of the land-mass; a trade which formed one portion of that which passed through northeast Iran. The Panjâb, however, was necessarily bound up with the Indic monsoon-watered region in its cultural patterns, rather than with the rest of the mid-Arid Zone. It contributed relatively little to Islamicate culture until quite late.

The Syr-Oxus basin, finally, like the Indus basin, was only less important for trade than the three leading territories; both contributed as neighbours to the importance of northeast Iran lying between them. Like the Panjâb, the Syr-Oxus basin carried only one portion of the long-distance trade that was further carried through northeast Iran—chiefly the great land trade between China and the Indo-Mediterranean regions. It possessed its own lesser Egypt in Khwârazm at the mouth of the Oxus; it possessed rich but arid irrigation areas in the upper Oxus valley and in the Zarafshân valley, a near-tributary of the Oxus; and even in the upper Syr valley, from which point set off also the trade northward. But its position was not so crucial in so many points as was even that of northeast Iran. Nevertheless, its role in Islamicate culture was only slightly less than that of the three key lands.

We have stressed the commercial resources of these lands: if long-distance commerce could strengthen the mercantile interests, or foster a cosmopolitan orientation, here is where it might be expected to happen. In such cities one might expect a minimum of uncritical allegiance to local custom, a maximum of the trader's calculation and resourcefulness, of his openness to pragmatic innovation. But the same routes that carried interregional trade could carry armies. In contrast to the peninsulas north of the Mediterranean, the trade routes, in their key sectors, were mostly inland even when passing along rivers.

Ever since Tyre—unlike either Athens or Carthage—found itself decisively vulnerable to massive armies from a vast agrarian hinterland, the cities of the region had developed a tradition of accommodation to imperial or at least territorial power; a tradition that could not readily be modified unless the circumstances that occasioned it receded fully enough to allow alternative patterns to mature. This tradition reinforced any cosmopolitanism that a market economy would encourage—the individual learned to feel himself at home anywhere that the imperial power reached, and to adjust himself to shifting circumstances; at the same time, such a tradition was necessarily more favourable to social interchangeability among the various towns and even countries that might be incorporated into an empire, than to the sort of local civic solidarity that would encourage individual cities, acting corporately, to take over power in times of breakdown in territorial authority. The resultant stress on personal resources and adaptability, together with a dependence on bargaining in an open market, would make, rather, for the combination of popular liberty with a tolerance of military authority that we find in the Middle Periods.

The Fertile Crescent and the west and northeast Iranian highlands together, then, were those lands in which, more than elsewhere in the whole Arid Zone, there was maximum access in the cities to profitable long-distance trade. And the whole mid-Arid Zone, at least, tended to follow the patterns set in these areas. They were influential by their very commercial activity: for instance, prominent men living along the trade routes would be known elsewhere more rapidly than their rivals in less frequented spots. But probably men living in these areas also found Islamicate traditions peculiarly congenial. Though the folkways of these particular lands could no longer be identified with the Irano-Semitic tradition of high culture in its Islamicate form, and other lands contributed creatively to that culture; and though the Islamicate cultural patterns proved appropriate to many widely diverse climes; yet it seems that in these lands, where the Islamicate patterns were primarily created, conditions long remained most propitious for their further development.

The precariousness of agrarian power in the mid-Arid Zone

But whatever weight we give to the relatively extensive and steady independent resources of a certain mercantile element within the cities, this would not of itself assure the key role that seems to have been played culturally by the mercantile classes generally in the region. I suggest that their resources could become significant only because, at the same time, the agrarian gentry classes were relatively insecure and unable to impose incontrovertibly their own cultural norms on society as a whole.

The classes that controlled the land for the time being did not always have (it has been made clear) the greatest power, even decisive power; nor were the cities in the greater part of Islamdom able to impose their own norms effectively on the gentry, or even able to form independent enclaves where they could escape the landed power. And an agrarian-based aristocratic cultural pattern always throve and always commanded more wealth than any other cultural pattern The weakness of the agrarian gentry was only relative and can be pinpointed: the courtly and agrarian cultural patterns had always to pay lip service to, and acknowledge the paramount legitimacy of, a cultural pattern more congenial to the market place and the city mercantile classes, and which in fact fully prevailed only among those latter classes. Islamicate high culture was not only even more urban than most citied agrarian cultures, where the gentry were more intimately associated with the land itself than usually in Islamdom; in its urbanness, Islamicate culture was also heavily conditioned by an urban populism which held a monopoly of cultural legitimation.

We can trace at least three components in the precariousness of the agrarian power which could lead to this result: its relative sparseness, especially as compared to the relative concentration of the mercantile cities; the precariousness of land cultivation and of control over the peasantry; and finally the increasing rivalry of the pastoral nomads. Each component became more serious as time went on.

It cannot be calculated, as yet, what proportion of the population of the mid-Arid Zone was urban, and whether this proportion was higher than in various parts of India or Europe; but it seems possible that in the vicinity of almost any given great city the number of wealthy men drawing their income from the land may have been less overwhelmingly larger than the number of wealthy men drawing their income from trade, including long-distance trade, than it was on the average (if not at special commercial junctures) in the less arid regions. In any case, the resources of the agrarian power tended to be scattered widely, one concentration of agricultural land sometimes being separated from another by long stretches of wasteland; large peasant armed forces, for instance, would have to be raised from widely scattered areas. In contrast, both the bourgeois of the cities and the upper class that rose among the pastoralists (who often proved allies to the urban classes through whom they traded their products), had relatively more effective resources than in many other areas. The cities were in more effective touch with each other, by a network of common trade and constant travel, than in some other areas: not usually to the point of military co-operation, but in offering mutual moral support and places of refuge. (And the lords of the pastoralists, with their mobility, could summon large numbers of herdsmen relatively quickly as soldiers.) Certainly the cities were overwhelmingly attractive culturally to the privileged elements among both pastoralists and agriculturists; they tended to denude the countryside not only of material resources for any high culture but of its human carriers, more than this occurred in many parts of Europe and probably of India in the same period. As long-distance trade became greater and as pastoralism was perfected and spread, the relative weakness of the agrarian power became more marked.

In some places in the Arid Zone, the dispersal of agricultural land has evidently resulted in helplessness on the part of the peasantry, who could not move freely in part because of the sheer problems of distance and lack of easily developed land. In much of monsoon-watered India, for instance, it was common for peasants to be opening up new tracts of forest land to cultivation and abandoning old tracts when they became less fertile; but peasants living on a restricted oasis were in no position to do this. Nevertheless, in most of the mid-Arid Zone peasants proved mobile enough; for other ways were found of moving from one place to another. This went so far as to constitute the second component in the weakness of the agrarian power.

Much agricultural land was always ready to go out of agricultural use, while other land came into use. Wherever irrigation was practiced, salinization could have this effect: too much irrigation without adequate drainage would make the ground water salty and raise its level to the point where its saltiness interfered with the roots of crops. Then the agriculturist must move on. Meanwhile, in other spots, new irrigation (often readily enough arranged by even a small group) might be bringing desert under cultivation. The attempt on the part of landlords or of rulers to extract too much surplus from the peasants could have the same effect. Much land was sufficiently marginal so that its cultivation was profitable only if rents and taxes were light; abandoning heavily burdened land for opening up new marginal land could repay the extra effort. Moreover, as we shall notice, especially after famines or pestilence there was likely to be empty land even in the more fertile areas, where previous cultivators had been killed off. And in some circumstances, peasants could even turn pastoralist to escape oppression.

In such circumstances, serfdom was almost impossible to impose in most of the Fertile Crescent and the Iranian highlands, however much the gentry might wish it. The peasants, however much they naturally loved their homes, could always go somewhere else and be welcomed. The danger of this was the recurrent theme of all essays on land management and government. This is not to say that sometimes peasant families did not live in one village for many generations, and that peasants were not badly oppressed, especially when they lived near towns. Sometimes, indeed, life even as a tenant cultivator might have its compensations; thus if turning over half of one's produce meant, in effect, working twice as much land as otherwise, the extra land might be crucially helpful for livestock and fuel. But in case of extreme provocation, or of disaster, or of any other critical circumstance, peasants could and often did find ways of asserting their independence.

Hence the landed gentry were not only relatively dispersed compared with the concentrated population in the mercantile cities; the class tended to be unstable, not being able to depend, in many areas, on a permanent peasantry or even on permanent agriculture. The tendency for the cities to dominate culturally the countryside was thus reinforced by instability in the rural scene itself.

The pastoralists as holding a balance of power

Probably the most decisive component in weakening the agrarian power, however, and hence in making possible the traits of Irano-Semitic culture that can be linked to the mercantile element, was the presence on a large scale of autonomous pastoralists as potential rivals to the agrarian gentry for power. From very early, nomadic pastoralism of various sorts seem to have played an unusually great role between Nile and Oxus; then with the development of complete horse nomadism and then camel nomadism, that region came to be the only one of the great citied cultural core areas in which nomadic pastoralism played a steady and major political role.

Especially in areas dependent largely on marginal quantities of rainwater, nomadization was a constant threat to agriculture. In the Arid Zone, where the large spaces forced the more adventurous herdsmen into social autonomy, herdsmen and cultivators came to form different social groups. As soon as this happened, they became rivals for areas where rainfall was sufficiently uncertain so that in some years raising crops would produce the greatest return but in other years crops would fail while herds might have grown fat. It might also sway the balance, that nomadic pastoralists could readily escape the rent and tax burdens that peasants could not resist. Once the herdsmen had asserted their supremacy—or, as might happen, the peasants had turned pastoralist—it was hard to reclaim an area for cultivation against their destructive resistance; and villages in the vicinity might so suffer from their raids as, in their turn, to be driven from cultivation. A large part of the Fertile Crescent was thus recurrently subject to nomadization, whenever there was no strong agrarian-based government actively to interfere.

On the other hand, even without governmental interference, the nomadization could reverse itself if social conditions were favourable. The nomads themselves, even when not under pressure to settle from some ruler, might find agriculture in their lands profitable once it was no longer cumbered by outside demands for revenue. But peasants of such antecedents could readily revert to pastoralism; a body of 'settled Bedouin' peasantry in the Jazîraḥ has been known to withdraw after generations to join their remote tribesmen in the Arabian interior. Thus the pastoralists provided further occasion for mobility on the land, besides contributing more directly to the reduction of agrarian resources.

But the effects of the presence of nomadism were not simply that the pastoral nomads were free, and that even when they became peasants they brought with them habits of freedom and indiscipline. To some degree, such habits probably were encouraged, both on the level of the peasantry and on that of ruling classes when a nomad element was at their origin. When the peasantry, as a result of pastoral antecedents, was tribally organized this was a check on the gentry; and when the army, for the same reason, was tribally organized this was a check on any central bureaucracy. But the freedom of nomads as such was extremely limited, being more a freedom of clans than of individuals; it could not have very extensive institutional consequences beyond such negative checks. And assimilation to settled life could and commonly did occur very rapidly once the nomads left their very narrow specialized sphere and attempted to cope with the more varied patterns of agrarian life, which presupposed horizons in some ways much wider than those of most nomads. (The connection some observers have made, between 'nomadic' habits of 'wandering' and the mobility of so many itinerant merchants, scholars, and Ṣûfîs, is, of course, merely a fanciful confusion between the distant but repetitive circuits of pastoral clans and the genuine roving of free individuals in a mercantile society.)

In addition to their free ways, pastoralists were known for their readiness in fighting. But the rivalry that pastoralists offered to the agrarian ruling classes did not rest simply on their military capacities either. The pastoralists did form an elusive source of military power, but a well-organized agrarian-based power with a peasant soldiery could defeat them readily enough on agrarian ground.

It was rather that pastoralist power formed a standing alternative always available in case any weakness appeared in the agrarian power and in any central government that was its expression. The pastoral economy (especially that of horse nomadism) had its own privileged elements, parallel to those in the agrarian economy, who could sometimes command the labour and the time of many common herdsmen, from whose herds they might raise levies, and whose manpower they could mobilize for military purposes, as the gentry made use of peasant foot soldiers. Moreover, the pastoral economy had its own relations with cities, again parallel to those of the agrarian economy. Indeed, to some degree cities could thrive on a largely pastoralist background much as they more normally throve on an agrarian background. Up to a point, agricultural production was necessary for both pastoralists and city dwellers; but beyond that point, the hides and rugs or blankets, the meat and milk or cheese offered by the pastoralists could, in principle, be as important a source of prosperity as additional agricultural products. Agriculture, rather than herding, is especially associated with urban prosperity in part, I surmise, for an administrative reason rather than an economic one:

pastoralism was normally a less efficient basis for taxation by city-based powers, and hence for the concentration of wealth and for the high culture that depends on concentrated wealth.

Then this broadly viable pastoralist economy, once established anywhere, tended to expand at the expense of a more purely agrarian economy. The system developed most complexly in the wide deserts or steppes, where agricultural oases were infrequent and agricultural production was widely marginal. In areas with denser agriculture and smaller ranges for pastoral movement—where mountains or agrarian valleys would interrupt the accumulation of large-scale power on the part of tribal chiefs, and agriculture was more profitable than herding anyway in large districts, independent pastoralist power was unlikely to arise on its own. But from the steppes it could spread into less favourable terrain, especially where there were considerable marginal areas in which nomadic herding would do better than village-based herding. In these secondary regions, of course, nomadism was carried by the ethnic groups—Arabs or Turks—that had developed it in the more open primary regions. In this way, the pastoral economy, with its own power structure, could become a rival of the agrarian even in a region relatively favourable to agriculture.

Though the agrarian economy and those who controlled it remained dominant, those who controlled the pastoral economy could yet be strong enough to determine the issue of any power struggle. In such struggles, the pastoralist chieftains, natural enemies of any landed gentry, might readily become the allies of mercantile urban elements; the mutually profitable alignment between the Quraysh merchants of Mecca and the Bedouin tribes often recurred, though in such combinations it was usually the tribal chiefs rather than the merchants that had the upper hand. Sometimes the pastoralist chieftains ended by gaining direct control of the agrarian economy as well, as happened to some degree in Iran under the Seljuḳs. But then their coming did not necessarily strengthen the agrarian cause which they took over, for it complicated the maintenance of agrarian high traditions. From the viewpoint of the gentry, it was not only peasant revolts but pastoralist incursions that had to be faced; and at a time of disruption, not merely new cadres from within the agrarian society, but pastoralist cadres from outside might have to be absorbed into the aristocracy, cadres who were ignorant of its agrarian roots.

In any case, whatever the political combination of interests that emerged, the pastoralist presence made the critical difference, directly or indirectly: in more than one sense, the pastoralist chieftains held the balance of power. Clearly, the agrarian establishment might have absorbed many waves of pastoralists without any serious structural effect had not the agrarian power been already weakened in its cultural appeal in the other ways we have traced. But a nomadic pastoral presence in a context of relative agrarian weakness and of mercantile strength could serve to shift the balance of cultural weight positively in an urban direction—where otherwise that presence might have been merely inhibitory; or else even just radically destructive (as it sometimes was, apparently, in the Sûdânic lands).[7]

We have investigated in some detail the relative strength of the mercantile cultural outlook in the mid-Arid Zone, nourished by long-distance trade and by imperial cosmopolitanism; and likewise the relative weakness of the agrarian cultural outlook, threatened by peasant mobility and pastoralist rivalry. Perhaps it is clearer now why the central lands of Islamdom developed a distinctive solution to the problem of ordering large-scale society under agrarianate conditions. But now I add a warning on the effect of the passage of time on these circumstances. It was only in part on account of events of the time that it was just in the Middle Periods that they had their fullest effect. In part, their effectiveness then was the continuing result of a secular regional process.

Nomadic pastoralism was significant in Islamdom in all periods, but it played a primary role only in the Middle Periods, especially after the incursions south and west of the Oxus by Oghuz Turks associated with the Seljuḳs (and the almost contemporary incursion of camel Bedouin, the Hilâl and associated tribes, into the Maghrib). This timing was presumably related in part to the long-term evolution of nomadic pastoralism, especially the horse nomadism of the Eurasian steppes, at which we shall look more closely in Book Four. Similarly, other circumstances affecting the balance between agrarian and mercantile authority and power that we have been discussing can be more or less dated: a certain secular deterioration in agricultural resources in the Arid Zone (which we shall also look at a bit in Book Four), and, of course, the cumulative development of Afro-Eurasian interregional trade. But the effects of these circumstances cannot always be correlated directly with datable events that visibly embody them, such as the Oghuz incursions. What affected the very texture of Islamicate culture was a cumulative process, which went on building up so long as the general circumstances we have been describing persisted.

The minimum political and social requirements of the society were ultimately determined by its ecology: that is, the natural and social resources available for the fulfillment of the various inescapable social interests at a given level of technique and organization. Over the centuries, those social institutions were reinforced, culturally, that most often proved capable of surviving such an ecological situation as we have described, and meeting its requirements. Then the resultant institutions of Irano-Semitic culture could outlast temporary shifts in the ecological basis of the society, maintaining a

[7] Fredrik Barth, *Nomads of South Persia: The Basseri Tribe of the Khamseh Confederacy* (London, 1961), gives an excellent analysis of typical nomadic pastoralism, though some of its conclusions, for instance on demography, would have to be modified for pre-Modern times. It does give, incidentally, illuminating information on the population area gradient, personal and ethnic mobility, and succession by prestige contest, all of which we will discuss in this chapter.

continuity of social pattern despite a relative shift in weakness or strength of agrarian, pastoralist, or mercantile elements. Even when long-distance routes shifted from one local site to another, or long-distance trade became less vigorous for a time, the overall cultural tendencies of the region could persist in their influence, already embedded to a degree in social institutions and in the sorts of expectations that prevailed. The process we have been describing was thus cumulative so long as the basic preconditions for it prevailed for the most part in most of the area most of the time. It reached its peak effect in the Middle Islamic periods.

In particular, the Islamic tradition itself was largely the product of the cosmopolitan and mercantile bias of society from Nile to Oxus. Both with its Sharîʿah and, as we shall see, in its Ṣûfî orders, it reinforced, in the face of temporary attempts at a more hierarchical or parochial structuring, the sort of free, open social structuring pressure to which it had itself responded. Yet even Islam could be made to serve a different tendency when that became strong enough.

For, despite the weight of institutional continuity, once any major enduring change supervened in the ecological configuration, either in its natural or in its social dimensions, then the process could begin reversing itself. Then a new pattern could begin to form on the strength of the same sort of human interests that had served to build up the first pattern. A reversal or even a major modification in any of the three components that made for the precariousness of the agrarian power could initiate a cultural process that would lead to a reversal of what I have described as the 'stalemate' between agrarian and mercantile powers. This in turn could lead to a reversal of the fragmentation and militarization of politics that characterized the Middle Islamic periods. After the advent of gunpowder warfare, such a modification seems to have begun to happen: the development of gunpowder weapons finally replaced the long-lost irrigated Sawâd agriculture as a support for strong central authority; moreover, the threat of nomadic power as a rival to established agrarian power was reduced. In the sixteenth century, then, some key features of the long-developing Irano-Semitic social pattern did begin to be reversed.

Population shifts and ethnic change

So much for the overall predisposing circumstances that made for what was distinctive in the region from Nile to Oxus in the Middle Islamic periods. Before we go on to study the internal organization of the several sectors of society, however, we must understand some points about the demographic movement of the region, which helped determine relations among different sectors in the population.

Under some circumstances, nomadization could occur in the form of a shift from one ethnic makeup to another; or, more accurately, from one balance among groups of different linguistic or other cultural heritage to another balance among them (for almost never was a whole population homogeneous in its linguistic and folk-cultural heritage). Such ethnic changes had diverse cultural effects. Nomadization was likely to be most enduring when it was accompanied by ethnic change. And when changes occurred rapidly, they could result in cultural ambivalence in areas where society was bilingual and hence 'bi-cultural'; this might make for greater receptivity to unconventional initiatives (this was probably the case in Anatolia for some time after the Turkic conquest), or for inhibition of more intensive cultural development. Ethnic changes further contributed both to the prevalence of ethnically diverse small bodies of population, which had little communication among themselves, and still less civic solidarity; and also to the widespread lingua francas that made possible the general use of a few highly developed literary languages. Speaking more generally, the speed and direction of ethnic variation could undermine the continuity of tradition in economic process and in high culture, or effect breaches in it. And continuity of tradition was a major social resource as a basis for prosperity or any high level of investment. For all these reasons, it could be crucial how ethnic variation took place. To understand this, we may invoke some far-reaching demographic principles, which will prove relevant also to understanding social mobility in countryside and town.

We cannot assume a Malthusian population pattern, such as tends to prevail modernly, where short of special restrictive practices population rises to the local limits of subsistence. There was usually unoccupied space for people to move into. But neither can we assume the more or less racialist image of population patterns that seems vaguely to underlie the casual remarks on population most commonly found: an image of 'virile' stocks with numerous offspring and 'degenerate' stocks with few, of 'vigorous' peoples forced to migrate by poverty or war and of conquered peoples apparently surviving only on the sufferance of the conquerors.[8] The presumption must always be that in any one area there was more continuity than discontinuity in biological makeup at any given time, except occasionally at the very highest social levels, unless the reverse can be demonstrated. But there was also an almost continuous process of population shift, which took place regardless of the presence or absence of prominent new ethnic groups. This process is perhaps the most important to keep in mind for most

[8] The notion that 'vigorous' stocks will be fecund, while 'degenerate' peoples will produce few offspring, may be natural—the vigorous male expects to beget lots of children. At any rate, a preoccupation with the birth rate as a sign of healthiness—rather than with the death rate, which surely has generally been the more significant variable—has been quite widespread. Even Henri Pirenne speaks this way in explaining the northwest European population increase in the eleventh century. To be sure, even the birth rate is already modified by those conditions that produce a high death rate; for hunger, disease, and even more subtle conditions can have their effects between conception and birth. The whole period from conception to weaning has always suffered a steady thinning out. The usual measurement, taken midway in this period, has been of limited relevance at best.

purposes; and I suppose that more spectacular changes can be construed as variations on what was happening all the time.

Differences in the growth of population seem to depend, in 'nature', on the incidence of pre-natal and infant mortality (differences in actual fertility probably play at most a marginal role), of normal early mortality among adults, and of abnormal mortality in times of calamity (in all regions, in the Agrarian Age, calamities drastically depopulated local areas from time to time); and secondarily, population varies with the incidence of what may be called 'social' control measures—the number of women withheld from sexual relations, and the frequency of contraception, abortion, and infanticide. It seems that when the 'natural' limits on population growth would allow population to increase beyond local social expectations, as a result of general good health or good fortune, then in reasonably stable societies 'social' means have been called on: delayed marriage or birth limitation. But in the Arid Zone, by and large, the latter means were frowned on; and moral policy, at least in the monotheistic traditions, aimed at maximizing births. We may presume, then, that the 'natural' limitations on population were usually sufficient—whether because long-established social exploitation had accustomed most of the population to relatively low levels of health and consequent high death rates, or because regional vicissitudes produced unusually abundant occasions of calamity. (Needless to say, the sparsity of means of subsistence, the aridity as such, is not at issue here: for every level of natural resources, however sparse, there is an appropriate level of population, which may be exceeded or may not be reached.)[9]

Despite the lack of any serious studies on pre-Modern demography in Islamdom (and there are very few even for other regions), I think I can discern two sorts of population shift in the pre-Modern Arid Zone. Whatever role an abundance of calamities played in preventing excessive population, a differential rate of death by calamities probably played a major role in the redistribution of population within the region. It was especially three major scourges that served to supplement normal mortality with special calamities: warfare, pestilence, and famine. But these scourges affected different areas differently. In almost any agrarian-based citied society, the population could be divided into three sectors: that of the cities, that of the citied countryside, and that of the remoter countryside; and on balance, these scourges hit the three sectors with decreasing force. This produced an area gradient in the population.

[9] Marcel R. Reinhard and André Armengaud, *Histoire générale de la population mondiale* (Paris, 1961), indicate by their omissions the fact that we have very little useful demographic theoretical apparatus for pre-Modern times. The work is sober and careful, yet on pre-Modern materials it is not only scanty but often naïve. Despite the title, its non-Western sections are not only marred by unperceptive uses of statistics, but so slight that they do not even provide the minimum context to introduce perspective into a work on the history just of Western population—which, incidentally, would have been a more honest title.

On the other hand, it was not so much a difference of exposure to calamities as a difference of exposure to normal mortality that differentiated between social classes. The more privileged the class, the better nourished; the lower, on the whole, its infant and adult female mortality; and hence (so long as social expectations called for the maximum number of births) the more numerous its surviving offspring. This produced a class gradient in the population. It was likely, therefore, that descendants of famous ruling families or conquering tribes, as well as of priestly or other learnèd families, would be disproportionately numerous not only among the privileged elements but in the population as a whole. Hence a conquest and military settlement, for instance, would result in some ethnic change beyond the actual numbers of migrants. However, the change was much less than might be supposed if one gave credence to all the claims of later figures to descend (in the male line) from early Arab settlers (especially from Ḥasan or Ḥusayn) or Sâsânian nobles or Turkic heroes.

Accordingly, there were two currents of population shift: in space, from the remoter countryside to the cities; and in class level, from the upper levels of society to the lower. Both had ethnic implications, which sometimes complemented and sometimes conflicted with each other.

Here we must spell out the population shift in space, the area gradient, for it had, perhaps, the most complex consequences. The urban population suffered most drastically from the three scourges; repeatedly, the cities were decimated. Warfare hit the cities most severely. Up to a point, indeed, the city walls protected people from minor banditries or even armed excursions, which ravaged the nearby countryside and sent the peasants into hiding. But when conquest did occur, which was often enough, the walls might form a prison, preventing people from escaping the fire and massacre that followed on a city's occupation. Pestilence likewise found its most ready victims in the massed population of the towns. Only famine was relatively mitigated in the towns, where such supplies as were stocked up tended to be kept, and to which imported supplies were first brought. In the long run (for these and probably other reasons as well), the cities appear not to have maintained their own numbers by reproduction among the city folk alone.

The scourges of warfare and pestilence were only less important in the countryside in the vicinity of towns. The effect of contagious disease was doubtless moderated there, but though the directly murderous effects of warfare were usually less intensive, invading troops destroyed crops and commandeered animals, further reducing the reserves with which the peasants could fight off famine. It was in the countryside that famine had its most immediate consequences when there was crop failure; for any surplus that the peasants could produce was normally drained off to the towns as revenue and the town population had first call on it. Only a highly developed bureaucratic government could maintain the granary reserves that would prevent starvation. The rural population, then, might not multiply to the point of using all the available land resources, and agriculture by and large, except in the immediate vicinity of cities, remained extensive rather than intensive. Nevertheless, the peasants usually more than reproduced themselves (just possibly—we do not really know—most peasants had a more balanced diet than the city poor). There was frequently a tendency, in any case, for the decimated city population to be recruited from the excess numbers of the countryside.

But it was in the remoter countryside that the three scourges were at a minimum. In the mountains relatively inaccessible to the city tax or rent collectors, in the steppe and desert where pastoralists were steadily on the move and could not be controlled, there was chronic petty warfare, but rarely the mass massacres which took place in more settled areas; and pestilence, I gather, was relatively less severe. Such privileged elements as existed there commonly lacked the multiple and specialized tastes which were served by the variegated city life, and so had fewer persons to support from the (doubtless smaller) surplus; and in any case, they were intimately involved with the ordinary people and could feel a personal responsibility for them in case of famine. In one way or another, mass mortality must have been less frequent, except where local resources were pressed to the limit. Though a shortage of men or of beasts could limit production for a time below its ecological limits, I gather that in the long run the Malthusian situation was more often approximated there than elsewhere, encouraging emigration.[10]

Comparatively, there was likely to be more space for additional producers in the citied countryside, where famine could strike long before the land was being fully used; and the land near the cities, likely to return more yield for a given amount of labour, could seem more attractive at the occasional moments when revenue collection was relaxed there. That mountaineers were hardier and nomads more mobile, not tied to defending a fixed investment in homestead and field, accentuated a tendency to migrate by giving the intruders an initial power advantage in any struggle that ensued. (Indeed, one of the commonest ways in which remoter populations entered citied society was as soldiers.) In parts of the globe where agricultural populations were dense and well organized and the areas relatively free of city dominance were rare, penetration from the remoter areas might be minimal or even reversed. In the Arid Zone, where the 'remote' areas were nearby in the hinterland of every denser agricultural area, population movement from them became quite important. Consequently, while the more adventurous or more desperate of the peasants near cities went into the cities to make up the steady losses there, the peasantry of the countryside itself was steadily recruited from the remoter areas.

[10] Sometimes one hears that mountain lands were 'too poor to support their population', which therefore had to emigrate. This, of course, is not the point. Rich or poor, if the population were not killed off or limited some way or other, it must infallibly become too numerous for the resources of any area.

This population area gradient normally had limited consequences in changing the cultural and ethnic composition of the population as a whole. The newcomers into the citied countryside were few enough at any given time to be assimilated into its cultural patterns and skills and its language. The same was necessarily true of migration from countryside to city. To some degree, there could be a tendency in the Arid Zone for those elements that had been represented in the remoter areas to become genetically predominant. This tendency would be reinforced to the extent that the newcomers tended to take over positions of authority and wealth by the impetus of their sometimes violent advent; for then it would benefit by the population current from better-fed upper-class levels to lower-class levels—especially where the wealthier males were in a position to take several mates and to control the cultural allegiance of their offspring. But such genetic effects need not, in themselves, have cultural consequences. (We must note that, presumably, genetic endowments do differ in culturally relevant ways from group to group, but that since at present we are ignorant of what these variations are, we cannot usefully refer to them in historical analysis.)

But at times the area gradient became steep—settled populations being badly thinned out and, simultaneously, the new groups being too dense to be quickly assimilated. Then visible ethnic change occurred. Thus during the Middle Islamic Periods the peasantry of the Syr-Oxus basin, of Azerbaijan, and of the Anatolian highlands came to be Turkic-speaking rather than Persian and Greek, as formerly. The settled pastoralists gained a relative preponderance, at least at key points, and the remaining Persian- and Greek-speaking elements there were gradually assimilated to the Turkic-speakers (presumably by way of bilingualism) rather than the other way round. Once bilingualism became common, which of the two languages would triumph would depend less on the proportion of the whole population preferring one language or the other than on the proportions at key points such as markets or town governments. Here again, the tendency for the upper classes to more than reproduce themselves would have consequences. Thus it was possible for the language of a minority to prevail, if the minority were dense enough and well enough situated.

Such a change in language necessarily carried with it shifts in folklore and in cultural traditions generally, for expectations fostered in the dominant folk tradition would have more prestige. It could perhaps make for a change or even occasionally a loss in craft skills. More certainly (in the case of pastoralists), it could make for an accentuation of tribal connections even among the peasantry and hence for a relative independence and willingness to revert to pastoralism under bad agrarian conditions. (If the new ethnic configuration reached the towns, in turn, it could produce an even sharper break in cultural continuity by putting in question the older high-cultural allegiance.)

In the Arid Zone, the population area gradient always tended to be somewhat steep. The very presence of large and relatively uncitied tracts of mountain fastness and pastoral steppe made the population movement from these areas to the citied areas always at least noticeable. Since population in the citied areas commonly was kept below the level at which all agricultural resources were fully used, there was always free space for new groups to settle in. Even when whole large areas did not adopt a new ethnic affiliation, yet several villages could form an ethnic enclave. The region from Nile to Oxus came to be dotted with groups of different ethnic backgrounds, stemming from various mountain or steppe origins, which were only gradually assimilated.

The converse of this was the extension of common lingua francas over vast areas of citied countryside. These reflected the constant tendency for the populations to be interchanged and mingle: thus over most of the vast zone from Egypt to the headwaters of the Oxus but two languages prevailed, Arabic and Persian, varied only in a minor way by dialects; and while Turkic was replacing Persian in the north, Arabic was replacing Berber tongues farther west throughout the Maghrib. Except where the population gradient was unusually steep, the language which ultimately became common to an area was that which was established in the towns, for this was the second language any active villagers had to know in addition to their own varying dialects; and hence was the common language when villagers of different backgrounds settled side by side. It was against a background of spreading linguistic uniformity that the many pockets of linguistic variety held out for a time—till they succumbed to the attractions of a more cosmopolitan medium (and were replaced by new linguistic pockets in turn).

B. THE A'YÂN-AMÎR SYSTEM

We are now to see more concretely how the a'yân-amîr system of social power developed and operated, first in the countryside and then in the cities. I hope that this description of the society in operation will make more plausible my analysis of the role, in its formation, of city-bred attitudes and a cosmopolitan outlook, traceable to the peculiar situation of the core lands in the mid-Arid Zone. We begin with the land. The foundation of any society on the agrarianate level was, of course, the agrarian relations holding on the land. It was the conditions of village life that made possible the combination in Islamdom of a free peasantry and military landholders, and that also determined, largely, what the consequences of such a combination should be.

The villages

Between Nile and Oxus, as almost everywhere in the Agrarian Age, the bulk of the population, even in the remoter mountains, lived in villages. A village might be large, embracing some thousands, all of whom either worked directly on the lands round about or lived from services directly rendered to the cultivators; or it might be small, only a handful of families in a spot where water was sufficient for a minimal area of cultivation. An individual cultivator with his family, isolated from others in the midst of his own lands, was not normally a viable unit, if only because the family could not defend its crops against even the slightest band of robbers. Moreover, some sort of continuing relations were necessary with a larger group, to provide an essential division of labour for such artisan work as was needed on the spot. Construction, tool repair, flour milling (not usually done at home between Nile and Oxus), even such amenities as bath-house bathing and the varied work of a 'barber', which included some surgery, required specialists. A village was also likely to have religious experts—either a Shar'î faqîh (who might teach school) or a Ṣûfî devotee or both. Each village was likely to have its own more prosperous families, who also exercised political leadership; in the fortunate village (free of absentee landownership) these might be the chief local landlords or moneylenders also.

The villagers might co-operate in such undertakings as clearing irrigation channels, or even in helping the disadvantaged among them get in the harvest. Many villages ordered their internal affairs through a village headman, generally named for life from one or two leading families and accepted by the consent of the more prosperous and influential men. He might be paid with a proportion of the crop of each cultivator, taken out at the time of harvest. (In some villages, other specialists, such as a barber or carpenter, might be prepaid in the same way.)

The villages were brought together in some sort of market: normally, this was in a nearby small town. (This was not a necessary pattern, but presupposed a rather developed market economy. In the Maghrib, for instance, travelling markets moved from open spot to open spot instead.) The town served in three ways. Such artisan work was done there as was more economically provided centrally than separately in each village. It also served as a place to exchange extra village produce for more exotic goods brought from a distance. Villagers commonly made use of several metal implements, of mood drugs, of sweets and trinkets, of medicines and charms, and even of some cloth for clothes and blankets that was not woven at home. (However, some of these things might be carried to the village by itinerant peddlers.) Finally, it was in the towns that the villager sold his surplus for cash when the revenue was being collected in that form. The towns, in turn, found a larger focus of trade in larger towns among them, which may be called the cities, and were generally the points where the court of the governor or of the amîr resided. The city craftsmen produced luxury goods which rarely reached so far as the villages. Towns and cities together made up only a minority of the total population, which was necessarily chiefly rural so long as the economy depended primarily on agricultural production.

Even within the villages, some men were decisively wealthier than others. In some villages—especially if controlled by a single landlord—a rough equality among the villagers themselves might be maintained by a periodic redistribution of land (so as to equalize any unevenness in fortune at one distribution by a new chance at the next); such land was held only on sufferance from the village or its landlord. But more usually, individual enterprise was allowed to have its way in holding land. Some acquired more land than they could cultivate personally, and rented it out to the less fortunate; correspondingly, many villagers rented in part or in whole from others.

Such differences in circumstance could become severe. Those who were better off acquired not only land, but funds of credit, in the form of money, which they rented out at high interest when a cultivator needed emergency advances (for instance, for seed, or to meet his rent or a tax levy). Once a man had to resort to such an advance, it was hard to pay it off, for the interest accumulated. Generations, barring fortunate rises, might find themselves the hereditary debtors of moneylenders. Many men ended up without any land at all, even rented, and did day labour for those who did have land. But, especially in areas where intervention by outside landlords was minimized, a large proportion of villagers, though not wealthy, were neither day labourers nor tenants, but owned at least part of the land they needed to support themselves.

Such villages were relatively openly structured, with status rather directly dependent on property acquired or maintained through the play of the market. In them affairs were controlled by the village notables (a'yân); and sometimes a landlord—often a military man—acted as final arbiter in case of disputes, if the disputes were not settled first by negotiation or outright fighting among blocs of villagers associated by ties of patronage with opposed notables. This was the a'yân-amîr system in miniature, which we will find writ large in the cities.

Revenue resources of the rich

The a'yân-amîr system of social authority, with the various arrangements made under it for appropriating the agrarian revenues, was, in principle, included in Max Weber's great analysis of forms of authority.[11] It might seem that I should use the categories that he developed—analyze the authority appealed to as approximating generally to the ideal-type 'tradition-based' (to use a less potentially confusing term than his simple 'traditional'; for authority *based* on tradition, on custom, may not be actually *traditional* at certain moments, when—for instance—it has become *traditional* to base authority rather on bureaucratic law); and analyzing the appropriation of agrarian revenues, in particular, in terms of 'patrimonial' authority and of 'sultanism'. Unfortunately, I cannot use his terms, first because his categories

[11] Max Weber, *The Theory of Social and Economic Organization*, ed. Talcott Parsons (Oxford University Press, 1947) is a partial translation from *Wirtschaft und Gesellschaft*, which itself was unfinished at the author's death in 1920.

do not fit well with what actually went on in Islamdom; but more fundamentally, because his basic schema for dealing with pre-Modern conditions is systematically faulty. (I have pointed out a far-reaching problem related to this in the Introduction in volume I, under 'On determinacy in traditions' in the section on historical method. Here, I refer to a more immediate problem.)

In all pre-Modern social orders, traditional custom and improvisation, its complement on the level of day-to-day decision, played a larger role than in the Modern social order; and the combination is quite noticeable in the Middle Periods in Islamdom in contrast to the more bureaucratic periods before and after. But (as I hope to show in Book Six) it is misleading to see reliance on traditional custom as the specific differentiating feature of agrarianate social arrangements (as well as of all still less complex ones) in contrast to Modern technical society. On every level of social complexity, legitimation is less tradition-based and more based in calculative rational-legal processes than it is on levels less complex. Legitimation in Modern technical society is less tradition-based than legitimation in society on the agrarianate level; but the post-Axial Period agrarianate social orders were in turn less tradition-based than the earlier agrarianate social orders; which in turn were less tradition-based than were pre-literate and pre-agricultural society. (Indeed, at every major cultural florescence there is an increase, at least temporarily and generally residually also, of reliance on calculative rationality rather than on traditional custom.) Hence in comparison with Modern technical society, any earlier societies may be called relatively tradition-based; but in comparison with earlier pre-Modern societies, the societies of the post-Axial Period, and especially the Islamicate society, may equally well be said to be based in rational-legal authority. And this is still true even of Islamdom in the Middle Periods, when sometimes a minimal level of institutional complexity can seem to be being approximated—which, if reached, would entail a maximal degree of reliance on traditionality (within limits imposed by the agrarianate social level). The feature that differentiates the agrarianate level of social order is neither that it was tradition-based (as compared with Modern technical society) nor that it was rational-legally based (as compared with pre-citied society), but that it was based, directly or indirectly, on citied exploitation of agrarian manual production.

Using the notion of traditionality as a point of departure, Weber constructed an 'ideal type' applying to virtually all pre-Modern society, in which the effects of immemorial custom and of personal improvisation were pointed up. In Islamdom, the patterns of assessing and levying agrarian revenues were often, on the local level, determined by custom felt to be immemorial (or by custom assimilable to such a standard, at any rate); hence in local detail they often answered fairly well to Weber's criteria. (It is in part for this reason that modern writers, finding remnants of pre-Modern ways chiefly on the local level, have tended to assimilate all agrarianate society to the 'tradition-based' type.) In certain other aspects of the a'yân-amîr system, also, custom and improvisation played a major role. But differences in these elements are not so determinative in setting off that system from its competitors in the world of that time as, for instance, differences in the role of the market and of personal freedom in regard to it. These latter differences come out more clearly, I think, if we start with the ways in which revenues from the cultivators reached the other classes.

Intervention in the villages by outside (and usually absentee) landlords was in fact very widespread. Sometimes the landlords were pastoralist chieftains; normally they were city men. For the cities were not primarily service centres for the villages. The towns and especially the cities derived their sustenance only in part from the artisan and trading services they rendered the village population by whom they were fed, and only in part from long-distance commerce. To a crucial degree, they lived on unreciprocated revenues levied from the countryside. The city populations were in large measure dependent, directly as servants or associates, or indirectly as caterers, on the privileged families to whom the revenues were allotted. Through these families passed most of the wealth of the society, whether their wealth came by way of taxes and was then distributed to them as courtiers by those in command, or whether it came by way of rents directly to landowners residing in the city (or to waqf endowments).

The gap in wealth and in standing between the ordinary villager and the privileged man in the city was severe; even the great families of the villages were likely to count for little in the cities unless they had special connections there. This gap was decisive: the manner in which the agrarian revenues were extracted from the villages and distributed in the cities determined the local social structure in each region and period. Hence the levying of revenue must be understood as a special process, to be abstracted from the mass of economic facts, for analytic purposes; and not to be confused with personal or social arrangements for the use of property within the village, though sometimes it was entwined with them.[12]

The process of collecting the revenues was regarded in the Sharî'ah law as falling under two heads. The law recognized landownership by individuals, on any scale or at almost any remove from actual land use, and saw arrangements between owner and renter as a question of contract, which was presumed to be between equals and was regulated in only secondary ways.

[12] Throughout this chapter, and in several subsequent ones, I have made much use of Ann Lambton's *Landlord and Peasant in Persia* (Oxford University Press, 1953); but I have not accepted two of her viewpoints in particular. I have not found it useful to suppose an 'original' condition of village organization (presumably established, in Iran, at the occupation by Iranian tribesmen); for in historical reality no cultural tradition begins from scratch, without considerable disequilibrium and diversity resulting from what had preceded. Nor have I been satisfied to regard the deterioration of the peasant's economic life—to the extent that it has happened—as the result simply of mismanagement. To a degree, mismanagement always occurs; but it is crucial to find what circumstances gave it more opportunities at one time than at another.

At the same time, it recognized that those who owned productive land owed dues to the common fisc of the Muslim Ummah, represented by the amîr; dues which were to be used for administrative purposes such as relief of the poor, defence of the community, support of religious scholarship, erection of public buildings, and police. Such a view of the revenue was forced. At best it answered to the ways in which a tradesman might be associated with the process. In fact, of course, the amounts collected in taxes were not restricted to the levels authorized by the Sharî'ah, nor did the whole relation between the classes conform to Shar'î norms. The Sharî'ah, that is, recognized some of the various individual relationships involved, seeing them from the viewpoint of contract where possible; but it did not face, as a whole (as for instance Mazdean doctrine, with its notion of social classes, had done), the overall process of shifting the rural surplus to the towns—the agrarian relationship as such.

Conventional Muslim religious thought went little further. It encouraged generosity by those in a privileged position, and stressed the equality of all men before God; but it could no more envisage a challenge to the overall agrarian situation than it could envisage a direct legitimation of it. Some of the more pious Ṣûfîs, however, did refuse to touch funds coming from an amîr, on the ground that they represented illicit gains.

The administrative tradition of the absolutism and of the ruling classes who succeeded thereto recognized the revenue process frankly and directly. Manuals for the privileged classes took it for granted that such classes were to be supported by the peasantry (*ra'iyyah*)—a conception which referred especially to the actual cultivators, but included all villagers indiscriminately in its sweep, unless perhaps men of religion; and sometimes even extended to the lower classes in the towns and cities. The privileged were even inclined to assert that the peasantry were obligated as a class to maintain production on their lands so as to provide for the revenues (especially the revenues for the fisc). They tended to think of the fisc, then, as being at the personal disposal of the amîr (as residually representative of absolute monarchy), or at most as intended primarily for the upkeep of his army and its officers. Correspondingly, they did not always distinguish sharply between levies on the basis of a peasant's personal contract with one of the privileged class as a landowner (rents), and levies on the basis of fiscal authority (taxes). Hence, for instance, it was often hard for legists, or central administrators either, to win practical recognition for the difference between an iqṭâ' assignment of actual landownership and an iqṭâ' assignment of the revenues which were due to the fisc. The recipients tended to behave alike in both cases.

The whole process of raising revenue was justified in these circles with greater or lesser reference to rationally acceptable norms. One justification for taking the revenue was economic in form: one portion of the crop was for him who provided the seed, one for him who provided the oxen, one for him who provided the water (that is, arranged for irrigation), one for him who provided the land (on the assumption that landownership was as much a contribution as the rest), and finally one for him who provided the labour; and since all but the labour required funds to provide, the man who had capital proved to have good reasons for taking most of the crop. On the other hand, a peasant who could save a little did have grounds for hope. But such a formula was rather theory than either law or even practice.

Apart from any such formula, men found more general justifications. It was understood that the privileged classes were to serve society as a whole, implicitly including the peasantry, as soldiers who would assure security to the villagers from marauders or invaders, and as administrators of justice; and in addition as patrons of religion. (These were the minimal functions that even the absolutism had been satisfied to fill.) But it was also clearly stated, often enough, that in any case the peasantry had no need of anything more than their subsistence; that they were crude, ignorant beings, scarcely more than brute animals, and were created to serve their betters.

This last was, indeed, a traditional attitude, having been transmitted for millennia; but it implied justification by right of the stronger more than by customary obligation, and carried with it little sense of custom-based restrictions on the stronger. In such circles, the inclination was often simply to find out what the cultivator could spare (of this, custom might be an index) and take that for the military class as a whole or for some member of it, without regard to considerations of ownership or of fixed rates of taxation. The faster the turnover in iqṭâʿ assignees, I would suppose, the likelier such an attitude. Against it, the peasants appealed, so far as they could, to limitations that might be justified as local custom.

Neither the attitude that the revenues were due only for services rendered nor the attitude that the stronger should take all was fully realized in practice. Respect for the Sharîʿah, on the part of the actual administrators who kept records, in itself helped ensure that the forms of contracts and of authorized taxation were always maintained, even if the substance was often evaded by the powerful. But there were further reasons for levying the revenues with a careful regard to individual obligations and legal niceties, such as the ruling military classes might have liked to disregard. In fact, despite the aristocratic theory of some manuals, and despite the enormous actual gap between extremes of revenue payers and revenue receivers, there was no sharp line at any one point setting off one class from another. Even within the villages there were men who could be regarded as relatively privileged, and who had higher connections; hence the process of raising the revenue for the cities could not be entirely disengaged from the distribution of wealth within the villages themselves. And both in the villages and in the towns and cities, many different sorts of people had an interest in how the revenues were to be levied; different persons stood to gain if different sorts of dues were imposed. These people could not be disregarded.

Where free contract alone, and not implicit status, was recognized at law, and where the conscience of the ruler was enlisted on the side of the law, all such interests had a chance to be expressed. In recurrent anecdotes, a poor peasant woman's rights were vindicated by the amîr against some usurping grandee; and sometimes this happened in actuality. Hence the revenues were levied, if by no means in accordance with Shar'î rules, yet according to stated decrees and formal contracts, as well as according to what the peasants claimed as custom for whoever undertook to work a given plot; with a careful eye to all the legal disputes that could arise if anyone took more than his share. This care for balancing multiple interests under sanction of freely assumed obligations was characteristic of the a'yân-amîr system.

Assessing the revenues

The actual form of levying the revenues, then, when once a central bureaucratic control broke down, varied in almost all the ways that might be conceived under agrarianate conditions, according to local political and economic circumstances. If circumstances changed, the forms of levying revenue did likewise. We may list five principal ways in which the levies might vary, each way of varying being more or less independent of the others. The revenues that came from the village to the privileged classes in the cities could come either to given individual members of the privileged classes—to rich merchants who held land or to 'ulamâ' or especially to soldiers—or they could come to the ruler's treasury (by way either of a salaried tax collector or a tax farmer on commission), and be distributed from there in salaries or grants (again largely to soldiers or sometimes to 'ulamâ'—or even to such hangers-on as poets). Variation on this score was essentially independent of a second variable: whether the revenues would be levied as rent (or other fee) on the basis of personal contract or as taxes on the basis of the authority of the ruler's fisc; though a strong ruler might prefer to make at least the soldiers dependent directly on the fisc. The individual who received revenue from the cultivator, either as taxes or as rent, might or might not have to send on a portion to the fisc, according to any special privileges he had been granted; though again a strong ruler might prefer to see the share of the fisc pass entirely through the fisc without any exemptions. Thirdly—whether on the basis of personal contract or on the basis of fiscal authority—revenue might be levied on the crops according to a prior fixed assessment, or according to a proportion of the yield (sharecropping). (Revenue was also raised to some extent by way of minor dues of innumerable sorts.) Fourthly, it might be paid in cash or in kind—or even in labour time; some peasants were required by the fisc, or by their rent contracts to contribute a certain number of days' labour to purposes often specified in advance.

A fifth major point of variation was that the man who received the revenue could have diverse rights over the source of his revenue. (This was relevant, of course, only where the revenue was coming direct to individuals

—chiefly when dues were paid under fiscal authority, though local customs and even long-term contracts as for leases might affect those who received dues by personal arrangements also, especially where the landlord was a tribal chieftain.) The recipient might be limited to simply receiving the money. He might have full authority over the use of the land—such that he could rotate shares in the land among the cultivators from year to year, acting locally as the owner. (Indeed sometimes the landlord, or rather—usually—his hired representative, undertook extensive land management and invested some of his revenue as capital for such improvements as irrigation works. Such things might also be done, of course, by large landowners local to the village.) His rights might or might not be hereditary, in the legal sense; and if not, they might, or might not, be transmissible to a son. Finally, he might have various administrative rights over the area in which his revenue was raised; and these rights might sometimes extend over a wide district, especially if his right to revenue was by fiscal authority over such a district, and so included the share that the fisc claimed in the revenue of lesser landlords. In theory, of course, administrative rights were not to be confused with rights to revenue, but it was sometimes convenient, or unavoidable, to leave them in the same hands.

There has been much discussion, on the basis of European notions of land revenue, which were built up in a society where personal status was much less fluid and legal rights much more readily schematized according to fixed status, about 'ownership' of the land in Islamdom: at what point should a given grandee be regarded as 'owning' a given territory, or should the ruler alone be regarded as 'owner', because he could so readily alter the rights which other grandees had in the land revenue? The difficulty has been that so often the revenue went directly to a given individual, but it was levied as taxes on the authority of the fisc—and such a recipient of the revenue had now one, now another set of rights over what happened on the land from which the revenue came. Such a situation cannot be handled properly in terms of the category of ownership, either Western or Shar'î. But there is no need to raise the question at all. Ownership, in the ordinary sense, was relevant enough at the level of the individual village, within which it was clear who could sell or rent rights to use land; but it was commonly an inappropriate category for describing overall revenue relations between the peasantry and the rulers.

The better sort of revenue-taker did limit himself to exactions traditional in his lands (and commonly made explicit when a new party arrived), and remitted part or all during times of hardship. But even traditional exactions left little to the peasant. And too many revenue-takers were quite unscrupulous. In a society in which status was not enduringly fixed, and each individual was expected to rise as high as his wits could carry him, the limits on ways of raising the revenue imposed by local custom were always in danger of being set aside. All sorts of trickeries and special exactions were used to extract a maximum revenue from the peasant, whether by local landlords, iqṭâʿ assignees, or tax collectors. Especially absentee landlords—whether receiving by contract or by fiscal authority—felt themselves little bound by such custom. Even when the custom was adhered to in the main, it might be violated in detail: thus a landowner might force a needy cultivator, contrary to custom, to sell the landlord his (the cultivator's) share of the crop at a low price, by threatening not to advance seed or other things the cultivator would need later. Such hard bargaining could be expected where so much depended on free contract.

Occasionally a pious ruler would decree the abolition of the more vexatious of the fiscal exactions, those most manifestly contrary to the Sharîʿah. But such exactions were commonly reimposed soon enough, if the abolition was taken seriously at all, by local decree or even by arbitrary action on the part of those in a position to exact them. Despite the Sharîʿah, many rulers did their best to constrain cultivation of the lands in their domain; and it was these same rulers who were most ruthless in inventing pretexts for seizing a maximum revenue, without always considering whether the peasant could survive on what was left. Such extreme behaviour was, of course, soon self-defeating; but the ruling elements regarded it as within the rights of whoever had enough power, even if not as wise or strictly legal.

But to a considerable degree local custom, allowing one arrangement but disallowing another, was able to maintain a viable balance between the claims of those who exacted revenue and the needs of the cultivators who produced it. At the same time, the policy of the amîrs' fiscal directors, who tended to keep in mind relatively long-term considerations, made for a certain continuity in overall development. Consequently, all possible forms of revenue-raising did not occur indiscriminately. Certain broad patterns can be traced in the raising of the revenue from one century to the next: patterns which, in the course of the Middle Periods, amounted to an increasing militarization of the process.

It was especially in villages near the cities, or along routes of travel, that wealthy city-dwellers were likely to be absentee owners or otherwise control the revenue. It was the revenues of such villages that were also most commonly regarded as at the disposal of the government—that is, in the last recourse, of the amîr and his troops. They were subject to arbitrary commandeering of supplies by an amîr and more especially by a great sultan who controlled garrisons at many cities, whenever he passed nearby with troops. It was accordingly such villages also that were likely to be assigned, on a more permanent basis, to individual military chiefs and their officers as iqṭâʿ, government assignments, from which the soldiers were supposed to be paid directly out of the resources of the villages, by fiscal right. In the course of such a development, the rights of the urban rent-recipients, from whom the iqṭâʿ holder took taxes as well as from any landholding peasants, were likely to be eroded. Gradually the important revenue-recipient became the iqṭâʿ recipient. The independence both of the civilian upper classes and of the local peasantry tended to suffer in consequence.

The iqṭâʿ system had originated (as we have seen) under the caliphs as a special bureaucratic device, when governors were allowed to make use of the revenues of state lands within their provinces, or tax farmers were made use of who paid in advance an agreed-on sum which they tried to more than recoup in collecting the taxes with a hired professional team. In both cases what was technically still direct payment to the fisc or a branch of it took on a form in which a powerful individual was in a position to turn fiscal rights to his own use. The system had been turned increasingly in a military direction after the breakup of the caliphal state, when the failure of the bureaucracy made more centralized collection of revenues less satisfactory; as the Middle Periods drew on, it went further even than the bounds Niẓâmulmulk tried to set to it: it became a common method of rewarding soldiers with property which, though revocable, yet might be passed on to a son; such a reward might be unconnected with any more central policy. If the bureaucracy still functioned well, it managed the tax collecting even when the revenue of a given spot was assigned in advance. But often the officer who held the iqṭâʿ was allowed to collect the taxes in person and could readily take whatever he found accessible, on the plea that he should have received a better-paying assignment but must make do with what he could find. Side by side with such assignments, the amîr continued to levy taxes directly into the fisc from unassigned areas.

If a particular government was relatively well established and the economy relatively productive, the taxes could be taken in the form of a rate on land resources (often partly in kind, for local convenience of logistics, but mostly in cash); under the iqṭâʿ system, this would mean that the iqṭâʿs were closely controlled by the bureaucracy. At the same time, iqṭâʿs would be changed frequently, either at the initiative of the bureaucracy or of a discontented officer, and would be in no sense heritable.

When the powers were relatively poorly organized, the taxes were simply a share of the actual produce—either in kind or in market value. The latter system produced a certain rough fairness, but made for fiscal unpredictability and seriously reduced the flexibility of the cultivators' or the local landlords' planning; it greatly reduced the value of any added increment of investment by the peasant, much of the yield of which would be carried off. But the system of shares was the more normal accompaniment of the iqṭâʿ system, and it was naturally the most common system in the Later Middle Period. The proportion was set, of course, at much more than the ten per cent laid down (more or less) by the Sharîʿah on Muslim land. As the control of the bureaucracy weakened, it became more possible, or perhaps more inevitable (in the view of an officer who did not like his assignment), that particular assignments be made indefinitely or for life; they might then be transmitted to an heir—not as divisible heritable property, but in the sense that people would expect a son or other relative to succeed to the officer's post and to his perquisites. But the assignment would remain revocable according to the fortunes of the officer's partisans at court, or even to the fortunes of the amîr's dynasty.

A tax system based on shares, such as accordingly tended to prevail, together with the assignment of iqṭâʿ lands to soldiers who could not know how long they would retain them, and hence mined them for whatever could be obtained from them quickly, would prevent much surplus from being built up in the villages themselves. In years of good production, this meant a certain opulence in the cities; in bad years, it meant famine in the villages. It also could mean reducing the variation in personal circumstances within the village, and the power of its aʿyân notables to make arrangements without regard to outsiders. This fact went to confirm the military power—and to undermine the counterweights to it—even in the cities—implied in the aʿyân-amîr system.

Refuges of the poor

Thus in one way or another, though increasingly at the expense of rural prosperity and civilian independence, the privileged classes extracted their revenue. But for the peasants, the problem was how to escape disaster from increasingly arbitrary exactions. When the agricultural economy had been expanding, new lands being opened up and greater irrigation projects resulting in more intensive production on the lusher lands, as had in the long run been the case in earlier millennia (and as continued to be the case in the better-watered regions, Europe, the Indias, and China), one escape from such an impasse was onto new lands, often protected by strong governments from the worst sorts of exploitation. In the mid-Arid Zone, the range of agriculture was no longer expanding, but (on the whole) contracting. The refuges of the poor were correspondingly less adequate in a long-term sense. In the immediate circumstances, however, the villagers had viable means of partially defending themselves.

First, the villagers regularly used means of direct resistance. Peasants had immemorial methods of concealing their produce from the tax collector, and sometimes prided themselves on being able to hold fast to their stories of misfortune and destitution even under torture. From time to time, when some inordinate oppression or some plausible prophecy led to despair or to a wild hope, peasants launched outright revolts—usually drowned in blood, but a warning to other landholders. There were also more indirect means of escaping the revenue collector. Many villages in remoter spots, often inherently less rich, but away from the immediate reach of large city garrisons or off the highroads followed by armies, managed to retain much of their produce at home, however inequitably it might be distributed there. Some favourably placed villages, in fact, were able to put up fortifications such that their storming, though quite feasible, would not be worth an army's while, considering the small returns the village would yield. In villages readily subject to over-taxation, in the period when bureaucratic control broke down, many smaller peasants commended their land to a wealthier local landholder, retaining practical control of it for a limited rental; the larger landholders often could resist importunate demands effectively.

Moreover, as we have seen, the last resource of the peasant—flight—was relatively easy. Though the total agricultural economy was no longer expanding, in the Arid Zone marginal land went relatively easily in and out of cultivation. Even if population became considerable, such land offered leeway. Either landless labourers or renters or even peasants who owned their own land might see fit to abandon the native village and go where land might be offered—or otherwise become accessible—on better terms. Especially with the high development of independent pastoralism, which supplied ever larger numbers to the peasant population by the working of the population area gradient, many peasants had links not too distant with the pastoral life. Sometimes, as we have noted, they could return to it, or could establish working relations with those who were still pastoralists. But more commonly, because of the loss of population to the great scourges, peasants were in short supply even on the better land; then there were other landlords or other amîrs who stood to gain by peasants' moves, or even rivalled each other in bidding for them. In such circumstances, attempts to prevent the moves could be successful only if force could be threatened against the rival amîrs.

Such mobility put a salutary limit on what those in power could exact from the countryside. Attempts to tie the peasants to their land or to bring them back if they fled commonly failed (save in a land like Egypt)—partly for the same reasons of governmental disorganization that made the taxes so often oppressive. On occasion, to be sure, mobility was quite involuntary. A very strong ruler could sometimes forcibly transfer large numbers of peasants (and even townsfolk) from one territory to another which he wanted to develop—commonly on the plea of punishment for rebellion.

Sometimes, however, peasants were forced clear off the land, which could no longer give them a return minimally sufficient for maintaining life. In flight from landlord or creditor or soldiery, the former cultivator could turn to recouping from the wealthy what he could no longer gain on the soil. He could himself turn soldier; there was always a need for soldiers, who were unlikely fully to reproduce themselves; then he could take part in the plunder, and possibly rise to be amîr himself, if he could pass for a Turk or if he belonged to one of the several other peoples which also formed regiments. If he disliked being a soldier, or if more soldiers were being discharged at the moment than hired, there were many channels open for a vagabond. A clever young man could become apprentice to numerous trades which were not so closely organized that one need have good connections to enter them—thus he might join a trade like jugglery or water carrying. Or he might join a robber band or become an outright beggar in the cities, asking for alms from those who had reason to be trying to win God's mercy by passing out pittances.

A surer refuge from the exactions of the powerful, if not from the disasters of nature, lay in the pastoral life, though this was normally not available save to those born to it. Every village had considerable livestock, for various animals—oxen or donkeys or camels or (more rapid) mules or even horses—were essential to ploughing and were used also for transport and for milk and hair; some villages had extensive flocks of sheep and goats herded, sometimes at a distance, by a village herdsman. But a peasant village was, by definition, tied to the tilled land, and its herds came home at least from time to time. The nomadic pastoral community, on the contrary, was organized on the basis of its flocks (of sheep or of camels); and though many of the nomadic pastoralists, especially in mountainous areas, also tilled the land, they could abandon such tilling at need. Hence the pastoralists would not easily be subjected to the levying of more than a token revenue.

Herdsmen organized in tribes and mobile within a reasonably wide range of relatively inaccessible pastures might be punished by a military expedition and prevented from harassing the towns or even the villages, but could not be well controlled in their own pasturelands. Such cultivation of the soil as they indulged in was not sufficiently crucial to them to make them vulnerable. (Hence any punitive measure lasted only so long as the punisher's act of power; in between such acts, the tribes were often in a position to force the nearby villagers, handicapped by immobility, to pay them off; thus the tribes could even take a cut in the cities' loot.) With the increase in herding in the region as a whole, as against farming, the proportion of people free from revenue-paying, among those who had little but what they could wring from their work, might in a sense increase. The freedom of the herdsman, however, was generally a group freedom: the individual was tied inescapably to a rigorous routine which moulded narrowly his thoughts and actions from birth to death. Unfortunately, moreover, his tribal chiefs in some areas might increasingly act like landlords themselves.

The peasant was a free man, and could often enforce his liberty. But that liberty could not guarantee him much advantage unless he had special gifts. The peasants were neither stupid nor heedless of their fate. They prudently respected custom, but were no slaves to it. When we examine closely the responses made by the peasantry to unusual crises or unusual opportunities, we find that the peasants—like other sections of the population—generally behaved resourcefully and shrewdly within the range of the information available to them. For instance, peasants responded with alacrity to changes in the market for agricultural products so far as these actually did affect them. But the peasants rarely found occasion to depart from practices of which they could predict the consequences. In the uncontrolled, open social situation, those persons who could gain a higher vantage point, through a military career or through some other path of advancement, as well as by mere birth, thereby gained a disproportionately large bargaining power, which they too were free to use; and they commonly used it in such a way as to vitiate effort on the part of the less fortunate. Time and again, a peasant's initiative in cultivating crops that required more investment of time and risk but would yield more return was ruined by thoughtlessly heavy demands for immediate revenue by those who could exact it. A military ruling group that could not be sure of their own tenure had little reason not to kill the goose that laid the golden eggs, as they were likely soon to lose the goose anyway.

We will take note later of one result of this social shortsightedness: a chronic and cumulative wastage of natural resources. Another result was a steady miserable wastage of human resources in poverty and insecurity. The misery was probably the greatest precisely where economic development had gone the furthest and hence exploitation could be most systematic. Not only were peasants between Nile and Oxus generally poorer than those, say, in northern Europe, where commercial involvement had long been less extensive; within the Nile-to-Oxus region, differences from area to area could show a like variation. In some cases, at least, in areas where agriculture was richest—that is, most commercialized and most profitable—the peasants themselves were less well-nourished and measurably feebler in body than those in 'poorer' areas with fewer market crops: in particular, such a contrast as that between the strength of the Anatolian backwoods peasants and the weakness of the peasants of the rich Fertile Crescent plains seems to have been a matter of economics more than of racial stock.[13]

The towns: the evolution of their organization

From the land, we now move to consider the social order in the towns. It is here that the peculiar situation of the core lands of the mid-Arid Zone made itself most strongly felt. The commercial advantages the mercantile classes had on which to build a relative cultural autonomy, and at the same time their tendency to a mobile cosmopolitanism rather than local civic solidarity, long made the cities the centres of the communal religious thrust; under the conditions of the Middle Periods, it was in them that the same persisting situation made for open social structuring, individual liberty—and militarization of political power.

Despite the revenue gap, in some ways the towns formed an extension of the social patterns in the villages: chief families in the villages were allied to town families, and the sort of daily relations among families or craft specialists that had grown up in the villages tended to be elaborated in the towns. (Indeed, some town residents were simply peasants, working fields near the town walls.) It is in village life that many of the clan rivalries or notions of propriety and justice of the towns were rooted. We have noted

[13] H. A. R. Gibb and Harold Bowen, in their study of Ottoman society, *Islamic Society and the West*, 3 vols. (New York, 1950–57), bring out several of these points better than do, as yet, any studies of an earlier period.

that the elements of the a'yân-amîr system were to be found in the more prosperous villages. Nevertheless, with an extensive differentiation of economic and social functions among different groups, town life introduced a much higher level of social complexity, and many institutions and problems unknown to the village. It is only in the towns that one can speak of the a'yân-amîr system in any full sense. There it emerged as a dominant social pattern. Despite a moment when a somewhat different pattern appeared possible, a distribution of power between a'yân notables and military amîrs was the steady background in the towns, against which the various attempts at state formation were erected.[14]

The towns offered social resources much more flexible than the countryside—and military rulers, under the iqṭâ' system, did not look for their main income from towns anyway; so that one might have expected to see arise vigorous municipal institutions able to protect the rights of townsmen. But it was impossible for towns to build up, in most cases, enduring bourgeois autonomy against a too-present land-nourished armed force; even though no strictly agrarian classes could countervail the towns, either. The very urbanization of society militated against an autonomy for the towns as such: the ruling element of the land was so closely tied to the towns that the countryside was largely assimilated into the political processes of urban society, so that city and countryside shared a common political fate. In any case, men who could not be tied to any fixed social status, even for an individual lifetime, were hard to bind into effective corporate entities. There was nothing closely corresponding to the European municipality or commune, with its carefully regulated grades of internal status, or to the Indian caste. Yet in their own ways the towns did build means of maintaining social norms and of achieving social goals: of mediating between the individual and a vast impersonal social environment.

The evolution of city life had paralleled the evolution of the caliphal state. In agrarian times, a number of types of city life were possible. The earliest cities between Nile and Oxus centred on a temple with its organized corps of priests, who controlled finances, learning, and all larger organization; any king had to work in conjunction with them, if indeed he were not high priest himself. This was an extreme form; it yielded to more complex patterns long before being in part superseded by the Hellenistic city. Among users of Greek, a body of merchant and landlord citizens (or, in the case of a 'democracy', a larger body including some craftsmen, whose patterns of time-use could in some degree be assimilated to those of merchants) centred less on any temple than on their theatre baths, and other common civic institutions

[14] Claude Cahen has written an important article on city autonomy, 'Mouvements populaires et autonomisme urbain dans l'Asie musulmane du moyen âge', *Arabica*, 5 (1958), 225–50; 6 (1959), 25–56, 233–65. His work has been of basic importance in all this field. Paul Wittek and Vasily Bartold have likewise thrown much light on social questions here and there even in their political studies; all of their work must be studied.

oriented to laymen; the theatre was a symbol of civic spirit rather in the way an American campus football stadium can be the symbol of a university spirit. As in the sacerdotal city, the city people were dependent directly and indirectly on the income from a dependent countryside; in the Nile-to-Oxus region, only landholders, of the country population, had any rights of civic participation in the Hellenistic cities alongside city-dewllers. But at the same time, the Hellenistic cities in that region, unlike the cities of an economically less developed period in the Greek mountains and islands and unlike the earliest priestly cities of the Iraq, had at most a very marginal corporate independence; they were incorporated into territorial kingdoms. What they still had was a strong autonomy; they selected their own officials and planned their own public works.

Under the later Roman empire this type of city too tended to be replaced. The city became the administrative centre of bureaucracies, imperial and ecclesiastical; the seat of a governor and of a bishop. The latter had wide local powers in the administration of justice and the arrangement of civic needs; the former held the crucial power, for now the city was no longer even autonomous, let alone independent; it was managed by appointees from the centre. After the weakening of the Roman empire, towns—throughout the Irano-Mediterranean zone—continued to be bureaucratically administered; but probably more loosely. One gets the impression of governments' allowing (in practice) a wide scope to individual initiative in both caliphal and Byzantine areas (at least in outlying towns, as in Italy). But we may distinguish developments special to Islamdom, where the relaxation of government control is unmistakable.

The sacerdotal city, the merchant-citizen city, the bureaucratic city, were but three notable types; each appeared more than once between Nile and Oxus, according to circumstances. In Marwânî times, at least two types of city had existed. There were those which were still dependent on an outside bureaucracy; in the formerly Roman provinces, the bureaucracy was represented largely by the bishops. Then there were the cities that grew out of the Muslim army camps. These were centred on a mosque, in which was represented the Sharîʿah; they were dedicated (so far as civic spirit went) to the ideals of the Hijrah: as the first Muslims had come forth from Mecca to Medina, Muslims came forth from nomadic wandering, which was of dubious moral standing, to form a single godly ordered civil community and to share in causing the godly order to prevail among mankind. Each town had significance as a body of believers set to its particular task; but it was not independent, nor even called to any autonomous development of its own life, for it was but a particular case of the common life of the whole Islamic brotherhood. The town was arranged internally according to the tribal origin of the inhabitants (or their affiliation, in the case of Mawâlî Muslims) —a matter of convenience rather than of any basic principle. Towns rivalled one another for repute as fulfilling ideals common to all: serving as a centre for the jihâd war, or elucidating the fiqh, or teaching ḥadîth reports; a town's greatest vaunt was the correctness of the qiblah of its chief mosque in being aligned toward Mecca.

The urban policy of the caliphal state as an absolute monarchy naturally had found the administered town most appropriate to its needs; the Piety-minded, on the other hand, took as their springboard the notion of the city as a *dâr al-hijrah*, a place to which Muslims came to put in practice the Islamic life. The two views of a city coalesced as uneasily as the corresponding two views of the caliphal state. With the dissolution of the Arab tribally aligned society, the centrally administered city might have become typical; but the caliphal bureaucracy collapsed also. In the Earlier Middle Period a distinctive Islamicate type of town developed, differing from any that had preceded.

In much of Europe, where an administered bureaucratic city organization lost the support of a territorial government it was eventually replaced by some sort of autonomous municipal government, frequently based on an elected commune set up by the more powerful citizens. In Muslim lands, such local corporate entities did not thrive. They presumed differential rights according to class and territorial status. That is, a man had rights and duties as member of a commune or of a municipality which an outsider could not have; and these rights were frequently based in turn on membership in a guild or other civic organization. Under Islam, with its cosmopolitan outlook, such parochial rights and duties were not judicially recognized. A person was not a citizen of a particular town, with local rights and responsibilities determined by his local citizenship; as a free Muslim he was a 'citizen' of the whole Dâr al-Islâm, with responsibilities determined by his presence before God alone. Legally, there was no true boundary line between the territory of one town and that of another, nor between a town and the surrounding countryside; and movement was free. Instead, the ever-present structuring of society according to lines of patronage by various sorts of notables, alongside voluntary associations of the less privileged, emerged from a secondary role to provide an almost complete basis of urban organization.[15]

Social structures of free men

From the perspective of any agrarian power, and from that of the amîr's court in particular, a city was a place to spend the land revenue. Hence the residence of a great amîr, accompanied by his dependants, virtually sufficed to ensure the existence of a city, and the merchant quarter could be viewed as an incidental, if necessary, adjunct to the residential quarters of those whose income came from outside the city. New cities were often founded in

[15] Ira M. Lapidus, 'The Muslim City in Mamlûk Times,' a doctoral thesis at Harvard in 1964, is a basic contribution to the study of urban life and especially the role of the notables (now published as *Muslim Cities in the Later Middle Ages* [Harvard University Press, 1967] but still dealing chiefly with Syria and Egypt).

just this spirit. It was common for a strong ruler to found a new city, as al-Manṣûr founded Baghdad and as al-Mu'izz, the Fâṭimid, founded Cairo. (Such an event was less common in the Earlier than in the Later Middle Period, but occurred from time to time in every period.) Such cities might be founded with an air of arbitrary fiat, with more regard to military or climatic advantages than to any economic need in the area; yet they did not want for inhabitants. For, to a degree, it was true that it was the concentration of agrarian revenues that made cities possible at all.

But a city founded without regard to economic considerations would not long survive. Generally, the many new foundations were economically useful. A large part of any town was normally built of mud brick, which was hard to keep in good repair; always a great many buildings were more or less in ruins. From time to time it seemed simpler to abandon the debris and move to a new site, a move which royal investment facilitated. Or rivers changed their courses, or ports silted up, and new locations had to be found to carry on old functions. New cities, then, did not necessarily imply increased urban life, but might be merely replacements for old and decaying cities (though often the old city persisted not far from the new, with a differentiation of function; thus Fusṭâṭ continued its own life, with its own distinctive cultural traits, alongside Cairo). In any case, a city had a life of its own. Its merchants and even its craftsmen need not feel dependent only on the beneficiaries of the local agrarian revenues. From the mercantile viewpoint, the agrarian element could come to seem itself almost an adjunct to the city as a whole.

It was the solidarity of the religious community that gave public life its sense of autonomy: its sense that ultimately the town belonged to those who made it up, not to a king, and that there were express limits on what the king or anyone else had the right to do there. But as ruling community, the Muslim community could not serve to represent simply the interests of its sector of the populace; for the ruler was a Muslim too. For any but the broadest Muslim interests, the Muslims—often with dhimmî participation—were articulated into more concrete groupings. The dhimmî non-Muslim communities, of course, exempt from ultimate political responsibility, functioned in a more directly communal way.

We may distinguish the typical Muslim population of the city into three elements. The amîr and his troops and dependents (including the remains of the fiscal bureaucracy) formed a substantial and wealthy part of any town. Sometimes, because of their control of the rural economy, the amîrs might intervene directly in the city economy, for instance as grain traders. But normally their role seems to have been more or less closely defined as providing a military garrison apart from the rest of the town. The ordinary city population, engaged in trade or manufacture or catering to those who were so engaged, formed a recognizable element over against the garrison and its dependants; they were organized increasingly in terms of their several economic functions. Finally, recognized and supported materially by both the amîrs and the ordinary townsmen were the religious classes, and most especially the 'ulamâ' scholars. The qâḍî judge of the Muslims and the subordinate Shar'î officers were technically appointed by the amîr commander, but they were normally appointed from within a restricted circle acknowledged by the town, and were able to function, on occasion, without reference to an amîr. The non-Muslim dhimmî population was aligned likewise into ordinary townsmen and the religious classes, of which the chief was at least confirmed by the amîr.

The establishments of the amîrs and of the 'ulamâ', as we have seen, were essentially independent of each other, forming alternative channels of authority. For some purposes, the 'ulamâ' represented the civic interests of the townsmen generally, or at least the Muslims, over against the amîrs. But they could do so only to a limited degree: partly because much of their financial support came from the amîrs, and partly because of their universal position: they represented the Muslim Ummah at large, and could not be identified with any particular local interests—interests that the Shar'î law they spoke for could not recognize. Consequently, the particular civic interests of the Muslim townsmen were expressed (at least frequently) through a third set of channels of authority. Though the townsmen did not form a municipal corporation to concert their common efforts against gentry or garrison, yet they were linked together in more limited and informal groupings, based on common interests, sometimes expressed in ties of personal patronage. These groupings were based on functional, contractual, or even natural bonds that made special juridical status for individuals in the group unnecessary, so that they need not invoke an alternative to the Sharî'ah for their legitimation. As the bureaucracy of the caliphal state lost power, such groupings became politically more crucial. But the genius of these groupings was not in the direction of formal organization; they depended too much on individual initiative.

Specialized urban groups of many kinds had been common between Nile and Oxus for many centuries (we know more about them in the Roman provinces, but clearly they existed elsewhere also). Those who worked in the same line of trade commonly had their shops near each other in the same market area, and (where bureaucracy was strong) were supervised in common by the government, which would impose a minimum of common life; in response to that supervision, they were likely to have a degree of common organization, sometimes amounting to regular guild life. The several quarters of a city, reflecting different crafts groups sometimes, or more commonly different ethnic backgrounds or religious allegiances only partly correlated with crafts, or even sheer accidents of political history, tended to be conscious of their existence as town quarters, and often vied with each other for reputation or power. Men's clubs might be organized for purposes of sport or for other social interests or else as a measure of solidarity and defence among the more isolated elements in society. We have little solid information about social organization. But so far as we can reconstruct the scene, all such groupings now came to play an increasing role in structuring the political life of the town.

These groups were articulated by two sorts of ties: by received custom, and by convention freely adopted for mutual benefit (even though not put in explicit contract form). The articulation was focused in the patrilinear family, in governing which the force of universal custom was overriding. Under agrarianate conditions, everything encouraged a close continuity of cultural outlook and social position between father and son: the father's religious allegiance was the son's, and the sons of the father's friends were friends of the son. This did by no means always happen; always sons rebelled to some degree against fathers. But it happened very often that the sort of family arose in which for several generations, from father to son or from uncle to nephew, the same sort of business reputation, the same sort of intellectual specialty, the same sort of moral dedication, the same sort of civic role—often on a repeatedly high level of competence—recurred in the one family. The possibility of this was increased to the extent that in upper-class families a man tended to have several sex partners, the sons from all of whom were treated on an equal basis—so that it was likely that among them at least one would prove to have the temperament and abilities requisite for maintaining the family tradition. In such families, solidarity was very strong. Personal success was participated in by the whole family—if a man was successful in business, not only his wife and children flourished with him, but his brothers and their children, and perhaps even his cousins. And misfortune was likewise shared—if a man were ruined by the chances of war or of court life, he could always turn to cousins more fortunately situated.

Around such families, as persistent, dependable units (we may conjecture from a few instances), the various city groupings were built. Continuity in a craft group could be assured by a few dependable leading families; and likewise in a city quarter or in a sectarian body. Around the wealthier men—and their families—as notables (a'yân'), a clientèle gathered, persons who served them in various ways, or were related to those who did; or persons, more generally, who could count on their protection and patronage in return for supporting them economically or socially. An element of customary expectations as to what sort of obligations a patron should undertake went into such relations too, as into family relations; but in those cases that we can trace—the patronage of a great man for a poet, the protection accorded by a prominent Ṣûfî master (pîr) to his neighbours, the association of a men's club with a rich merchant—the relations were built on a calculated (if not always stated) hope for mutual benefits, and ceased so soon as such benefits appeared unlikely to continue. It was not immemorial custom but mutually agreed convention that was the basis of the lines of patronage which tied together the urban community; though without the solidarity of family life at its core, such spontaneity and individualism on the public level might have been impossible. Accordingly, outsiders entered into the nexus of patronage with no difficulty, once they could demonstrate sufficient personal capacities to offer something in exchange for patronage.

The openness of these urban relations—their dependence on the personal initiative and the personal qualifications of the individuals so brought together, as well as on the immediate circumstances that occasioned them—was characteristic of the a'yân-amîr pattern, and determined its social resiliency and adaptability. This pragmatic spirit was reflected in the patterns of succession to office of all sorts.

Civic decisions: succession to office and common policy

Succession was normally expected to be within a given family: the continuity of family attitudes and even competence recommended such a course even when an office was by the amîr's appointment; and when it was self-perpetuating, a certain family loyalty provided an essential core of predictability. The amîr was expected to designate his own successor from within his own family, preferably from among his sons. Qâḍîs and village headmen were expected to be drawn from qâḍî or headman families. Even the head of a Ṣûfî order, who designated his successor from among his disciples, was encouraged to designate a son if one had become a disciple. But such family loyalty was pragmatic rather than prescriptive. Offices were felt as lifetime personal duties and were commonly the focus of a nexus of other personal ties, whether of patronage or of contract proper. It was hoped that a son would be more fully committed to all these ties than would an outsider, who would bring in his own inherited ties from his own family and disrupt continuity.

But within such limits of family continuity—and going outside them whenever family continuity would prove inappropriate—two principles of succession prevailed: succession by appointment and succession by contest. (I am making here an abstraction that might not have been recognized by the participants.) It was these principles that decided which son or which relative was to succeed. Either appointment or contest was normally limited to a small number of possible candidates—if not by family loyalty, then by the understanding that only men already raised to prominence in the group were qualified. When the caliph al-Ma'mûn attempted to appoint an outsider (al-Riḍà) as his successor, his choice was met with defection among the 'Abbâsids and those loyal to them, which he finally yielded to; when the Ṣûfî master Jalâluddîn Rûmî appointed as successor a favourite disciple who had otherwise no status among the other disciples, the appointee was ignored at Rûmî's death, and only the insistence of Rûmî's son, to whom the succession was offered by the group, reinstated him. Nevertheless, the leeway allowed to appointment or to contest could be decisive: among the possible candidates were likely to be strong men and weak, bold and cautious, those inclined to a forward policy and those inclined to consolidation. At each succession, a possible far-reaching question of policy was being made.

The principle of appointment was the only one recognized in the Sharî'ah except in the special case of the caliph himself. All Shar'î public duties were to be filled (if possible) at the personal command of the caliph—in effect, by his personal agents, whose acts he was responsible for; and when the caliph was not in question, then it was the amîr who should make the appointments. Such appointments from above could be revoked at will, of course. This concept was initially, perhaps, a moral and military concept of social organization; but in the context of agrarianate monarchy, it could be realized only in a strong bureaucracy. It was never carried out fully. In the Middle Periods, most important local offices, except in the amîr's court, were autonomous, like that of the amîr himself. The office was filled from within the body which it headed, and normally a man continued in office till he died. (Persons holding office in this way, by selection from below rather than appointment from above, were often called *shaykh*, elder, especially in religious contexts.) Here the principle of contest was at least potentially determinative of the succession.

Contest might be among sons of an amîr, to succeed to their father's position; among disciples (and sons) of a Ṣûfî master (pîr), to succeed to leadership in the Ṣûfî order; it might be among local scholars of a madhhab, to be recognized unofficially but potently as leader; or among guild elders, to be recognized as *shaykh*, master, of the whole guild. Very often, the contest was forestalled by designation by the predecessor. If the nomination by the deceased holder of an office was generally acceptable, it was effective. The effect of succession by designation was to assimilate autonomous succession to appointment from above. (This was, in practice, the rule accepted by Shar'î scholars for succession to the caliphate itself.) Sometimes it can seem as if succession by designation were the normal mode. But in several cases, it becomes clear that an incumbent, unless he was a specially strong personality, was not free to designate his successor. The most he might do was give to his favourite various advantages in view of the contest to come. The living insisted on their prerogative of selecting the successor. In such cases—and residually, whenever (even though it was allowed) no designation had been made—an outright contest ensued.

Normally, this was a contest for prestige. Such a contest may appear mysterious to outsiders observing it. But its chief mechanism, that of the 'band-wagon' appeal, is almost universal. It is clear that whoever wins will be in a position to favour his supporters; and doubtful persons will hasten to the side of any candidate who can give evidence of winning. Thus when Ibn-Rûḥ succeeded (by prior designation) the second wakîl, financial representative of the Twelvers' Hidden Imâm, at least one prominent member of the Twelvers' group refused at first to acknowledge him; he and his dependants stayed away from the new wakîl. But Ibn-Rûḥ was able to bring together sufficient visible support among the group on the day of his formal reception to convince the dissidents to accept him. Sometimes, however, the process has lasted for years; and unless there were strong pressures for coming to a single decision, it has often eventuated in a split.

Where either Shar'î law or immemorial custom prescribed only a bare core of expectations, and pragmatic individual initiative and bargaining determined a person's particular role for the most part, each succession tended to be a moment of uncertainty. A prestige contest often proved inconclusive: two factions might crystallize, neither of which was willing to concede to the other. Then, if the office was effectively indivisible, the prestige contest degenerated into an armed contest—unless this were forestalled by intervention (whether by appeal of the contestants or not) by an armed arbiter, the amîr. In this latter case, the principle of appointment from above might re-enter. (In some of the empires of later times, notably the Ottoman and the Indo-Timuri, succession to the emperorship was explicitly by armed contest in certain periods, and the incumbent emperor was not permitted to designate a son to succeed himself. Here the principle of succession by contest received an unusual formalization as a result of special circumstances.)

The crucial element in civic self-expression within a town was provided by the notables (a'yân), many of whom were raised to local eminence by the sort of contests we have referred to. Among the notables would be included any men who for their wealth or personal achievement, their seniority, and even their descent, to a certain degree, as well as for particular office, were known and respected within the relevant social body. They included the men who held major appointments from the amîr, of course, but most of them had standing independent of any amîr. (We must generalize from a few instances that have been studied.) Whoever was able to command, by wealth or by prestige, the respect or the clientage of a substantial number of more or less dependent persons was explicitly taken account of in reckoning the opinion that counted in making decisions. These men were not chosen arbitrarily; each commanded substantial effective support. If one were taking account of a town as a whole, the a'yân might form a very limited body: qâḍîs, Ṣûfî masters (pîrs), and other scholars, as well as the wealthiest merchants; and the heads of the dhimmî communities. In taking account only of a town quarter, a wider range of men, including the more substantial tradesmen, could be reckoned in.

At any given level, decision among these required a substantial consensus such that no serious division would result. But a consensus of some sort could commonly be attained. If, at the top, agreement might be slow, subdivision and further subdivision of the population at various levels made useful consensus relatively more feasible on the lower levels. And at such levels at least, neutral arbitration could sometimes be invoked. At levels that included a larger number of groups and hence a greater diversity of interests, common action was more difficult, just to the degree that it was facilitated at the lower levels. If no agreement could be reached, either an issue was left undecided, or factional disagreement had to be resolved by the amîr. (The frequent alignment of a town into two grand overall factions, of course, was a secondary effect; normally, neither faction had sufficient internal solidarity to hope to rule on its own if it could master or expel the other.) Nevertheless, in the face of the possibility of recourse to such an arbiter, ways were often found to achieve sufficient agreement for the social body to present a united front.

It was apparently by such agreements that Rayy (in 'Irâq 'Ajamî), freshly enthusiastic about the government of Maḥmûd of Ghaznah, resisted with its own militia the attempt of the Bûyids to reoccupy it; and that Balkh (just south of the middle Oxus), likewise satisfied with Maḥmûd's control, beat off the invading Ḳara-khânîs from the north without help from Maḥmûd. Maḥmûd recognized that such an action implied a form of social power potentially alternative to his own, and severely reprimanded the Balkhîs for their presumptuous action (they being mere 'subjects') against his enemies; he would have preferred to see them submit to the Ḳara-khânîs without risking a fight, and let him come and retake the city later. Indeed, the same sort of civic effectiveness allowed Kirmân to replace Maḥmûd's son Mas'ûd with a Bûyid on its own initiative; and Nîshâpûr, equally dissatisfied with Mas'ûd, to invite the Ḳara-khânîs (unsuccessfully) before finally receiving the Seljuḳs. However, none of these cities attempted to live without any amîr at all: it was a matter of choosing which one they wanted. Despite an occasional example to the contrary, such as Tripoli in Syria (ruled by a family of qâḍîs for a time), the a'yân depended on an amîr and his garrison to keep ultimate order.

The system of notables, with the pattern of consultation and consensus among them, was thus established at various levels within the social body. At the lowest level it represented immediate interest groups; at the higher levels it represented the most eminent among the non-Shar'î notables of the lower levels as well as among the interpreters of the Sharî'ah. This system, providing an informal yet well-understood position for interest groups on every level, seems to have made it possible for crafts groups (whether seriously organized as guilds or not), merchant trades, town quarters, and even a town as a whole to take decisive action as a body whenever it was called for. Without either a bureaucratic chain of command or an immemorial fixing of customary status (either for individuals or groups), the a'yân-amîr system made possible decisions that would be supported effectively by those concerned, despite the cosmopolitanism and personal fluidity of the expanding Islamicate society.

The fluidity of urban life

This loosely structured system of social power presupposed and facilitated social mobility of all sorts. The strength of personal ties to the constituent families and interest groups in the towns was more important than any overall structure or interests of the town as such. This made for a multiplicity of focuses of interest in a town; and for relative independence on the part of individuals, who could seek their own place in such a network of differing interests. This at once made for a social fragmenting of the town itself and for social involvement and solidarity among the several towns.

The fragmenting of civic life was felt even in the layout of the towns as they developed. The layout normally started out unified and even systematic. Erecting a new city was not necessarily the result of primarily economic foresight. Its immediate occasion was to provide unconstrained quarters for the ruler's administrative and military corps, and at the same time to display his power and splendour. Hence a new city, or at least its primary residential and official part, was made as spacious and luxurious as possible. New cities were commonly laid out with broad streets on a gridiron pattern.

But there was no organization that could maintain such a plan. Even a strong monarch could not maintain it against the pressure of individuals freely buying and selling according to unfettered right of contract. The city soon showed the effects. Very soon towns were split up into mutually closed quarters, and within each quarter most through streets were narrowed or cut off, and access left to devious little alleys. The few main streets were fed by culs-de-sac leading out of a solid mass of buildings, each of which was turned in upon its courtyard, facing away from even so much of a street as was the cul-de-sac. (Of course, some open space was generally reserved for special functions—a *maydân*, plaza, where soldiers might exercise; or at least a *muṣallà*, a reserved place beyond the walls, for special ṣalât at the *'îd* festivals.)

This resulted in part from unco-ordinated individual activity, in which private interests took precedence over any common public interest, which had no one particular civic body to support it. We have noted how the preference given by Shar'î law to individual rights over collective rights resulted in the steady encroachment of individual houses onto the roadways, so long as individual passersby were still not hindered, even though the Sharî'ah itself specified a minimum width to the roadways. The great houses of prominent individuals, as focus of authority, became more important than any more impersonal spaces, even than public squares. But the layout of the towns was also influenced by the interests of larger groupings. Hence the positive elements of urban organization in the Middle Periods reinforced tendencies already present under more bureaucratic rule. The town quarters came to be more or less materially self-contained, each with its own simple market for everyday needs, and with a wall separating it from other town quarters. Gates between the various quarters were shut at nights to increase security. This was not just a matter of reducing the area within which a thief might wander or flee detection; it reduced occasions of friction, especially when different quarters differed in religious allegiance. In a Jamâ'î-Sunnî town, a special quarter might be Shî'î; in a Ḥanafî town, one quarter might be Shâfi'î; and communal rioting was limited with the limitation of physical mingling or even access.

Corresponding to the fragmentation of the towns was the relative mobility of individuals from one social niche to another. Many townsmen travelled very readily. The prestige possessed by merchants, of course, encouraged the notion that travel was noble. But not only merchants, whose trade it was to move, but even craftsmen, who had valuable skills that might be rewarded where they were scarcer, moved from one town to another. Few were indisseverably tied to local establishments. (Nonetheless, some special crafts practiced exclusively at one or two towns managed to keep their members from carrying their secrets abroad.) Practically every well-known Muslim lived in many cities: soldiers travelled, by preference, in the way of conquest; scholars travelled to find new teachers and new libraries and also to find more appreciative audiences; even poets travelled to find the most bounteous patron. Consequently, the personnel of a given town—even the personnel of the groups of notables—tended to vary from time to time. But since the pattern was similar from one town to the next, strangers could establish themselves fairly readily on a personal basis. Such movement was not restricted, to judge by the notices I have seen, to the limits of linguistically or politically defined areas, but extended freely throughout Islamdom.

Naturally accompanying geographical mobility was social mobility. This characteristic trait of the region had far-reaching effects on Islamicate culture. Social mobility was relatively great even for the peasant. The shrewd and energetic peasant need not always leave the land, for often enough such men were able to better their position even within the village, catering to village needs with a craft or as peddlers, or even amassing a certain amount of land. But it was in connection with city life that social mobility was greatest. The sons of wealthier peasants were likely to have city connections, and might move to the city. But even fairly poor men, or at least their sons, once they got to the cities, had great opportunities.

Even in the towns, mobility was limited. As elsewhere, sons had the first opportunities in the lines of work and in the social circles of their fathers, if they were at all competent. In the Islamicate society, this was an effective advantage for the family as a whole, if not for all its members severally, because of the tendency for wealthier men to have more than their share of the surviving offspring, so that some of their sons were likely to prove capable; while the poorer families were more likely to die out. Here entered in, that is, the class gradient in the population, which favoured the persistence of upper-class families. What is more, there was considerable prejudice against men of trades regarded as inferior, which would be bound to hamper them. Just as the soldiery looked down on all civilians, and the kâtib bureaucrats looked down on all tradesmen, so merchants looked down on craftsmen, and craftsmen dealing in expensive goods (for instance, goldsmiths), or else relatively free of drudgery or dirt, looked down on men, such as weavers, whose trade was felt to be less attractive—and who might be presumed to want to do something better if they could. (Such differences even found an echo in the Sharî'ah—though only late, and not among the Shî'îs. Some jurists, distinguishing three levels of dignity among craftsmen, would not permit a goldsmith's daughter to be married to a mere tailor, or a tailor's daughter to a mere weaver; while occasionally men of the less respected trades were even handicapped in the reception of their witness at law.) The average man had little chance of rising in the world.

Nevertheless, the more privileged families had to earn their place anew in practically every generation. The survival of relatively numerous sons ensured that any one son would inherit only a fraction of the father's property, and there were special calamities that the wealthiest were subject to—not only if they basked too near the court, but simply through the fortunes of war, when plunder was best in the best houses. There were always opportunities for new men. A poor man, if endowed well above average, could find ways to make good.

For the more gifted, there were at least four major paths to advancement. With special good luck and sharp endowments, a man might make his fortune in trade: great merchant families did not commonly maintain their position many generations, but relinquished their role to new men. We have already noted that even a peasant might become a soldier; and good soldierly qualities could bring the most rapid rise of all. But other ways of rising were associated with religion and to some degree with education. To a limited extent, and with relatively limited prospects of a more diverse career, a young man could rise to social prominence and influence, if not (properly speaking) wealth, by way of becoming a Ṣûfî and being accorded eventually the rights of a pîr, a Ṣûfî master. Much more varied prospects opened to the 'âlim scholar. A religious education could allow the gifted man to rise not only to such ranks as qâḍî judge and muftî, but even to mingle in administration or have a career of less specialized learning.

Education was very widespread, by the norms of agrarianate times. Almost any gifted boy would know something of the meaning of reading and writing and have the opportunity, at the Qur'ân schools which were found even in villages, to master the rudiments that would then allow him to pursue his studies further, supported by a waqf endowment.

On the most elementary level education means literacy. But the usefulness of universal literacy can be exaggerated. Figures giving the percentage of literates in a population do not indicate dependably the proportion of the population that can be reached by written means. The use of letters can be quite widely formative of the social outlook once it has escaped the precincts of the temple and spread to the bazaars—where reading and writing services were generally available, and even those who could not personally read did receive verbatim the contents of written announcements and even of popular books. Letters can form the outlook of a population even more intimately when literacy has reached the family level: that is, when in most families at least one member can read. Even in the villages a significant degree of literacy existed. In the towns, at least in some classes, literacy at the family level was probably common. (Note that general urban literacy at the family level might be indicated—in terms of statistics of a modern type—by a 'national' literacy level of ten per cent—i.e., twenty per cent of all males.)

The Sharî'ah as a civic force

All the Muslim groupings that went to make up town life, however recent the advent of individuals in them to a given town, were held together internally, and, to a degree, across the lines that divided them, by three religiously sanctioned institutions in which all could participate. The first was the Sharî'ah law, which was sufficiently standardized that even differences among Ḥanafîs, Shâfi'îs, and Ja'farîs did not make much basic difference in common expectations from one to another on legally determinable matters; nor did differences of national background. The other two integrative institutions, the waqf foundations and the Ṣûfî ṭarîqahs, were themselves finally dependent on the Shar'î norms for their social viability.

The Sharî'ah was supported by deep-rooted public sentiment. The Islamicate social order presupposed a widespread loyalty to Islam, to the Muslim Ummah community—and hence to the obligations imposed by Sharî'ah law. This loyalty was not only a spiritual but a social virtue, in one sense a political virtue; perhaps even more so among the predominantly Muslim populations of the Middle Periods than among the Arabs at the time of the conquest, for whom loyalty to the Arab cause as such had been paramount, and Christian Arab tribes equal to Muslim ones. The solidarity among the Muslims as a body was felt very personally—in reporting natural disasters, for instance, a chronicler might note the number of fatalities in terms of 'Muslims' being killed, rather than simply 'people' or 'souls'. A joke was told of the bald man who found his cap missing when he emerged from the public bath; the attendant claimed the man had worn no cap when he came, but the bald man appealed for justice to the bystanders: 'You Muslims, is this the sort of head that goes hatless?'—for it was as Muslims that they were bound to defend a fellow-Muslim against wrong.

This sentiment for Muslim public solidarity was not institutionalized in the form of direct limitations on the ruler's power or tenure. Those who had created the Sharî'ah had been acting, in part, to neutralize caliphal power in favour of retaining power diffused in society at large. It was probably consistent with this aim that later Jamâ'îs refused to formulate any Shar'î method of deposing a caliph—or an amîr, conceived as his deputy—who transgressed the Sharî'ah; not even when it was asserted (as by the Ash'arî 'Abd-al-Qâhir Baghdâdî in the eleventh century) that the 'ulamâ' had, in principle, the obligation to depose an unjust caliph. For such a deposition would be, at best, a dangerous act. It surely seemed better to focus men's attention on so strengthening the Sharî'ah that the arbitrary interventions of the ruler would be as irrelevant as possible, rather than encourage rebellions that were unlikely to produce a perfectly just ruler in any case (and which, if successful, would enhance the new ruler's prestige as imâm at the expense of the ula'mâ'). Hence even when the office of caliph, in the Middle Periods, was retrospectively given a greater Shar'î role, the theorists did not repudiate the attitude of the Ḥadîth folk and Sharî'ah specialists, who had reduced the duty of each Muslim 'to command the right and forbid the wrong' to innocuous personal admonition.

But two other rules expressing the Muslims' political solidarity retained their full vigour: the overriding obligation of jihâd holy war to defend the frontiers of the Dâr al-Islâm against infidels, and the treatment of apostasy as treason subject to the death penalty. These obligations, which in Muḥammad's time had spelled out loyalty to a struggling new government, now marked the limits at which the social body would insist on its corporate identity—and beyond which it would refuse, if need be, to yield ultimate discretion to the government of the amîrs. The same spirit of insisting on a corporate Muslim identity for the social body as such was expressed in the popular hostility to dhimmî non-Muslims, which sometimes resulted in murderous riots just when the proportion of non-Muslims was dwindling to a marked minority. (It must be added that communalist rigourism only slowly extended to the point of forbidding infidels access to Muslim holy places; as late as the fifteenth century, the major shrine at Mashhad near Ṭûs, now closed to infidels by public sentiment, could be visited by foreign Christians without scandal.)

This Islamic social loyalty, this touch of 'political virtue', allowed for the formation of a Muslim public opinion, within a rather limited range of questions (such as fighting non-Muslim invaders); opinion that was more than merely an equilibrium among diverse particular interests. Everyone tended to take for granted this public opinion and to act on the expectation that it would have some sort of effect. It was this public opinion that gave legitimacy to the qâḍî's position, and endowed it with a degree of autonomy over against the amîrs. It was this public opinion, the only public opinion that could be certainly depended upon, that accorded the Sharî'ah and its 'ulamâ' their near monopoly of legal and moral legitimation even in the centuries when Ṣûfî mystics, offering an alternative form of devotional sensibility, were most widely respected. The power of this public opinion, and of its refusal to acknowledge ultimate legitimacy to non-Shar'î authority, was often illustrated in Muslim politics. The most famous occasion of this was probably the fall of the Sâmânid dynasty—when the 'ulamâ' helped persuade the people of Bukhârâ not to resist the advancing Ḳara-khânî forces, on the ground that fighting among Muslims was worse than the fall of a government.

The Sharî'ah was only one source of authority, though the most unimpeachable. It was enforced by Muslim public opinion only at a relatively general level of social activity. The universal reference of its rules, which paid no heed to local arrangements, and its highly idealistic and formalistic procedure were made possible by limitations on its applicability: not only did the amîr's military court take cognizance of administrative and criminal cases, dropping Shar'î procedure and sometimes even Shar'î substantive rules, as the caliphal courts once had done; at least as important, many local disputes within the groupings that composed a town (as well as the countryside) had always been settled on the level of a patron's decision or of negotiated compromise. Indeed, Shar'î justice, as individual justice, was often not to the taste of peoples who stressed local group adherence; they commonly withdrew their disputes from the courts and kept them within the range of family councils and guild or village arbiters. If they had to go to the courts, they were often glad if some 'corruption' were feasible, whereby local group privileges could be reaffirmed (or group rivalries gratified) in the face of the Sharî'ah and under its cloak.

We can list several sources of authority that might be appealed to, alternatively to the Sharî'ah. Bureaucratic regulations and precedents were honoured as far as possible by the kâtib clerks who attempted to maintain the forms of a centralized administration, and they honoured, in the same spirit, what may be called dynastic law—general ordinances laid down by a sultan or an amîr and respected by his successors. Local groups—such as men's clubs, or guilds—had their own rules, sometimes drawn up very explicitly. Such positive regulations must be distinguished from a source of authority even more pervasive, though always subject to change: local custom. Finally comes the fiat of the amîr, which must often, at least, be regarded as representing a sort of martial law, in that it expressed his authority as military commander and was normally exercised within the court itself, among persons who were admittedly under his command. (These last two sources of authority especially represent the relatively great reliance of the time on custom and personal improvisation, and the lesser reliance on impersonal calculative prescription.) In addition, of course, we must always reckon among the sources of authority a certain amount of charismatic initiative: initiative made possible by the purely personal prestige a creative figure may win for himself; and in the relatively fluid society of Islamdom, opportunities for such initiative often arose.

All these sources of authority gained their validity through the process of tradition: both explicit regulation and customary practice, and even the fiat of the amîr, were obeyed because of the common commitment of the carriers of a given tradition to its initial events and its continuing vitality. (Even the charismatic leader was normally only taking an unusually vigorous part in the dialogue to which one or another tradition was giving rise.) Yet none of these sources of authority, not even local custom, could endure the shock of temporary disgrace or defiance as could the Sharî'ah. In Hindu India, a village body might make a covenant among themselves and register it with a king, who would enforce it against their members; but among Muslims such a device was very unlikely—partly because the authority of any amîr was relatively transient, and partly because an appeal to the universal Sharî'ah was likely to invalidate any local corporate convention. The problem of legitimizing any extra-Shar'î institution for the sake of local exigencies can be illustrated with the calendar. Every society that depends in any way upon the land and its natural seasons must reckon time at least approximately by the seasonal year; if nothing else, the revenues must come due year by year after the harvest, when the peasant has the means of paying, and not at an arbitrary moment in some unrelated cycle. The Muslims, too, had to use a solar calendar for practical purposes. Every government established a solar calendar for fiscal purposes, which was then generally used for practical needs; but the only calendar legitimized by the Sharî'ah was the purely lunar calendar, which reckoned by twelve months rather than by true seasonal years. Hence none of these governmental solar calendars was accepted as more than a provisional convenience—and all of them fell into disorder because of neglect of such devices as the leap year that were required to keep them in a fixed relation to the seasons. All had to be reformed from time to time, and none could win a durable or universal standing. It was not only piety but a need for uniform reliability that caused only the Islamic lunar calendar to be used in broad contexts, as in history or diplomacy.

Nevertheless, the Sharî'ah did not merely inhibit other legal forms. Despite all its limitations, in its own proper sphere it had a vital positive function. Though largely ignored at court and among the peasants, it was consistently effective, in letter and in spirit, among merchants (even they, however, used much non-Shar'î commercial law); perhaps because they had to reflect a cosmopolitan outlook anyway. It was also the standard of appeal, no matter what the social class, wherever social continuity was required beyond the family or village level. For the purpose of a universal standard of legitimacy, then, it was essential that the Sharî'ah law vary as little as possible from place to place and even from time to time.

This was achieved only with difficulty, and was never achieved fully. What is sometimes called the 'rigidity' of Muslim law was not built into it with its first principles. Indeed, the principles taught by al-Shâfi'î had not only set aside local traditions but had put in question any continuity by way of mere custom. Such principles could have left the law open to unpredictable reinterpretation by every legist qualified to go back to Qur'ân and ḥadîth and reevaluate them for himself. Such a consequence was avoided and predictability assured by the device of expecting each Muslim to adhere to a given madhhab school of fiqh law. It was agreed among Jamâ'î-Sunnîs that any of several madhhab schools, going back to a great imâm such as al-Shâfi'î or Abû-Ḥanîfah, was equally acceptable. But a person should stick to one or another and not wander back and forth among them at convenience. Even jurists, then, were expected to abide by the decisions generally accepted within their chosen madhhab, and undertake their own *ijtihâd* inquiry only where there was still disagreement or where new questions had arisen.

Thus the Sharî'ah law was kept sufficiently uniform to serve the needs of the vast Muslim community, crossing all possible political boundaries: wherever a Muslim went, he could count on much the same law holding, and know that his rights won in one place would be respected elsewhere. Even when (as did happen, by principles developed in more than one madhhab school) explicitly local law (*'âdah*, 'custom') was applied by the qâḍî judges, it was always law that applied to every Muslim who happened to be in the area, not special law governing persons of a given status, such as local citizens.

But however universal a law was, if it was to remain applicable at all, of course, there must be change over the centuries. This was achieved through a recognition of the most eminent jurists of a given age not merely in one place but very widely, at least wherever their madhhab was taught; the fatwà decisions of such men served to keep the law up to date in the slow-changing Agrarian Age, by almost imperceptible increment, without undermining its universal applicability. Law guided by such fatwàs bears a limited analogy to Anglo-Saxon case law and the rule of stare decisis; but the argument was usually put only implicitly, in the posing of the question (to which the 'answer' was a simple yes or no); and such precedents were more freely ignored, each judge being independently responsible and not representing a continuing 'court'. Gibb has pointed out that the history of Muslim law is to be traced in the collections of such fatwàs rather than in the elementary legal textbooks, which changed far less but were less relevant to practical contingencies. (We will discuss some explicit ventures in maintaining the viability of the Sharî'ah in Book Four.)

There was a constant pressure for local patterns to be assimilated to the idealized Shar'î norms. This pressure made for a degree of social unity, especially in the lands which had been Muslim the longest. But diversity necessarily persisted, and even the pressure for Shar'î norms could produce distinctive local results. When the Sharî'ah replaced a given regulation of the 'âdah, the admittedly local custom, it could give rise to different results in different contexts.

The Shar'î family law, for instance, maintained a constant pressure in some areas—especially among matrilineal groups—toward the norm of patrilineal family relations with emphasis on the nuclear family. The point at which a given group started to make a changeover from matrilineal to patrilineal reckoning, as a result of this pressure, could be psychologically and socially very important; thus the very terms changed by which related persons called each other and according to which they categorized their relative closeness one to another. But with such a changeover, other pressures arose which gave it unanticipable effects. The sense of wider family solidarity could not be set aside in most agricultural contexts without risking social and economic dislocation.

In particular, it could be disastrous when land, as property, was divided up among a variety of heirs at every death; especially if parcels went also to girls, who would carry it out of the family on their marriage. Hence the Shar'î provisions gave rise to two sorts of arrangement. So far as they could not be avoided, they often led to cousin marriages: a man was expected to marry his father's brother's daughter, so that her portion would be kept in the family. (It may be that the frequency of such marriages as a form of endogamy among some Arabs made female inheritance possible in the first place.)[16] Such a marriage did not always occur, but in some areas there could be serious friction if it did not, with a sense of violated rights. Where such marriages were not adopted, it was desirable to withdraw land from the operation of the rules of inheritance altogether. An advantage of the iqṭâ' system was that it made this possible; inheritance could be of the iqṭâ' grant as such—indivisible—to the son alone. The erection of family waqf endowments had the same effect.

The qâḍî judge also presided, rather less directly, over the second institution that served to hold together the various social groupings: the institution of waqf endowments. Increasingly, most public institutions, from wells and fountains to madrasahs and mosques, came to be maintained through income from pious donations and legacies (usually rent-yielding land), administered as privately as they were established. Zakât, collected by public law, had been the original vehicle for financing Islam as a society; zakât continued as the main justification for a Muslim government's various urban taxes or as a ritualized form of personal charity, but no longer as the material foundation for most specifically Islamic concerns. Private waqf foundations largely took its place in this role. The properties set aside in waqf were guaranteed inalienable under the Sharî'ah and were very rarely touched by a Muslim ruler. There were waqfs to cover a host of contingencies of urban living. A Muslim traveller in Damascus tells of seeing a slave-boy stumble and break a precious vase he was carrying; the lad was in terror of his master; but passers-by reassured him: it turned out that there was a waqf established precisely to furnish funds for servants who got in trouble in such ways—the vase was replaced and the lad went home in safety. Through the waqfs, the various civic essentials and even amenities were provided for on a private yet dependable basis without need or fear of the intervention of political power.

[16] Germaine Tillion, *Le Harem et les cousins* (Paris, 1966), a fascinating study of rationale in Mediterranean family and honour patterns, suggests that cousin marriage is deeply rooted in the agrarian presuppositions at least of the whole Irano-Mediterranean region. Her work is not rigorously argued, unfortunately, and her historical reconstruction is fragmentary and thrown off by a Westernistic image of the world.

Finally, the Ṣûfî piety which had been developing in the High Caliphal Period furnished a pervasive set of spiritual presuppositions and sanctions which undergirded the whole pattern. Ṣûfism, as we shall see further on, became the framework within which all popular Muslim piety flowed together; its saints, dead and living, became the guarantors of the gentle and co-operative sides of social life. Guilds commonly came to have Ṣûfî affiliations. Men's clubs claimed the patronage of Ṣûfî saints. And the tombs of local saints became shrines which almost all factions united in revering. It is probable that without the subtle leaven of the Ṣûfî orders, giving to Islam an inward personal thrust and to the Muslim community a sense of participation in a common spiritual venture quite apart from anyone's outward power, the mechanical arrangements of the Sharî'ah would not have maintained the loyalty essential to their effectiveness.

The presence of Sharî'ah, waqfs, and Ṣûfî orders thus made possible the a'yân-amîr system as a viable universal pattern rather than just a provisional local arrangement town by town. But the a'yân-amîr system, in turn (with its rural foundation in a free peasantry and military iqṭâ's), allowed the Sharî'ah in particular to rise to the top, uninhibited by any one state's bureaucratic legalism; and so to maintain the universality of the whole society. As a result of this mutual reinforcement, no explicit civic unity was necessary in a town, either internal (as in the Sumerian priestly cities or in the Hellenistic merchant cities) or external (as in the bureaucratically administered cities). Even the dependent territory of a city could be ruled on the basis of village organizations tied by patronage to urban families. The only explicit unity was that of the Dâr al-Islâm itself; and that was actually effective.

Yet some residual central authority in a town was needed: an arbiter to enforce the peace if all the give and take of group rivalries and pious understandings should break into incurable internal fighting; to provide a regular army, above all a force of cavalry, which seemed to be needed in case of major invasion from outside; and to see, if normal ties broke down, that the revenues were collected from the villages.

The futuwwah clubs, town militias, and garrison government

Even such a need might have seemed about to be filled, for a time, from within the urban structure. On the basis of various urban ties, at the end of High Caliphal times began to develop what may be called a pattern of 'militia-autonomy'. In Syria, the Jazîrah, 'Irâq 'Ajamî, Khurâsân, and elsewhere, for a time various bodies of townsmen were organized on a more or less permanent militia basis. Sometimes these were sectarian groups (the Ismâ'îlîs formed one example, and Jamâ'î-Sunnî militia bodies were sometimes organized in opposition to them); sometimes they represented the lower-class elements in the towns but were more or less tied to the established authorities. In any case they formed centres of power to be reckoned with, if they could be effectively mobilized.

Some of the most important of these groups were explicitly lower-class. Many townsmen came to be organized in socially conscious bodies called most frequently, in Arabic, the *futuwwah*, or men's clubs, ceremonially devoted to the manly virtues. The word *futuwwah*, literally 'young manhood', expressed manly ideals of comradely loyalty and magnanimity (the term was taken from the Bedouin tradition but was given a special meaning when used to render urban notions; notions that had surely existed before the Arab conquest). In Persian, the corresponding term (*javânmardî*) also meant literally young manhood. (In Turkish, the term for a man of the futuwwah was *akhi*.) When we first come upon the term *futuwwah* in the sense of men's club, it is applied to upper-class organizations—as might be expected, so far as it was the upper classes who first took to speaking Arabic and using Arabic terms. But by the end of High Caliphal times, when the use of Arabic had become general, the term was applied more to men's clubs of the lower urban classes.

It has been shown that in the Byzantine towns, including those in Syria, the 'circus factions' were lower-class sportive men's clubs of the kind we find in Islamdom; they likewise had militia potentialities; they affected peculiarities of dress and were sometimes even referred to likewise as 'the young men'. Presumably the prominence of such organizations dates back to the emergence of the centrally 'administered' city. (As to such formations in the Sâsânian empire we have no information positive or negative.) Since such men's clubs were still active at the time of the Arab conquests, we may presume that there was a general continuity between them and the futuwwah, as in most other aspects of Muslim life, though we hear too little of lower-class life in the early Islamic centuries to trace their evolution as the population turned Muslim.[17]

These men's clubs were of several sorts; some seem to have been dedicated entirely to sports, and others more to mutual aid. Occasionally the members lived, or at least might eat, in a common clubhouse. They were formed among several different social strata; probably some were essentially youth gangs, bands of adolescents and young men asserting their personal independence, while (at least later) some were general tradesmen's associations. It may seem almost impossible to deal with all such groups under one heading, but it appears to me that there must have been an unbroken spectrum of such organizations, from one extreme form to another; and certain sorts of ideals

[17] The Byzantine factions are discussed by Spiros Vryonis in 'Byzantine Circus Factions and Islamic Futuwwa Organizations (neaniai, fityân, ahdâth)', *Byzantinische Zeitschrift* 58 (1965), 46–59, which also gives recent bibliography on the futuwwah. Vryonis seems to suggest, rather improbably, that Byzantine circus factions might have been imported into the Sâsânian empire. But since some of the factions' mannerisms (e.g., long hair) could be associated with Sâsânian culture, is it possible that there was already some continuity across the border?

and expectations were acknowledged by most of them, despite their variety. Moreover, historically we may single out a special role that this sort of organization played—well or poorly—in the Middle Periods; a role that might be played by futuwwah clubs of almost every sort. For it seems to have been in men's clubs, whatever their makeup, that the possibility of an urban militia lay if there was to be one.

The clubs all had in common an idealistic tone, a stress on unconditional loyalty of the members to one another, and some sort of private ritual. Their ritual became more elaborate with time, and it came to be very similar in all the futuwwah clubs by the end of the Earlier Middle Period, at latest. The most notable features of it were investiture of the initiate with special futuwwah trousers and other elements of distinctive dress, and the ceremonial drinking of salted water. In each town there were likely to be several independent futuwwah clubs, each of which kept jealously separate from the others, claiming alone to represent true futuwwah. Each such club, then, was closely organized into smaller units, within which the ceremonial life chiefly took place, and it was expected that each futuwwah man should be unquestioningly obedient to the head of his particular unit. (If a man did not get along with the head of his unit, there were even provisions for his transfer to another unit.)

The futuwwah clubs so strongly stressed the ties of mutual loyalty among the club members that other social ties might be disregarded; some clubs even insisted on their members cutting the ties to family, and admitted only bachelors; this would be specially true of those that could be called youth gangs. At the same time, they prided themselves on their ethical standards, particularly on their hospitality; those whose members were substantial tradesmen might be the first to offer hospitality to strangers in town. Probably they owed their strength in part to the need to overcome the isolation of the individual—resident or stranger—which liberty tended to bring with it.

The futuwwah naturally tended to supplement an interest in sports with a degree of military discipline; and such discipline was normally directed at least potentially against the established powers. Commonly futuwwah clubs might admit dhimmî non-Muslims; they might admit slaves and even eunuchs; but not a coward nor a tax-collector nor the henchman of a tyrant; that is, of an amîr. Futuwwah members readily took to bearing arms, allegedly to defend at need their futuwwah brethren. At times futuwwah clubs carried out military expeditions on behalf of their ideals—while at other times they carried out riots which frightened wealthier elements in a town. When riots did occur, some made a point of plundering only the houses of the rich—leaving what there was in the houses of the poor strictly alone. Even their opponents credited them with a strict code of honour in such matters. Some clubs undertook 'protection rackets': the well-to-do had to pay them for protection from the club's own attentions; and the club, in turn, would protect them from rival clubs. (Here they fulfilled a role, like some Bedouin tribes on desert routes, at a level to which the amîr's protection could not reach.) In the chronicles, the futuwwah clubs are often referred to by terms that imply banditry; nor did the futuwwah men always refuse to accept such terms for themselves. An honoured early Ṣûfî of Khurâsân was called by one such name, *'Ayyâr,* because of his futuwwah associations.

The futuwwah clubs seem to have represented most often just those elements not represented by the notables—the poorer and the younger men or those without good family connections, who, even if in relations of some dependence on more prominent personages, felt their own interests to be different from those of the well-to-do and the established. The futuwwah discipline emphasized the rights of human equality rather than those of cultural privilege, so dear to the kâtib clerks. Sometimes even the criminal or beggar elements of a town seem to have assimilated their organizations to the futuwwah; indeed, such elements were likely to be more tightly organized than were more established groups. Despite egalitarian inclinations the futuwwah was not necessarily always socially alienated. When the futuwwah clubs bore arms, they were linked sometimes with town volunteer militia groups apparently raised on a more general basis—the *aḥdâth*—which in Syria, at least, sometimes participated alongside the Turkic troops in their battles. Futuwwah clubs often represented or were associated with particular quarters of a town, and thus gained serious influence; then their chiefs might themselves become notables. But they always were potentially at odds with the established order controlled by the notables.

Such groups as the futuwwah were normally marginal to the urban life as a whole, even though sometimes influential. Even the poor did not always support them with political effect. The poor, even if not holding to the social doctrines of the privileged, always were inclined to mistrust an egalitarian appeal in practice, lest it merely pave the way for a new and less polished (and hence harsher) privileged group. But militia bodies based on the futuwwah could act with solidarity and independence. At times of political uncertainty, they could play an important and even a decisive political role.

In the Earlier Middle Period, this role seems to have increased. Already in the ninth century, the Ṣaffârids of Sîstân seem to have been leaders, in the first place, of a men's club militia organized to fight the Khârijî bands that were raiding in the area. Then when the Ṣaffârids swept out from Sîstân across Iran to take power from the 'Abbâsids' governors, the local men's clubs in the other Iranian cities seem to have given the Ṣaffârids important support. Between 950 and 1150, popular militia groups, including the futuwwah clubs, often determined events. The head, *ra'îs,* of the town militia even figured sometimes as head of the town itself. In Baghdad, it seems, these groups were held down by the more privileged classes; but in many provincial towns they formed a major official force for good order.

They not only brought solidarity and discipline to their members; they went on sometimes to provide a local source of civic discipline for the town as a whole.

But by 1150 such political power seems to have disappeared. The one exception seems to have been the Nizârî Ismâʿîlî state, unless perhaps, to a limited degree, the towns of Sîstân. The far-flung Ismâʿîlî state, so paradoxically cohesive and enduring in contrast to the formations of the amîrs, was based from beginning to end on the local Ismâʿîlî militias; in Quhistân, north of Sîstân, these were the militias of sizable towns, which never accepted outside garrisons. Doubtless the Ismâʿîlî revolt, which with its desperate tactics divided the city communities and so turned most people against Ismâʿîlism, had proved the decisive event that discredited not only Ismâʿîlism but also any other militia autonomy based upon the futuwwah.

Probably in any case, however, an extensive solution to the political problem on the basis of militia autonomy was out of the question. On some islands or remoter coasts around the Arabian peninsula, independent city-states did sometimes arise—for instance, on the island of Qays in the Persian Gulf (also accused of piracy). But most cities in the region had not the natural means of protecting their internal institutions from land-based agrarian interference until they could mature. Hence (I suppose) no general pattern of civic autonomy was developed (from which even the isolated towns might have profited). The fragmentation of the city social structure and the cosmopolitan links beyond any given town, which had resulted from age-old confrontations with territorial states and empires in the mid-Arid Zone, made sufficient local civic solidarity unattainable without some sudden major renewal of social forces. Ismâʿîlism, indeed, did offer just this at the time of the Nizârî revolt. But the required breach with the universal patterns of Islam—the demand for local civic isolation if need be—proved too great except for a handful of out-of-the-way places, not so very wealthy anyway.

As with the Ismâʿîlî case, so with the whole militia movement, the more advantaged urban classes, on whose co-operation all must finally depend, found too much was threatened that was precious to themselves. At least, I see no better way to reconstruct what happened than this. They found the militia groups, who were constituted of less privileged young men and resistant to imposed authority—in the spirit of the Sharîʿah law and of the futuwwah itself—too ready to side with the poor against the rich—and the notables could not expect, perhaps, given their own fragmentation and cosmopolitanism, to offer any alternative orientation to the movement. Certainly, in the freely mobile Islamicate society, they could not be sure of controlling any popular militia by ties of fixed status. Hence they could rely even less on their townsmen as soldiers than could the gentry on their peasants. (The caliph al-Nâṣir made an effort at reorienting the futuwwah clubs, rather later, on a still different basis, as we shall see; but his way would not have helped the city aʿyân become independent.) The notables seem to have preferred, at any rate, for filling the function of final political arbiter, the Turkic military garrisons, distasteful as they often were.

In such a society, if there were no central government, whence else could the requisite garrisons come? First, they could not be constituted in such a way as to represent the city as a whole on a legitimately legal basis; that is, on the basis of the impersonal and unlocalized Sharîʿah as such; for it recognized no special and localized social bodies such as the cities were in fact composed of. (Only the Ismâʿîlî Shîʿîs had found, in their imâm, an alternative to this Sharʿî impasse; but their alternative threatened, on this level, not only established urban interests but also the established ʿulamâʾ.) Garrisons might arise from within the faction-split city on the basis of more limited interests and without the universally conceded legitimation of the Sharîʿah; but, to judge by experience with the futuwwah, this could be only by favouring the many at the expense of the few. The garrisons, then, must be built of social elements from without the normal urban society; and it was these elements that were provided by the amîrs and their Turkic soldiery. And in fact, a town that by chance found itself without an amîr might seek one out and invite him to come; as happened once in Ḥumṣ in Syria when the amîr was assassinated and an Ismâʿîlî rising was feared. (On one level, the amîr filled a role like that of an Italian condottiere at certain periods; but different city structures determined different outcomes.)

As the pattern of garrison rule became established, the autonomous urban groupings, which had failed to replace it with a garrison of their own, became consolidated in other ways, as if to resist its encroachments. The most important of the urban organizations to develop were the trades guilds, which acquired effective strength in many areas in the Earlier Middle Period, or even later. Under the High Caliphate, after the weakening of earlier formations with the change of administration (and the piecemeal Islamization of their members), trades were associated, at least in many areas, only very loosely, and control by the government market supervisors was often exercised directly on individuals, without much reference to group responsibility. Such associations as there were now were strengthened, or else replaced by new stronger organizations, in forms that became almost universal in Islamdom by the end of the Later Middle Period.

But if the futuwwah men's clubs had failed to provide an independent militia for the cities, they did contribute to maintaining the autonomy of urban institutions against the garrisons that were established. Many of the guilds seem to have been organized as futuwwah clubs—and they maintained an appropriately independent spirit. The Islamicate guilds were not, as it seems sometimes they were in the later Roman empire, channels of government control, but fully autonomous expressions of the interests of their members, and commonly aligned, therefore, against the official powers.[18]

[18] It is not clear, however, that the guilds arose out of the Ismâʿîlî revolutionary movement, as suggested by Louis Massignon (article on *Sinf*, *Encyclopaedia of Islam*, 1st ed.,

The futuwwah guilds gained spiritual stability to support such a role through a close association with Ṣûfism. Even in the High Caliphal Period, many Ṣûfîs had adopted some of the futuwwah language for expressing loyalty and magnanimity, which they transformed into loyalty to God and radical magnanimity to all His creatures. Such an interpretation of the futuwwah ideals was ready, then, when the futuwwah was called upon to support spiritually the new guilds. Some writers interpreted the futuwwah as a sort of lesser Ṣûfî way for those unable to achieve the full mystical way. Sometimes futuwwah clubs came to have their own Ṣûfî ceremonies, after the manner of the social Ṣûfism which, as we shall see, developed in the Earlier Middle Period. And they might have Ṣûfî masters as patrons. By the end of the Middle Periods, the futuwwah had become, at least in some places, essentially the Ṣûfî dimension of guild organizations.

Military despotism and interstitial anarchy

In the absence of an extensive and self-perpetuating bureaucracy, or of any agrarian or bourgeois alternative, power was held on a strictly military basis. Such a situation opened the way to extensive arbitrariness and brutality. The brutality was not unmitigated; but it was a permanent feature of the society.

The justice of the court of an amîr (that is, the garrison commander, independent or not)—as compared to that of the qâḍî—was, I have suggested, in effect martial law: the amîr acted in his capacity of military captain—and primarily upon those who were admittedly at his command. Whenever the amîr found it necessary to intervene, he did so with the same priority for the security of the military authority that prevails in any martial law; the rights of the individual were taken into account only when the seeming needs of security were safely satisfied. At the same time, the power over any given place that an amîr could exercise was based on the immediacy of his military presence; that is, it was proportionate to his physical propinquity to the place.

In his immediate vicinity, then, the amîr's power would be arbitrary and unlimited: anyone at all prominent (and hence visible) in the city might feel his whims, for he need not work through the delays and correctives of an officialdom with its own standards of correctness. Here would be naked despotism; not the supreme indifference of the grand absolute monarch with an inherited and secure position who arbitrates among lesser men, but the personal intervention of a man whose strength rests on the perpetual vigilance

---

and elsewhere). They seem, in the High Caliphal and Earlier Middle Periods, to be continuations of the state-sponsored guilds of Roman and Byzantine times, but rather weakened by the social mobility of Islamic times. Gerald Salinger, 'Was Futuwa an Oriental Form of Chivalry?' *Proceedings of the American Philosophical Society*, 94 (1950), 481 ff., has an excellent discussion of autonomous urban organizations. The material is worked out, so far as it yet has been, largely in articles by Franz Taeschner and by Claude Cahen (see note 14 above), which are listed in J. D. Pearson, *Index Islamicus* (London, 1958—).

of his word and who, apart from his enormous present power, is not very differently placed socially from any other military leader. Even great sultans, ruling several provinces (or especially they, being relatively removed from any homogeneous local public opinion), ruling by martial law, tended to be drastically arbitrary, splendid in their moments of generosity, inhuman in their anger or their fears.

On the other hand, at such a distance from the amîr that it did not pay (in revenue returned) to despatch troops to enforce continuous obedience, there would be no proper government at all. This was anarchy; or, to be more exact, self-rule by strictly local units, by the acknowledged leaders in particular villages and particular tribes; and beyond the limits of the village or outside the tribal camp, the individual was on his own.

But anarchy also penetrated even the most highly garrisoned areas, periodically, in the shape of warfare. Among military governments, warfare was almost continuous. The greater sultans tried to exercise authority over the amîrs of all the cities in his reach. But this authority amounted chiefly, in many cases, to a share in their revenue, though it also could permit interference in other ways, especially in making the more lucrative appointments; that is, it was often simply that of one garrison commander over another. To retain such authority, the sultan had repeatedly to demonstrate his actual power. At any sign of weakness, one or another amîr would revolt—that is, refuse to send on any revenue, and try his luck at braving the sultan's anger. The sultan would send a numerically larger army to reduce the amîr. But with luck, the amîr might hold out against even a quite strong sultan till the sultan was sufficiently distracted by other revolts that he must make a favourable accommodation; or till he was removed by death (and his successor might prove weaker). Indeed, the death of a ruler was very commonly the signal not only for fresh revolts but for fighting over the succession; for power went to the captain who could command the most effective troops, and while normally this was one of the dead man's sons, different sons would have lined up different factions in their support, who must commonly fight it out. Finally, a ruler who had gained a certain amount of power was taught to feel it a test of his military prowess, even of his manhood, to be extending that power—and the wealth that came with power. A great sultan might attempt conquest at the expense of neighbouring sultans; or even a local amîr, if he owned allegiance to a weak sultan or to none, at the expense of his fellow amîrs.

Even more decisive in launching campaigns than greed or vanity on the part of a ruler was the economics of military life. The ruler necessarily kept as many troops as he could; and he could keep more than the revenue of his lands could regularly pay for if he could supplement the troops' income with opportunity to plunder. The ruler who offered extensive plunder attracted soldiers even from his rivals. Accordingly, the petty warfare that the amîrs carried on brought anarchy not merely to the battlefield itself, but to all the countryside and the towns. Anything in the path of the soldiers was likely to be regarded as fair game for plunder; and anything in the territories of the rival amîr was not only open to plunder but might also be wilfully destroyed when all movable goods had been plundered, so as to reduce the rival's resources—or even, by the perversity of human passion, to punish the rival's subjects for not betraying their town to the attacker. The normal accompaniment of war was rapine and fire: an anarchy much more serious, if more transient, than that which resulted merely from distance from the court.

It was the boast of the eulogists of some rulers that in their time a purse of gold could be left on a remote highway by an old woman and picked up again intact and safely by the same woman the next day. There was some exaggeration in such claims; but an alert and ruthless amîr could partly fulfill such hopes at least in the immediate vicinity of his power. If the amîr made a point of sending a strong and unbribable detachment against any independent robber band that might be reported, the main source of danger could be suppressed. Then in some Muslim areas a neighbouring village might be held collectively responsible for any other loss that occurred to travellers in their neighbourhood; for villages could usually act—or inform—against any purely local (and hence well-known) individuals who did not abide by the rules. This, however, depended on a strong amîr, jealous of his reputation, in firm control of his troops, and able to deploy them with the same readiness and minute surveillance as would be expected of police. Soldiers, bought as slaves or hired as adventurers, were more likely to turn, themselves, to molesting if the amîr's hand were at all weakened; for an amîr was himself dependent upon the troops' loyalty for his very position.

Wherever military despotism appeared, systematic brutality was likely to develop. The little military courts had the same need for sudden punishments and arbitrary wilfulness on the part of the ruler as had the great monarchies—on which, indeed, they tried to model themselves as far as possible. Lesser rulers might be restrained because the ruler was personally so close to his soldiers, but his actions could make up for such restraint within the court itself by increased arbitrariness among the subjects at large, which no remoter authority could curb. A military 'law' imposed the death penalty for slight offences, and the penalty was commonly exacted immediately, with no opportunity for passions to cool or new evidence to be discovered. (A great sultan, however, was likely to reserve final say to himself, as to the death penalty, staying the hand of subordinate amîrs.) At least as bad as sudden executions was the practice of torture. This was imposed either as punishment or as means of extracting information from principals or witnesses, and it could take exquisite forms in both cases. It was always possible for a man to die under torture, or to be maimed for life.

The Sharîʿah-minded still objected to such actions; their objections reflected both the humane aspirations of Islam and—more concretely—the sense of personal dignity of the various more independent groups, notably the Arab and Turkic tribesmen, who periodically contributed to the personnel of power. But for implementing their viewpoint in the form of respect for all Muslims there was little practical basis. The chief practical bases for reducing brutality in society on the agrarianate level were two, and neither of them was given much support by the Sharîʻah.

Within a clearly defined class, respect for personal dignity could be maintained on the basis of mutuality. When a city class was derived immediately from the socially better defined and more homogeneous life of a simpler society, the norms of that simpler life could be retained for a time within that class (hence a higher level of respect for the person often prevailed in areas newly citied than in older seats of citied life). Members of some aristocracies, accordingly, carried even into the anonymous complexities of city life a strong respect for each other's persons, and would respect each other's personal status however violently they fought each other. This was a specially marked instance of a more general phenomenon: throughout agrarianate-level society, even where tribal antecedents were lacking, it was normal that within any given social stratum—among the guildsmen of a town, for instance, or among villagers—brutality was curbed by carefully maintained custom. (Several of these considerations doubtless contributed, for instance, to the mutual respect of the citizens in classical Athens.) The Sharîʻah, of course, did not encourage such cliquishness.

But between classes—between master and servant, between rich man and beggar, between landholder and sharecropping peasant—there was no such solidarity. In these relationships, personal brutality—almost throughout agrarianate society—was tempered only by a sense of noblesse oblige on the part of the superior or by an effective solidarity on the part of the inferior. Rarely if ever—a possible exception was China for a time—did a universal and impersonal law achieve so general and immediate an application that it could control all relations of superior to inferior, eliminating most brutality and allowing people the luxury of being shocked by what was left.

As elsewhere, it was the less formal limitations, applied directly between the classes, that served in ordinary life in Islamdom. The general population could sometimes enforce recognition of its sentiments by riots, costly to the possessing classes. The tradesmen and merchants had a more dignified weapon for protesting any serious excess—a new fiscal levy or even the mistreatment of one of themselves: they could close their shops en masse, bringing town life to a stop and with it the victualling of the soldiery. Only a quite strong ruler might be able effectively to respond with force. (In many periods, merchants were virtually exempt from arbitrary interference.) Yet once again, the egalitarian doctrine of the Sharîʻah gave support neither to special nobility in the privileged nor to concerted resistance by the subjected.

But neither the solidarity that ensured respect for the person within a class, nor the pressures that were exerted between classes, could be depended upon within a military court, even a petty one. There, personal brutality knew almost no limits save what the monarch's personality voluntarily imposed. Unless he drove his subjects to the revolt of desperation by his unpredictability, the amîr's anger and vengeance could express themselves in the most inhuman savagery that the imagination could devise: tying a man to a stake and building a fire about him till he was consumed, or walling him with bricks to suffocate, or removing his whole skin while he was still alive. The chief limitation was that, in the case of a great officer, the ruler must take his victim by surprise, lest the man's own retainers support him in a revolt. Perhaps even more than in other pre-Modern regions, at many Muslim courts, especially the more powerful ones, such punishments were almost commonplace.

With the fall of the caliphal state as an empire, the problems of military despotism, latent so long as a general bureaucracy could still be effective, came to the fore. Already rulers such as the Bûyid military captains-turned-kings showed some incompetence in making work what was left of the bureaucracy in their regions, tied as they were to the immediate pleasure of their troops. All the more serious state formations of the period represented attempts, more or less successful, to rise above the level of local military despotism and interstitial anarchy. But by the end of the period this became more and more difficult in the central areas. Once the imperial structure was lost, it was very hard to regain; for the military conditions tended to perpetuate themselves as long as they satisfied the essential political requirements of the community. The hopes of the population for a great absolute monarchy that could curb the petty despotisms became the greater, as any less massive principle of control proved ineffective. Alternatively, the minds of the less patient might turn to chiliastic visions, which became common especially in the Later Middle Period.

C. DAILY LIFE

I hope I have emphasized the underlying ecological conditions, natural and cultural, that cumulatively made for the unusual balance of mercantile and agrarian interests in the pre-Modern Irano-Semitic culture; and that I have indicated how in the Middle Periods this balance was embodied in the a'yân-amîr system of social power and in the militarization of government it entailed. Now we must see how this worked out in the daily life of the cities. Both the strengths and the weaknesses of the system may be most readily seen in the patterns of economic investment that were associated with it, and to which it was probably conducive. Unfortunately, we know remarkably little of the productive economy of the period, but there seem to be enough indications to suggest a general and provisional picture.

International trade and economic investment

When the agrarian economy was no longer expanding in the Arid Zone, when the central bureaucratic state had collapsed and political power became militarized, long-standing tendencies in investment patterns were accentuated. We may distinguish three sorts of economic investment in the Agrarian Age. Those who wanted what extra funds they had acquired to yield them more yet could invest in land, in trade, or in industry. Free of ascriptive structuring, investment could tend to be put wherever the income would be greatest; but the same lack of structuring, in provoking military rule, had put effective limits on investment.

The amount of investment in land, on the part of others than the amîrs, was limited directly by the iqṭâʿ system (though by no means ruled out). Those who did invest in land tended to limit themselves, in intention, to receiving whatever revenue resulted from cultivation already going on; that is, the 'investment' was simply a purchase of rights to revenue, and not an actual use of accumulated funds on the land to make it more productive. But both Sharîʿah and state policy encouraged the use of capital to put previously unworked land under tillage. And something of this more productive sort of investment normally went with ordinary landholding, at least in the form of stocking seed or of maintaining irrigation works. Several considerations combined to keep productive investment in the land minimal. The iqṭâʿ system, as we have noted earlier, tended to discourage it in the lands reserved as iqṭâʿ—and not least when the fisc was strong enough to keep an iqṭâʿ holder unsure of his tenure. But the uncertainty even of ordinary landownership which the iqṭâʿ system produced, causing much land to be put into relatively safe waqf endowments, further discouraged investment. Family waqfs may have been kept up well enough, but at least waqfs in the hands of impersonal institutions, such as mosques or hospitals, tended to deteriorate for want of someone personally interested and responsible for them, to plough funds back into maintenance.

Investment in industry was limited more indirectly. Investment in manufacturing on a large scale had not been very widespread even in the prosperity of the High Caliphal Period in the region from Nile to Oxus. As we have noted, craftsmen preferred to operate singly or in small partnerships, with a limited amount of funds invested in any one endeavour, which meant limited opportunities for specialized investment. It was given still less encouragement in the Middle Periods.

The region could not, of course, dispense with industrial undertakings, and presumably some of these continued to be on a reasonably large scale. Parts of the Iranian highlands, especially in the northeast, were sufficiently rich in coal and iron and other metals; even the highlands north of the Fertile Crescent and in Syria had deposits on the scale required in agrarian times. Damascus steel was widely famous for its quality. Moreover, a certain degree of technological innovation, presupposing fresh investment, was taking place. We have noted the several new industries, such as sugar refining, paper making, and porcelain manufacture, which became important in the High Caliphal Period. We know rather less yet about such developments in the Middle Periods, but it seems, for instance, that windmills were carried westward within the Nile-to-Oxus region during this period; certainly manufactures associated with gunpowder steadily grew during the period; apparently gasoline distilling was introduced also, as well as the construction of elaborate clockwork mechanisms (mostly for show). (In some of these cases, some writers assume that because a particular invention is attested in western Europe a few years earlier than between Nile and Oxus, it must have come from the former to the latter region—which would presuppose a very rapid adoption of foreign inventions by the Muslims; this is, of course, possible, but in all these cases there is evidence that the full sequence of inventions from primitive to developed was continuous within Islamdom, and the scarcity of our documentation for Islamdom must make us cautious in assuming that the Europeans had even temporal priority.)

But there are indications that industry was handicapped. Many manufactured goods were imported both from Europe and from India, including fairly common metal instruments; and even from China. (Such importation was probably less for the core areas than for outlying lands, of course; when we hear that in Yemen scrap brass was collected to be sent to Keralam in India for remanufacture, we must recall that Yemen was commercially closer to Keralam than to Khurâsân or even to Syria.) The fame from Nile to Oxus of Chinese, Indians, and even Europeans as craftsmen was probably not unjustified economically. Perhaps especially in the Arid Zone, political conditions that could be tolerable or even favourable for merchants with movable investments could be prohibitive for industrial investment. We hear occasionally of merchant families being subjected to such demands for money by military rulers as ruined the merchants (this could happen also in the politically more stable regions of the hemisphere). But such short-sighted extortion was much easier to carry out against a manufacturer, whose assets were impossible to conceal or to move.

As we have seen, a good many manufactures were simply undertaken by the government in some places: not only the mint (making coins) and military manufactures, but the manufacture of fine cloths that required more varied raw materials than a single craftsman could find it easy to collect, or other luxury specialties. This did not usually make for far-sighted innovation except in such things as artistic style, which the court could appreciate directly. But private industrial investment, to be carried far, required a large-scale market and security of visible wealth. But a very large-scale market concentrated in the immediate vicinity of an industry was hard to find in the Arid Zone except where a great agrarian empire could concentrate wealth as its capital city. And the security of urban property, while never so uncertain as property in the villages subject to revenue collectors, clearly declined as military rule progressed. Even apart from soldierly rapacity, the repeated destruction of city property by war and even the transportation of skilled craftsmen by conquerors would tend to disrupt any tradition that was being built up. Industrial investment, then, was not the form naturally most favoured in the mid-Arid Zone; and the resultant emphasis on commercial investment did not make for civic conditions in which industrial investment was given even such encouragement as the population pattern of the Arid Zone might have suggested. It is possibly for want of an appropriate base in industrial skills and specialized tools that those Muslims who knew of printing, as it had been developed in China, and appreciated its advantages, were unable to introduce it in Islamdom save in very minor ways (e.g., for printing cards).

With investment in agriculture and in industry variously limited, investment by the city well-to-do tended more than ever to go into trade, at least until a family was so well established that it could risk trying to share in the land revenue. Local trade, in the vicinity of the towns and between one city and its neighbour, was substantial. As we have noted, even the villages, between Nile and Oxus, were probably, on the whole, less self-sufficient than those in India or much of Europe. And the grain trade made many fortunes. But, to judge by literary impressions, at least, the trade that bestowed both wealth and prestige in freest measure was the trade between one country and another, as well as the long-distance trade across Oikoumenic regions. Trade was consciously divided into two types: trade in staples, bulk trade; and trade in luxury goods, in which small quantities could produce a large return. Manuals in commerce might recommend that the merchant restrict himself to trade staples such as grains as safer than trade in luxuries, which might attract the attention either of robbers or of a ruler. Basic staples might be transported over very long distances according to demand, especially if poor local harvests sent the price up and attracted importers. But it was the luxury merchant who had the most alluring repute (and the longer the distance covered by the trade, the more it tended to be restricted to luxury goods). Hence the local social structure within a city, in which the wealthiest merchants played a major role, might become, if anything, more closely tied to the long-distance trade as the Middle Periods progressed, except where local conditions militated against this.

The facilities for long-distance trade were basically similar throughout the Irano-Mediterranean zone. From Nile to Oxus they remained well-developed during the Middle Periods, even though perhaps not always so spectacular as under the High Caliphal state. We have mentioned the private postal services that facilitated communication. The banking structure, which we have also noted in the High Caliphal Period, was presumably organized for the purposes of commerce, not of industrial investment; it made possible remission of moneys at a great distance much more readily than local long-term loans for investment. In India, at least, the financial entrepreneurs also arranged for some forms of insurance against commercial risks; this probably was done also between Nile and Oxus. The organization of camel caravans was professional and was generally, but not always, effective even in the midst of military anarchy.

We may miss the maintenance of highways, which was minimal. Highways in earlier periods had served two purposes, both in large measure military. They had served the needs of foot-soldiers in the day when well-disciplined infantry had proved decisive against horsemen still wanting the stirrup. In that period such enduring agrarian empires as the Achaemenid Persian and the Roman needed to transport their foot-soldiers rapidly over long distances. More important, highways served the needs of wheeled vehicles, which required a paved surface to move rapidly over long distances. The same empires transported their military provisions on wheels; and civilian land trade was likewise in wheeled vehicles. But with the supremacy of the well-mounted horseman from Arsacid Parthian times on, the speed of foot-soldiers was no longer so decisive. Soon after, even wheeled vehicles were superseded for long-distance transport in the lands between Nile and Oxus.

Carts and, in general, wheeled vehicles were displaced by the camel for most purposes in the Arab lands (the lowlands—around the Mediterranean as well as in Arabia itself); and carts were displaced even elsewhere in the Arid Zone, for instance in Iran, for long-distance trade. For the camel proved able to win out over any clumsier or less rugged form of transport on land. Accordingly, firm highways, which the earlier empires in the area had all maintained, gave way to relatively casual roads; for not only commercial but even military transport no longer had the sort of need for well-maintained highways that would make them worth the considerable expense they required. (That is, the decay of the highways was not, as it is sometimes pictured, the result of ignorant neglect, but of what by an economic calculus must be reckoned a technical advance.)[19] What was needed in the age of camel transport was adequate hostels at every stage of the journey, where water could be provided and goods safely stored overnight. These were well arranged along the main routes, and one of the most prominent buildings in any town was the caravanserai where the merchants found all the facilities they might call for.

Except in the realm of commerce, which continued to be socially crucial,

[19] This is at least partly recognized in 'L'Evolution des techniques dans le monde musulman au moyen âge' by Gaston Wiet, Vadime Elisséeff, and Philippe Wolff, in *Cahiers d'histoire mondiale* 6 (1960), 15–44; a convenient little survey of agricultural, urban, transport, industrial, financial, and military techniques in the Arab lands (despite its broader title); the article, however, shows no sense of development and is marred by a remarkable lack of sophistication, resulting in considerable misinterpretation. Its point of comparison is commonly the modern West. It expresses a naïve north-west European astonishment that in such lands as Syria the mould-board plough, designed for heavy northern soils, was not in use.

the overall pattern of the economy remained that of local subsistence in the countryside and individual craftwork in the towns, capped by extraction of revenue from the peasantry for the benefit of an increasingly military upper class and its dependants. As the Middle Periods advanced, complication of this pattern by extensive agricultural or industrial investment became increasingly difficult, though always sufficiently substantial to exhibit significant development.

Sex, slavery, and the harem system: the cult of masculine honour

The a'yân-amîr system and, more generally, the cosmopolitan tendencies of the mid-Arid Zone were reflected indirectly in the private life of the more privileged classes, which in turn helped to undergird the distinctive traits of public life. The slave household (or 'harem system') characteristic of upper-class Islamdom presupposed the social mobility of the society, the mingling of classes and the open and shifting lines of patronage among the a'yân notables. In contrast to upper-class households in the Occident or in Hindu India guaranteed by fixed social status, the Muslim household might preserve a reasonably fixed character only by way of slavery and female seclusion. The slave household contributed, in turn, to making the a'yân-amîr system work by avoiding the rise of private demands that might have required a more fixed structuring of the public realm. However, at least as important in giving rise to the slave household, presumably, was the underlying conception of masculine honour that it presupposed and embodied.

The most striking level at which the Irano-Mediterranean folk-cultural homogeneity showed itself was that of personal honour; particularly the man's sense of his status as a male, as this was expressed in social institutions. One must first describe these expressions of masculine honour in terms that may be applicable to many peoples, not only those that became Muslim; then, however, one can distinguish the points where the special conditions of Islamdom and especially of the Middle Periods seem to have evoked special effects—which in turn affected the Islamicate high-cultural life.

It is a tendency common in many societies, for the individual man to see his private life as a struggle to maintain his masculine honour. Probably this will be especially so when there are few other sources of assured status than sheer masculinity. Presumably in a society where social status on the basis of class was relatively precarious, sensitivity about a man's honour as a male was reinforced. Throughout the Irano-Mediterranean zone, the sense of male personal honour was often expressed in a pattern with two prominent features: formal vengeance and feuding between families or factions, and highly institutionalized—and drastic—sexual jealousy. However else the image of the ideal man might vary from class to class, it generally included an expectation that the ideal man would defend his honour with violence at these two points.

Even casual violence on the streets, when one man takes offence at another, seems to flare more readily in the Irano-Mediterranean zone than, say, in India or northern Europe. But what became socially significant in many areas was a conventionalized insistence on precedence, calling for vengeance upon violation, and issuing in a pattern of feuding. In contrast to the duel of European chivalry, the feud was not based on demand for recognition of fixed hierarchical status as a knight, say, or a peer, but on demand for acknowledgement of one's personal worth as a man and of the immediate power of the group of men whose solidarity one was able to command. The feud need have nothing to do with a cosmopolitan outlook. It was at its most highly developed among the Bedouin, where it served an indispensable social function, and it could appear in relatively isolated peasant villages with no Bedouin background (e.g., in Sicily), where it served a like function. But it was widely taken up in the towns and even the cosmopolitan cities—sometimes with a Bedouin or other pastoralist terminology (which was encouraged by a literary glorification of the pastoralist life, especially in Arabic). Sometimes the feuds were, in the original sense, clan feuds between two families or blocs of families, and this was naturally typical among settled Bedouin and among those peasants who assimilated themselves, for various reasons, to settled Bedouin. More often, in the towns, feuding took the form of splitting the town population (as we have already noticed) into hereditary hostile factions, whose pretext for differing might be political or especially religious, as in the common split between Ḥanafîs and Shâfiʿîs.

The expectation of masculine vengeance, when applied to an amîr or a king, reinforced the condoning by popular opinion of cruel acts of retaliation for slight faults, which marked the despotic courts. When applied to the notables of a town, it reinforced the tendency of a town to divide helplessly into multiple factions which prevented any common organization. A man's 'honour' was taken far more seriously than any sense of civic responsibility. At the same time, it doubtless reinforced the internal cohesion of the various channels of solidarity that did occur within towns, the futuwwah, the town quarters, the clientèle sharing the patronage of a notable. In all these ways, the spirit of feuding vengeance, by receiving an unusually high social status in Irano-Semitic life, reinforced the social tendencies that marked the Middle Periods.

But still more pervasive were the effects of institutionalized sexual jealousy. Formalized sexual jealousy, even more than the simple spirit of vengeance, fills the popular stories that appear, for instance, in the *Thousand and One Nights*. One can sometimes get the impression that the most important source of an individual man's personal reassurance was his absolute control over his womenfolk. A woman's 'honour', her shame, formed an important point in determining the honour of her man; indeed, perhaps the gravest insult to a man, which most insistently abridged his right to precedence and called for vengeance, was any impugning of the honour of his womenfolk.

And all sexual jealousy was expected to be subsumed into the pattern of defending one's masculine honour.[20]

A well-known pattern of institutionalized sexual jealousy was accepted in almost all citied agrarianate societies: sexual access to 'honourable' women was so severely limited to one husband that the most important virtue a woman could have was her sexual fidelity to him (and her avoidance of any sex act before marriage); while men until they were married, had sexual access only to a specialized class of 'dishonourable' women (prostitutes)—if, indeed, such were available at all. Nowhere was this pattern carried to such an extreme as in the central lands of Islamdom; from there the intensified pattern was gradually introduced elsewhere in Islamdom. The 'honourable' woman was expected to be excluded from any sort of contact with possible sex partners other than her husband; the whole pattern of family life and of social intercourse (especially in the upper classes) was geared to this exclusion.

Sex relations seem to have been thought of especially in two complementary aspects. They were a form of masculine triumph: the tendency to see the sex act as the domination of male over female was sometimes exaggerated into the victory of the male over a subjected female, his possession. That the female likewise received pleasure was fully recognized, to be sure; but her subservient role was clear when she was carefully trained by her mother in the skills of pleasing her lord in the sex act and so holding his affections. At the same time, the need for sexual privacy was exaggerated into a sense of shame about all things sexual. The male dared not allow his sex organs to be uncovered before other men; and, since women might be thought of as primarily objects of sexual pleasure, even the mention of a man's wife was regarded as indecorous. Women could be seen so exclusively as objects of possession and of shame that brothers were expected, in many circles, to kill a sister who had sex with the wrong man—sparing her husband (if she were already married) the need to act himself and the risk of arousing her family's enmity. We find the futuwwah men's clubs accused of encouraging such killings on mere suspicion of the girl's misbehaviour, without evidence.

A like attitude appears in a different perspective in the story of the saint at Shîrâz who was said to have married many wives, each of whom thought she was disliked because he never touched her—till one of them boldly asked him about it and he showed her the knotted flesh of his belly, which he said was the result of restraining himself from eating and from having sex. (One must add, for the record, that the man in question did have children.) The (male) narrator tells the story as an exemplary case of self-denial, and shows

[20] J. G. Peristiany, ed., *Honour and Shame: The Values of Mediterranean Society* (Univ. of Chicago Press, 1966), (uneven in value) brings out how universally in the Mediterranean the notions of male and female 'honour' are related to sexual jealousy. It speaks of the Mediterranean, but of course its points apply to the whole Irano-Mediterranean complex.

no awareness that from a feminine viewpoint it might equally illustrate selfish cruelty.

In marriage, then, the liberty and honour of the independent male seemed to require the subservience of the females, and with them of the children; as well as that of any dependent males. Accordingly, the pattern of sexual segregation, which (as we have seen) the Sharîʿah somewhat came to encourage, was completed by an institution which in its fullest form the Sharîʿah could not wholly approve: the 'harem system'. Something like the harem system was widespread in the Agrarian Age, particularly in its later centuries; it is as if the patterns of sexual jealousy usual to society on the agrarianate level naturally led to that as urban life became more complex and more mobile. In particular, in the Mediterranean peninsulas the upper-class Byzantine ladies, in a tradition that led back even to classical Greek times, were secluded in apartments not accessible to outside males, with much the same arrangements as prevailed among Muslims. But the Muslim form was the most severe.

Wealthy men not only had three or four wives by marriage, whom they kept secluded from masculine company; they had a whole household of female dependants, servants and also, among them, slave concubines; for each wife must be served by her own attendants, and a large establishment required many hands to maintain it before the days of household machines. All these, along with the children of both sexes, lived in a part of the house (by a good deal the largest part of the house), called the 'harem', which was not open to masculine visitors (except close relatives of the women involved). Thus a wealthy male had distinctly more than his share of dependent females, who had a world of their own in which women ruled over women, with the lone adult male as an often rather remote arbiter; or, often enough, willing tool of that woman who most charmed him at the moment. (If the male was dominant in the sex act, his dominance at home was sometimes very nearly reduced to that.) Though visiting males could not be admitted, visiting females could be admitted all the more freely, whatever their social station; so each man's harem-home was linked closely to a wide network of feminine life from most of which he was rigidly excluded and even his own portion of which he was necessarily rather aloof from.

The women's apartments, in these circumstances, tended to be the centre of intrigues: intrigues for the master's love—which often went to young slave concubines by preference—or for his respect (and monetary favours) or for his favouring of one women's children over another's (for though all the children were his, they were aligned almost in different families according to their different mothers). We have noticed some occasions on which such 'harem intrigues' governed the policy of rulers.

Sometimes, indeed, the intrigues included, as one component, the attempts of some neglected lady of leisure to find an admirer from among the men of the outside world. Accordingly, to remain master of his household, the man often took measures that went far beyond veiling and rigid privacy of the inner quarters—and which might also counteract, in some measure, his own helplessness to control his women's social life. The house might be so constructed that the rooms in which outside males were received did not even communicate with the private or 'harem' quarters; or the women's apartments might be locked and guarded. The purpose of such guarding was technically to maintain the chastity of all the female inmates, or, more precisely, to support the man's sense of sexual mastery by excluding all rivals. Such guards might be robust women or very old men; but already the Byzantines had learned to use, for a very similar purpose (though technically even their richest men could have only one legitimate wife), slave eunuchs; such would have much of the strength of men and, by reputation, more than their share of shrewdness, but presumably could not become sexual rivals.

The Sharî'ah law could accept (though it did not encourage) the use of slave concubines, even if with some limitations. The use of eunuchs was far more doubtful. Finally, in Shar'î eyes a free woman was (in principle) almost as free as a man, despite some ties of dependency. The whole atmosphere of servility and secrecy, founded on the use of slave guards, was seriously alien to the Shar'î sense of human dignity. It could also be disastrous for a ruling class. The advice of women kept in seclusion was, in any case, not such as to inspire their men with magnanimity, or even to curb them with practical good sense. Only an outstanding woman could so rise above her status as to be of serious help to her husband. Worse (as many have pointed out), a typical secluded woman could not give her sons, in their formative early years, the experience and guidance which would enable them to profit most fully from their later years of apprenticeship among the men. To the pampering that privileged children necessarily received from servants was too often added a petty and irresponsible direction from the mother. But the harem system itself made all this worse. That women kept deliberately ignorant might be able to move their husbands on points of policy which by chance touched the women personally is only a part of what makes a reference to harem intrigue figure sinisterly in the chronicles.

The harem system was fully developed only in the wealthiest households, but it was imitated as far as possible at lower social levels. However, on less well-to-do levels there was unlikely to be more than one wife, and the number of servants was limited. The situation, as it often developed, was probably well enough mirrored in several aspects of a typical anecdote from the poet Rûmî about a man who had an exceedingly beautiful slavegirl. His wife (who was the girl's immediate mistress, of course) made a point of never leaving the two alone together. But one day the wife was at the public bath for women—this was a valued occasion socially as well as hygienically; there she missed a bathing utensil, and sent the girl home for it. Too late she recalled that her husband was alone in the house. The girl had sped home and the pair had immediately proceeded to have sex; but in their eagerness they forgot to bar the door (the usual form of locking up, in a land where households were large and someone was usually within to unbar it at call). The wife came hurrying after the girl; as they heard her arrive, the husband pulled himself together and started performing ṣalât worship. But the suspicious wife pulled up his loose garment and saw the evidence, seed and all, that a moment before he had been engaged in something quite different (which indeed made him ritually unclean for the ṣalât till he had bathed); she slapped him and gave him an exemplary tongue lashing. I must add that Rûmî's point in telling the story was neither that the man was henpecked nor that his idea of sexplay was rudimentary (things the harem system surely encouraged), but that he was duly caught in a vain pretence.

Complementary to the harem system was a conventional pattern of homosexual relations, especially among males, that sometimes became highly formal. The exaggerated glorification of sexual jealousy and the system of sexual restrictions that expressed it entailed severe sexual repression, especially in youth, both of females and of males. This repression by itself would be likely to turn many to alternative forms of sexual satisfaction. Doubtless a sense of insecurity flowing from the social demand that the male prove his masculinity added pressures that might drive a youth unconsciously to avoid involvement with femininity and to welcome contact with the masculine. In any case, what is probably a natural tendency in most men, particularly in adolescence, to respond sexually to other men occasionally, as when women are not accessible, was exaggerated into a regular expectation or even, sometimes, a preference. Perhaps the militarization of the highest social classes contributed to this with its stress on masculine society. It was especially in the Middle Periods, in association with the military courts of the amîrs, that sex between males entered pervasively into the ethic and the aesthetic of the upper classes.

Not only those younger males who did not have access to free females and could not afford female slaves, but also married men with substantial resources would vary, in many cases, a sexual relation with a (perhaps too subservient?) female by having sexual relations with a male (perhaps more spirited?), especially an adolescent. As in some classical Athenian circles, it was assumed that a handsome adolescent ('beardless') youth or even a younger boy was naturally attractive to any full-grown man, and that the man would have sexual relations with him if the occasion arose (for instance, if the youth were his slave), alongside sex relations with his women. It even became conventional for a man to become enamoured of a youth in much the same way as he might be enamoured of a girl—and even for the youth to respond to his feelings; and for relations of jealousy to arise on this basis. The ordinary Muslim stereotype of such sexual relations answered to the idea of the sex act as an act of domination. The adult man, as the lover, enjoyed a youth (probably anally) who was, in principle, passive; and while the relation was only improper, at most licentious, for the lover, it was very dishonourable for the youth who was enjoyed, who thus allowed himself to be cast in a woman's role. (This attitude may be contrasted to that of the Spartans, among whom the intimacy with an older man was supposed to increase the youth's manly virtue.) Even relations among adolescent boys might take this form—some boys allowed themselves to be enjoyed and were dishonoured, while those who enjoyed them regarded themselves as manly.

Some persons are inclined to speak of 'degeneracy', and others of 'tolerance', where homosexual inclinations are publicly recognized without punishment. It must be recalled that most of the men who, following fashion, had occasional relations with youths continued to be interested primarily in women and produced numbers of children. And while those men, few in any society, whose personalities drew them into sexual relations with men by preference might have more open opportunities for sexual satisfaction, and even for relations more mutual than the stereotype would allow for, they could not easily take advantage of them without serious dishonour.[21]

Despite strong Shar'î disapproval, the sexual relations of a mature man with a subordinate youth were so readily accepted in upper-class circles that there was often little or no effort to conceal their existence. Sometimes it seems to have been socially more acceptable to speak of a man's attachment to a youth than to speak of his women, who were supposed to be invisible in the inner courts. The fashion entered into poetry, especially in the Persian. The narrative poetry, indeed, conventionally told of love affairs between men and women; but the person to whom lyric love verse is addressed by male poets was conventionally, and almost without exception, made explicitly male.

Private fears and pleasures

Sex was not the only area of repression and distortion. From villagers to amîrs, injustice and cruelty, ugliness and falsehood were abundantly built into the life that each individual inherited. They were often fixed in customary institutions which the kindliness of individuals could not set aside. Many anecdotes show that, if not too pressed by their own troubles, many

[21] Unexamined sexual assumptions have entered—usually rather unexplicitly—into Occidental impressions of Muslim mores so frequently that it is necessary to be as clear as possible as to just what is being referred to in the oblique remarks Western literature is full of. Perhaps it is becoming less necessary nowadays to point out that an inclination to have sex with other men—even when such sex is actually preferred to sex with women—need not imply effeminacy in any degree (though in some spectacular cases, especially with transvestites, it does so). It must still be pointed out, in some circles, that public display of affection between men, as by walking hand in hand, need not imply any sexual interest.

people were inclined to treat kindly even the animals that lived among them, down to the despised dog. But the dog's role in the village was to be watchdog (to alert people to any stranger's presence) and scavenger, and he was held to that role: dogs did not become pets; the children in the streets found it amusing to throw stones at them, and few adults would check them. In consequence, the dogs grew up curs, almost destitute of the endearing qualities that, in lands where they were better known as helpers in hunting or herding, made them so highly respected. Too many human beings grew up in much the same way.

People were often hungry and very commonly physically ill with a variety of endemic disorders. Eyes readily became diseased in childhood in those glaring regions and blindness was commonplace; old age was regularly marked by a series of bodily deformities, the least of which was a crooked back. People were repeatedly and chronically frustrated in even the low goals they dared set for themselves, and insecure against the still more devastating calamities of famine or pestilence. It has been found that modern peasant villages in the region can show a distinct profile of what current testing methods indicate as neurotic traits among the population, and the anecdotes we have from an earlier time imply severe crippling and mutilation of personality.

In desperation, villagers turned to all the imaginative devices they could invent in hope of breaking through their impasses. They used in abundance the petty tricks we call superstitions, in that their efficacy cannot be objectively shown, but they are resorted to for want of anything more likely, having emerged out of fears based on chance experience or analogy, or on a misunderstanding of real dangers. For instance, the subtle roles persons can play unconsciously in one another's lives were concretized in the notion of the 'evil eye'—that an envious person's glance could bring harm to the person he envied, and most especially to children; hence children might be deliberately dressed poorly, or referred to deprecatingly in company, to avoid arousing envy; and visitors were careful not to pay overmuch attention to them. Amulets of all sorts were omnipresent, including Qur'ânic phrases regarded as peculiarly potent; in particular, blue (a commonly available colour) was held to be efficacious against the evil eye. The powers of magic were held in awe, and anyone who got a reputation for it was sure to be feared—and courted. And since people were aware that piling superstitious precaution on precaution still sometimes did not suffice, and that even formal magic could prove impotent, they were constantly ready to try new tricks, or to credit a new magician if he were from a land distant enough. Townsmen readily shared the villagers' superstitions, being often enough desperate themselves; and the wives and serving girls even of the wealthy—who were often drawn from the lowest classes anyway—shared, for the most part, the same varied store of hopeful lore, and brought up the children on it. Perhaps the only class even partially free of practices based in this climate of petty magic were the merchants; and the Sharî'ah was relatively firm in its rejection of most such tricks.

It has been said that Muslims were 'fatalistic'; but such assertions, as commonly made, are misleading because they confuse diverse things under one term. If 'fatalism' means abandoning all effort to help oneself, on the ground that all that happens to one is fated, it is at best rare: no one fails to lift his food to his mouth, leaving it to fate. 'Fatalism' might mean, then, that a relatively large part of a population believes that only a relatively narrow range of possibilities are effectively open to the individual's choice. Certainly, despite their recourse to every trick they knew, most Muslims were pessimistic about their chances. But in itself this was simply a matter of a more or less shrewd estimate of reality; it had nothing to do with theology. But 'fatalism' refers most properly to an attitude taken to whatever, upon investigation, turns out to be in fact beyond one's control. One may resent such a fact impotently, or one may accept it, interpreting it as favourably or as nobly as one knows how.

In this last sense, Islamic religion, like any other, enabled a person to dignify his acceptance of the unavoidable with phrases that reminded him of his ultimate commitments—and even, sometimes, to turn his acceptance to good spiritual purpose in self-discipline or in refocussing of the attention. (Hence Ṣûfîs were especially fond of 'fatalistic' dicta.) In practice, references to fate among Muslims centred especially on two points. The time of one's death was 'decreed' and not to be changed by any amount of precaution—a 'fatalism' very common everywhere and particularly among soldiers, which had the advantage of rationalizing courage in the field even though it never hindered anyone from parrying a sword-thrust when he could. (In particular, the idea that death would overtake one at the appointed time wherever one was sometimes was used to justify failure to flee from plague; but most people avoided plague when they could.) And the amount of one's sustenance was likewise decreed; which notion had the advantage of rationalizing hospitality and generosity even when one's resources were limited, even though it alone never prevented anyone from accepting a job if he needed one to feed his family.

Accepting one's fate without complaining, particularly in these two matters, was inculcated in innumerable religious stories, including ḥadîth reports of the Prophet. It was told how the angel of death visited Solomon (as one of the prophets) in Jerusalem one day and stared intently at a man sitting next to him. When the angel was gone, the man asked who it had been; when he was told, he decided the angel's attentions were unwelcome, and set off at once on a trip to Baghdad so as to avoid his further notice. The next day Solomon chided the angel for frightening the man. The angel explained that he had been surprised to see the man in Jerusalem, for he had an appointment with him just a few days later in Baghdad. It must be noted, incidentally, that the 'fatalism' here inculcated has nothing to do with the divine predestination of the human will which the Jamâ'î-Sunnîs came to accept—more or less—and the Shî'îs to reject. Such pious stories were as common among Shî'îs as Sunnîs.[22]

In their need, in any case, the Muslims turned to whatever sources of help seemed to promise most; and this often meant practices certified by association with the high culture of the cities, which inevitably carried great prestige everywhere. As the ways of the city élites spread outward into the countryside, local superstition was supplemented with more sophisticated lore, even though this was distorted and debased often to the level of the economic and social means of the peasant. The skills of the Faylasûfs, once ministering to the wealthy only, came to be demanded even in the village; earlier priestly and folk remedies were supplemented by, or rather subsumed into, the repertory of the village *ḥakîm*, the physician-cum-astrologer who pretended to some touch of Galen and of Aristotle. Like his opposite number in the Hindu village, the sometimes barely literate *vaid* who tried to draw on the resources of high Sanskrit tradition, the village ḥakîm was sometimes more a magician than a philosopher; more a distributor of charms than of science. But a certain amount of genuine continuity between village practice and the best thought of Râzî and Ibn-Sînâ was established; and no ceiling was imposed on how much might be carried to the more fortunate village.

As commonly among people accustomed to poverty, it was rare that anyone gave up altogether the effort to make life endurable. People would lower their goals drastically rather than resort to suicide. And when not stricken by disaster, people did find ways to win pleasure from life. Most important, happiness need not always be found each person for himself. In the villages and even in the towns, much of the delight of life was found in group activities, in which the poorest could participate along with the most fortunate, and even the blind beggar had his share. Thus weddings were not a private episode in the lives of bride and groom, or even of their families. The role of the individual bride and groom was ceremonially central, but it was clear that the occasion belonged to all their friends as well. As at any other celebration, a whole village, or a neighbourhood in a town, danced with joy to the best music that could be hired locally, played games that tested the men's skills, and bought novelties from peddlers to please the women; and of course celebrated in drink. If the families were at all well off, they distributed largesse in the form of coins, often tossed at large into the streets for

[22] It has often been noted that among monotheists (among whom the problem of reconciling divine omnipotence and human free will is recurrent) a position that stresses divine predestination has commonly been associated with moral rigourism (which would seem to imply believing that a person can freely control himself if he tries). The point is that persons inclined to stress moral duty are the same ones who will be inclined to stress the supremacy of the moral God over the workings of amoral nature. As always, each really serious position on ultimate questions is derived independently from human experience, not by (supposedly) logical deduction from the formulations of positions on other ultimate questions. Hence predestination has been associated, in many cases, with the reverse of practical 'fatalism' at least as regards a person's efforts to improve himself.

the most needy, or the most shameless, to gather up. For such occasions, as on an occasion of hospitality, whoever had enough might sacrifice all his means—for the delight of the village was not only his delight but also his pride. If then he must go without food later as a result of his indiscretion, this demonstrated the ancient fact that human beings live by more than mere eating. However penurious his daily life might become, anyway, he would share in the next festivity arranged by another.

The wealthier classes had their own diversions—notably hunting, when not war (both of which were commonly enough at the expense of the poor). But even they shared in the festive occasions of the community, and their own festivities bore the same traits as those of the peasants, but on a larger scale; and small fortunes might be thrown about among the attendant mobs.

Like the medicine of the ḥakîms, such group occasions were steadily infiltrated by elements of the high culture, which the wealthiest even in the villages were, in a measure, exposed to. The reciters of epic literature, based on literary traditions, spread to the farthest corners the names of heroes who had won the imagination of the bourgeois—not without mingling them, sometimes, with oral traditions that were produced especially among the more adventurous of the rural population, Bedouin or tribal Turks. The Muslim religious festivals seem to have been carried to every village in rather the same way; that is, they likewise represented a contribution of the high culture to the perpetual attempt of the villagers to rise beyond themselves; though older festivals tied to the cycle of nature, such as the Nawrûz, the day of spring, were not readily abandoned.

The religious festivals, even when their main lines were laid down by the Sharî'ah law, came to have significance according to the needs of the life into which Muslims built those ceremonies. Not because of anything in the Qur'ân but because of its central place in the social calendar, the most important ritual obligation came to be felt as the fast of Ramaḍân: during one lunar month out of twelve (falling in different seasons of the solar year from time to time), the faithful (except those who were ill or travelling) must not eat, nor even drink water, from before sunrise till the sun sets; the whole community life during this month was reordered accordingly, to allow only the bare essentials of business to press on people at such a time. The nights were often times of even gluttonous celebration; though not with the more pious, who lit lamps in the mosques and recited the entire Qur'ân through, a specified portion each night. At the end of the month was a family festival, the 'lesser' 'îd (or *bayrâm*). The 'greater' 'îd, also largely a family festival, occurred at the time of the yearly pilgrimage to Mecca; but the 'lesser' 'îd was in practice often the greater, because of the build-up for it provided by the fasts and excitement of Ramaḍân.

But in addition to these 'îds, the *mawlid*, birthday (and simultaneously deathday) of the Prophet, was celebrated with almost as great ado. Moreover, the birthdays of major local saints (which, as we shall see, a socially active

Ṣûfî mysticism soon provided almost everywhere) became occasions for all in a wide district to gather at the saint's tomb for a blessing and also for an outing and a fair. These lesser occasions were foci of pilgrimages, serving more local functions such as the ḥajj pilgrimage to Mecca had once served within the Ḥijâz. In the ḥajj itself, every wealthy Muslim planned to participate as a major life's excursion, not only for piety but for adventure and perhaps learning or personal retreat; and even occasionally as a political expedient.

The Muslim who was comfortably off should give part of his substance to the poor. The minimum amount of the zakât, or yearly legal alms, was theoretically fixed in the Sharî'ah; but the piety of it came to be associated not with the legal dues often collected rather arbitrarily by Muslim governments, but with private voluntary giving, notably at the 'îd (and directed—with Qur'ânic authority—especially to needy relatives). It thus became part of the festive sharing that bound a locality together.

The greater shrines to which pilgrimage was made, finally, served as places of asylum for those who must flee their homes—on account of a crime committed, or suspected, or of a great man offended. Society could be cruel, but it provided points of escape from its worst cruelties for those fortunate enough to find them. And under the protection of religion a man could retain his dignity as a Muslim even when, in desperation, he must take refuge with God's saints at their tombs.[23]

[23] One ought to make a comparison with Byzantium in the same period, where the persistence of the empire with its bureaucracy and its laws had pervasive effects in a setting otherwise somewhat similar; Walter Kaegi has suggested such contrasts to me. Others who have contributed to clarifying the drafts of this chapter have been Donald Levine and Lloyd Fallers and especially Reuben Smith, whose experience and comments have been helpful throughout the work.

III

Maturity and Dialogue among the Intellectual Traditions, *c.* 945–1111

The new social order of the Middle Periods differed not only politically from the society of the High Caliphate, but in all aspects of its culture, in religion, literature, art, and science, as well as in economic life or the patterning of social classes. The culture of the High Caliphate gradually became classical, an inherited model to look back to. The great schools of fiqh which it had developed became accepted as the only possible ones; the Sharî'ah was no longer an adventure but a heritage. The canons of Arabic literary criticism and of grammar, which the scholars of Kûfah and Baṣrah and Baghdad had quarrelled about, came to be a semi-sacred inheritance, to be learned and believed; and the top literature of that older time was held unsurpassable in its kind, particularly in those countries where Arabic continued to be the chief cultural language. Formal political theory never abandoned its attachment to the caliph, not only after the end of the actual caliphal state, but after there was no longer even the title of caliph in Baghdad. New creative effort, accordingly, new life adapted to the new conditions, took this heritage for granted and went into new channels of activity.

Pressures for overall intellectual conformity among Muslims had been growing as Islamicate culture matured and as norms seemed to be established in various fields; and as pressures for a more concrete social conformity within a dominant élite ceased to be relevant to Muslim life as such. The Ḥadîth folk had their own ideas of what was public propriety in things intellectual; but so did many other groups, and these groups did not always disagree enough to cancel each other out. Even Faylasûfs could encourage respect for the great masters among disciples obviously not mature enough to strike out on their own—disciples who, when they became mature enough, might have gained the habit of intellectual accommodation. But during the Shî'î century, any more external, social pressures for such conformity were partly neutralized. The various Shî'î rulers, of course, were unwilling to enforce standards that were largely associated with Jamâ'î-Sunnî 'ulamâ'; nor were they interested in imposing the views of the Shî'î 'ulamâ' upon subjects who were mostly Sunnîs. By their neutrality as well as by their rather heterogeneous personal patronage, they helped foster intellectual pursuits. The Jamâ'î-Sunnî rulers also mostly maintained old habits of general tolerance. Under the considerable peace and administrative continuity that were still maintained in large areas, therefore, external conditions for intellectual life continued not very dissimilar to those under the High Caliphate.

In the Shî'î century and just after, the consequence was a series of serious intellectual confrontations. In the High Caliphal Period, Islamicate scholarship and science had flowed in a number of largely separate streams. The Shar'î scholar, the adîb, and the Faylasûf by no means lived in separate worlds; there were important intellectual contacts among them, increasingly as time went on. But the story of the intellectual development of each group can be told, in the main, separately from that of the other groups. This was much less true of the Middle Periods. In the tenth and eleventh centuries, all the different intellectual traditions were well matured—that of the adîbs, that of the Shar'î 'ulamâ', and also that of the Hellenic-Syriac philosophic and scientific tradition which had so long depended on an active work of translation and adaptation. Each tradition was ready to look beyond its own roots. Now, in particular, the Hellenists and the 'ulamâ' fully confronted each other and the result was as stimulating in the intellectual field as the confrontation of the absolutism of the adîbs with the Shar'ism of the 'ulamâ' had been frustrating in the social field.

Out of these dialogues among mature traditions, with their assumption of a minimal Shar'î pattern as already given, and out of the relatively decentralized and emancipated social context generally, grew two forms of intellectual independence that were, though not unparalleled in other times, yet specially distinctive of the period. On the level of imaginative literature, we find the expression of a human image that was relatively secular, in that the writers were not primarily preoccupied with coming to terms with the challenge of Islam. Then in more explicit speculation, where the assumption of Shar'î dominance was more pressing, we find a growing pattern of free esoteric expression of truths.

By the end of the eleventh century, the political milieu was no longer Shî'î. (And fewer of the intellectuals were of the old Shî'î families.) Moreover, pressure for conformity on a Jamâ'î-Sunnî basis was gaining governmental support. But the confrontations had borne fruit. And just as in social and political life the various elements of urban society had worked out effective patterns consistent with the supremacy of the iqṭâ'-amîrs, so in intellectual life by then, ways had been found to accommodate in practically all fields of thought a certain intellectual supremacy that had to be accorded the madrasah-'ulamâ'. So was ushered in the intellectual life of the Middle Periods, in which the intellectual traditions were relatively interdependent. The graduates of the madrasahs themselves eventually tended to blur the lines between the kalâm of the 'ulamâ', the various sciences of the Faylasûfs, and even adab of the old courtiers. The Faylasûfs, in turn, adjusted their thinking, at least in secondary ways, to the fact of Shar'î supremacy. And speculative Ṣûfism penetrated everywhere.

The new learning at its best displayed a depth of maturity that contrasted with the enthusiasm of some earlier endeavours, which sometimes can seem one-sided or naïve. The best thinkers were not simply working out the consequences of the particular insights of their own immediate tradition, as often before, but now came frankly and honestly to grapple with the best insights that any accessible tradition could offer. The intellectual resources offered by the various pre-Islamic traditions had been fully assimilated, and the consequences of the several channels of inquiry opened up in the High Caliphal Period were being explored.

The Persian heroic tradition: Firdawsî

The old Iranian historical tradition had long since been incorporated into Islamicate history in an Arabic form. In its original Pahlavî form, it was becoming increasingly inaccessible. But now, with the relaxation of pressures for close integration of Muslim culture in a single ruling class around a major capital city, it became possible for the historical consciousness which the Iranian tradition presented to become a major component in the human image of a large section of the Muslims—those for whom Persian was becoming the primary language of culture. For the time being, this meant the Muslims of the Iranian highlands and the Syr-Oxus basin; eventually, it was to mean the greater part of the Muslims everywhere. The revival of the tradition took the form of translations from the Pahlavî into the new Muslim Persian; and most especially of a grand epic work by Firdawsî, the *Shâh-Nâmah,* Book of Kings.

Each social milieu tends to carry more or less consciously an ideal image or what a man should be like (to which an ideal image of a woman is generally correlated). Some historians have brilliantly analyzed cultures in terms of these human images. In some cases this works well. The camel Bedouin had presented, in the old Arabian poetry, a very clear-cut human image of this sort: the ideal Bedouin man should be uncompromisingly loyal to his clan and his guests, fearless, tempered, and resourceful, and beyond this careless of the morrow and correspondingly generous with whatever he had at the moment. Muḥammad's little community, so far as it found expression in the Qur'ân, had a different ideal image which stressed propriety and responsibility.

In more ordinary life, apart from isolated, homogeneous groups like the Bedouin or from dynamic new movements like Muḥammad's, the ideal human image is rarely so sharply focused. To be sure, every form of piety in the great religious traditions necessarily presents in more or less generalized terms an ideal human image for its devotees—the scrupulous servant of the law among the Sharîʿah-minded, the self-transcending lover of God among the Ṣûfîs, for instance. And every social class, the more so the more homogeneous its life patterns, likewise presents an ideal human image, sometimes very highly articulated: thus the adab literature of the High Caliphate outlines a clear image of the ideal kâtib clerk and courtier, who should be of well-placed birth and certainly of good breeding, who should have a varied literary culture at call, and be smoothly adaptable to any demands which the courtly life might make on him. But since few men were simply Sharî'ah-minded, for instance, without at the same time aspiring to the status of kâtib or of tradesman or of landed gentry; or, correspondingly, few men felt themselves exclusively as a kâtib, say, without some inclinations towards piety of a Sharî'ah-minded or a Ṣûfî or an 'Alid-loyalist bent, such ideal human images tended to be diluted and dispersed in their practical effects, each man justifying himself by whatever image, of those honoured in his milieu, best fit his temperament. Hence it is a dubious temptation, to try to characterize in terms of an ideal human image not merely a small isolated culture, but a great and varied people or an age of history or even a whole civilization.

Nevertheless, an ideal human image may play a role outside the specialized milieu to which it might initially be proper, and this role may be sufficiently potent in some periods to affect the overall social development. The image cultivated by a privileged class, provided its life is highly visible to others, may play a secondary role in the self-conception of members of other classes and may even be decisive in the formation or the self-justification of exceptional or creative individuals. Or it may be an image proper not to a current privileged class but to an idealized past or to a potent religious current, which captures the imagination even of those not directly affected. Such a human image is likely to be carried in generally received legends or in artistic literature, as was the camel Bedouin image among the city folk of the High Caliphate, markedly in contrast though it stood to the expressed human image of the privileged courtly classes. In literary form, it may have a subtly pervasive influence even when few individual men would own it as determining their sense of what they ought to be personally.

In the Islamic Middle Periods, as the whole population from Nile to Oxus shared in a common culture in which the religious dimension as such was only one of the common ingredients, the image of the adventurous hero as the ideal man came to play such a role. It was received especially in the ruling circles, where the prevalence of political insecurity and of individual military initiative must have made it congenial, but also in other circles, even among the bourgeois. Its effects can be traced even in the formulation of other human images, those of the Ṣûfîs and even of the Sharî'ah-minded. This image of the adventurous hero found its most influential form in the Iranian heroic tradition; but it also appeared in other forms, inherited and even newly invented.

For Arabs, and among those who adopted some form of Arabic speech, the heroic age was that of the pre-Islamic Bedouin of the Jâhiliyyah. Other possible sources of heroic vision were rejected. To some degree, the legendary kings of the pre-Islamic Yemen were included in the Arab vision, but they did not become folk heroes nor did their alleged remote conquests set the tone for an Arab self-image. Old Yemenî kings had supposedly conquered as far as India or the Oxus basin, but the Arab populations did not see themselves as heirs of these exploits: the feats of the early Muslims themselves threw all other such feats into the shade. As to any heroes of the Aramaeans of the Fertile Crescent, from whom the Arabs in the most influential Arab region were in fact mostly descended (subject to the effects of the population are gradient), these did not provide any strictly heroic tradition. The Aramaeans, under Roman and Sâsânian rule, had long since ceased to have an independent ruling element able to take the kind of initiative which is the stuff of hero-worship. Such ancient heroes as Gilgamesh were long forgotten, at least in any recognizable form; the heroes of the Aramaeans were religious figures: mighty prophets and saints, like Saint George who slew the dragon. These heroes of the settled populations remained imaginatively not quite satisfying.

The religious figures persisted, of course, under Islam; but for a sense of strictly human heroism, the men of the Fertile Crescent and of Egypt were glad to turn to the Bedouin, who represented for them a visible independence from agrarian authorities, and whose heroic image had been deeply imprinted on the Arabic language itself from the first. ʻAntarah, pagan poet and fighting man, was typical of these Bedouin heroes, whom the Arabs of village and city dreamed of. Son of a Bedouin chief by a Negro slave-girl, he had not been acknowledged by his father and was left a slave. In a crisis, his father told him to charge the foe; but ʻAntarah declined, on the ground that a slave was not fit to fight, till his father freed and acknowledged him. Thereupon he saved the day—and went on to many more exploits. On the level of literature, this heroic image was represented in the poetic tradition of the qaṣîdah ode and its related brief verse forms, and otherwise chiefly in popular tales conveyed by wandering story-tellers with relatively little refinement.

Among the Iranians, on the contrary, the heroic tradition of the Sâsânians was vividly alive, despite their defeat, and needed no supplementing from Arab or Turkic nomads. The Pahlavî literature was rich in stories of heroic men who engaged in superhuman exploits of hunting, war, and demon-killing, and indeed in gallant chivalry and love, under the aegis of royal majesty and surrounded with fabulous wonders. Whether based ultimately on historical events or on mythical archetypes, or even on sheer inventive fiction, these themes were taken from the ancient horseman culture of the cow-herding Iranians—the chief hero, Rustam, was a cowboy, and the lasso was not the least of his weapons. The herdsman themes were joined to themes taken from the life of the court of the great monarch, in which a world-dominating royal splendour took first place; here in Persian literature in the time of the amîrs the royalist element which had been lacking in the Arabic literature of the High Caliphate was restored. But urban and mercantile themes were strictly subordinated, despite the urban life of most of the more cultivated listeners at least in Islamic times.

In Pahlavî, these themes took the form of historical narratives and of romances; in the new Persian, all such were put into the *mas̆navî* form (a long couplet poem). The poet who did most to give the heroic tradition literary status among Muslims was Abulqâsim Firdawsî (*c.* 920–1020), who lived in Ṭûs, in Khurâsân, under the Sâmânids and, at the end, under Maḥmûd of Ghaznah, to whom he dedicated the final form of his epic. The *Shâh-Nâmah,* Book of Kings, is his one great work; it is an inordinately long epic poem covering several thousand years of myth, legend, and history, from the dawn of civilization in Iran to the Muslim conquest. It embodies—with close fidelity to the Pahlavî chronicles which Firdawsî used as sources—all the famous events (actual or legendary) the memory of which could give Iranians a sense of ethnic identity; even its language contributed to the sense of Iranian identity by excluding as many non-Iranian, that is Arabic, words as possible, though spoken Persian already included a great many such words. As the Arabs of the lowlands identified with the Bedouin heroes of the time before Islam, so the Persians of the highlands identified with the ancient figures presented in Firdawsî's work. It became the almost canonical presentation of the old Iranian heritage among Persian-speakers and was subsequently respected as a model of the truly heroic wherever Persian became the language of culture.

Covering so great a span of time, the *Shâh-Nâmah* necessarily takes on an episodic structure, in which quite distinct stories are strung one after the other. It is tied together by preoccupation with the dignity and the fate of the kingship (which began, in the legend, with the first man himself), as the kingship was adorned or abused by various men who occupied the kingly status; it ends with the end of the Iranian kingship at the advent of Islam. In pursuance of this theme, the epic concentrates on only a few chief periods, skimming lightly over the ages between. Within these periods, the story is made less discontinuous by the presence of a number of long-lived men: several of the kings are made to live hundreds of years, but especially the hero Rustam outlives many kings and appears again and again throughout a major part of the story.

Rustam is the greatest hero in the book; he fights indomitably, ever placing his loyalty where it should go—and first of all to his father Zâl (only less of a hero and only less long-lived than himself), who is heroic ruler of Zâbul in the Afghân mountains, and generally loyal vassal to the great king. Rustam is tied by family relations to other major heroes; the hero Gîv is Rustam's brother-in-law and also his son-in-law. One of the greatest of Rustam's exploits is his conquest, single-handed, of the *dîvs,* demons (superhuman beings with evil powers) whose great stronghold was Mâzandarân (south of the Caspian): the king, Kay-Kâ'ûs, has foolishly allowed himself to be captured by them and blinded with all his men; Rustam comes to the rescue, liberates the army of Iran and its king, and restores their sight with the blood of the chief of the slain demons. Yet Rustam does not do this quite single-handed: he is accompanied by his faithful horse, Rakhsh, who performs feats worthy of a hero's mount. At one point, Rustam is sleeping in the open with Rakhsh tethered nearby. A demon appears in the form of a lion to attack him, and Rakhsh whinnies a warning; but so soon as Rustam awakes, the demon vanishes; when this happens again, Rustam is angry at being interrupted in his rest and threatens (in the manner of impulsive heroes) to kill his steed if he does it again. Accordingly, Rakhsh has to fight and overcome the demon-lion himself.

One of the major themes of the work is the quarrel between Iran and Tûrân, which latter is identified with the lands north of Iran across the Oxus. (Tûrân was eventually identified with the Turks.) Kay-Kâ'ûs is a king of the Kayânian dynasty (vaguely answering to the Achaemenids and pre-Achaemenids of actual history) who allows himself a number of follies—including the attempt to fly to heaven in a basket borne by eagles. He drives his handsome son, Siyâvush, into exile in Tûrân out of jealousy; the perennial king of Tûrân, Afrâsiyâb, is persuaded to have him killed. Siyâvush's son, Kay-Khusraw, on ascending his grandfather's throne, becomes one of the best-loved kings of the Kayânian dynasty. But one of his chief purposes is to avenge his father's death. His pursuit of revenge is made to account largely for the unending quarrel between Iran and Tûrân. Rustam is again his great pillar of strength; but finally Kay-Khusraw is alienated from Rustam and orders his son Isfandyâr to arrest Rustam and bring him to court. Isfandyâr and Rustam are friends, but the duty of the one and the dignity of the other force them to fight, and Rustam kills his king's heir. Rustam is subjected to other moments of tragedy. His death duel with his own unrecognized son has been taken over into English poetry by Matthew Arnold in *Sohrab and Rustum*.

Mazdean religion necessarily plays a great role in the *Shâh-Nâmah*: Ormazd appears in the poem as Creator-god, and Ahriman as the Devil; Mazdean months are cited for dating, and Mazdean angels are invoked. But such religious terms seem not to evoke any sense of the Zoroastrian tradition as bearing religious values; rather it evokes a sense of the exotic remoteness of the scene and its separation from the normal responsibilities of humdrum present life: a 'pagan' element present in so many heroic traditions. It helps make the story more explicitly human, almost as if freed of divine sanctions or moral standards, and hence makes the heroic deeds themselves more identifiably human in their passion and motivation, despite the magic and wonders threaded through them. When Firdawsî wishes to bring the reader back to the level of daily responsibility and to a recognition of the subordinate place of human wills in a cosmos ruled by God, he freely invokes the language of Islam, as at the beginning of the story of Bîzhan and Manîzhah, where a sober mood highlights the free romantic sequence: a princess of Tûrân kidnaps her Iranian lover and takes him back to her palace, where he is discovered and consigned to a pit from which Rustam must rescue him.

The maturity of Arabic letters

During the Earlier Middle Period, despite the cultivation of Persian verse and of Iranian traditions, Arabic remained the favoured vehicle for serious prose. Most writers still looked for recognition throughout Islamdom, which was possible only in Arabic. Moreover, by now Arabic literature could take for granted established classical norms and the variety of genres that had been developed in the High Caliphal Period; it could also take for granted the essential norms of Shar'î Islam. Especially during the first century or so, the best writers were able, using the familiar forms with assurance, to evoke a pageant of human life at once vivid and independent of over-insistent moral or communal pre-commitments.

The newly developed Persian prose of the time was relatively free of the classical critical norms and can strike one as very informal; doubtless in part because those who wrote it did not aim at so universal and timeless an audience as did those who wrote in Arabic, but intended it for limited and often practical purposes. Like Persian poetry of the time, which was meant even more than Arabic poetry for a courtly embellishment and abounded in qaṣîdah odes in eulogy of one or another amîr and in courtly romance, the prose was centred on the courts. A favourite genre was the 'mirror for princes' sage advice to rulers in the form of maxims and of instructive anecdotes. Niẓâmulmulk, the great vizier, composed a guide to royal policy for the Seljuḳ sultan Malikshâh which marshalled its examples of royal wisdom and unwisdom with such directness and force that it long remained a favourite work. Rather more personal was the *Qâbûs-Nâmah* (written in 1082–83) of Kay-Kâ'ûs, himself hereditary old-Iranian ruler of Ṭabaristân, the south coast of the Caspian. Kay-Kâ'ûs seems to have been a venturesome man, and is said to have enlisted for jihâd holy war in his younger days as far as India. His much-read work, directed to his son, is more concerned with the private life of a nobleman than with actual ruling, though it does touch on state policy too. He assumes that his son cannot be dissuaded from drinking, so advises him to drink only the best wine and listen to only the best music, so that the drinking will have grace in it; and to avoid drinking in the morning or on the eve of Friday (out of respect for the day of community ṣalât worship), so as to gain a bit more sobriety, and to reassure men as to his piety. He gives equally practical advice on buying slaves, horses, —and lands; for even great lords and kings were expected to put their funds into real estate to ensure their personal incomes, and rulers might own buildings and even blocks of shops in every town in their domains. (I will say more in a later chapter about Persian poetry, but I must recall that already at this time it had defined its major genres and was reaching greatness.)

In contrast, formal Arabic literature (composed, of course, as much by Persians as by Arabs) was still mostly oriented away from expressly royal and aristocratic themes. Even when it presented a heroic human image, it was not that of the chivalric lord beloved in Persian. The image of the hardened but sensitive Bedouin fighter and lover still dominated poetry. In prose, the human image presented was not usually a heroic one. Yet even there, a new genre was created at the end of the tenth century which presented a curiously urbane heroic figure: the eloquent and undefeatable scoundrel in the *maqâmât*, a genre of rhymed prose, saj', recounting a series of episodes in which the hero plays one trick or another. The maqâmât genre reflected the varied aspects of the interests of an adîb. Badî'-al-Zamân (d. 1007 at the age of forty) of Hamadhân in 'Irâq 'Ajamî is credited with inventing the genre as a medium to display his flashy verbal talents, which he liked to rout rivals with by sheer skill of eloquence and wit.

In a series of word-pictures, scenes in the life of its worldly hero, the classical maqâmât pictured the escapades of a clever man who enjoys playing pranks, especially if they yield him money. The saj', itself very carefully constructed for verbal effect, was intermingled with pieces of shi'r verse produced according to the most exacting rules of the critics. All the finesses of grammatical and lexicographical lore were displayed in verbal fireworks as interesting as the stories themselves. Equally enjoyable for the reader were the often witty references to curious or recondite bits of learning. A contrast with our psychological novel, which also classically deals with a hero's adventures, confirms the ornamental intention. The maqâmât dealt not with the inner development of the person but with the various sides of the figure he presents to the world; their concern was above all with delicacy and even virtuosity in the handling of words and of erudition. In contrast, our novels frequently reduce precision in the play of words to a minimum and make no appeal at all to the reader's stock of learnèd lore.

Yet the maqâmât genre carried a fascination not unconnected with the figure of its hero as a personality. Once invented by Badî'-al-Zamân Hamadhânî, the genre always featured the same pair—the adventurous, brilliant impostor who always gets away with his plans, however outrageous, and the narrator, a lay figure who is often duped by the hero and sometimes shocked by him, but yet admires him for his gifts and his daring. The greatest work of maqâmât was that of Abû-Muḥammad al-Qâsim al-Ḥarîrî (d. 1122), an unobtrusive grammarian of the Iraq who was persuaded by friends to produce his one great triumph, designed to show proper usage of all the more recondite points of Arabic form. It is one long display of virtuosity; for instance, some passages are written exclusively with letters which in the Arabic alphabet are undotted—that is, omitting half the letters of the alphabet (a like effect as if one wrote an English sonnet without using curving letters—i.e., using only A, E, F, H, I, K, etc.). Yet the work has unceasing charm even for the non-grammarian; indeed, it can even be read with pleasure translated into an alien tongue, where most of its tricks disappear.[1]

Abû-Zayd, its scoundrel hero, is at his most typical in a simple begging episode: invited to join a company of men for an evening on the strength of his conversational gifts (for the men are connoisseurs of good talk), he tells them movingly that he has just found a long-lost son but dares not discover himself to him because he has not the means to bring him up properly; whereupon they raise a large sum for the purpose; but afterwards the narrator (who was one of the company), asked by Abû-Zayd to go with him to cash the checks that had been given, finds too late that the son is imaginary, and the money will be used for drinking. In another episode, the narrator, travelling in hopes of improving his fallen fortunes, meets Abû-Zayd at a caravanserai and is persuaded to let Abû-Zayd marry him to the daughter of a wealthy family staying in the same caravanserai; Abû-Zayd's eloquence carries all before it; but at the wedding feast he distributes sweets drugged with a sleeping potion and calmly gathers up all the guests' property before heading off into the desert—leaving the narrator (alone undrugged) to get out of the scandal as best he may. Once again, the narrator comes across Abû-Zayd parodying the conventional sermons at the wedding of two impudent beggars in the midst of a festive company of beggars and thieves. At the same time, Abû-Zayd often shows a streak of lofty piety, confirmed in a scene on pilgrimage at Mecca, when it turns out that he preaches as movingly as ever but, for the duration of the pilgrimage, he has sworn off receiving money of any kind. At every juncture, the narrator (and with him the reader) is helplessly attracted to Abû-Zayd and becomes an accomplice with him—ostensibly because of the overwhelming beauty of his language, but also surely because of the unvanquishable freedom of his vagabond life. On occasion, indeed, Abû-Zayd applies to himself the language of a fighting Bedouin hero—but he is a sophisticated hero, tamed to the dimensions and taste of a kâtib clerk or a merchant.

The more elegant side of the maqâmât, the virtuosity with language, reached its peak in the epistolary art of the time. Badî'-al-Zamân Hamadhânî was noted also for his brilliant letter-writing. State epistles, composed in rhymed prose, were collected by amateurs, and their authors were the object of jealousies that were not limited to the high official position they gained, but were aimed also at their artistic reputation. Al-Ṣâḥib b. 'Abbâd (d. 995), a vizier under the Bûyids at Rayy (near present Ṭihrân in 'Irâq 'Ajamî), was patron of many writers and the object of many panegyrics, grateful or hopeful; he was the most profuse benefactor of letters in his century. But he was as proud of his epistolary art as he was of his patronage of writers (to say nothing of his considerable fiscal and military exploits), and his rivalry for

[1] The German imitation of al-Ḥarîrî by Friedrich Rückert suggests the possibilities: Friedrich Rüchert, ed., *Die Verwandlungen des Abu Seid von Serug; oder Die Makamen des Harin* (Stuttgart, 1864).

fame in both respects with a predecessor vizier at Rayy, Ibn-al-'Amîd, was the talk of critics and gossips alike for long after.

But the delight in fine language penetrated every field. Inquiry into the qualities of the Arabic language was carried far beyond ordinary grammar almost into metaphysics. Ibn-Jinnî (d. 1002) elaborated a system of higher etymology, trying to show not only how every Arabic word was derivable from a basic meaning in its triliteral 'root', but even that the several roots might themselves be related in meaning on the basis of common letters.[2] His work was used later in the development of a philosophic attempt to see all the individual Arabic letters, as well as the roots they could combine to form, as bearing implicit meanings—and as sharing among them all the essential elements of meaning of which human language can be composed. Such notions were then used in a variety of religious and even scientific contexts as well as for a sophisticated species of soothsaying, in the *jafr*, books of dark sayings of multiple applicability.

Abû-'Alî al-Tanûkhî (939–994) exemplifies at once the moralizing of the age and its delight in sheer wit. (The number of famous writers is so great, I must simply mention a handful here also at random, and al-Tanûkhî has been partly translated into English and his anecdotes graphically illustrate the life of the times.) He was associated with an old Arab tribe and served as qâḍî under Bûyid rule in the Iraq; he regretted the decadence of the times. His writing illustrates the mingling of the Shar'î and the literary traditions: he used the device of an isnâd documentation in introducing his anecdotes (leading back, of course, only to the eyewitness, commonly a contemporary or else a generation or so earlier) and maintained that his was a sober moral purpose in telling them; yet he wrote with an eye to entertainment as well as edification. Like Jâḥiẓ, he avoided boredom by frequent changes of pace or even of topic without confusion, and he was quite conscious of his own literary mastery. He criticized earlier works of a like character (and even title) to his, on which his own were largely modelled; and later opinion sustained him with many imitations. His sense of the literary art becomes explicit when he recounts a long anecdote about a usurping king in India who vindicated his royalty by asking his critics to name, one after another, the royal ancestors of the dethroned king, till they reached the usurping conqueror who founded the old line, whereupon the new king pointed out that he himself was in that founder's place with regard to his own line; to which al-Tanûkhî counterposed a pithy Arab equivalent, that a Bedouin boasted to his rival, my line begins with me while yours ends with you.

Despite all the preoccupation with style, the influence of the tradition of Falsafah was increasingly felt in literature. Both geography and history, essential disciplines for an adîb, were still composed with mastery; and

[2] This notion—apparently by way of Hebrew scholarship and an obscure nineteenth-century French development thereof—became a prime inspiration for the work of the provocative modern linguist Benjamin Lee Whorf.

probably the most important historian after al-Ṭabarî was more a Faylasûf than a Shar'î scholar: the Persian Abû-'Alî Aḥmad Ibn-Miskawayhi (d. 1030). Ibn-Miskawayhi wrote on medicine and chemistry; he earned his living as librarian for viziers at Baghdad and then at Rayy (under Ibn-al-'Amîd). But he became best known for his work on ethics and history. He wrote (in Arabic) several works on ethics conceived in the Aristotelian manner, tracing the golden mean with but little reference to the Sharî'ah; one of these became the basis for the most famous later Persian treatises on ethics. As a historian, he was a moralizer. He wrote essentially in terms of reigns, not at all, however, in the grandiose manner of the Sâsânian tradition, but with an independent and perceptive eye to the practical lessons to be derived. With a Faylasûf's interest in society as a whole, he traced not so much, like al-Ṭabarî, the course of the Muslim community and its conscience as the decline of good agrarian administration in 'Abbâsî and Bûyid times.

The penetration of Falsafah lore and attitudes into the general educated consciousness proceeded more by way of general writers, winning an audience by the delight of their style, than by relative specialists like Ibn-Miskawayhi. Abû-Ḥayyân al-Tawḥîdî (d. 1018) was a Shâfi'î in fiqh, a Mu'tazilî in kalâm (following the teaching of al-Jâḥiẓ); he hewed closely to the example of al-Jâḥiẓ in his style—and though he was not always simple, he was always fresh and clear. More precious to him than his fiqh and perhaps even than his kalâm, however, was his interest in Falsafah. He popularized all sorts of learnèd lore, even some elements of Ṣûfism; and in his very miscellaneous books of popularization, the philosophy of the Faylasûfs was often prominent. One of his major works was a report—presumably not verbatim, but probably not invented of whole cloth (as some of his reports were)—of the learnèd conversations that took place at the home of one of his masters in Falsafah, Abû-Sulaymân al-Sijistânî, whom he revered, though he respected few men. (A teacher of al-Sijistânî and of al-Tawḥîdî himself was Ibn-'Adî, the great Christian disciple of al-Fârâbî.) Al-Tawḥîdî was much interested in logic, and at one point he reports a discussion between a prominent Faylasûf logician and an equally prominent Arabic grammarian on the parallelism between logic and grammar. (Grammarians of the time were eager to attempt new systems; one of al-Tawḥîdî's masters so mingled rules of logic in his grammar that it became virtually unintelligible, but al-Tawḥîdî explains that this was not because of the use of logic but because the master used a system of logic of his own invention, differing from that of Aristotle.)

Al-Tawḥîdî's career is instructive. Son of a date merchant and evidently never very well-to-do, he expected his literary talents to win him eminence and wealth; but though he sat at table with viziers, he never seems to have satisfied his ambitions. Unlike Ibn-Miskawayhi and some others who found relatively secure posts and pursued their studies in quiet, al-Tawḥîdî led an embittered and sometimes stormy life. Much of the time he earned his living, as many scholars did, as a private copyist (such were hired to produce better manuscripts than resulted from the booksellers' group dictations, but al-Tawḥîdî complained that the close work ruined the eyes). Some despised him as a dilettante who wrote on many subjects and mastered none; some accused him of free-thinking opinions—he was once exiled from Baghdad for writing a book that seemed to undermine the authority of the Sharî'ah (rather like al-Ḥallâj, he suggested an inward spiritual pilgrimage that would be the equivalent of the ḥajj pilgrimage to Mecca if one was unable to undertake that). Even al-Ṣâḥib b. 'Abbâd, the bountiful vizier at Rayy, rejected him after three years' hospitality; probably not so much because of al-Tawḥîdî's outspoken opposition to Shî'ism (the vizier was a Shî'î sympathizer) as because of his impudence and intractability—for though al-Tawḥîdî sometimes wrote fulsome flattery of an obvious insincerity, he made it clear in practice that he felt himself the vizier's equal. Later, he wrote a scathing attack on both al-Ṣâḥib and his predecessor, Ibn-al-'Amîd, who had also failed to reward him sufficiently, in which he exposed their weaknesses and even exaggerated them—as he himself admitted, excusing himself on the ground that they had been unjust first. The book was prized for its magnificent phrasing and use of words, but the story went that it was so virulent that any who possessed it were subject to bad luck. Al-Tawḥîdî's life-long search for a maecenas seems to have been only briefly fulfilled for a time in Baghdad. At one point he burned all his writings in despair. Late in life, he retired to Shîrâz, in Fârs, and seems to have been sufficiently well accepted there to teach in quiet.[3]

The most eccentric figure of the time, and for many moderns the most appealing, was Abû-l-'Alâ' al-Ma'arrî (973–1058). After an education in Aleppo, he spent most of his life in the small town Ma'arrah, in northern Syria, his birthplace. At thirty-five he paid a long visit to Baghdad and surveyed the varied literary and philosophical life there, but returned home to find his beloved mother dead. Thereafter he lived in retirement, never marrying and maintaining an ascetic personal life to a great age. In his later years he was blind but well supplied, the most prominent of the a'yân notables of his town, revered by the people and surrounded by students who came from a distance to hear him lecture.

His prose epistles are tissues of manifestly insincere praise (which no one took amiss, since the acknowledged point of the praise was only its elegant play of ideas—except when it proved subtly barbed) mingled with personal information that was sometimes more rhetorical than informative. Yet each epistle is a work of art. To read it, one must first plot out the sequence of thought, often not clear at first sight. Then one can appreciate the balancing of epithets and similes, one image bringing its complement into unexpected

[3] Ibrahim Keilani, *Abû Ḥayyân al-Tawḥîdî: introduction à son oeuvre* (Beirut, 1950), is one of those minor studies of an individual which, by relating him to other persons of the time and noting their interests and affiliations also, can throw some light on a whole period.

relief; thus he may top a standard static simile with a seemingly slighter one which, being more fresh or vital, in fact gives sparkle to a conclusion: 'so long as the mountains remain firm and the salam-tree has leaves' or 'like a bubble in a pond or a raindrop in a mountain tarn'. And one can savour the citations from a vast store of Arabic literature, which a well-read reader might identify, and the rare words, to recognize which would tax his skill and perhaps tickle his vanity. To feel the music of the words, of course, the letter in Arabic should be read aloud. Then, like good conversation, it fitted excellently into the decorative refinement of a well-appointed home.[4] His poetry was more famous than his letters: he was one of the few major poets in Arabic after al-Mutanabbi' (in an age when poets in the more Iranian parts of Islamdom were turning to Persian instead). It was constructed on much the same pattern, full of precious or intricate turns of thought and recherché words. He named his great collection of verse from the later part of his life, the *Luzûmiyyât,* after its self-imposed requirements in meter and rhyme, even more exacting than those imposed by the critics.

Al-Ma'arrî's viewpoint on life likewise imposed standards few could meet. He roundly condemned the injustice and hypocrisy he saw about him, denouncing in detail whoever fell short, 'ulamâ' and rulers and ordinary citizens. He saw so much of human shortcoming, indeed, that he regarded living itself as a misfortune and took pride in having done no one the injury of begetting him. He ridiculed most formal religious dogmas. Placing all the formal religious allegiances on a level, he called truly religious only those persons who were helpful to their fellow-creatures, regardless of beliefs. But he was careful to disguise his utterances just enough to defend himself, if need be, against any charge of explicit impiety. As corollary of his morality of mutual helpfulness among creatures, he taught harmlessness even to animals and was himself a vegetarian. On this subject he had a considerable correspondence with a chief Ismâ'îlî dâ'î of Egypt under Fâṭimid rule. The dâ'î was sober and concerned enough, but when it became clear that he was failing to comprehend the ethical issue, al-Ma'arrî relapsed into his typical pose of paradoxical frivolousness and played with him, till the dâ'î gave up trying to make sense of him.

Science mature: al-Bîrûnî

The maturity of literature brought a freedom to use established forms for a great diversity of purposes. Correspondingly, when in the realm of scientific and philosophical studies multiple older traditions had been fully assimilated, scholars were freer to explore quite new sorts of questions or to rethink basic

[4] David S. Margoliouth has translated al-Ma'arrî's *Letters* (Oxford, 1898), which are necessarily less inaccessible to the non-Arabist than his verse. Unfortunately, sometimes Margoliouth spoils the imagery, as when he substitutes a common English proverb for a rare Arabic one.

questions anew while at the same time retaining the advantages of all that was soundest in the tradition.

Not all currents of the pre-Islamic Irano-Semitic intellectual heritages were able, so easily as the Iranian heroic tradition, to gain open and popular acceptance. But the more practical sides of natural science did almost as well. With the passing of hospitals and observatories from dhimmî to Muslim hands as the bulk of the population became Islamized, it became normal for natural scientists to be Muslims; and as hospitals and libraries came to be endowed increasingly on the basis of waqf, often independent of current rulers, the Muslim scientists in turn found themselves part of the overall Jamâ'î-Sunnî establishment, often subject to the oversight of qâḍîs and of the Shar'î 'ulamâ' generally. But by this time the tradition of natural science was so highly sophisticated that fairly ready accommodation could be found with such an establishment. Scientific studies generally continued strong. One limitation: in the Earlier Middle Period, the régimes of the amîrs did little to encourage massive investments in large observatories and the like, nor did the 'ulamâ' encourage devotion of waqf moneys to such ends. Except for a well-financed reform of the civil (solar) calendar under Malikshâh, scientific work proceeded quietly, with few spectacular moments such as can be cited earlier or again after the Mongol conquest. (The high quality of much work done then suggests that any reduction in institutional complexity that was occurring was not intellectually disastrous.)

Science, save perhaps in the field of medicine, remained most often an expression of the spirit of high play: to solve a new equation was to win a game. Men were interested in paradoxes—in the solution of seeming dilemmas, in the achievement of the seemingly impossible.[5] An old Greek tradition of inventing automata, gadgets which would do the unexpected, producing illusions or counterfeits or juggleries, was perpetuated and added to. The operations of waterpower, mirrors, levers, gears, clockworks, or any other devices which can have seemingly disproportionate powers when ingeniously used were hidden within artistically decorated cabinets. Ismâ'îl al-Jazârî produced (1205) a widely read compendium of such automata, which was carefully illustrated; what he presents was intended more for amusement than for labour and presupposed a high mathematical culture, which ordinary craftsmen would not be expected to have anyway.

Nevertheless, major developments were taking place, and some scholars were philosophically serious about their task of understanding reality. The developments were commonly less dramatic than the reorganizations of scientific knowledge in the High Caliphal time, but perhaps more fruitful in the long-term cumulation that is required for science. A scholar still felt his primary task was just to gain as much understanding himself as possible,

[5] Rosalie Colie has presented the spirit of such delight in 'paradoxes' in her studies of sixteenth- and seventeenth-century Occidental natural science: *Paradoxia epidemica: The Renaissance Tradition of Paradox* (Princeton University Press, 1961).

which meant above all absorbing what had already been learned: without printed bibliographies and indexes and journals, this alone could be a lifetime task, even within a given specialty. But once the natural science traditions of the Greek and also Sanskrit backgrounds had been fully expounded in Arabic, and the most sophisticated forms of them had emerged as generally recognized, a comprehensive, disciplined view did become possible. The great syntheses made it much easier and made it possible for personal research to be more than mere duplication of effort. Hence investigators could go on to make more innovative contributions.[6]

New contributions commonly remained on a level of detail which retrospectively seems almost petty. For instance, after Muḥammad al-Khwârazmî had composed his synthesis on algebra, it was more possible to see where the gaps lay in that field; but the gaps were necessarily felt at first in terms of individual mathematical cases. Among others, a certain geometrical proposition, necessary in further proofs, and which had been posed already by Archimedes, became a fruitful point of departure. Already shortly after the times of al-Khwârazmî, the proposition had been identified with the solution to the equation $x^3 + a = b x^2$; it had been proved geometrically, with the aid of recourse to other Greek geometrical treatises on conic sections by the end of High Caliphal times. But several differing proofs were possible and at least two more were found in the succeeding century. In the course of such work, individual solution by individual solution, the significance of the use of conic sections and the relation of geometrical and algebraic proofs became clearer. By the time of 'Umar Khayyâm (d. 1123—this is the man whose poetry was metamorphosed into English by Fitzgerald), who himself traced carefully the history of the problem just mentioned, a lucid terminology and an extensive set of techniques had been worked out for dealing with equations in first, second, and third degrees—though in higher degrees, equations considered were only sporadic. (As among the later Greeks, irrational solutions were admitted, but not yet negative ones.) 'Umar Khayyâm produced a comprehensive and systematic algebraic study, including many new solutions; though even within the first three degrees he still omitted a number of possible positive solutions. It was on the basis of his new individual solutions as much as on the basis of his synthesis, however, that algebra could push further still.

In chemistry, after the corpus of Jâbir was set forth, already in the eleventh century can be traced the beginnings of a quantitative analysis, rather than a merely qualitative one; but, as far as we know, this was abortive and not taken up again until the eighteenth century, and then in the Occident.

[6] It is for this reason that even popularizations like that of Ibn-Rustah (transl. Gaston Wiet), *Les Atours précieux* (Cairo, 1955), served a scholarly purpose—even though this one made no distinction between natural facts and conventional facts such as that a circle has 360 degrees or that the earth's centre is at Ujjain, just as a modern publicist will treat 'Europe' and 'Asia' as if they were units in natural geography.

More fruitful was the development of stills which produced condensation of the distilled vapour outside the stillhead; these seem to have appeared simultaneously in the thirteenth century in Islamdom and the Occident. In optics, al-Ḥasan b. al-Haytham (d. *c.* 1039—he had produced one of the solutions of the above-cited equation) took important steps toward understanding the light spectrum—the rainbow and artificial rainbow effects. Ibn-al-Haytham was the first to use the camera obscura for experiments. Born in Baṣrah, he served the Fâṭimid caliph al-Ḥâkim; but at one point he seems to have aroused expectations in his master that he could regularize the all-important flow of the Nile; on failing to do so, he was disgraced. He earned a living, at least toward the end of his life, by copying manuscripts. His general study of optics became the basic text of that science and was used through the time of Kepler, in Latin translation, in the Occident also.

In astronomy, occasional Muslims were innovative in ways that appeal especially to modern students: it was suggested that the earth turned on its axis (to account for the diurnal round of the heavens and so simplify planetary motions); this was rejected after careful calculations of the speed of the winds that should result, if the atmosphere was thought of as independent of such motion. It was even suggested that the earth moved around the sun. But this latter theory could not be supported by observations of changes in the position of the fixed stars during the earth's yearly course nor by the ever-improving observations of planetary motions so long as circular orbits were presupposed; much as was Copernicus' theory later, it was rather an attempt at a more beautiful schematism than at a more exact rendering of facts, and was rejected.

The most attractive figure of the period was Abû-l-Rayḥân al-Bîrûnî (973–after 1050), from Khwârazm, a 'universal man' of science. His first major work (1000 CE but added to and corrected from time to time) was 'Remaining traces of bygone ages', an extensive chronological study, handled from a mathematical viewpoint but bringing out a sense of historical sequence which put Muslim history into a broad perspective. He was patronized by the last of the Sâmânids at Bukhârâ and early travelled as far west as Rayy; but he returned to Khwârazm and served the last of the autonomous local Khwârazmshâhs as scholar and also as diplomat till Maḥmûd of Ghaznah took over. Maḥmûd brought him to Ghaznah, where he served as court astrologer—though he seems to have rejected privately the possibility of judicial astrology, as a system of predicting actual events. His scholarly work was supported adequately by the court, though he did not always cater to its tastes: for a long time he refused to write in Persian, holding to Arabic for scholarly work. (His own language, of course, was Khwârazmian—Iranian but not Persian.) For his monumental work on astronomy it is said he was offered an elephant-load of silver and refused. At one point he reckoned up a hundred and thirteen treatises that he had written, to which he added a number written in his name by scholarly friends (presumably based on his material); among his treatises were studies of gems and of drugs and of questions in mathematics and in physics.[7]

His most remarkable work was a survey of Indian life (1030 CE) based on studies carried out when he went with Maḥmûd on his expeditions. In this he included especially a study of the Sanskritic philosophical systems (for he learned Sanskrit) made from almost an anthropological viewpoint; that is, he did not so much look for truth in the systems as for an understanding of

Muslim Belles-Lettrists, Scientists, Philosophers, and Theologians, 945–1111

950	Death of al-Fârâbî, Faylasûf-metaphysician holding for élitist attitudes, well grounded in Hellenistic traditions
956	Death of al-Mas'ûdî, well-travelled and erudite writer, 'philosophical' historian
965	Death of al-Mutanabbi', last great poet in older Arabic style, paragon of subtlety in poetic allusion
c. 970	Collection of the Rasâ'il of the Ikhwân al-Ṣafâ', comprehensive compilation of 'scientific' and metaphysical knowledge
994	Death of al-Tanûkhî, adîb, historian in the adab style, courtier
1000	Death of al-Muqaddasî, well-travelled and literary geographer combining information on languages, races, and social behaviour
1008	Death of Badî'Zamân al-Hamadhânî, called the 'Wonder of the Age'; founder of maqâmah style of rhymed prose and genius of it
1013	Death of al-Bâqillânî, jurisprudent and Ash'arî mutakallim, systematizer of Ash'arî kalâm
1018	Death of al-Tawhîdî, popularizing Faylasûf, courtier, adîb
c. 1020	Death of Firdawsî, Persian epic poet
1030	Death of Ibn-Miskawayhi, adîb, 'philosophical' moralist and moralizing historian, Faylasûf
1037	Death of Ibn-Sînâ, Faylasûf synthesizing Hellenistic and Prophetic sources for knowledge, casting Falsafah positions into Islamic terms, vizier
c. 1039	Death of Ibn-al-Haytham, astronomer, optician, mathematician patronized by the Fâṭimid caliph al-Ḥâkim

what it was made the Indians think as they did. He was highly conscious of the cosmopolitan nature of the Islamicate culture: he found the Greek and Islamicate traditions as one in the face of the alienness of the Indic thought-world; but he stressed the greater expanse of Islamdom as compared with the regions open to the ancient Greeks, and accounted partly on this basis for the greater extent and sophistication of some Islamicate scholarship, notably

[7] R. Ramsay Wright translated al-Bîrûnî, *Elements of Astrology* (London, 1934), but mistranslated the scientist's very carefully phrased disclaimer about the possibility of actual astrological prediction.

in the field of geography. He passes for a good Muslim, but he was an admirer of that very independent Faylasûf, Ibn-Zakariyyâ' Râzî.

Falsafah and the problem of spiritual experience: Ibn-Sînâ

The ending of the High Caliphal state was perhaps more significant for the more strictly 'philosophical' side of Falsafah, in which the total sense of the cosmos and of the place of human beings in it was being assessed, than for more positive scientific inquiries. Here also the great synthesis of al-Fârâbî made it more possible to see where the gaps were. But the times themselves raised new questions. In an age when the caliphal state no longer seemed to offer the option of a philosophically ordered society, and when a Sharî'ah-minded Islam was enforcing its norms on all, the personal and social mission of Falsafah had to be envisaged anew, and in particular its relation to the ruling popular religion.

The most intriguing attempt at this, done in the years following 983 CE, was that of the Ikhwân al-Ṣafâ', the 'Pure Brethren'. They formed a fellowship of men at Baṣrah and probably another at Baghdad, dedicated to enlightening and spiritually purifying themselves and to propagating their ideas in the various towns of Islamdom, quietly winning as much of the population as possible to ways of truth and purity and so raising the level of society. They produced an encyclopedia of the sciences of rationalistic Philosophia as a handbook for this purpose. This encyclopedia, which is all that really remains of the association, shows that they were associated with the Bâṭiniyyah among the Shî'îs. (If it is true that the Faylasûf Abû-Sulaymân al-Sijistânî was one of the brethren, as we are told, then they did not insist exclusively on a Bâṭinî approach.) The encyclopedia looks to an imâmate that should represent divine cosmic rationality among mankind, and delights in finding hidden symbolisms in Qur'ân and Sharî'ah. But its teaching was more explicitly Falsafah than that of the great Ismâ'îlî dâ'îs in Egypt, whose political leadership the brethren, or some of them, may have respected. It presented in an essentially independent way, without pre-commitment to any sectarian organization, the myth of the microcosmic return (more or less as it had been developed among the neo-Platonists, but Islamicized): that is, the idea that the world in all its complexity emanated from the ultimate One, which was expressed in cosmic Reason; and that all this complexity was resumed in human beings as microcosms, who by purifying their individual reasoning powers could reascend in intellectual contemplation to the original One.

The Ikhwân al-Ṣafâ' suggest an exciting vista. To the extent that the group represented Ismâ'îlî inspiration, it apparently meant a new departure in Ismâ'îlî idealism. They clearly had more than personal aims: they wanted to leaven Muslim society in a new way by transforming the lives of individuals. What was distinctive in their effort was the idea of mutual enlightenment and support in little groups of studious friends everywhere, evidently without insistence on doctrinaire uniformity. Nothing much seems to have come of this project. The encyclopedia did become very popular, and continued so till the end of Islamicate civilization, popularizing one aspect of Falsafah culture. But even it did not lead into further intellectual or spiritual developments. It was not intellectually well disciplined. There was little trace of the work of al-Fârâbî here; the ideas mostly derived from a wide range of Hellenistic schools, without rigorous integration. Hence the problems raised were not sharply posed.

The Ikhwân al-Ṣafâ' point up, by contrast, the strength of the work of the greatest Philosopher of the time, Abû-'Alî Ibn-Sînâ (called, in Latin, Avicenna; 980–1037), during whose childhood they were at work. Ibn-Sînâ did build upon al-Fârâbî (and upon Aristotle as al-Fârâbî had made him known). In doing so, he also found that in the post-High Caliphal age, Falsafah was not accounting for political and social, and even personal, reality unless it made sense more explicitly than had al-Fârâbî (his chosen guide to Aristotle) of *religion*—in particular of the Sharî'ah; and then of the religious experience which went with it. But he rejected the Bâtinî path which had interested his family. And his work proved capable of opening up great new intellectual resources—though not of transforming society.

Ibn-Sînâ was born near Bukhârâ (in a Shî'î family of officials), and learned all he could as a youth in the Sâmânî court libraries. He tells us that by the age of eighteen he had devoured libraries in his reading and had acquired all the book-learning he was to have, at least in the various disciplines of Falsafah. He was already practicing medicine with success. He made a point of entering the service of munificent courts, but he did not want to go to Ghaznah, and when al-Bîrûnî and others were taken off by Maḥmûd, Ibn-Sînâ took refuge from Maḥmûd's importunities at ever more distant courts in western Iran. There he became vizier for the most successful of the later Bûyid rulers, going with him on his campaigns. In the midst of all this, he found time to compose both numerous small treatises and two great encyclopedic works in his two favourite fields, medicine and metaphysics.

Al-Fârâbî had attempted to account for Islamic revelation and its Sharî'ah law in rationalistic terms, yet like al-Râzî he was still relatively independent of Islam as an intellectual force. With time, such aloofness became less feasible. In his metaphysics, Ibn-Sînâ was the harbinger of a Falsafah that would be more closely integrated with the Islamic tradition as such. Acknowledging the importance of the Sharî'ah as it had been developed, he took far more pains than had al-Fârâbî to justify not merely the general principle of the need for a prophetic legislator but in particular the revealed legislation ascribed to Muḥammad. He expounded elaborately the social usefulness of the various Shar'î rules for the masses and even for the élite—with the understanding, in the latter case, that the 'philosopher' as sage could dispense with details for overriding reasons. Thus he defended the usefulness of ṣalât worship as a discipline of the attention even for the 'philosopher', but he allowed himself wine on the ground that he found it helpful and knew how to avoid excess—the danger of which among the masses had been the ground for the Prophetic ban of it.

But he was also concerned with the psychology of revelation itself. Al-Fârâbî had left prophecy to the imaginative faculty, which rationalistic Philosophers did not take very seriously as compared to the rational. Ibn-Sînâ presented an analysis in which being a prophet would seem to presuppose being an ideal 'philosopher' too and having even fuller access to truth than the best 'philosopher' who remained on the level of discursive reasoning. He came to this by way of accounting for the mystical experience of the Ṣûfîs, with whose spiritual experience he had to come to terms in any case. Making use of the neo-Platonist system of logico-rational emanations from the One down to the world of compound beings, he explained that it was possible for the soul to have immediate intuitions of the cosmic Active Intellect governing events of this world, more immediate than those perceptions to be gained by deductive demonstration. The evidence, in effect, was the ability of Ṣûfîs to arrive at certain insights in which they got beyond conventional presuppositions and came to what had to be admitted was a philosophic point of view without the use of syllogism and rational category. These intuitions could be translated into images by the imaginative faculty, and so presented to others by either Ṣûfîs or prophets. The prophet was he who was perfected in this way in the highest degree.

In the course of this analysis, Ibn-Sînâ was led to invoke a psychology that proved congenial to later Ṣûfîs themselves. He asserted that the human mind was not reasonable simply by participation in the universal Active Intellect, as al-Fârâbî had held; that is, by its effective recognition of the rational universals underlying all transient appearances, a recognition which 'actualized' the potential intellect in each individual. Ibn-Sînâ insisted that the potential intellect in each individual was a distinct individual entity; it was immaterial and hence rational and indestructible, no matter how inadequately it had been 'actualized'. He supported this thinking in two ways. He cited such phenomena as autosuggestion and hypnotism and interpreted them as showing the direct action of the soul on its own body and on others, rather than as showing the intervention of disembodied spirits, as some in the Hellenic tradition had done; and he made unprecedentedly persistent use of the principle that distinguishable concepts must answer to distinguishable entities—a principle implicit in the faith of the Hellenic Philosophic tradition that human reason must find its analogue and its fulfillment in cosmic harmonies. By means of such practical evidence and of such normative principles, he established the independence of the soul from the body as a separate substance—differing here not only from Aristotle but also from Plotinus. This principle allowed for an individual survival after death (as against merely a general 'survival' in the ever-present Active

Intellect) and permitted an otherwise essentially Aristotelian system to accommodate itself to the Muslim (and Platonic) doctrines of the afterlife by spiritualizing it. But it also helped more speculative Ṣûfîs to make more sense of their own experiences of a self which remained their own distinct self and yet was somehow beyond the world of time-and-space limitations.

Such an approach was supported with a comprehensive reinterpretation of every relevant point in the Philosophic system, from the process of intellection to the nature of existence. The reinterpretation was focused in the doctrine of God. God was made to remain a simple being, as was required by rationalistic Philosophy; yet that being was assigned traits more consistent with an actual object of human worship. A careful analysis of the primary divine attributes showed that, if one used the proper logical distinctions, they could all be retained as identical with the divine essence (as Necessary Being). And it could even be shown that the ultimate simple God of universal rationality could be expected to 'know' not merely universal essences as potentialities in His rationality (as Philosophers had generally supposed), but even particular individuals or events—though only 'in a universal way', as a particular eclipse must be 'known' implicitly if one knows all the celestial essences and their possibilities of combination and interaction. It was in pursuit of such analyses that Ibn-Sînâ developed his complex doctrine of existence (*wujûd*), set over against essence. Taking Aristotle's logical distinction between what a thing is and the fact that it is, he assigned the distinction an ontological role: existence is something superadded to an essence, by which it can be asserted. The import of this ontological role emerges strikingly in a derivative distinction, that between necessary and merely possible existence, which for Ibn-Sînâ marks the difference between God and the creation; for by making God's existence be of a radically different sort than any other, this distinction sets God off as more than merely one point in the total system of nature, as He can seem to be for Aristotle.

The most impressive achievement of Ibn-Sînâ was to make the system of Aristotle more serviceable both for the understanding and for the disciplining of religious experience. But it seems to me that this was not so much by way of adapting it to Islam, as by way of making use of the metaphysically solid work of Aristotle to support the life-orientational dimension of the Philosophic tradition itself—the religiousness in it that had already been prominent in Socrates and Plato and that was less congenial to Aristotle. He was doing more soundly what the sort of Philosophers that the Ikhwân al-Ṣafà were following had done less soundly for want of an adequate reckoning with Aristotle. He did this, in part by invoking some of the religious values of the Abrahamic prophetic tradition as represented in Islam, and notably its stress on divine transcendence. To this degree, his was a real synthesis between the two life-orientational traditions, in both of which he seriously participated. But the Philosophic life-orientation tradition remained primary: he continued to find ultimacy rather in the rational harmonies of a universal nature taken as normative than in the challenging historical events the Abrahamic communities took as revelatory. Thus the mission of Muhammad remained for him primarily a political event, wfth little ultimately orientational significance for the true 'philosopher'; and he denied any future moment of bodily resurrection—save in his works ior tne general public, where belief in such resurrection was recommended only as a point of 'faith', that is, of religious allegiance. Most of his adaptation to Islam, in fact, continued to be just what was called for when one envisaged Islam as a legitimate political and social order.

Thus Ibn-Sînâ went further than al-Fârâbî in recognizing the institutional religious tradition in two ways: by granting a somewhat more dignified role to the Islamic revelation in particular; and by allowing more philosophical space to the sense of ultimate relation between person and cosmos which marks religious traditions generally—including the more religious aspects of the Philosophic tradition. Accordingly, Ibn-Sînâ's philosophy, unlike al-Fârâbî's, became the starting point for schools of speculation in which the values associated with Ṣûfî mystical experience were primary. The Ṣûfî study of the unconscious self eventually came to presuppose the terminology of Ibn-Sînâ.[8]

Later, Ibn-Sînâ became a bone of contention. The strictest Peripatetics, notably Ibn-Rushd, quarrelled with him on points of logic as of metaphysics, preferring to hold by al-Fârâbî.[9] But not only the Ṣûfîs but also many later men of kalâm disputation founded their philosophy upon him, and he became the starting point of the greater part of later Islamicate rational speculation. The attitude among later Ṣûfîs to Ibn-Sînâ's work is summed up in a surely apocryphal anecdote: Ibn-Sînâ and a great Ṣûfî met and talked together for a long time; when they emerged, Ibn-Sînâ reported of the conversation, 'All that I know, he sees'; and the Ṣûfî reported, 'All that I see, he knows'. To what extent Ibn-Sînâ himself would have welcomed the constructions later put on his work by the more mystically inclined is not clear.[10]

[8] The later commentators of Ibn-Sînâ interpreted him, accordingly, in Ṣûfî terms. It is not entirely clear how far this was justified by Ibn-Sînâ's own thought. Henry Corbin, in *Avicenne et le récit visionnaire*, vol. 1 (Tehran, 1954), maintains the Ṣûfî tradition. Anne-Marie Goichon, in *Le récit de Ḥayy ibn Yaqẓân commenté par les textes d'Avicenne* (Paris, 1959), contradicts him. At least on the level of the immediate meaning of the story in question, Goichon seems to have the better of the argument in insisting that it can be most unequivocally understood as remaining strictly within the Aristotelian tradition of Falsafah as enlarged by Ibn-Sînâ himself.

[9] S. M. Stern gives an illuminating example of this Faylasûfs' dislike of Ibn-Sînâ in the physician (and travel writer) 'Abd-al-Laṭîf: 'A Collection of Treatises by 'Abd al-Laṭîf al-Baghdâdî', *Islamic Studies*, 1 (Karachi, 1962), 53–70. (Cf. for the same point, in the same journal, D. M. Dunlop, 'Averroës (Ibn Rushd) on the Modality of Propositions', pp. 23–34.)

[10] The 'mashriqiyyah' wisdom, which Ibn-Sînâ refers to in some logical or metaphysical connections but does not clearly expound, seems to be a key to part of this question. (The word is sometimes misrendered 'Oriental' philosophy, as if Ibn-Sînâ shared the notion that Greece was somehow 'Occidental' and Iran 'Oriental' and this should be reflected in philosophy.) The point at issue is his attitude to mysticism. It has been

The kalâm of the madrasahs: triumph and inanition

During the formative generations of the Earlier Middle Period, kalâm, as a speculative method, only gradually won through to independent maturity, and still more gradually won the respect of many Sharî'ah-minded 'ulamâ'. As it matured, its relation to Falsafah metaphysics became its great problem. The original Mu'tazilî school of kalâm continued to be represented both among Jamâ'î-Sunnîs and especially among Twelver Shî'îs, and made progress even outside Islâm: many Jewish scholars professed a kalâm that was Mu'tazilî in substance. But the more creative labour was done in the schools of al-Ash'arî (associated with the Shâfi'î legal madhhab) and al-Mâturîdî (associated with the Ḥanafî). The Ḥanbalî and Ẓâhirî and (at first) Mâlikî scholars tended to stay aloof.[11]

It was a Mâlikî qâḍî, however, al-Bâqillânî (d. 1013), who did the most to popularize the Ash'arî system in the Fertile Crescent. He set forth with

---

extensively debated whether the term means 'eastern', in the sense of Khurâsân or else Jundaysâbûr against Baghdad, or 'illuminative'. In the former case, it would refer merely to certain practices and logical teachings on which Peripatetic schools differed; in the latter case, it could refer to the mystical implications of certain ontological points which were undeniably included in its scope anyway. Cf. Carlo Nallino, 'Filosofia "orientale" od "illuminativa" d'Avicenna', *Rivista di Studi Orientali*, 10 (1923–25), 433–67; Louis Gardet, *La pensée religieuse d'Avicenne* (Paris, 1951), p. 23; A. M. Goichon, *Le récit de Ḥayy ibn Yaqẓân*, cited above; and Henry Corbin, *Oeuvres philosophiques et mystiques de Shihabaddin Yahya Sohrawardi*, 1 (Tehran and Paris, 1952), Prolégomènes. Possibly Ibn-Sînâ intended a pun. Ibn-Sîna's disciples certainly took it in the sense of 'illuminative', and supposed that he intended a mystical implication; but this may not have been in his mind.

The rendering with 'orient', which Henry Corbin likes, is legitimate only if 'orient' is remembered clearly to refer to the sunrise, taken metaphorically—not to any geographical sector of mankind. If, later, Suhravardî took over the same notion and linked it especially to Iran, this resulted simply from the chance that he felt that the Iranian tradition—not some generalized 'East'—happened to expound the nature of illumination.

[11] George Makdisi, 'Ash'arî and the Ash'arites in Islamic Religious History', *Studia Islamica*, 18 (1962), and subsequent issues notes that the usual notion that Ash'arism became 'orthodox' (whatever that may mean) at an early date is based on a small number of Syrian and Egyptian Ash'arî writers of the Later Middle Period, who were in fact trying to maintain a thesis rather than simply presenting a well-known fact. His excellent and important article helps clarify the way in which scholars have been misled by relying on a particular local Sunnî Arab tradition for scholarly understanding of what Islam was and was not. (It also makes it less necessary to rely on such amateur efforts as Asad Ṭalas, *L'enseignement chez les Arabes: la madrasa nizamiyya et son histoire* [Paris, 1939], filled with errors.)

Unfortunately, Makdisi does not himself altogether escape the effects of the scholarly pattern which he has helped to show the pitfalls in. He seems still to accept the conventional image of Islam as being from the start Jamâ'î-Sunnî and Sharî'ah-minded, its tradition being essentially the tradition of the ḥadîth; only introducing the new point that Ash'arî kalâm was long not accepted among most of the ḥadîth-minded 'ulamâ'—at least in Syria and Egypt (he does not go much further afield) well into the Later Middle Period. His larger misconception is reflected in, and perhaps was reinforced by, his use of the term 'Tradition' for a ḥadîth report. The inconveniences of such a notion of 'traditionalism' are analyzed in the section on usage in Islamics studies in the Introduction in volume 1.

comprehensive clarity such doctrines as atomic creation as conceived by the school. Perhaps his popularity resulted in part from his bold application of reasoning to the revelatory events as unique events. The Ash'arîs were developing a close analysis of just what sorts of reports of such events could be relied on: how widespread a report must be, for instance, for it to be accepted without a detailed authentication of each of the alleged witnesses. The revelatory quality of the events themselves, once properly evidenced, also needed study. Al-Bâqillânî is especially associated with the doctrine of evidentiary miracles, which he saw as a practical indication of prophethood even though they had no metaphysical standing.

In particular, he stressed the special importance of the inimitable Qur'ân—whose literary style, Muslims believed, was such that no one else could produce a work that could properly compare with it—as the chief evidentiary miracle of Muḥammad. As a revelatory fact it had the unique status not only of being the undeniable residuum of what had happened in the Ḥijâz, but of being perpetually accessible. By way of a detailed analysis of its style, he tried to show what it is makes the Qur'ân humanly compelling as a concrete phenomenon.

But al-Bâqillânî's work was oriented to polemic within the tradition of kalâm, without serious care to challenge minds outside the tradition. It sometimes seems naïve: he seems even to have insisted, countering the Ash'arîs' opponents' intolerance with its equivalent, that he who believed for no good reason was no sound believer; that therefore those who did not accept (Ash'arî) kalâm were not even true Muslims. This point some Ash'arîs tried to show by arguing that just as correct proofs of a thesis showed that the thesis itself was correct, so false proofs of a thesis entailed the falseness of the thesis itself; hence the correct proofs of orthodox positions, which the Ash'arîs thought they had found, were as important to admit as the original positions. This specious argument seems to have been set aside by the time of Imâm-al-Ḥaramayn Juvaynî (1028–1085), who used subtler methods than his earlier predecessors. His purpose was still polemic within the tradition, and he continued to present the atomistic doctrine and all that was associated with it; but he did so in a more rationalistically philosophic spirit. There is nothing naïve about his work. Inevitably, it dominated the Ash'arî school of his time. Yet possibly it fulfilled its task less appropriately than did the work of some earlier kalâm scholars.

Juvaynî inherited the religious questions he occupied himself with and even the basic viewpoints that he publicly represented. His father, originally from Juvayn, had become head of the Shâfi'î legal madhhab in Nîshâpûr in Khurâsân; when he died, the son succeeded him in his teaching post at the madrasah, though he was only eighteen at the time—clearly, his unusual gifts were already apparent. He had also studied with an Ash'arî teacher. A recognized scholar from the beginning, Juvaynî did his chief work in clarifying the basic principles of his two traditions—Shâfi'î fiqh (which he defended against other madhhabs) and Ash'arî kalâm. But at least in kalâm, his outstanding gifts allowed him to carry forward the inherited tasks to what could seem a point of completion.

At the same time, he witnessed the last major effort of the Ḥadîth folk to suppress kalâm disputation altogether. The Seljuḳid Ṭoghrïl-beg's vizier, al-Kundurî, ordered that all Mu'tazilî teaching (in which he included other kalâm as well) cease, and Juvaynî had to leave home; but in Mecca and Medina, where he took refuge, he gained such a name—though still in his twenties—that his followers subsequently called him 'imâm of the two holy cities', *Imâm-al-Ḥaramayn.* When Niẓâmulmulk came to power as Alp-Arslân's vizier, however, Juvaynî and the other scholars of kalâm were without difficulty restored to favour; only in a few places, notably Baghdad, did Ḥadîthî resistance against them remain effective.

In Juvaynî's work in kalâm, two traits stand out. If one contrasts Juvaynî's work with earlier work—with the writings ascribed to al-Ash'arî himself, for instance, or even with later pieces—one is struck with the degree of sophisticated detail to which the disputation on every controverted point had been refined. But this refinement and precision express, in turn, a second trait: an awareness of the intellectual standards in logic and metaphysics maintained by the Faylasûfs. Though he was not arguing expressly with them, yet their categories were everywhere present.

Juvaynî recognized, for instance, that the old Ash'arî attempt to maintain God's omnipotence was less than satisfactory by rationalistic standards. It could be objected to their doctrine of *kasb* (that humans morally 'acquired' their good and bad works even though God was the sole cause of them), that it was unintelligible; and once it was no longer acceptable just to state whatever could be deduced from revealing facts, whether it could be seen to fit into a harmonious system or not, then that a point was unintelligible meant that it could not be regarded as proven. This Juvaynî acknowledged. His solution was to try to define what he could call a middle position between sheer determinacy and indeterminate free will, in which the words answered to the demands of the Ḥadîthî insistence that only God could really make or do anything, while the conditions appended to them virtually satisfied the Mu'tazilî insistence that people could not be responsible for what they could not choose to avoid.

Often what seems to be happening in his work (as his doctrine of kasb) is a return in substance to the early, more common-sense positions of kalâm, those of the Mu'tazilîs before the rise of Ḥadîthî piety forced a modification. For instance, in asserting the divine attributes (such as God's eternity), Juvaynî insisted that God does have them (as the Ḥadîthîs said)—they are not merely modes of his being, as for the Mu'tazilîs; yet they are not based on anything added to his being: which comes to the same. (He acknowledged rather apologetically that he had deviated here from earlier Ash'arîs.) And Juvaynî even allowed for metaphorical understanding of some attributes, when linguistic usage could be found in support, though far less readily than did the Mu'tazilîs.[12]

But actually Juvaynî had added something to the Mu'tazilîs' stance. If one compares Juvaynî's doctrine with Ibn-Sînâ's on the same point, one finds a rather similar concern with finding formulations that will define an effectively worshipable God without sacrificing what seemed necessary—for a rationalist—to define His transcendence. One can suppose a sequence of intellectual needs: that for the earlier Mu'tazilîs, still consciously carriers of the Qur'ânic mission to a conquered world, the God of worship needed no closer definition, and what was called for was simply a defence of the essentials of Islamic monotheism; and then for the Ḥadîth folk, for whom certain traits of that monotheism were more nuanced, God's transcendence was sufficiently guaranteed by insisting on His incomprehensibility; whereas for the more rationalistically inclined, once the issues had been well posed, the transcendence which a monotheistic sense of the numinous called for had to be reconciled with the ultimate rational harmonies a rationalist tried to see in the cosmos. In such a task, the Faylasûfs inevitably posed the most sophisticated standards then available. Juvaynî's concern with them is illustrated by his interest in the three-term Aristotelian logical syllogism, though in practice he usually used the more convenient two-term form of argument that had been customary in kalâm, in which some of the logic was left implicit.[13] He established the subsequent form of an Ash'arî treatise by introducing serious prolegomena on the nature of abstract reasoning.

I have the impression that in the very moment of its triumph, in the act of perfecting its own tradition, the Ash'arî kalâm was near losing sight of its very purpose: the rational defence of a non-rationalistic kerygmatic position, in which key individual events are held to have revealed more about what life and its commitments mean than can any universal uniformities of nature. Juvaynî could no longer understand, for instance, why the doctrine of 'commanding the right and forbidding the wrong' should ever have been given the special treatment the Mu'tazilîs and earlier Ash'arîs had given it as a primary doctrine alongside the unity of God and the prophethood of Muḥammad. For them, it had dealt with the historical commitment of the

[12] The new edition of the *Encyclopaedia of Islam* omits mention of a modest and not very perceptive, but useful, opuscule on Juvaynî, Helmut Klopper, *Das Dogma des Imân al-Ḥaramain al-Djuwainî und sein Werk al-'Aqîdat an-Niẓâmîya* (Wiesbaden, 1958), including a translation of the latter.

[13] He rarely used the syllogism form itself; it was left to Ghazâlî to take advantage of its logical efficiency (see W. Montgomery Watt, *Muslim Intellectual: The Struggle and Achievement of al-Ghazâlî* [Edinburgh University Press, 1963]). Ibn-Khaldûn contrasted the kalâm of the earlier period as the 'old way' to the kalâm of the flowering of the Earlier Middle Period as the 'new way' (for he disliked seeing Falsafah diluted with kalâm, and preferred the kalâm left relatively naïve if there must be kalâm at all) and he has been followed by modern scholars. For an analysis of what is involved, so far as we know it (for the work of the older kalâm is largely lost), see Louis Gardet and M.-M. Anawati, *Introduction à la théologie musulmane* (Paris, 1948), pp. 72–76.

faithful; but for Juvaynî, typically of his time, it seemed to deserve no more than a minor place among the other rules of fiqh, covering the ways one Muslim should admonish another on an everyday basis. A viewpoint was beginning to be adopted—and not only by Juvaynî—that could receive its fullest and freest expression only in Falsafah or its equivalent. To be sure, the revelatory value of events that can only be 'heard about', not reasoned out from recurrent experience, was still given exclusive credit. But even the proofs offered for prophethood were touched with a rationalistic spirit.

We may say that from the time of the Ḥadîth folk on, with their cautious view of Muslim political responsibilities, the kerygmatic force of Sharîʿah-minded piety had been being reduced in favour of a greater degree of ritualistic 'paradigm-tracing' piety: that is, Muslims were more inclined to articulate the patterns of proper Sharʿî life into an enduring, almost natural cosmos, in which the Qurʾânic message was an eternal datum almost as much as it was a challenging event. Such a mood could call for a timelessly rationalistic outlook. But there may have been also a more directly intellectual reason for the shift.

Without a more general doctrine of history as such—that is, without a general form for reasoning effectively about events as morally committing rather than as merely exemplifying natural possibilities—any more satisfactory method of reasoning expressly appropriate to the problems of prophethood was presumably out of the question. If such methods can ever be found, one may speculate that they could not have been expected in an agrarianate-level society anyway. There, the strong kerygmatic tone of Islamic thinking, in which certain historical events were explicitly vested with ultimate values, had issued in communalism, in which the Sharîʿah was reinforced by way of exclusive group loyalties—so that the Qur'ânic event became intellectually more isolated even than in the Qur'ân itself, where it appeared as one in a long chain of revelatory events. No general doctrine of meaningful historical events could arise in such a context. That is, there could be no pattern of rational analysis to rival the refined Philosophic doctrine of nature. Hence the more the kalâm was rationally elaborated, the more it came into competition with Falsafah, and the more it could seem threatened with futility in such a competition. Henceforth in all the great figures in kalâm disputation one can see clearly what was only implicit in Juvaynî: to the extent that they took kalâm seriously at all, it was in the form of modifying the conclusions of Falsafah so as to bring its analyses into accord with Islamic community loyalties.[14]

[14] For those who cast the history of Islamicate civilization into the form 'what went wrong with Islam?', there have been two answers on the level of intellectual history: that Muslims failed to give full effect to the Greek heritage, or that they allowed the Greek heritage to inhibit unduly their own more concrete and historically-minded (kerygmatic) heritage. I am not, here, siding with those few who take the second view, of course; I am not clear that anything more did go wrong with Islam than with any other tradition. I am only trying to state one problem that arose. As we shall see, the resolution of this crisis represented by Ghazâlî, though it produced its own problems as all resolutions do, cannot be regarded as marking an intellectual failure of Islamicate civilization.

Ghazâlî's re-evaluation of the speculative traditions: kalâm and Falsafah

It was only with Juvaynî's disciple, Abû-Ḥâmid Muḥammad Ghazâlî (1058–1111), that the kalâm came to make full use of the resources of Falsafah and was able to meet it on its own terms. But it was also with Ghazâlî that it received its rudest discounting as a means to truth. For Ghazâlî, the crisis in kalâm finally led beyond kalâm to a new approach to religion generally, on both personal and social levels.

Abû-Ḥâmid Ghazâlî and his brother Aḥmad (almost equally famous as a Ṣûfî) were born at a village near Ṭûs in Khurâsân and were supported through their schooling by a small bequest left in trust by their father, whose brother (or uncle) was already established in the city as a scholar. Both boys had outstanding minds, and Abû-Ḥâmid particularly rose fast. At about thirty-three years of age, in 1091, the aged Niẓâmulmulk made him director of his Niẓâmiyyah madrasah at Baghdad. There, as a teacher of fiqh law as well as of kalâm, he won great prestige even with quite Sharîʿah-minded men. His innovations in kalâm itself were incisive.

But he became personally dissatisfied with his very acceptable expositions. At length he found himself crippled by a persistent crisis of personal doubts, which coincided with but can hardly be reduced to a political crisis at Baghdad among Ghazâlî's friends after Niẓâmulmulk's assassination. Suddenly he left his post at the Niẓâmiyyah madrasah (1095) and fled his public, retiring secretly to Damascus and Jerusalem. (He even left his family behind, providing for them by way of public waqfs.) Only years later did he re-emerge, with a sense of personal mission, to teach publicly. Therewith he attempted, and carried through, a more fundamental revision of the foundations of Islamic thinking than a mere sprucing up of kalâm. Such was his prestige that his opinions, fitting in well enough with the trend of the times to be sure, carried great weight; and while the development that followed was not all due to his work, it may be understood through an analysis of his line of thought.

Ghazâlî wrote a schematic little book in which he summarized the attitude he took (worked out in detail in other volumes) to each of the major traditions of life-orientational thinking in his time, *Al-Munqidh min al-ḍalâl*, the *Deliverer from Error*.[15] This was put in the form of a sketch of his own life; but it was not a straight narrative autobiography. The intimate autobiographical form was foreign to the Islamicate reticence about personal matters, and the *Deliverer* dealt, in fact, with intimate matters. Ghazâlî himself points out that he feels it impossible to describe all the living details relevant to his conclusions. The book did describe certain crucial moments in his experience. But this was done rather in the manner of the schematic

[15] *Al-Munqidh min al-dalâl*, translated by William Montgomery Watt in *The Faith and Practice of al-Ghazâlî* (London, 1953); his is a better version than is an earlier one, but still more fluent than exact sometimes.

autobiographies popular among those Ismâʿîlîs whom he wrote so many works to refute, as a dynamic statement of faith in terms of the facts of his own life.

The work began by presenting the intellectual helplessness of the human condition in itself. He described how earlier in his life he came to doubt not only all religious teaching, but even all possibility of dependable knowledge of any kind. He had overcome the problem for a time but then, at his personal crisis, he doubted the validity of all that he was teaching of religious lore; he could be healed only by accepting a moral decision to withdraw and lay new bases for his life through Ṣûfî practices. The classical ʿulamâʾ scholars, whether exponents simply of ḥadîth and fiqh or exponents of kalâm as well, had discussed proper belief as if (once it was correctly established) it were simply a duty which a good man accepted and a bad man rejected. Ghazâlî made it clear that this is not a matter of simple choice; doubt is beyond a person's deliberate control, and sound thinking is like sound health—a state of being rather than an act of will.

In particular, a state of total doubt, where one thinks about whether one can or cannot think, is existentially not so much an error in logic (which it is) as a mental disease. If it has blocked one, one must be restored by receiving fresh vitality from God, rather than by a syllogism. But even less drastic states of doubt, if at all radical, require more than purely intellectual instruments for their healing. When doubt and error arise in religion, they must be looked on as diseases to be cured rather than just as sins to be condemned. The various available intellectual paths must be explored not merely for their informative value but as possible means of curing people of error. Hence, in principle, the Sharîʿah-minded objection to kalâm simply as an intellectual luxury cannot stand; the question becomes whether kalâm can cure anyone of error. It was on this basis that Ghazâlî depreciated kalâm.

Ghazâlî continued to be a major exponent of kalâm, but he ultimately took, in the *Deliverer*, an attitude toward it that departed minimally from the feeling about it of such Ḥadîth folk as Ibn-Ḥanbal (whom indeed he made a point of citing favourably in a relevant context). He denied that it led to any positive truth in itself. It was no use at all to the ordinary person whose faith was still sound (and such a person should be protected from exposure to its doubt-engendering argumentation). It was of use only with those who had come to doubt the truth and adopt errors that must be corrected. And, even as a corrective of errors, its function was limited. Its use was to confute various more or less trivial heresies, by showing that they are untenable on their own grounds; accordingly, it started from any assumptions admitted by the heretics, without needing to question whether such assumptions be sound or not. But this made it appropriate only to such doubters as had not pushed their doubt in a truly philosophic direction. Kalâm was useless for the truly independent mind. Thus Ghazâlî assured kalâm a necessary but not very honourable niche in Islam. (Al-Ashʿarî had seen kalâm in a somewhat similar light, but did not draw such weighty conclusions.)

In contrast, Ghazâlî allowed Falsafah great honour and even a basic role. This was muted by his attack on the crowning glory of its system, that is its metaphysics, which he insisted was false and dangerously misleading. But he attacked its metaphysics in the name of fidelity to Falsafah itself. He insisted that the very sort of reasoning that allowed Philosophy its triumphs in the natural sphere, in mathematics and astronomy, for instance, no longer served if one turned to seeking out absolute truths beyond the natural sphere of the mind and senses; that the Faylasûfs had been unfaithful to their own principles in making the attempt. (His masterly and minutely argued work, *Tahâfut al-falâsifah*, 'The Incoherence of the Philosophers'[16] is devoted to showing that the arguments the Faylasûfs used on the level of metaphysics lack the indubitable cogency the Faylasûfs pride themselves on elsewhere; that, indeed, other equally sound arguments could lead to other positions, even orthodox Muslim ones, though they would admittedly not prove these latter either.) While rejecting Falsafah metaphysics, he held, therefore, that Muslims should accept the findings of the Falsafah sciences in their proper sphere—knowledge of nature—contrary to the attitude of many Sharî'ah-minded persons. Moreover, he went on later to apply to the Islamic tradition itself a basic principle of Falsafah, that truth must be ultimately accessible to and verifiable by any individual human consciousness; he did not, however, call the principle 'Falsafah' at that point.

Yet even so, his attitude to Falsafah was informed by the spirit of the Ḥadîth folk. The Ḥadîth folk were radically utilitarian: a man should be concerned with living and believing correctly for the sake of divine blessings in this world and salvation in the other; he should not meddle in what does not concern him, and should seek knowledge only for its use as a guide to living, not out of idle curiosity. Ghazâlî used precisely such criteria in defining the scope and value of the Falsafah sciences: they were to be cultivated so far as they are useful, but the speculation of Falsafah was not to be tolerated merely because of its beauty. And, consistently enough, if the perils in Falsafah for any given person outweighed its utility, such a person should not be permitted to study it, lest he be led astray by the tempting delusions of its metaphysics in that point which is most important of all: correct religious belief. Therefore only qualified scholars should be allowed to dip into philosophic and scientific writings.

On such a basis, the populist sentiments of the Ḥadîth folk were vindicated, in that Falsafah was declared dangerous because it could not be properly

[16] Translated into English by Sabih Ahmad Kamali (Pakistan Philosophical Congress Publication No. 3, Mohammad Ashraf Darr, Lahore, 1958). The bulk of it is also translated as a part of Ibn-Rushd's answer to Ghazâlî's book, *Tahâfut al-tahâfut*, 'The Incoherence of the Incoherence', translated by Simon Van den Bergh (Unesco Collection of Great Works, and E. J. W. Gibb Memorial Series, London, 1954).

understood by the average man, whose religion was both sufficient and of paramount importance. Yet, as in the case of kalâm, an exception was made in the condemnation, a niche was found for it. And because of the inherent consequence of Falsafah, the niche turns out to be of moment, for it implies, as the exception for kalâm did not, an élite in the midst of common mankind: not an élite in anything essential to religion, of course, but yet an intellectually privileged minority.

The debate between kalâm and Falsafah seems to end with both forms of speculation rather heavily discounted. But Ghazâlî had a broader perspective in mind than the men of kalâm had normally had. His intention was to build a comprehensive foundation for effective religious life in an age which, as he put it, had degenerated not only from the simple purity of the pristine Medina but even from the relatively high moral standards of the scholars of al-Shâfi'î's time. The new age needed a new religious awareness and commitment. This new religious life required a new intellectual basis; and in this, Falsafah was to play a larger role than Ghazâlî directly acknowledged in the *Deliverer*. Then it required a new pattern of religious teaching and guidance built upon that basis. (From Ghazâlî's viewpoint, of course, what was new in either case was merely that what could be left implicit in better times had to become explicit in his generation.)

Ghazâlî's quarrel with the Ismâ'îlîs

The *Deliverer* embodies the key points of his intellectual foundation for the new life. If kalâm gives correct answers but on a trivial foundation and if Falsafah rears a sound foundation but cannot yield correct answers to the crucial questions, the remedy for the disease of philosophic error and ultimate doubt must be sought outside either apologetic or rationalistic intellectual analyses. In the *Deliverer,* Ghazâlî suggested, in effect, a twofold solution. Ultimately, he had recourse to Ṣûfism.

But for ordinary persons who have had the misfortune to lose their childhood simplicity of faith, he recommended a course based upon universal human capacities and leading to historical authority. He introduced this approach through a refutation of the position of the Shî'ah, more precisely that of the Ismâ'îlî Shî'îs of his generation, who were then launching their great revolt against the whole Jamâ'î-Sunnî order of the Seljuk amîrs.

Ghazâlî's listing of the major traditions of life-orientational thinking of his time, to which the *Deliverer* is devoted, can be surprising at first sight: kalâm, Falsafah, Ṣûfism, and the doctrine of the Nizârî Ismâ'îlîs; he assures us that truth must be found among these four schools of thought or nowhere. Three of these a modern person may generalize readily enough as theology, philosophy, and mysticism; but the fourth is a single doctrine held within a single sect—and even if one takes it as symbolic of authoritarianism generally, as if that were a way of seeking truth distinct from, say, theology, one might suppose authoritarians were to be found closer at hand, such as the Ḥanbalîs. Other Shî'îs, even other Jamâ'î positions, to say nothing of non-Muslim religious traditions, are ignored. The prominence assigned to the Ismâ'îlîs, which reappears in many of Ghazâlî's works, has been explained as due to his dislike of authoritarianism—perhaps there was danger in attacking authoritarianism more directly, though he did directly oppose the imposition of conformity upon qualified scholars in deciding legal points. More cogently, it has been seen as a response to the urgent threat posed by the Ismâ'îlî revolt. But the confrontation with Ismâ'îlî teaching is too intimate, and is taken up in diverse forms too repeatedly, to be accounted for in a purely external way. He refuted the Ismâ'îlîs over and over, I think, because he found something in their position to be persuasive—persuasive on a level with the other three positions he lists.

I think what this was may become clearer if we characterize the four schools of thought as forming, in their mutual contrasts, a comprehensive schema of life-orientational possibilities. Two of the schools represent exoteric, public positions, in which the seeker takes the whole initiative and his process of thinking can be followed at will by anyone else. Kalâm was founded on dialectical argument on the basis of commitment to a historical revelation; Falsafah was founded on demonstrative argument on the basis of the timeless norms of nature. The other two schools represent esoteric, initiatory positions, in which part of the process of coming to understanding does not depend simply on the seeker and cannot be reproduced at will. The Ismâ'îlîs appealed to a privileged historical institution, the imâmate and the community that had been built around it. Like the men of kalâm, they insisted on a kerygmatic vision, but that vision was on an esoteric rather than an exoteric plane. The Ṣûfîs appealed, as mystics, to privileged individual but potentially universal awarenesses. That is, like the Faylasûfs, they appealed to present normative experience, not to any kerygmatic event; but again on an esoteric plane.

Each of the four spots in the schema (which is, of course, my schema, not Ghazâlî's) was represented by the tradition that seemed best to exemplify it. (I would assume, for instance, that for this purpose the Ḥanbalîs would appear—so far as they offered any argument at all—simply as a case of imperfect kalâm, better represented by the Ash'arîs.) Ghazâlî does not, finally, adopt one of the four positions to the exclusion of the others. Both the kerygmatic and the non-kerygmatic, both the exoteric and the esoteric have their place. What he adopts from Ismâ'îlism (without admitting as much, of course!) is elements that help show how a kerygmatic tradition can be validated on the basis of a more or less incommunicable personal experience, in which the historically revealed authority comes to be acknowledged without external proofs. Much of this viewpoint emerges directly out of the passages devoted to refuting the Ismâ'îlîs, when he argues that Muḥammad himself fills the role of infallible imâm; but the viewpoint is consummated only in the role that he gives to the Ṣûfîs—who are assigned a function in validating a kerygmatic, historical vision as well as a more properly inward mystical role.

As it found itself losing out in the attempt to win the allegiance of the masses, Shî'ism was forced into two alternative postures: accommodation, represented especially by the Twelvers, who often tried to win tolerance from Sunnîs as a minor deviation; and defiance, expressed especially by the Ismâ'îlîs. It was in this latter posture that the Shî'î position could become intellectually most challenging. The Ismâ'îlîs seem to have developed at that time a peculiarly trenchant simplification of the all-Shî'ah doctrine of *ta'lîm*: of the necessity for exclusive religious authority in an infallible imâm. One of their leaders, Ḥasan-e Ṣabbâḥ, argued with telling subtlety a position which may be summed up thus: that for absolute truth, such as religion seemed to require, a decisive authority (an imâm) is needed, for otherwise one man's reasoned opinion is as good as another's and none is better than a guess; that this proposition itself is in fact all that reason as such can furnish us with; finally then, that, as no reasoned proof could demonstrate who the imâm was (only that he was needed), the imâm must be he who relied on no positive, external proof of his own position, but only on pointing out explicitly the logically essential but usually only implicit need; and as it was the Ismâ'îlî imâm alone that made so unconditional a claim, he thus stood as his own proof—by fulfilling the need in the act of pointing it out.[17] (This was, in effect, to point to commitment to the Ismâ'îlî community itself and to its revelatory teaching. For, of course, it was not the imâm in person that anyone found, but his authorized hierarchy; and then the truth the seeker would find was not merely the solution to a logical dilemma, but a moment of existential recommitment posed in logical form.)

Ghazâlî rejected this case for ta'lîm authoritarianism, partly by pointing out its inherent elements of self-contradiction (he showed, as with kalâm and Falsafah, that they could not prove their case, even though it might not be disproved); but primarily by putting forward a slightly different interpretation of reason. He granted that reason shows the need for an authority beyond reason; but he maintained (in effect) that reason could not only establish the need, but could at least begin to recognize when the need had been fulfilled: that is, it could recognize the true imâm not merely through a logical impasse but through his positive qualities as a teacher. This true imâm, he claimed, was none but the Prophet himself, whose teaching would be found valid in each person's own life. The need for an authority, of course, arises from the general human need for spiritual guidance; and Ghazâlî maintained that if a person followed closely the advice and example of the Prophet, he would find in time that the spiritual needs he had confronted were being

[17] For an analysis of this doctrine and of Jamâ'î-Sunnî responses to it see my *The Order of Assassins: The Struggle of the Early Nizârî Ismâ'îlîs against the Islamic World* (The Hague, 1955).

met. In this way he could recognize a prophet, just as he could recognize a physician as a man able to meet medical needs. Indeed, the very personality of Muḥammad in its kindness and concern, as it shone through Qur'ân and ḥadîth, would prove itself. (This was to invoke a sense of Muḥammad's prophethood as comprehensive as al-Shâfi'î's, but closer in feeling to the 'Alid-loyalists' sense of heroic personality than to the legally exemplary figure posited by al-Shâfi'î.) Not unrelated to this appeal to personal experience was a secondary appeal made elsewhere to the very fortunes of the Muslim Ummah, which had come historically to be the dominant community (so it seemed) among mankind.

The Ismâ'îlîs were right (Ghazâlî admitted implicitly and sometimes explicitly) in denying that any particular proof (for instance, any miracle) could indicate the man of true authority; and they were right in pointing rather to the authority's self-validation as head of the saving historical community, which would be discovered because it answered an inner need otherwise unmet. But the truth would be recognized not by way of a single existential dilemma but by cumulative experience, which the Ismâ'îlî argument did not allow for. The experience Ghazâlî pointed to, both personal and historical (that is, derived from the history of the Islamic community as a whole), was such experience as every human being went through at least to some degree; therefore, if any person were fully honest with himself and serious in his search, he could discover who was the needed authority and, by following his teachings, be as sound in faith as any. What was needed, where doubt had sprung up, was healing grace from God, sincere endeavour on the part of the individual, and warning and encouragement by those who had come to the truth.[18]

Here the Muslim community at large played a central role (as the Ismâ'îlî community did for Ismâ'îlîs). It guaranteed the truth for those of its members who were not afflicted with doubt and so need not think for themselves. And it provided the stimulus and guidance needed by those who were seeking. (It was perhaps this appeal to the living community that made Ghazâlî—and many later Ṣûfî-influenced scholars—somewhat careless of proper isnâd documentation in citing ḥadîth reports. It was the present community, not that of Marwânî times or even Medina times, that played the role of guarantor.)

In this way, the populist spirit of the Ḥadîth folk, as well as its kerygmatic

[18] The Christian theologian Paul Tillich, in *Dynamics of Faith* (New York, 1956), gives an existential interpretation of faith which, I believe, can be helpful toward understanding what men like Ghazâlî have been confronted with and have achieved. Tillich's great merit is to have clarified certain common confusions which have led to misappreciation of some religious writers. But in particular he sketches, from a modern perspective, the essentials of how reason leads to the need for ultimate faith but awaits revelation to carry it further. Though Ghazâlî cannot be called an existentialist in the modern sense, Tillich's analysis makes more sense of Ghazâlî's position (and the Ta'lîmîs') than do some less sophisticated readings: it is not a matter of supplementing reason in its own realm but of complementing it in total experience.

vision, was maintained—for no man's religion need be essentially better than another's; and revelation and the holy community were made indispensable. But at the same time, the basic principle of the Faylasûfs, validation by universal human experience, was tacitly given its due among an élite.

Yet for the most perceptive, the cumulative experience that would verify the presence of the Prophet must be capped with an ingredient that Ghazâlî did not mention immediately in the *Deliverer*; for it need not be pointed out in advance for the general point to be made to the satisfaction of any but his most demanding readers, and these latter would perceive it themselves from what he had to say about Ṣûfism and prophecy. That is: the requisite cumulative experience must include some touch of prophesying itself. One must be able to perceive the ultimate truth, in however slight a measure, in the same way the prophets perceived it, in order to verify definitely that they were prophets—just as one must be in some slight measure oneself a physician to judge of physicians. One must know what it is, to have not merely knowledge about the truth but immediate acquaintance with it as prophets had. Otherwise, the cumulative experience would still allow only a superior sort of kalâm, merely probably in its conclusions. A further way to truth was called for, beyond kalâm, beyond Falsafah, beyond even an ordinary pursuit of an authority that would meet the needs that reason disclosed.

This lay in the Ṣûfî experience. When Ghazâlî fled from his public eminence at Baghdad into retirement at Jerusalem, his purpose was to explore more deeply the Ṣûfî way. He did not have major mystical experiences, but he had enough to convince him that there was indeed a sort of awareness that could not be reduced to Aristotelian syllogism and yet carried its own conviction; enough, indeed, to convince him that the claims of more advanced Ṣûfîs could be trusted.

For him this had the consequence that the Ṣûfîs' certification of the Prophetic message in its essentials was also to be trusted. And in Ṣûfî experience he thus saw the challenge, posed by the Ismâ'îlîs, finally met. It was through the psychological teachings of the Faylasûfs, particularly Ibn-Sînâ, that Ṣûfî experience could be so interpreted. Ghazâlî interpreted prophecy not as an unparalleled event but, in the Faylasûfs' terms, as a special natural species of awareness which merely took its most perfect form in Muḥammad. This awareness was of the same sort as the Ṣûfîs gained, though of a much higher degree. Hence Ṣûfîs were in a position to recognize full-scale prophecy when they saw it. Indeed, he went further. Just as prophetic awareness took a minor form among Ṣûfîs, so it might even be genuinely echoed in analogous experiences of ordinary people. Ghazâlî cited especially the sort of awareness that can come through dreams; which, however, Ghazâlî (like some of the Faylasûfs) saw not as revealing unconscious forces, as moderns do, but unforeseeable external events—though perhaps the practical difference is less than it might seem. Thus though the Prophet was long since dead, a touch of prophecy was always present and accessible in the community—as it was for the Ismâ'îlîs with their imâm.

The intellectual foundation of Ghazâlî's mission, then, was an expanded appreciation of Ṣûfism. Kalâm was relegated to a secondary role; and the most valuable insights of Falsafah and even of the Ismâ'îlî doctrine of ta'lîm authority were subsumed into the re-valorized Ṣûfism, which now appeared as guarantor and interpreter of even the Shar'î aspects of the Islamic faith.

Ghazâlî recognized the dangers attendant upon Ṣûfî freedom and warned against them—the Ṣûfî, for all his special graces, must not imagine himself exempt from the common human obligations of the Sharî'ah. The inward spirit (the bâṭin) must not be allowed to displace the outer law and doctrine (the ẓâhir). But the bâṭin of the Ṣûfîs was indispensable. The Islamic faith could not ultimately stand without the continuous re-experiencing of its ultimate truths by the mystics. They did not merely know about truth on the Prophet's authority; they knew it directly, personally, within themselves. In every generation they alone could bear witness, to those willing to listen, to the truth not merely of such fragments as an individual might chance to verify in an ordinary lifetime, but of the whole of the Prophet's message. Thus the Ṣûfîs were assigned a crucial role in supporting the historical Muslim community as a body, as well as in guiding personal lives. (This was probably one reason why Ghazâlî was so insistent that Ṣûfîs were subject to the community law—only so could they serve the community as witnesses to its mission.)

Spiritual ministry and the gradation of knowledge

Having established an unimpeachable intellectual basis, appropriate to his age, on which the new religious life should be built, Ghazâlî had to work out a new pattern of teaching and guidance in which the consequences of his intellectual re-evaluations should be put into practice. This was probably central to his thoughts from a very early time.

Ghazâlî had long wished to become a religious and spiritual guide to his people. His restless exploration of every sort of opinion, his attempts to achieve Ṣûfî experience (which had begun even before he was raised to the Niẓâmiyyah madrasah at Baghdad), the doubts he was repeatedly tormented with, all seem to have been directed not only toward achieving a personal religious certainty but also toward giving him a sound basis for religious leadership. Before his retirement from Baghdad he had spoken of founding an independent Ṣûfî doctrine of his own. But it is perhaps even more consistent with his sense of mission that Ghazâlî was so persistently interested in intellectual method, much more so than in systems of ultimate truth for themselves—which could hardly be put in publicly accessible terms anyway. Even a work of his that has the appearance of Ṣûfî speculation on the cosmos, the 'Niche for Lights', is devoted primarily to elucidating ways of understanding words and symbols and doctrines. (Hence attempts to reduce his thought to a set of cosmological conclusions are bound to miss the point of it and succeed only in making him look self-contradictory.) One of the achievements he was proudest of was a test to settle how far one can go in taking the Qur'ânic images metaphorically as the Faylasûfs and the Ismâ'îlîs were wont to do; he was rather naïvely sure that the justice of his 'scales' could not be denied and would settle most disputes if attended to.

During his years of retirement—during which he travelled a good deal, though probably settling down finally in Khurâsân—he seems to have matured his ideas of what role he could play in the Ummah. He never resumed his chair at Baghdad, the most prominent teaching post in Islamdom; perhaps because of the danger of assassination by the Ismâ'îlîs, whose revolt was still in full course; but probably also because his conception of his mission was no longer compatible with an outward career so prominent and controversial. Ghazâlî does seem to have regarded himself as called by God to the office of *mujaddid*: the renewer of Islamic faith that Muslims had come to believe God would send at the start of each new century of the Hijrah. In 1106 (499 of the Hijrah) he accepted the call from a son of Niẓâmulmulk, himself now vizier, to teach publicly again. But he did so only in Nîshâpûr, not far from his home in Ṭûs, and ceased when his patron was assassinated. His teaching was such as required not so much a spectacular confutation of opponents as a pervasive influence, at many levels, of a very personal sense of life. It could be done as well at home and through his writings.[19]

His masterpiece is the *Iḥyâ 'ulûm al-dîn*, the *Revival of the Religious Sciences* (composed in Arabic, as was the *Deliverer*). Under Ṣûfî inspiration, it interprets the whole Sharî'ah corpus as a vehicle for a sober inward personal

[19] Farid Jabre, *La notion de certitude selon Ghazali dans ses origines psychologiques et historiques* (Paris, 1958), has studied the structure of Ghazâlî's thinking with great care, and his works are the best point of departure for further study on him. (He is more penetrating than W. Montgomery Watt in *Muslim Intellectual*, see n. 13 above, a work which is too brief to allow Watt to counterbalance his oversimplified psychology of how people hold ideas with a close analysis of the data from the viewpoint he adopts; but Watt's work remains useful.) Jabre gives considerable bibliography. In his main theses, Jabre seems to me sound: Ghazâlî surely was committed throughout to the validity of revelation, and the certainty he was seeking was not a validation of intellectual processes for supporting it, as such, but rather a state of the soul to which such processes might or might not contribute. Yet I find Jabre's picture not very human: he makes Ghazâlî unduly singleminded. A continuing commitment need not be incompatible with times and moods of intense doubt—and what is doubted is just the themes of the tradition to which one is committed; that one has come to certain conclusions early does not preclude a repeated rediscovery of them in the course of one's life, and the rediscovery may make a crucial difference. If Ghazâlî writes as a physician to heal others' doubts, if he stylizes his manner to meet the reader where he is, one must not take the resultant doctrinaire posture too literally. And perhaps Jabre does not sufficiently credit the degree to which critical rationality can enter into the understanding of historical revelation as well as of recurrent experience. My own understanding of Ghazâlî is a development from that of Duncan B. MacDonald.

regimen. Every Shar'î rule is interpreted ethically and given a devotional dimension such that it can become the starting point for inner purification. The social implications of the Sharî'ah become, if anything, more attenuated than before. (Ghazâlî relegated political life explicitly to the amîrs and wrote a manual for kings—in Persian—in the Iranian tradition.) Ghazâlî was not writing for a judge or a *muḥtasib* supervisor of markets, but for a private person concerned for his own life or charged with the spiritual direction of others. Some advice he gave presupposed a man (not a woman) whose trade allowed him a fair amount of leisure during his day: a scholar particularly, though also, at need, a kâtib or merchant or even a craftsman working on his own account. Only a person whose time could be largely devoted to religion could afford to make use of the Shar'î life to the full as Ghazâlî interpreted it.

But the social implications of the *Revival* are nonetheless important: as Ghazâlî pointed out in the *Deliverer*, the sort of life led by the men of religion could become an influence to form the lives of Muslims generally. Thus indirectly the *Revival* might influence many more than the religious scholars. In the *Revival* he grades society into three classes: those who believe the truths of religion without questioning; those who learn reasons for their beliefs—who are especially the religious scholars (particularly the men of kalâm); and those who directly experience religious truth, the Ṣûfîs. This is a distinction not merely of knowledge but implicitly of moral function. For each class could teach those below it and might serve as an example to them. The Ṣûfîs, whose direct perception of truth was held to be akin to that of the prophets themselves, might have a mission, as Ghazâlî did, to infuse the religious forms of the time with spiritual life. It follows that the Shar'î men of religion had the responsibility to receive the Ṣûfî inspiration so far as they could and to spread the inward spirit of religion, and not merely the outward doctrines, among the populace generally. Thus the high evaluation of Ṣûfî experience as a vindication of truth had social consequences which Ghazâlî did not quite dare spell out but which he himself provided a living example of.

One may suspect that in a society where personal relations counted for so much, especially on the local level, such an outlook was eminently practical as a social programme. To a large degree, I think, it was in fact approximated in subsequent centuries, as we shall see in the next chapter, though the Ṣûfîs often had more direct influence on the populace than they did on the Shar'î scholars. In this sense, the work of Ghazâlî may be said to have given a rationale to the spiritual structure that supported society under the decentralized political order, the order that resulted in part from the work of his patron Niẓâmulmulk.

But such a programme presupposed a more or less hierarchical religious life, a gradation of men of religion from the viewpoint of their role in spiritual ministry to the Muslim community. This might be justified on the basis of the ancient principle that Muslims were to be graded—in point of dignity, at least—according to their degree of piety. But a hierarchism based on the special sort of insight to which Ṣûfîs had access required, in turn, a crucial principle which would have horrified the early Muslims. Religious knowledge itself must be graded. Though the full and sufficient validity of the faith of the ordinary person was carefully safeguarded, much knowledge that was important, even in a way essential to the community, was not accessible to him; nay, it should be kept carefully concealed from him lest, misunderstood, it cause him to stumble.

This principle finds broad application in the *Deliverer from Error*. Thus the writings of the Faylasûfs should not be studied by the weak-minded lest, through respect for the writers, they be misled into sharing the writers' infidelity. But still more important, those who have not entered on the Ṣûfî way under proper guidance should not be informed of the secrets that Ṣûfîs discover; they must receive only the general witness the Ṣûfîs can bear, that they know the faith is true. Ghazâlî was one of those who maintained that al-Ḥallâj's error in declaring 'anâ 'l-ḥaqq', 'I am the Truth', lay not in the sentiment itself, which represented a legitimate Ṣûfî ḥâl state, but in having uttered it publicly where it could confuse common people; for this he had to be punished lest the common people suppose that blasphemy was to be tolerated.

Indeed, in the very principle of using whatever argument might be most weighty with a given audience, Ghazâlî already illustrated what this tendency could mean on the level of common discourse. In the *Deliverer* itself, for instance, he appealed on occasion to the supposed miracles of the Prophet as evidence of his prophethood where he was speaking to those who might be expected to be convinced by miracles, though from other passages it is obvious that he had no real use for such 'proofs'. For the *Deliverer* was a book of kalâm in Ghazâlî's sense—thus an *instrument* rather than a piece of information: the Arabic participle 'deliverer' in the title is intentional, for the book was designed to deliver from error by whatever means might be appropriate, rather than to state positively truth as such. Positive truth must be come to, as he makes clear, not by argument but in personal growth. In the tactical details of his argument, indeed, Ghazâlî hardly went beyond a practice that is always tempting to the dialectical polemist. But in endorsing more generally the principle that one is to keep concealed the more profound truths from all those unworthy of them, giving (in effect) the appearance of a simple orthodoxy despite one's own internally more complex approach, he endorsed a far-reaching ambiguity in religious truthfulness. He did not invent the principle of concealment. The Ismâ'îlîs had systematically interpreted in this sense the general Shî'î principle of taqiyyah, of precautionary dissimulation of faith; and the Faylasûfs and especially the Ṣûfîs had developed a practical form of the principle which Ghazâlî was here taking over. In his writings it was generalized and legitimized as a basis of religious ministry.

In the end, the basic position of the Ḥadîth folk had been maintained in certain fundamental respects; Falsafah and Ṣûfism both were re-evaluated in the light of Sharîʿah-minded sentiment. Yet the introduction of Ashʿarî kalâm was almost a trifle to what was now being offered the ʿulamâʾ. Elitism in an extreme form was being superimposed upon Islamic populism. This had potential consequences Ghazâlî could hardly have envisaged. The tastes and needs of almost everyone might be accommodated within the limits of toleration of such a new Sharʿî system. At best, the ground was laid for a full and varied intellectual as well as spiritual development with the blessing of Islam. But it might open the way to centrifugal licence. For it was done at the price of sacrificing the common and open exchange of opinion and information on which the ʿulamâʾ had depended for re-creating, in some measure, the intimate common life of Medina, and which the Sharʿî movement itself had presupposed in its search for the Divine will.

With the establishment of the international Islamicate social order, however, there had come into being new ways of ensuring the unity and even the discipline of Muslim society. The autonomous, private institutions of the towns depended on the Sharîʿah, but also on other structures; and among these (as we shall see) were the forms of organization that came to undergird popular Ṣûfism itself, which proved, in its flexibility, appropriate to the private and indefinitely varied character of the local institutions. By the end of the formative phase of the Earlier Middle Period, then, Muslims were ready for such a pattern as Ghazâlî offered. His moral authority seems to have been widely accepted even in his lifetime. And some such intellectual synthesis among kalâm, Falsafah, and Ṣûfism as he expressed became, in effect, the starting point of the intellectual flowering of the Earlier Middle Period.

Obscurantism and esotericism

During the ‘Shîʿî century’ there had been a liberty of opinion within the Muslim community very rarely found in any citied land in the Agrarian Age. But with the advent to authority of men owning the same allegiance as the majority of Muslims and recognizing the same ʿulamâʾ scholars as authoritative, the temptation to try to enforce conformity in opinions became strong. Those who distrusted the results of unfettered private inquiry by persons not trained to come to the right answers were often in a position to prevent dangerous ideas from having a public hearing; those who disagreed with the more popular positions could find themselves persecuted. This had happened before, as when Qadarîs and Manicheans were persecuted and then (with less violence) the Ḥadîth folk, but from this point on, with the advent of substantial unity of allegiance in a population turned predominantly Muslim, the tendency became commonplace.

Even apart from its social utility, a pressure for conformism is always with us. It has high origins. Human beings, unlike other animals, live at least as much by what they do not see as by what they do see: unlike the signals of animals, their very words are symbols of what is not there. The symbolic picture people make for themselves of the world is not an incidental curiosity but the mainstay of their personal orientation. Hence people everywhere have been afraid of being forced to listen to new ideas that contradict the notions on which their lives have hitherto been guided. Even if they reject those ideas, the very process of finding good reasons to reject them may be laborious and troubling; but what is worst, for most people, is the possibility that others may actually accept those new ideas—leaving the adherents of the older notions isolated and unsupported. To allow unpopular ideas to be aired freely requires a great deal of fortitude and social discipline on the part of any who might be in a position to suppress them.

This is true everywhere; but in societies of a monotheistic allegiance, this natural inclination to intolerance has been reinforced by the demands of communalism. As we have noted, the notions of one moral God and one morally decisive lifetime have been completed, in the monotheistic traditions, by the notion of one morally normative community; and in Islam this tendency reached so strong an expression that the law of the religious community, the Sharîʿah, was granted to be the only basis for fully legitimizing any social action. It was the religious community as such, through the Sharîʿah, that guaranteed social morality and hence the very existence of society. But if the safety and good order of society depended on the strength and coherence of the religious community, then everything else must, at need, be sacrificed to this. Even pity for an honest but misguided man should not divert one from one's duty to prevent him from corrupting society with his misguided ideas. For all practical purposes, the moralistic outlook of a monotheistic religious tradition readily led to *communalism*: to the exaltation of loyalty to the community and its acknowledged symbols (and especially its doctrines) even at the expense of all other values.

In such an atmosphere, even personally magnanimous men, able to resist the impulse to protect their own intellectual security by silencing a threatening voice, might become persecutors. For they might feel it their duty to support intolerance for the sake of others who could not endure the threat so easily. Hence the societies that adopted the monotheistic traditions have been unusually vulnerable to giving vent to self-righteous persecution of anyone who dared voice unpopular ideas. The point of view had come to be generally accepted among the Muslims; and now it was no longer so inhibited by divisions and doubts within the bulk of the community, which had made its application impractical. It was felt to be an act of piety to burn books that contained dangerous ideas, and to exile or even kill those who composed such books or taught them to others.

Just whom the ban affected, however, continued somewhat to vary even within the circle of Jamâʿî-Sunnî agreement, whenever one group locally got the upper hand. In Baghdad in the eleventh century the Ḥanbalîs still controlled the mob; more even than in the later days of the High Caliphate, they were able there to prevent those with whom they disagreed from teaching publicly. It was other Sharî'ah-minded men elsewhere that persuaded the sultan Toghril-beg to attempt to suppress the Ash'arî kalâm—cursing the Ash'arîs in the mosques and persecuting their leaders, such as Juvaynî. The Ḥanbalîs were even able to force conformity on those of their own allegiance who were sufficiently curious to listen to teachers of other stripes. A major Ḥanbalî authority in Baghdad who went privately to hear what the Mu'tazilîs had to say, without adopting their views, was forced (not without some threat of mob violence) publicly to recant such behaviour; he had to humiliate himself before a rival Ḥanbalî teacher, who had been able to carry the crowds with him against the 'innovations' of a man who would even listen to the opposition. But the Ḥanbalîs were only slightly more intolerant than others. Where the Ash'arîs were themselves in favour they were willing, provided they had the power, to persecute others. Reproving the Ḥanbalîs of Baghdad for their intolerance, which had erupted into riots between the Ḥanbalîs and some pro-Ash'arî Shâfi'îs when a prominent Ash'arî Shâfi'î tried to teach publicly in Baghdad, Niẓâmulmulk noted that in Khurâsân the Ḥanafîs and Shâfi'îs, recognizing each other indeed, joined together to allow no other teachers to be heard. In Baghdad the Ḥanbalîs had to be tolerated because of their popular appeal, which was supported privately by the caliphs; but clearly Niẓâmulmulk regretted that this was necessary. In other cities, other traditions held sway. It was said that in Khwârazm the Mu'tazilî 'ulamâ' were so strong that they could forbid a non-Mu'tazilî from staying the night in the town.

If the more zealous of the Sharî'ah-minded 'ulamâ' had had their way, no Muslim would have been allowed to learn about anything that was not certified as religiously edifying by the 'ulamâ' themselves: or, to put it unkindly, ignorance of everything beyond the most essential practical skills and the uncritical lore on which community was founded would have been insisted on as a virtue, and even chronicles and belles-lettres would have been barely tolerated. The range of knowledge that would have been accepted was probably narrower than in any other major citied society—even in the Christian Occident, the church, which (in the monotheistic manner) made itself guardian of morals and protector of society from dangerous ideas, tolerated among its clerics (especially in later centuries) a considerable body of relatively useless knowledge stemming frankly from the tradition of pre-Christian paganism. But in practice, provided certain rules were observed, Muslims were free to learn almost anything with only a minimal risk of penalization; much less risk, on the whole, than was run by their opposite numbers in the Occident. This was made possible by the pattern of gradation and concealment of knowledge, of which Ghazâlî was an exponent. After the end of the High Caliphate it rapidly became a general pattern for all thinkers who did not conform to the narrow range approved by the official 'ulamâ' scholars. All the more imaginative sides of intellectual culture in Islam, that is, tended to become esoteric.

The esoteric did not claim to be in competition with the normal, generally accepted exoteric truth; rather, it was to complement it. In the exoteric culture, that of the Sharî'ah-minded circles through which the Islamic community was admittedly preserved, all the prosaism called for by a populistic, moralistic orientation was allowed free play. Only the matter-of-fact, historically documented data which in principle every individual could assimilate was regarded as 'ilm: significant knowledge. Knowledge could be extremely refined and detailed, as was the ḥadîth corpus and the criticism of it, which called for encyclopedic memory and for keen critical discriminations; it could even be extremely intricate, to the point of splitting hairs in academic niceties as often happened in the more hypothetical exercises in fiqh jurisprudence. It could even involve extensive logical sequences, assuming remotely abstract premises, as among those willing to accept kalâm argumentation as being within the Shar'î range; but such premises must be prose-clear, the logic must proceed by unshaded alternatives of yes or no, and in any case (of course) the conclusions must be consistent with positions accepted by the community on grounds of soberly documented historical revelation.

There was no room for the confusing recognition that the same verbal formulations might have different implications in different contexts, that different formulations might express different but equally meaningful perspectives, or generally that the subtleties of good taste, as against sheer information and rules of right or wrong, might have a role in human truth and wisdom. Anything not evident in the stated formulation of an idea was not to be considered. Even poetry (which, in a starkly limited classical form, as we have noted, was accepted in Sharî'ah-minded circles) was treated as a series of statements of fact—to be judged as proper or improper—statements cast in a technical form which could also be judged proper or improper, right or wrong.

Esoteric truths, on the contrary, are just those that are not public. Whereas the 'ilm knowledge of the Sharî'ah-minded ought to be accessible in principle to anyone who could listen and memorize what he heard, as befitted populistic moral standards, esoteric 'ilm could be come by only through initiation—through a private relation between master and disciple. And only those specially qualified could be initiated, and in turn must not promiscuously divulge the secrets. Even if the uninitiated came across a work of esoteric truth, it would not, in principle, be intelligible to him, though he might mouth its words uncomprehendingly. Here there was room for every sort of subtlety and ambiguity, provided a tradition welcomed it. In fact, esoteric lore was not always wiser than exoteric, but it was commonly more colourful.

In principle, any truth that could be called esoteric was by its nature selective: no matter how hard a master might try to help an unqualified disciple understand, his efforts must be in vain—the disciple must possess a nature adapted to receiving the truths, or they would be lost on him. But the masters of esoteric lore have generally taken pains to make sure that if a work should fall into improper hands, its more delicate points would not be even half-understood—and so misunderstood; they have so written that the barriers imposed by nature were further reinforced by art. This was not merely to avoid persecution but also to avoid untoward consequences among the uninitiated themselves. The realm of public knowledge and truth has been conceded without contest to the exoteric teachers, and their exoteric students have been protected from contamination with the esoteric by the esoteric masters themselves.

There were three major sorts of lore cultivated among Muslims that now were treated as esoteric: the metaphysics and some natural sciences of the Faylasûfs; the interpretations of revelation made by the Shîʿîs; and the personal discipline of the Ṣûfîs, together with their visions and speculations. All of these sorts of lore had tended even earlier to be treated as esoteric in some measure. But in Islamdom in the Middle Periods they were given a more consistently and comprehensively esoteric treatment than often before, or even, I think, than was usual in other societies of the time. Much lore requires inherently special capacities for its comprehension—good taste in music, for instance; or acuity of judgment in metaphysics or even physics; or even intuitive perceptivity, as in medicine or astrology—yet such lore could be treated as exoteric, open to whoever took time and pains enough, or at least not guarded from outsiders. It was not only several fields of that sort, but much lore that might be relatively easy of access, that was treated as esoteric and hence privileged lore if it did not come within the limits fixed by the Sharîʿah-minded; it was to be protected by being made artificially difficult of access.

The modern contrast between the scientific and the occult was exceptional before the Technical Age. Not merely a populistic utilitarianism but the venturesomeness as well as the élitism of the scientists themselves made for a contrast between the sober public realm and the scientific. An esoteric treatment of the scientific understanding of nature goes back very far, to its ancient association with the magical arts. Even since the Axial Age, at least some of the sciences of the Faylasûfs had always been treated as esoteric; for instance, chemical studies—associated in the popular mind with the search for unnatural gold and with magic generally—had been cast into symbolical terms and withheld from the common gaze. Moreover, precisely the most abstract of the sciences—metaphysics—had come to be taught more or less esoterically to protect it from the jealous exponents of the monotheistic traditions; at least in the sense that positions unwelcome to most Muslims were cautiously disguised. By Earlier Mid-Islamic times, sciences might be private in two degrees. All of them were private in the general sense that their books were often composed with mental reservations and they were not

Types of Muslim Esoteric Élitism

Faylasûf Élitism	Sectarian Élitism, Particularly Bâṭinîs	Ṣûfî Élitism
Forerunners rejected by Râzî, but developed by al-Fârâbî (elements) and Ibn-Sînâ (principles)	Principles of taqiyyah and discipline of ghulât under Ja'far Conspiratorialism of the Ismâ'îlîs and other bâṭinîs	The argument over al-Ḥallâj, the position of al-Junayd
Ibn-Ṭufayl: Falsafah élitism modified by Ṣûfî experience		
Ibn-Rushd and the Spanish school most fully represent this attitude in practice		Al-Ghazâlî's élitism: taqlîd for ordinary believers; kalâm for ordinary doubters; taqiyyah for Ṣûfî 'ârif
The Ibn-Ṭufayl–Ibn-Rushd positions affect also Jews	Taqiyyah of Nizârî Isma'îlîs: after qiyâmah: unbelievers do not truly exist	
Later Spanish Faylasûfs and Ibn-Khaldûn	Merge in Ṣûfî ṭarîqahs	Ṣûfî matured positions: Ḥallâj was wrong only in his public avowal; pîrî-murîdî discipline and the silsilah

taught in public institutions such as the madrasahs, but by master to private disciples screened for their qualifications and reliability. Then some sciences —notably chemistry and also the arts of explicit magic—were kept more jealously secret, and might even be rejected as immoral (if not as ineffective) by the relatively less esoteric Faylasûfs. But in practice, no very sharp line between the two degrees of privacy was drawn, and persons given to any sort of Falsafah were likely to delve into its most esoteric corners.

Ṣûfism was, in principle, even more restrictive. (It was the pervasive importance of Ṣûfism that did most to give an esoteric tone to Islamicate culture.) The lore of inward self-analysis depended almost necessarily upon a master, who should guide the dangerous process and guard against premature over-estimation of his achievements by a novice. Without the institutional control of a church, this process had to be handled esoterically and the *murîd* was treated as an initiate, not permitted to teach others what he was learning till expressly authorized by his master. Here again, there were degrees of the esoteric; theosophic cosmological doctrines which served to interpret the deeper ranges of self-perception were kept especially secret and often rejected by less daring Ṣûfîs. But even in point of inward discipline, it became a commonplace for ardent Ṣûfîs to reject the ever re-formalized patterns of conventional Ṣûfism as in turn having become exoteric, and turn to a further esotericism within Ṣûfism.

The Shî'î esotericism did not analyze or manipulate nature, nor did it deepen awareness of the self; rather it dramatized history and the present world in historical perspective. This dramatization, as we have seen, was an expression of social protest: it was chiliastic; that is, it looked to promised historical events that should reverse the present historical situation in favour of the oppressed lowly—or those of them who clung to the true loyalty and did not sell out to the established order. The present historical and social situation, then, was constantly re-evaluated on the basis of such hidden expectations. It was this posture of resistance that made it necessarily esoteric—as chiliastic movements had tended to be earlier in the monotheistic tradition. The general public was the enemy or the dupes of the enemy and must be guarded against. The Shî'î doctrine of taqiyyah, precautionary concealment of one's true allegiance, answered to a persistent tendency among earlier chiliastic movements to form closed and often secret bodies of the elect.

Shî'ism as a whole, of course, even Ja'farî Shî'ism, was not necessarily very esoteric: the Sharî'ah-minded 'ulamâ' scholars among the Shî'îs, even when they included the doctrine of taqiyyah dissimulation in their legal system, or acknowledged some hidden references in the Qur'ân to the imâms, could be as prosaically exoteric as any Jamâ'î-Sunnîs. But the spirit of 'Alid loyalism, at least among Shî'îs and perhaps among some Jamâ'î-Sunnîs, if taken seriously, could call for an initiatory atmosphere, in which only those truly capable of the loyalty required of the elect should be told the truth. There was a persistent pattern of inner Shî'ism which professed to teach the real truths (for instance, the cosmic role of 'Alî) back of the external doctrines of Twelver and even Ismâ'îlî 'ulamâ'—and which kept itself secret even from the official Shî'îs. Even so, all Ja'farî Shî'ism, to the extent that it carried a dramatic sense of the persecuted suffering of the house of Muḥammad and those loyal to it, did adopt at least the outer forms of esotericism by way of taqiyyah.

All three forms of esotericism tended to overlap and interpenetrate one another. A Shî'î historical sense found its way not only into alchemy by way of the Jâbir corpus but also into astrology; and both Shî'î historical drama and the occult lore of the more radical Faylasûfs provided terminology and symbolism, at least, for the Ṣûfîs. Moreover, groups in society that were in some way set apart from the established régime of the amîrs and a'yân and 'ulamâ'—notably the rising crafts guilds and other solidarity groups in the towns—commonly were themselves secret and initiatory and shared at least some of the same lore with these broader esoteric movements.

But at the same time, the imaginative social and cultural life which was thus given an esoteric status became relatively inaccessible to the ordinary outsider. Even within Islamdom this was so: the most important channels of social mobility were usually through the military establishments of the amîrs or the Shar'î establishment of the 'ulamâ'—all heavily exoteric. It was only with very special charisma, for instance, that a mere wandering Ṣûfî, even if he became a pîr and had his own disciples, could gain a high place in society. It was the prosaic, exoteric culture that was the chief vehicle of success. It was against the disapproving eyes of just such successful men that the representatives of all sorts of esoteric lore protected themselves, by writing or teaching in a manner calculated to throw an observer off the scent. But to later outsiders, attempting to evaluate the Islamicate culture, the richest of its works have remained singularly hard of access.

The esoteric posture of these several cultural elements was taken up only in part as a defence against persecution. But whatever its motives, it did succeed, for the most part, in guarding them against the obscurantism of the more extreme of the Sharî'ah-minded. If the bigoted wanted to eliminate someone who refused to conform, their task was not easy. It was necessary to persuade, not a single established persecuting authority, as in the Occident, but a number of authorities, each of which might have reasons for hesitating before damning a given work or its writer. A single Shar'î scholar might give his fatwà sentence, but if others of equal standing refused or even abstained, the decision of the first could not be regarded as binding. In any case, the amîr had to decide for himself, once the 'ulamâ' had declared that killing a given dissenter would be legitimate, whether he really ought to. If there were even a minority in his court who favoured the accused, they could suggest practical reasons for lenience. When all dissenting statements were cast in esoteric form, explicitly acknowledging the correctness of the received exoteric doctrines which the esoteric lore was merely to complement or interpret, it became easy to find excuses for doubt about a dissenter. No one denied the official positions; the question was simply whether what else a person said did in fact contradict those positions. But if writing was done with sufficient obscurity, guilt could never be proved beyond a reasonable doubt.

Throughout the Middle Islamic Periods, individual Ṣûfîs and Faylasûfs and Shî'îs were executed, sometimes very cruelly; but such an event usually resulted from a momentary political constellation unfavourable to the accused. Most of the outstanding representatives of esoteric culture died in their beds. Meanwhile, the Sharî'ah-minded guardians of the single godly moralistic community maintained a frustrated tension with the sophisticated culture of Islamdom, which they could successfully condemn but not effectively destroy. The resultant sense of threat to the integrity of Islam from high-cultural compromises persisted as an undertow in all exoteric Muslim life. Wherever the 'ulamâ' became unusually strong, the life of the high Islamicate culture was put in doubt.[20]

[20] Gustave von Grunebaum, conceiving the intellectual development of these centuries in rather different terms from what I have used here, describes the flourishing of free humanistic thinking and the communal religious reaction thereto and compares this to rather similar developments of the same period in Byzantium, in 'Parallelism, Convergence, and Influence in the Relations of Arab and Byzantine Philosophy, Literature, and Piety', *Dumbarton Oaks Papers*, 18 (1964), 89–111.

IV

The Ṣûfism of the Ṭarîqah Orders, c. 945–1273

While intellectual life was being transposed into its Middle Period forms, Ṣûfism was being prepared to play a larger role, both social and intellectual, than it had played in High Caliphal times. The ultimate outcome of the new direction of intellectual life was displayed in a largely Ṣûfî context, as had been foreshadowed by Ghazâlî.

The popularization of mysticism

The prominence of Ṣûfî mysticism in the life of Muslims was part of a more general popularity of mysticism in the Afro-Eurasian Oikoumene. Fully developed mysticism, as we know it in Ṣûfism, can scarcely be traced as a culturally cultivated practice before the Axial Age (though of course elements of mystical practice have been a part of religious life as far back as we can trace it). By the end of the Axial Age, explicit mystical movements were influential in the Greek, the Sanskritic, and even the Chinese spheres, and probably also in Irano-Semitic circles. Except possibly in India, they were mostly marginal to the main cultural currents. But the traditions then established have persisted.

It was very gradually in the post-Axial periods that a developed mysticism came to be taken for granted as a normal ingredient in popular religion. We have noticed in Book Two that the development of Ṣûfism roughly coincided with the development of a high love mysticism also among Christians and even Hindus. This growth of a mysticism of loving devotion seems to be correlated even in India with the increasing popularity of mysticism among large sections of the population and not merely among specialists of a strongly ascetic temperament. But the popularity was, if anything, more general than the emphasis on divine love. In China, the popularity of mysticism may have reached its peak in the Sung period—roughly the Earlier Mid-Islamic period. In western Europe, Christian mysticism became more widely accepted and more intellectually influential right into the sixteenth century; then modern technicalization pushed it into obscurity. It was in the lands of Indic heritage and in Islamdom that mysticism became most pervasively popular; there it continued so into the nineteenth century, being an established background both of popular cults and of high-cultural creativity.

We know relatively little about Christian mysticism within Islamdom in this period, and almost nothing about Jewish. But we have some idea of the general development among Jews. It shows a close relation to the general development and particularly to the Islamic. Jewish religious life developed jointly in Islamdom and in Christendom; the records that have been studied are mainly from west Christendom, but the point of origin of many movements seems to have been between Nile and Oxus. In the early post-Axial centuries and well into the Islamic period, Jewish mysticism was focused in what has been called the 'Merkabah' movement: this was expressed in the form of descriptions of a frightening inward journey to the throne of God, who was, above all, august and wondrous. With the introduction of the Kabbalah movement in the thirteenth century (on the Christian side of the line in Spain and Italy), we find something much closer to mature Ṣûfism. The Merkabah mysticism had already included many of the elements that lie in the background of Islamic mysticism—notions of a Gnostic type, for instance. But with the Kabbalah mysticism, the Merkabah traditions were re-evaluated with more emphasis on a personal loving relation to God. And therewith came, though later than in Islam, many (but not all) of the elements that characterized Ṣûfism in the Middle Periods: notably a use of Philosophic terminology, even though the Kabbalists remained much closer than the Jewish Philosophers to Torah and Halakha law, just as the Ṣûfîs remained closer than the Faylasûfs to Qur'ân and Sharî'ah; and a tendency to form the basis for popular religious life—for instance, of popular folklore—a tendency which came especially late among Jews, being given a major impulse in Palestine in the sixteenth century. How much these developments were inspired by the Islamic we example cannot tell. To some degree, at least, they show an independent evolution.[1]

Some scholars have tried to correlate the rise of mysticism with the collapse of great empires and consequent political insecurity; or, more precisely, with the displacement of a cultural élite from political power and its withdrawal into inward compensations when it could no longer fulfill itself in external action. To a degree, such a correlation will hold insofar as mysticism became generally stronger after the collapse of the great empires of the early post-Axial centuries. But it is far from clear that it was largely the descendants of displaced political élites that turned to mysticism; among Muslims, many mystics were of a craftsman background. Until the Technical Age brought a recession of interest in it, first in the West and then elsewhere, it is easier to correlate the secular rise of mysticism with a growing complexity and sophistication of civilization generally, whatever the special conditions that might govern its fortunes temporarily here or there. Some traditions, like the

[1] Gershom Scholem's magnificent *Major Trends in Jewish Mysticism* (Jerusalem, 1941), is based largely on manuscripts from Italy and Germany and hardly professes to say much of Judaism in Islamdom except where there were direct contacts—as with exiles from Spain.

Jewish, have shown a greater resistance to it than others; but on the whole the more the population at large has been integrated into the high-cultural traditions that originated in the Axial Age (often at the expense of local nature and tribal cults), and the more those high-cultural traditions have been exposed to alien and cosmopolitan influences, the more flourishing mysticism has been.[2]

In the Irano-Semitic traditions, mysticism had been well established by the advent of Islam, though not as a dominant force. In the early centuries of Islam it received a new vitality (as did the other dimensions of Irano-Semitic piety), and by the Early Middle Period it was ready for whatever tasks might be required of it.

It was in the Seljuk domains that some of the greatest impulses were given to a reorientation of the piety of Islam on the basis of Ṣûfism. The orientation of Muslim piety to historical considerations had gradually become less intense with the end of the High Caliphal age. At the same time, the less temporally insistent pattern of Ṣûfism gained increasing respect. The time of formation of the international society was a formative age for a new, popular Ṣûfism also. Earlier than most of the 'ulamâ' scholars, large numbers of the masses came to accept the Ṣûfî pîrs, master holy men, as their guides in matters spiritual.

Then men like Ghazâlî (d. 1111), who combined a mastery of the teachings of the 'ulamâ' scholars on Sharî'ah and kalâm with a respect for the independent wisdom of the Ṣûfî mystics, helped to make Ṣûfism acceptable to the 'ulamâ' themselves. By the twelfth century it was a recognized part of religious life and even of religious 'ilm knowledge. Thus gradually Ṣûfism, from being one form of piety among others, and by no means the most accepted one either officially or popularly, came to dominate religious life not only within the Jamâ'î-Sunnî fold, but to a lesser extent even among Shî'îs.

From this point on, Islam presented persistently two faces: one, Sharî'ah-minded, concerned with outward, socially cognizable behaviour, accepted as their care by the Shar'î 'ulamâ'; the other mystical-minded, concerned with the inward, personal life of the individual, accepted as their care by the Ṣûfî pîrs. Often the same religious leader was at once pîr and Shar'î scholar, or at least took both sides of Islam very seriously; just as most of the Muslim public respected and took guidance from both pîrs and 'ulamâ'. Always, however, there were those who accepted the one face of Islam as genuine and mistrusted the other, or even rejected it as spurious. A third stream of piety was also carried forward from High Caliphal times: 'Alid loyalism with its chiliastic vision. Sometimes it was merged with Sharî'ah-mindedness, in the

[2] So far as I know, there is no sober world history of mysticism which could put the several traditions into a context where common circumstances and interrelations could be balanced against local diversities to yield a serious insight into the overall relation of mysticism with civilization. This gap is typical of our want of world history generally.

Shar'î 'ulamâ' of the Shî'ah; sometimes it contributed to Ṣûfism, when its esoteric notions proved illuminating; from time to time it emerged as a positive independent force. But it almost never gained socially legitimizing force in itself independent of the Sharî'ah, and never rivalled Ṣûfism in enduring popular appeal.

The Ṣûfism of this period was no longer simply the individual piety of mystically inclined Muslims, but developed first an elaborate lore and custom based on the relation of disciple and master, and then, after 1100, a whole social organization, that of the *ṭarîqahs*, Ṣûfî orders, side by side with that of the mosques and the regular 'ulamâ' scholars. The experience and teachings of the earlier Ṣûfîs under the High Caliphate had been taken, from the tenth century on, as the foundation of a new, more complex Ṣûfî pattern, with its own conventions; and about these, by more or less legitimate derivation, was built a comprehensive system of theosophic thought and of pious activity. It was this which became popular in the eleventh century. In the course of the development that followed, in the blossoming of the Earlier Middle Period, it came to be that every sort of devotion, whether mystical or not, found a place in the new system if only it could be built around some aspect of mystical practice as a core.

The human outreach of the mystics

It can seem paradoxical that the subjective, ineffable, extraordinarily personal experiences of Ṣûfism could become a basis for social life and become historically decisive; that the most personal and esoteric form of piety should be the most popular. This is in part due to the effective way in which mystical forms and language can sanction elements of religious life downgraded by a strongly kerygmatic approach. Age-old nature and personal cults could be transferred with considerable ease to the one form of the faith which—however reconditely—recognized in saintly men a special nearness to God. The saints (and even the more homely gods) of earlier religious traditions reappeared here. And intellectuals could recover, under the cover of mysticism some of the flexibility of outlook that a kerygmatic moralism would deny them.

But mysticism had social potentialities built into it even apart from the special circumstances of a kerygmatic allegiance. The challenging character of even sporadic mystical experiences can be such that a person feels inhibited from pursuing or even discussing them. But if the barrier is got past and they become the conscious objects of cultivation, then, however private they still remain, they take on comprehensive implications. The moments of one's living in which the distortions in sense of proportion and relevance occasioned by anger or lust or fatigue or mere bias are cleared away are felt to afford the most valid perspective on actuality, by any criterion of validity which is available to us. Such a moment, further intensified in its clarity, is at the heart of everyday mysticism; and also of the more spectacular ecstatic sorts of mysticism (at least so far as these are incorporated into historical mystical traditions), though there the experience may be heightened in emotionally complex ways. Dispassionateness, broad perspective, even immediacy of acceptance of what we are, do not properly bring positive knowledge, of course, though often such an experience is formulated as if they did; but they bring a point of view, a moral posture, from which to see the meaning of any positive knowledge one may have. If such experiences carry authority and are found relevant to the ordinary course of living—the decisive criterion of mysticism from a historical viewpoint—then their consequences will be unpredictable and may invade any sphere of human activity. Once their validity is accepted, they must determine all of life.

Those who go far in clarifying and purifying their consciousness of themselves and of existence about them, then, will have a transformed relationship to the human beings among whom they live. In the case of some hermits, in any religious tradition, this has amounted to an almost total withdrawal, either in stern indifference to the fate of any transient beings or (no doubt more often) in keen awareness of one's own remaining pettiness and unreadiness to be of real service to others. One of the most persistent forms this withdrawal has taken has been celibacy, which assures of itself a certain degree of social isolation. Celibacy has appealed to the spiritually minded for diverse reasons, ranging from defensive prejudice against a frightening sexuality, when it had been hedged socially with excessive taboos, up to a sober recognition that the impassioned self-assertion let loose in the sex act could be incompatible with unremitting self-control and dispassionate clarity.

Many Ṣûfîs withdrew to the point of becoming full hermits; others, without going so far, did adopt celibacy, if not as a universal ideal then at least as appropriate to their own spiritual needs. But neither the hermit's isolation nor even simple celibacy became normative for Ṣûfism. Celibacy normally carries with it rejection of family duties and of more than marginal responsibility for the economic production of the community (often it has implied mendicancy); hence men concerned with responsible social order have commonly been sceptical of it. The overwhelming weight of the Islamic tradition bore against it: a ḥadîth report represented Muḥammad as saying there was no monkhood in his community, with the implication that celibacy was contrary to Islam. Accordingly, while the celibate temper could not be excluded from among serious Muslims, the Islamic religious context ensured that it was restricted to a secondary role; even those Ṣûfîs who adopted it were often apologetic about it. Many Ṣûfîs taught that ideally any sort of total withdrawal from social relations ought to be a temporary discipline rather than a permanent status.

If total withdrawal was avoided, then whether celibacy was adopted or not, the readiest way for a mystic to bring his experience into relation with others has been by way of preaching. Some might be restrained by humble despair of being able to remove the darkness of others while still too benighted themselves. More frequently, among those who seek to clarify themselves, their meditations have seemed to lead them, above all, to preaching; they have reminded themselves and others monotonously or eloquently of the triviality of everyday worries and enthusiasms in the face of life and death, using all imagery at their command, notably that of Hell and Paradise, to arouse their listeners. But different traditions have encouraged more specialized forms of outreach. The Manichean holy men, for instance, were teachers; but they had rejected most of worldly mankind, seeing them as objects of pity and kindness who, however, lay irreparably in the outer darkness unless they took the crucial step of becoming Manicheans; it was only to the faithful themselves, therefore, that the holy men could extend their special guidance, helping them to come toward the purity the holy men themselves had gained.

The Ṣûfîs had inherited the populist outlook of the Ḥadîth folk, with its tenacious sense of the dignity of common people and of their conceptions. Some of them, indeed, expressed this in a socially conscious activism. The number of leaders who rose from meditations of a Ṣûfî type to lead militant men in attempts to reform the government and mores of society increased as Ṣûfî piety became increasingly prevalent. But the more typical Ṣûfîs looked to a different approach. Perhaps their awareness of their own weaknesses led them to a tolerance of others' weakness when others were willing to recognize that weakness (a tolerance which did not diminish their condemnation of the arrogance of the mighty). Like the Manicheans, they sought to teach individuals. But they were not sectarian: they no more attempted to reform doctrines than institutions.

Ṣûfî ministry and pîrî-murîdî discipline

Many Ṣûfîs devoted much time not only to public preaching but also to helping others to work through moral problems as they came to them and to find as pure a life as they personally were capable of. In doing so, such Ṣûfîs sometimes made little even of differences in religious allegiance. Thus a figure like the great pîr (master) Niẓâmuddîn Awliyâ in the late thirteenth century in Delhi acted as father-confessor to Muslims of all classes, and even to some non-Muslims (he was ready to see some merit even in Hindu ways); he stressed forgiveness of enemies, insisted on moderation in enjoyment of the goods of this world (though not on the asceticism he himself practiced), stressed responsible behaviour in the work one had taken up (but forbade government employment, as involving too much corruption), and required explicit repentance if a follower slipped into sin. His was looked on as the next power in the kingdom after that of the sultan, and from Delhi he commanded the free allegiance of Ṣûfî pîrs over much of northern India.

Such men and women gradually won enormous popular respect. Among the more perceptive, the respect was given for the moving effect of their preaching and still more for the moral purity of which they gave evidence in their persons. Living in poverty (many made a rule of consuming or giving away by nightfall whatever they earned by their trade or were given by followers during a day), scorning the niceties of courtly fashion and the competition for financial and social advantage of the urban tradesman, they had the same kind of moral appeal for concerned men that the Manichean holy men had once had: in their persons, at least negatively, they filled the long-standing Irano-Semitic dream of a pure life over against the injustice that seemed built into city life on the agrarianate level. Moreover, their purity was not always entirely negative. Some Ṣûfîs made a point of trying to implement the spirit behind the Muslim social ideals. In particular, they perpetuated the spirit of protest which had already led some of the early heirs of the 'Piety-minded opposition' publicly to remind the caliphs of their duty; sometimes they were more urgently and dramatically aggressive, in upbraiding rulers who fell short of the ideal, than had been those more propertied and hence more circumspect legists.

But the Ṣûfî piety, tolerant of human weakness, did not generally separate itself from common beliefs and from the sensibilities of the common people; unlike the Manicheans, the Ṣûfîs were willing to accept as valid at least externally whatever religious notions they found about them. Partly in response to this tolerance, popular respect for the Ṣûfîs was often expressed in wonder tales. The moral respect which the perceptive conceded to them was transformed, in the minds of wider circles, who required a less subtle formulation of it, into a deferential awe expressed in tales of ordeals endured and marvels performed. It became the rule that while no given Ṣûfî seems to claim miracles for himself in his own writings, every Ṣûfî who had earned the honour of those nearest him was soon ascribed all sorts of miracles by those at any distance from him, miracles ranging from simple acts of outstanding perceptiveness of others' mental states, through feats of healing and of telepathy and telekinesis, to more imaginative feats like flying from Delhi to Mecca for a nightly pilgrimage. And such tales were then accepted by the Ṣûfîs themselves (as they accepted other popular beliefs)—as regards their respected predecessors, that is.

The Ṣûfî pîr who came to be the most widely revered of all pîrs as a preacher to the population at large was 'Abdulqâdir Gîlânî (1077–1166). He came of a family of *sayyids*, alleged descendants of 'Alî, in Gîlân, south of the Caspian, and like many sayyids he was encouraged from boyhood to take up religious studies (especially since he was already having visionary experiences). As a youth, his mother gave him the whole of his share of the inheritance (in the form of eighty gold coins sewed up in his coat) and sent him off to get further religious training in Baghdad. He set out with a caravan, and on the trip occurred an incident that typified his saintliness for later generations. His mother had made him promise never to tell a falsehood. The caravan was accosted by robbers; but Gîlânî was poorly dressed and was almost overlooked. One of the robbers did ask him casually, however, whether he had any money about him; whereupon he avowed having the eighty gold coins, though they were effectively hidden. Astonished at such honesty, the robber took him to the chief of the robber band, to whom Gîlânî explained that if he had begun his quest for religious truth by telling a lie, he could not expect to proceed very far in that quest (already, in the Ṣûfî manner, he identified true knowledge with moral rectitude). It is said that the robber chief was converted on the spot and abandoned his wicked life: the first of many won by the saint.

At Baghdad, Gîlânî selected as his spiritual guide a man who was a syrup vendor by trade, and who was extraordinarily severe in disciplining him. When his studies were completed, he continued the disciplines on his own: he would often stay up the whole night in worship (a regimen that normally implied a nap in the afternoon); on such nights he would often recite the Qur'ân from beginning to end (a common exercise among the very pious). Or he went off wandering in desert areas. He continued a long course of spiritual austerities, first at a town in Khûzistân (in the lower Mesopotamian plain) and then back in Baghdad, until he was about fifty years old. By then he had become known in Baghdad. Having achieved the spiritual maturity he was seeking, and under what he believed was divine guidance, he undertook to teach the people. He was given a madrasah college of his own, where he lectured on all the standard religious subjects, Qur'ân, ḥadîth, fiqh jurisprudence, etc. At the same time, he got married; hitherto he had regarded marriage as a hindrance in his spiritual quest, but now he regarded marriage as a social duty, for which Muḥammad had given the example, and appropriate to a man in the public eye. He took four wives and had a total of forty-nine children in the course of his long life; four of his sons became known as religious scholars like himself. Despite his public life, he continued a part of his austerities: thus he normally fasted in the daytime, according to the rule set for the month's fast of Ramaḍân, all year round.

His teaching and especially his public preaching became extraordinarily popular at Baghdad. His madrasah college soon had to be enlarged, and he took to preaching (on Friday and Wednesday mornings) in the *muṣallà* prayer grounds outside the city, normally reserved for the mass worship at the 'îd festivals, for there was no other place large enough to hold the crowds. There too a special building was constructed for him. Visitors to Baghdad made a point of coming to hear him. After midday worship he gave out fatwà decisions on points of Shar'î law and ethic; sometimes requests for fatwàs were sent him from distant lands. (He followed the Ḥanbalî school of fiqh, which in Baghdad was still very popular and was associated at once with Shar'î rigour and concern for the religious good sense of ordinary people.) He received large amounts of money from those who made him their channel for charity, as well as waqf endowment funds; in addition to individual alms, he distributed bread to any of the poor who came for it, every day before evening worship.

Gîlânî is said to have converted many persons to Islam, and to have won many Muslim sinners to repentance. He put his spiritual teachings in such a form as to illuminate the everyday moral problems of the tradesman; they were little tainted with speculation that the Sharîʿah-minded might take offense at. The perfect saint whom he described was a humble man content with whatever God might assign him either in this world or in the next. Some of his sermons were collected by one of his sons and given the title of 'Revelations of the Unseen'. One of them sketches ten virtues which, if they become well-rooted, will lead to full spirituality. Each of the virtues is at least seemingly very simple, accessible to anyone. (None, however, is required by Sharʿî law.) But each of them is inward-looking and can lead far if carried through consistently, with all implications followed up. The first is not to swear by God either truthfully or falsely: a point that would undercut a practice very common among Muslims (and often commended as pious) of invoking God on every occasion, and would require a habitual self-control that would, as Gîlânî says, lend dignity to a man; but which would also force him to take the more seriously any reference he did make to God. The second virtue is not to speak any untruth even in jest; the third is not to break a promise. From this point on, the virtues become more obviously comprehensive, though they retain a starting point of concreteness: not to curse or harm anything (this in a climate where cursing what one supposes is displeasing to God was considered pious); not to pray or wish for harm to anyone; and, attached to that, not to accuse anyone of religious infidelity; not to attend to anything sinful; not to impose any burden on others—and here Gîlânî notes that if this becomes habitual, it will give a person the strength equitably to perform the Muslim duty of admonishing people for good and against evil; not to expect anything from human beings; and finally to notice only the points in others where they may be superior to oneself. If a person so lives, his secret thoughts and his evident words and actions will be at one.

Sharîʿah-minded scholars, eager to accuse the dissident of religious infidelity, were also sometimes very popular preachers; but the comprehensive humanity with which a Ṣûfî could preach gave the Ṣûfî tradition an often spectacular advantage. However, it was not perceptive preaching alone that won for Ṣûfism its leading role, or even personal example, but the institutional forms that it took. Both the popular appeal of Ṣûfism in this period and its social role in the Earlier Middle Period were most enduringly based on a particular form which the ministry of the Ṣûfîs took, *pîrî-murîdî*, the relationship of master (*pîr*) and disciple (*murîd*). This produced at once a needed discipline and a vehicle for public outreach.

The mystical life claims to offer freedom in its purest form: freedom from inhibitions, from prejudices, from commitment to any habits or regulations as such. To be sure, the freedom, if genuine, is guided simultaneously by the spirit of universality and truth which is the source of the freedom. But superficial acquaintance with Ṣûfî principles, without the deep inward growth which they presupposed, could lead not to freedom in truth but to license in passion. There was no hierarchy to control, no sectarian fellowship to rule the individual Muslim believer, who was expected to come before God personally and directly. Consequently, the discipline necessary to prevent freedom degenerating to licence must be applied on a strictly personal basis. The master-disciple relationship has been developed in many religious traditions; in the Ṣûfism of the Earlier Middle Period it became the keynote of the whole system.

Each aspirant to the Ṣûfî way was expected to put himself into the hands of an established pîr (Arabic, *shaykh*), whom he was to obey at all costs—even if it meant contravening the Sharîʿah itself. The pîr master undertook to guide his spiritual progress, suggesting his patterns of meditation, watching for blocks that might arise within his personality against full yielding to truth, and applying such discipline as might be necessary to keep him from going in too deep. The young man must leave his soul's salvation entirely in his master's hands; and the prudent doctrine arose that the pîr could intercede before God for his disciples. The phrase was used, as also later among Jesuits, that the disciple should give up entirely his own will and be to his master as a corpse to the man who washes it. Only when the disciple, murîd, was sufficiently mature to be trusted to himself could he leave his pîr; when the moment arrived, the pîr bestowed upon him a *khirqah*, a special cloak, in principle torn and patched as an emblem of poverty, to show that he was now a true Ṣûfî. Even then, each disciple remained attached throughout life by bonds of loyalty to his master.

The disciples willingly spread abroad their masters' fame, if only because it added to their own standing. Such persons as had only begun to tread the path and had given up when it proved too arduous were perhaps especially likely to proclaim the superhuman virtue and power of a master whom they could not understand. The pîr master became the centre of a little community whose peripheries might become more reverent in just the degree to which they did not achieve the central purpose of the spiritual fellowship but gazed on it from afar. The general respect for the Ṣûfî holy men was reinforced and given tangible content by the awe of the disciples and the would-be disciples.

Ṣûfism as institutionalized mass religion: the techniques of dhikr

In this way there developed by the eleventh century a new pattern of religious life supported by mass piety. Thereupon, though the Ṣûfî heroes of High Caliphal times remained ideal heroes of the new movement, a galaxy of new figures arose and the movement as a whole was transformed. In the later part of the Earlier Middle Period, the new Ṣûfism had its period of greatest bloom. The 'ulamâ' scholars, who had been wary of the early Ṣûfism of an élite, were mostly persuaded by the early twelfth century to accept the new Ṣûfism of the masses, in conformity with their populist principles, and to try to discipline it. Then with their acceptance, around the latter part of the twelfth century the reorganization of Ṣûfism was completed with the establishment of formal Ṣûfî brotherhoods or orders (*ṭarîqah*). (The development of these orders came later in some areas than in others. Like the erection of madrasah colleges and the integration of kalâm disputation into Shar'î studies, the formal organization of Ṣûfî orders seems to have appeared earliest in Khurâsân, though it soon spread everywhere.)

The distinctive marks of the new Ṣûfism, were two: its organization into these formal 'orders', *ṭarîqahs* (of which more shortly); and its concentration on a formal method of mystical worship, the *dhikr*.

Each ṭarîqah order normally had its established pattern of meditation (the heart, indeed, of its 'way' to God), centring on a devotional practice called *dhikr*. This was originally simply one form of internal 'remembrance' of God, consisting of set recitations which were sometimes contrasted to more open meditations called *fikr*. Something of the contrast emerges if one renders *fikr* 'meditation', and *dhikr* 'invocation'. The dhikr made use of forms of words or even syllables to be chanted or otherwise held before the attention, designed to remind the devotee of the presence of God. Sometimes the syllables used were to be accompanied by special controls of the breath, so as to make possible more intense concentration. Such practices readily became the nucleus of a fully developed ritual.

With the popularization of Ṣûfism as the most important vehicle of serious inward religious experience in the region from Nile to Oxus, from which control by any ecclesiastical hierarchy or rivalry from sacramental mysteries had disappeared, Ṣûfî ways became adjusted to more than one sort of religious aspiration. One such aspiration was the achievement of religious ecstasy. Dhikr had presumably originated as a method for recalling a wandering attention and perhaps for controlling ordinary consciousness as part of a larger programme of self-awareness. In some circles, it now was turned into a method of achieving ecstasy directly—that is, the overwhelming euphoric state of consciousness which mystics had always regarded as a great grace, and often as a significant basis for mystical knowledge, but which sometimes now was felt to be an end in itself.

A sophisticated array of techniques was developed for producing the desired results: breathing and posture were carefully prescribed, and the dhikr formula was to be uttered with attention directed to particular parts of the body at particular moments of the breathing. Pattern and limit were set upon the process in the form of regulation of the frequency of uttering, or (at more advanced states) sensing, the formula: the rosary (it was introduced from India—as were perhaps some other techniques at this time) was used to keep track of the frequency. Since it was acknowledged that without genuine moral intention, the recitation could not in itself be effective, concrete content was sometimes retained in the recitation by having the murîd disciple keep before his closed eyes the image of his pîr, as exemplar of ideal humanity and, as such, as representative of God to the murîd. The psychic processes to be anticipated as a result of the exercises were eventually described in detail in technical manuals: for instance, certain colours of light were expected to appear mentally at certain stages of the process. Sometimes a very high degree of organic self-control could be achieved. Of course, proper use of the dhikr presupposed an accompanying intense development of ascetic techniques also, which made possible the requisite focusing of the mind. All these matters of technique were similar, often in great detail, to the techniques of similar religious exercises found among Eastern Christians, in certain Hindu and Buddhist Indic traditions, and elsewhere, though probably they were not so highly developed as in the more advanced of the Indic traditions.

Each devotee was to maintain a private dhikr recitation, as assigned him by the pîr, but in addition all might come together in dhikr assemblies, where commonly the formulas would be chanted aloud in a group. Often the immediate effect seems to have rested on a type of hypnotic autosuggestion. In principle, any ecstatic response to the stimuli of the chanting should be spontaneous and individual; a man might rise from the circle and fling himself about, or faint, or shout; in practice it very early became widely accepted that all present should associate themselves to some degree in the more explicit ecstatic activity aimed at, once it had begun, as a form of psychological solidarity whether each was inwardly impelled or not.

In the Middle Periods, such techniques of the dhikr recitation were ever more highly elaborated in the manuals used by the various ṭarîqah orders. Perhaps more important, the dhikr came to take precedence over other forms of meditation, and in particular the group dhikr became the most prominent activity of ṭarîqah Ṣûfism. Many writers ceased to describe the dhikr and the results it could produce as merely a means of readying the heart for response to a divine grace that could not be achieved by any sort of technique in itself; they wrote as if the dhikr practice could lead, by way of simply human initiative, to a state of consciousness which embodied all the cosmic harmony that was to be desired. Pîrs continued to insist on a 'Way' which should include moral growth; indeed, without this, an ecstatic moment, if it could be achieved, might yield only an abortive sense that something was there to be found, without the means of finding it. But it was the special ecstatic moment that was really sought. Everyday mysticism, with its comprehensive moral discipline, was often neglected in favour of ecstatic mysticism. Eventually, purely physical techniques of stimulation were to be used to produce more easily a state of consciousness regarded as the equivalent of what more ascetic techniques of self-control produced. Nevertheless, despite the prominence of dhikr recitation in a relatively specialized form in ṭarîqah Ṣûfism, the most respected Ṣûfîs generally continued to be those who might, indeed, make use of the dhikr techniques for the sake of focusing the attention, but for whom such techniques were by no means an end in themselves, and who retained the broad moral vision of the classical Ṣûfî masters.[3]

A great many Ṣûfîs made use of some sort of music in their assemblies for dhikr recitation, especially the singing of devotional songs by expert singers. The music was designed to heighten the sensibilities and intensify the concentration. This use of 'listening', *samâ'*, was the point that aroused most doubt among the 'ulamâ' scholars, who seized on such music (music being frowned upon in any case) as a singularly dubious means of spiritual discipline; sometimes they suspected that the good looks of a lad who sang might move hearers as much as words he uttered about God. Some Ṣûfîs, the more Sharî'ah-minded, consequently avoided its use. Some, on the contrary, looked on it as peculiarly emblematic at once of the Ṣûfî's freedom and of God's beauty. Music often inspired ecstatic movements, which in the Mevlevî ṭarîqah, founded by the Persian poet Jalâluddîn Rûmî (d. 1273), became a highly formalized whirling dance (whence the Mevlevîs are called the 'dancing' or 'whirling dervishes').

The dhikr sessions came to supplement (and sometimes to supplant) the ṣalât worship. Accordingly, in addition to the ordinary mosque, each Muslim community now had its *khâniqâh* (Arabic, *zâwiyah*), where the Ṣûfî pîrs lived. There they instructed and housed their disciples, held regular dhikr sessions (often for a fairly wide congregation), and offered hospitality to wandering Ṣûfîs, especially those of the same ṭarîqah. These institutions, which had some of the same functions as a European monastery, became basic centres of social integration. They were mostly restricted to men, but in the Earlier Middle Period there were occasionally some for women also.

In addition to the regular murîd disciples, the preaching and even the dhikr sessions attracted many laymen only partly associated with the ṭarîqah order, who followed a modified form of its way for help within the limits of ordinary life. Eventually, sometimes a whole guild came to be associated with a given ṭarîqah and its pîrs. It was through such followers that the Ṣûfî khâniqâhs were financed.

The worship at the mosques never ceased to be associated in some degree with political authority; it was a state function. The khâniqâhs were eminently private from the very beginning. Even when endowed by an amîr,

[3] Louis Gardet has been very keen, but perhaps somewhat ungenerous, in analyzing the later developments of dhikr; cf. his portions of *Mystique musulmane* (Paris, 1961) written with G. L. Anawati. For a different appreciation of the possible role of ecstasies in human inward development, consider the Buddhist views brilliantly summarized by Edward Conze in *Buddhism, Its Essence and Development* (New York, 1951).

they retained this air. When the khâniqâhs became the foci of the more private, personal side of worship, they reinforced the fragmentation of Muslim societies in apolitical social forms (and at the same time, as we shall see, gave these forms legitimacy and spiritual support). With the decline of the caliphal state and the rise of the international order, the Shar'î zakât alms, which had been the original means of financing Islamic religious activities through the central treasury, were effectively replaced by the waqf foundations; zakât alms became an incidental personal obligation, on which few or no religious institutions were dependent. Even mosques, though properly to be supported from taxation money, benefited by wawf endowments. But these were far more important for institutions like madrasah colleges and khâniqâhs which ultimately depended almost exclusively on such funds; this was true especially of the khâniqâhs, which in this way expressed the apolitical mood of the times even on the religious side.

The tarîqah orders

Both dhikr worship and the khâniqâhs in which it was housed were given public credit on the basis of adherence to one or another recognized *ṭarîqah*. The ṭarîqahs (literally, 'ways') were loosely organized bodies of pîrs and murîds following well-defined and even hierarchically controlled 'ways' of mystical discipline, each with its rituals, its chiefs, and (of course) its endowments. These were founded on the relationship between master and disciple, as this relationship had been formalized in the previous century or so. In principle, every aspiring young Ṣûfî (as murîd) attached himself to an established Ṣûfî pîr (or shaykh), who was himself the disciple of another and greater pîr; whose own training had come through a line of pîrs reaching back, ordinarily, to the Prophet. (Members of the general public were assimilated into this discipleship as lay murîds.) Thus a sequence of teachers handed on one to the other, in pîrî-murîdî relationship, the secrets of spiritual life that had supposedly been first enunciated privately to select companions by Muḥammad.

This sequence was called a *silsilah*: it amounted to an isnâd documentation translated into organizational practice. Each major ṭarîqah traced its form of the Ṣûfî doctrine and practice, especially its dhikr, back to some proximate founder, from whom it usually took its name, who in turn was connected by his special silsilah sequence, via one or more of the great Ṣûfîs of High 'Abbâsî times, to one of the great figures of the time of the Prophet, usually 'Alî. Many Ṣûfîs seem to have welcomed some of the conceptions that had been developed on the esoteric side of 'Alid loyalism, and most specially the notion that 'Alî had received secret teachings from Muḥammad for which most of the first Muslims were not qualified; but the Ṣûfîs identified those secret teachings with their own traditions. In this way they provided a Jamâ'î-Sunnî context for some elements of 'Alid-loyalist esotericism (to the

Filiation of the Ṭarîqahs and Their Founders, 945–1273

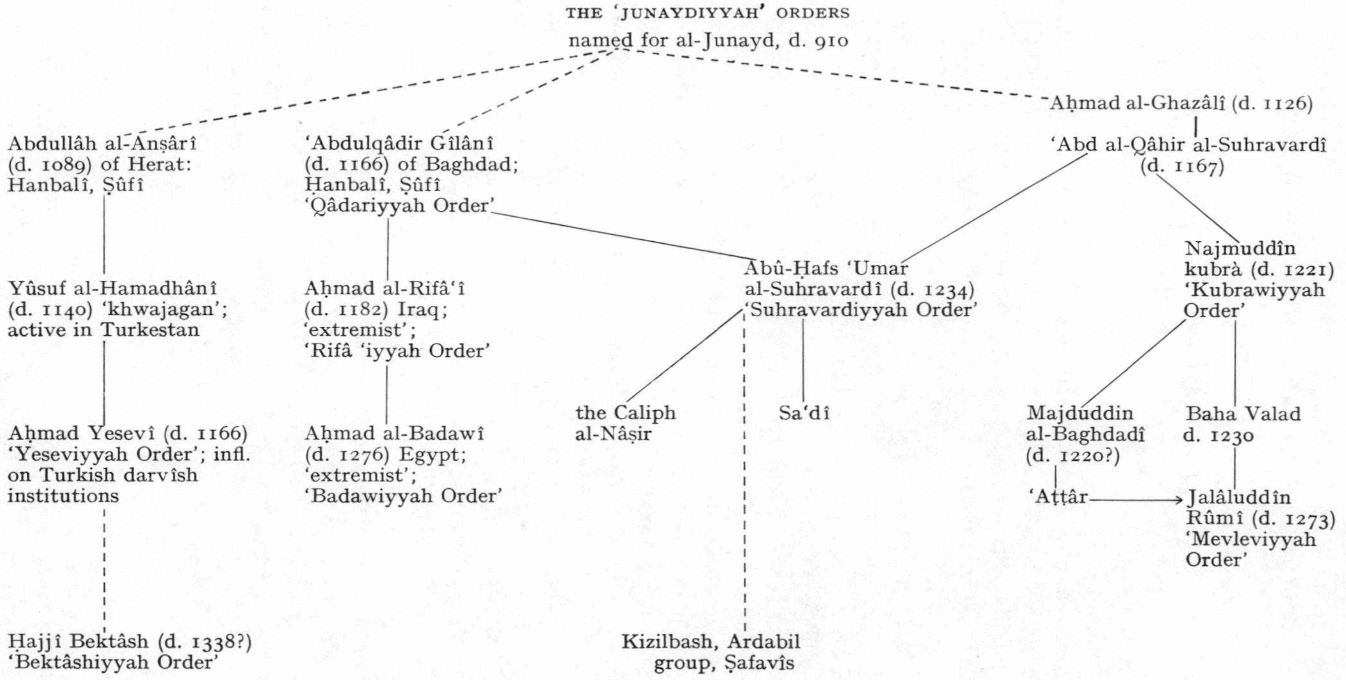

annoyance of those ʿAlid loyalists who clung to a Shîʿî partisan position) and at the same time provided a means of explaining how their own teaching could be traced back to the Prophet. (The use of a silsilah was exactly parallel to the use of the isnâds with which the Ḥadîth folk had earlier connected their own ideas to the Prophet, one might add. In each case a form of piety which, on the face of it, could be identified neither with the common piety of earlier Muslims nor with the Qur'ân did, nonetheless, represent the development of elements more or less present from the first; and the citation of a more or less plausible sequence of witnesses fixed and, to be sure, exaggerated the relationship.)

All followers of a given ṭarîqah order continued to acknowledge more or less loosely the headship of a spiritual or (more often) physical descendant of the founder, his successor, *khalîfah*, who took charge of his khâniqâh or his tomb. Sometimes the relationship was chiefly ceremonial—all whose Ṣûfism was traced to a given founder would try to come together at his tomb on the anniversary of his death, for common remembrance and spiritual renewal. But sometimes the holder of central authority kept very tight control over all the pîrs who acknowledged him. Succession to the position of the founder normally carried with it control of endowments of considerable size; and even though most pîrs declined to use such funds for personal or family luxury, even their distribution in charity entailed choices, including the choice of agents of distribution, which necessarily helped determine the position of many followers among their fellows. Such considerations increased the importance of the selection of a successor to a great pîr (and they account, in some cases, for the disciples, preferring succession by a son of the pîr, if a suitable one were available; for he would be most likely to be neutral among the factions that tend to divide any group of men, even those attempting to cultivate the mystical way).

Too often the death of a pîr without very clear designation of a successor led to splits in the ṭarîqah order, in which two leading disciples divided the other disciples between themselves and each pronounced the other a renegade.

The central pîr appointed not only that khalîfah who was to be his direct successor but, often enough, a number of khalîfahs, qualified to lead the work in one way or another; often these were sent to towns where the pîr's interpretation of Ṣûfism was not yet being taught, and where the khalîfah was authorized by the pîr to carry out a preaching mission, both to touch the general public (morally and financially) and to train local disciples. So long as the central pîr's authority was acknowledged, the khalîfah in another town could not himself appoint khalîfahs without at least tacit authorization, nor could he move to another town where more rewarding prospects beckoned unless his master approved.

The most famous and perhaps always most widespread of such ṭarîqah orders was the Qâdiriyyah, which traced its silsilah through the preacher ʿAbdulqâdir Gîlânî. He himself does not seem consciously to have founded any order, or to have appointed a successor in that sense. But he had bestowed the khirqah cloak, in recognition of spiritual maturity, on many disciples. After his death, one of his sons took his place at his assembly hall and as administrator of the endowments that had accumulated in his name. Eventually not only his disciples but their disciples in turn looked to his authority and to the authority of his successors (khalîfah) at his tomb in Baghdad for guidance in the mystical way. So, an originally charismatic leadership was institutionalized.

What came to matter was the authority of the founding figure rather than his insights. And at this point, it was not only practicing mystics but insecure aspirants and even the general public that had to be impressed.

Gîlânî's standard biography, written a century later, makes him a supreme miracle-worker; omitting all his practical work and teaching, in favour of an imaginary exalted figure in which the common person could take refuge for intercession and consolation.

The catholic appeal of Ṣûfism

An even larger clientèle than those interested in either preaching or dhikr was sooner or later brought into the Ṣûfî orbit. The Ṣûfî pîrs, especially when dead, became the centres of a direct popular cult, which must be distinguished from the mystical cult as such. The people at large did not fail to look for the intercession of the Ṣûfî saints, in whose human sympathies they found a much more believable compassion than in the remote Oneness of God. If the saint could intercede for his murîd, so could he for any devout petitioner. And experience predictably bore out the devotees' hopes: even apart from the chance fulfillment of wishes that will always be recalled when all disappointments are forgotten, the subtle effects of confidence and sometimes the vitalizing presence of a potent man could indeed work wonders. Even alive, a Ṣûfî pîr might receive a higher reverence than was accorded to any other man except a king. It was not only the murîd, seeking spiritual illumination, but the common Muslim, seeking God's favour through the favour of the pîr, who paid his court to and sought spiritual advice from the well-known representatives of Ṣûfism. The dhikr sessions of mystical worship among disciples were no longer private ceremonials, but might be attended by numerous ordinary people with no mystical tendencies at all, for the sake of pious edification or a sheer blessing.

But after his death, the saint's soul must be yet freer of the trammels of individual flesh. To the tombs, women came for a blessing that they might bear children, and sick people that they might be healed. The tomb of a famous pîr became a centre of local and even international pilgrimage which no pious Muslim failed to visit respectfully when he came into its vicinity. The celebration of a great saint's birthday at his tomb site became a major local festivity, in which every inhabitant took part. At last, not only in the towns but in the countryside, the peasants looked to the shade of some local ascetic, who had received the khirqah cloak of some prominent order, as the protecting genius of the village, and honoured his tomb as the locus of his blessèd power.

In such ways, a tradition of intensive interiorization re-exteriorized its results and was finally able to provide an important basis for social order. Perhaps more than their peers in any other major cultural environment, the Ṣûfîs succeeded in combining a spiritual élitism with a social populism—even though, to a considerable degree, at the expense of a certain vulgarization, beginning at the level of the dhikr recitations and extending out to the level of popular superstition. (The contrast to the Faylasûfs—even the astrologers and physicians—who likewise cultivated a certain élitism, is striking; yet it is not obvious, in principle, that it must be more difficult to popularize some adaptation of natural science, with the moral concomitants assumed to go with it at the time, than to popularize mysticism, that most elusive of experiences.) Ṣûfism provided a wide field of free development for the exceptional individual, as we shall be seeing; it also provided a vehicle for expressing every aspect of popular piety within Islam.

For a long time after the advent of Islam as dominant religious allegiance, the shrines of the populace, the holy places where ordinary people were able to find access to a special sacredness to grace the routine events and crises of their lives, mostly remained in the hands of the non-Muslim dhimmî communities. (The mosque, of course, was no shrine in this sense, but rather a place of public assemblage: it answered more nearly to the agora than to the temple of the ancient Greeks.) Shî'î piety was early able to develop a limited number of shrines in the form of the tombs of descendants of 'Alî; in some areas, as in Syria, Muslim converts could share unashamedly with those who remained Christians in the cult of such shrines as the reputed tombs of ancient prophets, recognized in both traditions. But it was only with the spread and general acknowledgement of ṭarîqah Ṣûfism and its myriad saints that it became possible to produce (or to Islamize) Islamic shrines everywhere, and to every purpose—shrines where one could pray for the pressing needs of every day: women for sons or men for good harvests; for rain or peace or love or healing.

This popular outreach was prepared and defended by a reasoned adjustment to Sunnî Sharî'ah-mindedness, which served to explain the appeal Ṣûfism had for all classes. Long before Ghazâlî, Ṣûfîs had been at pains to insist on the full and even rigouristic observance of Sharî'ah rules by mystics. In the eleventh century, the Ash'arî scholar al-Qushayrî (d. 1074) was notable for analyzing mystical states consistently with Ash'arî kalâm and hence in such a way as to reassure the Sharî'ah-minded. This sort of argument the 'ulamâ' scholars proved willing to accept, or at least wink at, so soon as it became clear that the whole Sharî'ah-minded structure as such was being left intact and accorded respect in the only sphere, that of outward social acknowledgement, where the Sharîʿah-minded principles (ultimately concerned above all with social order) inescapably required it.

But the usual justification of Ṣûfism with regard to the Sharîʿah did not depend on dialectical subtleties or even on rigoristic rules, but on a frank division of labour. It was explained (perhaps borrowing a bit from some Ismâʿîlî teachings) that the Ṣûfîs dealt with the inward side (bâṭin) of the same faith and truth of which the Sharʿî ʿulamâʾ scholars were concerned with the outward side (ẓâhir); and that both were completely valid and necessary. In all respects, the inward paralleled the outward, complementing it, not contradicting it. The ʿulamâʾ taught the Sharîʿah, the 'way' of daily life; the Ṣûfîs taught the ṭarîqah, the 'way' of mystical life. The ʿulamâʾ possessed ʿilm knowledge, essential information transmitted outwardly from person to person through the isnâds of ḥadîth reports; the Ṣûfîs possessed *maʿrifah* (again, a synonym of *ʿilm*), a different sort of knowledge, not that of report but that of experience, gained by adherence to the silsilah which, like the isnâd, also led back to Muḥammad. But the ʿulamâʾ looked to the *prophethood* (*nubuwwah*) of Muḥammad because they were concerned with outward law; the Ṣûfîs looked to the *sainthood* (*wilâyah*) of Muḥammad because they were concerned with inward grace. The ʿulamâʾ taught islâm, submission of humans to God's majesty (*jalâl*), which is perfected in *tawḥîd*, the profession of God's unity; for the Ṣûfîs this was essential, but only a first step; they taught the way to *ʿishq*, love of God's beauty (*jamâl*), which is perfected in *waḥdah*, the experience of God's unity (or even of unity in Him). No person could attempt the Ṣûfî way until first confirmed in the way of the ʿulamâʾ, for the one presupposed the other.

By Jamâʿî-Sunnî principles of recognizing diversity as legitimate, no man could question the islâm of another if he professed the shahâdah declaration and followed the essentials of the Sharîʿah law, whatever his inner motivation, or the variations in secondary matters which he adhered to. (Shîʿî Sharîʿah-mindedness, less catholic in principle, and in any case attached to its own special saints and its own intercessors in the persons of its imâms, was less ready to accept Ṣûfism.) Once a reasonably Sharîʿah-minded Ṣûfism came to be accepted (more or less from the early twelfth century), all varieties of Ṣûfism came to have a cloak, and in subsequent centuries even forms most alien to the Sharîʿah temper were given wide tacit recognition.

The various ṭarîqahs differed enormously in the sort of meditation and dhikr recitation they cultivated, the emphasis they laid on individual mystical experience or on simple asceticism, the attitude they held toward the Sharîʿah or toward Muslim governments (some had as little as possible to do with either, while some were very rigidly Sharʿî), and so on. There was indeed an attempt to distinguish off Sharîʿah-observant ṭarîqahs from less acceptable ones. In great measure, however, the fact of being organized in ṭarîqah form and tracing one's discipline to respected ancients through a silsilah was commonly sufficient to establish the right of a group of Ṣûfîs to public recognition; thus, for instance, a Shî'î group, condemned by the 'ulamâ' scholars for their heresy, could gain toleration by presenting themselves in the form of a Ṣûfî ṭarîqah, into whose private doctrines it was not proper to enquire. (In this guise the remaining Nizârî Ismâ'îlîs were to find solace after the destruction of their state in 1256.) Only a minority of the 'ulamâ' maintained a struggle against the Ṣûfî torrent.

Ṣûfism as a mainstay of the international social order

In this Ṣûfism, the international ties which the Sharî'ah provided, and which the madrasah colleges helped maintain in concrete form, were given a strong moral support. In the first place, the ṭarîqah orders were many of them international and at least at first there was a certain subordination of pîrs and khâniqâhs at a distance to the headquarters of the head of the order—usually at the founder's tomb. In this way, the several ṭarîqahs formed a flexibly interlocking network of authorities, which paid no attention to the political frontiers of the moment and was readily expandable into new areas.

Moreover, the Ṣûfîs tended to be as naturally tolerant of local differences as the Shar'î 'ulamâ' tended to be naturally intolerant. The 'ulamâ' had to concentrate on matters of external conformity, as dictated by the Sharî'ah, in order to maintain the legal and institutional framework for social unity. It was they who pulled for a central cultural tradition into which all Muslim peoples must be drawn. For the Ṣûfîs, on the contrary, externals were secondary. For many of them, especially by the Earlier Middle Period, even the difference between Islam and other traditions such as Christianity was of secondary importance in principle; of still less moment were the various differences in social custom within the community of Muḥammad. What mattered was the inner disposition of the heart of God. Hence the Ṣûfîs were prepared to allow every sort of difference in the mere customary behaviour of day-to-day life. Many of them wandered incessantly in remote parts of the Dâr al-Islâm, as unattached poor *darvîshes* (Arabic, *faqîrs*—mendicant holy men), while a learnèd qâḍî, if he moved about, usually did so with circumspection and was slowed down by his possessions. The Ṣûfîs knew much of the world, and with their lenient sanctity they could cushion the shock of the rigorous demands of the 'ulamâ' for uniformity.

Finally, the Ṣûfîs contributed to solving a pressing political problem among the Muslims. The Sharî'ah law afforded legitimation on a universal basis, on the assumption that nothing mattered legally but relations between individuals, equal anywhere in the world. But actually in Islamdom, as elsewhere, relations were conditioned by local groupings, such as town quarters and guilds and men's societies, in which an individual's special status in the group, as apprentice or master or client or notable, mattered as much as his universal status as a Muslim. Something was required, as a basis for assuring legitimacy in these relations and so providing a moral check on their operation, more universal than the authority of sheer power; something that could tie them into that Islam which was the moral basis of individual lives. Like the Sharîʿah, the spiritual authority of the Ṣûfî pîrs and the ethic they preached proved able to relate the conscience of ordinary men to the institutions they needed, but in a way that allowed an individualized status to particular personal and group relationships.

As, in the Middle Periods, futuwwah men's clubs and crafts guilds came to carry a larger part of the burden of maintaining social order, many of them were permeated with a Ṣûfî spirit. Sometimes they might adopt the patronage of a given pîr or of his ṭarîqah order, sometimes they adapted the forms and something of the moral norms of a ṭarîqah order to their special body. The life of a man in a given trade, for instance, should form a total moral pattern in which the techniques of the trade were only one aspect; and it must be learned gradually from those more experienced in it. Ṣûfî principles allowed for just such a process, and for special personal ties between master and disciple, and among disciples, which carried recognized moral obligations and privileges. And they allowed for a distinct moral posture by the special group toward the world at large, based on generosity and loyalty. Principles of universalism in religion could even solve the problem of the presence of Muslims and dhimmî non-Muslims sharing a common guild.

The Ṣûfî tie at once deepened the local moral resources, and tied them in to a system of brotherhoods in some ways as universal as the old caliphal bureaucracy had been, which had disappeared. The refusal of some Ṣûfîs to permit any association with the amîr's court served to underline the alternative social outlook. It was as if the court were carefully quarantined so as to minimize its influence. Thus Ṣûfism supplemented the Sharîʿah as a principle of unity and order, offering the Muslims a sense of spiritual unity which came to be stronger than that provided by the remnant of the caliphate. They developed, as we shall see shortly, a picture of the world which united the whole Dâr al-Islâm (and even the lands of the infidels) under a comprehensive spiritual hierarchy of pîrs, which was all the more effective, imaginatively, for being invisible; they could replace even the caliph himself with a supreme pîr master, whose authority was felt though his name was unknown. The individual khâniqâhs and saints' tombs to which the faithful could come for spiritual guidance and consolation from God-dedicated men were part of an inclusive holy order—not merely the order of a given ṭarîqah, but that of God's chosen men throughout the world.

Thus the whole body of the Muslim people came to be united in a common pattern of piety, which in its rich variety could provide a home not only for mystics properly speaking, but for ascetics and for those whose chief interest was in esoteric speculation; for those who sought God through warm personalities; and at last for the simple, superstitious villager, who transferred his ancestral usages, which had once been given a Christian or a Hindu veneer, to a Muslim tomb. Indeed, such piety tended to bridge the gap between Muslim and infidel. Not only in their lifetimes were Ṣûfîs commonly tolerant of differences in the outward rites of faith, but after their death their shrines often attracted devotees of every spiritual allegiance—even if the alleged Ṣûfî tomb were not, in fact, simply an older place of worship renamed. Many Sharî'ah-minded Muslims, seeing the stern message of divine confrontation exchanged for what was in fact a complete mediationism, and seeing the old spiritual egalitarianism exchanged for a very marked hierarchism, were indeed troubled; but most of them salved their consciences with a recognition that, now that it had been generally accepted by the community, the new order was sanctioned by ijmâ' consensus. This, loyal as they were to Muslim unity, they could not venture to gainsay.

This interpersonal and social role of Ṣûfism was explained and guided by a body of teachings that went beyond the bare analysis of inward states to an analysis of the role of the mystic in the world. And these teachings, in turn, reinforced the Ṣûfî role and gave it a degree of that legitimation so necessary for durability. On the popular level, they allowed the unsophisticated imagination to grasp something of the human potentialities the mystics had discovered. On the learnèd level, they served to broaden and rationalize the perspectives of mystics and non-mystics alike.

Ṣûfî speculation: the myth of the microcosmic return

Mystical experience, if the sense of freedom it brings is not to run out into mere euphoria and wilful imaginings, which would invert its moral essence, requires two auxiliary practices. It requires discipline, as we have seen; in exploring his unconscious, the beginner murîd must be under the watchful control of one more experienced than himself. It also requires some sort of conceptual analysis: to speak intelligibly about the murîd disciple's fears or blockings or dreams, the pîr master must use categories and concepts designed to make the murîd's condition graspable by his conscious mind, at least by way of a first approximation. Hence mystics must turn to a certain amount of speculation. And just as, once there was a personal discipline, it readily expressed itself in social forms, so once there was speculation this also was soon expressed intellectually in the form of social discussion; first in the field of psychology and then overflowing into all fields of study interdependent with psychology—that is, into practically all fields of study. Just as the socialized personal discipline could become a basis for a total social outlook, so the socialized speculation could become the basis of a comprehensive intellectual life.

Ṣûfîs could not be content to let their analysis rest with a relatively straightforward description of the stages of their mystical progress. Their experience

Ṣûfîs of the Earlier Middle Period, 945–1273

fl. 961	al-Niffarî, 'intoxicated' wandering darvîsh who wrote an analysis of his ecstatic experiences
Eleventh century	Ṣûfism well established in the lands from Nile to Oxus; beginning of 'systematizing' era
1021	Death of al-Sulamî, moderate Ṣûfî; wrote—in addition to a Ṣûfî exegesis of Qur'ân ('first' Ṣûfî exegesis by al-Tustarî, d. 896)—the 'first' register of Ṣûfîs
1049	Death of Abû-Sa'îd b. Abî'l-Khayr, influential preacher, presumed writer of quatrains (rubâ'iyyât), sometimes called 'first' Ṣûfî poet in Persian
1072	Death of al-Qushayrî, 'classical formulator' of Ṣûfî doctrine
c. 1075	Death of al-Hujvirî, wrote systematic treatise on lives and doctrines of Ṣûfîs, 'first' treatise on Ṣûfism in Persian
1089	Death of 'Abdullah al-Anṣârî, Ḥanbalî anti-kalâm Ṣûfî writer in Persian poetry and prose, systematizer
1111	Death of Muḥammad al-Ghazâlî, systematizer of knowledge, harmonizer of Ṣûfism with Sunnism, writings of great importance to later generations
1126	Death of Aḥmad al-Ghazâlî, brother of Muḥammad, popular Ṣûfî teacher emphasizing love
Twelfth century	Ṣûfism becomes popularized at all levels of society; beginning of Ṣûfî 'Orders' (ṭarîqahs)
1130	Death of al-Sanâ'î, 'first' great Ṣûfî (Persian) poet
1166	Death of 'Abdulqâdir Gîlânî, Ḥanbali anti-kalâm revivalist preacher; Qâdariyyah order organized about his teaching
1167	Death of 'Abd al-Qâhir al-Suhravardî, uncle of Abû-Hafs 'Umar, for whom Suhravardiyyah order is named, important teacher
1191	Death of Yaḥyà Suhravardî 'al-Maqtûl', Faylasûf, cosmologist, executed for heresy, founder of Illuminationist school (Ishrâq)
c. 1200	Death of 'Aṭṭâr, Persian writer of important Ṣûfî allegory
1221	Death of Najmuddîn Kubrà, student of 'Abd al-Qâhir al-Suhravardî, Kubraviyyah order organized about his teaching; possibly directly influential on father of Jalâluddîn Rûmî
1235	Death of Ibn-al-Fâriḍ, most important Arabic language Ṣûfî poet
c. 1235	Death of Abû-Hafs 'Umar al-Suhravardî, student of 'Abd al-Qâhir al-Suhravardî and of 'Abdulqâdir Gîlânî, pîr of the caliph al-Nâṣir and of Sa'dî
1240	Death of Ibn-al-'Arabî, cosmologist, one of the greatest Ṣûfî theoreticians, developer of Ishraqî ideas
1273	Death of Jalâluddîn Rûmî, one of the four or five 'greatest' writers in Persian, author of the Mas̄navî; Mevleviyyah order organized about his teaching

demanded a total picture of the universe different from the notions common among mankind: special mystical experiences in themselves seemed to call for such a picture, which was further needed if they were to make sense of their lives as their experience had transformed them. Hence to psychical analysis was, before long, added theorizing about the cosmos in which the psyche found itself.

Exploring the meanings that given symbols can bear seems to form a major part of any comprehensive attempt to make sense of oneself and the universe. For when one tries to present ultimate cosmic and moral insights, one is at the limits of conceptual discourse; that is, at the point where the terms in which logical sequences issue are, strictly speaking, indeterminate (e.g., the finiteness or infinity of the universe, the causal determinacy of all sequences at once, the value of any valuation). Here logical deductions produce antinomies. Hence one must speak (if at all) in symbolic images that evoke emergent associations rather than fix propositions; and this is done most richly in what are called mythopoeic forms, adumbrating truths after the manner of myths, which tell in multivalent images truths about life that every hearer can grasp at his own level of understanding.

All ultimate life-orientational thinking must turn to indeterminate, evocative images. But those who count on explicit intellectual resolutions, whether by way of analyzing nature or by way of asserting history, may be ill at ease with their ambiguities. The inward orientation of mystics, on the contrary, can find such images spontaneously congenial. Mystics must be open to the many levels of meaning behind any outward action or impulse. It is no accident that the term 'mystical' initially referred to finding supposed hidden meanings in external texts or acts; an inward penetration of one's own consciousness can go hand in hand with a penetration of formally received ideas to implications latent in them. Mystics have always found a major medium for expressing the inexpressible in a symbolical deepening of scriptural passages, which are at least as open as any other writings to such a procedure. Correspondingly, in independent composition: where the Sharî'ah-minded turned by preference to at least ostensibly historical forms of writing, and the Faylasûfs to abstract exposition in which the ultimate indeterminacy was disguised, the Ṣûfîs most naturally turned to frankly mythopoeic forms of expression.

The rich heritage of mythic figures in the Irano-Semitic tradition had already been made use of in the Qur'ân. Already Muḥammad seems to have conceived his mission in terms of patterns that were present in the monotheistic tradition: a heavenly book of which extracts could appear on earth as scriptures, angels as intermediaries between the Creator-god and human beings, the sending of prophets on explicit missions. All these elements implied a rather elaborate cosmic structure which, already in the Qur'ân, carried overtones suggesting a cosmic drama more integrated and involved than the prosaic Sharî'ah-minded commentators were willing to allow when they reduced everything to arbitrary individual acts of God.[4] The Bâṭinî speculations had already developed further just such Qur'ânic elements. The Bâṭinîs had interpreted the figure of Muḥammad as a link in a great cosmic action, in which an initial disruption of God's order was being repaired —carrying forward a cosmic myth common to many monotheistic traditions. The Ṣûfîs now used fundamentally similar symbolic myths (including some of the ideas set forth among the Bâṭinîs) to develop their own interpretations on a less sectarian, more universalistic basis than had the Bâṭinîs.

The Ṣûfîs found, as their pre-Islamic and Islamic mentors had often found earlier, that many of the historic religious symbols made sense on both the personal and the cosmic level if sensitively followed through in their implications; moreover, that it was possible to unify them in what may be called the 'myth of the microcosmic return', and that it was possible to invoke this myth so as to apply the findings about the unconscious to the cosmos as a whole—and conversely to illuminate the self from what could be understood of the cosmos. The sense of communion with God which some of the classical Ṣûfîs had spoken of, in which individual and cosmic meanings converged, thus led readily to a teaching of Gnostic type which combined old Hellenistic and Irano-Semitic elements with a new outlook appropriate to the Islamic setting. In this teaching were combined special notions of the place of mankind in the cosmos, and of the place of the saint among mankind. The Ṣûfî myth of the microcosmic return was being worked out during several generations of Ṣûfîs, beginning with later High Caliphal times, but it took full form only in the Earlier Middle Period.

It had long been believed that the human being was the 'microcosm', the 'world in miniature', in which were combined to their fullest fruition all the elements of the 'macrocosm', the universe. Thus water, in itself, stands futile in the sea; or air, in itself, floats pointlessly over the hills. These things seemed to exist only for the sake of supplying the liquid that pulses in the veins and the breath that moves in the lungs of a being that can fulfill the plan of God by knowing and worshipping Him; that is, of a human being. To the pre-Modern mind, a rational universe implied purposiveness in all its parts and in its totality; the purpose, the *raison d'être*, as it were, of all the elements, so ran the Ṣûfî doctrine, was the human being, in which they were combined to best advantage. This was the meaning of being human in our wondrous world. We may call 'a myth of the microcosmic return' any myth

[4] George Widengren, 'Muḥammad, the Apostle of God and His Ascension (King & Suri,V)', *Uppsala Universitets Årsskrift*, 1950 and 1955, points out that much of this pattern goes back to pre-monotheistic traditions, and shows that important points of the legend of Muḥammad, notably his heavenly ascent, can be paralleled in earlier Hebrew materials. In using this sort of philological analysis, however, one must bear in mind that these Irano-Semitic traditions could persist only so far as they fulfilled current functions in the Islamic context; unfortunately, Widengren takes the reports of the Ghulât, and even of Muḥammad, too much at face value without historical criticism, and hence sometimes makes the religious life he describes look like mechanical repetition of inherited motifs.

that tries to show how the cosmos is fulfilled through an individual's self-fulfillment; that self-fulfillment being seen as a return, on a new level, to cosmic origins. Among the Ṣûfîs, such a myth was built up only gradually, achieving its fullest form in the work of Ibn-al-'Arabî (1165–1240).

The myth of the microcosmic return explained—in the allusive, paradoxical way that a myth can 'explain' at all—how our shifting, unstable world comes to be so; and with the same stroke, how the soul comes to find itself longing always for something beyond its present reach. The Ṣûfîs quoted a ḥadîth report that God said, 'I was a hidden treasure, and I wanted to be found.' Therefore He created the world; projecting rationality into existence, and with it a vast proliferation of differentiations—stars and planets and rocks and chemical elements—expressing all the various potentialities inherent in total rationality. Within all this proliferation, then, he created complexities in which the elements were combined together ever more fully: plants and animals; till finally he created beings in which all the differentiations came to a focus, in which every sort of rational possibility was comprehended: human beings. Such beings were capable at last, in their reflexive consciousness (in which they could take up again all that exists and trace everything back to its source), of becoming conscious of the origin of it all, of God himself—of discovering Him through and beyond all the wondrous proliferation of existence which expressed His potentialities, and returning to his presence. In this way, they could even become mirrors for God himself, where He could see His potentialities displayed. Another, more universally accepted, ḥadîth, modelled evidently on a passage in Genesis, was 'God made Adam in his own image'—implying a correspondence between humanity and deity which the Sharî'ah-minded had some trouble explaining away.

All things then, were created to make possible the ultimate vision of God; all things are driving, inarticulately or with lesser or greater glimmerings of consciousness, toward realization of God; the secret moving force of all that move, all animals even and especially all human beings, is God. All love is divine love, however blindly misdirected onto unworthy objects; all worship is worship toward God, though it shortsightedly comes to rest too soon, on mere idols.[5]

In this comprehensive vision, everything in God's creation had its place: even the Devil, Iblîs. According to one view (fully developed by the end of the eleventh century), the reason for Iblîs' refusal to bow down before Adam (as the Qur'ân reports) when Adam was created was pride (as the Qur'ân states) only in a very special sense. God had commanded all the angels to bow down before a mere creature, under penalty of being banished and condemned to Hell. All the other angels complied with the command and remained in God's presence. But Iblîs, said some Ṣûfîs, obviously loved God

[5] Hans Jonas, in 'Immortality and the Modern Temper', *Harvard Theological Review*, 55 (1962), 1–20, shows very perceptively some of what can still make sense for Moderns in the sort of notions embodied in the myth of the microcosmic return.

even more than did the other angels, and he was confronted with a tragic dilemma. Either he must dishonour God by bowing down to something lesser, or he must disobey God and accept the penalty. But if one interprets God's command as presenting a choice: bow down and stay in Paradise, or refuse and be condemned to Hell—it can be seen that the perfect devotee of God could make only one choice. He must refuse to bow down to a mere creature even if the consequence was banishment from the presence of God and assignment to the role of devil. In the end, Iblîs' unique steadfastness would be rewarded when he would receive the highest place in Paradise. Such a story exalts a total love for God above even the commands of God set forth in the Sharî'ah law; but it also suggests how even the work of the Devil himself, as he inspires people to the lesser loves that veil them from the love of God, indirectly an effect of the universal striving toward God of all creation, including the Devil.

The quṭb saint as cosmic axis

But if the cosmic purposiveness were to be complete, they felt, then one must posit something more than the imperfect human we commonly see—we must assume that somewhere there is the 'perfect man', in whom this cosmically culminative human role should be brought to perfection. There must be a person who fulfills human nature (the distinctive feature of which is rationality) by knowing all things and above all knowing God totally. Who but the perfected Ṣûfî saint, with his divine communion, fits this requirement? Accordingly, it came to be believed that some one of the Ṣûfî pîr masters was the *quṭb*, the pole, or axis around which the whole universe revolves—in Aristotelian terms, the final cause of all sublunar existence: the 'perfect man', for the sake of whose perfection all the elements of nature, and indeed even all other humans, exist. It was never known for sure who, in any given generation, was the quṭb saint of the time; his authority was total, but it was secret. Muḥammad had been this perfect man in his time, of course; but the natural world could never exist without the perfect saint, even though his mission now no longer included prophecy.

This conception was grounded in older Irano-Semitic and Hellenistic theorizing, and was deeply influenced by Shî'î conceptions of the sinless imâm, ever present (even if hidden) as guarantor of the faith. But it was also rooted in the practical relationship of pîrî-murîdî. Following the quṭb in saintliness was a large hierarchy of lesser saints, in pyramidal ranks one below the other, down to the ordinary murîd, studying Ṣûfism at the hands of the village pîr. Each figure in the hierarchy bore, to the one above, the relation of murîd disciple, and must obey him; and was in turn pîr master to those below. The preacher 'Abdulqâdir Gîlânî was considered to have been the quṭb in his time. Niẓâmuddîn Awliyâ told how a saint flew over Gîlanî's worship service one night, without doing obeisance, and was immediately cast to the ground.

There is much that seems intangible, or else absurd, about this invisible hierarchy as it was imaginatively conceived by the faithful. The higher saints in the hierarchy shared in some degree in the cosmic role and the resultant dignity and powers of the quṭb himself. This cosmic role included giving support—as its teleological 'cause'—to the existence of the world itself, and Ṣûfî imagination painted this relation to the world in vividly active terms. The highest saints were said to move perpetually—at least in spirit—through the world, seeing that it was kept in good order; we even hear of their flying bodily across it once a night. The greater saints were responsible for perfecting the lesser. We hear how Shams-e Tabrîz, for instance, a major saint and friend of the poet-saint Jalâluddîn Rûmî, attracted in Damascus a Frankish youth who was destined to be a member of the invisible saintly hierarchy, but did not yet realize his own position. The saint (knowing the youth) engaged him in some frivolity (gambling, in fact) in which the youth lost his temper and struck the saint—only to be impressed, as the saint's true status happened soon after to be revealed upon the arrival of some disciples, with horror at what he had done; so that he was converted and sent back to western Europe to become the ruling secret saint there.

But in fact all this grandiose activity was but a corollary of what was always granted to be the central role of the saint: to come to consciousness of God. In this basic task, not only the top saints of the hierarchy but every pîr—even every murîd—shared according to his own measure. The assumed universal hierarchy of the saints was very real to those who sought to tread the mystical path. It imaged forth an essential feature of each man's inner search. They were each bound with all other pious Muslims in a common, if imprecise, obedience, the first and most visible step of which was submission to one's own pîr (and to the greater pîrs of his ṭarîqah order). There might no longer be a caliph with power in the ordinary political sense. But there remained a true spiritual caliph, the immediate representative of God, who bore a far more basic sway than any outward caliph.

The Ṣûfîs were fond of referring to Muḥammad's alleged saying, after a campaign, that his people were now returning from the lesser jihâd (holy war) to the greater jihâd—the struggle against one's own passions. This referred initially simply to the importance of the moral life. But all Ṣûfîs would agree that the only sound foundation for success in the 'lesser' jihâd was discipline in the 'greater'. And this was pre-eminently the province of the quṭb and his saints, who thus implicitly became commanders in the jihâd—even when there was no outward war.

The Ṣûfî thinker who perfected the myth of the microcosmic return, Ibn-al-'Arabî, presents us with a legal analysis, worked out in terms of fiqh, of the authority of the invisible caliph, the quṭb. The quṭb, he says, is a mujtahid, not in the ordinary way as having acquired sufficient 'ilm knowledge by study, but by direct acquaintance with the same spiritual sources that the Prophet himself drew on for legal decisions. The quṭb is the true caliph (*khalîfah*); but not so much khalîfah (representative) of the Prophet as khalîfah of God directly (though he can expound only Muḥammad's revelation and not a new one); accordingly, his authority is more direct and more cogent, even in points of 'ilm and Sharî'ah law, than that of any caliph at Baghdad—and than that of any qâḍîs and muftîs the caliph can appoint or stand guarantor for among the 'ulamâ' scholars. He was more like the Shî'î imâm, except that his position was defined without reference to historical disputes and without need to reject the associates of Muḥammad in the Shî'î manner. The invisible quṭb, then, without prejudice to any lesser role played by a caliph in Baghdad, was the true caliph of the Ummah community, as it expanded from ocean to ocean. He ruled through his invisible hierarchy, the *abdâl* saints, and finally through his more visible representatives, the pîrs. Their blessings and warnings, which amîrs generally did respect, were to be guaranteed not just by a personal sanctity but by an all-Muslim spiritual structure which was to take precedence ideally even over the Sharî'ah law of the 'ulamâ'.

With such an approach to the role of the pîrs, it could be explained, and accepted by even the most sober of Ṣûfîs—and, with them, by most of the Sharî'ah-minded 'ulamâ'—how it was that the accomplished Ṣûfî mystic was not a friend of God in vain. Already in the High Caliphal Period, miracles, which always had been ascribed to the earlier prophets, were being freely ascribed to Muḥammad himself, as the greatest of prophets. (The highest miracle was always the inimitable Qur'ân, an evidentiary miracle of special potency, since it was ever-present.) But the Ṣûfîs felt this was not an arbitrary decoration granted by God to enhance the position of His prophet with the impressionable multitude. The Prophet had obviously been the quṭb of his time—the perfect Ṣûfî, freed of all accidental and self-centred restraints. It was in virtue of this cosmic position that he could do whatever was needful to fulfill his mission. Along with the title *quṭb*, pole, an equally important title for the perfected saint was *al-ghawth al-a'ẓam*, the 'supreme defender'. Then by the same token any other great Ṣûfî too, as a 'friend (*walî*) of God' (an expression commonly rendered 'saint'), must be granted miraculous events. The 'ulamâ' of the Earlier Middle Period eventually came to accept this claim, for the most part, with only one reservation. Like the Ash'arî, al Bâqillânî, they were careful to distinguish between the fully evidentiary miracles (*mu'jizât*) of a prophet, which corroborated his teachings, and the merely incidental wonders (*karâmât*) which attended on a saint. For the more intense Ṣûfîs, this distinction was as secondary as was often the letter of Prophetic law itself.

Ṣûfism thus became a vast complex of practices and theories and hopes, in which every class shared on its own level and to its own intentions. This whole personal and social and imaginative complex, then (not merely some of the theories embodied in it), became the starting point for the creative works in philosophy and literature that Ṣûfism inspired and carried with it throughout Islamdom.

Ṣûfism as metaphysics: unitive doctrines

During the fuller mutual confrontation of intellectual traditions in the Earlier Middle Period, Ṣûfism, like the other traditions, maintained its essentially independent intellectual identity. Indeed, as a tradition it became more self-contained; for elements of other traditions were more fully integrated into it. Eventually Ṣûfîs went beyond psychological analysis and mythical cosmology to systematic exposition in the form of metaphysics. This was worked out by intellectualizing Ṣûfîs who surely did have mystical and even ecstatic experiences but whose greatest interest often seems to have lain in philosophizing.

Once the Ṣûfîs came to espouse a distinctive metaphysic, that metaphysic became the most influential form of speculation among Muslims generally. Just as Ṣûfism offered a spiritual cement for the social order—and (as we shall see) the most ennobling themes for literature—so Ṣûfism, especially the new intellectualizing expression of it, served more than any other movement to draw together all strands of intellectual life. Nothing was so congenial to it, indeed, as an atmosphere in which each truth was carefully suited to the spiritual state of the recipient. Its speculation was founded upon a Gnostic or neo-Platonist type of world-view, favoured by many Faylasûfs already, and wedded at the very core to the full apparatus of Jamâʿî-Sunnî ʿilm (and sometimes Shîʿî ʿilm as well, for Ṣûfîs were eclectic) in the cause of making intelligible the Ṣûfî mystical experience, and through it the whole social and intellectual life of Islamdom. Al-Qushayrî, Ghazâlî, and others had made Ṣûfism palatable to the Sharîʿah-minded on condition it accepted Sharʿî restrictions. This condition the proper Ṣûfîs never went back on in the letter, but their great creativity led them very far from Sharîʿah-minded doctrine in spirit, once having attained house rights.

The combination of mysticism with metaphysics is paradoxical (however common it has become in some contexts). Mystics are at ease with myths, but any approach to discursive analysis seems to contradict the ineffability of mystical experience and especially of those ecstatic experiences from which a mystic's most comprehensive sense of reality seems to flow. In fact, in reading any metaphysics produced by mystics or in a mystical context, we must always bear in mind that it will probably tend to the mythopoeic. The Ṣûfî metaphysicians handled questions formulated much like those of the Faylasûf metaphysicians, but they handled them with much greater imaginative freedom. (Sometimes their metaphysics has been set off as 'theosophy' in distinction from metaphysics limited to supposedly 'public' premises—or from theology based on revelations or public access. But it is doubtful whether a sharp line can be drawn in principle; for any metaphysics requires, in fact—like that of the Ṣûfîs—a generous dose of imaginative commitment, however much a given school may try to limit its own imaginative resources as did the Faylasûfs.)

Yet mystics may conceivably make a distinctive contribution to the sort of questions metaphysicians would like to study. Whether or no their drive toward detachment from personal engagements and prejudices allows them to escape, in a measure, from that plague of any serious philosopher, unconscious precommitments, yet certainly the sort of experiences they go through, both the moral discipline of the self and the probing of the consciousness, are such as to open unusual perspectives on any more general questions. Nor can it be taken for granted that reality is wholly subject to reproducible public observation and statistical measurement such as most metaphysicians hope to base themselves on. (Even phenomena such as those called 'extrasensory' may be real enough without being subject to ordinary expectations of repetitiveness and so of public analysis.) And mystics, with their intensive discipline of consciousness, may be in a favourable position to be sensitive to any less predictable dimensions of reality.

In any case, the Ṣûfî metaphysicians must be read with two sorts of warning. Both Ṣûfîs and Faylasûfs tried to describe reality on the basis of what was required to make moral and aesthetic sense of the universe as we confront it. (Neither granted that it might ultimately not make sense.) But whereas the Faylasûfs tried to use only premises (especially logical or mathematical premises) that at least appeared to command inescapable human assent, the Ṣûfîs often backed up their statements with an appeal to special experience (even when they were contradicting another Ṣûfî who had also appealed to such experience); not reckoning with just the lowest common denominator of experience in anyone, but taking into account the seemingly extraordinary. Secondly, the same trust in the process of immediate experiencing left the Ṣûfîs free to regard no given verbal formulation as absolute, such that other points could be derived logically from it directly; any given formulation was felt as an image indicating one aspect of a truth (often regarded as accessible only at a given level of experiencing), which need not be incompatible with contrasting complementary aspects, though the formulation of those aspects might appear contradictory. One can scarcely tie down a true mystic to any unequivocal assertion about ultimate matters unless one allows him also its opposite in a different context.[6]

Mystics have, in fact, been concerned especially with one sort of intellectual problem, which has led them to favour one sort of metaphysical formulation:

[6] Eugene T. Gendlin, *Experiencing and the Creation of Meaning* (Glencoe, Ill., 1962), points out the degree to which it is legitimate (from the viewpoint of the modern phenomenological tradition) to recognize that live conceptualization is in continuous interplay with subjective experiencing and is in fact falsified when frozen, apart from that experiencing, into mutually exclusive categories. This sort of modern analysis is helping us to appreciate the intellectual claims of many writers whom Westerners, at least, in an overly positivistic mood, had for two or three centuries discounted as wanting in logical rigour.

what may be called, generally, 'unitive' formulations, answering to 'unitive' mystical experiences. Philosophically inclined mystics, with their ecstatic experiences of feeling at one with all, have had pressing reasons, even more than other philosophers, for conceiving all existence as fundamentally one—for insisting that the multiplicity and change we see about us is somehow illusory. They have not insisted on its illusoriness merely in the manner of a scientist who might reduce everything to a mathematical field of forces—or, as in kalâm disputation, to an ever newly created range of atom-moments, though Ṣûfî metaphysicians were glad to make use of such an idea. On the basis of experience that they have been convinced is privileged as a medium of observation, a medium as valid as is external light to the senses, they have found it necessary to assert, in some sense or other, that nothing is real but what can be identified as divine. When it is pointed out, in the Qur'an, that 'everything is perishing except His face', this has suggested to them not mere transience of things otherwise perfectly real, but some far-reaching falsity in our perceiving them as if they endured at all; only God's face, His essence, is not subject to this falsity.

For Ṣûfîs, the metaphysical problem par excellence, then, became to analyze just what such an experiential observation could mean: in what sense of such terms as 'real' and 'God' can one say that nothing is real but God? Sometimes scholars apply summary terms to the various solutions, calling a writer a 'pantheist' (because he seems to define 'God' so as to include all that most people would call 'real'), or a 'monist' (because he seems to say that all that appears—however complex—is of one divine substance); but such tags are of marginal help in understanding these writers. One must recognize that they were trying to find ways to express a persistent insight which may be called 'unitive', and their problem was to express this insight without inconsistency with other insights similarly grounded in experience and of equal validity; for instance, with the insight that human beings are morally responsible—seemingly vitiated by an assertion of the unity of everything in God.

Among the most influential intellectual figures in the century or so following Ghazâlî were two great Ṣûfî metaphysicians. At the end of the twelfth century—a generation rich in Ṣûfî thinkers—they developed two contrasting forms of unitive doctrine, which not all Ṣûfîs accepted but which grew increasingly influential with the centuries. Shihâbuddîn Yaḥyà Suhravardî called *Shaykh al-Ishrâq*, master of Illumination (d. 1191), on the basis of a fairly straight Aristotelianism as prolegomena, developed a philosophy of Divine Light as the sole substance of being. Ibn-al-'Arabî (d. 1240) elaborated the Ṣûfî myth of the 'perfect man' as microcosm in the direction of a total ontology.

In contrast even to Ghazâlî, and still more to the earlier Ḥadîth folk, neither was historically minded. Though each had something to say about world history, their universe was essentially timeless, as was their religion.

For them, the great, concrete Muslim state had disappeared from philosophy as effectively as from the political map; their thought was diffused, by their admirers, from Morocco to Java in a society which likewise tended to ignore the undependable frivolity of military politics. But the thinking of these Ṣûfîs was nonetheless Islamic. Like the piety of the High Caliphal Period, it took off from the Qur'ân, bringing into focus potentialities in that document that had not been much explored before. If we regard the challenge laid down by the Qur'ân as summoning above all to *tawḥîd*, 'unity', to affirming (in thought and in life) the unity, the singularity of the Divine and its moral demands, then it is understandable that this challenge can take shape, for a contemplative mind, in the summons to affirm the moral unity of God's creation, to understand the whole as an expression of cosmic unity, in harmony with which one's life is to be ordered. At least for the pre-Modern mind, in such a perspective, the variables of history can become secondary concerns, more relevant as examples and illustrations than in themselves. Instead of historical commitment, intellectually, such a summons would call for a unitive metaphysic to tie the whole together. It was as a deeper probing of what was necessarily implied in the common Muslim's assertion of tawḥîd, God's unity, that Ṣûfîs saw their own thinking.

What is more, something of such a mood can be felt in the Qur'ân itself precisely in its most eloquent moments. One of the most striking passages in the Qur'ân is the 'Light Verse' and what follows (XXIV, 35 ff.)—which is, in the first instance, an eloquent contrast between God's guidance of humans and his abandonment of them, but which also implies an interpretation of the divine presence that invites to a unitive idea of total reality. The opening phrases of the passage run as follows:

'God is the light of the heavens and the earth; the likeness of His light is a niche wherein is a lamp (the lamp in a glass, the glass as though it were a glittering star) kindled from a blessèd tree, an olive neither eastern nor western, whose oil would almost shine out even if no fire touched it; light upon light. God guides to His light whom He wills. God poses likenesses for people; God has knowledge of everything.'

The immediate reference of these lines is to the light provided by God's guidance (as becomes especially clear from the later contrasting lines which speak of 'darknesses one upon another' encompassing those who reject God's guidance). The light is the light of divine revelation. But the characterization of God himself as light is explicit. And if one sets the passage against its cultural environment in Muḥammad's time, this fact carries weight. If the passage is read with continuity, it appears that the lamp that serves to exemplify God's light is in fact the lamp of a monastery in the desert, whose retired monks are commended for their piety. And in the monotheistic tradition which those monks represented, the description of God as light was commonplace, going back at least to the Gospel of John. Wherever the term had appeared, it had carried implications of a deeper understanding of the relation between God and his creation than was implied on the surface of the Hebrew creation story.

Certainly, the phrases quoted can all be understood on a relatively immediate level as describing revelation. Every word counts even on this level: the full impression of brilliance and purity, of detachment from any local or transient involvement, and withal of perfect security and dependability, requires every touch in the elaborate simile. Yet the impression remains of a reconditely elaborate statement which would seem to describe more than merely the purity and dependability of God's word; an impression which seems to invite (as so often in the Qur'ân) the further consideration which the Qur'ân itself often suggests. And indeed if one begins to study the phrases closely, one finds it quite possible to see there a symbolic or mythic image of God's way with heaven and earth. Ghazâlî, arguing closely, tried to show that consideration of the semantics of the term 'light' confirms this. He maintained that intellectual understanding carries, more accurately than does physical seeing, the connotations implied in an ultimate moral usage of the terms; hence 'light' applies more properly to our relation to God as revealer than to our relation to the material sun. But the course of his argument leads one to surmise also that no sharp distinction can be drawn between God's relation to us as revealer and his relation to us as creator and sustainer. Both can be equally implied in the simile of light. (After all, presumably God's very being can be known to us, in any case, only through His own revelation and in terms appropriate to that revelation.)

Yaḥyà Suhravardî: the metaphysics of light

Ghazâlî did not carry his analysis so far as to establish a general doctrine of ontology. But such work as his prepared the way for more developed metaphysics among the intellectually curious; notably for Yaḥyà Suhravardî's use of the concept 'light': the universal light by which and toward which all things grow. For Suhravardî, revelation becomes generalized to include not merely divine guidance of human beings who submit, but all divine direction of the universe. (This sense of it is already present in the Qur'ân, which presents God's guiding the bees and the ants in their accustomed ways as some sort of revelation.) That is, at every level of being, and not only on the level of human moral consciousness, God intervenes to draw creatures toward His own norms: in this sense, His is a universal light toward which all things grow.

But all things also grow by means of that same light. For revelation that is so pervasive cannot be distinguished from God's actual sustenance of the creatures (at least on any level below the highest human level). Both guidance and sustenance are God's creative action: in a relatively gross form, it is by that action that we perceive outward images; in its proper reality, that action constitutes the ultimate substance of all things in their infinite differentiation. The darkness of inert materiality is merely potentiality, into which the actuality of Light can shine, producing all that appears. Thus everything is an expression of a single divine energy, called light from its most tangible pure form.

This is given meaning, then, by the conception of the microcosm, the human being who fulfills the purpose of creation in his consciousness, which Ṣûfîs found almost inescapable if they were to make sense of the whole. With that conception one defines a universal purpose, ultimately the same both in the differentiation of creation outward from God and in the return of that creation on a higher level back to its true oneness in God: the self-fulfillment of the light in total awareness. The human responsibility is to allow the light in oneself to shine fully, and hence in unity with the ultimate light; otherwise it will be swallowed up in darkness instead.

Suhravardî claimed that the wisdom he was presenting was nothing but a restatement, guided by mystical inspiration, of the unitive wisdom of ancient ages, which had been obscured by the Faylasûfs since Aristotle (and of course never was known to the ordinary adherents of the prophets). He avowed himself the reviver of Plato as against Aristotle, and even of an ancient Iranian—perhaps Manichean esoteric tradition as against the standard exoteric Mazdean doctrine; and both the Platonic and the esoteric Iranian traditions he traced back to the Hermes of the Hermetic corpus (a late Greek collection of mystical and symbolical speculations which was thought to be far older than Plato or Pythagoras). Indeed, Suhravardî's thinking shares much with that of the neo-Platonists and of others who looked to the yet more esoteric strains of the Hellenic heritage. They had started with the same unitive problem as he had, and some of their most essential writings had been long accessible to any Muslim concerned with such questions. But his work presents a new vision of his own, reinterpreting in a fresh integration the heritages he cited. And however much it was guided by the neo-Platonists and other Philosophers, it expressed also a new and personal confrontation with the prophetic tradition, particularly in its Islamic form. I believe that Suhravardî was responding vitally to the life challenge embodied in the Qur'ân.

His system is tightly worked out—nothing fails to support his distinctive vision. His unitive metaphysic is based on an eagerly argued identification of three seemingly different sorts of clarity: that of logical rational consciousness; that of the formal essences of whatever is (the distinctness of which makes things intelligible to the mind); and that of the physical medium of perception—light, which he interpreted as energy (especially as thermal energy), and in which he included seemingly related phenomena such as sound waves. Thus he integrated the whole physical universe into his vision. He supported his system on many psychological and physical observations, and ultimately on an appeal to the inherent 'nobility' of things; taking it for granted, for instance, that the less noble cannot be the cause of the more noble.

(He expected to be understood, moreover, only by the noble of soul; among the prerequisites he listed for studying his book was a gentle mild asceticism, which included vegetarianism.) But he argued it out by way of an incisive technical re-evaluation of the analyses and categories of Aristotle (as understood by Ibn-Sînâ).

He defined five of the ten irreducible 'modes of being', identified by Aristotle, in such form that they could be made variants on Aristotle's mode 'relation'. So throughout: he redefined various Aristotelian notions in a highly abstract form, so that the common-sense cases envisaged by Aristotle could appear as but special cases of much more general categories—other cases of which would be found beyond the sensory realm in the realms of mystical experience. In this way he identified, particularly, the 'forms' of Aristotle's system with the 'ideas' of Plato's thought: Plato and Aristotle were seeing in different perspectives the same fact, that each sort of thing had an essential reality given transcendently (so Plato) but embodied in the individual thing (so Aristotle)—because that thing itself was essentially transcendent.

But this reconciliation of Aristotle and Plato was not, I think, designed primarily to show their philosophic harmony: Suhravardî insisted that Aristotle's system was of a lower order than Plato's (and hence more accessible on an exoteric basis), and even sometimes simply wrong. Suhravardî used the ideas of both philosophers to lead up to a sense of essences different from what could be found in either Aristotle or even Plato, though allied to both. For he interpreted them both by way of the old Mazdean teaching about angels: that every substance and every person had its guiding angel, a personified ideality of form which was not merely a metaphysical abstraction but represented in everything a personalized, dynamic aspect. This Mazdean inspiration was genuine and served his purpose well. However, the result was not Mazdean either. Though he introduced the Mazdean angels to represent the organic vitality he felt in all being, he used them in a context that remained Hellenic: for instance, the greater angels were identified with the intellects of the neo-Platonic system and so with the planets as envisaged by Ptolemy, contrary at least to known Mazdean tradition. Though we know little of the particular variants of the Mazdean tradition to which he appealed, it is conceivable that sometimes he used Mazdean terms arbitarily, almost as decoration. It was neither a justification of the Philosophic tradition nor fidelity to an esoteric Mazdean one that moved Suhravardî, but his own experience as a Muslim mystic.

The spirit of the whole was identifiably Suhravardî's own, and as such Islamic. This fact was expressed in his eschatology. The Qur'ânic challenge was not interpreted kerygmatically but in terms of an ever-present natural situation in which the Prophet is merely an exemplary figure. Yet a strong sense of final judgment remained, as in the Abrahamic tradition, and that judgment was not interpreted dualistically in the Manichean manner but consistently with the Islamic appeal to total divine lordship.

I think it was especially by way of his third form of clarity—the visible light itself—that he introduced the Qur'ânic challenge. The rationality and the formality of the Philosophic traditions were essentially abstract and timeless. Visible light, in contrast, is in some sense concrete, even contingent. It is in the actuality of the light itself that we can feel the Qur'ânic urgency in Suhravardî's thinking. Thereby Suhravardî combined the moral decisiveness of the monotheistic tradition, for which a person's single lifetime was decisive, with that sense of the unity of nature which is expressed in the ancient doctrine of the gradation of souls among all species and of reincarnation among them. Suhravardî saw souls as a multitude of irreversibly individual lights (energies), which get entrapped in dark (latent material) bodies; their first entrapment is the least onerous, being in a human body capable of self-purification; but if (at death) they have not become pure enough to escape from the darkness and rejoin the heavenly light, they are doomed to ever darker entrapment as they are reborn in lesser beings.

For Suhravardî, Falsafah, even in its metaphysics, must be taken seriously; it was indeed a preparatory discipline of the soul, as the Faylasûfs had claimed, and not a merely useful set of natural sciences as Ghazâlî had presented it. But it prepared for something utterly beyond its own intellectual reach—for the unitive insights that mystical experience made possible. On the other hand, mystical experience without the underpinning of the metaphysical understanding offered by Falsafah could lead the speculative mystic sadly astray. Such an attitude toward Falsafah was to characterize permanently the 'Ishrâqî' school of mystical philosophers who were to build on Suhravardî's foundations.

However, a work like Suhravardî's cannot be left merely at metaphysics. Ṣûfî philosophy such as his afforded an inexhaustible channel for personal exploration. The great book *Ḥikmat al-Ishrâq* (*The Wisdom of Illumination*), of Yaḥyà Suhravardî, for instance, is markedly unified by its prevailing Ṣûfî themes, the exclusive reality of the Light and the crucial character of the soul's ascent in the Light. Yet at the same time it carries the reader through very diverse fascinating realms of thought. In its earlier part we explore a series of problems in physics and other parts of natural science, diverging curiously and pertinently from Peripatetic orthodoxy. In like manner, he analyzes a number of points of abstract logic, answering the philosopher in us as well as the scientist (if we may distinguish the two moods). But all this is mere propaedeutic to the major, more strictly mystical part of his work. Within this work we have interwoven, on the one hand, cosmic speculation—the relation of the beings of earth to the heavens and to time itself; and, on the other hand, the psychology of spiritual development. At every point Suhravardî is, if not always original, at least incisive and fresh. But what is perhaps most charming about the work is the grand aesthetic vision that is built up out of its many details—some of which seem to be present indeed chiefly for the sake of the elegance of the cosmic vistas which are painted. The whole world in all its parts is seen, under Suhravardî's perspective, as a wondrous whole in which the individual soul has a great and meaningful part to play. His chief work has much of the literary appeal of a dramatic epic.

The works that have made Suhravardî famous were published already when he was in his thirties. He was an intellectually self-confident young man, eager to persuade the rulers of the world of his opinions, and travelled widely, accepting court patronage. At about thirty he settled at Aleppo in Syria (whence he was called Suhravardî Ḥalabî, the Aleppine), where he was caught in a Sharî'ah-minded revivalism which had been evoked in part by the Crusades. Those Shar'î 'ulamâ' who were hostile to Ṣûfism, at least to speculative Ṣûfism, were able to win the ear of Saladin, whose son was amîr at Aleppo, and Suhravardî was executed at thirty-six or thirty-eight on suspicion of being in league with the Ismâ'îlîs to overthrow Jamâ'î-Sunnî rule.

Ibn-al-'Arabî: the metaphysics of love

Even more widely influential than Yaḥyà Suhravardî was his younger contemporary, Muḥyi-l-dîn Muḥammad Ibn-al-'Arabî (1165–1240); often called Ibn-'Arabî), whom we have already met as theoretician of Ṣûfî legal independence. (He is commonly known as *al-Shaykh al-Akbar*, 'the Greatest Master'; like many other Muslim teachers, he is thus referred to by a title of respect rather than by a proper name.) Suhravardî was very systematic, and concerned himself above all with the structure of the cosmos and its processes, all conceived in the one manner, as Light. Muḥyi-l-dîn Ibn-al-'Arabî was also intensely concerned with the problems of unitive metaphysics on the level of cosmology; but he was at least as much concerned with the problems raised by the perception of cosmic unity for personal experience. The result was a rich and far-ranging synthesis of philosophical learning and mystical lore.

Ibn-al-'Arabî had begun his career in Spain. He revered his Spanish teachers (two of whom were honoured women Ṣûfîs); but he found the intellectual resources of Spain provincial, and the Berber government (after the collapse of the party kings) ill-disposed toward esoteric speculation. He set off on a ḥajj pilgrimage, and travelled in Egypt, Arabia, and Syria widely before finally settling in the city of ancient prophets' tombs, Damascus, where his own tomb was later added to the attractions for the pious. In a series of stays in Mecca he composed (or at least initiated) the greatest among his numerous works, the vast *Futûḥât Makkiyyah* (*Meccan Revelations*), which he regarded as divinely inspired, though he did not claim technical prophethood. His writings were intensely allusive and deliberately made confusing, all his phrases being so turned that it would be impossible to interpret him with assurance in any simplistic way. (He insisted that his true doctrine could be known only if one pieced it together from scattered references in the whole of the *Revelations*). Nevertheless, even in his lifetime they were highly prized, and subsequently (as interpreted orally by his disciples, but also directly as written works) they became the most important single source of Ṣûfî speculation.

Ibn-al-ʿArabî was more fully in the main stream of avant-garde Ṣûfî thinking in his time than was Yaḥyà Suhravardî. He corresponded with a major disciple of Najmuddin Kubrà (d. 1220) of Khwârazm on the Oxus (founder of the Kubrawî ṭarîqah and a leader of local resistance against the Mongols), who is said to have popularized metaphysical speculation among Ṣûfîs. Another contemporary, at Shîrâz, developed a dialectic of love very like his. But Ibn-al-ʿArabî developed a more comprehensive synthesis than any.

He willingly made use of every pattern of conceptualizing that had been known in Islamdom: not only earlier Ṣûfî mythopoeic writings, but Ashʿarî and Muʿtazilî kalâm disputation, the Bâṭinî speculations of the Ismâʿîlîs, and of course the various strands of the older philosophical heritage, including the neo-Platonist notion of creation by divine emanations. Ibn-al-ʿArabî had a very wide personal culture, which allowed him to use such references effectively. But his learning was more literary than either scientific or historical. He saw all questions from a metaphysical angle, and was not seriously concerned with positive science. It is typical that he took up the common notion that Falsafah studies had originated with the Hermes of the Greek Hermetic corpus (identified with the Biblical patriarch Enoch—whom Muslims knew as the prophet Idrîs), just as the Sharîʿah-minded studies were supposed to have originated with the prophet Muḥammad. He regarded differences among Faylasûfs as representing different interpretations of Idrîs' revelation just as differences among Sharîʿah-minded ʿulamâʾ represented different interpretations of Muḥammad's revelation.

But Ibn-al-ʿArabî relied also on his personal experience and taste. It is just as typical of him that he legitimized the synthesis that he made of Falsafah metaphysics by appeal to his private experience: he claimed that he himself had talked with Idrîs in a vision, and so was in a position to settle the Faylasûfs' disputes. Such a claim could be both honest and meaningful, I must point out, so long as it was only speculative questions that really mattered to him; for the comprehensive reconciliations he was accustomed to find in such questions, which made allowance for all possible positions, were, in fact, guided ultimately by a personal moral judgment (that all insight carries some truth, and all truth is one); and they seem to have emerged for him (at least at some stage of his mental process) in the form of dreams and ecstasies. Ibn-al-ʿArabî himself recognized, in a somewhat different form from the Faylasûfs, that any revelation arises (like all moral action) from the essence of the person receiving it, not from an arbitrary external event; his descriptions of revelation must be read in the light of this.

If Ibn-al-'Arabî's work can be treated as having a single focus, that focus was the perfecting of the myth of the microcosmic return as vehicle for a complete and systematic metaphysical doctrine at once of cosmology and of mystical psychology. Ibn-al-'Arabî became known especially for the ontology implied in this myth. His formulation of the problem of unitive metaphysics is summed up in the phrase *waḥdat al-wujûd*, 'the oneness of existence', which interpreted all that is or might be as manifestations of the various 'beautiful names' of God, His attributes, as understood by way of the experience of mystical love. Every name indicated potentialities in God's essence, the realization of which through God's self-objectification in love constituted existence. Thus God was many and the universe one—or, to put it with a specious clarity, the One reality was at once one and many in different perspectives. (The meaning of terms like 'oneness', 'existence', the 'names of God', and perhaps especially 'love', must, of course, be understood only in the total context of Ibn-al-'Arabî's thinking; needless to say, no deduction is authorized from his general doctrine beyond what is present in the elements that go to compose it in his own work.)

It was in the microcosmic return that true oneness was realized. This return, it seems, begins for Ibn-al-'Arabî in the very moment of creation. The individual beings become actual only in at least a rudimentary desire or 'love'—the loving response of the individual potentialities to the evocative love of the divine Actuality for these potentialities which are expressions of Itself. Hence all beings are at once wholly self-determined, for they are still fulfilling their several individual potentialities, however full is their response to God; and yet exist only as moments in God's love of his own self-fulfillment. Divine love is so universal that it will eventually dissolve even Hell—which is anyway merely a false, properly a limited, point of view on the part of incompletely actualized potentialities. (To use modern terms, we may say that such a conception accounts for the imperious fact that our conscious wills presuppose for their very self-definition, as capable of detached choice, a point of reference beyond the determinate natural order; and at the same time the conception provides a perspective in which, however petty our choices, however blind, they are not arbitrary defiance of the natural order and meaningless, but are to be seen as gropings within a range of responses the potential meaningfulness of which is infinite.) For whatever a man loves, by his very existence he is inchoately loving God; his most self-centred passions are but misplaced piety.

The scholar Massignon has pointed out that Ibn-al-'Arabî was dealing with the same contrast that was a central theme of the Ṣûfî al-Ḥallâj, executed at the end of the High Caliphate. Al-Ḥallâj likewise saw human nature as playing a cosmic role as mirror of the divine nature and its attributes, with which it was united in longing and love. But al-Ḥallâj felt intensely the contrast between the ultimate unity, which ought to overcome all separation, and the ineluctable separation of lover from beloved, sundered by a radical gulf. The tension between ultimate unity and felt separation was a point of the human condition, not to be finally resolved this side of death. On the contrary, for Ibn-al-'Arabî the contrast was readily understood as a logically necessary relation—and it might seem as if the tension it bespoke were as readily resolved. Of course, the tension remained, on its own level. But it is true, I think, that Ibn-al-'Arabî found the religious challenge more insistently elsewhere, in the universality of cosmic potentialities—potentialities that he himself found fulfilled in his own comprehensive visions.

A major difference between the two mystics was the use of systematic metaphysics by Ibn-al-'Arabî where al-Ḥallâj used chiefly what can be called poetic myth. But still more important is the difference in devotional posture. For Ibn-al-'Arabî, in an age when Ṣûfism need not be an unexpected isolating personal mountain-peak experience but offered a broad and even varied pattern of great expectations to almost any aspirant, it may have been more possible to cultivate an unanguished, contemplative universal vision, perhaps more aesthetic than moral in tone.

This sort of expectation was expressed most clearly in Ibn-al-'Arabî's teachings about the 'perfect man', the quṭb saint. The divine oneness was most especially realized in the oneness of the perfected saint with God—of the saint who fulfilled God's purpose of self-knowledge, since in him also all cosmic complexity—the reality of all God's names—was itself fulfilled. Every prophet was such a 'perfect man', as were the quṭb saints when there was no prophet; the type of the 'perfect man' was Muḥammad. And every individual should strive for that same goal. Through the oneness achieved by the 'perfect man', the oneness of God himself was to be understood, and the illusoriness of all multiplicity so far as it seemed not to participate in this oneness. On such a basis, even the separation of the soul from God was not a dread chasm but a chance of viewpoint. The soul's own calling was more imperious: to fulfill itself in total awareness and response.

Ibn-al-'Arabî also, like Suhravardî, made use of the notion of the divine Light as medium of total consciousness; but only as one way of approach among others. Somewhere in his work, one feels, can be found every possible unitive approach, all integrated with his central insights. For most Ṣûfîs, his comprehensive solution of the unitive problem in terms of actualization through love was to prove definitive.

With Ibn-al-'Arabî and the Ṣûfî metaphysicians of his time, the Islamic tradition has seemed to many to have become practically unrecognizable. As in Yaḥyà Suhravardî, there can seem little trace of anything truly Qur'ânic in Ibn-al-'Arabî's religion. The repeated references to the Qur'ân can seem like window dressing.

One of his most famous works, the *Bezels of Wisdom* (*Fuṣûṣ al-ḥikam*), is, in effect, a Qur'ân commentary ordered not by sûrah chapters but by the various prophets mentioned in the Qur'ân. In the section on Moses, Ibn-al-

'Arabî has a delightful exegesis of Moses' conversation with Pharoah as reported in the Qur'ân (sûrah 26). When Pharoah asks Moses *what* is God, he is actually testing him; for Pharoah too has esoteric knowledge, though he uses it perversely: if Moses responds correctly with a description of God's essence (His *what*ness), the courtiers will take him for a fool; but when Moses responds rhetorically with a description of God's action instead—as lord of creation—Pharaoh shows that Moses has not given a straight answer; and then when Moses defends his position with a reference to God's outward power (according to Ibn-al-'Arabî's exegesis), Pharaoh claims to oppose Moses by virtue of representing outward power on earth, a power necessarily itself derived from God. Ibn-al-'Arabî even uses a pun in his exegesis. What he writes is subtle analysis of the relation of God's being to various creaturely manifestations of it, but it all seems remote from the spirit of the Qur'ânic story of Pharaoh's stubborn refusal to honour the Creator-god.

Ibn-al-'Arabî, however, was very sophisticated in his methods of exegesis. He accepted the rules laid down by Ghazâlî limiting metaphorical exegesis of Qur'ân and ḥadîth reports; he was glad to acknowledge literal meanings and the authority of Arabic linguistic usage. But in addition, he saw 'parallel' evocative implications in the texts, which he made the basis of a search for the bâṭin, inward, meanings of them. In fact, it can be argued that if one pushes far enough the implications of recognizing evil human power in a cosmos ruled by an omnipotent Creator-god (the obvious subject of the Qur'ânic text), just those dilemmas will arise that Ibn-al-'Arabî was here exploring. Nor need it have been merely for convention's sake that Ibn-al-'Arabî used a Qur'ânic text rather than some secular one through which to pursue his study in depth. The whole Qur'ân is suffused with a mood of ultimacy, and its cryptic style makes every verse call out for further exploration in some such vein. The Qur'ânic challenge must have been real to him just as it was to Suhravardî. Ibn-al-'Arabî was not merely a part of the Islamic tradition in the sense of participating vigorously in its latter-day dialogue; he was also committed directly to its creative moment of departure.

As with Suhravardî, it was in a non-kerygmatic aspect that the Qur'ân appealed; but Ibn-al-'Arabî was less concerned with the finality of Judgment that impressed Suhravardî. He dealt most eagerly with two great themes of the monotheistic traditions: the omnipotence of God; and the phenomenon of prophethood, the personal role of the man of revelation. Most Muslims had insisted (in contrast to the Christian tradition) on rejecting any limitations on God's power that would define what He could not do or must do; and on the human (and universal) character of the men who reveal God; and such emphases were rooted in the Qur'ân. In both points, Ibn-al-'Arabî was very Islamic and contrasts to neo-Platonists or Manicheans or any earlier representatives of a myth of microcosmic return. His doctrine of God's unity is oriented not so much to the moral or rational purity of God as to His omnipotence and omni-effectiveness. Apparent evil is neither imperfection nor opposition nor even the unavoidable result of freedom, but a veiled expression of God's majesty. And his doctrine of human prophethood—expanded to include the doctrine of the 'perfect man'—is equally central to his thinking.

Ibn-al-'Arabî's doctrine of prophethood and the 'perfect man' is related to an earlier moment in the monotheistic tradition—that of Christianity—in his treatment of Jesus in the *Bezels of Wisdom*. There he comes precariously close to accepting a doctrine of the divine and human 'two natures' of Christ that is almost incarnational, though persuasively based on Qur'ânic passages. But in his very assertion of the divine presence in Jesus' healings, for instance, he effectively insists on the humanness of Jesus as a man. His point was not to exalt Jesus as unique, but to show how the divine presence appears in any prophet—indeed, in any man formed to be revelatory spokesman for God. With his analysis of Jesus he helped to show that divinely formed spokesmen for God must always arise—though after the advent of the most perfect one, Muḥammad, they must be called saints rather than prophets. And the role of these saints was to guide the saving and saved community, as ever in the Abrahamic traditions; though invisibly and with little reference to outward history.

In solving the unitive problem by way of the myth of the microcosmic return and of the constitutive power of love, Ibn-al-'Arabî concerned himself necessarily with all the problems that arise in the mystical relationship of the soul to the divine, and particularly with the relationships implied in the term 'love'. This notion was empirical as well as theoretical. As the individual personality was laid bare and deepened in the mystical experience, it found itself responding ever more intensely to something that seemed at once beyond itself and also the very core to which its self-stripping was leading. The intensity of response, especially in ecstatic experiences, could be spoken of only in terms of love; but what could be the meaning of passionate love by a self which was losing more and more of its selfhood, for a beyond which seemed at the same time its truest inner self? Put in cosmological terms, what could be the meaning of a love between God and an expression of His attributes? To such a question, Ibn-al-'Arabî wrote answers in terms of myths, of straight Qur'ân commentary, of subtle metaphysics, and, most favouredly, of love poetry each line of which carried metaphysical implications—explained in Ibn-al-'Arabî's own commentary to the verses. Out of the cumulative mass of exposition, or perhaps out of a single line or a single image which met the condition of an individual reader at a given moment, answers emerged richly enough to enthrall generations of Ṣûfîs.[7]

[7] The Ṣûfî tradition of Ibn-al-'Arabî, like that of Yaḥyà Suhravardî, is still alive and ought preferably to be learned in apprenticeship to the present masters. Titus Burckhardt is one modern writer who has studied with some of them and has been translated from French into English, *An Introduction to Sufi Doctrine*. Unfortunately, he rejects a historical perspective as essentially irrelevant; yet does not refrain from making untenable judgments of an essentially historical character. More philological scholars have

Ibn-al-ʻArabî's work did not merely settle questions that had arisen in Ṣûfî experience. It was also a starting point for further questioning. If the whole of life truly was so much of cosmic loving, everything in life could become quiveringly important—and all received ways could be put in question; even Ṣûfî ways. Ibn-al-ʻArabî's sense of human destiny was thus hugely expansive. It could be used in relatively private ways, to explain the tremendous impact of mystical experience. It could also be used in more public ways, to justify what might otherwise seem utopian hopes for the human future. We shall see that in the Later Middle Period it was often combined with a Shîʻî chiliasm in the cause of justice or of freedom. And it could also set off the odd individual onto unpredictable paths of his own.

Ṣûfism as poetry: Jalâluddîn Rûmî

Despite the popularity of metaphysics, the most popular and most frequent literary expression of the Ṣûfî vision took the form of actual poetry. Besides Ibn-al-ʻArabî, some other Arabic poets wrote compositions expressing, in the forms made familiar by ordinary love poetry, the Ṣûfî experience of divine love; and many Persian poets did the like. But in Persian, in addition, a series of poets arose who expressed not only certain mystical experiences but the whole Ṣûfî vision of life in poetic form, especially in long narrative couplet poems (in Persian, *mas̄navî*), sometimes called epics. The greatest of these Ṣûfî couplet poems was the *Mas̄navî-e Maʻnavî*, the *Poem of Inner Meanings*, composed in the years just following 1258 by Mawlânâ Jalâluddîn Rûmî (1207–1273) at Ḳonya in central Anatolia. (He is most frequently known as 'Mawlânâ', 'our master', according to the custom of preferring titles of respect to simple names.[8]

---

gradually built up a different sort of understanding: Ignaz Goldziher in the chapter on Ṣûfîs in *Richtungen der islamischen Koranauslegung* (Leyden, 1918); Tor Andrae at several places in *Die person Muhammeds in lehre und glauben seiner gemeinde* (Uppsala, 1917); and especially H. S. Nyberg, in the long introduction to *Kleinere Schriften des Ibn al-ʻArabî* (Leyden, 1919), who analyzes his technical terms, their functions in his metaphysic of divinity and cosmos and microcosm, and the origins of the notions he used; and A. E. Affifi, *The Mystical Philosophy of Muḥyid-din-ibnul-'Arabi* (Cambridge University Press, 1939), who shows how effectively Ibn-al-ʻArabî developed a 'pantheism' in which everything was truly itself and yet also truly God, but who is sometimes too preoccupied with logical consistency, in necessarily trans-logical realms of metaphysics, to see what is actually going on. Louis Massignon in *La passion d'al-Ḥallâj, martyr mystique de l'Islam* (Paris, 1922), has some keen observations; Reynold Nicholson, in *The Idea of Personality in Ṣûfism* (Cambridge, 1923), shows where some problems lie in interpreting his substantive meaning. The most brilliantly subtle of the scholarly interpreters is Henry Corbin, *L'imagination créatrice dans Ibn-ʻArabî* (Paris, 1958), who, however, is an apologist for a certain mystical form of Shîʻism and is undependable as to historical actuality. The most comprehensive modern study is contained in several solid works by M. Asin-Palacios, notably in *El mistico murciano Abenarabi*, 3 vols. (Madrid, 1926–27); he looks at him from a friendly Christian viewpoint.

[8] The Mas̄navî is available in an English prose translation by Reynold Nicholson, *The Mathnawí of Jalálu'd-din Rúmí*, 8 vols. (London, 1925–40) (E. J. W. Gibb Memorial Series, n.s. vol. 4). which is not very readable but is reasonably accurate. The various

Rûmî's family had migrated from Balkh near the Oxus to Anatolia (the Seljuḳ kingdom of Rûm, whence his name); there and in Syria Rûmî lived out the time of the Mongol invasions. His father had been a Ṣûfî pîr, and though he died while Rûmî was still young, Rûmî's teachers made sure that he got a good training not only in the Shar'î disciplines but in his father's Ṣûfî tradition. The great inspiration of his life was his encounter with a wandering Ṣûfî pîr of dubious antecedents (some said he was a son of the last Ismâ'îlî imâm of Alamût), Shams-e Tabrîz, a wildly unpredictable man who defied all conventions and preached the self-sufficiency of each individual in his search for the divine. We see Shams-e Tabrîz largely by way of the wonder-tales collected about him two generations later by a disciple of Rûmî's ṭarîqah, Aflâkî. In these tales, Shams' wondrous power generally results in the withering or death of someone who has failed to recognize Shams' high station (and with it the possibility of any man's reaching such a station); wonders of healing or of restoration to life are notably absent. Shams led an ascetic life, but felt himself free of the Shar'î law, even in its most sacred points. Aflâkî tells us that a very spiritual murîd disciple once happened to make Shams angry, and found himself struck deaf; even after Shams pardoned him, though the deafness ceased, the murîd continued to suffer a stop in his spiritual life—till one day he proclaimed in public, 'There is no god but God and Shams-e Tabrîz is the prophet of God.' At this blasphemy the people raised a turmoil, but Shams saved the murîd (by roaring so, that the man who was attacking him died on the spot); then explained to him, 'My name is Muḥammad; you must say *Muḥammad*, for people recognize gold only when it is properly minted.' In his personal devotedness to Shams-e Tabrîz, Rûmî found a paradigm of his love of God: a participation, on a concrete level, in that free responsiveness to ultimate beauty in which he discovered the meaning of his life.

But meanwhile Rûmî's poetic gifts and passionate ecstasies (and his learning) had already gathered about him a group of admirers and murîd disciples, some of whom were shocked, or jealous, at seeing their master abandon himself to a disreputable stranger. Shams was driven away—and Rûmî sent off in search of him, and finally persuaded him to come back. But not only some of the murîds were dissatisfied; many of the townspeople of Ḳonya were outraged by Shams' contemptuous manners. Shams' last stay with Rûmî in Ḳonya was terminated by a riot, in which he and one of Rûmî's sons were killed. Rûmî eventually found a substitute for Shams in one of his own murîds, to whom the great couplet poem, the *Mas̄navî*, was dedicated; of him also some of the other murîds were scornful—or jealous—but at the master's behest he was admitted as khalîfah in the master's place

verse translations of Rûmî are afflicted with the doctrine that the poetic effect is the main thing to try to imitate rather than the ideas in their nuances. But Nicholson's prose is an example of how heavy a translation can be if literary considerations are ignored.

on his death; though not till after the murîds had offered that position to a surviving son of Rûmî's (himself a murîd), who refused.

On the favourite's death, that son finally did become khalîfah, and proved a worthy and effective pîr. It was he that organized Rûmî's followers into a regular ṭarîqah order, called the 'Mawlavîyah' from Rûmî's title 'Mawlânâ', or more commonly (using the Turkish form) 'Mevleviye'. In their dhikr services, the Mevlevis made use of the poems of Rûmî, set to music of course. In particular, they developed to a high art a form of whirling dance (hence they have been called in English the 'Whirling Dervishes'), done in groups, largely to set tunes played on a reed pipe. The dancing could lead to a state of ecstasy. For those well grounded in the symbols of circularity and dedication embodied in the form of the dance, and well matured, as well, in their spiritual growth, this ecstasy could take on high spiritual meaning. The ṭarîqah became very popular, eventually, among the more sophisticated classes in the cities of the Ottoman empire.

But Rûmî was not only the inspirer of a ṭarîqah order of unusually poetic and artistic lineaments. His poetry became prized even by non-mystics wherever Persian was used. Some of his verse—notably the dîwân collection which he ascribed to Shams-e Tabrîz by way of honouring him—was in the form of brief lyric pieces of a set form, called *rubâ'iyyât,* four-liners. The most important of Rûmî's works was his *Mas̄navî,* the long poem in rhyming couplets in which he attempted to set forth every aspect of mystical perception and aspiration, and which has been called 'the Qur'ân in Persian'. Without going very far in the theosophical speculations that had recently been developed by Suhravardî and Ibn-al-'Arabî, it presents, in its many anecdotes, most of the fundamental viewpoints that gave ṭarîqah Ṣûfism its power.

The *Mas̄navî* is an endless chain of anecdotes (commonly familiar ones) interspersed with more general moralizing observations—in form, then, very like a great deal of the Qur'ân. And as with the Qur'ân, what makes it live is not merely the beauty of the words chosen, but the turns to which the stories are put and the challenging meanings they are made to carry. Some stories are told on at least three levels, narrative, moral, and metaphysical. The obvious level is that of sheer narrative—but this is subordinated, sometimes to the point that it is hard to follow unless one knows the story in advance. The second level commonly points a moral lesson. In one story (I, 3721 ff.) 'Alî drops his sword when the infidel he is fighting spits at him; the moral, as the story is told, is simply that the true saint will not allow a selfish anger to enter into the motive for his acts. Hence when 'Alî felt an affronted anger rising in himself, he had to stop fighting; as a natural man, subject to passions, 'Alî explains to the astonished infidel: 'When you spat in my face, my fleshly soul was aroused and my good disposition was corrupted'. The infidel is converted at the sight of 'Alî's self-control.

But Rûmî is not normally content to leave the story on that level. He presents also what may be called a metaphysical level, expressing ultimate relationships of being. Hence elsewhere in the story, 'Alî is teaching the infidel a lesson on the place of the human soul in a moral cosmos. It turns out that 'Alî's ceasing to fight was not so much an act of direct self-discipline as a symbolic gesture to show that it is not anger that motivates him in the fighting. Explaining his inner posture, which has resulted from his complete submission to God, he says to his opponent: 'Since I am free, how should anger bind me? Nothing is here but Divine qualities. Come in!' It is not just anger that the story condemns, but any response, 'good' or 'bad', that does not come from God. It is not always easy to distinguish between the immediate moral of a story and its ultimate teaching, for the immediate moral will generally be found to lead directly into the metaphysical level. Thus anger is a legitimate instance of that individually-oriented consciousness that is to be transcended in God. But the real significance of the story is the larger, subtler significance, which must not be confused with what appears at first sight: anger is to be transcended not because it is a vice but because it is individually oriented.

The form of the stories reflects their intention. Rûmî draws no sharp line between his general comment and the speeches of the characters in the stories; there is no attempt at naturalism. The modern translator who thinks he must insert quotation marks around direct discourse cannot settle clearly on what is 'Ali's speech and what is Rûmî's comment. Even where it is unambiguous that someone in the story is speaking, he may speak more as representing a particular metaphysical situation than as a recognizable actor in the story: thus the infidel who was fighting 'Alî suddenly (and even before conversion addresses 'Alî as 'you who are all mind and eye'—taking an attitude quite inappropriate to an enemy who, on the anecdotal level, had merely been baffled, but appropriate to the inward relation of one who (unconsciously) is seeking (not merely an explanation of the one act but) Truth itself, to one who has found it.

Again, it is this intention of pointing to a metaphysical reality beyond the immediate morals of the stories that explains why the several stories are interwoven as they are. Almost every main story is interrupted by a number of other stories; but this is frequently not in the manner of the *Thousand and One Nights*, where a character in one story tells the subordinate story. Rather, in Rûmî the added stories form a running commentary further illuminating the basic theme at hand, or else complementing it with an alternative theme that must also be kept in mind. Occasionally the conclusion of a first story is inserted in the middle of a following story (e.g., II, 3336); in such a case, the conclusion of the first story may carry (in harmony with the mood of the second story) a quite different implication from the rest of it—so that unexpected light is thrown on the first story as a whole by a hidden connection, so brought out, with the second story.

It is tempting for bewildered first readers, trying to find a clue to what can seem an exotic and alien thought-world, to reduce all of Rûmî's stories to the monotonous refrain: all is God—the ocean is God, 'Alî is God, the pîr is God, the wine is God, and the wine-drinker; all truth is to know just this. (And the more or less passive Muslim commentators, concerned only to clear away superficial stumbling-blocks and to start the reader on his own exploration of the text, abet the unwary reader in this reduction.) Whatever truth there may be in this from one point of view, it does not begin to exhaust the meaning of Rûmî's work. His work is addressed to a living, complex individual, and is meant to confront him time and again throughout his complex life; and this process can never be really completed. Rûmî intended to illuminate the Islamic conscience of his time; and however much he valued the particular ecstatic experiences of the mystic, his poem is an interpretation of all aspects of life so far as they enter into moral awareness. If the message of the *Mas̄navî* is to be summed up quickly, it can perhaps be described as a summons to go beyond the routine. The ideal human image which he presents is profoundly allied to that of Firdawsî's *Shâh-Nâmah*, which had celebrated the old Iranian heroic legends in a form that captured the imagination of most of Islamdom in the Middle Periods. Rûmî too celebrates the adventurous and undaunted hero, faithful and unvanquishable; but the fields of struggle of his heroes are not ordinary battlefields, but the inner soul on the one side, and the whole cosmos on the other.

Accordingly, Rûmî must present innumerable facets of the spiritual life; for instance: the relation of pîr and murîd disciple, the relation of the supreme saint to nature as a whole and to mankind in particular, the relation of the insights of the spiritual élite to the ordinary religious teachings of the masses; the role of the mind and the emotions in spiritual growth, the place of sin in a spiritual life, and more generally the meaning of evil within and outside of human beings; and so on through all the questions that must arise if a person takes seriously the challenge to live beyond himself. But Rûmî would be untrue to his own vision of the unity of all reality if he set about isolating and classifying these various themes. However convenient it may be for our analysis to pigeonhole such separate points of inquiry, they cannot be truly understood nor lived out as a serious of separate doctrines. The meaning of any one theme is fully clear only as it can be grasped in terms of all the others.

The overall pattern of Rûmî's poem is formed by this fact. It may suggestively be contrasted to Dante's *Divine Comedy*. Dante's work is like a mountain, with a fixed, closed structure. On the lower slopes you take each path as it leads you higher; as you go on, more and more of the overall shape of the mountain becomes clear to you. Finally at the top you see the whole displayed in order. Dante's last line contains the whole poem in nucleo. Rûmî's poem, in contrast, is fluid; it is like a river. Its structure is open and indefinitely extendable. As you float down a river, sooner or later everything is displayed to you—rapids and still ponds, towns and farmhouses and woods;

but provided you stay with it for a long enough stretch, it makes fairly little difference where you start and where you stop. Or, to change the angle of view a bit, if you stand in one spot in the river, sooner or later the whole of it will appear to you where you are—every stick that floats in it, every drop of its water will pass by your feet. Similarly, at every spot in Rûmî's poem the whole is present by implication. One theme is placed at the centre of attention; but the other themes are at least implicit in the wording, brought in (as often in the Qur'ân also) by incidental references, by overtones, by comments, by whole inserted stories. Rûmî thus never allows a theme to be analytically isolated; the form of the poem reflects his sense of organic continuity. A Western reader may feel the anecdotes to be interminably expanded by extra verbiage and the poem as a whole to be shapeless. He must rather dip into the waters and feel all their varied ripples as they flow by.

Mystical life as human triumph

Rûmî's generation followed after the generation of the great Ṣûfî metaphysicians like Ibn-al-ʻArabî. Without adhering closely to any one of their systems, he (like many other Ṣûfîs of the time) accepted their unitive speculation as a legitimate part of Ṣûfism. It served to justify a Ṣûfî outlook more expansive than in an earlier age; one in which was felt the full effect of the triumph of Ṣûfism as a frame for popular piety. In his *Maśnavî*, Rûmî illustrates magnificently all the varied aspects of Ṣûfî thought and feeling vital in his time.

In Rûmî's *Maśnavî* a mood is dominant that was typical enough of much of the Ṣûfism of the ṭarîqah orders, but stands in contrast to most of the moods expressed in the Ṣûfism of an earlier time: that is, the unlimited glorification of human potentialities generally and of the power and achievement of the perfected saints in particular. The endless weeping of a man like Ḥasan of Baṣrah plays but a minor role in Rûmî's world: the great saint is still likely to be an ascetic; but if he weeps it is likely to be not fear of hell that moves him, but his distance, bound to the earth, from God. The esctatic Bâyazîd Bisṭâmî, who produced such glorious utterances expressing his identification with God, turns up more congenially in Rûmî's writing than does the sober and cautious Junayd, the pivotal figure in High Caliphal Ṣûfî teaching.

Rûmî took very seriously the idea (already at least implicit in Junayd, but not made much of) that every human being is, at one level or another, already involved in the mystical quest for God; indeed, is likely to receive intimations to lead him on if he is at all open. This quest was seen not merely as the calling of the most pious, but as the calling of all creatures, even in the midst of their perverseness when they mistake petty creaturely goods for the true good to which they are being called. The *Maśnavî* starts with an image at once universal in that all who listened to music knew it well, and yet special to the Ṣûfî musical dhikrs, where the reed flute was commonly used. 'Listen to the reed, how it tells a tale, complaining of separations—saying, Ever since I was parted from the reed-bed, my lament has caused men and women to moan. I want a bosom torn by severance, that I may unfold [to such] the pain of love-desire: everyone who is left far from his source wishes back the time when he was united with it.' All who hear the mournful tones of the reed flute respond because they themselves know in their depths the same sorrow of separation from the divine source, even though most people ignorantly turn their enjoyment of the music to much lesser ends than that of awakening their ultimate longings. But for those who truly understand their own condition, the reed flute is sweet and poignant with the sweetness and poignancy of that longing love which comes of separation from one's own reality.

But the *Mas̄navî* calls not merely for recognition of one's inmost longings. It demands an active response. Ordinary people scold Majnûn for going distraught for love of Laylâ when there are many damsels as fair that he may freely choose among (v, 3286 ff.). Yet he cannot remain passive at home but must rush out into the desert to wander. We must break with the conventional. Indeed, as in the case of the infidel who spat at 'Alî, and so released an action of forgiveness in 'Alî which resulted in the infidel's conversion, even sin can prove to be a means to God if the soul is ready. (The approach to God may even result from the punishment which the sin entails: Rûmî tells (II, 3284) of the mole who lived blind inside the earth, but came out one day to steal something and was eaten by a bird in punishment for his theft—and as he was transformed into the bird, came to rejoice that now he could fly high above the earth and sing God's praises.)

Rûmî does not, indeed, recommend sin as such; but sin is not so bad in itself as the separation from God it results in. A man boasted (II, 3364) before one of the prophets that God was very merciful to him, for he had sinned often but had never been punished. The prophet (knowing the man's heart) answered that in fact the man had been punished most grievously: repeated sinning had inured him to sin, so that he was now subject to his sinful wishes and was incapable even of desiring God. The unforgiveable sin was to have small expectations: without need, 'God does not give anything to anyone' just as he gave no sight to the underground mole, '. . . therefore quickly augment your need, you needy one, that the Sea of Bounty may surge up in loving-kindness' (II, 3274, 3280).

It was on the level of everyday mysticism that, in a practical sense, everyone could have high spiritual hopes. Despite the exaltation of ecstatic mysticism over everyday mysticism as the renown of the Ṣûfî pîrs spread, everyday mysticism remained fundamental. Perhaps it even took on a peculiar importance for those many moderate adepts who had no great bent for special mystical experiences but who found the pîrs to be the natural guides of their seeking, and not merely heroes to adore. Rûmî stressed the continuity that prevails through all stages of mystical life, showing it not only in his style but more explicitly. The sequence of casting aside appearances and external concerns leads by slight gradations from the most superficial checking of one's self to the most ecstatic moments. Rûmî compared the process to a stream of water: when it flows very slowly, it can hardly be seen for the débris upon it; as it moves faster, the lighter débris sinks, and the grosser twigs and leaves part to make the water visible; as it goes ever faster, all such traces of the surface life disappear in the torrent.

An incidental consequence of this sense of the universality of spiritual longing was a willingness to recognize a genuine, if misled or distorted, worship of God in all religious intention—even in idolatry. The external Shar'î worship among Muslims was itself an inadequate substitute for full inward devotion to God; hence the even blinder worship performed in other religious forms was not decisively worse. All human beings were launched on the same one quest, less or more consciously.

But if all men were, in some sense, incipient mystics, clearly most had not gotten very far and must depend on the more advanced to carry them even the little distance further that they might actually hope to go. The perfected pîr was the means whereby ordinary men and women could rise spiritually—not merely in the sense that the pîr could give them good advice and guide them day by day in their spiritual experience, but in the sense that the pîr embodied the spiritual quest for the others. His very presence was necessary to the validity and effectiveness of the others' quest: the blind gropings of the weaker were justified by the success of the stronger; what is more the weaker could participate on a certain level in that success by identifying with the pîrs obeying them, and accepting their pre-eminence.

Like 'Alî when he startled the infidel, the pîr rouses the soul to its true mission. Rûmî tells (II, 3210 ff.) how Ibrâhîm b. Adham, the king who abdicated to become a wandering darvîsh, was discovered sitting in rags on a beach one day by a former captain of his. The captain was secretly shocked, and Ibn-Adham knew his thoughts: he threw the needle, with which as a good darvîsh he was mending his cloak, into the water and asked to have it back; whereupon a host of fishes emerged offering him each one a golden needle. He explained to the captain that the traces of his spiritual condition that could become visible so were like a few leaves plucked from a grand orchard and brought to be displayed in a town. The captain repented his obtuseness, exclaiming, 'The fish recognize the pîr, while we are afar: we are damned in our lack of this fortune, and they are blest!'—and went off distracted with longing for God. The pîr becomes the touchstone of the ordinary person: all depends on how he reacts to the challenge posed by the existence of the pîr.

Indeed, humans can come to the truth only by way of the pîr—the greatest of pîrs having been Muḥammad, of course (e.g., I, 1529 ff.). All true islâm is supposed to be at least elementary mystical awakening; thus when an ambassador from the Romans found the caliph 'Umar living humbly despite his vast power, and was converted at the sight, Rûmî interprets this as the response of a murîd disciple to the inward truths of a pîr, in this case 'Umar (I, 1390 ff.). As 'Alid-loyalist esotericism had taught, Muḥammad had had a spiritual message behind the explicit revelation, which only a few, like 'Alî, had learned—though those few included all the major Jamâ'î-Sunnî heroes, like 'Umar, as well. To benefit from this message, at least indirectly, one must turn to a pîr.

Pîrs were not merely the means whereby other humans came to God. As the perfect human beings, they were the reason why the universe had been made: not merely as the specially obedient creatures of God, who give Him pleasure, but as the metaphysical goal of all the universe, including other human beings. When perfected, they were necessarily sinless, for their transformed nature was incompatible with sin (that is, separation from God) and would transform what seemed to be sin into holiness. Rûmî tells (II, 339 ff.) of a pîr who was found in a wine tavern with a cup in his hand—but on investigation, the cup was found to contain pure honey; when the pîr exclaimed that he was in pain and required some wine as a medicine (which was permissible), it was found that all the wine had turned to honey: the pîr could not have wine even if he wanted to. Indeed, a pîr could sin only by contradicting himself, the touchstone of sin in all mankind, since sin was whatever hindered people from ascending to that position in which the pîr was, and to which the pîr was the means of ascent. 'Sins are made sinful by the disapproval of pîrs', Rûmî says (II, 3351), hence what a pîr (if he be true) approves cannot, by definition, be sinful.

Rûmî insisted that what mattered was the triumph of the pîrs over all the evil and sinfulness in the world, and the possibility all people had of sharing in that triumph by recognizing the pîrs: but he did not deny the existence of evil and sinfulness. He devoted many stories to elucidating its existence, and reconciling it with the mood of moral triumph. He tells, for instance (II, 2604 ff.), that the caliph Mu'âwiyah was once awakened from sleep and could not tell how till he spied a man crouching behind the door, who had to admit that he was Iblîs (Satan). Iblîs thereupon explains that he has awakened Mu'âwiyah so that he will not miss the ṣalât worship, which is due shortly. But Mu'âwiyah will not be put off by such a show of virtue on the part of Iblîs, and presses for a true explanation. Why should the Devil, that is, sinful impulses, move one to a good deed? What is the role of sinful impulses in a person's life? Iblîs thereupon attempts to show that he, Iblîs, is in fact not so bad as he is reputed, so that a good deed on his part is not out of place. His arguments resume, in effect, the various explanations that had been given for the existence of sinfulness in God's world—and especially the explanations that had occurred among Ṣûfîs.

The poetic fancies in this story seem to tumble over themselves in disarray as Rûmî utters them, and here, as elsewhere in the poem, most of Rûmî's themes can be found alluded to in at least a line or so. But if one follows out seriously the implication of each tale, not letting oneself be tied to the immediately apparent meaning but being guided by the mood set in what comes before and after, then the themes turn out to succeed each other appropriately enough. Sometimes, as in this story of Mu'âwiyah and Iblîs, they even build up a reasonably complex argument, though the form of the argument is determined by the dramatic situation into which the argument is set, and which must never be lost sight of.

Iblîs first notes that all that God has created must be fundamentally good—reflecting His beauty (jamâl); but an integral part of that good is the power, the terrifying majesty, the splendour (jalâl) of God: which casts the shadow (Rûmî notes elsewhere) that makes clear the brilliance of the light. It was Iblîs' role, among all the angels, to be fascinated with the splendour of God, rather than with the benevolent beauty of Him—and therefore to provide the opportunity and impetus to sinful defiance which brings out God's terrible majesty as response. Yet Iblîs is no less a servitor of God for that. 'Since there was no play but this on his game board, and He said 'Play', what more can I do? I played the one move that there was, and cast myself into woe.' With the growth of ṭarîqah Ṣûfism and its emphasis on the universal love of God, sometimes at the expense of the sterner aspects of the mystical experience, some of the growing number of more or less amateur mystics had been tempted by the implications of Iblîs' argument—that since everything is from God and is good in its own way, the sin one encounters cannot really matter if one's heart is turned to God. But Mu'âwiyah, the vigorous caliph, is not satisfied with such a tendency to indifference. It might seem a logical conclusion from considering the problem of evil by way of general principles, but it does not answer to the experience of the vital act in its personal integrity, where choice is decisive. Mu'âwiyah admits the abstract validity of what Iblîs says, but denies that it applies to the case at hand, where Mu'âwiyah is to perform a personal act; for in fact by Iblîs' temptations innumerable individual hearts have been morally wrecked.

Iblîs then directs himself precisely to the case of personal decision. He presents himself (and the impulses that he represents) as no cause of sin—he is only God's tester: 'God has made me the test of lion and cur, . . . the test of genuine coin and counterfeit.' The evil lies only in the objects tested—not in Iblîs nor in God who made Iblîs: accordingly, an impulse to sin can be like a mirror in which the good man's goodness will appear as readily as a bad man's badness. But for a mystic, an inviting implication of such an attitude can be that to the pure, anything at all will be pure: that a given act of 'sin' is evil only so far as it reflects an evil disposition in the man himself. Iblîs' passive explanation of his presence could lead the mystic to depend on his inner virtue to turn all his impulses to good, without mistrusting them; could be a temptation to spiritual pride. Mu'âwiyah responds by appealing to God to protect him from the deceits of Satan: even Adam fell, who taught the names of all things to the angels; human logic is impotent against the deceitful heart. Finally, then, Iblîs complains that he has been made a scapegoat for people's own faults—implying that there is no objective natural propensity to sin at all, and that sinfulness, while it does always threaten, could be set aside by an act of sheer will. This notion may undercut one's spiritual pride in a state of grace that would seem to make sin no longer a problem. But it invites to a purely human self-reliance. Mu'âwiyah, who knows by his mystical experience that he must rely on God's grace and not on his own powers, now appeals to the ultimate spiritual criterion of the mystic, the sense of inward taste. Thereby a sound suggestion, one that will prove satisfying however much experience may test it, can be distinguished from one that rises from the limited perspectives of momentary self-will. (But lest just anyone feel invited to let his feelings be his guide, at this point is inserted a story of a qâḍî judge whose dispassionateness alone made him a sound judge; the interested parties, though they know more facts, cannot judge at all.) The true mystic is safeguarded by his inward taste from succumbing to the temptations Iblîs has presented. Confronted with this final test, Iblîs is forced to admit the true reason for waking Mu'âwiyah in time to get to the ṣalât worship. If Mu'âwiyah had slept through the ṣalât, he would have sighed deeply in his disappointment; and such a sigh, worth many a ritual ṣalât, Iblîs wished to forestall.

At this point, Mu'âwiyah, now speaking as master of the situation, sheds a rather different light on sinfulness. Often in mystical lore, God appears in the guise of enemy, or at least of opponent in a contest—mystics with access to the Hebrew Bible have loved to comment on Jacob's wrestling with an angel. In such a context, sinfulness is an incident in the struggle God is making for the human soul, and in the latter's resistance. Here, sinfulness can become almost a function of human greatness, a real and very dangerous by-product of the fact that humans are nearer to God than are the other animals or even, perhaps, than angels. Mu'âwiyah goes so far as to suggest that the Devil and God are playing much the same game at different levels. He tells Iblîs to go hunt lesser prey: Iblîs is a spider and should weave his snares only for flies; he, Mu'âwiyah, is no fly, but a white falcon; none but the King (that is, God) is great enough to hunt him. In becoming the prey of such a huntsman lies true human triumph.

V

The Victory of the New Sunnî Internationalism, 1118–1258

Under the blessing of the comprehensive Ṣûfî spirituality and supported by high intellectual sophistication, in the Earlier Middle Periods we can see growing a new Jamâʿî-Sunnî cultural synthesis. It was no longer the mere set of accommodations of High Caliphal times. The Jamâʿî position itself was no longer largely a political compromise as in early ʿAbbâsî times; a certain unity of orientation among the now primarily Muslim people is borne witness by the relative thinning out of Shîʿî intellectual life. More fundamental was an international spirit, tolerating wide differences of tongue and clime, and welcoming everywhere all that was Muslim from anywhere (within limits of heresy which the Sharîʿah-minded attempted, with mixed success, to lay down). This spirit was consonant with and was reflected in the international political order such as it had been formed by about 1100, resting on the enterprise of the amîrs and the multiple autonomous ties of interest in the cities.

After that time, there were further experiments in international state formation; but unless they fitted in with the new international and Ṣûfî-oriented Sunnism, they seem to have been doomed to futility. Purely locally oriented sectarian movements scarcely reappeared. The more broadly based Shîʿî dissent was not to be overwhelmed; but after its most intense effort of all, that of the Nizârî Ismâʿîlîs, the twelfth century saw the end, for a time, to any active Shîʿî campaigning (except in the Yemen). Most of the Jamâʿî-Sunnî states were not supported by any large political idea. Yet in most areas, despite the rivalries of the amîrs, political life did maintain a degree of continuity and a breadth of scale above the minimal local level called for by the urban-agrarian symbiosis; presumably in part because of the constant pressure of Muslim society for social order.

The successor-states to the Seljuḳs

The Seljuḳ state had never been a highly centralized absolutism; it had early reached that point of no return, where state resources were so far committed to private interests among the amîrs that, when in difficulties, no central authority could muster enough resources to impose a will for reform upon the amîrs generally. We have seen how the state power tended to be distributed among the amîrs, who emerged as almost their own masters in the strife that followed Niẓâmulmulk's death. Sanjar (1118–57) was the last of the 'great Seljuḳs', who claimed some sort of control over all the Seljuḳid house in the several Seljuḳ provinces in the central lands of Islamdom.

Sanjar kept his seat of power in Khurâsân and passed most of his life trying to assert supremacy everywhere else. He sent expeditions against the Nizârîs in Quhistân and against various local rulers north of the Oxus who were supposed to have submitted to him but who ignored him whenever he seemed to be weak. He also had to suppress gestures of independence by other Seljuḳid amîrs. His most persistent opponent was the ruler of Khwârazm, the lower Oxus valley (as in earlier dynasties, that rule was still called king of the country, 'Khwârazmshâh'). The first of the current dynasty had been a servant of the Seljuḳids appointed as governor, but his descendants made pretensions to independence. The most ominous of Sanjar's wars were with the Ḳara-Khitay, a pastoralist-based power whose rulers had taken on Chinese culture, and who controlled part of the trade route between the Oxus basin and northwest China. Their power seems to have been wider than that of the Ḳara-khânî Ḳarluḳ Turks who had defeated the Sâmânîs from the same direction: and although—or perhaps because—they left defeated local rulers in possession, only exercising general oversight, their power was quite tenacious. By 1141 they were able to defeat Sanjar as close to his base as Samarqand, and became lords of all the Oxus basin.

But most immediately decisive to Sanjar's fate was the rebellion of his own Oghuz tribes—those Turks who had remained pastoral and had gradually ceased to play any role in the Seljuḳ state and armies. Driven to desperation by the tax-gatherers who served Sanjar's professional slave-corps troops, a group of them offered resistance; then they appealed over the head of the local governor to the sultan himself, as the head of all Turks. But Sanjar was persuaded to be rigorous and make an example of them—presumably to end once and for all the independent spirit of the pastoral nomads who had won a privileged position in Khurâsân with the Seljuḳ success, but who must always have irritated the agrarian bureaucracy. Instead, when battle was joined, the Oghuz defeated Sanjar's army (1153), took Sanjar captive, and held him for years in honoured captivity—protecting him as their chief from his 'evil' advisers—while his state crumbled. The Turkic pastoral element had entered Iran permanently and henceforth must be taken into account. Meanwhile, the destructive wanderings of the Oghuz added to the general collapse, for they felt licensed, after the ruin of Sanjar's army, to loot and burn at will, and looted and wrecked several cities.

The lands of Iran and the Fertile Crescent can be divided, in this period (as often), into two political zones: eastern and western. In eastern Iran and the Syr-Oxus basin, the dominant Muslim power after Sanjar's fall was that

The Age of Sunnî Triumph, 1118–1258

Maghrib and Spain | Sudan | Egypt and Syria | Arabia and East Africa | Anatolia and the Balkans | Iraq, Caucasus, West Iran | East Iran and Transozania | Central Eurasia | North India | South India and Malaysia

1117–57 Sanjar, last great Seljuḳ, rules Khurâsân; in his time the peak of pre-Ṣûfî Persian poetry

1150+ Death of Sanâ'î, a founder of Ṣûfî Persian poetry

1185+ Death of Anvarî, master of the panegyric qaṣîdah in Persian

1117–1258 Caliphate (and other small dynasties) essentially independent except as they must bow to occasional superior power in a neighbour

1229 Death of Yâqût, authoritative geographical compiler in Arabic

1127–73 Zengids, dynasty founded at Mosul by a Seljuḳ general, unites Syria and eventually Egypt against Crusaders

1143–76 Nûr-al-dîn at Aleppo, attempts to order his society in terms of 'ulamâ' ideals

1106–43 'Alî b. Yûsuf b. Tâshfîn (and family till 1147) tries to maintain the Almoravid régime of 'ulamâ' bigotry against Almohads

1130–1269 Almohads, a reforming dynasty in North Africa and Spain, replacing Almoravids; introduce Ghazâlî's thought and synthesis of Ṣûfism with 'ulamâ' orthodoxy; patronize Falsafah if it be kept private

1185 Death of Ibn-Ṭufayl, a teacher of Ibn-Rushd

1126–98 Ibn-Rushd (Averroës), leader of the Spanish-Moroccan Aristotelianizing Falsafah; the great commentary on Aristotle

1165–1240 Muḥyi-l-dîn Ibn-al-'Arabî, leading exponent of Ṣûfî monism, a Spaniard who later went to live in Egypt and Syria

1171–1250 Ayyûbids in Syria and Egypt, restore Sunnism to Egypt, based on the work of men like Niẓâmulmulk and al-Ghazâlî: madrasahs, khâniqâhs

The Age of Sunnî Triumph—*continued*

Maghrib and Spain | Sudan | Egypt and Syria | Arabia and East Africa | Anatolia and the Balkans | Iraq, Caucasus, West Iran | East Iran and Transoxania | Central Urasia | North India | South India and Malaysia

1169–93 Saladin the Ayyûbid throws Crusaders out of Jerusalem (1187, battle of Ḥaṭṭîn)

1191 Death of Yaḥyà Suhravardî 'al-Maqtûl', Illuminationist Ṣûfî speculator, killed for heresy

1148–1215 Ghûrid dynasty, in Afghan mountains, controls eastern Iran and (after defeating Ghaznavids in 1186) the Panjâb

1161–86 Ghaznavids, a purely Indian dynasty in the Panjâb

1193 Ghûrids from the Panjâb take Delhi

1150–1220 Khwârazmshâhs, who from the northwest corner of Transoxania gradually enlarged their domains to cover most of Iran, eliminating the remains of the small Seljuḳ dynasties

1203 Death of Niẓâmî, poet of romantic mas̄navî epics (Persian)

1199–1220 'Alâ'-al-dîn-Muḥammad, Khwârazmshâh, whose ambition to restore a great Iranian monarchy conflicted with al-Nâṣir

1180–1225 al-Nâṣir, caliph at Baghdad, attempting to reorganize Islam under his own leadership in terms of futuwwah chivalric orders

1220–1369 Age of the Mongols; at the beginning their raids disrupt political patterns and ruin the economy in Transoxania, Iran, etc.; later their pagan governments there keep Egypt, Anatolia, and Delhi under constant threat; when Islamized both in Muslim and some non-Muslim lands, their activity becomes part of a larger expansive tendency throughout the Dâr al-Islâm at the time

1220–31 First great Mongol raids, till the death of Khwârazmshâh heir in Azerbaijan; enormous destruction of cities; political center of much of Eurasia fixed at Karakorum in Mongolia

1227 Death of Chingiz Khân, whose enterprise organized the vast destruction

Maghrib and Spain | Sudan | Egypt and Syria | Arabia and East Africa | Anatolia and the Balkans | Iraq, Caucasus, West Iran | East Iran and Transozania | Central Eurasia | North India | South India and Malaysia

1205–87 'Slave Kings', sulṭâns of Delhi ruling whole Ganges valley after fall of Ghûrid power

1266–87 Balban, last upholder of Turkish élitism in India

1225 Almohads abandon Muslim Spain, which is soon reduced to the small Naṣrid kingdom of Granada (1232–1492)

1228 (–**1535**) Ḥafṣids in Tunisia, succeeding Almohads, maintaining a remnant of Spanish cultural tradition

1269 (–1470; and to 1550, in form of Waṭṭâsids): Marînid dynasty replaces Almohads in Morocco (had ruled in hills since 1195), and in Algeria after end of Ziyânid rule there (1235–1393)

1231–56 Continuing raids and Mongol overlordship of local Iranian and Arab rulers; flanked by Delhi sultanate in east, Ayyûbids in Egypt, and Seljuḳs of Anatolia (1077–1300)

1224–1391 Golden Horde Mongols in lands north of Caspian and Black Seas (called Ḳîpchaḳ); soon converted to Islam; disputing heirs last till 1502 (Russian conquest)

1227–1358 Chaghatay Mongol khâns of Trans-oxania, converted to Islam *c.* 1340

1250–1382 Bahrî Mamlûks, Turkish military rulers in Egypt and Syria; political insecurity but economic prosperity

of the Khwârazmshâh with whom he had quarrelled. Khwârazm was an area naturally wealthy as an irrigated delta land, relatively secure from attack across surrounding deserts, yet along an increasingly important trade route northward toward the Volga region. It was naturally autonomous in its national political tradition and the solidarity of its bourgeoisie. The new Khwârazmshâhs seem to have adopted the national ways along with the national title, and to have maintained good relations with the cities. The importance of Khurâsân had lain in its being at the crossroads of trade routes on a fertile plateau; but this very situation could expose it to disruption at a time when large-scale government was breaking down. Khwârazm, to its north, became its rival as political centre for the whole region. The Khwârazmians came to terms with the Ḳara-Khitay power, which was overlord of the Zarafshân and Oxus valleys, paying it tribute; but acted on their own account in Iran. There they shared with the Ghûrid power (which was replacing the Ghaznavîs on the eastern rim of Iran) the task of taming the Oghuz tribes and restoring prosperity in Khurâsân itself. The Khwârazmian state was (in effect) the successor to the Sâmânî, but the bureaucratic traditions of the area had been weakened under the Seljuḳs and during the Oghuz depredations, and were not fully restored.

In western Iran and the Fertile Crescent, the chief power was nominally that of the Seljuḳids of 'Iraq 'Ajamî, the immediate heirs there of Alp Arslân and Malikshâh and Muḥammad Tapar. Actually, the power in the region was divided for roughly a century among ten or eleven chief dynasties and many lesser ones, most of them claiming some relation to the Seljuḳ authority. These dynasties, compared with the Seljuḳs in their prime, can seem petty, and they were not major powers. Yet they were not mere city states: potentially, they could command considerable resources. Many of them controlled territories (even excluding dependent but autonomous dynasties) the size of European lands like Switzerland or larger, though much less densely settled; they could support substantial courts, which did offer handsome patronage to poets. However, even the internal control within these states was not tight—local amîrs seem to have had considerable range of discretion. And a large proportion of the resources available to the courts was used in destructive wars, both among the states and within each of them. At best, the administrative efficiency of the several governments varied with the personality of the ruler.

This situation resulted directly from the circumstances of the amîr-a'yân system with its iqṭâ' assignments. Among these states, the preferred ruling title was *atabeg*, literally 'father lord' in Turkish. The title referred to the guardians appointed for minor princes of the Seljuḳid line who were nominally set over garrisons in one or another province; the atabeg (usually a Turkic slave-officer) was at once tutor and vicegerent to the young prince. But in the political circumstances of the time, the atabegs naturally became the actual rulers. In the system of rule by amîrs, the only effective power was that of the military garrison on the spot. The corollary of the amîr system, on the level of a relatively large-scale power, therefore, was that the army captains ruling a province in the name of a prince were substantially autonomous. The result was that the atabegs, as powers behind the throne, preferred to have the minors under their control succeed to nominal authority, rather than a grown Seljuḳid prince. And there tended to be not just one Seljuḳid minor and his atabeg; unless one amîr clearly outweighed all the others in power, there were many successions disputed among contending minors—

who often did not long outlive their maturity. Eventually, the title *atabeg* came to be used by rulers who had disencumbered themselves of their Seljuḳid prince—or who had never even been an atabeg in the proper sense—who founded dynasties with little more than nominal relations to the Seljuḳids. The political situation within the states corresponded to the manner in which the atabegs rose to power: the dynasty's authority was limited to direct military control, and had to be constantly reimposed if lesser amîrs were to be kept in abedience, as well as being defended against the encroachments of other atabegs.

It was in western Iran and the Fertile Crescent, the central territories of the old absolute empires, that the breakdown of bureaucratic control and the militarization of landholding had gone the furthest; and it was in these lands that the atabeg states developed. In eastern Iran, as we have seen, the Khwârazmshâhs ruled a rather better controlled empire (despite some fraternal strife). At the same time, in more out-of-the-way areas of the mid-Arid Zone—the bulk of Arabia or even southeast Iran—power tended to be still more localized. The ports were independent, either with essentially republican (oligarchic) institutions under their leading families or under the leaders of a tribal formation of the hinterland; though sometimes one town would dominate several others. Inland, the deserts were controlled by tribal confederations.

Even in the agricultural Yemen, ports such as Aden tended to be ruled in local independence; while inland, the country was divided between quarrelling dynasties among whom the Zaydî Shî'îs at Sa'dà in the north generally held a strong place. The whole Ḥijâz was ruled traditionally by one or another family of *sharîfs* (descendants of Muḥammad) at Mecca, commonly under the suzerainty of the power in Egypt or sometimes Syria. In 1174, however, a Turkic garrison from Syria—carrying institutions derived from the atabeg system—brought much of the Yemen under its control (as well as the Ḥijâz); under this Ayyûbid dynasty and later under its successors, the Rasûlids, the Shâfi'îs in the Yemen were somewhat more integrated into the ways of the central areas.

The Nizârî Ismâ'îlîs, of course, ruled themselves, in Quhistân and locally elsewhere, by means of their civic militias. Egypt, as always, was a strongly centralized state, remaining till 1171 under Fâṭimî control.

The series of Seljuḳid princes and their atabegs that succeeded Muḥammad Tapar in 'Irâq 'Ajamî did at first manage to force several other provinces to accept their supremacy at least in the sense of sending tribute. But they had little solid strength. As long as Sanjar lived, the disputed successions at Iṣfahân and latterly at Hamadhân in Kurdistân, which became the capital, were settled by the 'great Seljuḳ', though not till after the local armies had done their share of fighting each other. During this period, a major Seljuḳ policy objective was to keep the caliphs at Baghdad in subjection—in part because of the symbolic value to the Seljuḳids of being the primary lieutenants of the caliphate. They deposed and exiled more than one caliph. However, in 1157, at the same time that the death of Sanjar removed his waning authority from his back, the Seljuḳid at Hamadhân was forced to give up a siege of Baghdad and acknowledge the caliphs as exercising an independent power in the Mesopotamian plain. The caliphs could rely on their independent prestige against the weakened amîrs; but they emerged merely as one power among others. Then from 1161 the Seljuḳid princes at Hamadhân fell under the control of the atabeg of Azerbaijan, who had built up his provincial power there to the point of being able to intervene effectively against more home-bred atabegs. The last Seljuḳid prince tried to establish an independent authority in 'Irâq 'Ajamî and so far succeeded in resisting the atabeg that the Khwârazmshâh was called in to help to reduce him; he was killed in battle at Rayy in 1194, and the last Seljuḳid of the main line disappeared, replaced for the moment by agents of the atabegs of Azerbaijan.

Besides the Seljuḳids of 'Irâq 'Ajamî, the atabegs of Azerbaijan, and the resurgent caliphs, there arose, in the west Iranian and Fertile Crescent region, independent lines of considerable authority (as may be seen from the map) in Fârs; in Kirmân east of Fârs; in Lûristân, the mountains north of Fârs; in Kurdistân; in Armenia; in Diyâr Bakr of the Jazîrah; in Mosul of the Jazîrah; in Damascus. Even several lesser (or more ephemeral) dynasties, such as the Arab line at Ḥillah in the Iraq, played a significant military role. These major dynasties did not all stay put, of course, and rival lines indulged in fraternal strife; but most of them lasted at least a couple of generations. Aleppo and, for a time, Damascus had their own Seljuḳid princelings at first. In Kirmân also the ruler was an independent Seljuḳid—controlled usually by his own atabegs. Not all the rulers of other families took the title *atabeg*, but almost all were of Turkic origin.

The Seljuḳids of Kirmân had been autonomous ever since the Seljuḳ wave of Oghuz had carried one of the Seljuḳid cousins there in 1041, though they had been forced to submit to the authority of the 'great Seljuḳs'. Kirmân was on a north-south trade route that sometimes rivalled Shîrâz in Fârs, and at first the rulers there had been strong enough to control the seaports and even the coast of 'Umân. But eventually the same military disruption supervened as in other states, and in a period of great disorder the new Oghuz elements that had defeated Sanjar overran the land and expelled the last Seljuḳid from Kirmân in 1186, setting up their own chieftain in his place.

Because of the literary importance of Shîrâz, some of the rulers of its province, Fârs, have had an adventitious celebrity. The Salghurid dynasty there will serve as a sufficient further example of the politics of the region at the time. The heads of a Turkic pastoralist group who had revolted more than once against the Seljuḳs of 'Irâq 'Ajamî, the Salghurid family took possession of Shîrâz in 1148, defeating the atabeg of the Seljuḳid prince there.

But before long they were forced to pay tribute ot Hamadhân. They adopted the title *atabeg* to distinguish themselves from lesser amîrs. But their tributary position did not save them from repeated internal warfare. After the fall of the Seljuḳs in 1194, they became tributary to the victorious Khwârazmians. But for eight years until 1203, a contest was carried on between brothers for the atabegship which left the economy of Fârs exhausted. The line continued, however, right through the Mongol conquests.

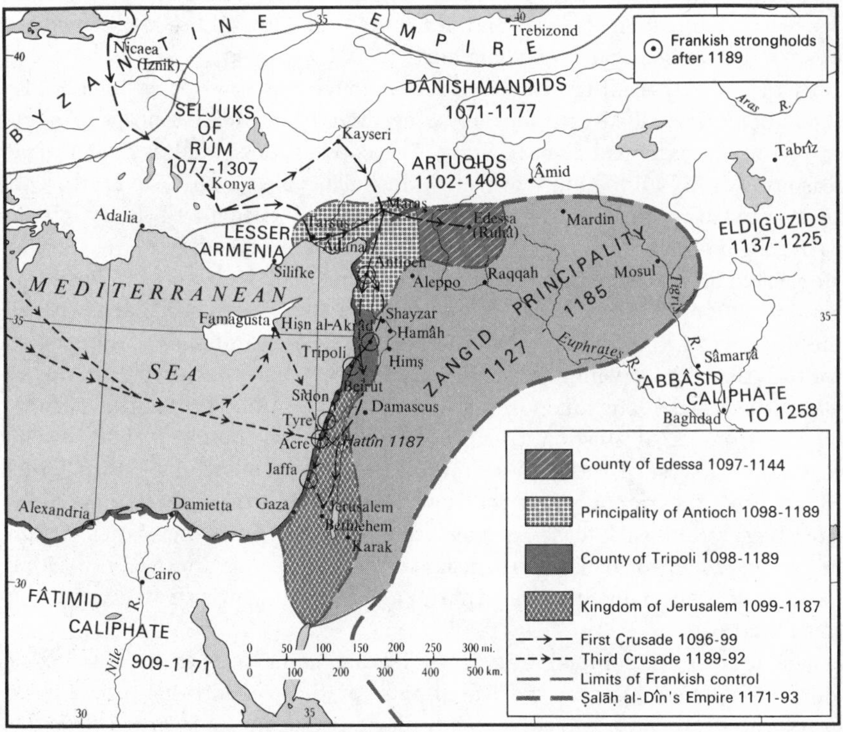

The Crusading period in Syria and Anatolia

The Crusades and the Zengid-Ayyûbî restoration

The worst results of the military system of the age lay in the continuous internecine warfare among the various sultans and atabegs and amîrs, with its intermittent ravages. But it was in the defence of the Dâr al-Islâm against an external enemy that the weakness of the fragmentation of power in local military hands showed itself most dramatically. It was also here that the resiliency of the system, its potentialities of eventually evoking strong leadership and effective cooperation, showed up best.

This danger and the response to it occurred chiefly in the Muslim lands along the Mediterranean coasts, in Spain, the eastern Maghrib, Egypt, and Syria. The Earlier Middle Period was a time of vitality and expansion for

Islamdom, but it was this also for the Latinizing peoples of western Europe. The expansion of western European activities was on a much more limited range, but was founded in a rapidly growing economy as the northern hinterland of the west Mediterranean was being developed as never before; it engendered considerable force for a time. Where in High Caliphal times the Muslims from the Maghrib and Spain had raided all the northern shores of the Mediterranean and occupied ports from time to time in Italy and Gaul, in the eleventh century the movement was reversed; the Muslims were driven out of Italy and even of Sicily and of northern Spain, and the Maghrib coast was itself harassed and even some ports at last occupied.

In the twelfth century this Occidental movement was at its height. In the expeditions called Crusades, drawing directly on north European manpower, it was extended even to Syria. Thereupon it presented (for ideological reasons, largely) all the more westerly Muslim peoples with a severe threat. In the twelfth century, in fact, the Italian and Catalan Christian cities, battening on the burgeoning trade of the north, achieved as near a mastery of all the Mediterranean sea lanes as the Muslims had had before. The naval dominance of the Occidentals proved permanent (perhaps in part because the opening of the Sûdânic lands as Muslim hinterland proved much less fruitful than the opening of northern Europe); but their political threat was turned back along an enduring defensive line, by the thirteenth century, by a resurgence of Muslim strength. This resurgence involved, both in the east and the west of the Mediterranean, the development of political forms which used the resources of the new international order with maximum effectiveness; in each case, it gave new leadership to the Jamâ'î-Sunnî 'ulamâ' and helped to eliminate or neutralize the various alternative Islamic movements, especially Shî'î and Khârijî, along all the southern Mediterranean shores.

The process of political fragmentation had gone farther in Syria than almost anywhere else: in the last decade of the eleventh century almost every important town had come to have its independent amîr, only nominally under the primacy of a Seljuḳid prince whose effective power was limited to Aleppo. The amîrs were jealous of each other but doubly jealous of any outside interference from the Iraq or Iran. When there swept in upon them the troops of the Western allies of the Byzantine empire, they could plan almost no united defense; each amîr held out in his own town in the hope that sooner or later the storm would blow over and the unexpected show of initiative from the Christian power would burn itself out. One by one some of the most important towns fell.

From the point of view of the Byzantine empire, the first Crusading expedition was a contribution to its standing goal: to regain all the territories once held by the Christian Roman empire; and more particularly, it was a riposte to the Turkic occupation of most of Anatolia that had gradually followed upon the recent Seljuḳ victory at Malazgirt in 1071. The West

European peoples readily became enthusiastic at the idea of retaking the holy city Jerusalem from Muslim rule; their enthusiasm had been stirred now by the still more recent loss of Christian territory to Muslims. Taking advantage of that enthusiasm, the Byzantines regained large parts of Anatolia in the wake of the Occidentals; but they left to the Crusaders themselves such parts of Syria as the latter could conquer, to be held as Byzantine vassals. The Occidental adventurers, under various commanders, largely French, were willing enough to let Byzantium take over Anatolia, and so repaid the entrée it had afforded them; but they rejected the idea of being vassals in Syria. There they fought on their own account. Favoured by the unusual disunion of the Syrian amîrs and supported effectively by the navies of the Italian trading cities, they were enabled to murder and plunder straight down the Syrian coast. Exultantly, they massacred indiscriminately the population of Jerusalem in 1099.

In the next few decades they established a series of little Latin principalities which the Muslim amîrs were for some time powerless to counteract, though the infidels were even holding Jerusalem, one of the holiest cities of Islam. The Crusaders did not form a single strong state, having refused Byzantine leadership, the only strong central leadership available. But with the support of the Italian fleets, they were able to hold all the Syrian ports. In addition, they controlled considerable territory inland in the extreme north and in the south. In the north, they held a number of cities along the old frontier zone between Islamdom and Byzantium, partly in co-operation with local Christian Armenian groups that distrusted the Occidentals less than they did the Byzantines. In the south, they held Jerusalem; and that name attracted thither a steady stream of soldiers of fortune, who enabled the Crusader king of Jerusalem to annex, for a time, most of southern Syria and even an outlet south to the Red Sea. The quarrelling amîrs at Damascus, Aleppo, and the lesser towns between were on the defensive.

The Occidental settlers (called 'Franks' by the Muslims) attempted to set up an idealized Occidental feudal régime. At the same time, culturally they were being rapidly assimilated into Islamicate life. They made little contribution to that life, of course, save in the field of military architecture. Their judicial duels and their primitive medicine struck Muslims and local Christians as absurdly crude. Few Occidentals even learned literary Arabic. But they did enjoy the luxuries of the outward life. Soon the older settlers lived what could appear to be a largely Islamicate life, to the astonishment of newcomers from Europe. These newcomers were numerous enough at all times, however, to prevent complete assimilation and eventual conversion.

Only toward the middle of the twelfth century did some Muslims begin to overcome the parochial quarrels among the amîrs of the various cities sufficiently to gain an effective vision of joint action against the Crusaders. It was always easier for an amîr to expand at the expense of a neighbouring Muslim, where basic loyalties were not in question, and troops defeated in one or two engagements could be absorbed into the new order. When non-Muslims were fought, the very existence of the threatened group, both of the soldiers and of the whole privileged class, was at stake; hence resistance was necessarily more persistent.

The amîr Zengi, son of a Turkic slave officer of the Seljuḳs, rose rapidly under Seljuḳ atabegs till he was himself appointed atabeg at Mosul in 1127. He had sufficient success in extending his own power within the Muslim-held area in the Jazîrah and northern Syria (occupying Aleppo already in 1128, on the failure of the local line), to enable him to gather extensive material resources for an assault on the Crusader positions. He also won a good name with the 'ulamâ'. In 1144 he took Edessa (Ruḥà), capital of the most exposed of the four main Crusader states; but he died in 1146. As was typical among atabeg families, two sons thereupon established themselves as amîrs, at Mosul and Aleppo. The line at Mosul claimed a vague leadership as atabegs, but was preoccupied with concerns that drew it away from confrontation with the Crusaders, for instance, with an attempt to displace the Salghurids from Fârs. It was Nûr-al-dîn at Aleppo who succeeded to Zengi's zeal for the jihâd against the Crusaders.

Nûr-al-dîn was an eager *ghâzî*, but at least as eager to be a model ruler in terms of the new Jamâ'î-Sunnî ideals. He created no centralized state, but built his power on co-operation between the Turkic garrisons and the urban leadership. He used his resources for building all sorts of welfare edifices—mosques, hospitals, caravanserais, madrasahs—as well as for recapturing places held by the Crusaders. Though tolerant within the wide scope then allowed by the Jamâ'î position, he was as severe against such heresy as went beyond those limits as he was against tolerating Christian rule in what had been Dâr al-Islâm. He was especially concerned to see the Sharî'ah integrally enforced, and imposed this on occasion even against the outcry of citizens who felt it offered far scantier protection than a more summary law. Thus he won the solid support of the 'ulamâ' as well as the loyal respect of his soldiers. These served him well in taking the chief remaining independent Muslim city of Syria, Damascus, and turning the united resources of Muslim Syria against the Crusader kingdom of Jerusalem. From the Occidental point of view, Jerusalem was ill-supported from home; but from a Muslim perspective, the continual flow of special help from Europe made it strong beyond what it could count on locally, especially the naval help from the Italian cities, which now were outshining Muslim naval power. The resources of the Shî'î Fâṭimid dynasty in Egypt were at their lowest ebb, and far from being able to threaten either the Sunnî or the Christian position in Syria, Egypt now became the object of rivalry between the two Syrian powers. In 1169, Nûr-al-dîn succeeded in placing his own lieutenant in control of Egypt, as vizier to the boy-caliph, in return for Syrian military support. Thereby a potent Muslim combination was created which outflanked the Crusaders decisively.

Before the potential resources of Egypt could be brought to full readiness, Nûr-al-dîn died (1174). At this point, the same loyal Jamâ'î-Sunnî spirit that had erected the state threatened to ruin it, for in loyalty to Nûr-al-dîn the pious Syrians supported his weak son against his lieutenant in Egypt, Ṣalâḥ-al-dîn b. Ayyûb (Saladin), the ablest successor. Saladin had been a rather reluctant soldier, even bookish in his youth, but had loyally followed his father and brother in the Zengid service. Now he showed himself a worthy continuer of Nûr-al-dîn's policies. After a time, he was able to win over Muslim Syria despite numerous initial disadvantages, notably that he was no Turk but a Kurd (of west Iranian highland origin), ethnically alien to the bulk of the military corps. Saladin tended to make Egypt a primary base of operations. He was able to restore, in territorial extent though not yet in effective power, something like the state of early Fâṭimî times, fostering the same patterns of trade. He maintained careful relations with several distant Muslim rulers and especially with the caliphate; but he got little help save bodies of private volunteers. He also made friendly arrangements with Greek and American Christian powers, arrangements that were probably at least as useful as his correspondence with Muslim rulers. Without otherwise making any more basic changes in political structure than had Nûr-al-dîn, and still founding himself on an appeal to the ghâzî spirit of the troops and the Jamâ'î-Sunnî ideals of the urban leaders, he took Jerusalem (whose population was spared, in conscious contrast to the Crusaders' behaviour) in 1187, and soon reduced the Crusader states to a few seaport towns.

A joint expedition of the kings of France and England along with a major German expedition, all supported by the power of the Italian cities, was unable materially to reverse this situation, though it prevented further Muslim successes. Saladin was hampered by the irregular resources of his varied troops, and the Occidentals by quarrels among their nobility. The resulting warfare is memorable chiefly for putting in relief the contrast in personalities between Saladin and the English king Richard, the dominating Occidental figure. Even the Occidentals respected Saladin for his unfailing chivalry and his fidelity to his word. This did not prevent them from repeated displays of bigotry and treachery; most notably when they retook Acre on terms (the chief accomplishment of the joint expedition) and Richard had the garrison massacred, including women and children, though they had surrendered on a pledge that they could be ransomed.

On his death (1193), Saladin left his power to his sons and brothers as amîrs of the chief cities; but first his brother (al-'Âdil, d. 1218) and then his brother's son (al-Kâmil, d. 1238), both capable men, were able to dominate the various family amîrates, holding themselves the crucial resources of Egypt. Only after 1238 did the cohesiveness of Saladin's Ayyûbid dynasty fully break down. In 1250, the dynasty was replaced in Egypt, and within a decade or so in the other provinces, by the leaders of its slave-soldier corps

(Mamlûks), who restored the Egyptian-Syrian state on a somewhat new principle.[1]

One of the effects of the Crusades was at least a local increase in Muslim communalism. There was an active debate as to whether pacts with infidels had to be honoured. Saladin held they were valid; but some 'ulamâ' argued they were not. (The weight of opinion among the Latin Christians decided that such pacts were not to be held to.) In any case, the presence of the Latins stimulated riots against dhimmîs, who tended—quite unfairly—to be associated with the Crusaders in the mind of the populace. Perhaps a more important effect of the Crusades was a disruption of Muslim commerce in Syria and hence in the Levant generally. The naval superiority of the Italians was consolidated by control of the chief Syrian ports. But the vigour of Occidental commerce there apparently did not make for an integrated economy in the region as a whole. Even after the last Crusaders were ejected, the Syrian coastal cities did not recover fully their prosperity.

Reforming states in the Maghrib

The political evolution in the farther west proceeded independently of the outcome of the Seljuḳ glory. It had long been independent of 'Abbâsî power and had experienced little united regional authority. Nonetheless, there was a similar political climate, especially after the transient general subjugation by the Fâṭimid caliphs, which had broken the Ibâḍî Khârijî power. There also Islam was felt as commanding a wider allegiance than any prince could offer; there also the tendency was for each city to act as an autonomous nucleus within a universal nexus of Muslim social relations. There too the pastoral tribes (Berbers) were in a position to dominate through their superior solidarity. But a combination of religious zeal with tribal power succeeded in erecting a pattern of state formation that was durable in its overall structure, though subject to interruptions and other weakness.

The west Mediterranean provinces, independent of the 'Abbâsî empire, had tasted the central intellectual and spiritual developments of the High Caliphal Period only at a certain remove. The Ibâḍî rule at Tâhart had indeed fostered the development of Khârijî law; but its liberal spirit would have left much unchanged in the actual Berber life. The Idrîsid dynasties farther west were only tinged with Shî'ism and left Berber tribal life even more intact than did the Ibâḍîs. But by the eleventh century, Islam had become very deep-rooted and was being actively spread southwards into and even beyond the Sahara. The Islamic presence had become the most important spiritual force.

Ibn-Yâsîn, the leader of a group of militant devotees who had established

[1] Of all the writing that has been done about Saladin, the most perceptive piece is surely H. A. R. Gibb's 'The Achievement of Saladin', *Bulletin of the John Rylands Library*, 35 (1952), 44–60, reprinted in his *Studies on the Civilization of Islam* (Boston, 1962), pp. 89–107.

themselves in an armed *ribâṭ* (jihâd war outpost) as far south as the Senegal river, converting or subduing the population there, was able to persuade (1056) the chiefs of the Lamtûnah Berber tribe to support his efforts at reform. The followers of the movement were called the *Murâbiṭs*, as devotees in the ribâṭ. They imposed a puritanical rule on the far western Sahara and then on all the western Maghrib (founding Marrâkash as their capital). They favoured the most rigid faqîh legists, who brought into full force the Mâlikî legal madhhab (at least in the towns), which had been becoming the most popular in the western Mediterranean. The state they built up was based on cities but supported by tribal military power from the surrounding mountains. It was more solid than any the western Maghrib had known, and disposed of relatively concentrated resources. Hence when the Spanish Muslims found themselves, under their numerous city-state rulers, threatened with Christian power from northern Spain, the tradesmen and the faqîhs were eager to have the Murâbiṭs cross over and defeat the Christians; and when that had been done they forced the various Spanish princelings to abdicate (1090) in favour of Murâbiṭ power.

The Murâbiṭ state, then, was not a mere predatory amîrate. It was founded on a demand that the Maghrib should enter into the full stream of the Shar'î life of the central lands of Islam; and it extended its power on the plea—like that of the Zengids in the east Mediterranean—that Muslims must close ranks against the Christian threat.

But there were already new streams of thought developing in the Nile-to-Oxus region itself. The writings of Ghazâlî, who tried to reconcile the increasingly popular Ṣûfism with an intellectualized Sharî'ah-mindedness, had been burned by the faqîhs under the Murâbiṭs. The same writings stimulated a new reformer, Ibn-Tûmart, after two generations of Murâbiṭ rule had left the earlier wave of reforming zeal much weakened (and the government's military power dissipated). By now, the petty legalisms of the Mâlikî faqîhs which had doubtless been a cosmopolitanizing influence in the Maghrib, seemed intellectually shallow and perhaps behind the time. Ibn-Tûmart's reforming zeal laid as much stress on puritanical detail as had Ibn-Yâsîn's, though preferring the Ẓâhirî madhhab to the Mâlikî, but he encouraged a wider intellectual perspective. (He shows traces of Falsafah and even Shî'î influence.) Retired to the Moroccan mountains, he declared himself *Mahdî* and called his followers the true monotheists, *Muwaḥḥids*.

Ibn-Tûmart died in 1130, but he had gained the support of his own Berber tribal bloc, the Maṣmûdah, and had gathered a core of brilliant leaders. Their chief, 'Abd-al-Mu'min, as khalîfah, successor to the Mahdî, organized an effective campaign against the Murâbiṭs. In more than twenty years of war (to 1147) the Muwaḥḥids occupied almost all the Murâbiṭ territory. The Muwaḥḥid campaign had itself contributed to the Murâbiṭ weakness that was yielding bits of Muslim Spain to the Christian powers. But with Muwaḥḥid victory, what the Muslims had retained in the south of Spain was safeguarded for two or three generations. On the mainland the Muwaḥḥids extended their sway even beyond the area to which the former dynasty had reached, conquering eastward in the Maghrib to Tripoli. They brought to an end there, as they had in Spain, the local Muslim weakness which had been inviting aggression and even occupation by Christian forces from Italy and Sicily.

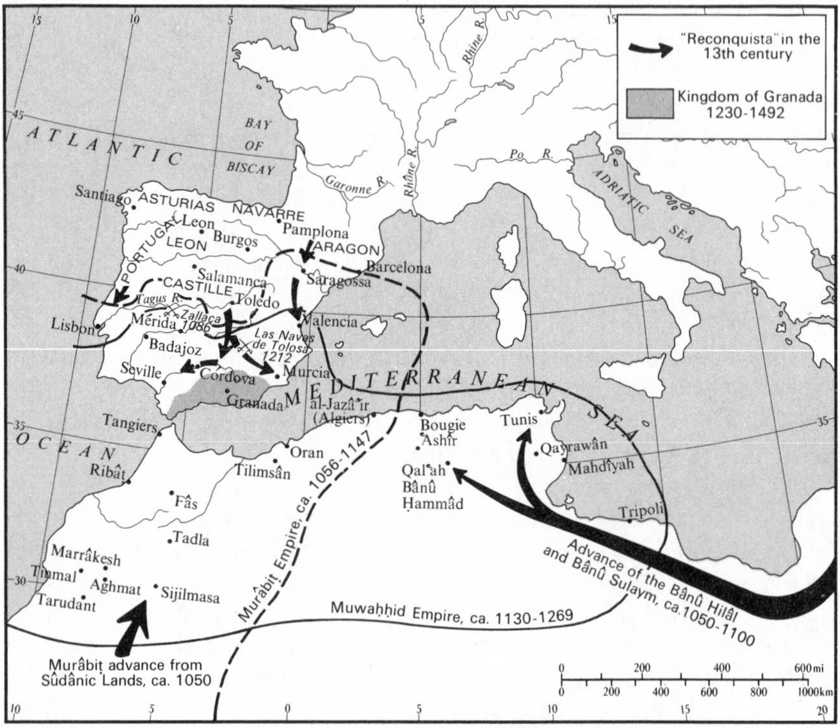

The Murâbiṭs and Muwaḥḥids

The pattern of reformist Berber political power thus gained a new lease on life. The Muwaḥḥid ruling family soon turned out to have broad intellectual interests and encouraged covertly a significant movement of Spanish philosophy, which we shall see more of. Nevertheless, the state continued to be founded (despite the hostility of Ibn-Tûmart to Mâlikism) upon an alliance of puritanical faqîhs in the cities and relatively crude Berber pastoral tribesmen. Architecture flourished in a solid, vigorous form. But courtly art and literature were given relatively less encouragement than earlier in Spain or than in, say, the contemporary Iran. Even while a degree of philosophy and serious art was encouraged, a tradition developed of mistrust for the worldly polish that was associated with Islamicate culture further east. Henceforth, ideas stemming from the rest of Islamdom were generally suspect. In Spain, at least, the state was little loved by the polished classes, but was supported ardently by the 'ulamâ'.

Early in the thirteenth century, the dynasty began to lose power. In 1212, the Muwaḥḥids were disastrously defeated in Spain by the Christian kings; soon they withdrew from Spain, whereupon the Christians took Cordova (1236) and Seville (1248). A single tiny Muslim state survived in the mountains at Granada (from 1230), paying tribute to the Christians. Muwaḥḥid officers established independent rule here and there, as at Tilimsân in the central Maghrib in 1236. The most important move was that of Abû-Zakariyâ' Yaḥyà the Ḥafṣid, governor of Tunis and the eastern Maghrib, who denounced the Muwaḥḥid ruler (1237) for deviating from proper Muwaḥḥid doctrine. He very nearly restored a strong central authority to the region, but could not consolidate his power. By 1269, the Muwaḥḥids had been replaced in the western Maghrib itself by the Marînid dynasty, of fresh tribal origins, which beat back the Ḥafṣids but was unable long to revive the greatness of the Muwaḥḥids (though it appealed implicitly to their heritage). Under the auspices of Murâbiṭs and Muwaḥḥids, however, the Maghrib had become the centre of Mâlikî Islam and had established its own comprehensive variant of the Islamicate high-cultural tradition. And the Maghrib remained Muslim.

The spread of Islamicate civilization beyond its original territory: into Europe

Although in the Mediterranean basin the weakness of the new international social order resulted in at least temporary recessions of the Muslim frontiers, on the whole Islam as a faith, and even Muslim polity, was expanding enormously in this period. Indeed, the high degree of decentralization in every social institution seems to have favoured a ready expansion of these institutions wherever an opportunity presented, whatever the apparent political situation. By and large, the Muslim society flourished grandly in its post-caliphal form. Even where Muslim rule was absent or had been overthrown, Islam often continued to flourish, although thrown on its own. In Spain and Sicily, indeed, the Muslim minorities at last withdrew when unable to re-establish their rule; yet in many other other areas it is precisely from this period that dates a significant body of Muslims under non-Muslim rule—for instance, in China. In short, Islamdom found itself able to maintain itself and its society apart from all governmental support altogether. It is this ability that made possible the remarkable expansion which now took place, and which was often, but not always, accompanied by political supremacy.

During almost three centuries following the initial spread of Muslim rule under the Medinese and the Syrian caliphs, the boundaries of Muslim territory had varied little; almost identical with the boundaries of the caliphal power and its successors, they had advanced in some places, notably in

Sicily, on the south shores of the Caspian, and in the Afghân mountains; but about as often they receded, as in Gaul and Spain and, most important, in all parts facing the Byzantines of Anatolia in the tenth century. In the many centuries after 945, on the contrary, there was an almost constant expansion of the area in which the religion and even the civilization flourished, often with no dependence on any previously Muslim state; an expansion which has indeed continued, in some senses, down to our own time.[2] The expansion proceeded in almost all directions: southward across the Sahara into the Sûdânic lands of Africa; southward and eastward into the coastlands of the Indian Ocean in East Africa and Malabar (in India) and the Malaysian archipelago; northward into the vast regions north of the Black, Caspian, and Aral seas and as far east as China. One of the most active centres of Islamization, from the tenth century on, was the Bulghâr state, centred at the confluence of Volga and Kama (near the later Ḳazan). But perhaps the most significant directions in which Muslim rule expanded were west and east into the rich core areas of civilization which were southern Europe and northern India. We will be reviewing most of this expansion in a larger sweep in Book Four, but here we must deal with the political evolution of Islamicate society in these two key areas.

After the end of the eleventh century, when the long-standing barrier of the Taurus mountains, which had normally marked the boundary between the Byzantine empire and the caliphal state, was breached by Seljuḳ troops, inner Anatolia gradually became Muslim under the leadership of Turks. (The Anatolian coasts and all the Balkan peninsula eventually followed, so that all remaining areas of Greek culture east of Sicily came under Muslim rule.) Also in the eleventh century, the Panjâb had been occupied, in northwestern India (under Maḥmûd of Ghaznah); then, at the start of the thirteenth century, the Ganges plain too, including the key areas of the old Sanskrit civilization. By the end of the century, almost the whole of India was more or less under Muslim control. In these two areas, Europe and India, Islamicate culture was to become almost as creative as in its homelands between Nile and Oxus.

On both sides of the Nile-to-Oxus region, the frontier zones between Islamdom and its two great rival societies were marked off for a long time,

[2] The term 'expansion of Islam' applied most appropriately to this latter movement. It is sometimes applied to the first Arab conquests; but they formed an 'expansion of Islam' only in a very limited sense. What then 'expanded' was, of course, not the full Islamic faith (and culture) of history, but the kernel of a faith then in the course of establishing its historic identity: it had no previous established area from which it was expanding (neither the Ḥijâz nor Bedouin Arabia can bear that character). In any case, it 'expanded' as to area controlled but not, during the conquests themselves, as to numbers (save chiefly in the case of the Berbers). The Arab *conquests* are better termed just that, and the term 'expansion' of Islam reserved for the later more massive movement. It is Western ethnocentrism, seeing the whole in terms of that movement which carried Islam into Spain, France, and Italy, that has occasioned the less satisfactory usage.

both emotionally and socially, as pronouncedly special districts. In each case, the effective frontier area, where the societies were in direct contact by land, was a fairly small zone. In each case, it was inhabited by warlike populations. But the history of the frontiers was rather different.

The frontier with Europe, till the battle of Malazgirt (1070), was normally in the eastern Taurus mountains and the mountains northeastward from them. This was the most famous zone of historic enmity, where the 'Abbâsid caliphs had led yearly expeditions against the Byzantine emperor, the most powerful of infidel kings. Great prestige was attached to the jihâd war in that zone, and men travelled to take part in it from as far off as Khurâsân, sometimes in great unruly bands. On both sides, the governments recognized a special status for the frontier districts and organized special bodies of troops to defend the more settled hinterland against raids from the other side—and to raid, themselves, when they could. These troops were partly organized from the local population; partly volunteers, adventurous men glad to enlist in a good cause; and partly mercenaries recruited from everywhere. On both sides, Turkic soldiers were used; on the Muslim side they came from north of the Oxus and were, of course, mostly Muslims; on the Christian side they came from the Black Sea region and were Christians. On the Christian side, Armenian highlanders played a specially great role; they moved from the northern Armenian territories all along the mountains to the south. On both sides, romantic epics were composed, in Greek and Arabic, about the fighting and its heroes. A few generations of continuous fighting, with neither side permanently gaining ground, sufficed to give both sides a reasonably similar frontier culture, so that individuals or even small bands might change sides, when discontented, without great difficulties of adjustment.

By the eleventh century, the Byzantine side was becoming the weaker. The main parts of Anatolia were thoroughly Greek and adhered to the official Chalcedonian church; but disaffection had shown itself even in the form of religious allegiance: the frontier Armenians stubbornly clung to their religious independence as Gregorian Christians, despite the attempts of the Greek church hierarchy to subject them; and heretical movements had become popular even among the Greeks themselves. There was a period when the militarization of landholding and of power might have seemed to be progressing in Byzantium rather as it had been in Islamdom. But it seems that now the agrarian economy was being undermined not by military decentralization but by its remedy—an excessive bureaucratic power, which required ever more revenue to meet its steadily growing commitments. When further taxation threatened to be disastrous, the bureaucrats were even inclined to reduce military expenditure so as to curb the rival military powers while balancing the budget; thus alienating not only peasants but soldiers. The catastrophe came at Malazgirt, and once the main army was broken, no way was found to restore the old frontier. The Armenians preferred to set up independent little states, ignoring the Byzantine state; and much of the frontier population (including Turks) seems to have gone over to the Muslims.

Thereupon a new frontier zone developed in the twelfth century. But it proved to be merely a zone of Muslim advance. The Byzantines had regained, at first with the help of the Crusaders, the coastal regions; but the Muslims, now mostly Turkic, held the interior. Between the two, in the highlands inland from the sea, the Greeks held the cities, while Muslim raiders made the countryside increasingly untenable. The Muslims were organized in several little raiding states, whose political strength lay in their ability to attract ghâzîs from the Muslim hinterland for the jihâd war. Anatolia was a land of hope for Muslims who wanted to improve their lot, and found themselves free to move; and especially for nomadic pastoral clans. In the new frontier zone, gradually agriculture was greatly reduced, and the Byzantine government became ineffective. While many of the Christian peasants remained on their lands, the church hierarchy withdrew from the unsafe and unprofitable districts; gradually the cities became sufficiently isolated to find it profitable to make arrangements with the Muslim raider bands.

The new frontier zone was never stabilized like the first one, but proved to be a shifting line along which power was passing increasingly to the Turkic Muslims. Behind the line, at any given time, the Muslim Turkic population, pastoral or settled, was sufficiently dense, as compared to the decimated Greek Christian peasantry, to maintain their own identity, and gradually the peasantry—and still later, the towns—were attracted into its cultural orbit. As the line advanced, the new areas were assimilated to the older ones. By the end of the thirteenth century, the Muslims had reached the sea and its many harbours. There they took to ships and raided under sail—not the last time that piracy was to mark a frontier zone between Islamdom and Christendom. But once the primary frontier with Christendom at the Taurus had been breached, henceforth there was no obvious stopping place; the social situation in all the Greek territories was rather similar. In the fourteenth century the Aegean too was crossed, and then the Balkan mountains, and finally even the Danube.[3]

Once sufficient numbers of civilian Muslim cadres—merchants and tradesmen, administrators, and men of religion—had been attracted into Anatolia, a formal Islamicate state could be set up. One family of Seljuḳid chiefs, with headquarters at Ḳonya (Iconium), had retained a nominal overlordship over the various Muslim groupings in the peninsula. Some of these groupings formed strong little states, based on ghâzî troops, which could defy Seljuḳ authority; moreover at first the Seljuḳids of Ḳonya turned their interest primarily toward gaining a position in the Fertile Crescent among the rest

[3] Some writers make a great deal of the moment when the Muslims first occupied land on the Balkan side of the Aegean, saying that now 'Europe' was entered. Such an idea, like the artificial delimitation of 'Europe' that it presupposes, is merely silly.

of the Seljuḳid family. But after 1107, when the Seljuḳ empire was clearly breaking up into small units anyway, the local dynasty accepted the idea of basing itself on the growing resources of a cultivated Muslim life in Anatolia itself. Some of the petty Muslim states around about were subdued, and Ḳonya became the centre of a state in the Iranian style, the sultanate of Rûm (i.e., 'Rome', the Christian empire of which Anatolia had been the richest part). The Rûm Seljuḳs fought the Byzantines in western Anatolia as one state against another rather than as ghâzîs; border raiding was partly superseded. After 1204, when Crusader troops intended for Jerusalem took Constantinople instead and occupied Aegean territories as a more promising field for easy exploitation than hostile Syria, the Muslims readily reaped part of the benefit. They seized some coastlands, enough to make Ḳonya a station on the Mediterranean–Black Sea trade route.

At Ḳonya, Persian and Greek as well as Turkish were used, and the arts of Islamdom flourished as well as in the older territories. The Rûm Seljuḳ architecture is famous, but Ḳonya's greatest claim to fame is the poet and Ṣûfî Jalâluddîn Rûmî, whose shrine has remained the most important building in the city. Even the Rûm Seljuḳ arms prospered for a time just when the other Seljuḳ states were being torn apart; the local dynasty renewed its interest in the lands of old Islam, came to terms with the Byzantines, and expanded its power eastward. But by the mid-thirteenth century it was already in difficulties. In any case, most of the Muslim ghâzîs preferred to pass beyond Ḳonya to its vassal states that were growing up on the newer Anatolian frontier. In 1243, Ḳonya had to submit to the Mongols, and the dynasty never regained independence or greatness.

Into India

We know a great deal less about the frontier with India than about the frontier with Europe, though for Islamicate civilization in the long run the passage into India was the more important of the two. The frontier zone was for a long time in the mountains of the Kabul river basin (for Sind, where Muslims had ruled since the eighth century, was isolated by the Thar desert. There various principalities of Indic religious and cultural allegiance held out in greater or lesser dependence on Muslim power. There was no one great opponent like the Byzantine emperor, and anyway India was culturally far more alien to the Irano-Semitic traditions than was the Hellenic Mediterranean. The frontier was less famous and fewer ghâzîs went thither. Gradually much of the population was Islamized, accepting the more dynamic cultural lead in their region. Presumably, this enabled the Sâmânîs (in the later tenth century)—sending Turkic garrisons into the area under Maḥmûd's predecessors—to carry direct Muslim rule to the edge of the mountains, to the passes commanding the Indic plains. Then, once many of the mountaineers had become Muslim and were led by well-organized Turkic troops in the name of a jihâd war that could override local feuds, the plains were at their mercy. No second frontier zone had to be established. Indeed, each stage of the conquests in India was earlier and more sudden than the corresponding stage of the conquests in Europe.

The first important descent into the plain was overwhelming, as we have seen. The genius of Maḥmûd of Ghaznah doubtless made it more sudden and devastating than it might have been otherwise; but at least the Panjâb was historically open to such overwhelming descents, once people from the highlands and the north were sufficiently united; there was no reason to await the slow progress that was required in the mountainous Greek territory, which was as rigorous in climate and terrain as the territory from which it was invaded. However, the Panjâb was separated from the rest of India not by a sea full of harbours, like the Aegean, but by a hundred-mile stretch of open plain, flanked by desert and mountains. The strip of plain offered no special incentives, perhaps; at any rate, the Muslims were restricted to the Panjâb (except for raids) for most of two centuries after its conquest. There much of the population began to turn Muslim. Throughout the Indus basin there was considerable Buddhist population, especially, it seems, in classes (perhaps mercantile classes) that were at odds with the ruling Hindu castes; the Buddhists may not have been unfriendly to the Muslims and some of them, at least in Sind, may have converted fairly soon.

In the rest of northern India, the clans that had ruled for some centuries (later, at least, collectively called *Râjpûts*) continued their own internecine strife, and their political traditions presumably became steadily more tied with commitments that made effective deployment of revenue resources more difficult. Only at the end of the twelfth century, under the Ghûrid dynasty from the Iranian mountains, was there a new thrust into the Ganges plain. Then, again, advance was phenomenally rapid. We have seen how the Ghaznavid house was reduced to its Panjâb province by the Ghûrids. In the 1170s the Ghûrid ruler appointed his brother, Muḥammad, governor of Ghaznah and encouraged him to raid in India. At first he raided Ismâʿîlîs, established for a time in independence at Multân, and Hindu states not too far beyond; but finally, in alliance with a Hindu ruler, he reduced Lahore and replaced the last of the Ghaznavid dynasty. Then he undertook the conquest of the Ganges plain, beginning in 1191. By the end of the decade, he and his captains (mostly Turkic slaves) had conquered as far as the western parts of Bengal. The Râjpût ruling castes were massacred—or slew their womenfolk and sacrificed themselves in hopeless sallies as a chivalric gesture.

In 1206, Muḥammad of Ghûr (who had meanwhile become sole ruler) was assassinated and no Ghûrid was able to claim power. His captains fought among themselves for control of their provinces. But the conquests remained under Muslim occupation. The Turkic ex-slave Quṭbuddîn Aybak became sultan at Lahore and ruled also the Ganges plain, but had little opportunity to settle a policy. When he died in 1210, his freed slave Iltutmish, in turn,

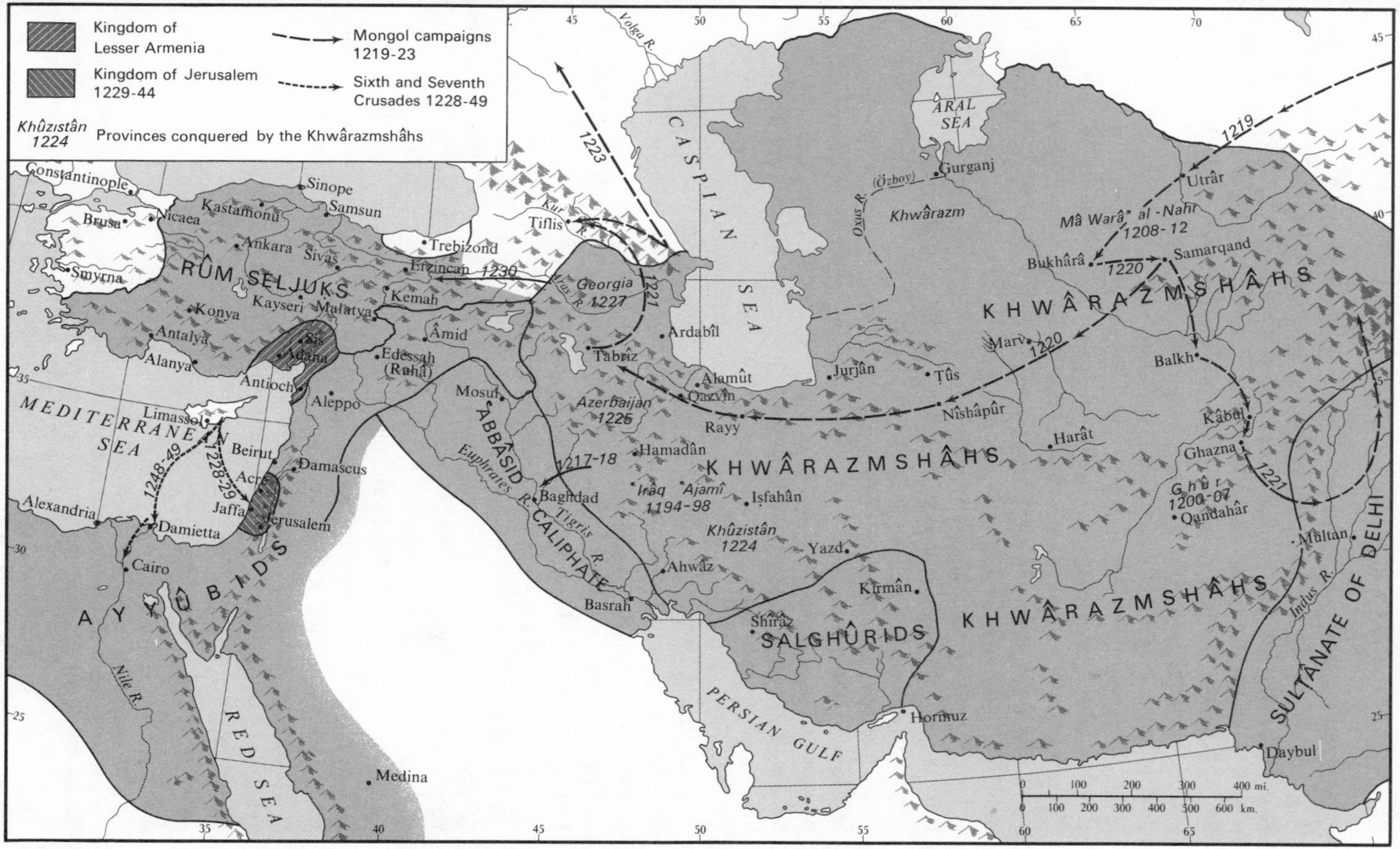

The central Islamic lands in the early thirteenth century

became sultan at Delhi, which had been captured only a few years before; it was he that organized the sultanate. The sultans were chiefs of a tightly organized oligarchy of Turkic captains, who formally limited their sultan's power. They were rather like the Mamlûk oligarchy in Egypt; like them, they were jealous of sharing any power with outsiders, particularly with non-Turks, Muslim or no.[4] As with the Mamlûks in Egypt, at one point their sultan was a woman: Iltutmish recognized that his sons were incompetent and nominated his daughter, Raẓiyyah, who indeed did prove her ability to rule well (and even to command on horseback in battle), having had some administrative practice already under her father; but after three years, the perpetual conspiracies of captains who were ill at ease under a woman general succeeded in doing away with her (1240).

The régime was conscious not only of its Turkicness but of its Muslimness. But—as had earlier Muslim governments in the Indus basin—it readily extended dhimmî status to its infidel subjects and made use of them in many capacities. The Muslims, particularly in the first wave of conquest, wrecked and looted Hindu temples; eventually, few earlier temples survived in that part of India. But the bulk of the population (unlike that of the Panjâb) remained Hindu even after centuries; except in eastern Bengal, where the lower classes—who had perhaps been partly Buddhist at one point—later turned Muslim while the higher castes remained Hindu.

In neither Anatolia nor the Panjâb—nor, then, in the Ganges plain (or later in the Balkan peninsula)—was there any serious movement for the restoration of non-Muslim power, even when the centre of Islamdom was overrun by infidel Mongols. The Christian peasantry seems to have had no fond memories of the Byzantine empire. As to Indian society, it was so divided by caste that it did not easily unite behind new claimants to rule, once the old ruling caste was gone. As we shall see, the Muslims filled the role of the Râjpûts, with the one difference, that, unlike the original Râjpûts they had their own cosmopolitan ties, in the perspective of which Hindu society was a local phenomenon, to which they did not deign to assimilate. In both Europe and India, Islam represented a socially flexible allegiance which the most vigorous persons locally could adopt; and though they might be barred from rising within their own communities, as Muslims they could rise almost indefinitely. Once the Muslims were established, the territory remained Muslim-ruled, and the Islamicate civilization became increasingly dominant even among non-converts—down to modern times, when the role and the very existence of an Islamicate culture have been put radically in question.

[4] The dynasty is commonly called the 'Slave dynasty', but unlike the Mamlûks of Egypt, these Turks did not make a habit of preferring a sultan's slave to his son; if Aybak and later Balban and his family are to be included with Iltutmish and his family in one group, it should be under the name of the 'Albari' sultanate, for they were all Albari Turks. Cf. Ram Prasad Tripathi, *Some Aspects of Muslim Administration*, 2nd revised ed. (Allahabad, 1956), a well-informed summary.

Both in the Panjâb-Ganges plain and in Anatolia, as in Islamdom itself, the period preceding the Muslim conquest had been one of long-run weakening in the central powers. In both areas, the advent of Muslim rule seems to have been associated with an increase in urban prosperity. And in both areas, the urbanization, in which both Muslims and dhimmîs participated, was carried out under the auspices of a distinctly Islamicate (i.e., Irano-Semitic) social and cultural pattern. The 'lands of old Islam' held enormous prestige for the new lands as models and as sources of expertise. It was as if Islam offered a relatively viable answer to problems that were besetting all these areas in this general period.

One must add that the bulk (though not all) of the ghâzîs on each frontier were Jamâ'î-Sunnîs, and religious minorities were not popular among them. Islam in both Europe and India was to be predominantly—though again not entirely—Sunnî. Indeed, in all the areas into which Islam began to spread in this period Sunnism predominated, in most of them far more completely than in India and Europe. Shî'ism retained any marked strength only in the central lands of old Islam.

The caliph al-Nâṣir, the courtly futuwwah, and the Khwârazmshâhs

In central Islamdom, most of the successor states to the Seljuḳs paid little heed to the Christian offensive in the Mediterranean, eastern or western. Nor were they more than marginally impressed by the spread of Islam itself, west or east: these new territories merely added themselves to the already vast diversity of Islamdom. In the core of the old caliphal lands, after the fall of the last Seljuḳid, the Muslim political conscience staged a more domestic drama.

Perhaps the last serious effort at finding a new political idea on which to build the unity of Islamdom as a whole took place in the early thirteenth century under the guidance of the caliph himself. As we have seen, even the ideal of an all-inclusive Seljuḳ sultanate had failed, and it was especially in the most central areas of Islamdom that the atabeg system produced maximum fragmentation of authority. It was among these rulers, whose claims, even at their widest, were personal and ephemeral, that the caliph al-Nâṣir tried to inject a new element into political life, an element that might have caused just the qualities of personal leadership, which the atabegs often displayed, to make for co-operation or at least peaceful competition rather than always for hostilities.

Among these many provincial rulers, the caliphs regained their independence at Baghdad, and were able to pursue a reasonably consistent policy of consolidating their control in the Iraq because of the unique authority that still clung to their title. Under the caliph al-Nâṣir (1180–1225), the caliphal government was able to annex a certain amount of territory beyond the Iraq itself. But it was clear that it could not dream of restoring the lost caliphal power on the old basis.

Al-Nâṣir reigned forty-five years. He shared, at least at first, in the violent ways of the time: he had his first two viziers executed, and caused the head of his enemy, the last Seljuḳid sultan, to be publicly displayed at Baghdad. But he also established many waqf foundations, especially for the benefit of the poor. And despite his sober financial husbandry (which some of the lettered public did not approve if it meant a less liberal patronage of such men as poets), he attracted an outstanding circle of advisers, some of whom were widely respected. Thus he had the opportunity to try out fully a far-reaching programme which he conceived for unifying the Muslims on a new basis. Early in his reign he was already launching some of his more characteristic policies. He seems to have developed his programme consistently till the end. It did not produce all the results presumably intended, but it had ramifying effects.

It is unfortunate that Ibn-al-Athîr, the most urbane of the general historians of the time, failed to see the genius of al-Nâṣir as he also failed to see that of Saladin. We are forced to reconstruct the picture from diverse indications.

Two levels may be distinguished in al-Nâṣir's policies. He expanded his own direct rule in neighbouring territories by relatively conventional military means. But at the same time he was extending his influence very widely in Islamdom in ideological forms. In his thinking, the role of the caliphate was given a much more important role than that of mere certifying agency, but also a role quite different from that envisaged for an ideal caliph by the latter-day theoreticians of a Shar'î society. Al-Nâṣir's two levels of policy were closely interrelated, but we may consider them separately.

Profiting by the weakness of the last Seljuḳs, al-Nâṣir consolidated the power of the caliphate in the Iraq and even in part of the Jazîrah. He ruled his provinces rigorously, maintaining public security; but he could not, of course, restore the original productivity of the Sawâd. He also worked actively toward the destruction of the remnant of Seljuḳ power that had so long overshadowed the caliphate, and was still potentially the strongest single power in the area. This he undertook by way of alliances. First, he was allied with the Khwârazmshâh Tekish (1172–1200); the caliph assisted his expedition into western Iran, where the last Seljuḳid was destroyed (1194). Thereupon, al-Nâṣir and Tekish quarrelled. The Khwârazmshâh asserted his own control in 'Irâq 'Ajamî, and evidently expected the caliph to be subservient to him as previously to the Seljuḳs. When Tekish withdrew, al-Nâṣir's army secured the submission of Khûzistân and even of the adjoining parts of Iran (1195). Tekish returned and drove the caliph's forces out of Iran, leaving him, of his late conquests, only the Khûzistân lowlands.

It became clear that the Khwârazmshâh, who now adopted the title sultan, was proving capable of replacing the Seljuḳs with a power newer and less handicapped by vested commitments. Al-Nâṣir turned against this new power too, and constructed a new system of alliances among the lesser powers. The most important figure in the alliance was the atabeg of Azerbaijan, who was enabled to regain control of Hamadhân in 'Iraq 'Ajamî—and again to regain control when his lieutenant there rebelled (and tried to go over to the Khwârazmshâh).

Al-Nâṣir's most spectacular diplomatic victory was to integrate even the head of the Nizârî Ismâ'îlî state into his alliance. The young heir to the Ismâ'îlî imâmate at Alamût in Daylamân decided to become a Jamâ'î-Sunnî on his advent to power, and to take his people along with him, so ending the implacable hostility that had isolated the Ismâ'îlîs. But this would be impossible without the co-operation of the Jamâ'î-Sunnî rulers. Al-Nâṣir assured this by silencing those Sunnîs who remained sceptical of the imâm's conversion: no easy feat even on the part of a caliph. The Ismâ'îlîs obeyed their imâm in this move implicitly, presumably on the basis of taqiyyah dissimulation (though the ruler himself was perfectly sincere). At first allied politically to the Khwârazmshâh, the Ismâ'îlî ruler came round to the caliph. He materially helped the atabeg of Azerbaijan in the wars in 'Irâq 'Ajamî—once in a joint military campaign, and once by sending an assassin.

But more significant than the caliph's campaigns and alliances was his experiment with the futuwwah men's clubs. The writings of al-Nâṣir's friend 'Umar Suhravardî are the most important source for understanding the ideological side of al-Nâṣir's policies. 'Umar Suhravardî (1145–1234) was founder of a Ṣûfî ṭarîqah order that quickly became very prominent, and author of a widely popular manual of Ṣûfî ways, the *'Awârif al-ma'ârif*. In his Ṣûfism, 'Umar Suhravardî was conservative: he mistrusted the speculative orientation of his avant-garde contemporaries. In contrast to his contemporary and fellow-townsman, the Ṣûfî metaphysician Yaḥyà Suhravardî, he was very strong for the Sharî'ah and its related disciplines, and explicitly opposed to such speculation as either the Faylasûfs or the more adventurous Ṣûfîs indulged in. Nevertheless, he was tolerant of all kinds of Ṣûfîs; and, for himself, always moderate—both in his claims for Ṣûfî achievements and in his demands upon those who would follow the way.

He saw Ṣûfism as a way to perfect devotion, in which one can fully enjoy the divine Beauty, one has previously but glimpsed. With unfailing good sense, he advised a Ṣûfî regimen that was practical to this end: he encouraged living in a khâniqâh lodge without trying to earn one's bread, as more within the spiritual means of most serious devotees than trying to pray all night and work all day (and less subject to temptation than being a wandering beggar). He left the point of celibacy up to the spiritual adviser. Yet he said the wandering beggar Qalandars, who were generally loose in Shar'î matters, were honest but satisfied with the relatively low spiritual stage they happened to have reached. Throughout, at the same time, he allowed himself a creative breadth of view. He seems to have been the most important collaborator of al-Nâṣir in his policies; he was sent on key diplomatic missions. He had clear political ideas.

'Umar Suhravardî taught the primacy of the Jamâ'î caliphate, as capstone of the structure formed by the Sharî'ah. The caliph must, in person, be the ultimate guarantor of the Islamic religious and social order. But in contrast to such theorists as al-Mâwardî, Suhravardî did not see the caliph as then delegating his authority to a great sultan, who should wield it on the basis of effective military power. But neither could he expect to see the caliphate renew its central bureaucratic power as of yore. Rather, he seems to have hoped that the caliphate could work through just those multiple and decentralized institutions that had become the true loci of power in the Middle Periods.

The caliph, as head of the legal structure created by the Sharî'ah, must first of all be the chief of the 'ulamâ' scholars as interpreters of the law. But he could be this not from outside the body of independent 'ulamâ', making them his servants. Rather, he must be one of the 'ulamâ' himself, and become the chief of the 'ulamâ' according to the standards of the 'ulamâ'. Indeed, al-Nâṣir undertook to be an active teacher of ḥadîth reports, as Suhravardî makes a point of showing us by citing al-Nâṣir as the latest link in the isnâd documentation of some ḥadîth reports he uses. Al-Nâṣir made a point of getting himself certified as a legitimate faqîh in all four Jamâ'î-Sunnî legal madhhab schools still recognized at Baghdad: the Ḥanafî, the Shâfi'î, the Ḥanbalî, and the Mâlikî. Such a policy also served, incidentally, to underline the equal legitimacy of the four madhhabs, and to encourage them to admit each other's validity.

The caliphate was not only the focus of the Sharî'ah; it was also the focus of the Ṣûfi ways. For Ṣûfism was but a branch of the Sharî'ah: it was the way appropriate to the spiritually strongest of the community, but just as much authorized by Sharî'ah as any less difficult way. But al-Nâṣir's role as chief of the Ṣûfî way was expressed less in purely Ṣûfî terms than through an institution more directly involved in social responsibilities: the futuwwah men's clubs. We have seen how these clubs were the most prominent channel for expressing lower-class interests in the towns, and how, after failing to provide militias on which town autonomy might have rested, they were increasingly pervaded by Ṣûfî teachings and Ṣûfî connections. Suhravardî taught that the futuwwah was a part of the Ṣûfî way, set off (by Abraham) precisely for the ordinary folk for whom the full Ṣûfî way was too hard; accordingly, futuwwah, too, was an integral part of the Shar'î way, and was to be ultimately focused in the caliph. But here, too, al-Nâṣir's policy was not to command from without, but to join the futuwwah clubs himself and achieve leadership from within them.

Though the futuwwah clubs had not been allowed to reach the dominating position as police bodies in Baghdad they had sometimes achieved in other towns, yet they had been important enough to inspire some earlier Baghdad dignitaries with the idea of joining them, in the hope of bringing them under some control. This was surely one of al-Nâṣir's hopes: that by controlling the sometimes turbulent futuwwah from within, he could be surer of controlling Baghdad as a city. He had himself initiated into one of the futuwwah clubs, two years after his accession as caliph, by a saintly pîr in great repute among the futuwwah men. Then he began initiating others himself—courtiers and also lesser personages; and even foreign amîrs. Only in 1207, after twenty-five years as an initiate in the futuwwah, was he ready to consolidate the position he had gradually gained. He declared that he was the head of all futuwwah clubs both in Baghdad and everywhere, and that any clubs that did not acknowledge his headship were banned, and not to be recognized as true futuwwah. He went rather further, in his encouragement of mutual tolerance among Muslims, with the futuwwah than with the 'ulamâ': the several obedient futuwwah clubs were told, as integral parts of the Islamic Ummah, to recognize each other's validity. We have a work on the futuwwah, written in al-Nâṣir's time and favourable to al-Nâṣir, which reflects the attitude taken: the futuwwah clubs should not quarrel among themselves; they should carefully hold themselves within Shar'î limits; and (since Islam was the basis of their solidarity with the other Shar'î institutions) if they must include non-Muslims, this should be only on the understanding that they would be good prospects for conversion.[5] In fact, while he lived, al-Nâṣir does seem to have succeeded in keeping the futuwwah clubs and other factions from violence in Baghdad.

Al-Nâṣir's efforts at conciliation among Muslims went beyond the Sunnî 'ulamâ' and the futuwwah to the Shî'ah. After the Ismâ'îlî revolt, many of the Shî'îs who remained loyal to the Twelver tradition were eager to identify themselves socially with the Jamâ'î-Sunnî community.[6] In any case, Ṣûfîs especially were willing to take up 'Alid-loyalist notions; Suhravardî, for instance, says that Adam was to propagate the Sharî'ah, while Seth, his son, was to propagate the Ṣûfî way as the inner truth of the Sharî'ah—a notion of the relation between the two patriarchs that we first come upon among the Ismâ'îlîs, who projected back to all the great prophets the special relation they recognized between Muḥammad and 'Alî, who propagated the inner meaning of Muḥammad's Sharî'ah. Though Suhravardî was strongly Jamâ'î-Sunnî in his outlook, he and al-Nâṣir evidently extended their conciliatory tendencies to the Shî'î tradition and also to Twelver Shî'îs themselves (we have noted how al-Nâṣir was able to bring the Ismâ'îlî Shî'îs as a body into the Sunnî fold through their imâm). Al-Nâṣir, in fact, showed on several occasions his strong leaning toward 'Alid loyalism, and a special respect for 'Alî; he built the shrine at Sâmarrâ over the spot where the Twelfth Imâm was said to have disappeared. (He was even accused of being a Shî'î.) It was

[5] Deodaat Anne Breebart's dissertation, 'Development and Structure of Turkish Futūwah Guilds', Princeton University Ph.D. thesis, 1961, has been very useful to me, though it shows remarkably little historical perceptivity.

[6] A Twelver Shî'î treatise of the twelfth century, *Kitâb al-naqḍ* by 'Abduljalîl Râzî, approved by the local leader of the Twelvers, sometimes goes to great lengths to reassure the Sunnîs that the Twelvers are within a common fold.

through such circles that 'Alid-loyalist ideas were permeating Sunnism generally.

The futuwwah (and ultimately the ideas of Ṣûfism, which legitimized the futuwwah) served also as vehicle for leadership of the caliphate in a third sphere, besides that of Sharî'ah law and that of popular urban institutions: the sphere of direct political power. This had been the sphere in which the caliphs had once been supreme; but now this sphere, too, like the others, was fragmented and decentralized. Here al-Nâṣir demonstrated his full membership in the class of amîrs (as in the 'ulamâ' and in the futuwwah) by his own military control in the Mesopotamian plains and by his effective webs of alliance. But he required more than local power, however great, or even than the abstract dignity of caliph, to assert his actual leadership among them. This he did by way of an upper-class, more especially a courtly, version of the futuwwah.

The futuwwah into which al-Nâṣir initiated his well-to-do followers had in common with the lower-class futuwwah (in addition to its ceremonial) above all its practice of sports. The futuwwah men trained homing pigeons (and al-Nâṣir tried to control this training in the interests of official information services); they practiced archery and other military games; as well as competing in such more bourgeois skills as wrestling. In the latter games, at least, every class could share. The appeal of al-Nâṣir's futuwwah was doubtless partly the glamour of engaging in such sports ceremonially and under such high auspices as that of the caliph himself. But among the courtly futuwwah initiates there could be a further advantage to the organization, comparable to the purpose of mutual aid in the lower-class futuwwah. The futuwwah ties could establish more formal lines of patronage through which disputes could be reconciled and individuals be assured greater security of personal status, countering the tendency in Islamdom to drastic social mobility. This may have been important even within the court at Baghdad. It probably played a part in the extension of al-Nâṣir's courtly futuwwah to other courts.

Al-Nâṣir's system of alliances was strengthened and extended by his initiating other rulers into his futuwwah club. Such initiations began before 1207, when he formally declared his general leadership, and were widespread after that. Al-Nâṣir, as head of the futuwwah club to which most of the Muslim rulers belonged (except for the strong rulers whom al-Nâṣir opposed and who formed a danger to all the others also), was in a position to be active mediator in their quarrels; and he did intervene, with greater or lesser success, as far away as Syria. Potentially, this could make for greater stability among these powers. Al-Nâṣir's role was at best marginal. Saladin had desired him to send major bodies of troops to help in the struggle against the Crusaders, and made it clear the caliph could take over the political leadership in that struggle; but al-Nâṣir sent only a token force. Al-Nâṣir clearly did not envisage an attempt at re-establishing the caliphate as a general monarchy in Islamdom. But the possibility of his mediation probably made itself felt everywhere; he never lost the respect even of Saladin.

After al-Nâṣir's death, his policies lasted during the next generation. His grandson, al-Mustanṣir (1226–42), still did a little mediating in Syria; even later, the futuwwah, under 'Abbâsid auspices, still played a part in the Mamlûk court of Egypt in the second half of the thirteenth century. In the futuwwah manuals of the guilds of subsequent centuries, al-Nâṣir was cited as the great master of the futuwwah.

His programme seems to have remained largely a personal effort, significant above all for what it tells us of the possibilities serious Muslims could envisage of healing their political disunity and the military anarchy it produced. Yet it cannot be dismissed as simply quixotic. After the possibility of an urban militia autonomy had failed, at the beginning of the twelfth century, with the Ismâ'îlî revolt, any further effort at a political pattern which should answer the needs of Islamdom must take into account the actuality of the amîrs along with the more autonomous urban elements and the over-arching Sharî'ah. This al-Nâṣir's effort did. It accepted the decentralized organization of the time with its dependence on relations of personal patronage and contract. That it was not entirely impractical may be suggested by the degree to which al-Nâṣir's successors, surely less gifted men than himself, were yet able to maintain at least traces of it even after the intervention of the Mongols in the region, which decisively altered the political situation it presupposed.

However, al-Nâṣir's diplomacy had nearly failed, already, against a contrasting but yet more romantic dream on the part of the Khwârazmshâhs, and especially of Muḥammad (1200–1220), son of Tekish, al-Nâṣir's first Khwârazmian opponent. Muḥammad took advantage of political movements north of China which weakened the Ḳara-Khitay power, to throw off its yoke and seize control of the Oxus basin area. Then Muḥammad used his forces for extensive conquests throughout Iran. He seems to have dreamed of restoring the absolute monarchy in the ancient Iranian manner, at least to that degree to which the Seljuḳs had seemed to do so. Such a restoration was, indeed, the only evident alternative to al-Nâṣir's policy of multiple rulers. Certainly al-Nâṣir, with his system of alliances among so many lesser rulers, was his most important opponent. Muḥammad went so far as to find an 'Alid to set up as a counter-candidate for the caliphate, whom he intended to install in Baghdad; but an unseasonably early winter made him postpone his campaign against Baghdad (1217). Then his plans were brought to an unexpected end even before al-Nâṣir's death.

The really serious blow to any future that al-Nâṣir's reconceived caliphate might have had came not from the Khwârazmians but from the central Eurasian steppe. It is doubtful if Muḥammad's edifice could have proved very strong anyway, though it was, for a few years, very extensive. He offered no means of counteracting the military decentralization of the time. Indeed, he does not seem to have attempted to restore the bureaucratic basis for extensive rule; rather, he further undermined it.[7] In any case, his career was cut short before a final decisive contest with the caliph. On the Khwârazmshâh's eastern frontiers, the Mongol tribes were building an enormous nomad-based state. His pride deliberately insulted them and they swept down upon his territories in 1220 with unprecedentedly ruthless and wholesale destruction.

Muḥammad fled without lifting a hand. His capital attempted resistance without him, but in vain. The Mongols pursued his more valiant son, Jalâl-uddîn, across Iran from the Panjâb to Azerbaijan. Wherever Jalâluddîn took his little army, he could set up as amîr (when for a moment the Mongols allowed him to breathe a bit) simply by the strength of his hardened military forces. But then the Mongols came. For ten years, Jalâluddîn's pride and charm brought disorder, plunder and romance to land after land till he was killed.[8] (His leaderless troops remained as a body, wandering as far as Syria, plundering or hiring themselves out to anyone interested.) By the time the Khwârazmian dynasty was finally ended so northern Iran had been devastated.

Cities like Bukhârâ were heaps of rubble and of corpses. Some cities, like Ṭûs, never were rebuilt. Large numbers of refugees, including many learnèd men, had fled to Syria and Egypt, to India, or even to the Ismâʿîlî strongholds in Quhistân, where the new allies of the caliphs treated them with generosity. The caliph at Baghdad had been spared. Henceforth, however, the dominant political fact in the central Muslim areas was the presence of the infidel Mongols, and all the courtly play at futuwwah proved irrelevant. The amîrs negotiated or fought or submitted, each garrison for itself.

The Mongol catastrophe

The comparative freedom of the Islamicate society from the political framework which had been its original matrix was tested by the West Christian movements of the twelfth century, when considerable Muslim territory in the Mediterranean was subjected to Christian rule, in Spain, Sicily, and Syria; but it was tested far more deeply in the thirteenth, when the most active centres of Islamicate culture, all the lands between Syria and Delhi, were conquered by the Mongols.

Nomadic pastoralist societies had developed wherever peasant agriculture did not find the terrain or the political resources to establish or maintain itself. The pastoralist society of the Arabian peninsula had been closely

[7] Cf. V. Bartold, *Turkestan down to the Mongol Invasion*, 2nd ed. (London, 1952), a magnificent study of underlying forces.

[8] His secretary, Nasawî, wrote in Persian a delightful account of his adventures, which has been translated into French, *Vie de Jalal al-Din Manguberti*, 2 vols. (Paris, 1891).

dependent upon the surrounding citied lands, as we have noticed. The pastoralist society of the Eurasian steppes was built on a vaster scale and was more complexly related to agrarian societies. The steppes were on the whole better watered than Arabia; the steppe nomads made greater use of horses than of camels, and were perhaps more self-contained. Nevertheless, the steppe nomads did engage in constant trade, throughout their terrain from north of the Black Sea to north of China, which depended on the goods of the cultivators and townsmen; especially they were involved in the inter-regional trade that passed across central Eurasia from China to various termini at the western end. It was in part constant mutual rivalry for grazing lands, but at least as much direct and indirect relations with the great trade routes, that kept the various tribal formations astir and led them into large-scale adventures.

Periodically, as in Arabia, nomadic tribal groups were combined under a single leadership; to the extent that such combinations were able to dominate and exact tribute from towns, for instance those at oases along the trade routes, they were able to grow still further; sometimes they created substantial nomad empires, fattening on the labour of town and country alike. Such formations were exceedingly unstable. But with the increasing spread of citied agrarian life they had naturally become increasingly common and increasingly powerful (that of Attila and his Huns was an unusually outsized example). Since the early centuries CE, it had been the received policy of the Chinese government—often the most powerful in the world, and perhaps the most exposed—to break up such formations; when it was strong, it extended its military force, and still more its negotiations, across the greater part of the steppe, as far as the Caspian Sea. (When it was weak, however, such nomad régimes had been able for long periods to extend their sway over north China itself.) Since the conquest of Syr-Oxus basin, the caliphal state and its successor states had likewise had an interest in keeping nomad formations under control, though they undertook it far less systematically.

In the twelfth century, no Chinese state and far less any Muslim one was in a position to perform this office, and nomad-based empires like that of the Kâra-Khitay thrived. These were, however, relatively tamed by close contact with the urban populations that had come to play a very important role throughout the area. In the first years of the thirteenth century a new formation arose, based on Mongol tribes far to the north on the very edge of the forests north of the steppe; its leadership had had at most only distant and hostile contact with agrarianate civilization. By 1206, Chingiz Khan had become chief of a wide grouping of Mongol tribes. Within a few years, he dominated much of northern China and eastern central Eurasia; when Muḥammad Khwârazmshâh defied him in 1219, he already possessed a massive force, controlling many centres of urban culture, from which he drew much skilled personnel. The conquest of the Oxus basin area was a matter of months, and very shortly the whole of Iran had acknowledged his sway. By his death in 1227, yet other areas, notably the Volga plains and much of Russia, had felt his blows. Under his son, Ögetey (1227–41) the empire continued its headlong expansion, overwhelming the rest of north China and making a general sweep of eastern Europe as far as into Germany (whence the Mongol withdrawal was purely voluntary).

Three traits were distinctive of this latest steppe power; the unprecedented extent of its activity, such that it could retain under a central control mighty expeditions simultaneously at opposite ends of the steppe; the unique ferocity of its campaigns; and its effective and intensive use of the technical resources of urban life. The three traits were interrelated, all depending on the world-historical situation then of the steppe region as a whole.

The wide extent of the conquests was partly ensured by the genius and regulations of Chingiz Khan; but it was made possible at all by the degree to which, in the previous thousand years, some sort of urban influence and even control had been converging about and into the steppe areas from China, from the Nile-to-Oxus region, and from Europe, so that awareness of distant lands and lines of communication already existed. Even in such remote areas as the upper Yenisei and the valleys south of Lake Baykal, the number of settlements that can be called towns was increasing in the centuries just before Chingiz Khan. And alternative long-distance trade routes were evidently becoming more widely known. The Mongols did not conquer blind but spied out every land they were coming to. This convergence of citied advance in the steppe was crucial to the other two traits as well.

The omnipresence of the agents of urban life helps account for the Mongols' ferocity. Again and again, almost the entire populace of a city was massacred without regard to sex or age, only skilled artisans being saved and transported away; even peasants were involved, being used as a living mass of rubble forced ahead of the army to absorb arrows and fill moats. With the population dead, the buildings would be levelled with the ground. To be sure, not all cities were so treated, though sooner or later (since any were so treated that revolted after once submitting) an appalling number were. The cumulative effect of independent accounts from Chinese, Muslim, and Christian lands confirms the impression that the Mongols loved destruction for its own sake, and often seemed unmoved even by the loss of revenues that such destruction would mean, once the area had submitted. Despite the abuse of the peasantry, the total population loss cannot have been great, for most towns were small and always recruited from the countryside anyway. But the break in high-cultural traditions seems to have been unusually severe in some cases, as compared with ordinary warfare.

In any case, the terror was unprecedented. This was the primary purpose of the ferocity, which the Mongols exploited with high adeptness at psychological warfare, and which secured the economic submission of vast tracts at the mere threat of the Mongol presence. The ferocity was, then, a deliberate technique. But it expressed violent emotions also; certainly on some occa-

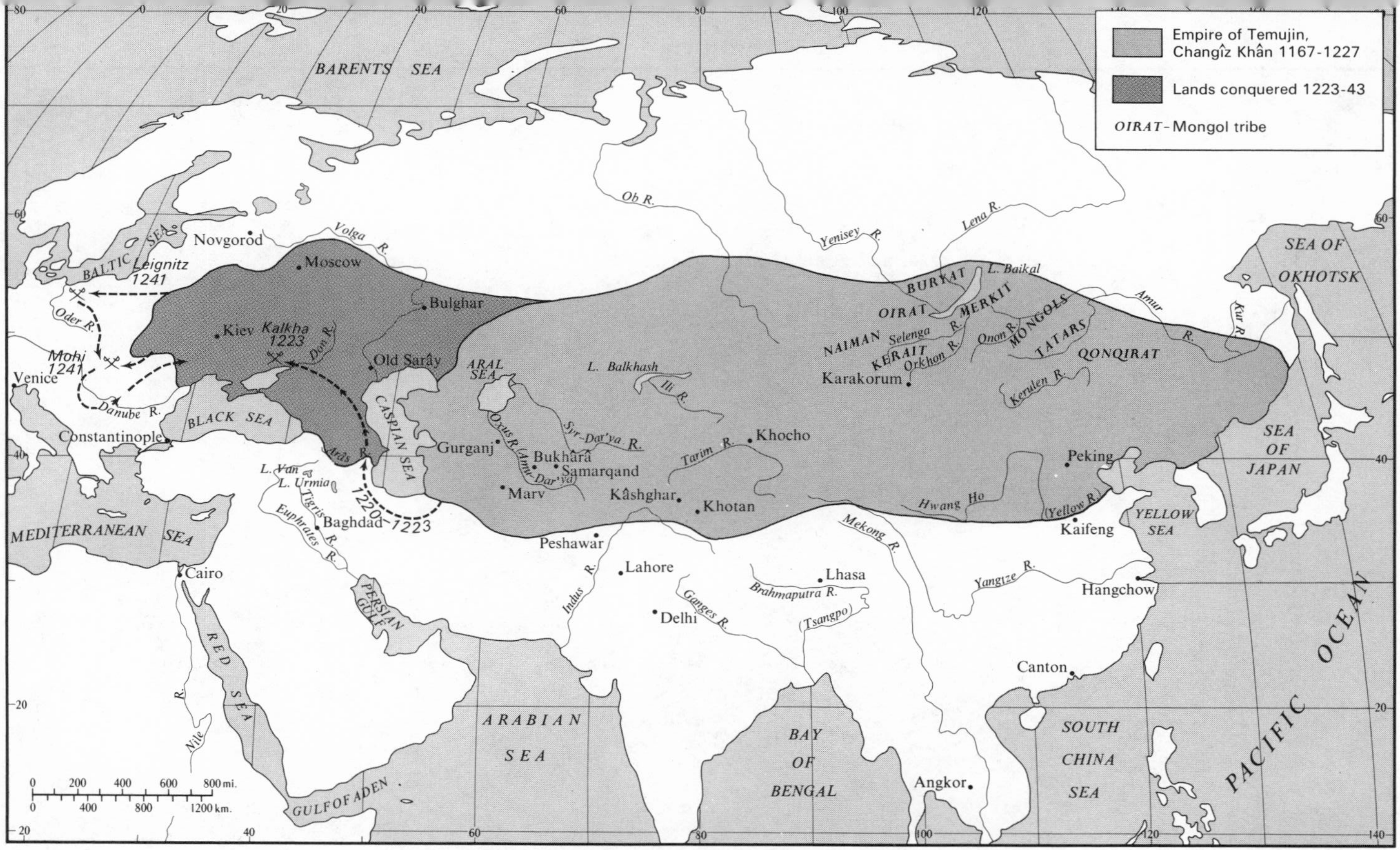

Mongol expansion, mid-thirteenth century

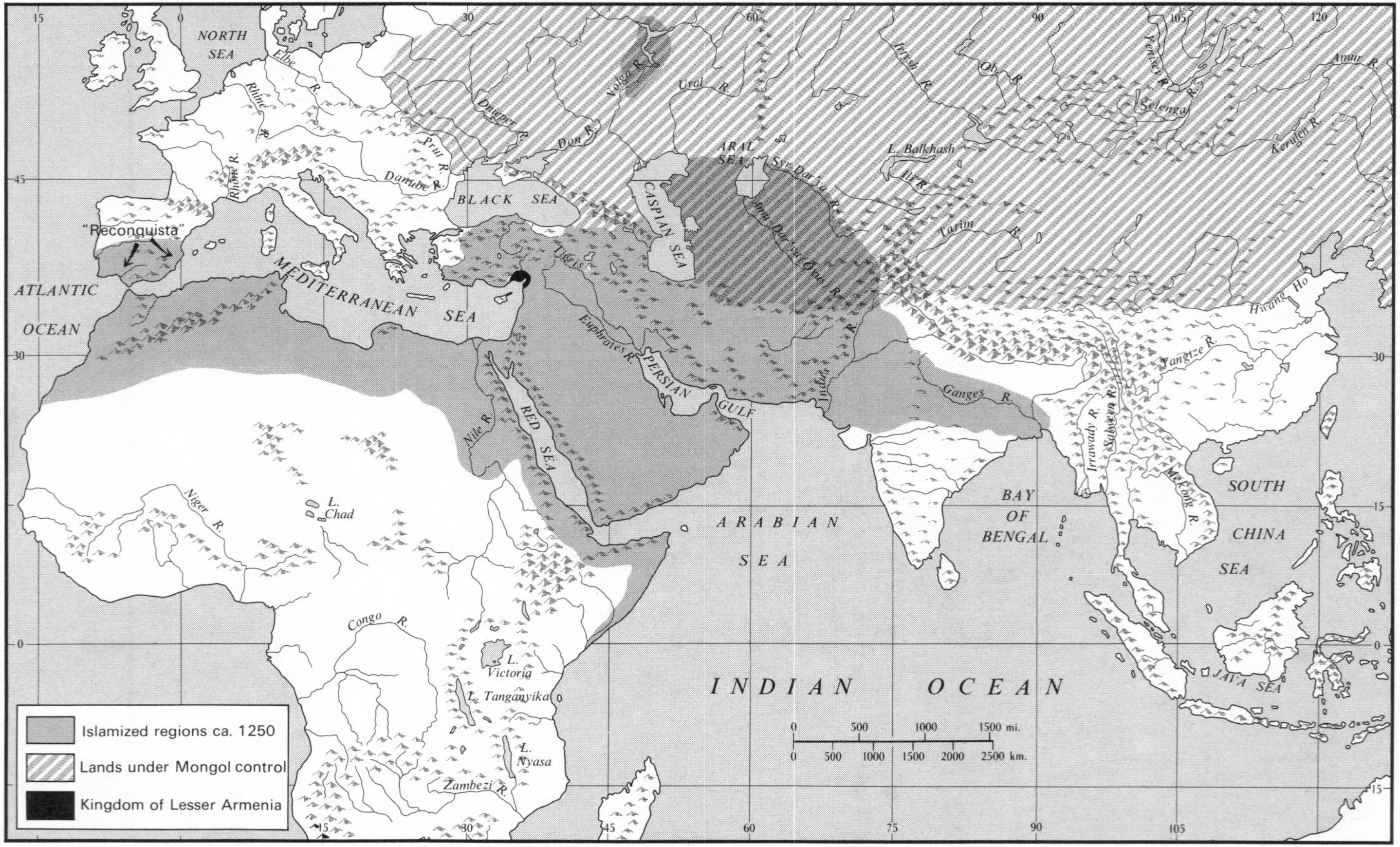

The spread of Islam to 1250

sions, when the chance death of a member of an élite Mongol tribe unleashed furious vengeance; and one may suppose on most other occasions. With the advance of citied influence, many pastoralists were no longer overawed at the splendours of cities; they had taken their measure and could use them, but could also hate them. The mixed expectations pastoralists had of 'city slickers' must have been widely diffused. The ferocity, then, was at least in part the other side of the urbanity with which Chinese engineers were employed to build siege machinery, Uighur scribes (from the central part of east-west trade route) were made to keep elaborate records, and officials were chosen, to administer the conquered countries, from lands as culturally distinct from what was administered as possible—Muslims and Europeans in China, Chinese and Tibetans in Iran.

After Ögetey's death, the next great central ruler was Mengü (1251–57), who launched two major expeditions to round out the world empire in the most important directions. (He seems to have postponed the case of western Europe, as of India, as less urgent; he sent only threats.) One, under Ḳubilay, was to subdue southern China. The Chinese resisted more stubbornly than any other people, but by 1279 they were overwhelmed, and from China further expeditions were sent, as to Java and Burma; the only land to resist successfully was Japan. The other expedition, under Hülegü, was to subdue the rest of the lands south and west of the Oxus; it had a much easier task. The Iranian amîrs hastened to show their continuing homage.

Sunnî ambassadors in Mongolia had urged the destruction of the one Shî'î state, that of the Nizârî Ismâ'îlîs of Alamût, scattered in its many strongholds from the Syrian hills to the wastes of Quhistân. The Ismâ'îlîs were scarcely politically dangerous any more; they could do little but defend their own prized freedom; but they doubtless offered a tempting example to independent-spirited villagers, and even so late as the mid-thirteenth century they provided hospitality for scholars and scientists, even those who were not Ismâ'îlîs, a fact that may have influenced some of the more rigoristic 'ulamâ'. (One such scholar was the Twelver Shî'î philosopher Naṣîruddîn Ṭûsî, who began his political career by sacrificing his Ismâ'îlî protectors, continued it by encouraging the destruction of Sunnî Baghdad, and crowned it, as counsellor of the Mongols, with protection and favours to the Imâmî Shî'î communities of the Iraq.) Hülegü obliged the amîrs, and in the course of several years—and with considerable difficulty—his huge army besieged and captured most of the tiny Ismâ'îlî rural strongholds. Alamût, more out of mismanagement than out of necessity, gave in on terms in 1256, but the terms were violated and the Ismâ'îlîs massacred.

Then the Mongols portentously moved on to Baghdad, in 1258, where the caliph (alone of the amîrs between Delhi and Cairo) still tried to maintain his independent dignity; one battle wiped out the caliphal troops in their splendour, and the walled city fell with far less trouble than an out-of-the-way little Ismâ'îlî fortress. It was thoroughly sacked. Henceforward there was no caliph at Baghdad to act even as a certifying agency for the amîrs, but for the time being this was irrelevant; such of them as were not displaced were proud to receive their titles at the hands of the infidel Mongol world rulers.

Hülegü was supposed to carry the Mongol supremacy westward to the Mediterranean lands. In Anatolia, the Seljuḳid dynasty of Rûm submitted (and was permanently weakened), but Byzantium itself was never seriously threatened. In Syria, the Mongols met the embattled Mamlûks, the slave-soldiers of the late Ayyûbid dynasty of Egypt who now ruled directly in their own name. Under the leadership of the Mamlûk Baybars, in 1260, the advance Mongol expedition was decisively defeated, and later engagements repeated this verdict. Soon after, the Mongols began an attempt to subdue India. For a time they were able to control the Panjâb, but the new Muslim sultanate of Delhi steadily resisted them and kept them out of the rest of India. The Muslims of the Volga basin had already been overrun in 1237–38, when the cities of the Bulghârs had been wrecked.

After the death of Ögetey in 1257, the several Mongol domains functioned as independent empires, though for another generation or so most of them recognized the headship of Ḳubilay and his house in China. In each empire the Mongols themselves formed a privileged upper stratum, such as the Arabs once had formed; they assimilated, in addition to the small core of Mongols, most of the Turkic steppe nomads who had joined with them, as a privileged stratum almost as high. Somewhat analogous to the sunnah of the Arabs, the Mongols brought with them their Yasa, a code based on old pastoralist practice, but ascribed to Chingiz Khan, who had no doubt contributed important provisions and a new spirit; this governed their relations among themselves. They were tolerant of all religions, even patronized most of them; but on the whole felt themselves superior to any, though many of them brought along Buddhist monks, and Buddhism was especially favoured. For two or three centuries in most of the areas where they went and, in places, much longer, the Mongol tradition was looked to unquestioningly as the norm and ground of all political authority. Yet they founded neither a new religion nor a new civilization. By the end of the thirteenth century or in the first half of the fourteenth, all the Mongol empires west of the Altai mountains had been converted to Jamâʿî-Sunnî Islam.

VI

The Bloom of Persian Literary Culture and Its Times, *c.* 1111–1274

High-cultural life by the end of the Earlier Middle Period was reflecting the a'yân-amîr system of social order, with its fragmentation of political life and consequent lack of major central monarchical courts around which to build continuing monumental traditions—and its multiplicity of petty courts to patronize what became the fashion in a more scattered way. All cultural and artistic life bore the impress of this situation. It was under such auspices in particular that the new social and cultural synthesis of the Middle Periods found its most elegant fruit: the poetry of a new dominant literary language, Persian. And the Persian tradition itself, even later, reflected the atmosphere of short-lived rival courts in which it developed.

The rise of Persian had more than purely literary consequences: it served to carry a new overall cultural orientation within Islamdom. Henceforth, while Arabic held its own as the primary language of the religious disciplines and even, largely, of natural science and philosophy, Persian became, in an increasingly large part of Islamdom, the language of polite culture; it even invaded the realm of scholarship with increasing effect. It was to form the chief model for the rise of still other languages to the literary level. Gradually a third 'classical' tongue emerged, Turkish, whose literature was based on the Persian tradition; it was almost as widespread in use geographically as was Persian, but in most places it was used in more limited social circles, and it never reached the level of Persian as a major cultural vehicle. Most of the more local languages of high culture that later emerged among Muslims likewise depended upon Persian wholly or in part for their prime literary inspiration. We may call all these cultural traditions, carried in Persian or reflecting Persian inspiration, 'Persianate' by extension.

There were, at the same time, large areas in which Persian was little known: notably in the Arabic-speaking lands west of the Iraq and in the new Muslim lands south and west of them. For some purposes, we may distinguish there an 'Arabic zone' to be set off from the 'Persianate zone' to north and east. But this 'Arabic zone' is distinguishable less by a common positive tradition not shared by others, than by a common ignorance of the Persianate tradition. This ignorance only helped to cut off that portion of Islamdom from the most creative currents that were inspiring the majority of Muslim peoples.[1] (It could even be said that Islamicate civilization, historically, is divisible in the more central areas into an earlier 'caliphal' and a later 'Persianate' phase; with variants in the outlying regions—Maghrib, Sûdânic lands, Southern Seas, India, the North—some of which did and others of which did not share deeply in the Persianate phase. But this would risk oversimplification.)

Persian and Arabic as literary vehicles

In High Caliphal times, the language of all aspects of Muslim higher culture—administration, scholarship, and belles-lettres—had been Arabic throughout the empire. The personal language of large portions of the ruling class was Arabic also; but the ordinary people long retained their older languages for everyday purposes. In most of the western parts of the empire, where Semitic dialects (hence related to Arabic) were already widespread, these older tongues (together with the Hamitic) gradually gave way to Arabic. Not only in the already Semitic lands surrounding Bedouin Arabia, but even in Hamitic Egypt, by the close of the High Caliphal Period, Arabic was being adopted, in a modified form, as the ordinary language. In the towns and lowlands of the Maghrib, Latin and probably local Semitic (Punic) dialects gave way to Arabic, which then began to make steady inroads on the (Hamitic) Berber of the more rural and mountainous areas; even the Latin (or Romance) dialects of Spain yielded at least to a bilingualism with Arabic in the cities and never offered serious cultural competition to it among Muslims.

In the wide highlands north and east of the Tigris, however, Arabic never replaced the local tongues in any large areas. At best it became a second tongue in cities. Most of the populations here were Iranian and, as we have noted, the most important Iranian language, Pahlavî, had a well-developed literary tradition dating from Sâsânian times, which (Arabized) even enjoyed a certain respect under the Baghdad caliphs. But because of its cumbrous script and its priestly and aristocratic associations, among Muslims it was replaced by the new Persian in Arabic script; though Pahlavî continued to be widely read, new writing in it was restricted to the fast diminishing number of Mazdeans; Muslims who cultivated it might be suspected of indifference to Islam. The modern literary Persian was a modernized and simplified literary form of Pahlavî, corresponding to the Iranian actually

[1] It is this contrast between Arabic and Persianate zones that Toynbee perceived in distinguishing an 'Arabic' from an 'Iranic' civilization. But he much exaggerated the isolation of Syria and Egypt as core of the 'Arabic' civilization. Anything of interest done there was attended to in the Persianate zone, and (so far as Arabic was the vehicle) much that was done in the Persianate zone was appreciated in Syria and Egypt, if not further south and west; see e.g., *A Study of History* (London and New York, 1934), vol. I, pp. 67–71. Incidentally, the Arabistic bias has led some, identifying Arabic and Islamic, to see the reduction in the scope and vigour of Arabic in its most loyal centres as an eclipse of Islamicate culture generally.

spoken in wider cultured circles. It took its standardized literary form in the Earlier Middle Period. Of the several potential non-Arabic literary mediums, this was the only one with a wide enough audience in the lands of the caliphate to rise above the level of purely local use and rival Arabic itself.

This Muslim Persian was first used for poetry—the form of composition that demands the fullest mastery of a language, and hence is hardest to pursue in a language not one's own. By the tenth century, at the Sâmânî court, it was being used for prose works also—notably for translations, from the still dominant Arabic, for literate persons for whom the alien Arabic was too difficult. It quickly displaced the old Pahlavî almost wholly as a medium of new Iranian culture. But poetry always maintained a pre-eminent place in Persian letters, perhaps even more than in Arabic; partly because some types of scholarly prose always continued to be pursued primarily in Arabic even when, after Mongol times, Arabic had lost almost every other trace of its former general priority in Iranian lands.

At first the new Muslim Persian developed very much under the influence of the Arabic of the High Caliphate (itself, of course, partly of Pahlavî inspiration). Poets were expected to be able to compose equally in Arabic and in Persian. In many ways both poetry and prose continued to have much in common with the Arabic. Poetry in particular was used, as in Arabic, primarily for oral recitation; and the individual line was expected to stand up by itself as a verbal gem, even apart from the whole poem. And as in Arabic, since the poem was not to be responded to privately in the study but publicly at a recitation (for instance, at the court of an amîr), what won praise was not new, personal themes but the delight of unexpected variants on established themes. Likewise, as in the Arabic tradition, verse was interspersed in prose, commonly enough, so as to produce contrasts in timbre. Prose again followed to a considerable degree in the footsteps of Arabic in its choice of topics and in its tendency to run into rhymed prose, saj'.

Nevertheless, Persian literature soon took its very independent way. In poetry, for instance, metres were designated by the same terminology as had been used for Arabic; and indeed the new Persian poetic forms seem to have had little to do with the old Pahlavî verse form, which seems to have been based (rather like the English) on stress and on syllable counting. Like the Arabic (and the Latin), the new Persian verses depended on patterns of syllable length. Yet even so, the Persian metres were substantially different in pattern and in tone from the Arabic metres. The established Arabic 'metres' were in fact, as we have noticed, often groupings of several related metres under a single name, some variants being markedly different from others. Even when Persians used metres under the same name as those used in Arabic, the variant might differ from that more usual in Arabic; and some Persian metres were so different that new names had to be invented for them. Moreover, the spirit in which the metres were used differed. The originally free, almost impressionistic use of metre and rhyme of the Arabic (which had been only disguised under the host of minute rules devised to contain it) was replaced by a genuine firmness and regularity (which did not really need rules, as it leapt to the ear). The metre often retained a syllable-by-syllable fixity throughout a piece, though not invariably, and the rhymes likewise tended to be exact in the sense one expects in the West—and even to become elaborately multisyllabic. Scansion of verse was, as in Arabic, according to syllable length; many of the same formal criteria were used in the critical discipline of composition; but the weight of interest went to a largely different set of considerations.

For one thing, the content of Persian poetry was rather more varied than that of Arabic. This fact was reflected in the formal genres most favoured in Persian, most of which were much rarer in the Arabic. Only the monorhymed qaṣîdah ode, especially as vehicle of courtly panegyric, retained a high place in Persian similar to its theoretical supremacy in Arabic (though the classical sequence of topics, starting with the deserted camp site, had disappeared). The Persians did far more with stanza forms of verse than the Arabs, despite the Spanish influence among the latter. But they developed, above all, three outstanding genres. The nearest the qaṣîdah in form was the *ghazal*, a short monorhymed lyrical poem, usually on love or wine, terminating conventionally with some mention of the poet's pen-name, or *takhalluṣ*. Alongside the ghazal, an epigrammatic form, the rubâ'î (quatrain), was used for impressionistic effects. It has left its mark on English verse in Edward Fitzgerald's *Rubaiyat*, properly *rubâ'iyyât*, the plural of *rubâ'î*. Technically this was the equivalent of the first two lines of the qaṣîdah, with the internal rhyme of the first line; but each hemistich was taken independently—so that it amounted to four lines with the rhyme pattern *aaba*. As in the case of any poetic form whose essential appeal lies in its brevity, the force of the rubâ'î had to come from a single beautifully made point, disciplined by exactitude of verbal pattern.

Finally, the Persian poets gave themselves unwonted freedom in the mas̱navî (couplet poem), a form of verse in rhyming couplets that could be extended indefinitely and was governed by little in the way of formal requirements except for a persisting uniformity of rhythmical pattern, and which therefore was eminently suited to every kind of dignified narrative. Narrative took on an independent position more readily than it had in Arabic. Under the guise of the mas̱navî, the Persians versified moralistic tales, long romances, and legends and history on an epic scale; the Persian equivalents of the novel are to be found as mas̱navîs, where Arabic was more likely to use a mixture of prose and brief verse passages for such a purpose. Indeed verse of various sorts was found to be so flexible that the fine prose essay, typified by Jâḥiẓ, was less cultivated in Persian than it was in Arabic.

Persian poetry, both in its verse patterns and in its subject matter, has proved more congenial than Arabic poetry to modern Western tastes. It has even proved easier to translate into Western languages. Many attempts have been made to translate not only the anecdotal poets, such as Jalâluddîn Rûmî, but the more lyric poets (notably Ḥâfiẓ), whose material is inherently as untranslatable as that of their Arabic counterparts, who have been attempted less often and with less popular success. It must be noted that any translation omits much of value, and many translations import very alien elements into the poet's work—diction and metres and even rhymes far from the poet's own. The most popular of such translations, Fitzgerald's *Rubaiyat of Omar Khayyam*, exemplifies the dangers as well as the creative possibilities. While the original poems are separate, brief entities, ordered alphabetically in a dîwân, a collection of a poet's work, Fitzgerald has put them into a sequence which, however loosely, tells a continuous story—and so denatures the original perhaps even more than do his free renderings. Such re-creations of poetry are to be commended when they are intended to enrich the receiving literature, as Fitzgerald's was. But they do not serve well as study translations for understanding the original writer and his culture. As to less inspired verse translations, they neither produce a good new piece of poetry nor serve, as a prose translation can, to give the writer's thought.[2]

The poetic image: panegyric, romantic, and lyric

As in Arabic literature of the High Caliphal age, poetry was designed for public recitation, not (in the first instance) for private meditation; it was expected to adorn a courtier's life, almost like fine clothes. The consequences in Persian were comparable to those in Arabic literature: an emphasis on precision of form and familiarity of substance, so that no unexpected context will interfere with an appreciation of the virtuosity in handling received form and theme—and, incidentally, avoidance of any purely personal private reference that would detract from the common public decorum. (A comparable concern for public effect in Soviet art seems to have produced a comparable emphasis on individual virtuosity.) As in Arabic, in Persian also, of course, a great poet could rise above the limitations so imposed, could indeed make use of them to build the greatness of his poetry.

Panegyric poetry was quite frankly praise of patrons, often of parvenus. If Modern Westerners are ill at ease with elaborate praise of living individuals—especially those dubiously worthy individuals who commonly are in a financial position to be patrons—it is in part because they are less given than their ancestors to formal courtesy even in everyday social intercourse (and none less so than those who use English). We no longer pretend to be the

[2] It is taking a long time for the principle to be received, that for different purposes, different sorts of translations are required, and that even scholars can benefit from several sorts of translation. Meanwhile, partly for want of recognition of what standards are appropriate to different purposes, the general level of translation remains low—by any standards. For minimum standards for translating for the purposes of historical study, see the Note on Translating in the Introduction in volume 1.

The Classical Persian Belles-Lettrists to 1291, with a Few Arabic Writers [Arabic names in brackets]

fl. 930s	Rûdaqî, Sâmânî poet, first important poet in 'New' (Islamic) Persian language
c. 974	Death of Bal'amî, Sâmânî vizier, translator into Persian of Ṭabarî's *History*
c. 980	Death of Daqîqî, Sâmânî poet, sympathetic to Zoroastrianism, began a *Shâh-Nâmah* which Firdawsî incorporated into his version
c. 1020	Death of Firdawsî, composer of the epic *Shâh-Nâmah*
c. 1039	Death of al-Unṣurî, panegyrist at court of Maḥmûd, 'Arabic style' poetry and influences strong
1049	Death of Abû-Sa'îd b. Abî'l-Khayr, 'first' Ṣûfî poet in Persian, user of quatrains (rubâ'iyyât)
1060	Death of Nâṣir-e Khusraw, Ismâ'îlî writer of qasîdahs, speculative treatises, travel account
1092	Death of Niẓâmulmulk, vizier to the Seljuḳs, composer of *Siyaset-Nâmah* (Mirror for Princes), a ruler's handbook
1122	Death of 'Umar Khayyâm, mathematician, astronomer, Faylasûf, and writer of quatrains
c.1150	Death of Sanâ'î, 'first' great Ṣûfî poet
1144	[Death of al-Zamakhsharî, Mu'tazilî exegete]
1153	[Death of al-Shahrastanî, heresiologist, mutakallim]
1150s	[Death of al-Idrîsî, geographer at Roger II's court in Sicily]
c.1191	Death of Anvarî, panegyric poet in erudite style, satirist
c.1200	Death of 'Aṭṭâr, Ṣûfî writer and allegorist
1203	Death of Niẓâmî 'Ganjavî', poet of the five 'epics', the *Khamsa*, of romantic themes
1229	[Death of Yâqût, encyclopedist]
1234	[Death of Ibn-al-Athîr, historian]
1235	[Death of Ibn-al-Fâriḍ, Ṣûfî poet]
1273	Death of Jalâluddîn Rûmî, Ṣûfî composer of the *Mas̄navî*
1274	[Death of Ibn-Sa'îd, Andalusian poet and adîb]
1282	[Death of Ibn-Khallikan, compiler of biographical dictionary]
1286	[Death of al-Baydawî, exegete]
1289	Death of 'Iraqî, ecstatic Ṣûfî poet, influenced by Ibn-al-'Arabî
1292	Death of Sa'dî, moralist prose writer and poet

most humble servants of persons we scarcely know, even in prose. We are ill at ease when the same sorts of courtesy are spelled out and elaborated in Persian verse.

It was not only in panegyric but in many sorts of Persian verse—publicly recited in a hall where ceremonial precedence (even if only of a relatively transient military variety) determined everyone's fate—that formal courtesy formed the starting point for the most elaborately cultivated language. But it was most obviously so in panegyric. This normally took the form of a qaṣîdah ode, but sometimes it took the form of a eulogistic chronicle of a king's deeds, preferably in mas̄navî couplet form. Like modern advertising, panegyric was produced for money—for the gifts with which a proper amîr showered those who praised him elegantly; but unlike much advertising, it was not done with intent to mislead; for everyone concerned knew that the panegyric made no pretence to a balanced account of a man and his deeds; poets were deeply respected for their ability to evoke an elegant image of greatness; if this could be tied to the actual circumstances of the amîr to whom it was dedicated, so much the better. To be sure, excellent panegyric might actually enhance an amîr's reputation—that is why he paid for it—partly because the ability to attract and hold a really great poet argued both taste and power, or at least wealth; and partly, yes, because people are prone to prefer a glorious fiction to a dubious actuality.

In the panegyric, as in polite conversation, conventions reigned. (These conventions could not be peculiar to any one dynasty and its traditions—no one dynasty was so deeply rooted—but were transferable indefinitely to any man in power at the moment.) A king was ruler not just of one city but of the world; he was also always victorious over mighty enemies. A king was the sun in splendour, a lion in prowess; he must personally destroy people and animals on as large a scale as possible. He was also, however, generous—the loot which he gathered in was not stored up in treasuries but was distributed with a free hand (to the poor, and especially to the soldiers and courtiers and to the poet), on the assumption that he could always go out and get more. Preferably, also, he had a long line of ancestors honoured for the same qualities. Men of lesser rank were allowed somewhat comparable compliments, appropriate to their status (the poet must take care not to praise a courtier so much as to anger the ruler, who would not tolerate excessive poetic honours to his servants any more than he would tolerate undue ceremony for them in court). Given these conventions, the poet was free to invent the most subtle conceits, in which the music of words combined magically with plays of implication in their meaning. Panegyric had one great advantage over love-poetry, its most important rival in the way of stock subject matter: whereas in matters of love, delicacy did not allow a man to touch on any details that could remotely betray the individuality of his belovèd (a gentleman does not talk about his women), in matters of public glory, the poet could bring in actual episodes that had occurred in the life of his subject, so adding both piquancy and variety. Hence a really great panegyrist was regarded as the greatest of poets.

Probably the greatest of the Persian panegyrists was Awḥaduddîn Anvarî (d. *c.* 1191), a favourite of the Seljuḳid sultan Sanjar. He was trained at a madrasah in Ṭûs and was reputed learnèd not only in kalâm but also in logic and mathematics and especially astronomy. As a young man he turned from his scholarly studies to writing poetry as a more remunerative career. (The biographers typically put this in the form of an anecdote impossible in its details but graphic in its mood: one day he saw a richly dressed man riding a horse richly caparisoned and surrounded by servants, and asked what his trade was; on learning he was a poet, he compared his lot with that of a poor scholar like himself, wrote a qaṣîdah ode that very evening, and the next day presented himself to Sanjar with the ode, which won him a permanent place at court.) His chosen career did bring him money and fame and also the quarrels and disappointments that go with a lust for money and fame. He did not forget his scholarship, however, for he filled his poems with scientific allusions which laymen sometimes found it hard to follow. In 1185, it seems, his science got him into trouble (along with other astrologers): an unusual conjunction of planets was interpreted as foretelling great windstorms; but the day of the conjunction was utterly becalmed, and the whole year was one of extraordinary calm—so that the astrologers, and especially the proud poet Anvarî, were disgraced. By then he had been complaining for years, since Sanjar's death perhaps, of lack of munificent patrons; in any case, he retired to Balkh, renouncing any further panegyrics and devoting himself to piety. Even at Balkh the quarrels he had indulged in pursued him: it is said that a rival composed insulting verse against the people of Balkh and ascribed it to Anvarî, whereupon the Balkhîs paraded him through the streets in dishonour and he was rescued only by the intervention of highly-placed friends.

Anvarî had some hard words for the falsehood and ignobility entailed in being a courtier and writing panegyric, and he did compose a few qaṣîdahs not devoted to praise of a patron (or to ridicule of his rivals); he is famous for a moving elegy on the destruction wrought in Khurâsân by the Oghuz tribes after their defeat of Sanjar. Nonetheless, he was known chiefly by his panegyric qaṣîdahs. One of the most famous illustrates how direct and fluent he could make the most preposterous statements. It begins: 'If [any] heart and hand be sea and mine, it is the heart and hand of [this] great lord'—abounding in generosity. Other lines run 'You are in the world and yet are greater than the world, like the deeper sense hidden in a word. On the day of fighting, when by the blaze of your lances even the dust is clothed in smoke, the bridles of hope slow down, tired, while the stirrups become heavy with death.'

The obverse of panegyric was insult poetry. If the poet had decided to break openly with an enemy—possibly because he had not paid him enough for his praises before—there were no limits on the coarseness of his language; for he was no longer bound by the etiquette of the court. His frank purpose was to be offensive. Some insult poetry was extraordinarily refined in the shading of its scurrilities, and a good poet knew how to make the most of whatever weaknesses were publicly attributed (truly or falsely) to his subject, who as a prominent figure was necessarily subject to the gossip of envy. But simply to associate the name of a man with gross accusations (however incredible) was—as in ordinary Irano-Mediterranean life—to besmirch his honour; and if he proved unable to avenge the insults, his honour was diminished by that very fact. Hence insult poetry proved a potent weapon of hate, and the perpetrator exposed himself to terrible punishment if he ever fell into the clutches of the butt of his words. More than one talented poet, who had been presented with bags of gold for a single evening's recitation, was finally put to death with refined tortures.

We may cite an insult poem by the great panegyrist Khâqânî (1106/7–85), who is known for the obscurity of his verse, which even Persians can find hard to unravel because of its recondite and erudite references. Khâqânî was inordinately vain and quarrelsome, exalting his own poetry above that of any of the great poets who preceded him. The poet with whom he had been an apprentice, and who had given him the honour of his daughter's hand, warned him against such tendencies in a poem itself not gentle—for it suggested that his mother had not been faithful to his father. Thereupon Khâqânî turned viciously against his master. He accused him of every vice, including sexual relations with boys, graphically described, and in particular of being an Ismâ'îlî heretic (the Nizârî Ismâ'îlî revolt was yet recent and still not resolved). About that time, Khâqânî left his home town permanently.

Panegyric poetry (and its reverse) enjoyed tremendous prestige, but romantic poetry was at least as popular. It commonly took the form of mas̄navî verse. Tales of fighting and of love, preferably told of figures long since dead but well known to all the audience, at least by reputation, offered opportunity for most of the turns of image that were prized in panegyric, though without the added spice that came from tying the verse to current actual events. As in panegyric, the conventions of courtly courtesy were maintained, and the most private experience was generalized by way of brilliant but impersonal images. The historical figures invoked were largely taken from pre-Islamic Iranian lore—occasionally from pre-Islamic Arabian lore—and were, in effect, fictive figures; only the very broadest lines of the inherited story need be adhered to. (The situation was very like that in classical Greece.) But though the stories could be varied considerably, the attitudes presupposed in the characters had to be those acceptable to courtly life. Thus the masculine hero had to be watchful of his honour—his right to precedence—against all attacks; this honour could be sullied either through his own weakness—if he let a challenge go without silencing the challenger—or through his women, if his presumed sexual jealousy were offended.

Hence normally the heroes had to behave in orthodox fashion, both in love and in war; a personal response to the moral or sentimental questions that might rise was out of the question. However, there was, for the case of love, a major alternative available in the notion of the sublimated, servient love of a man for a woman whom he cannot possess physically, but whom he idealizes as the embodiment of transcendent beauty, and to whom, accordingly, he remains faithful. But within these conventional limits of form and treatment, a great poet could show not only his virtuosity but his sensitivity and perceptiveness.

The greatest of the romantic poets was Niẓâmî of Ganjah (Kirovabad) in Azerbaijan (1140/1–1202/3), who seems to have lived soberly, faithfully, and humanely, and whose poetry is capable of inspiring such sentiments in others. We know the Ṣûfî pîr whose guidance he sought. Though he dedicated his greater poems to various ruling amîrs, he avoided panegyric. He is best known for five long mas̄navî couplet-poems, which in retrospect are collectively known as the 'quintet', and which inspired attempts by later poets to produce comparable 'quintets' of mas̄navîs. One of these five mas̄navîs is didactic, with Ṣûfî elements; but the other four present themes which became popular with other poets partly as a result of Niẓâmî's example. It is Niẓâmî's treatment that has given these themes their most persistent overtones in subsequent Persian literature.

Alexander of Macedon (called Iskandar Rûmî, the European) had appeared already in Firdawsî's epic among the rulers of Iran; Niẓâmî reworded his story with a greater eye to the unity of the story within itself, not without overtones pointing to the ultimate human quest in general. Perhaps most memorable in such a presentation of Alexander is not his more historical exploits but his legendary quest to the ends of the earth for the water of life —as Niẓâmî presents it, to a land of almost transcendent darkness.

The story of the lovely Shîrîn and the Sâsânian emperor Khusraw Parvîz is also in Firdawsî; but again Niẓâmî stresses the romantic colour. Persian painters have loved to depict the scene at which Khusraw first sees Shîrîn— she is on a trip and has stopped to bathe in a stream when Khusraw, on a trip in the opposite direction, chances to ride by. Niẓâmî exploits fully the pathos in the story of her other lover, Farhâd, who, to gain her hand, is set the task of hewing a way through the rock of the great mountain Bihistûn (on which the Achaemenids had carved their inscriptions); and who faithfully proceeds with his labour for years, till when he is almost done Khusraw has someone send him a false report that Shîrîn has died; whereupon he kills himself. By the code of honour, no other solution to the story was possible; the lord Khusraw must triumph. But Niẓâmî also portrayed, subsequently, a love in which the lover who truly triumphs is he who has renounced his object. The story of Majnûn (the 'madman') and Laylà, his beloved, comes from ancient Arabian lore; Laylà is given by her father to another, but Majnûn refuses to renounce her and wanders distraught in the desert, befriended only by the wild beasts. When her husband dies, she comes to him, but he is too crazed to know her. Niẓâmî tells us they were finally united in Paradise. Though Niẓâmî's treatment is not primarily a Ṣûfî work, as were some other treatments of the theme, yet it bears a Ṣûfî stamp.

The last maṡnavî of Niẓâmî's quintet deals again with a figure from Firdawsî, the Sâsânian emperor Bahrâm Gûr, famed as a hunter and fierce as the wild ass he hunted. The greater part of the story, however, moves into a realm yet further removed from history, being made up of seven fanciful tales retold by seven princesses whom Bahrâm Gûr has wooed (on the basis of the beauty of their portraits) and won; the princesses represent the seven regions of the world—in this case, India, China, Turkistan, the Slavs, Iran, Rûm (Europe), and the Maghrib (the Arab lands and Negro Africa both being omitted in this list)—so expressing both the glory of Bahrâm Gûr and the romantic wonder of the exotic.

Yet further removed from the formal courtesy of the court was the language of lyric, normally expressed through the rubâ'î quatrain or the ghazal, short poem. Here we are in the realm of private sentiment rather than of public honour. Yet etiquette still held here also, for the poetry—by the very fact of being shi'r poetry, uttered for an audience—was not really private. In such poetry the tones of feeling could become extraordinarily delicate; and since practically everything depended on the images used, comprehension of the poetry depended on recognizing the force being given to each image. A beautiful face is regularly called a full moon; a straight figure called a cypress tree; a passionate and hopeless love finds its image in the singing nightingale (bulbul) who is fancied to be in love with the unapproachable but supremely beautiful thorn-girt rose. The ancient Iranian monarch Jamshîd (as presented by Firdawsî) possessed a wondrous cup in which he could see all that went on in the world; a single reference to this cup might evoke many overtones derived from the whole story of it. (Jamshîd also invented wine.) Another ancient Iranian monarch, Farîdûn, might be invoked to symbolize long life and fortune: as a young man he avenged Jamshîd against the monster Zaḥḥâk, who had deposed him; then he ruled the world for a thousand years in good fortune; but in his old age he divided his realms among his three sons, two of whom slaughtered the third and were killed by his avengers; so that Farîdûn spent his last days staring at his son's three skulls. These references and similes are taken for granted; what counts is what the poet can do with them, how well he can make his references to them serve his turn in constructing a deft expression of emotion. The commonest subject for a ghazal was naturally love (always, by convention, the love must be for a young man or a boy—the poet, as a man, being the lover: to have mentioned loving a woman would have been undecorous). (There were women poets, but they were rare.) But many other topics naturally were taken up—the charms of wine, in the first rank, or even the expression of sorrow; more than once a poet mourned a wife or a son untimely lost with haunting tenderness.[3]

Ṣûfism and worldly wisdom: the simplicity of Sa'dî

Persian poetry and even Persian prose became increasingly influenced by the imagery of Ṣûfism. This was already true in the poetry we have been describing, which was oriented to worldly sentiment. It was yet more true in poetry intended to express not etiquette or sentiment but enduring wisdom. For some generations after the downfall of the High Caliphal state, Persian literature was not overmuch marked by any religious concern at all. Such religious spirit as was present in Firdawsî, for instance, reflected a simple, generalized Islam: the acceptance of God's will as supreme; the sentiment was sufficiently undifferentiated so that it could readily enough be conveyed even when he was using Mazdean terminology. But when the Ṣûfî-oriented society of the Earlier Middle Period had been fully formed, from the twelfth century on, increasingly Ṣûfism was the inspiration of more and more of the important poets.

These celebrated Ṣûfî devotional values in the more lyrical short forms, ghazals and rubâ'î quatrains; in the looser mas̄navî couplet-poem they sometimes expounded Ṣûfî theory and metaphysics at length. Such poets did not represent any established hierarchy; what they produced did not become monumental liturgy, but expressed the spirit of personal initiative and improvisation that marked the rise of Ṣûfism as a decentralized popular movement. But the poets became immensely popular and at least after their deaths often received some of the honours of a Ṣûfî saint themselves; indeed, men who were primarily Ṣûfîs, like Rûmî, sometimes contributed to this poetry. (No doubt the excellence of the poetry contributed somewhat in turn to the prestige of Ṣûfism.)

The poets learned to handle the language with great grace and imaginative splendour. The ecstatic character of Ṣûfî attitudes and aspirations lent itself to poetic rendering; numerous stock images were developed—sometimes borrowed from more mundane poetry of love and wine—and used with all kinds of subtlety. In their verses, the raindrop, as the individual soul, entered the ocean of God's universality in a thousand slightly differing ways; the nightingale repeatedly sang his love to the rose of divine beauty, but hardly more often than the moth gave up its life out of passion for the candle's flame—the all-consuming and yet all-impelling fire of God's majesty. Eventually, almost every poet, whatever his theme, tended to borrow these pregnant images and to invest even a plain mundane theme with something of the overtones of Ṣûfî inwardness. The diverse elements might be merged as intimately as perhaps they ought to be in the living heart. Eventually (as

[3] Helmuth Ritter and J. Rypka have added to their edition of Niẓâmî's *Haft Peykar* (Prague, 1934) a thorough cataloguing of Niẓâmî's metaphorical symbolism.

we shall see), with a master poet like Ḥâfiẓ, it becomes difficult (or, more correctly speaking, irrelevant) to try to sort out the mundane from the spiritual elements in his work. This use of Ṣûfî thought was not unjustified, given the inherent tendency of Ṣûfîs to see every mundane object or passion as the reflection of a transcendent reality and of a love that unconsciously sought God in His manifold creation. Such poems, however gross their apparent themes, have been interpreted by unimaginative latter-day scholars as pure religious allegory: thus even in the piquant verses ascribed to 'Umar Khayyâm, some later scholars have mechanically glossed whatever could be understood as Ṣûfî imagery, and denied any sensuous intent.

Later Persian poetry was so much influenced by Ṣûfism that even expressly mundane parodies might imitate a Ṣûfî manner. An occasional bit of Ṣûfî-oriented sentiment was taken for granted.

Farîduddîn 'Aṭṭâr (d. 1190) is the most honoured (apart from the Ṣûfî Jalâluddîn Rûmî, who learned much from him) of those poets who wrote in a wholeheartedly Ṣûfî vein. 'Aṭṭâr was not himself, it seems, a full-time practicing Ṣûfî, and some of his verse does not seem to be dedicated especially to Ṣûfism; but the bulk of it is devoted to honouring the Ṣûfîs and glorifying their doctrines. 'Aṭṭâr's most important writings take the form of mas̄navî couplet-poems, which tell a single frame-story embellished by numerous incidental stories which form the heart of his work. Many works written by others have been attributed to 'Aṭṭâr, and the problem of identifying which are really his is even knottier than with most poets, but there is no doubt that the greatest of those attributed to him are his own.

Perhaps the most famous tells allegorically of how the birds all set out to find the great magical bird, the Sîmurgh (a feather of which, dropped in China, had been enough to set every painter there at vain endeavours to recapture its beauty); they pass through many desperate adventures on the way—symbolizing the adventures of the human spirit on the mystical Way—till only thirty of them are left at the end; there, reduced by their travail to practically nothing in either soul or body, they discover themselves again, purified, and the Sîmurgh at the same time, in a giant mirror: for the Sîmurgh turns out to be their own image (*sî murgh* in Persian is 'thirty birds').

In prose, 'Aṭṭâr collected anecdotes about all the great Ṣûfîs before his time in a book almost as popular as his mas̄navîs. The stories are hopelessly uncritical, filled with marvels and unrealisms; but they are all warm and lively, and teach the lessons of Ṣûfism more effectively than any treatise could do. 'Aṭṭâr also produced an extremely popular book of wisdom literature, the *Book of Advice* (translated into many Islamicate languages), a didactic compendium of wise sayings, meant as a reminder to everyone of how best to cope with the world. But in this field he was surpassed by the beloved Shaykh Sa'dî.

The most popular of Persian poets was Muṣliḥuddîn Sa'dî (1193–1292) of Shîrâz, capital of Fârs. He travelled widely in Arab lands and elsewhere—

even, perhaps, into India—but eventually returned to Shîrâz, where he wrote, about 1257, his two most famous books of poetry, the *Gulistân* and the *Bûstân*. Both titles mean 'garden'; both books are collections of tales which are the sweet flowers in the garden. The *Gulistân* tells the story proper in simple prose and ornaments it with comments in verse; the *Bûstân* puts everything into mas̄navî couplet verse. Both books are didactic—Sa'dî wants to teach about life in an entertaining way; no abstruse or far-fetched complexity is admitted to dim their elegant clarity. The stories are arranged loosely under headings such as 'on kings' and 'on generosity'. However, Sa'dî does not develop a logically comprehensive scheme for interpreting life: the message of the books may be got at, whatever the order in which the stories are read. Sa'dî wrote much other poetry, but these simple collections have most endeared him to all generations.

Sa'dî tries, in those books, to present a rounded wisdom to guide living in this world. Accordingly, he offers advice on every level: from the level of immediate shrewdness to the level of ultimate purposiveness. When he comes to his most profound understanding, this is inevitably cast into Ṣûfî terms. Thus he tells of a drop of rain that fell into the ocean and saw itself as nothing in that immensity, but was taken into an oyster and became a famous pearl. On a more practical level, he tells how Abraham wanted to refuse an evening's hospitality to a guest who turned out to be an infidel, but was reproved by God, Who had given sustenance to that infidel for a whole lifetime. And just as he frowns on communal exclusivism, he rejects dependence on external ritual, telling of a pious man who performed worship at every step he took on his ḥajj pilgrimage and was tempted by the Devil to think well of his own piety—and was barely saved from Hell by a vision in which he was warned that well-doing would have been more excellent than any number of acts of worship.

What well-doing might be is illustrated, likewise in a Ṣûfî rather than a Shar'î vein, by the pious man in whose house a thief found nothing to steal, and who threw a blanket on which he himself had been sleeping into the thief's way, that he might not leave empty-handed; and by the pîr who reproved one disciple for informing on a fellow-disciple's public drunkenness by having him go bear home his drunken comrade, who had fallen asleep in the gutter, and so share his ignominy. Sa'dî was willing to exalt the saints' piety by tales of miracles, for instance telling of one who, when refused boat passage because he had no money, crossed a river on his prayer rug. Yet he could also advocate ungenerous behaviour in those in whom generosity was simply naïveté: while he commended the holy man who gave himself as surety for a debtor and spent years in prison when the debtor fled, he condemned the mercy of the vizier who saved from execution a boy who had been part of a captured robber gang, so as to bring him up properly in his own home; for when grown, the boy turned against his benefactor and resumed his robber ways. Many of Sa'dî's tales purport to recount his own adventures when travelling as a Ṣûfî darvîsh. After his death, Sa'dî was regarded as a great Ṣûfî saint, and was surnamed 'the Shaykh', the old master, par excellence.

The lessons Sa'dî taught and the wisdom he preached made no pretence to originality. Indeed, wisdom is seldom original. What Sa'dî aimed to do was to put the old truths well. He phrased in unforgettable images the truths that people always know and yet spend a lifetime learning. These are truths which are apparently simple and even obvious, and which even youngsters are aware of in some degree, and yet which, with each year of increasing age and further experience, each person seems to know as he had not known them before. Already in the ancient Cuneiform literature—as in most other literatures—writers had tried to put such wisdom in a clever nutshell, in a memorable, definitive form wherein the mind could see its own sagest reflections as in a mirror. The Hebrew Bible contains elegant examples of the genre. This has been called 'wisdom literature' and has always been popular even with the most sophisticated. Sa'dî's is one of the most cherished attempts at this in the whole Irano-Semitic tradition.

Prose: plain and fancy in Persian and Arabic

Persian literature appealed not only to Persian and other Iranian-speaking people, but also to the Turks who came into power as soldiers and amîrs almost everywhere in the Earlier Middle Period. The centre from which they came into political power, whether farther east toward India or farther west toward Europe and Egypt, was the Iranian plateau; there their leaders learned to use Persian as a courtly tongue, which they carried with them most places they went. Consequently, while Arabic remained the language of science and religious scholarship, Persian became in wide areas the language of polite intercourse and of poetry. Persian writers were given wide opportunities in this way; we have noticed that one of the greatest of them, Jalâluddîn Rûmî, did most of his work under Turkic rule in Anatolia far to the west of his Iranian birthplace. And a major Persian poet was Amîr Khusraw of Delhi, far to the east, who gloried in his Indian homeland and even experimented with verse in the local Hindi tongue, but used Persian for all serious work.

Arabic during this period continued to be a major literary tongue, but it was increasingly restricted as to the area where cultivated circles used it for belles-lettres; even in the Fertile Crescent some rulers, notably in the Iraq, eventually preferred Persian. Partly because Arabic literature had already produced so much as to inhibit new ventures, but perhaps even more because of its loss of social status, few new genres or even new ways of handling old genres were introduced. Ṣûfism, while equally prevalent in Arab lands, did not achieve a like poetic embodiment. One Arab Ṣûfî poet, Ibn-al-Fâriḍ of Egypt (1181–1235), stands out for his uniquely ecstatic Ṣûfî verse; few others achieved much standing. In prose, on the other hand, Arabic continued to produce many major works, partly because religious scholarship still was expressed in that language even in the Persianate zone; some works arising out of the circle of religious scholarship deserve to be included as works of belles-lettres. In a certain sense this was the milieu even of the greatest work of Arabic literature of the Earlier Middle Period, Ḥarîrî's *Maqâmât*; for whatever its literary excellence, it was largely intended as an exercise in grammatical and lexical subtlety.

In the Sharî'ah-minded studies, the great task was to produce definitive treatments in the main fields. Of many almost equally memorable names, I pick the most interesting one. The most important figure in Qur'ân studies and in grammar in the period was Maḥmûd al-Zamakhsharî (1075–1144) of Khwârazm, a Mu'tazilî like other Khwârazmians. He spent some years in Mecca, but returned to Khwârazm for most of his life. The Mu'tazilîs had always made more of the Qur'ân than of ḥadîth reports; hence it is not strange that it was a Mu'tazilî who produced the greatest Qur'ân commentary after Ṭabarî's. He analyzed grammar and style with great precision as well as searching out philosophic implications (and incidentally, of course, giving a Mu'tazilî interpretation of all anthropomorphisms). The commentary proved popular everywhere and later evoked an equally popular rival commentary (by al-Bayḍâwî) containing much of its material but expurgated and adjusted for those who had rejected the Mu'tazilî doctrinal positions in favour of the Ḥadîthî ones. Al-Zamakhsharî also produced a grammar of Arabic that became standard for its clarity, and published works in lexicography and related subjects, collections of proverbs, and even some ḥadîth studies; he also composed poetry. Like his fellow Khwârazmian, al-Bîrûnî, he rejected the use of Persian for scholarly purposes, but had to learn it and teach beginners in it all the same; he even composed an Arabic-Persian lexicon.

The field of history, of course, called for ever new efforts. Most writers in this field, Arabic or Persian, were chroniclers of dynastic wars or of the learnèd men and women of a city. Their purposes, as always, were primarily entertainment and pious edification, though some justified their work as containing examples for statesmen to emulate or avoid. Hence often it is hard to draw a line between the chronicler and the teller of wonder tales. But implicitly, at least, a historian was trying to establish the record which pinpointed the true place and dignity both of living families (honoured in great ancestors) and of those vanished people whose deeds entered the horizon of living men by way of their monuments or of the popular tales told about them; as well as the dignity of past and present generations, as compared to the greatest men of old. Some historians were quite conscientious in their mission to provide such a basis for perspective on one's own time and place.

Among these, 'Izz-al-dîn Ibn-al-Athîr (1160–1234) stands out for the thoroughness and lucidity of his two chief works (in Arabic), despite his prejudices, which we have already noticed, against both Saladin and al-Nâṣir. He composed a detailed account of the Jazîrah and Mosul under the Zengid atabegs, monumental in its kind. He also composed a general history: in its earlier parts it was mostly a résumé of Ṭabarî's history (selecting the most devout rather than the most subtle interpretation of an event where there were alternatives); then it was continued in annal form down to Ibn-al-Athîr's own time.

The contrast in manner of composition between the two works illustrates the contrast between the two periods. Where Ṭabarî, centring his attention on the caliphate, had drawn on various collections of reports about the Muslim conquests or the fitnahs or other all-Muslim concerns, collections often reflecting the perspectives of tribal blocs or religious factions, Ibn-al-Athîr drew partly on local archival material and partly on various local chronicles rather like his own history of the Zengids. He had access to archival material (and to personal accounts by participants) as a scholar and even by way of family connections. He was born at a small town in the Jazîrah and travelled some, settling in Mosul as a private scholar. His brothers were more active. His elder brother was perhaps as widely respected as a scholar as himself, dealing with Qur'ân, ḥadîth, and grammar; unwillingly, he accepted a high fiscal post at Mosul; when he retired, he turned his home into a hostel for Ṣûfîs. His younger brother wrote a long-famous work on prose style and was employed to draft fine documents at several courts (being vizier for a time at Damascus) and finally at Mosul. In such a milieu, Ibn-al-Athîr had access to both gossip and inside information; but he was also deeply committed to the régimes in which such scholars as himself—and what they stood for—were paid such high respect. Lacking the stature of Ṭabarî, he became a partisan and was not above manipulating his information, on occasion, so as to make his favoured rulers appear in a better light.[4]

Two major tendencies in style affected Arabic and Persian letters of the time alike. The more obvious was that of recherché verbal elaboration, which had been latent in Arabic even from the time of Jâḥiẓ, but now developed more fully. This tendency, of course, was at least as strong in verse as in

[4] H. A. R. Gibb, 'Islamic Biographical Literature', in *Historians of the Middle East*, ed. Bernard Lewis and P. M. Holt (Oxford University Press, 1962), pp. 54–58, brings out the persisting preoccupation of historians with the continuity of the Ummah as represented in the carriers of its culture, especially its religious culture—a preoccupation that culminated, among the Ḥadîthî scholars in the Arab lands, in comprehensive biographically conceived histories; notably those of Ibn-al-Jawzî (1116–1200), *Mir'ât al-zamân*, and Shams-al-dîn al-Dhahabî (1274–1348), *Ta'rîkh al-islâm*. This volume contains other useful papers, for instance those by Claude Cahen, 'The Historiography of the Seljuqid Period', pp. 59–78 (more revealing of the nature of the historical writing than he claims), Halil İnalcîk, 'The Rise of Ottoman Historiography', pp. 152–67, and Bernard Lewis, 'The Use by Muslim Historians of Non-Muslim Sources', pp. 180–91, though both the quality of the volume and its coverage (centring on the east Mediterranean lands) are exceedingly uneven.

prose. It entered the tradition of Persian verse simultaneously with or a little later than the Ṣûfî outlook, a little later than it did Arabic, carrying a drive for verbal elaboration and conceptual cleverness of the kind that (during the early days of Persian literature) had reached a peak in Arabic poetry with al-Mutanabbi'. Each writer felt the need to outdo his predecessors. Rûdaqî, Sâmânî court poet, had made liberal use of similes and metaphors; but later Persian critics could despise him as too straightforward and unadorned, too prosaic to delight the mind. In its earlier stages, the fertility of verbal invention and imaginative conceits which this demand brought forth made for subtlety and charm. Pushed too far, in the Later Middle Period, it often made for over-ornateness.

But it was especially as the drive for elaborate preciosity affected prose that it has troubled Western readers; the more pretentious historians, Arabic and Persian (but not such scholarly authors as Ibn-al-Athîr), began to adorn almost every sentence in an account of a battle, say, with often far-fetched metaphors and similes. This sort of tendency has been even more oppressive in Persian than in Arabic, since Persian taste was being first formed in this period. As compared with the Arabic, the Persian tradition as a whole came to be wanting in the light essay and to be weighted toward the moralizing and the ornate, even in its soberest accounts. In the Earlier Middle Period, however, this sort of writing (provided one is well enough read to enjoy the allusions) remained within easy limits and graced an essay without becoming its prime preoccupation.

One must distinguish from ornateness certain traits of the prose of the period that may seem equally unpalatable to some modern readers. The use of hyperbole was an established form of representation. As we have noticed, the forms of civil courtesy often required an exaggerated deference toward powerful individuals and also toward private scholars or artists whom one wished to honour, even when no panegyric was intended. It was possible to describe first one individual, then another, in superlatives which, if taken literally, would be mutually exclusive; such hyperbole had its own rules and could sometimes be subtly differentiated to produce a nuanced effect. Often, however, hyperbole seems to have been simply a manner of heightening effect without much concern for a precision that was unattainable anyway, given the impressionistic and personal state of most information in the period.

Anecdotes, except where intended as a part of serious biography, were commonly exaggerated. In modern fiction we try to minimize the distortion needed by any art, and leave more fanciful distortion—whether grotesque or grandiloquent—to children's fairy tales. In pre-Modern literature, anecdotes were commonly 'fairy tales' neatly tailored for adults. Even when a story might be literally true, a point was made, by preference, by illustrating the extreme case rather than by understating. We hear of a slave who was so gentle toward all living things that he kept his brethren in the futuwwah club waiting for a meal till a group of ants should have moved off the tablecloth, lest by dumping them sooner he hurt them or make them lose their way. The implication of the tale was not that every man should do likewise, but that if one man could go so far, others might at any rate show consideration for the helpless in a somewhat lesser degree which—by comparison—might seem easy to attain. With the same intent, we hear of a man who, when he found that his newly wed wife was marred by smallpox, to spare her embarrassment feigned eye trouble and then blindness, and maintained the pretence consistently until her death.

Even in the literary treatise on government of Niẓâmulmulk, honoured by generations of men of taste, ethics in government were illustrated by the extreme case rather than the case calling for a nice judgment; so that the examples he cites are mostly more charming than realistic. Niẓâmulmulk was an effective administrator and fully understood the value of reserves in a treasury and of maintaining a budget; but to enforce the lesson that the sultan should not treat the income of the government as wholly at his personal disposal, he tells an improbable story of the caliph Hârûn al-Rashîd and his wife Zubaydah (consciously recasting history in the process). After receiving a reproof from a number of impoverished Muslims who claimed they were entitled to a share in the treasury, since it belonged to the Muslims and not to the caliph personally, al-Rashîd and Zubaydah had identical dreams, in which they were turned away by Muḥammad, at the Last Judgment, for having used the Muslims' treasury for their own ends. They awoke in terror; next day, al-Rashîd proclaimed that any person with a claim should present himself, and vast sums were issued in gifts and annuities. Zubaydah matched her husband out of her personal treasury by making, forthwith, all those benefactions that duller historians do record her as making in the course of a lifetime.

On at least two points, the sense of decorum of the day—and not only in Islamdom—has seemed crude to some modern readers. Though unwarranted boasting was laughed at, no shame was usually seen in a legitimate assertion of one's own prowess and virtues (but modesty in such matters was an honoured trait). And despite the excessive precautions that were taken to keep women out of men's sight and even men well clothed, there was no more hesitancy at speaking of sexual activity than at speaking of eating: both were described with equal frankness whenever the narrative called for it. Perhaps this is partly because, in a segregated society, male conversation did not need to take into account the presence of females. (Of course, there was also a considerable literature that was unmistakably pornographic, designed exclusively to titillate.)

The esoteric style in literature

A second major tendency was by its nature less obvious, yet socially and intellectually more important. This was to write in a disguised or indirect manner, leaving many points tacit. The wise conclusion of Ghazâlî, that one must write with the level of one's audience in mind and not disclose dangerously confusing truths to the masses, had literary effects even more subtle than its effects on Ghazâlî's own *Munqidh*, in which he argues unashamedly, but not always avowedly, from the reader's chance opinions. As we have seen, for Faylasûfs and Ṣûfîs and 'Alid loyalists, a certain gradation and concealment of knowledge became normal. It could seem but common sense, especially in life-orientational questions, to write in such a way that one's full intentions need not be immediately clear to every reader, so that readers could draw their own conclusions according to their own level of need. And this approach could apply, whether one had an explicitly esoteric intent or not. In any case, it had significant effects on literary style. The tendency was becoming endemic in all serious prose and even verse, so that one must think twice, in reading any piece of work, before assuming that nothing was intended that is not explicitly stated.

This is especially true wherever Ṣûfism had an influence. I have spoken of the tendency to exaggerate anecdotes whenever a literary effect was intended. To some extent what I said of the moralizing tales of general literature applies also to the wonder-tales told of ancient prophets and Ṣûfî saints, which amounted to a regular genre of literature. Wonder-tales were expressions, normally, of enthusiastic popular belief. But they could be taken seriously by a cultivated audience, which could discount them like any other sort of exaggerated tale; and then they could take on more recondite implications as one more sort of indirect writing. In an atmosphere in which Faylasûfs and Ṣûfî metaphysicians wrote hiddenly for the initiate, the Ṣûfî poet Jalâluddîn Rûmî was quite explicit that his *Mas̃navî*, also, must be read esoterically. He cites (II, 3602 ff.) a ḥadîth report that Mary and Elizabeth had met when both were pregnant, and in their wombs Jesus and John had bowed to each other; then he notes that the Qur'ân seems to make the report impossible by asserting that Mary met no one during her pregnancy. After suggesting a rationalizing answer (that the two women were present to each other in spirit), he boldly suggests that such explanations are irrelevant at best; that what matters is the meaning of the stories, just as what matters in animal fables is not the possibility of animals talking, but the morals the fables point. And then he warns the obtuse reader that, if he insists on taking the poet's stories literally, they are so constructed that such a reader will be deliberately misled by them. He tells how a grammar teacher who had used the paradigm sentence 'Zayd hit 'Amr' was asked by a pupil why Zayd should hit 'Amr. When his attempt to explain that the names were mere names in a paradigm failed, he gave an explanation more suited to the pupil: the name 'Amr has, in Arabic, a silent letter; 'Amr was hit for 'stealing' that letter, which did not belong to him!

To write indirectly was perhaps easier then than now. All who had read at all had read much the same books and shared many of the same intellectual presuppositions. Hence a new contribution to intellectual dialogue could safely leave a great deal unsaid. Moreover, far fewer books were accessible than since the advent of printing; if any one book was taken seriously at all, it would be read with great care, perhaps even memorized. The need for cautious reading was accentuated by the imperfect state of most manuscripts, which did not allow for rapid eye movement: probably a large proportion of the reading was reading aloud or at least lip-reading at a slow pace, and presumably each sentence might be weighed for possible implications. In any case, every important book was supposed to be read by any serious student orally with a master who knew the book from his masters and explained it—in principle on the basis of an oral tradition transmitted from the author himself. Accordingly, an author had every reason to be less than explicit where too explicit a formulation in black and white might cause difficulties. If I am right that already al-Ṭabarî had left many of the implications of his history intentionally inexplicit, the pattern of partially tacit composition began very early.

The effects of this indirect style were compounded in an important genre of the time, in which an esoteric approach was especially appropriate. I refer to what I call 'mythic-visional' writing: such works of evocation as, unlike science, are primarily moral interpretation of experience already given; yet unlike more fragmentary rhetorical or lyric writing, attempt a comprehensive vision of the totality of life; and unlike even the most comprehensive fictional novel, do this by way not of imagined example but of direct, if symbolic and mythic, description of the world as a whole, or some sector of it. In Modern times, fascinated with the triumphs of our specialized natural sciences and with the subtle psychological observations of our novelists, there has been less call than once there was for such a genre. Hesiod and Genesis appear to many as merely historical curiosities. Writers like Boehme or Swedenborg attract us little and even Dante is commonly read now for merely lyric delight. And we scarcely know what to make of Yeats or Teilhard or Toynbee. But some of the most important works of prose of the Islamic Middle Periods were of a mythic-visional type, which tends to get misread and so miscomprehended and undervalued.

Such writing may express a heroic vision of life, as in ancient epics where men wrest a mortal grandeur from an inscrutable fate; or a unitive vision of life, where the meaning of the individual life answers to some meaningfulness in the cosmos, as in the scriptures of the confessional religions and especially in the writings of the mystics. In either case, what may be called archetypical symbolism often recurs. The point of this symbolism must be grasped, if not on the level of universal human unconscious images, then at least on the level of deeply appropriate interresonances of forms of being, usually selected and preserved in enduring traditions. To the degree that any given mythic writing is effective, it is likely to be woven upon such interresonances and to be rooted in such traditions.

We have already mentioned several pieces of Islamicate mythic-visional writing: symbolic tales by Ibn-Sînâ, cosmological descriptions by Yaḥyà Suhravardî and by Ibn-al-ʿArabî. Some alchemical literature could be placed here and probably some astrology, as well as much more Ṣûfî writing. The genre was a literary form (in a broad sense); but since it dealt with life-orientational questions, it was also a means of discursive communication—thus some mythic stories were recast by a series of authors, each of whom implicitly contrasted his own interpretation of the story—and therefore of human life as such—to that of his predecessors. For instance, Ibn-Sînâ's tale of the voyage of a traveller (the soul) into exile in the west (the sunset realm of unilluminated material actuality) was taken up by other writers with a different emphasis. And despite the difficulty for us of being sure of what it was Ibn-Sînâ himself meant, because of his indirect manner of expression, a real dialogue does emerge from one rendering of the myth to the next.

But to the obstacles placed in our way by the tendency of such writing to be indirect and partially tacit, or even frankly esoteric, are added other obstacles to our comprehension. First, such writings always presuppose a great deal of special information which an editor must give in footnotes—about chemical or astronomical or psychological teachings of the time, or about legendary themes that are made use of. But even when such information is assimilated, a larger problem remains: learning to read such a work in its own terms. If a work of fiction were to be read as biography and so judged, its whole point would be missed: the reader would complain of the want of much essential information and of the inclusion of so much inessential detail, and if he found out that the persons described did not exist at all he would dismiss the whole as a hoax. Likewise, mythic-visional writing will be misunderstood if it is read simply as lyrical outpourings, or as pseudo-science or metaphysics, or as fiction.

Though Dante did not mean his localizations to be taken literally, yet if he had learned that the solar system is in fact heliocentric, he would have felt that his *Paradiso* had in some degree been proved false; for the sense of a closed and hierarchical universe was crucial to him. He was trying to describe the cosmos as a concrete whole. His history and cosmology formed the core of his description of real people and real places, not a backdrop for airy lyric or for fiction. If we read his work in the latter ways, we effect a transposition that he would rightly have been unhappy with. And we would be equally wrong to read it as science; he himself did not intend it as that, but as an interpretation of a reality which he envisaged according to the best science available. His work requires a special mode of perception, in which its claims to deal with the real cosmos are done justice, but on a mythic level to which the criteria of science are less directly relevant than he realized. Such a perspective can be even more needed with the corresponding Islamicate writings.

Finally, even when these obstacles to reading can be overcome, a further question seems to arise: how many such visions of the world can one person seriously assimilate? A full appreciation of the outlook presented in such a work would carry the reader outside the work itself into the life and cosmos which it is attempting to interpret; each such work presupposes that the reader will be willing to see not only the work itself but his whole life, at least provisionally, from the one angle of vision. This cannot be done in a casual reading. Perhaps most persons cannot expect to do more than to glance at such a work, wonderingly, from outside.

Unfortunately, the Muslim commentators are generally of little help in overcoming such obstacles. Even when they understood, themselves, they commonly restricted themselves to explaining references that an unlearnèd reader might miss, and handled the main ideas rather mechanically. Such an approach need not indicate obtuseness; it might be adopted deliberately by one who was ready enough to clear away, in writing, minor philological details; but who believed that a more serious understanding could not be gained except in oral intercourse with a master and upon a background of relevant personal experience. It is possible that the recent tendency among modern readers to accept more readily the paradoxical and the obscure will make it easier for us to appreciate the Islamicate heritage. Meanwhile, the indirect style generally and the mythic-visional genre especially have entrenched the esotericism, and added to the inaccessibility for us of the high-cultural achievements of Islamdom.

The philosophy of the isolated wise man: Ibn-Ṭufayl and the Spaniards

While the most striking developments in the imaginative life in the century or so following Ghazâlî were in Ṣûfî speculation and in the flowering of Persian literature, more prosaic intellectual activity was developing solidly the leads opened up in the century before. This intellectual life showed the mature effects of a military régime of amîrs and of the integrative social role played by a Sharîʻah independent of them.

In the context of the Sunnî synthesis, where the social primacy of Sharîʻah-mindedness was conceded as autonomous basis for a society otherwise ruled by the amîrs, the Faylasûfs found themselves integrated into an overall tradition in which the Sharʻî Muslim character of society as a whole was taken for granted. Following a path already prepared by al-Fârâbî, they commonly accepted this as a fait accompli and argued that it was the best available society and creed for the vulgar herd. Any latent thoughts of transforming society seem to have been given over, and Philosophers' aims were definitively restricted to satisfying the curiosity of an élite. There were even attempts to suggest that the 'true philosopher' could be self-sufficient entirely by himself, without the society even of other philosophers, contrary to the Aristotelian conception of the human as a social animal.

Ghazâlî had defined a place for both Falsafah and Ṣûfism alongside the

Sharîʿah. He had gone beyond Ibn-Sînâ's attempt to find a place both for the Sharîʿah and for Ṣûfism within the framework of Falsafah, above all in that he asserted the validity of historical and personal revelatory experience—prophetic and mystical—as distinct from and above and far beyond anything that could be achieved by abstract reasoning from nature. In this way, Ṣûfism became the intellectual cornerstone of his Islamic synthesis and it remained so in the central Islamicate lands.

Muslim Philosophers and Theologians in the Early Middle Period, 1111–1274

1111	Death of Ghazâlî, limitor of Falsafah, harmonizer of Ṣûfism and Sunnism
1138	Death of Ibn-Bajjah, Andalusian vizier and physician-Faylasûf, interested in the union of the soul with the Divine
1185	Death of Ibn-Ṭufayl, Andalusian secretary and physician-Faylasûf, author of allegory *Ḥayy b. Yaqẓân,* mysticism as culmination of Falsafah
1191	Death of Yaḥyà al-Suhravardî, Faylasûf, cosmologist, founder of Ishrâqî school building on Ibn-Sînâ
1198	Death of Ibn-Rushd (Averroës), Andalusian qâḍî and physician-Faylasûf in a strong Aristotelian manner rejecting Ibn-Sînâ (Avicenna) and Ghazâlî
1209	Death of Fakhruddîn Râzî, anti-Muʿtazilî mutakallim, supporter of Ashʿarî positions, teacher and preacher, well versed in Falsafah
1269	Death of Ibn-Sabʿîn, originally Andalusian Aristotelian-style Faylasûf, turned Ṣûfî
1274	Death of Nasîruddîn Tûsî, Faylasûf, astronomer, codifier of Imâmî Shîʿî teachings; served the Assassins and Mongols

The political experience of the Maghrib and Spain was somewhat less discontinuous and the development of a Sunnî synthesis took a rather different form there, centring more closely on the court of the great dynasty. When the Muwaḥḥids sponsored a more sophisticated intellectuality to overlay the Sharîʿah-mindedness of the ʿulamâʾ of the Murâbiṭs, they did so at first on the basis of Ghazâlî's work. But it was rather his Ashʿarî kalâm and even his interest in Falsafah, more than his Ṣûfism, which seems especially to have attracted Ibn-Tûmart. When, then, the Muwaḥḥid state proved able to form a reasonably enduring political tradition controlling at least the urban network of the Maghrib and Spain, the Faylasûfs found an excellent vantage point as friends and high ministers of the new rulers.

Falsafah had come as late to Spain as any other intellectual fashion, for little was to be inherited from the local Latin past. In the time of the party kings, it had been introduced especially in the form of the positive sciences.

Under the Murâbiṭs the local Falsafah tradition was maintained despite dynastic hostility—but not without a certain sense of isolation. Ibn-Bâjjah, of that age, was known for his study of the proper regimen of the isolated 'philosopher' in an unphilosophic society which he knew could not be made philosophical.

The first great Faylasûf under the Muwaḥḥid dynasty, Ibn-Ṭufayl, has left us a study which developed that theme in a more comprehensive sense. In his philosophical tale, *Ḥayy b. Yaqẓân,* he set out to explain what the 'illuminative' (or 'eastern') philosophy was which Ibn-Sînâ had referred to as different from the received Peripatetic, but had never fully expounded. In his introduction, he refers to Ghazâlî and Ibn-Sînâ as the two masters—Ghazâlî being, in a sort, the patron sage of the dynasty and Ibn-Sînâ being the greatest exponent of Falsafah in Islamic terms. In effect, he defended Ibn-Sînâ's interpretation of Islam against Ghazâlî. He conceded to Ghazâlî the crucial importance of *dhawq,* of direct and incommunicable personal experience, as an essential ingredient in the search for truth, to be distinguished from any possible results of discursive reasoning (identified with Falsafah). Here was a basis for the philosophy of illumination: the philosophy which should expound the Ṣûfîs' mystical experience. But he reserved such immediate experience to the highest levels of a sequence of intellectual development in which philosophical discursive reasoning was the main body and the natural preparation for the highest phases.

In his tale, he tells of a man (Ḥayy b. Yaqẓân, 'Alive son of Awake') whose organism germinated by spontaneous generation out of mud in which the elements and temperaments were perfectly balanced. The man grows up (cared for at first by a deer mother) on an island by himself and by stages learns to provide for himself and then to speculate and philosophize, in the Falsafah sense. He becomes aware of his place in the cosmos as a rational being and develops a sensitive ethic, which even includes vegetarianism; an ethic based not on any social relations but on his natural status, set between the self-moving, changeless planets and the unthinking, passion-moved creatures about him. Finally—by the perfection of his organic composition—he reaches the heights of philosophical awareness, whence he proceeds on into ecstatic contemplation as a continuation of that awareness proper to the most perfect nature, which his is. We have here a presentation of human potentialities which makes a place for mystical experience and even credits it with a significant role in truth-seeking beyond the level of demonstrative discourse. But he has insisted that even on points of metaphysic his hero was able to argue himself into fundamentally sound truth, and his hero's mystical experience is clearly but the perfection of the philosophizing on which it was necessarily founded. Our lone human being, then, has achieved perfection through fulfilling Philosophia, entirely on the basis of the operation of the Philosopher's ever-present, eternal and rational natural forces—the same forces that accounted for his very origin by spontaneous generation.

But at this point in the tale, we are led to another nearby island, which in contrast to the island of natural Philosophy is the island of prophetic revelation. At the very beginning of the tale we had, in fact, heard of that other island, for an alternative possible origin for our hero was suggested—that he was inopportunely born there to a lady, who set him out to sea in a box. On that island of human frailty, it seems, humans can be born only from other humans, historically-bound descendants of Adam. This is not the eternal world of the Philosophers' nature but the created world where the human race is supposed to have had its origin at a given moment by the fiat of the Creator—and where the greatest truth people are capable of is that of the images of prophetic revelation designed to keep them in order. After a futile and, indeed, dangerous attempt to open the eyes of the men of that island to their true potentialities as human beings, our hero decides that it is best that they be left in their ignorance after all, lest a few words of truth merely make them unruly. He returns to his own island and his own blessèd destiny.

The real Philosopher could not withdraw to another island, but otherwise he could follow the example of Ibn-Ṭufayl's hero within the society of the Muwaḥḥid empire. That is, he could isolate himself in his own Philosophic awareness, and leave the rest of mankind to pure revelation and its exegetes, without any middle ground. Ibn-Ṭufayl, accordingly, scolds al-Fârâbî for not concealing Philosophic views (for instance, on the afterlife) carefully enough. His own tale, appropriately, was itself more or less esoteric in form: the reader is forced from the beginning, with the alternative stories of the hero's birth, to choose how he is to read it—what attitude, in particular, he will take to the island of revelation and its presuppositions.

Ibn-Rushd and the distinction between philosophy and religion

The conclusion was worked out most fully by Ibn-Ṭufayl's disciple, Ibn-Rushd (1126–98; called by the Latins, 'Averroës'): under dynastic protection, Falsafah and Sharî'ah were to share the field exclusively between them. On this basis, Ibn-Rushd rejected much of Ibn-Sînâ's attempt to give Philosophic standing to Ṣûfî experience and to prophethood; he went back to a stricter Aristotelianism, which allowed him to take a more uncompromising stand against allowing any purely intellectual dignity to Islam as such, whether in Shar'î or Ṣûfî form (though he did allow a certain natural gift of wisdom to the Prophet). This renewed Aristotelianism also allowed him to turn Ghazâlî's attack by withdrawing to a narrower front (much of Ghazâlî's great assault on Falsafah had been against exposed positions of Ibn-Sînâ).

Ibn-Rushd preferred to defend himself by cautiously shifting some primary categories. Thus he argued that every particular thing in the world was indeed originated by God, as Ghazâlî said was required by the Qur'ân, and not eternal; but that neither the notion origination nor the notion eternity properly applied to God's relation to the whole world. And he countered the demand that God know not merely universals but particulars, by saying that neither of those two sorts of knowledge was appropriate to God's knowing; His knowledge was of a still more comprehensive kind than either. That is, in really ultimate questions, where Ghazâlî had denied the applicability of abstract argument at all, Ibn-Rushd preferred to say that the alternatives deriving from finite experience were not relevant, and a proper Philosopher should use terms sui generis on that level. These, one may say, had the virtue of not being refutable, as their meaning could hardly be known.

On such a basis, he could deny any inconsistency between the rational conclusions of Philosophia, even as to metaphysic, and the mere images presented in revelation; but only so long as he could treat the images as just that, and therefore as subject to whatever interpretation was needed. Hence the fully demonstrative reasoning of Falsafah could claim validity as a sophisticated alternative to simple acceptance of the Sharî'ah and its associated notions; but any analysis that made the images more than arbitrary substitutes for Philosophic ideas must be rejected. Any argumentation (kalâm) short of true demonstrative Philosophia was merely misleading people into thinking they were coming to rational truth; it stirred up controversy where persons were not ready for pure reason and diluted their faith in the images of revelation.

Accordingly, the Muwaḥḥid policy of his time was justified: while privately at the court the speculations of Falsafah were cultivated among the few who were believed capable of them, yet publicly, intellectual speculation was frowned on. Falsafah itself was not to be published among the masses and kalâm and speculative Ṣûfism were not to be tolerated at all. Muwaḥḥid obscurantism, which persecuted all sorts of deviation from Sharî'ah-mindedness (including the dhimmî non-Muslim communities when they seemed too comfortable), was perhaps to be moderated but was not fundamentally to be reversed. Ibn-Rushd himself was grand qâḍî and chief censor.

This philosophical viewpoint was sufficiently vital to be adapted, almost simultaneously with Ibn-Rushd's work, to Judaism, though the Jews and their Halakha law, which corresponded to the Sharî'ah law, did not control the government. The Halakha, in any case, was given by Muslim rulers a role within the Jewish community answering to that of the Sharî'ah among Muslims. Maimonides (Ibn-Maymûn, 1135–1204), like Ibn-Rushd born at Córdova, and only slightly later, proved one of the greatest masters of Jewish thought of all time. Writing partly in Hebrew and partly in Arabic (but then in Hebrew characters), he presented a Philosophical analysis of Jewish faith which extensively influenced, for instance, Thomas Aquinas in his subsequent analysis of Christian faith. That analysis, like Ibn-Rushd's and unlike Aquinas' (and unlike the thinking of many Jews of western Europe, who though writing in Hebrew wrote as Occidentals rather than as

Islamicate thinkers), rejected kalâm, speculation in the service of revelation; he insisted on a simple acceptance of Torah and its traditional commentary for those unable to rise to his own heights. Appropriately, he regularly condemns 'the Philosophers' for errors the best Philosophers did not make, and never acknowledges the character of a Philosopher even when taking most distinctively Philosophical positions (for instance, in carefully leaving the way open to asserting the eternity of the universe).

In the Maghrib and Spain, a political tradition similar in form to the Muwaḥḥid lasted through the fifteenth century. The distinctive features of the Maghrib were set by then: large isolated cities set off against a tribal Berber background with no smaller trading towns in the hinterland; Arabic high culture under the rule of dynasties dependent on Berber pastoral power; and, perhaps in consequence, an unusual social conservatism, sceptical of any private deviation as an intellectual luxury. With this social and political pattern persisted the tradition of a Falsafah aloof from other intellectual currents and at least intending to maintain an alliance with the most rigoristic representatives of Mâlikî fiqh (a rapprochement which the latter did not often reciprocate). The great Ṣûfî development did come to the west Mediterranean and flourish there, but (as ever) later than in the central lands; and it achieved dominance only by adapting with unusual abandon to the Berber tribal demand for visible focuses of piety, provided by living saints and even hereditary holy families (Marabouts).

The form of Islamicate culture known to the Occident from Spain in the High Medieval Age was thus wanting in much of the intellectual middle ground on which the great central tradition was being built. For the Occidentals, Ibn-Rushd (Averroës) was the major representative of Arabic philosophy, the writer of the great Aristotle commentary. As to the later Islamicate philosophy, it did not exist for them (except perhaps indirectly by way of one or two later Occidental thinkers who read the original Arabic).

As a direct consequence, later Islamicate philosophy has also not existed for many modern Western historians. This is partly because translation into Latin ceased before later writers became popular in Spain—if they ever became popular there at all. It is also because much of the more creative philosophy of later times did not present itself as Falsafah in the sense of an independent tradition still set off, as in the High Caliphal Period, in sharp contrast to the other intellectual currents. From the perspective of Spanish Falsafah, this meant a betrayal of true philosophy.

A most far-reaching consequence of the viewpoint of the Spanish school of Faylasûfs and particularly of the work of Ibn-Rushd was felt much more in the Occident than in Islamdom: the notion that 'faith' and 'reason', as alternative grounds for belief, characterize two categorically contrasting fields of inquiry, 'religion' and 'philosophy'. Wherever there exists a canonized body of statements alleged to be from a supernatural source, some contrast between 'faith' and 'reason' can arise: do you believe the sacred text or do you believe what you can reason out for yourself on the basis of natural observations? But in itself, such a contrast is superficial.

Because of their dependence on particular prophetic pronouncements made at particular historical moments, the Abrahamic traditions had set off such canonized texts (as reporting prophetic revelations) with unparalleled rigour. By Muḥammad's time, faith in the Creator-god was very often identified with believing the scriptures as His revelation, and this attitude sometimes appears in the Qur'ân. As we have noticed, with the Mu'tazilîs this identification of 'faith' with belief in certain theses as found in the sacred text became the foundation of their intellectualistic outlook. The early Faylasûf al-Kindî, moving in Mu'tazilî circles, found it quite feasible, accordingly, to take over the notion already developed among Christian Philosophers, that 'revealed doctrines' were parables of Philosophic truths that happened to come to us through special channels which could be taken 'on faith'. But we do not yet have here the full later distinction between 'reason' and 'faith' as grounds for different intellectual disciplines. The Philosophical metaphysicians (at best) merely had a more demonstrative way of doing the same thing as the Abrahamic theologians.

On this level, a contrast between the Philosophic tradition and the Abrahamic need have little to do with any contrast between reason and faith or revelation. One can argue that the theologians who reasoned from prophetic revelations were merely taking into rational account evidence which the Philosophical metaphysicians had irrationally overlooked. The Ash'arîs, though they modified the Mu'tazilî definition of 'faith', retained the Mu'tazilî demand for belief in revealed statements. Yet they recognized that the faith in revelation that they called for took the form of correct reasoning from explicit evidence—from historical evidence that had to be verified as carefully as any other sort of evidence; and they accused their opponents of reasoning not from evidence but from their own wishful thinking—their passions. When they contrasted *aql* and *naql*, reasoning and transmission, they were contrasting, properly speaking, not natural evidence to supernatural authority, but subjective conjecture ('reasoning') to (one kind of) objective evidence (transmitted reports). The contrast could be applied, within Shar'î thinking, to arguments about the interpretation of Qur'ân and fiqh, as well as in any other realm; but if the two terms were applied to different realms of inquiry, then all historical studies, including grammar and prosody, were (quite properly) studied under the heading not of 'reason' but of 'transmission', for the latter referred to any evidence of past events or usages, including reports of revelatory events, among others.

In contrast to later distinctions between 'religion' and 'philosophy', then, it can be argued that, on the level of life-orientational thinking, any system is based on both reason and faith. Reliance on transmitted reports, as such, does not exclude or even set special limits to the use of reason; rather, it seems tacitly to imply a choice of the sort of evidence one is to reason about

—a choice on the basis of what it is one puts one's faith in. That is, the men of kalâm were reasoning from a historical event they trusted to be revelatory, but others—the Faylasûfs—might reason from a natural pattern they trusted to be normative. In that case, each party was using reason about something taken on faith. But if the men of kalâm would have been unhappy at being thus placed on a level with the Faylasûfs, the Faylasûfs, basing their outlook on an appeal to abstract reason as such, could not accept such a contrast at all. Rather, they contrasted the independent exercise of the mind (on the basis of an ever-accessible nature) to unreasoning submission to a given text (dating from a contingent and therefore not truly knowable event).

Al-Fârâbî had crystallized in two ways the Muslim form of the old accommodation between Philosophia and the Abrahamic tradition: partly by stressing the autonomy of the various disciplines of Philosophia from any overall life-orientational commitments, partly by reserving the Philosophical vision for a special élite. But for him, the Philosophical metaphysic was still just a superior way of understanding the same problems to which the Abrahamic tradition gave more imaged answers. Ibn-Rushd now systematically drew more substantive conclusions from the Philosophers' felt contrast between the independent mind and blind 'faith': he not only reserved rationalistic Philosophia, identified with philosophic thinking as such, to an intelligent élite, but restricted the incompetent masses to unquestioning submission to established texts of limited scope, to be taken 'on faith'. The position of the Ash'arîs, that the texts themselves had to be reasoned about as evidence, was ruled out. 'Religious' thinking, i.e., thinking in the prophetic traditions, was restricted to sheer legal deduction from Shar'î texts—Qur'an and ḥadîth—given in advance by faith. Dealing only with law (including law about what could be *stated* about God), such thinking thus even answered different sorts of questions from Philosophia. In this way, both Philosophia and the Abrahamic tradition were to give up certain claims: Philosophia readily gave up any life-orientational role for the masses, even an indirect one (that was left to 'religion'); while the Abrahamic tradition was to give up claims to understand the nature of metaphysical reality, which was reserved to Philosophia.

In Islamdom, where the overriding claims of mysticism could not be fitted into such a dichotomy, Ibn-Rushd's division played a secondary role at most. But in the Occident, where intellectual life was dominated by a highly organized church basing its authority on revealed texts, the contrast was accepted—by way of the 'Averroists'—with this serious difference: Christian theology, which had an ecclesiastical status as crucial to the church as fiqh was to the 'ulamâ', was not shunted aside, like kalâm, but took the place of the properly textual Shar'î studies as the 'religious' side of the division. Yet the division was still seen as separating two different realms of truth, answering largely different sorts of questions. This gave articulate form to a distinction (already implicit anyway as a result of the tension between the Abrahamic and Philosophical traditions) between two fields of life-orientational thinking: the Philosophic tradition became 'philosophy' based on 'reason' about 'nature'; the Abrahamic tradition became 'religion' based on 'faith' in authoritative 'revelation'. The Averroists prudently asserted that where they conflicted, 'reason' must give way. Others found ways to deny any conflict, but accepted the convenient idea of two differing fields of inquiry even though defining the fields variously.

When such a distinction has been applied retrospectively by modern Western scholars to earlier periods and other cultures, it has predictably resulted in distortions and confusions; but this fact has not prevented it from being so generally taken for granted latterly that even in modern Arabic the term *falsafah* refers not to a particular school of thought but to philosophic thinking generally—as does *philosophy* now in English—in a confused contrast to dogmatic 'religious' thinking.

The union of Falsafah and kalâm

In the more central Muslim lands, especially in Iran, the madrasahs, which started out devoted to fiqh and to a few ancillary studies recognized as useful by the Ḥadîth folk, eventually became the centres of a Sharî'ah-mindedness recast on broader lines than were common in the Maghrib. The rights that kalâm and Ṣûfism and even Falsafah had won (at the price of recognizing a limited status and a certain obligation to silence) had opened the way for what was called 'rational' (*'aqlî*) inquiry to flourish even in the madrasahs side by side with the collection and sifting of authoritative reports from the past (which was set off as *sam'î* or *naqlî*, 'transmitted' study). Falsafah as such never gained much popular acceptance and consequently could not be used with full freedom; resistance to kalâm, however, fell away. Consequently such scholars as were inclined more to Falsafah than to Ṣûfism, but were not prepared to become explicit Faylasûfs, developed their speculation under the heading of kalâm; for instance, as extensive prolegomena to the defence of particular Sharî'ah-minded positions.

After the time of Juvaynî and Ghazâlî, kalâm presented a new face. Old issues, such as free will versus predestination, that had once aroused the intractability of the Ḥadîth folk, were increasingly glossed over in the name of reason by their successors, and all the resources of Hellenistic learning tended to be accepted as compatible with Islamic 'ilm, provided only a few points of indubitable heresy were avoided. By the time of Fakhruddîn Râzî (d. 1210), kalâm was treated very much in the spirit of Falsafah, with great sophistication as to the intellectual presuppositions of abstract inquiry. The Sharî'ah-minded man of kalâm (*mutakallim*) still set himself off from the Faylasûf, and opposed certain of the latter's most characteristic conclusions—e.g., the eternity of the world. But the mutakallim's universe of discourse now included the whole range of Falsafah with its intellectual sophistication.

The earlier Ash'arîs had opposed the Mu'tazilîs on Mu'tazilî grounds, Muslims fighting Muslims over the interpretation of the Qur'ân, the whole discussion remaining essentially within the limits of theological dogma. Now the later Ash'arîs were opposing the cosmopolitan Faylasûfs, whether Muslim or not, on the seemingly neutral human grounds set forth by Falsafah itself. Even so, the historical and populist framework set by the Ḥadîth folk asserted its primacy and imposed its limits so long as kalâm as such, defence of supposedly revealed doctrines, retained their primary allegiance.

In such a context, even those thinkers who refused the limitations of kalâm in principle, the conscious Faylasûfs, found it possible to weave the special problems of kalâm into their work. It becomes difficult to distinguish who should best be called Faylasûf and who mutakallim; for they dealt with like questions and often came to like conclusions.

Naṣîruddîn Ṭûsî (1201–74) was much inclined to Falsafah but did not withdraw into the Spanish philosophy of the isolated wise man; if he withdrew, it was into sectarianism, identifying himself with the Shî'ah (and availing himself of its special principle of concealment, taqiyyah). By the early thirteenth century, the Nizârî Ismâ'îlî movement had been brought almost to a standstill politically, but not intellectually. Writing as an Ismâ'îlî, he produced theological tracts for them which justified their latest position and then remained standard for centuries. When the remains of Ismâ'îlî power collapsed, he emerged as a Twelver, writing Twelver Shî'î tracts, and gained great renown in this his (no doubt) truer allegiance.

Ghazâlî, in his recasting of Jamâ'î-Sunnî thinking to make a place for the studies of Falsafah and to introduce Ṣûfism as culminating principle, had confronted Nizâri Ismâ'îlî doctrine and allowed it considerable impact. A curiously, though perhaps accidentally, analogous role was played by Ṭûsî in Twelver Shî'ism and by Ismâ'îlism in Ṭûsî's thinking. The Ismâ'îlîs, when their revolt had collapsed, had eventually turned to spiritualizing their mission. Rediscovering an imâm (1164 CE) among themselves, they had attempted to live the life of spiritual resurrection even in the body: which meant a life in which the attention was focused, by way of the imâm, solely on transcendent values, and all things of daily life were to be seen from this viewpoint. In this effort they were aided both by earlier Ismâ'îlî teachings and by the writings of the Ṣûfîs, to whose endeavour their own was patently similar. Later, in the time of the caliph al-Nâṣir, their imâm (proclaiming himself a Sunnî, 1210) refused to be used in this manner, and the Ismâ'îlîs had to develop a spirituality centred on a veiled imâm—almost a hidden one like that of the Twelvers—and in so doing necessarily moved even closer to the Ṣûfî pattern. It was at this stage that Ṭûsî lived among them. He helped them to work out this latter phase of what was, in effect, an accommodation between Shî'ism and Ṣûfism.

As a leading (and politically privileged) Twelver Shî'î after 1256, having gone over to the victors when the Mongols took Alamût and massacred the

Ismâ'îlîs, Ṭûsî brought together three traditions. With his Twelver allegiance, to which he dedicated much of his political influence, he combined both a keen interest in Ṣûfism and an ultimate allegiance to Falsafah. He was the first major Twelver Shî'î to do either, though some such combination had been common among Ismâ'îlîs; after his time, and following his lead, the combination became common among Twelvers.

Ṭûsî did not renounce kalâm, but adopted the Mu'tazilî position which had come to prevail among Twelvers. But more important to him was his defence of Ibn-Sînâ, whom he seems already to have regarded, like most of Ibn-Sînâ's major commentators, as nearly a Ṣûfî. Like Ibn-Ṭufayl, he took up Ghazâlî's challenge to the Faylasûfs by directly defending the master—in contrast to Ibn-Rushd—and used his Ṣûfî orientation to support his defence in a way that stressed more comprehensively than did Ibn-Ṭufayl the validity of traditional religious experience and hence of the religious community as a Philosopher's spiritual home. His treatise on ethics, inspired, like other Islamicate ethical treatises since Ibn-Miskawayhi, by Aristotle and the categories implied in his golden mean, was strongly philosophical and yet envisaged a popular and even religious clientèle. (We shall meet Ṭûsî again in Book Four as a natural scientist and a patron of natural science.)

Whether in stark individualism or in ambivalent sectarianism, Falsafah protected itself with the veil of secrecy: Faylasûfs, even if they saw a role for Philosophical insights at a broader level, agreed with Ghazâlî at least in this, that true Philosophia in its own nature was not for the common man. Ibn-Rushd, as private thinker a loyal Aristotelian, as qâḍî could condemn as dangerous heresy too popular a promulgation of Aristotelian ideas. Nor was Naṣîruddîn Ṭûsî any more willing to allow the ordinary populace to experiment with actual philosophic freedom.

Visual arts in the Earlier Middle Period

It was only with the end of the High Caliphal state that the visual arts in Islamdom took on traits recognizable as Islamicate for the next thousand years. By the later part of the Earlier Middle Period, what is distinctive in Islamicate art was already well developed. Like literature and intellectual life, it bore traces of the fragmentation of political life and even of the relative autonomy of urban cadres.

In the centuries when the confessional religions were rising, the higher arts of the peoples from Iran through the Mediterranean basin (which once had breathed almost everywhere the spirit of Hellenism), had broken away from the idealized naturalism of the pagan Greeks and had found ways to express other sentiments—in foremost place, of course, the trans-natural aspirations of the newly prevailing religions. In painting, for instance, the moulded musculature of the old Greek figures, or the elaborate casualness of their robes, was abandoned for a quicker narrative, in which the simple lines of the figures did not interfere with the vigorous colour, but made the story of the picture all the more clear and direct. In painting and mosaic there resulted eventually the style which we associate with the earlier Byzantines; something not too different, if less elegant, was done in Latin Europe, too, and what we know of the depictive art of Sâsânian Iran shows a similar spirit. At the same time, there was a move in many areas, for instance in Egypt and Syria, toward a strongly non-naturalistic stylizing in any graphic art where the figure was not of central importance. In architecture, the new spirit showed in the love of domed structures (such as Hagia Sophia at Constantinople), with their sense of artificial internal space, as against the Classical columned temple, where the simple rectangular spaces could more readily seem an extension of the natural space about them. Cumulatively, by the time of Islam's arrival, the visual arts were developing their own stylized, imaginative world, full of strong colour and a strongly narrative symbolism.

The advent of Muslims as the wealthiest patrons of art reinforced this tendency. To the extent that there was a certain breach with the old ruling classes, a higher proportion of nouveaux riches than usual, the ancient imperial styles lost the advantage of inherited taste. As we have seen, under Muslim rulers who moved freely from one province to another, often carrying artisans with them, the local styles of Egypt and Syria mingled with the inherited traditions of the Jazîrah and the Iraq and all the Iranian lands. The egalitarian and iconophobic tendencies of Sharîʿah-minded Islam, however, true to the heritage of populistic monotheism, further militated against even the symbolically monumental manner which the arts in Sâsânian times had still cultivated even in religious images. The result was, at first, an active reshuffling of design elements, with the loss of some symbolically figural styles, but with the addition of few distinctively new motifs (unless one include the architectural scheme of the mosque itself). The mosque, to be sure, required adaptation of old patterns to a new layout: the large oriented rectangular area appropriate to the ṣalât; but except for liberating artists from symbolic expectations associated with older temple forms, this was not in itself aesthetically creative. In art generally, the High Caliphal Period remained one of ferment and exchange, of wrestling with problems rather than of many decisively new results.

The ferment of the period did eventually yield, however, several distinctive decorative forms and artistic themes. Hence in time (after the bulk of the population in the central areas became Muslim), more identifiably Islamicate sorts of visual art emerged. One can never speak of a single Islamicate style of art. But one can find points of contact—in common motifs and in formative problems—among the Islamicate styles. In the decentralized international art of the Earlier Middle Period, each area developed its own styles; yet people moved about with sufficient freedom so that elements of technique and solutions to artistic problems tended to be shared very widely. Artisans themselves might move, or they were brought by amîrs into new provinces as the amîrs themselves moved about, or sometimes they were carried off by conquerors to adorn their headquarters. However different the styles from Spain to Bengal, they were visibly Islamicate. Apart from the subtly perceptible outcome of the intershading of a common fund of techniques, the Islamicate character of the art is most readily seen in a limited number of traits. First among them is the intensive use of calligraphy as a central decorative theme, even in architecture. To this are related other traits, less universal: a frequent use of 'overall' patterns, intricately interweaving design elements symmetrically integrated over a large surface; or of complex ordered symmetry, even apart from any given surface. The most important sort of 'overall' pattern was the arabesque, which we shall discuss further in Book Four.

In the Earlier Middle Period, when such Islamicate art became first fully disengaged, it was sometimes combined with a special tendency not repeated later, though it left its mark on the later tradition: a tendency to what may be called 'bourgeois' art—art patronized by and, indeed, commissioned by the wealthier urban elements below the level of the amîrs. For a time (1150–1300?), it was such art that formed the fashion at least in some areas. This seems to have followed, temporally, immediately upon the period during which what we have called the abortive 'militia autonomy' had allowed a considerable role to local urban militia bodies; it continued for some time, with increasing rivalry from other forms, as more absolute power was gained among the amîrs and their garrisons; and disappeared finally in the Mongol period, when the military power undertook systematic patronage of the high culture.

However, even apart from any identifiably bourgeois patronage, the art of the period showed several traits that set it off from the monumental art, heraldic or hieratic, of previous ages, with their established courtly or temple traditions. The figural art, for instance, is uncompromisingly narrative in effect—even when, as it occasionally does, it includes Ṣûfî or other symbolism. In the painting of this period, as we see it on ceramic pieces and in book illustrations, the figures have become stylized, like their backgrounds; but they often stand out very sharply; for they are meant, above all, to tell a story. Their poses are unmistakable. But unlike some Byzantine hieratic art of a similar heritage, they are not meant to impress with their awesome presence; even when one has a face-on confrontation with a figure, the purpose is not to facilitate worship but to designate a character.

Often enough, the paintings burst with a sense of humour. We have a medical manuscript, for instance, in which the master teaches his disciple in the most improbable postures: he leans casually and pensively against a long pillow which is balanced on its point and sticks up into the air as if held by magic; while the book-stand from which he has been reading has one of its two legs clear off the platform on which it sits, resting on air; the disciple, about to leave, turns back in some uncertainty. That these arrangements were not accidental is shown by another painting by the same artist in which the pillow and the book-stand are handled less extremely, but which makes almost the same points—though here both master and disciple are more intent on their business. In other paintings—of animal tales or human scenes—the humour is generally more subtle and is expressed through the bold, slightly unfinished lines themselves. The illustrations to certain manuscripts of al-Ḥarîrî are as full of delight in the common life of city men as is al-Ḥarîrî himself.

The construction of the mosques reflected in a most direct manner the development of the Muslim social order. Lacking a priesthood, the mosques long maintained more a civic than a hieratic appearance. In the High Caliphal Period they were fundamentally large oriented courtyards, the centres for common discipline and for public information among the Muslim class of a town which the Muslims as a body controlled. As more of the town became Muslim, however, the big mosques tended to be subdivided by way of minor architectural elaboration—rows of pillars, miḥrâb niches, and so on —in ways that suggest that different Muslims worshipping there were identifying with their own quarters of the town more than with the government of the town as a whole. (I am told this sort of thing first appeared in eastern Iran and also in Spain.) In the eleventh century, the mosque design came to be relatively fragmented by way of such details. Only a good deal later—presumably with the rise of stronger central authorities after the Mongols—did the mosque come to be seen as an aesthetic whole.

A sign, perhaps, of the Muslim sense of individual independence, as against an anonymous corporate institution, appeared not long after the visual arts became distinctively Islamicate: the signing of the artist's name to his work. In fields much honoured, like poetry or calligraphy, Muslims had always liked to know who did a given piece of work: in principle, there was no anonymity. But in the High Caliphal Period (before many of the artists were Muslims, to be sure), signatures were rare, whether of painters or ceramicists or architects. In the twelfth century, such signatures became very widespread.[5]

[5] Oleg Grabar has done some preliminary investigation of such matters, on which I am relying (oral communication).

VII

Cultural Patterning in Islamdom and the Occident

For Western readers, Islamicate institutions can be specially illuminated by a comparison with Occidental institutions of the same period, as well as by consideration of what the Occidentals found to learn or borrow from the Muslims. Such a comparison can suggest assessments of potentialities in the two cultural sets as well as suggest long-term directions of movement in them, which may help us understand why this or that seeming possibility was not taken into account at this or that juncture. But at this point in our studies, it is hard to sort out the properly ecological circumstances from the expressly cultural commitments that enter into such comparison. It is perhaps even harder to sort out the cultural commitments that have contributed to social patterns in particular ethnic groups—local ruling classes, relatively compact nations like Egypt, and even whole language blocs like the Iranians. Inevitably, many comparisons have been attempted by scholars as if such elements could be sorted out. Perhaps the most important function of such a comparison as we can attempt is to suggest an alternative viewpoint to complement and perhaps correct the various current comparisons, usually superficial and often invidious or self-congratulatory on one side or the other.

The Earlier Middle Period, particularly the twelfth and thirteenth centuries, roughly equivalent to High Medieval times in the Occident, is the first period during which a comparison of the Occident with Islamdom can be particularly fruitful; up till that time, the Occident had been, on the whole, too backward to compare with one of the major centres of civilization. It is not only the first but also the best period for such a comparison. A comparison drawn later, in the sixteenth century, say, would be of interest for understanding the background of Modernity, but would lose value for purposes of illuminating the two traditions *as such* because the Occident had then entered one of those periods of major florescence relatively rare in agrarianate times, while the Islamicate lands were witnessing more normal historical conditions. After about 1600, the basic conditions of agrarianate historical life itself began to be altered in the Occident, and comparisons after that date therefore introduce considerations alien to any direct comparison between two cultures as such.

Islamdom and the Occident in the thirteenth-century world

Since the rise of the confessional traditions in late Roman and Sâsânian times, the Afro-Eurasian Oikoumene had not changed in the most fundamental conditions of its social life. Civilized culture was everywhere still carried primarily by privileged classes in cities, living ultimately from the labour of a great majority of chiefly illiterate peasants in the countryside. Cultural and intellectual innovation was everywhere still a secondary aspect of cultural life; the prime object of all institutions was the preservation of what had been attained rather than the development of anything new. Not only arts and crafts, but life-orientational and scientific thought, while not (as in pre-citied times) a matter of oral tribal lore, and no longer (as in citied times before the great Axial Age flowerings) the initiatory privilege of special priestly orders, nevertheless remained primarily a matter of personal apprenticeship from generation to generation on the basis of a limited number of classical texts among a small minority. Any possible historical action in any such fields could still not escape the presuppositions of society of the agrarianate level.

Yet within these limits, much that was only slightly less fundamental had changed by the thirteenth century. In these changes Muslims had played a primary role. Much change was the direct outcome of the force of Islam itself, which had had major consequences not only from Nile to Oxus but throughout the Indo-Mediterranean regions. Much change was the result of cumulative processes in which Islam and the culture associated with it were only one force among many. But even here the presence of the Muslims had often been of determinant importance. The most evident changes had been those that followed from the cumulative further development of the overall Oikoumenic complex of citied life. As compared with a thousand years before, by the year 1300 the area of civilized interaction had expanded in all directions. Cities had arisen in the Sûdânic lands, in northern Europe, in the lands south of the older China, in Malaysia, and they not only traded at long distances but added their own products to the trade, and sometimes even their own ideas. In the heart of the steppe, the Mongols themselves were becoming Buddhists and were well launched on the path to abject dependence on Chinese merchants and princes to which they had sunk by a few centuries later. In the Indian Ocean basin, trade no longer depended simply on a few northerly markets, but was active along all the shores.

In the same thousand years the technical competence of human beings in the Afro-Eurasian civilized zone had markedly increased. 'Greek fire' had been invented and then gunpowder; the compass had been put to work on all the seas; paper had spread from China to all regions, and printing was in use in the Far East and at least some of its elements were known elsewhere. Innumerable lesser inventions and discoveries had been made in the field of practical and of artistic technique, in the cultivation of plants and animals, in abstract scientific knowledge; some were of local application and some of general use; some of the most spectacular originated in China, but every region could be credited with some; and all (whether taken up elsewhere or merely adding to a local complexity) cumulatively contributed to a heightened level of availability of human resources everywhere in the Oikoumene. It was indeed, in part, some of the new discoveries that helped make possible, directly and indirectly, the expansion that had taken place in the area of civilized interaction; and this expansion, in turn, added to the potential sources of new discoveries. As in each millennium that had preceded, cumulatively the pace of history had quickened. (Whether mankind was *progressing* is a different question.) Here again, Islamdom shared at least as much as any other society in the overall development.

There was a third field of change during the previous millennium, less tangible than the geographical and technical accretions. This was a broadened and deepened experience with philosophical and religious life. Not only from Nile to Oxus but in all the major citied regions the rich creations of the classical Axial Age had been deeply assimilated, marvellously differentiated, a thousand and one of their possible implications worked out minutely. The labours of Ghazâlî and Ibn-al-ʻArabî in appreciating and integrating the Irano-Semitic life-orientational traditions, as they had developed by their time, were matched in differing ways in the other regions by figures like Shaṅkara and Râmânuja in India, Chu Hsi in China, Michael Psellus and Thomas Aquinas in Europe, all roughly (as world history goes) contemporaries. At least as important as any intellectual formulations was the maturing of traditions of personal experience with various aspects of the mystical life, and of institutions (usually monastic) which embodied these traditions, a maturing which had taken place likewise in all the great Oikoumenic regions.

Within this wider and more sophisticated world, Islamdom occupied an increasingly central and already almost a dominant position. The nature of this dominance has been misunderstood. The peculiar notion of some modern Western writers, that before the sixteenth century other societies, such as the Islamicate, were 'isolated' and were brought into the 'mainstream' of history only by such events as the Portuguese invasion of the Indian Ocean, is of course ridiculous: if there was a 'mainstream', it was the Portuguese who were coming into it, not the Muslims; the Muslims were already there. But the contrary notion, also found among Western writers, that in the High Caliphal Period Arab or Islamicate culture was the greatest in the world, that Córdova or Baghdad were incomparable centres of wealth and learning, is almost as poorly founded. It springs equally from the unconsidered assumption that the Occident was the 'mainstream' of world history and culture. Compared with the Occident, in the High Caliphal Period, when the Occident was still rather a backwater, Islamdom looks magnificent; but such a comparison says nothing about its relative position in the world; the Baghdad of the caliphs was merely on a plane of relative equality with Constantinople in eastern Europe and with the metropolises of India or China. (In the Earlier Middle Period, when the Occident was more developed, Islamdom looks less strikingly glorious in comparison; but most of the change in appearances is due to a change in the level of the Occident, not in that of Islamdom.) The well-known cultural superiority of Islamdom, then, was not absolute in the world at large (in the Earlier Middle Period, surely it was in China, if anywhere, that would be found the maximum economic and cultural prosperity); it was relative to the developing Occident.

Yet in certain respects, Islamdom was indeed pre-eminent in the Oikoumene. For the configuration of regional lettered traditions in the Oikoumene had, in the course of the other changes, itself subtly changed. In the Axial Age three great lettered traditions had been launched in the Indo-Mediterranean zone, the Sanskritic, the Irano-Semitic, and the Hellenic, in relatively close relations with each other but in rather tenuous relations with the fourth lettered tradition, the Chinese. The same four traditions still formed the matrix of all high culture; but their pattern had been altered now in three ways. First, the Irano-Semitic traditions had loomed much larger under Islam. In the early post-Axial centuries, the Irano-Semitic lettered traditions seemed almost ready to be submerged under waves of Hellenization and even of Indicization. By late Sâsânian times, these traditions were asserting full autonomy, and under Islam the Irano-Semitic heritage was clearly established on an equal level with the others—or more than an equal level; for by 1300 already the other two heritages were being submerged, at least in their original core areas, by the Irano-Semitic in its Islamicate form. Already by then the whole core area of Sanskritic culture was ruled by Muslims, and in the following centuries even independent Hindu states in the region learned more and more to live in an Islamicate world, even adopting some Islamicate patterns at least on superficial levels. By 1300 also the Anatolian peninsula was Muslim-ruled, and within a century so was the Balkan peninsula; of the homelands of Hellenic culture, only southern Italy and Sicily were not regained for Islam—and at this point, at any rate, Sicily even under its northern conquerors still retained strong traces of its earlier Muslim past and of its Islamicate surroundings. In short, by way of Islam almost the entire Indo-Mediterranean citied zone of Axial times, together with a wide hinterland, was already or was about to be united under the aegis of a single society; even though locally the Hellenic and the Sanskritic traditions maintained a certain limited vitality—a vitality visible especially in religion (and not too different from that maintained locally by the Irano-Semitic traditions at the height of the less extensive Hellenic dominance).

But there were two other events complementing this rise toward hegemony of the Irano-Semitic traditions: the potent burgeoning of China and the independent maturing of the Occident. Even at the height of Islamicate power, in the sixteenth century, when the greater part of the Oikoumene seemed to have become, if not Muslim, then at least a series of enclaved societies surrounded by Islamdom, still even then two citied societies stood out relatively impermeable to Islam: the Far East of China and its neighbours, and the Occident of Europe, part of the region grounded in Hellenic traditions. But neither of these societies played the same role as it had in Axial times. The Far East, of course, like the other societies had been doing its own expanding, and from a relatively small area along the Hoang-ho and the Yang-tze its lettered traditions had come to dominate a wide zone from Japan to Annam. But more important, in the T'ang-Sung period (from the seventh century) impulses from the Far Eastern region had impinged increasingly on the other parts of the Oikoumene; we have already noted, from the very moment of the advent of Islam down to the Mongol conquests, the relative ascendancy of Chinese art and trade between Nile and Oxus (and latterly, even some political impact); an ascendancy only limitedly attested for Sâsânian times.

The Occident was at first far less wealthy or cultivated, and impressed the imagination of the Indo-Mediterranean peoples generally less than did the Chinese. But its rise represented an even greater shift in the old Oikoumenic configuration. If one can think of the Occident proper as a complex of independent Latin-using and papacy-owning peoples set off from those under Byzantine leadership, one will see that the Occidental traditions arose on essentially new ground, in lands northwest of Rome rather than southeast of it in the terrain of the old Hellenic traditions. This in itself was nothing new—throughout the hemisphere, new areas were modifying in some measure the culture of the core area from which their lettered traditions were derived; thus in further India the Indic traditions maintained an independence, in a different form, after the Ganges plain was overrun by Muslims, just as the Hellenic traditions did in northern and western Europe. But the Occident developed a much more vigorous cultural life than any other such outlying region—indeed, it came to function almost like a fifth core-area, a fifth centre of persistent and comprehensive cultural innovation and radiation. After establishing its explicit independence in the eighth and ninth centuries (of course, always within the overall cultural commitments of the Christianized Hellenic tradition), by the twelfth and thirteenth centuries it was imposing its influence, economically, politically, and even culturally, on eastern Christendom, both north among the Slavs and south among the Greeks.

The Far Eastern and the Occidental traditions equally resisted the Muslim expansion—though both learned something from Islamdom as well; but the Occident was much closer home and even, in a few isolated cases, proved strong enough to roll back Islam from territories where it had long prevailed. One may thus say that in contrast to the situation a thousand years before, when four more or less equal core-areas had coexisted, now there was developing a three-cornered conflict among the most active cultural traditions:

the Islamicate in the whole of the old Indo-Mediterranean zone; the Far Eastern, newly making itself felt abroad; and the new Occidental variant of the Hellenic tradition. The conflict rarely became explicit. The Occident made at best sporadic attempts to act together (as in the Crusades) as a joint political power in its relations with outsiders. The Chinese empire was resisted by Japanese and Annamese. In the vast middle, Muslims, for all their emotional solidarity, acted even less often in concert. But the effective course of the conflict can nonetheless be traced. At the Mongolian capital, Karakorum, representatives of all three blocs had been present and intrigued against one another; if the Tibetans or the Russians seemed for a time to form secondary but independent sources of social power or cultural influence, this soon proved to be transitory or at least closely limited in scope. The Occidental cultural complex was certainly, at first, much the weakest of the three; but it grew steadily stronger, till in the sixteenth century it was competing on a level of full equality with both the others.

In 1300, the Occident could be compared to the dark horse in a race—if it were not that there was no race, or at least no very conscious one: for world hegemony, the presumable goal of any such race, was rarely pursued consciously even on the level of religious allegiance; nor is it clear that world hegemony was a necessary or even likely unintentional outcome of the cultural conflicts I have mentioned—or of any historical forces at work before the seventeenth- and eighteenth-century transformations changed the basis of all such conflicts. The Occident, comprising the lands of Latin expression in the western part of the European peninsulas, had a very limited territory and, by its remoteness, was limited in its contacts with other cultures: it had close contacts only with its former mentors of Eastern Christendom and with the Muslims. It had done very well by itself within these limits. From the viewpoint of urban life, much of it was newly opened frontier land; much of its intellectual resources consisted of material adapted or translated from the Greek (and Hebrew) or, latterly, from the Arabic. Yet in High Medieval times high culture, as well as all aspects of economic life, came to a great flowering in the Occident: a flowering comparable to that of contemporary Islamdom in the Earlier Middle Period, and even more striking because of the much lower point from which the Occidental cultural development started. For the first time in Oikoumenic history, the culture of a great new area, not a mere minor extension of one of the older cultural core areas, had drawn abreast of the old core areas in independent fullness of cultural sophistication and originality.

Yet even so, the Occidental cultural horizons remained more limited than those of Islamdom, if only geographically. After the final defeat of the Crusades, despite occasional merchants and missionaries who travelled great distances in the Mongol time (as did men from most other regions), Occidental culture was confined to its own little peninsulas. Thomas Aquinas was read from Spain to Hungary and from Sicily to Norway. Ibn-al-ʿArabî was read from Spain to Sumatra and from the Swahili coast to Kazan on the Volga. Even so late as the sixteenth century, the central position and vast extension of Islamdom still assured it at least the apparent pre-eminence which it was beginning to acquire by 1300. In contrast to any other of the major cultural core areas, that of Islam was in direct and active contact with all the major Oikoumenic regions; and not only in the neighbouring core areas but in some more outlying regions, Islam was becoming dominant politically and even culturally. If less industrially developed than the Chinese, the Muslims yet were more widely influential than any other bloc in shaping the cultural interchange and even the political life of the whole Oikoumene. But it was not merely the geographical centrality of the Muslim heartlands that put them in a pre-eminent position. It was the cultural and social mobility of the Muslims, their cosmopolitanism, that allowed them to take full advantage of their central position. Within the setting of agrarianate-level Oikoumenic society, the Islamicate culture was maximally adapted to an expansive and dominant role. It was to maintain this role, becoming steadily more dominant in the Oikoumene, until the Oikoumenic historical circumstances were totally altered—at the hands of the Occidentals.

The sources of Occidental strength and growth are the object of one of the most intriguing inquiries of world history. The sources of Islamicate strength and persistent vitality pose almost as great a world-historical problem, and one perhaps equally intriguing. To compare the two societies at their most nearly comparable stages can help to show to what degree the strength of each can be ascribed to its particular cultural composition, and to what degree to the overall circumstances in which its peoples found themselves.

Islam and Christianity as frameworks for religious life

The attractiveness of Islamicate culture and much of the potency of its institutions stemmed largely from the distinctive structure of the Islamic religious expectations as they had been developed by the Earlier Middle Period. It will be clear by now that the romantic notion that has prevailed in some circles, that Islam was the 'monotheism of the desert', born of the Bedouin's awed wonder at the vast openness of sky and land and their overwhelming unpredictability, is unhistorical. Islam grew out of a long tradition of urban religion and it was as city-oriented as any variant of that tradition. Like the other confessions, Islam was practiced by many unsophisticated people and among them it could appear very unsophisticated. Even at its most sophisticated, it usually retained, like the other pre-Modern religious traditions, a number of culturally primitive traits in its cult and its myth. But it stands out among those traditions for its relative sophistication and its freedom from the age-old compounded intricacies of the nature cults.

So far as any religious structure can be called 'simple', that of Islam can be. Its central formulations have been singularly stripped and direct and its essential cult has been plain to the point of austerity; the central challenge of its spiritual experience comes forth with almost blinding elemental immediacy. This is a simplicity not of naïve 'primitiveness' (pre-literate and other parochially limited systems are rarely if ever simple anyway) but of single-minded sophistication which integrates all the diversity of experience through a few potent and comprehensive conceptions; and then discards all that is circuitous and irrelevant, all that hangs over from a time when perceptions were less broadly generalizable. This relative urbanity of Islam can also be interpreted as a relative rootlessness, being cut loose from any particular local setting and its local involvement with nature. It is traceable to the mercantile orientation of Islam and in turn reinforced the cosmopolitanism of the society which had produced that orientation. Along with the advantages it afforded Islam in making for social and cultural strength, it brought disadvantages too, of course. But both advantages and disadvantages, strengths and weaknesses, were proper to a highly advanced stage of agrarianate social development.

The stark simplicity of the primary Islamic affirmations was but one expression of its overall urbanity. This lay not so much in any one feature of the tradition as in the whole structure of it: that is, the mutual interrelation of the various sub-traditions that went to make up Islam as a whole. Almost every trait to be found in any one religious tradition will be found somewhere in almost any other, if not in a mainstream then in some persistent variant of it; especially where the traditions have received high development among large populations. Thus may coexist social conscience and inward cultivation, moralistic austerity and cultic splendour, stress on transcendence and stress on immanence. But traditions differ as to what form these varying experiences and perceptions are expected to take, and as to which will be granted the greatest prestige; as to what sorts of temperament will be encouraged by those who stand relatively neutral in the community, and what sorts will be, at best, tolerated. It is this, the interrelation and subordination of different elements, that forms the structure of a religious tradition and gives it its distinctive effect as a body. Though such interrelations will change during history in response to the new insights and possibilities developed in the ongoing internal dialogue, yet to a large degree the common commitment to the initial creative events and to the succeeding dialogue, as it has unfolded, assures great continuity in such structuring under even widely varying circumstances.

Since Christianity and Islam share common roots and even much common symbolism, the striking contrast between the ways in which such common elements are lined up in the two traditions can bring out the diversity of their meaning in the two contexts. In particular, comparing such structuring in Islam and in Christianity can bring out the consequences of the persistent primacy in Islam of a sense of personal moral responsibility. But at best such a comparison is full of pitfalls. To evaluate in any way a pattern of ultimate orientation seems to imply judging one ultimate standard by another—or by a standard less than ultimate. In our case, to see either religious tradition from the viewpoint of the other (the commonest procedure) amounts inevitably to showing the one as weak in the other's strong points. To judge them both by a standard alien to either (sometimes attempted in reaction) is to risk missing just those points that are most distinctive and for that very reason incommensurate with any more common human norms. Yet, fortunately, human life is not divisible into watertight compartments. Apart from such explicit physiological defects as colour-blindness, the sorts of experience accessible to one human being are at least in some measure generally accessible to other human beings, so that there are no ultimate barriers to mutual comprehension between different cultural frames of reference—at least so far as such frames of reference are open to diverse temperaments within their own ranks. Hence what is called a phenomenological approach—such as a comparison of the structuring of comparable elements in two traditions—allows at least an opportunity of genuine appreciation, and will guard maximally against the effects of the inevitable precommitments of the inquirer.[1]

Despite the tremendous variety of religious orientation that has arisen in different sects or orders within the Christian tradition, a central theme has retained its hold on Christian imaginations under all sorts of circumstances, a theme ever presented to them anew especially in the writings of Paul and of John: the demand for *personal responsiveness to redemptive love in a corrupted world.* An equally wide variety of religious orientation has arisen among Muslims of different allegiances and ṭarîqahs, and among them also a central theme has retained its power under the most diverse circumstances whenever the Qur'ân has been taken seriously: the demand for *personal responsibility for the moral ordering of the natural world.*

These themes have been presented in contrasting cosmologies. Christians have seen the world as first corrupted with Adam, thenceforth to be patiently redeemed by a loving God, tirelessly forgiving His people so soon as they respond to His grace, and finally revealing Himself most fully among them as a perfect Life of suffering love, to which they need only respond with love, to be saved from the corruption and made whole. Muslims have seen the world as the proper sphere of Adam's vicegerency; when Adam strayed into error, he turned to God for guidance and was guided; rather than a source of taint in his descendants, he is a model to them. Thenceforth, God continued the guidance through a series of prophetic summonses to a total pattern of living; finally He revealed His transcendent unity most clearly through a perfect Book; if people allow it to remind them of what they are if left to

[1] This is not to say that one can actually dispense with those precommitments. On the inevitability and, indeed, the creative value of Christian, Westernistic, and other high-level precommitments, particularly in Islamic studies, see 'On scholarly precommitments' in the section on historical method in the Introduction in volume I.

themselves, they will turn to Him and His guidance will enable them to live right and to rule the world in justice. The central event of history for Christians was Christ's crucifixion and resurrection, which most decisively evoke a sense of God's love in him who opens himself to their impact, and lead him to respond to others in the same spirit. The central event of history for Muslims was the descent and preaching of the Qur'ân, which most decisively evokes a sense of God's majesty and his own condition in him who opens himself to its impact, and leads him to reflect and submit himself to its norms.

For Christians, the Law, the necessities imposed by social living, is transcended as people are liberated, in loving response, to act through the inward power of God's free spirit; the Sermon on the Mount provides a standard of true living. For Muslims, the laws and customs of humans are reoriented toward a universal justice; humans, stirred out of their petty neglectfulness by confrontation with God's words, are to act as the vicegerents of God in the whole creation; the jihâd, the struggle for social righteousness, provides a standard of true living. For Christians, the kind of religious experience most honoured is the acceptance of redemptive grace, which means a process of rebirth, of inward transformation. For Muslims, the kind of religious experience most honoured is the acceptance of prophetic vision, which means a process of chastening, of concentrating his attention, of inward refocusing. Christians share their experience in a redemptive fellowship, a special sacramental society, the church, which is to be in the world, redeeming the world, but is not of the world; within which, normally, some have been ordained to offer again the tokens of God's love to the rest in recurring reenactment of Christ's sacrifice. Muslims share their experience in a total society, comprehending (in principle) the whole of human life, the Ummah, built upon standards derived from the prophetic vision; comprising a homogeneous brotherhood bearing a common witness brought to mind daily in the ṣalât worship and impressively reaffirmed en masse each year at Mecca.

It is impossible to compare directly what profundity of human awareness may be encouraged by giving primacy to one or the other of such interpretations of life. Each has encouraged its distinctive areas of intensive probing. Christian writers, facing the stark reality of evil, have found layer beneath layer of meaning in suffering and death. It is notorious that Christians have not solved the logical problem of suffering—not on the level of evident formula, that is; surely this is precisely because they have probed it too deeply to be content with a pat answer. Yet the mark of the matured Christian has undeniably been his vital joy. Muslim writers, accepting the consequences of purposefulness in the creation, have spoken on many levels to the person who finds himself facing solemn responsibilities—as father in a family or judge in a city or seer for a great community. It is likewise notorious that Muslims have not solved the logical problem of free will on the level of past formula, for all the disputes about it. Yet the mark of the matured Muslim has ever again been seen to be his human dignity.

As compared to the Christian tradition, the Islamic seems to have held closer to the central lines of the old Irano-Semitic prophetic tradition, especially as represented in the Hebrew prophets with their emphasis on direct human moral responsibility. To persons for whom the tragic sense of the classical Greek drama, focusing on irreducible evil, raises the most telling ultimate questions about human life, the Islamic tradition, where such problems have been kept to one side, may seem to lack a crucial profundity which may be found in the Christian tradition. Others distrust too encompassing a preoccupation with what is sombre or poignant or obscure as tending to tempt people to neglect what lies before them direct and clear. Such may feel the Islamic tradition to be more manly and more balanced, and even a sounder point of departure for any profundities that may be ventured on. They may agree with the Qur'ânic description of Muslims as forming a middle community, avoiding extremes.

Enduring religious commitments in the two cultural patterns

The prime norms of a society must not be confused with the multiple actuality of the various standards and expectations actually effective in its cultural life. Peoples do not differ nearly so much in practice as may seem if one judges either by the obvious difference of symbolic detail whereby they fill the demands of daily behaviour, or by the standards given primacy in their high culture, and so embodied in their literature and in the more formal events of law and social intercourse among especially the privileged classes. Any persistent cultural pattern is likely to be making sense in terms of the calculable interests of those who practice it. Hence it is doubtful if one should say of any given major society (though it is often said) that such and such practical alternatives were closed to it because of such and such unalterable culture traits. If, in the long run, a given society failed to develop along a line which might seem to us advantageous, this is generally to be explained in terms of the practical options open to members of the society at the time: one can expect to find that in fact, given the total situation, the necessary steps were not sufficiently advantageous to sufficient numbers in any given generation to make them worthwhile. One need not invoke the dead hand of the past, supposedly exercised through traditionally imposed attitudes, religious or not. In a history such as this, therefore, the interests of particular groups and the problems of particular periods are put in relief.

Nevertheless, those norms that are given primacy in prestige, on the level of high culture among the privileged classes, have a pervasive and enduring efficacy. In a crisis, they underlie the ideals that imaginative individuals will bring to bear in working out new ways of action; they offer a guide that aspiring groups in the society can make use of as they try to approximate to the privileged classes' ways; above all, it is these norms that confer legitimacy. Other things being equal, those ideas, practices, and positions of power or authority that are recognized generally as legitimate can survive times when their current expression or implementation is temporarily weakened; for each person expects that the others will support them, and so he will be guided more by the positions' long-term prospects of strength than by a short-term weakness. A dog is obeyed in office: even a fool will be obeyed for a time if he is recognized as legitimate ruler. Hence norms given cultural primacy and legitimizing some cultural forms at the expense of others have a pervasive influence so long as the traditions that support them retain their long-term relevance. A global comparison between two cultures, as in this chapter, will necessarily bring out any more persistent constants of this sort that can be perceived.

It is not only norms in the sphere of ultimate commitment, but also in other spheres, artistic, intellectual, and socio-legal, that mould the climate of a society. The straightforward moral appeal of the Islamic religious tradition was complemented on the social level, in Islamdom in the Middle Periods, by what may be called a 'contractualistic' pattern of determining legitimacy in social organization. We may subsume the whole a'yân-amîr system of social power under this more abstract principle. This pattern contrasted as sharply to what may be called Occidental 'corporativism' as did Islam itself to Christianity. The norms of social organization cannot be derived directly in either case from the religious orientation as such; nor the reverse. Yet they were not unrelated. The manner of their relationship is itself a point of contrast between the two societies.

In the case of Islam, life-orientational and societal norms were directly co-ordinate in our period. Both the social norms and the religious seem to have resulted from the same long-term circumstances in the Irano-Semitic core area, and the line of development taken by Islam then reinforced the corresponding social expectations. In any case, the monotheistic communal tendency in Irano-Semitic culture necessarily made for casting society into forms conceived as religious, unless religion were to be isolated and neutralized entirely. Yet Islam has proved consistent with quite different social forms and standards from those of the Irano-Semitic core area in the Middle Periods. Accordingly, we must see Islamicate contractualism not as the result of Islam but as largely a tendency parallel to that of Islamic moralism itself, though perhaps unrealizable without the support of Islam.

As to Christianity, the social pattern and the basic thrust of religious ideals were less closely interdependent. The Occident was obviously only one society among several in which the Christian tradition formed the spiritual and intellectual foundation, and the other societies were very differently organized from the Occidental. Early Christianity, in any case, gave no such primacy as did Islam to social considerations; hence it was all the more acceptable, even in a religious perspective, for each region to produce a form of Christian society congenial to itself. At the same time, the Occidental patterns of social expectation were at least consistent with a Christian approach to the world—Christian in a general sense, that is, not in a sense limited to the Occidental form of Christianity. We may probably go further and say that they cannot be fully understood without reference to the persistent Christian challenge we have outlined. Accordingly, in both Islamdom and the Occident we may identify cultural constants, even on a level where the searching conscience may rest, and see contrasts between the two traditions in respect of them; and these constants may extend broadly over many dimensions of the culture and be expressed on a highly abstract level.

A purpose of our comparison is to counteract premature assessments, if we cannot rule them out altogether. To this end, we must bear some things in mind as presuppositions of both societies. We must make our contrast against the background of any common necessities or commitments that would produce a common pattern of which the individual regions would be developing variant forms. Here this is not a matter simply of a common agrarianate substratum, but of a common dynamic situation, with an active historical dimension.

Apart from the broadest possible lines of what minimally distinguished any agrarian land tenure and any urban-based government, there were no norms of social organization evidently common to all agrarianate-level society. Yet there was one widespread tendency with its own norms which, if allowed full play, could determine legitimacy in a wide sphere: the tendency to subordinate everything to a great territorial bureaucracy. Such a tendency could be traced back at least to the great empires that arose in each of the core areas at the end of or soon following the Axial Age. Where it prevailed, agrarian relations were regulated, at least, by bureaucratic oversight from the centre of imperial government, cities were administered from there, even crafts guilds or monasteries were likely to be subject to imposition of rules and even rulers from above. This was the organizational side of the absolutist ideal, invoked in the name of peace and equal justice against the tyranny of the strong. In significantly differing forms, such a pattern dominated many sectors of social organization to a great degree in the Byzantine and the Chinese societies long after the fall of the early post-Axial Age empires.

But territorial bureaucracy, though universally present in some degree, was more usually limited in its overall social effects by equally potent alternative sets of social expectations. In the Occident and in Hindu India, any tendencies toward territorial bureaucratic domination were inhibited drastically by systems of deep-rooted particularism. These two rich agricultural regions, flanking the central lands of Islamdom on either side, had in common not only the obvious reverence for images (which Muslims called idolatry) but also, less obviously, a somewhat comparable social organization. In both societies, from the time of the Râjpûts and of feudalism, innumerable social bodies maintained or developed their private (caste, or corporate and estate) laws and customs, and were integrated among themselves less by any commonly recognized authorities than by an intricately hierarchical system of mutual obligations, in which every social unit retained its indefeasible autonomy.

Occidental corporativism, Islamicate contractualism

With the fall of the High Caliphate, most of such bureaucratic authority as had prevailed in Islamdom disappeared, but it was replaced not by a system of particularisms but by a unitary—or unitaristic—pattern of legitimation that made Islamdom unique among the major societies: what we shall call a 'unitary contractualism'. Under this head, we are to consider more formally and abstractly the open structuring of Islamic society which we analyzed more substantively in the chapter on the social order. Its implications may come clearer if we contrast them to what in the Occident may be called 'hierarchical corporativism'. Neither the Islamicate nor the Occidental patterns were fully elaborated in the Earlier Middle Period—rather, they were in process of formation: the most creative moves of social organization were in that direction. That is, the patterns were at the peak, at that time, not of their formal prestige but of their historical vitality.

The contrast between 'contractualism' and 'corporativism' will recall, in some of its aspects, the famous contrast between society and community, Gemeinschaft and Gesellschaft. Especially 'contractualism' suggests status by achievement rather than status by ascription. As compared with most preliterate and even peasant life, both the 'corporativism' and the 'contractualism' here described are in the direction of Gesellschaft: both are subject to impersonal, formal norms, within a community impersonally and formally defined, and in both, the contractual principle plays a significant role. Yet as between them, Islamicate contractualism had many features which suggest a greater emphasis on the sort of legitimation in which personal achievement counts high and relations are fixed by contract more than by custom. But even the Islamicate pattern never escaped, historically, the presuppositions of agrarianate-level society; it never approached the level of impersonal achievement-oriented evaluations that has been associated with modern technicalized society. The contrasts between such things as Gemeinschaft and Gesellschaft, status by ascription and by achievement, decision by custom and by rational calculation, are always matters of degree; the end result of even the most drastic shift in such directions always seems to retain, in a new form, elements of ascription and custom and personal community, so that in a new historical setting it in turn can seem (to use another term in a popular but misleading way) 'traditional' rather than 'rational'. Here what matters is less the degree of 'rationality' than the distinctive functioning.

In the Occident, ultimate social legitimation and authority were conferred not on personal relationships nor on a given power structure but on *autonomous corporative offices* and their holders as such. That is, legitimate authority was ascribed primarily to such positions as kingship, vassalship, bishophood, burgherhood, electorship, membership in a guild; these offices were autonomously legitimate in that fixed rights and duties inhered (by custom or charter) in the office, in principle, without authorization or interference from any other office; and they were corporative, in that they presupposed established social bodies, limited in membership and territory, and themselves autonomous, within which the holder of an office was to exercise its duties: kingdoms, municipalities, dioceses, duchies. Such autonomous public offices have occurred everywhere, especially in ritual functions, but also otherwise, usually in more or less incipient forms: for instance, in the Muslim qâḍî, the village headman, the grand vizier. What was special in the Occident was that this sort of office became the leitmotif of the whole conception of social legitimacy. These offices then, were felt to carry authority insofar as they *fitted into mutual hierarchical relations within a fixedly structured total social body*: that is, they were to be constituted and exercised in accordance with established rules of feudal tenure or ecclesiastical obedience or privileges of estates; these rules, in turn were to be binding both on superiors and inferiors, and presupposed a closed system of mutually recognized individual rights and duties which wove together the whole of papal Christendom, under the leadership, perhaps, of pope and emperor.

The hallmark of Occidental corporativism was its legitimism. For every office there was one predetermined 'legitimate' holder and any other was 'illegitimate', in the eyes of legitimists, no matter how long and firmly he had been established. A monarch was 'legitimate' if he came to power according to the fixed rules that applied to that particular office, however incompetent he might be—an infant, or insane; otherwise he was a 'usurper', however sound or popular a ruler. Even a man's sons were divided into 'legitimate' and 'illegitimate' ones, according as their origin satisfied the rules of the system; though personally he might make no distinction in his care for them. To be sure, there were many disputes as to which claimant to an office was in fact the 'legitimate' one, but that one or another was indeed 'legitimate' and the others not seems never to have been doubted. At first sight this might seem a peculiarly irrational Occidental aberration, but elements of the approach, in a milder form, are to be found very widely spread in societies. But the Occidentals carried it to its logical extreme—while the Muslims systematically excluded it almost altogether.

This corporativism was an admirable way of envisaging social relations, elegantly worked out and to a remarkable degree effective in practice. It has been compared to a Gothic cathedral, the form of which was also worked out in High Medieval times. Both the 'corporative' tendency in government and the art of the Gothic cathedral, as well as several other sorts of artistic and intellectual works of the time, seem to reflect a common sense of fitness as to form. Restating our description of hierarchical corporativism in slightly more general terms, we may say that those who articulated the norms of the time seem to have seen satisfying order in a pattern of *autonomous fixed units arranged in hierarchical mutual relations in a closed and fixedly structured whole.* Writers cast allegorical poems and even scholastic treatises into such a form, and something of the same feeling is traceable in the honour paid to demonstrative geometry as a model discipline and to the syllogism as a form into which to put thoughts even when they were not very syllogistic in content.

In Christian thought, in any case, the spiritually significant events of history were seen as having miraculously unique status within a total sequence of sacred dispensations, set off self-contained from ordinary history. This answered to the sacramental organization and the redemptive, supernatural, role of the church. The Occidentals now stressed even more than other Christians the autonomous corporate unity and hierarchical structure of the church and of its history from the time of Adam.

Wherever a sense of fitness was called for, especially wherever validation and legitimation were consciously required, such a sense of style could come into play: in art, in theology, in government, in etiquette, even in science. It determined at least the form in which legitimation was made, if it did not always make a great difference in substance. And this sense of style could have sufficient effect upon practice to affect related activities, where there was a less conscious demand for legitimation; for certain types of expectation tend to prove mutually compatible, and so reinforce each other. Thus could be achieved, at least for a few decades in a portion of northwestern Europe, on the level of public expectations, a relatively homogeneous style ('High Gothic') in a wide range of activities. This style had been being prepared and formed, in some of its aspects, for some centuries; and elements of it, at least, proved sufficiently attractive to colour a great part of Occidental culture for a long time after; but it may be regarded as peculiarly distinctive of the High Medieval Occident.

The Occidental side of the comparison, just sketched, will (I hope) take on substance from the reader's independent knowledge of the Occident. The Islamicate side now must presuppose all that has been said in this work. We will start by characterizing schematically an overall style answering to the 'High Gothic' in which our sketch of the Occidental side culminated. Then we will go on to characterize the religious and the social order, in particular, in terms of the overall style.

In Islamdom, the elements that went to make up a corresponding style do not seem to have come to quite so sharp a focus as in the High Gothic period in northern France, but there too a distinctive style, partly prepared earlier and largely persisting in later times, was especially characteristic of the Earlier Middle Period, though (as in the Occident) never prevailing exclusively. To Islamicate 'contractualism' in the social sphere, the most appropriate analogy in the visual arts is doubtless the arabesque-type patterning, including geometrical and floral interlacings as well as the arabesque proper, which came to full maturity under Seljuḳ rule, more or less contemporaneously with the Gothic cathedral. To put the overall style in a formula corresponding to what we used for the Occident, the sense of good order demanded a pattern of *equal and transferable units satisfying a single set of fixed standards in a field penetrable to several levels and universally extendable.* The indefinitely repeated rhythms of the arabesque, where often a bold obvious pattern was superimposed on a subtler pattern at first barely noticeable, answered to such a sense of form, as did the maqâmât in prose and several genres of verse, notably the symbolic mas̄navî. Something of the same feeling is traceable in the honour paid to historical knowledge and the passion for ḥadîth isnâd and Ṣûfî silsilah. Geometry, so beloved in the Occident, starts from a minimum set of premises and develops by a hierarchy of set deductions to definitive conclusions, closing the argument in autonomous self-sufficiency. In contrast, the indefinitely expandable corpus of historical reports, each documented and certified on a level with all the rest, allows the seemingly chaotic variety of life's reality to be reduced to manageable order without arbitrarily setting bounds to it either in extent or in depth of meaning.

The Islamic religious sense of the equal and co-ordinated responsibility of all possible individuals for the maintenance of moral standards in the natural world was probably not unrelated, from the beginning, to the orientation out of which grew this Islamicate sense of style. But it was especially after the fall of the High Caliphal state, among Jamâ'î-Sunnî Muslims, that this atomistic dimension of Islam became most explicit. It was justified in kalâm disputation and it was deepened into more inward levels by the general spread of ṭarîqah Ṣûfism, with its silsilahs of independent pîrs bringing spiritual truth to each according to his capacities.

It was the enduring balance between Sharî'ah-mindedness and Ṣûfism, developed in this period on this basis, that made it possible for Islam to appeal to every sort of temperament without sacrificing its egalitarianism and its moralism. One can claim that, to maintain the church and its hierarchy, Christians sacrificed both prophetic vision and mystical liberty in some measure. That is, they were limited both in any direct confrontation with the old prophetic themes, for the prophets were largely reinterpreted as mere harbingers of Christ, and in an independent growth of mystical experience, which had to be restrained within the sacramental discipline of Christ's church.[2] In contrast, Muslims had no single organizational authority over even particular sectors or local groupings of the Islamic religious establishments, unless by arbitrary and temporary superimposition. They looked, for

[2] Such a contrast has been stressed by Henry Corbin in several works, including his *Histoire de la philosophie islamique* (Paris, 1964). It has also been hinted at in less scholarly circles, as by Aldous Huxley in *Grey Eminence* (New York and London, 1941), and elsewhere. Such writers have taken a personal position which not all may share. But that this was a problem posed by the special structure of Christianity, and that it called for a special solution (successfully or not) will be more widely granted.

the subtlety which sensitive persons demand, not to the guided diversity of a church but to direct personal deepening, individual by individual as he was capable of it. Hence the tacit mutual toleration of 'ulamâ' and Ṣûfîs. Yet so effective was the correlative insistence on a unitary set of fixed standards, that, unlike Buddhist monks or Brahmans, say, the 'ulamâ' could not develop freely independent standards, but were under effective pressure to maximize communal uniformity. The whole development of the contractualist sense of social order in this period, which expresses the same overall style, was made possible by the corresponding developments in religion. And as in religion, so in the social order the seeming simplicity required considerable social sophistication to become so effective; it was no sign of primitiveness.

The hallmark of the Islamicate social order as embodied in the a'yân-amîr system might seem to be—over against Occidental legitimism—what can be called its 'occasionalism', the impression it can give that everything was improvised as the occasion arose, that almost no weight was given to established position and precedence once their immediate force was gone. This was the institutional expression of the general tendency to exalt individual liberty at the expense of any fixed status. As in the sphere of art, of course, such a principle was not inconsistent with an elaborate surface formalism, adaptable to any substance. If Occidental legitimism sometimes led to self-evident absurdities, this Islamicate 'occasionalism' could be reduced to the arbitrary rule of violence. Yet Muslims insisted regularly that the candidate for a post be at least theoretically qualified for it—and a deposed caliph could be effectively disqualified by blinding, unlike an Occidental king. And such principles allowed Islamdom, in any case, to make good its tremendous expansive vitality—not merely to conquer but for the most part to hold what it had conquered. Here, too, there was method in the madness.

In contrast to the hierarchical corporativism of the Occident, what I have called the 'unitary contractualism' of Islamdom meant that ultimate legitimacy lay not in autonomous corporative offices but in *egalitarian contractual responsibilities*. That is, legitimate authority was ascribed to actions that followed from responsibilities personally undertaken in such roles as that of amîr in a town or imâm in the ṣalât or ghâzî on the frontier or husband in a family. The model that defined public duties thus in the form of personal responsibilities was the ingenious Shar'î principle of the reduction of all social functions to either *farḍ 'aynî*, a duty incumbent on every individual, or *farḍ kifâyah*, a duty incumbent on only so many as were required to fulfill the function—though until the function was fulfilled, potentially incumbent on anyone. Thus public duties, as a special case of personal duties, came under the same sort of rules as any others. If those who fulfilled such duties made any agreement in the course of their labours, that had the same status in Shar'î law as any personal contract. (We have seen an example in such arrangements for succession as that attempted by al-Rashîd in dividing the caliphal state.)

This personal, contractual, principle was extreme in the opposite direction from the corresponding Occidental principle of public, corporate offices. One may say that most commonly in the great cultures some special status is allowed to acts or property and the like ascribed to a social body, such as the state, but that such status tends to be looked on as a special case of a more inclusive moral law which applies, in principle, to persons as such. The status of royalty seems to have been such among the Sâsânians, where the royal *khvarnah,* as a supernatural aura, set off the monarch from other men, but only so long as he was divinely deemed fit to rule. The Occidentals tended to push the special status of public acts to an extreme point, in their emphasis on the fixed autonomy of an office; a point where there should be an unbridgeable cleavage between private and public realms, private and public law, such that the conclusion could eventually be drawn that the state had its own norms not subject to the ethical considerations applying to private actions. The Muslim principle, in contrast, denied any special status to public acts at all, stressing egalitarian and moralistic considerations to the point where it ruled out all corporate status and reduced all acts to the acts of personally responsible individuals.

It is incorrect, in this perspective, to refer to these as 'private acts', since the antithesis public-private in social activity is precisely what the Muslims denied while the Occidentals carried it to an extreme. Of course, what I am speaking of here is a highly schematic perspective, of limited reach. On neither side was the contrast carried out fully in the Earlier Middle Period. Moreover, in some perspectives the difference between Occident and Islamdom dwindles to the accidental.

In both cases, one can describe what happened, when the bureaucratic absolutism disappeared, as private possession of public office. Among the Muslims, some sense of a public realm with its own norms did not disappear. For instance, the position of the caliph, as certifying agent legitimizing other rulers, retained an echo of that sense of a bureaucratic public order which had been maintained in High Caliphal times; from this centralizing perspective, the rights of an amîr and of an iqṭâʿ holder were public rights in private hands. In any case, it was always realistically recognized that a king, at least, must act for his own safety—for public reasons—in ways repugnant to proper ethics. Yet both iqṭâʿ holder and amîr were thought of as individual men in direct relations with other men—and this fact affected the manner in which they could raise revenue, their relations to other officeholders, and even the succession to their office.

Among the Occidentals, the devolution of authority to a multiplicity of autonomous offices had threatened to wipe out that very distinction between private and public which had been inherited from earlier times, and to which the eager lawyers were trying to give such a broad effect in the new setting. For a time, feudal relationships, for instance, could have been interpreted in a highly contractualistic sense. But the most characteristic drive was to reinterpret the devolution of offices and the whole feudal system in a corporative sense, in which it was the office, not the man, that was autonomous. Thus, on principles utterly alien to Islamdom, even rights to the kingship of Jerusalem could be bought and sold. However unrealistic in some ways, then, the two principles we have contrasted make explicit certain attitudes that were singularly formative in the two societies in the period.

These personal responsibilities of office in Islamdom were conceived on an egalitarian basis: in principle, they might be assumed by anyone who was qualified, once he became a Muslim, whatever his antecedents; in strict theory, they were not heritable. There were traces of inequality both in Sharî'ah and in custom. Descendants of Muḥammad were given a peculiar status in certain marginal cases—they could not receive certain alms but were entitled to the special benevolence of all Muslims, and they were expected to marry among themselves. With more disruptive results, various military groups were pleased to erect themselves into closed privileged corps as long as they could. But the social pressure was such as to break open or break down such closed corps, as no other elements in society seriously acknowledged the legitimacy of their pretensions in the long run.

Above all, these personal responsibilities were, even if not exactly contracts, contractual. The Sharî'ah envisaged many relations as contractual, but the mood of the time went beyond the Sharî'ah. Whether an independent position of authority was legitimized by appeal to personal charisma or to explicit law or to custom, it was conceived as established by mutual agreement and as assuming mutual obligations between one individual and others.[3] On a relatively private level, this amounted sometimes to a relation of personal patronage—a type of relation that played a major role in such a society. Sometimes it was put into a full legal contract; notably marriage was seen not as a sacrament giving ascriptive status but as a contract subject to reversal if satisfaction was not delivered. And just such a viewpoint prevailed on the public level.

Even in the case of the caliphate, the Jamâ'î-Sunnî theory was that the next caliph, designated by the key notables of the Ummah, or by the most notable one of them (the reigning caliph), was to be confirmed by the *bay'ah*, the act of acceptance by the notables generally on behalf of the whole community. That is, it was not enough simply to submit to the established ruler when occasion arose; the individual Muslim must explicitly assume his side of the relationship. (The Shî'î theory, which made the designation stem back to divine action, still demanded that the believers personally offer their act of acceptance to the imâm; this is part of the meaning of the ḥadîth report that 'he who dies without knowing the imâm of his time dies an unbeliever'—a report which Jamâ'î-Sunnîs also could accept.) The acceptance of an amîr

[3] J. Schacht, 'Notes sur la sociologie du droit musulman', *Revue africaine*, vol. 96, nos. 432–33 (1952), brings out nicely the degree to which the spirit of contract suffuses the Sharî'ah and even other sorts of Muslim law.

by his soldiers and by the community at large in the persons of its notables and the acceptance of a Ṣûfî pîr by those who sought his spiritual guidance, were on the same model; always it was a contract-type arrangement which had to be renewed personally with each new holder of authority and was properly binding only on those who had personally accepted it. (Too often Western scholars have vainly tried to reduce Islamicate transactions of this sort to Occidental legitimistic categories and found themselves baffled. The bay'ah was analogous to the Occidental oath of allegiance but was not its equivalent either in form or in function.)

Then these responsibilities of office were exercised under *a single set of fixed legal standards, universally applicable* so soon as a minimum of Muslims were present, and, at least Ṣûfîs would add, meaningful at once on an obvious, mechanical, level and on ever deeper levels according to the spirituality of the person concerned. Though the Sharî'ah varied in practice not only from legal madhhab to legal madhhab but from century to century, yet the constant interchange of viewpoint was bringing the madhhabs ever closer together—there was conscious pressure to avoid any really drastic discrepancies—and the gradual evolution of legal standards tended to be more or less common throughout Islamdom. As great a legal uniformity, at least on some levels, was achieved in Islamdom as ever has been in a pre-Modern society, despite its unprecedentedly wide spread. The Sharî'ah law was applicable wherever Muslims were to be found in sufficient numbers, being dependent on no territorial establishment nor even on any official continuity of personnel, but only on the presence, among Muslims committed to it, of someone at least minimally versed in it to see to its application. If in a new Muslim community it was not at first very perfectly applied, every visiting Shar'î scholar from any other Muslim land would contribute to perfecting it, preventing it from deteriorating to a purely local customary law. Without any new enactments, the system was extendable to include ultimately the whole of mankind.

Communal moralism vs. *corporative formalism in law*

The contractualism of the Islamic Middle Periods presumably grew out of the mercantile-oriented communal tradition of the Nile-to-Oxus region and can be seen, from our vantage point, as its culmination. The mercantile tendency had favoured, on the intellectual level, the moralistic, populistic, factualistic bent which we have already analyzed in the Sharî'ah-minded circles; on the institutional level, it favoured a unitary contractualism in the same way. In sum, what had happened was that, with the powerful crystallization in Sharî'ah-minded Islam of the most extreme populistic and moralistic tendencies of that tradition, the monotheistic religious community ceased to be a merely subordinate social form and became the major form through which social legitimation was expressed. The religious community was almost—though not quite—liberated from dependence on an agrarian-based state; so that its communal law, built on its communal presuppositions, and not that of any territorial state, assumed the persisting primacy that accrues to whatever possesses exclusive legitimacy. It was not quite liberated: the ultimate sanction of force remained critical, and was left in the hands of the state. But the role of the state was as far reduced, especially in the basic sphere of law, as it ever has been in citied high culture.

This was made possible, however, because the monotheistic tradition was gathered—at least as to the active sectors of society—into a single community allegiance. Each of the other monotheistic communities to be found within the core area of Islamdom—pursuing an evolution already begun before Islam—became juridically self-contained like the Islamic community itself. But without the overwhelmingly predominant position of the Islamic community throughout the region, the juridical autonomy of bishops or of rabbis must remain secondary. It was the universality of the Muslim community that could make it outweigh an imperial bureaucracy. Without the potent appeal of Islam with its summons to personal responsibility, the Islamicate contractualist pattern could hardly have succeeded despite the favourable conditions between Nile and Oxus.

Each of the two patterns of legitimation, the Occidental hierarchical corporativism and the Islamicate unitary contractualism, had consequences which are not immediately evident from the overall guidelines here sketched. To be sure, often Occidental and Islamicate practice were more alike than the contrast would suggest; nor was everything in which they differed attributable to this particular contrast. Yet each pattern not only facilitated some sorts of social relations but also set limits to the development of others. Normally these consequences were such as reinforced the same tendencies, arising out of the ecological setting of the core area of each culture, as had produced the pattern of legitimation in the first place. But at least in secondary details, the pattern of legitimation could itself logically entail consequences otherwise perhaps unnecessary.

The demand for a rule of law, as against arbitrary rule, took a moralistic turn in Islamdom as against the formalistic turn the same demand took in the Occident. As so often, each system pushed toward a contrasting extreme. Some formalism is found in almost all legal systems, especially those connected with cultic ritual. This was pushed in the Occident to the point of sanctioning those trials by technicality which have sometimes been the glory of its law courts, when they served to defend an unpopular position, but have more often been their shame. (Some Westerners seem to have confused a formalistic pattern in law with independent objectivity and predictability as such in law, looking to the Roman legal heritage with its formalistic bent almost as if it alone fully deserved the status of 'law'; even though they would decry those excesses of formalism and literalism which even Occidentals have recognized as such.) The Sharîʿah may seem to some to have exaggerated in a contrary direction. Law is a natural field in which to emphasize moral values to the exclusion of even the most practical considerations of other sorts, but the Sharî'ah law perhaps went further in this direction than most systems. In its law of contracts, the actual intent of the parties was usually preferred (in principle) to the verbal form; perhaps the Marwânî-age insistence on living witnesses as guarantors of any written contract retained its vitality in part as a means of assuring the primacy of intent. More generally, there was a tendency to insist on equity even when a person seemed willing to renounce his own rights.

The secondary institutions of law were moulded to the respective legal patterns. The Occidental advocate was expected to argue the case of one party against the other in disputes, making the most of even a morally dubious case, often on the basis of his knowledge of technicalities. Such a stance might seem morally unsound, but it ensured that special circumstances in each particular case were not overlooked. The Muslim muftî might be as concerned as the Occidental advocate with the ambiguities of practical situations. But he was expected to give priority to eliciting and settling the decisive moral issue impersonally as it arose in such situations—advising the judge rather than either one of the parties concerned. In principle, he should not know who was on which side. The Occident saw a luxuriant growth of legal fictions—notably corporative ones, in which a corporate body was accepted as a legal entity on a par with persons, so as to exercise the autonomous rights attached to offices when such offices clearly pertained to a group as such. Such legal fictions as the Sharî'ah encouraged (especially the ḥîlah 'tricks' used in commerce) were not essential to the law but incidental to its application; their function was normative, safeguarding a standard toward which the reality might, with opportunity and goodwill, be moved.

Modern Westerners have tended to see the moralism of Muslim law as a major defect. So far as, in its insistence on personal responsibilities, it denied any independent sphere to public law over against private, they feel, it had no means of legitimizing and hence taming the public reality. Because of the unconditioned universality which, at least in pre-Modern times, was ascribed to any serious moral code, a moralistic law was relatively rigid and incapable of adaptation to varying conditions of time or place. Finally, in renouncing formalism in some respects (by no means all) it lost a technique which in the Occident often proved useful in preserving the rights of the individual, whether used wisely or foolishly, from interference by public opinion or by state power, however benevolently intended.

Yet the Muslims' extensive mobility among social milieus and across geographical and political boundaries was made possible by that same Sharî'ah, and in its own way (together with the freedom of inner interpretation that went with it) ensured a wide range of personal liberty. Nor could the law have ensured this mobility without a high degree of legal fixity. This fixity was, indeed, constantly threatened by the fact that not all Muslim law in any one place was Sharî'ah law; but the Sharî'ah successfully maintained its central position and was kept adequately integrated through changing conditions by the judicious recognition of latter-day fatwàs by jurists respected throughout the Dâr al-Islâm. Because of the independent position, then, which the relative fixity of the law gave to its interpreters, both 'ulamâ' and Ṣûfîs were in a position to hold the political powers within bounds—never in so wide a sphere as desired, yet never without substantial effect.

In Modern times, both of the legal patterns have had to be modified. Occidental formalism has latterly had to give way even to sociological considerations as to what legal concepts mean in social reality, while Muslim moralism has been forced to retreat before the new organized power of the state and the impersonal requirements of the machines.

The Occidental formalistic law was doubtless appropriate to the corporative Occident. There a person's status was determined by his position in various bodies intermediate between the individual and the total society. As a member of such bodies—municipalities or estates or the church—he enjoyed special liberties, defined historically according to the situation of the particular body; he had not so much the rights of a man, or even of an Englishman, as those of a burgher of London. Despite the attempt to invoke ancient Roman law as if it could form a universally applicable code, such particularistic rights could not in practice be defined on universal principles but depended on the historical events which gave rise to them, such as the granting of a city charter. The greater the formalism with which such rights were interpreted, the more secure they were from interference in later circumstances when the original power relations might have changed. The Muslim moralistic law was equally appropriate to Islamicate contractualism, where ascriptive status was minimized, at least in principle, and the decisive ties were those of contract and of personal patronage. What mattered to the Muslim was not particular liberties but a more generalized liberty, based on his status as a free Muslim. Such a position was best guaranteed by principles which could apply everywhere and always, without prior covenant or special historical connection.[4]

Contractual vs. *formalistic status in civil and personal roles*

Because the autonomous corporative office was so crucial in the Occidental system, succession to office was likewise fixed and formalistic. In the Occident, the question who would succeed to a self-perpetuating (i.e., non-appointive) office was governed by rules specific to the office and as formalistic as was the

[4] That Sharî'ah law was grounded in the principle that liberty was to be presumed as the natural human condition, and was not to be abridged without reason, has been presented effectively by David de Santillana, 'Law and Society' in *The Legacy of Islam*, ed. Thomas Arnold and Alfred Guillaume (Oxford University Press, 1931), pp. 284–310.

law generally. Some posts were hereditary; here normally a fixed rule of unilinear succession held, so that as soon as a baby was born in the relevant family, one could calculate under just what circumstances he would succeed: normally according to the rule of primogeniture, which during High Medieval times was being made to cover not only succession among sons but any contingency of kinship. Other posts were subject to vote; in this case, the voting was collegial, that is, a fixed body of electors was admitted to the electoral right, which in turn had to be exercised in a fixed manner to be valid. Thus succession had a formal and fixed element even when not hereditary. (It must be recalled that collegial voting was a very different sort of process from modern mass voting, which perhaps has almost as many affinities with Islamicate prestige contests.) In High Medieval times the rules were still being perfected and disputes in both kinds of succession still occurred, but normally the claim of the disputants on each side was legitimistic: that is, not that their candidate was necessarily the best but that he was the legitimate one, and that the opposing candidate, however personally excellent he might or might not be, was usurping.

Westerners have been so accustomed to such a type of succession that they have expected to find similar characteristics in non-appointive offices elsewhere too. Often even scholars have read primogeniture into the fact that it was often an eldest son who proved most appropriate to take over his father's office. A certain respect for the elder brother is perhaps almost universal; in the Occident this was hardened into a rule, but in Islamdom, though the feeling was potent, it was not allowed any formal recognition. More sophisticatedly, some Westerners have tried to find an alternative scheme of fixed succession such as seniority, which will sometimes fit the facts a bit better. Sometimes they have labelled 'usurper' a candidate who rose to power by rebellion. Then (since the exceptions to such 'rules' prove disconcertingly numerous) they have complained of the irregularity of Muslim succession and its failure to follow a fixed rule which would supposedly have obviated succession disputes. But in Islamdom, formalistic succession by unilinear heredity or collegial voting was rare at best, not because Muslims were less inclined to rationalize their social arrangements but because the contractual spirit called for a different sense of legitimacy in successions. Succession was open to some choice or even negotiation: to the fixed succession of the formalistic Occident we may counterpose the succession by contest of the contractualistic Islamdom, where a personal responsibility was to be undertaken by the best man.

It did not necessarily contravene this principle when contest was forestalled by designation by the predecessor; it was as if he who was already charged with a responsibility had likewise the responsibility of seeing that his charge would be carried on by someone suitable. Otherwise, of course, contests were to be settled by consultation among the notables felt to be representative of the affected social body. It was the very point of succession by contest, to adjust various group interests according to current actualities—and this could be done only with a certain amount of bargaining. Then if formal contract was invoked it was, of course, at the final stage, in the form of a rubber stamp. Consultation should obviate an armed contest, but if not, then an armed contest seems to have been felt to be a misfortune rather than an actual breakdown in the social process.

An incidental—but essential—consequence of this approach was (on the whole) the elimination of utter incompetents. It was even a legal requirement that the candidate had to be at least minimally qualified; occasionally, at least in religious contexts, this was insisted on to the point of formal public examination by the notables. It was rare (though not unknown) for a child, a woman, or a physically incapacitated man to be accepted for long unless he had a powerful protector; for, as the political ruler was essentially an amîr, a military commander, a woman was disqualified insofar as she was not qualified to be a soldier at all. Analogous considerations prevailed in other fields of action.

In the process of consultation, the Islamic principle of universality had its way. For the most part those were recognized as notables who had achieved positions of great personal responsibility and had ties of mutual obligation with a large number of people; and thus a largely common set of considerations as to what bestowed status was received throughout Islamdom and was applicable immediately wherever Islam penetrated. Since decision required not a mathematical majority as such, but a more substantial consensus, no exact lines of inclusion and exclusion had to be drawn, for no vote had to be taken. Because there was no fixed electorate, the Islamicate prestige contest has looked mysterious to some outsiders. But its chief mechanism (that of the 'bandwagon') is used in many contests settled by mass voting. In Islamdom there was no set voting to cut short the contest before its natural term, so that it might take some time unless appeals were made to arms or to an amîr.

Even on the level of family law, we find in the Occident the sense of fixed, autonomous status, formalistically defined. In families in which any sort of office was hereditary, of course, the status of family members had to be defined in such a way that the principle of primogeniture could hold. This already called for the special exaltation of the man's primary sex partner as his only proper wife, and her children, therefore, as sole heirs to the exclusion of his other children. As we have noted, the Sharîʿah looked to the opposite extreme from this, placing all the man's free sexual partners on the same level, as well as their children, and governing their position by contract, giving none of them an indefeasible status such as an undivorceable materfamilias could have. (As with collegial voting, so with 'monogamous' marriage, the old Occidental pattern was even further, in some respects, from modern international patterns than was the Islamicate.)

But the contrast between the Islamicate and the Occidental patterns of marriage went beyond what could be deduced from the relative positions of the wives in Sharîʿah and in canon law. The contrast that springs to the eye between upper-class family life among Muslims and among Occidentals is that between the segregated slave household of the harem system, and the wife-centred servant household of the Occident. In each society the husband and father was the dominant and in theory even despotic figure who had final power of decision; and in each society the wife in fact often ruled the husband. But the differences in norm of expectation did produce differences in practice.

In the Occident the 'legitimate' wife presided; she was hostess to her husband's guests, and if he had other sex partners, they had to have separate establishments as 'mistresses', for she would not tolerate them in her domain. The attendants of the household were free servants at the least and, in feudal courts, often persons of high status themselves. The peasants were tied servilely to the soil and subject to the grossest indignities from their legal masters, but household slavery had practically died out. Thus the hierarchical principle prevailed even in family life: the closer to the top, the higher the rank, while even the servile mass at the bottom were governed by their own fixed rules.

In Islamdom, the egalitarian principle surely accounts in part for an opposite situation. Well-to-do men, themselves of no birth, surrounded themselves by preference with the only sort of persons whose dependence could be counted on: slaves; and where all classes mingled socially, their wives could not assert their inaccessibility by the aloofness of a hierarchical rank but preserved it rather by a rigid female segregation. If there was more than one sex partner, all shared the household alike, and none was hostess save to her own friends, who, however, might be drawn from any social level she chose. The peasants were legally and usually factually free men, while in the homes of the wealthy, slaves were preferred to free servants, though not necessarily treated any worse, and steadily emancipated. We may suggest that slavery by import (as against a more home-bred peasant serfdom) was retained in Islamdom partly because of the relative access of the wealthy Muslim cities to frontier areas of the Oikoumene where captives were available; but primarily because an egalitarian and socially mobile society seemed to require, in an agrarian age, such a class to set off those who momentarily had risen to the top.

Both in Occident and in Islamdom, a correlative of the social system was a good deal of arbitrary and destructive military activity. Military power was limited in its effects in the two societies in quite different ways. In the Occident, the military were rooted in the land and their activities were increasingly being formalized, even idealized. The barons could indulge in persistent petty warfare and indiscipline, harassing peasant and townsman in a steady stream of quarrels which rules about suspending local hostilities for weekends could barely alleviate. But it was with difficulty that they could combine really massive armies under one chief for general indiscriminate slaughter; to concentrate power in one hand, the chances of fixed succession, modulated by dynastic marriages or even by purchase of succession rights, were as important as outright political and military skill. No ruler extended his sway far beyond his hereditary lands, generally rather small tracts at best. It was already a sign of new times when, in the fifteenth century, the duke of Burgundy gathered together so much arbitrary force that he could destroy the city and the entire population of Liège, pursuing those few who escaped the flames into the woods, tracing them by their tracks till they should all be killed. And even that duke found himself so bound by custom that to the end he was frustrated in his attempt to take the title of king.

In Islamdom, in contrast, the military were city men and little bound by parochial prescriptions. Nowhere was mobility more drastic than among the soldiery, whose members could rise to the highest social peaks, and could campaign for distances incredible in the Occident. Local captains seem to have been kept under some control on this basis, so that private quarrels among the military did not immediately issue in warfare; there was extensive peace on a local basis, times when the greatest alarms were raised only by bandits. (But in remoter areas, pastoral tribal chiefs could play the role of robber barons.) But aggressive concentrations of power like that of the duke of Burgundy were almost commonplace, and looting and massacring of cities took place more readily—and from the Mongol times on, in the Later Middle Period, became relatively frequent.

In religious and intellectual life, the differences between the two societies were complementary to the differences in the role of political authority. In the Occident, the noble was at once the political ruler and the focus of all social life; and the cleric was his brother or his cousin. Scholarly life was largely channelled through the church, which was highly organized along lines parallel to and interweaving with the secular establishment. In this hierarchical context, every intellectual question was likely to turn into a question of formal heresy, i.e., of institutional loyalty; heresy could be a life-or-death question in a way that was unlikely in Islamdom even if the question was formally raised there. However, at the same time, the Philosophical tradition played a more integral role in so hierarchical a structure, its more abstractly normative traditions forming the core of formal education for the clerics. This is partly because the Latin lands continued to look to the Hellenic tradition in general for their high-cultural inspiration, but surely the educational pattern was perpetuated, in part, also because it was suited to the relatively closed, fixed structure of the church, which could justify a hierarchical social structure with a hierarchical vision of the cosmos much in the manner of the Ismâʿîlîs. Esoteric studies did exist, but they played a relatively marginal role. When the mystic, Eckhart, was condemned for talking too freely of subtle matters to the common people, his guilt was violation of common prudence, not of an established doctrine of concealment. Subjects like alchemy, of course, did receive a directly esoteric treatment.

In Islamdom, the 'ulamâ' and the amîrs stood aloof from each other. And even where learning was institutionalized in madrasahs, the 'ulamâ' retained a broad independence among themselves. In both Islamdom and Occident, formal education was devoted largely to normative disciplines rather than to empirical. But the most respected Muslim education was more oriented to explicit cultural norms. This was consistent with the historical, communal emphasis of the Abrahamic tradition. But it surely reflected also the basis on which the 'ulamâ' maintained their common discipline, by common legal norms rather than by any common lines of command. The Occidental sequence started with the trivium (essentially study of linguistic norms) and went directly on to the quadrivium (essentially study of mathematics), in which the content tended to refer to natural studies like astronomy and music rather than to historical studies; while law and theology came last, as specialized professions, accompanied by medicine as an integral part of the central studies. In contrast, the madrasahs stressed first what was essential for everyone—ritual, law, theology, all essentially historical subjects. Matters like literary criticism were secondary, and mathematics and logic received attention last of all. Medicine and astronomy were studied quite independently of the madrasahs, patronized by the amîrs' courts, while the philosophy and psychology of the Ṣûfîs were learned at still another centre, the khâniqâh. And the learning of these more élite centres tended to be systematically esoteric.

Much later, travelling in the Ottoman empire, a French diplomat and scholar was impressed with the degree to which the Muslims were personally more gentle and sober than their opposite numbers in the Occident; even animals were treated with relative humanity.[5] The scholar was perhaps influenced by a desire to reform his own compatriots. In any case, it is fairly evident that by most standards, Islamicate society must be accounted more urbane and polished than the Occidental in the Earlier Middle Period, both in intellectual life and in day-to-day security. But it was also more subject to arbitrary interference and even to catastrophe.

Resources for historical action

Human excellence has been held to lie on the one hand in contemplation, in maximum awareness of reality and its meaning both in the cosmos at large and within one's self; and on the other hand in action, in free initiation of new sequences of events on the basis of a rational estimate of their consequences rather than of habit or custom. As we have learned to see it, our world is in fact in such continuous transformation that just as genuinely free action cannot take place without the highest contemplation, so genuinely true contemplation cannot take place without the most incisive action. If this

[5] I refer to the well-known Turkish Letters of de Busbecq, tr. by E. S. Forster (Oxford, 1927).

is so, the distinction between the two forms of excellence can become artificial. Yet modern Westerners have seen, at least retrospectively, the genius of their Occidental heritage to have lain in giving maximum scope to human initiative and action, while they have often been willing to grant the palm for contemplative excellence to others. At the same time, the Islamic can seem the most activist of the great pre-Modern heritages. Even those superficial observers who have claimed that Islam led necessarily to fatalistic acceptance of whatever might happen as God's will, have also stressed the pride and fanaticism of Muslims, especially as expressed in implacable prosecution of the holy war. Both societies, then, have had some repute for a bent to action. But what were the channels through which free human action could be undertaken in each society?

In some ways, freedom was greater in Islamdom than in the Occident. Islam was relatively tolerant—not so much in willingness to accept other religious bodies (in this, Islam did much better than Christianity but even so was intolerant by non-monotheistic standards)—but rather tolerant on the personal level. Diogenes and his tub would have been more readily tolerated in the Islamicate society than in the Occidental. In the latter, he would have had to show some proper status, not simply as an individual, but as member of some order or corporate body; if he had claimed a moral mission, he would have been under the jurisdiction of the ecclesiastical hierarchy; if he went naked in public, he would be duly disciplined by the church authorities. In the Islamicate society (unless he was a dhimmî unwilling to convert) he would have had but one legal status, that of a Muslim; he would, indeed, be subject to the discipline of the market overseer, the muḥtasib; but if he claimed a moral mission, he would have had a good chance of passing freely as a mad darvîsh, to be troubled by no authority but that of his chosen pîr. (As a dhimmî, of course, he might run into greater difficulties with his communal authorities.) The Occidental pattern as a whole made for great social continuity, but militated against mobility—against geographical mobility, because the all-important offices were tied to particular localities; against personal initiative, which the guilds systematically discouraged. As in Islamdom, development did take place, but as much despite the system as through it.

The immediacy of the individual human being vis-à-vis society as a whole thus made for important freedoms. But it exposed persons to certain dangers against which the rights of corporate bodies afforded a surer buffer in the Occident. Even in Islamdom, the individual adventurer, relatively free as he might be, was wise to associate himself with some recognized group—Ṣûfîs of some ṭarîqah, 'ulamâ' at some madrasah, merchants of some trade, or, at a less respectable but almost equally protected level, members of a futuwwah brotherhood, or beggars or thieves of some town quarter. In such groups membership was largely self-chosen and the discipline imposed might be very lax. But the strength of such groups against arbitrary interference by the amîr was correspondingly less. And those who wished to undertake a new sort of enterprise—for instance, investment in a new type of project—could be hard put to it to find a place in any solidarity group which would resist a tyrant's hand. Such undertakings could and did get launched without being smothered by the jealous rigidity of guild regulations; but they could and did find themselves taxed out of existence or even plundered by shortsighted amîrs so soon as they became sufficiently prosperous to attract notice.

Yet in Islamdom there remained wide personal liberty for a man to make his own choice within a reasonably predictable framework and in a range that was relatively broad, given agrarianate-level social conditions; and even to make choices differing greatly from those of most other men. Such freedom was essential for a further sort of freedom of action—freedom of historical action, freedom to initiate new ideas and teach them, to suggest and help carry through new policies and patterns in social life, more generally to set about consciously to modify the conditions within which life was being carried on. But for this, in addition to simple personal freedom, there must be appropriate channels for individual initiative on the social level. The nature of such channels differed, even more than on the purely personal level, according to the pattern of legitimation.

In the High Medieval Occident, one of the most intriguing scenes, from the viewpoint of the development of human self-awareness and self-determination, was that in which the pope solicited suggestions from all Western Christendom on what to do about the presence of Islam, when the Crusades seemed to be failing. Serious persons responded and among the conventional exhortations were some relatively far-sighted projects, including plans for reforming the church itself in the name of making action against Islam more effective. Relatively little came of most of these plans, yet they were intended and received seriously. For such an approach to historical problems was not an isolated occurrence but was grounded in the Occidental pattern. The great church councils, in which a hierarchically limited number of autonomous holders of episcopal office gathered to consider and vote on matters of dispute, formed a model of such consultation. But the spirit was more general. If each particular establishment had its own autonomous rules, they had once been shaped and could be reshaped anew; moreover, it was the office of bishops and popes, kings and emperors, to make sure that all was going well in their jurisdictions and concerned individuals might hope that good advice might find favour with them.

In China, the custom of private memorials offered on public problems was even more highly developed than in the Occident and more effective, in the context of the most powerful and the most rationally considered bureaucratic government in the world. In Islamdom, such channels for initiative and reform were not so available. After the collapse of the caliphate there was no central establishment from which reform might be expected to proceed, and to have permitted serious institutional initiative to the amîrs would have been to disrupt the unitary pattern across Islamdom on which Muslim contractualism depended. When Malikshâh asked for advice from his courtiers, what he wanted and received was not projects for solving particular institutional problems but general precepts to guide his conduct as an absolute monarch, which with little change would apply to any ruler. It would seem as if a primary intention of those who developed the self-contained Sharî'ah, which gave such little scope to initiative by a caliph, was to reduce the realm of free political action to a minimum—looking to the security of trade rather than to the adventures of an aristocracy of any sort. In any case, at courts where status was not ascriptively assured, but depended on personal relations with the ruler, serious reform movements, which always threaten vested interests, could not be mooted without the personal support of the ruler, who otherwise would be moved by rivals to eliminate the reformer without ado.

The social activism which nonetheless the Islamic spirit did call for was expressed, in the Middle Periods, above all through a repeated and many-faceted drive for Sharî'ah-minded reform. This ranged almost imperceptibly from the revivalist sermons of preachers who assailed the manners and morals of all classes, including, at their most daring, the amîrs themselves, to the full-scale revolts of reformers who tried to implement the hope for a mahdî who would fill the earth with justice as it has been filled with injustice. The career of Ibn-Tûmart illustrates both extremes. Though such reform movements were not able to bring in the millennium, they cumulatively went far toward reinforcing the independence and effectiveness of the Sharî'ah and of the institutions under its protection. Reform projects of a more particularized sort became more important in Islamdom in subsequent centuries, but military venture with wholesale revolt continued to pose an ideal for reformers, to which the most zealous approximated as best they could, and which was realized again and again.

It is not easy to choose exactly comparable figures to point up the contrast between the two societies, since so often the career through which a man could arrive at a position of influence presupposed quite different steps in the two settings. But both 'Umar Suhravardî and Bernard of Clairvaux were men mystically inclined yet of conservative piety; and from their positions as spiritual advisers they were drawn into the major political ventures of the day, where they played an influential, if not always successful, role. Both were confronted with the long-standing injustice of agrarianate life and in particular with the licence of innumerable military powers let loose by the disappearance of central bureaucratic authority. Both represented the response to such a situation by a monotheistic conscience. The truce of God, imposed in the Occident with elaborate regulations and special courts, was not Bernard's invention, but he helped make it effective; it may be compared to the attempted disciplining of the futuwwah men's clubs to which Suhravardî contributed, and the control of the amîrs by way of personal involvement therein. Each approach enlisted the highest motives of those concerned, yet in a form adapted to the social order and to the sense of form developed in the two societies. The truce of God invoked the hierarchy of the church in favour of specially protected days and civil statuses. The futuwwah reform invoked the Shar'î duties of Muslims by way of a network of personally assumed obligations. Each approach had some success, but did not prove an adequate solution.

Since here I have been comparing two societies on the level of high culture and of the most abstract possible patterning on that level, we must be reminded that such patterning is of limited relevance to the course of actual history. The fact that, for an artificially stilled cross-section of history, one can formulate phrases that indicate a wide formal presupposition seemingly underlying the various aspects of a given culture must not be construed too substantively. People's minds are not necessarily set differently. The congruence results from the fact that in each complex of cultural traditions, the several particular traditions must mesh, must gear. At any moment there must be at least a temporary equilibrium among various temperamental tendencies and cultural traditions such as those in art, science, or politics, developing autonomously but interdependently. This need for congruence, moreover, is concretized in the human ideal images that tend to prevail in key high-cultural circles; for each such image is necessarily one human whole. But this image and the equilibrium it may answer to need not be taken as a 'causal' drive 'underlying' the particular cultural and historical facts subsumed under it, though it may, in turn, help mould them.

Such pattern abstractions have their use, but they can lead to seeing historical developments as the logical outcome of a closed circle of concepts seemingly presupposed in the high-cultural thinking of a society. The civilization as a whole (on the high-cultural level) is thus made analogous to a particular ethnic group (with its folk culture) in having collective patterns of expectation which mould its social and historical possibilities; though the attempt to trace such patterns even on a simple ethnic level is generally premature. Such conceptualistic interpretations of civilized history have been congenial to certain philosophers and to many philologians, for it seems to allow them to see the whole process of history simply through deepening their perception of the texts at hand. But they fail to grasp the play of interests at all levels that undergirds the formulations as well as the historical process generally; and especially to allow for the difference between high-cultural formulations and the unarticulated springs of human action at all class levels. Hence they scarcely allow for the rapid cultural changes that so often ensue when new opportunities are opened up. In particular, they tempt people to read back artificially into the Occidental past various lauded traits of Modernity in the form of supposed seminal conceptual traits in law, science, aesthetic form, etc.; in this way, some writers have produced an exaggerated notion of the Occidental genius, and falsified the relation of both the Occidental and the other heritages to the advent of Modernity.[6]

Islamicate influence on the Occident

Cultural exchange between Islamdom and the Occident in High Medieval times was drastically one-sided. In a limited number of cases, Muslims learned something from the Occidentals: for instance, in the art of fortification in Crusader Syria (though even in this same art, the Crusaders learned from the Muslims also). But by and large, Muslims found almost nothing that they thought worth learning from the Occident, though even from the more remote China they were already by the Earlier Middle Period adopting techniques and occasionally even more abstract ideas. In contrast, Occidentals were absorbing cultural practices and conceptions of many diverse sorts from Islamdom, and this absorption was of far-reaching importance to the growth of their culture. This was largely due, of course, to the superiority of Islamicate cultural competence, at least at the beginning of the period. The contrast was then exaggerated further by the pre-eminence of Islamdom in the Oikoumenic configuration. Contact with the Occident was peripheral for

[6] The most brilliant interpretation of Islamicate culture as resulting from a closed circle of concepts is that of Gustave von Grunebaum, expounded in his many books and articles, all of which are worth reading. It is no accident that he exemplifies at its best what I call (Introduction, vol. 1) the Westernistic commitment or outlook, which commonly envisages Western culture in just this way. In his 'Parallelism, Convergence, and Influence in the Relations of Arab and Byzantine Philosophy, Literature, and Piety', *Dumbarton Oaks Papers*, 18 (1964), 89–111, at the end especially, it becomes clear that in his analysis, the formative assumptions of Islamdom (and Byzantium) are derived at least in part negatively, by way of contrast (what Islam *lacks*), from certain contrary formative assumptions he ascribes (in the Westernistic manner) at once to the West and to Modernity. This method almost assures in advance that 'Eastern' cultures, as lacking what he finds unique to the West, will turn out to be essentially alike, but will be separated from each other just by what they have in common—that is, in his view, by a dogmatic claim to completeness, which also has suppressed their occasional glimpses of a Western-type or (preferably) Western-inspired rationally open humanism. The formative assumptions he sees in the West, on the contrary, turn out to be central to what is most distinctly human. For instance, he refers to these assumptions as 'the attitude toward the world into which man grew during the Renaissance'; here 'man' cannot refer to the biological species type (as in 'man has thirty-two teeth') nor even to mankind collectively (as in 'the unity of man') but (as so often in Westernistic literature) makes grammatical sense only as referring to a long-lived mythical being, 'Man', who has personally undergone a series of crucial experiences in successive historical periods, and who is identical with that primary figure of Westernistic myth, 'Western Man', whose cultural traits as finally unfolded are held to be the highest and most human yet achieved.

All this assumes an organic fixity in each cultural tradition, represented in a personified ideal human image, which merely unfolds in time its inherent potentialities. On the limitations of such determinacy in the traditions, and the difficulty of comparing the development of the Occident and Islamdom on the basis of seminal culture traits, see the section on historical method in the Introduction in volume 1.

Islamdom, and no more important or even less important than contact with eastern Europe, Hindu India, or any other of the various regions with which Muslims were in close contact. For Occidentals, eastern Europe and Islamdom were the only alien societies accessible, and the western outposts of the Muslims in Sicily and Spain, of relatively minor import to Islamdom at large, loomed very close and large in the Occident.

The influence of the Muslim presence was twofold: as a source of ideas and as a challenging presence. First, it brought about more or less explicit adoption of given cultural practices. Sometimes this was direct, as when the works of Abû-Bakr al-Râzî were translated into Latin and used in medical treatment. Sometimes this was more indirect, by way of what has been called 'stimulus diffusion'. It seems likely that descriptions of Islamicate windmills, introduced from further east into Mediterranean Islamdom by the beginning of the period, were the occasion for the appearance of windmills in the Occident by the end of the period. But since the arms of the mill were spread horizontally among the Muslims and vertically in the Occident, clearly what passed was the basic idea and not the complex practice of building windmills in its particulars. Much of the Islamicate influence on the Occident was in some degree of this indirect sort.

Indeed, the diffusion of cultural details was subject to diverse limitations. Items which could find no ready niche in the new society, however efficient and useful in the old, were not adopted. Camel transport, though very effective, was not adopted in the Occident partly because of climate, but also partly because even in the most southerly parts the ox sufficiently filled the relevant niche and a change would not have brought enough advantage to pay. What *was* adopted was likely to be transformed, even when contact was direct and the practice immediately imitated. Even technical details, when taken over, often had to be rethought and adjusted so as to fit into the technical context of the new society. If, as it appears, the Gothic arch was suggested by corresponding arches in Islamicate buildings, in any case the way it was used and hence also the details of its construction were very different in a cathedral from what they were in a mosque; the total effect and meaning of the arch were entirely new.

This high selection and rethinking was even more important when it came to the properly aesthetic and intellectual levels. Here, for the most part, Occidental imitation and adaptation of Islamicate material was restricted to what was rooted in traditions already largely shared by the Occident, at least on a rudimentary level. Thus the romantic poetic tradition of the troubadours seems to have depended directly on the somewhat prior corresponding tradition of Islamicate Spain; but this went back ultimately to older Hellenistic traditions, long since partly echoed in Latin, and seems to have received its immediate forms from local Romance tendencies common to Spain and Gaul. Though some elements of the tradition are probably traceable to old Arabian motifs or at least to the local work of Arab Muslims, clearly a large part of it was congenial to moods and forms already found in the Occident.[7] It is this tendency for the culture to adopt from abroad only what was already half-known that has sometimes made it difficult to sort out Islamicate 'influences' in the Occident from indigenous growths. (It has also contributed to the notion in the modern West that the Islamicate intellectual culture offered nothing but originally Greek ideas, perhaps slightly further developed.)[8]

Perhaps as important as the actual number of technical methods, pieces of information, and books that the Occidentals learned from the Muslims (or from Jews of Islamicate culture), was the confrontation with Islamdom as a historical fact. Many of the books that the Occidentals got from Islamdom they could have gotten from the Greeks themselves—and later did; whereas the sort of insight that could not have been gotten from the Greek tradition was largely overlooked by the Occidentals anyway. What perhaps mattered most was the stirring of the imagination and the challenge to the ingenuity of Occidentals who, in the full flush of their increasing economic prosperity and the rising cultural level associated with it, found themselves looked down on and hemmed in by a society which shared none of their overt assumptions and yet was obviously, at least at first, culturally and politically superior. The Muslims posed a challenge to the Occident such as the Greeks of Byzantium, long respected but latterly overcome and almost despised, could not.

The distant contact in Syria as a result of the Crusades does not seem to have had much effect on the Occident in terms of direct borrowings; but the very fact of the Crusades' being undertaken shows the tremendous stimulus that the Muslim presence formed, and the very process of Crusading—their one great joint effort—taught the Occidentals more sophistication, perhaps, than they could ever have borrowed from their unwilling Syrian hosts. The political greatness of the papacy owed much to its leadership in those wars. In Sicily, where Occidentals ruled over subject Muslims and Greeks of high culture, much was learned on the factual level; but possibly the greatest impact on Occidental cultural and political life was made by the Latin rulers of the island, notably by Frederick II. The Latin rule there was unique in the Occident for its bureaucratic solidity—required because of the high-cultural level of the local population and their intimate relations with Muslims as well as Greeks; and this in turn made possible the unique role of Frederick II as disturber and ultimately inspirer of other Latin princes. The third locus of Muslim-Occidental relations was the Spanish peninsula, where

[7] S. M. Stern has shown that a specifically Arabic intervention in the process of developing Romance verse in both Spain and Gaul (whether among Muslims or Christians) is possible, perhaps even likely, but not yet demonstrated.

[8] H. A. R. Gibb, in 'The Influence of Islamic Culture on Medieval Europe', *Bulletin of the John Rylands Library*, 38 (1955), 82–98, offers a suggestive study of how a high-cultural tradition tended, in pre-Modern times, to maintain its own genius despite great influence from the outside. He is speaking only of diffusion and not considering the more contextual effects of the sheer presence of the alien culture and its challenge.

imitation and adaptation of Islamicate ways was at its height, and whence they were most regularly spread over Europe. Here perhaps more than anywhere else it was the tremendous prestige of Muslim learning that persuaded Occidentals to study works in Arabic that they did not trouble to study in the original Greek, though by 1204 Latins were thoroughly at home in the Greek-speaking countries where the Greek books were to be found.

Though the most important influence of the Muslims on the Occident may have been the stretching of the imagination which they encouraged, yet the particular points of cultural adoption were crucial in Occidental growth as it in fact did take place. Even the Greeks were translating works from Arabic and Persian, for they were the most vital languages of the age this side of Chinese. Perhaps most important were technological borrowings. Crafts and manufacturing methods, commercial methods of organization and even political methods (in Sicily), and agricultural skills could be taken over fairly directly. By and large Islamdom, especially at the start of the Earlier Middle Period, was more advanced technically than most of the Occident; however, by the twelfth and thirteenth centuries the two societies were growing on roughly the same level and it is then sometimes hard to know in which society a new development came first. In some fields, such as the steady improvement in the uses of gunpowder, it may well be that corresponding inventions were made roughly simultaneously but independently, as the technical level came to be ready for it in both areas at once. As yet the history of the Occident is better documented in these matters and often new inventions can be attested slightly earlier there; this may be the case for certain complex kinds of stills and for the use of the compass. But in many other cases, such as the manufacture and application of the many items which, like alcohol, still bear among us names derived from Arabic, the priority is sufficiently clear. The wide range of Occidental dependence can be suggested by a random and very partial list of English words derived from Arabic (though many of these words came to Arabic in turn from Persian or Greek): orange, lemon, alfalfa, saffron, sugar, syrup, musk, muslin, alcove, guitar, lute, amalgam, alembic, alchemy, alkali, soda, algebra, almanac, zenith, nadir, tariff, admiral, check-mate.

In natural science, especially in mathematics, astronomy, medicine, and chemistry, but to a degree in all the fields then cultivated, the Occidentals frankly acknowledged their debt to Arabic books, which they eagerly translated throughout much of the High Medieval period. In the process, classical Greek texts took on an Arabic dress (the 'Almagest' of Ptolemy retains in Latin the Arabic article *al-*) and numerous Muslim writers, not only Ibn-Sînâ ('Avicenna') and al-Râzî ('Rhazes') but many lesser men, became commonplace Latin authorities. Astronomical tables compiled at Muslim observatories were authoritative. (We still use the Arabic names of many stars.) Only those works that had been produced by the early twelfth century were translated, for by the time the translations into Latin ceased, the most recent writings were not yet well enough known to have come to the translators' attention. Discoveries made in Islamdom after about that date had to be remade independently in the Occident later.

This was not, of course, a matter of 'bringing back to the West' its own heritage, meanwhile 'preserved' by the Arabs: the Latin Occident had played almost no role in building up the Hellenic scientific corpus even at the height of Roman power, and the Occidentals can less properly be called its heirs than can the Muslims, in whose lands much of the scientific corpus originated. And when the scientific heritage was finally carried to the new territory in the northwest, it did not die out (as some Westerners have supposed) in its homelands in the eastern Mediterranean and between Nile and Oxus; at least at first, the scientific productivity of the Occident did not markedly improve on that of Islamdom, and after High Medieval times it may have declined again for a time to a level below that of Islamdom. Nevertheless, the Occidentals did prove apt scholars, able by the end of High Medieval times to continue the tradition on their own without further reference to the work being done in Arabic and Persian; and though for a time there was a partial lull in Latin scientific work, the tradition persisted and later led to the great scientific transformations of the seventeenth century.

The problems of Philosophical metaphysics received in the Occident, as in Islamdom, a more sustained and socially organized attention. Here too the most important texts came at first by way of Arabic; translations initiated a great Aristotelian revival. But both the Aristotelian and the Platonic traditions had been rooted with sufficient solidity in Latin in imperial days, though chiefly by way of secondary writings, so that the impetus that came from Arabic brought nothing radically new. The new writings were made to serve a dialogue that was arising before they were introduced. Thus the position of Ibn-Rushd (Averroës) in Islamdom had justified an accommodation of the private wisdom of the Faylasûfs to the social supremacy of the Sharî'ah, at the expense of any properly theological speculation; in Christendom, his attitude, under the name of 'Averroism', served rather to justify an accommodation between a radically rationalistic Philosophy and Christian theology itself. The most important consequence of the translations from Arabic was to raise Occidental thinking to a higher level of sophistication. Even here, then, despite the obvious transference of particular texts, the influence of the presence of Islamdom, great as it was in the form of cultural diffusion as such, was even greater in the form of the challenge to the imagination posed by the very existence at such close range of Islamicate sophistication. Provided the particular texts were not so alien as to be totally unintelligible—that is, given that the Islamicate heritage had much the same roots as the Occidental—it mattered perhaps relatively little which particular texts the Occidentals came upon, compared to the fact that they were exposed emotionally to a society in which texts of high sophistication prevailed at all.

In the fields of the Abrahamic tradition and of mysticism, at first sight there seems to have been no Islamic influence at all. Ghazâlî (called 'Algazel') was known for his exposition of the Falsafah metaphysic rather than for his Islamic refutation of it. Probably religious experience as such was not shared. Rare was the Occidental who had a serious enough acquaintance with Islam for such influence to be imaginable; most Occidentals who wrote about Islam repeated the most grotesque misinformation, designed purely as encouragement for the faithful against a foe they should regard as despicably irrational. But on the level of metaphysics, among a few, contact was possible. It has been suggested that certain Christian mystics, notably Raymond Lull of Spain (1235–1315), who indeed was one of the rare souls that did know something of Islam, may have learned something from their Muslim counterparts, and so from Muslim metaphysics later than Ibn-Rushd; though they could scarcely acknowledge the fact, if they were themselves aware of it. Lull's thought was marked by a boldness and breadth of vision not without affinities to that of such men as Ibn-al-'Arabî, of whom he must have known; and especially by way of Giordano Bruno, Lull was one inspiration of the much later imaginative ebullience that ushered in Modern times.

In the field of aesthetic culture, the penetration of Islamicate themes and methods is harder to trace than in the technical and intellectual fields. Some prose fiction was translated directly. But art, above all, transforms whatever it feeds upon. Specialists have traced the introduction of numerous lesser motifs at one point or other from Islamdom in architecture and in what in the Occident are called the 'minor' arts. The elaboration of musical instruments was given a great impetus from Islamicate models, and even poetry, as we have seen, at its Medieval peak in the troubadours, probably made use of old Arabic traditions. Both popular tales and pious legend, which formed the substratum of much of the best prose, were nourished in part from Islamicate sources. Some of Dante's materials have been shown to bear striking analogies with certain Islamicate materials—notably some points in a description of Muḥammad's ascent to Paradise—which were available in Italy at the time on the basis of translations from Spain. But here again, the heart neither of Dante's poem nor of the Occidental aesthetic culture generally was seriously touched by the alien details. Probably in this realm also the most important consequence of the Islamicate presence was its challenge to the imagination.

By the end of the Earlier Middle Period, the Occident had become a significant force in the life of Islamdom. The Occidental efforts at conquest in the east Mediterranean had been mostly turned back, and they had been limited in the west Mediterranean to a line somewhat north of the Straits of Gibraltar, efforts to cross the seas having failed. For two centuries the Occident was not to advance again. But Occidental culture had become independent of Islamicate resources and had pulled abreast of the Islamicate in sophistication. The Occidentals of Italy and Spain retained the dominance over the Mediterranean seaways and their commerce which they had gained in the Earlier Middle Period. Thus they blocked in the west Mediterranean that expansion which characterized Islamdom everywhere else, and which elsewhere expressed and probably reinforced the genius of its social order.[9]

[9] The most accessible study of Islamicate influence on the Occident is *The Legacy of Islam*, ed. Thomas Arnold and Arthur Guillaume (Oxford University Press, 1931). The 'legacy' in question is not that to modern Muslims but that to the Occident, rather prematurely conceived as the heir to a moribund Islamdom. Not all the chapters are relevant to this theme, but many are. The best is by H. A. R. Gibb, 'Literature', pp. 180–209, who brilliantly traces what influence can be found in Occidental literature. The chapter on the visual arts, Thomas Arnold, 'Islamic Art and Its Influence on Painting in Europe', pp. 151–54, is also useful, but less discriminating as to what 'influence' really means. H. G. Farmer has a useful chapter, 'Music', pp. 356–75. The studies on the natural sciences, e.g., Max Meyerhof, 'Science and Medicine', pp. 311–55, all suffer from the misapprehension that what can be traced into the Latin was substantially the whole of Islamicate science; this means that they leave untouched some serious questions about Occidental selectivity, but they are good so far as they go.

BOOK FOUR

Crisis and Renewal: The Age of Mongol Prestige

Indeed, she had quite a long argument with the Lory, who at last turned sulky, and would only say, 'I'm older than you, and must know better.' And this Alice would not allow, without knowing how old it was . . .

—*Lewis Carroll*

PROLOGUE TO BOOK FOUR

The fourteenth and fifteenth centuries, which chiefly concern us here, can be set off (if one will) from the Earlier Middle Period, studied in Book Three, as displaying not so much basically new social conditions or new historical tendencies (though such do occur) as unwonted continuity. By the time of the Mongol invasions in the thirteenth century, the international Islamicate society had been fully formed. Ṣûfî ṭarîqah orders had been organized, Persian literature had developed its most characteristic forms, the expectation of rule by military amîrs was general, the patterns of continuing Islamic expansion were set. In absorbing and converting the pagan Mongols who occupied the central Muslim territories, the international Islamicate society demonstrated its strength; and in the following two centuries it continued to develop in most respects along the lines laid out in the Earlier Middle Period. What is most obviously new in this period is this very fact of continuity, of a relative lack of basic social innovation. We come to a society which—however unstable it was in its political expressions—was relatively stable (as citied societies go) in its underlying expectations and expressions of social and cultural life. Our interest, then, can focus on what happened to the persisting cultural patterns under such relatively stable conditions. It can be a study in conservatism.

Such a period should be, so far as this is so, relatively unexciting. Even as a study in conservatism, it is nonetheless both important and instructive. It can be instructive in so far as it allows us to witness a relatively complete working out of the patterns established in the Earlier Middle Period, uncomplicated by many intrusive elements. If, as I have suggested, it is in the Middle Periods that we see, if at any time, features specific to Islamdom as a society, then it is especially in the Later Middle Period that these features may come clear. Not unexpectedly, many literary presentations of Islam and its ideals which became standard date from then. At the same time, some of the most outstanding figures of Islamicate civilization were active in this period and reflected its continuity and its Islamicate traits.

Nevertheless, it would be a mistake to consider the period as entirely, or perhaps even primarily, a period of continuity and of unfolding of implications already inherent in earlier creative life. There was a range of new elements in the historical situation at this time. The very expansion of Islam, which continued fairly steadily throughout this period, helped almost imperceptibly to change the presuppositions of Islamicate cultural life as a whole. The Jamâʿî-Sunnî religious synthesis of the Earlier Middle Period was sharply challenged by a revived radical Shîʿism, by extremist tendencies within Ṣûfism itself, by philosophical intellectual independence, and even by a neo-Sharʿî reaction. The most important single source of new ways was the Mongol conquest. In destroying the vestiges of the caliphal state and overwhelming many Arab and Iranian cities with unprecedented physical destruction, which commonly eliminated many of the carriers of the highly cultivated traditions of the craftsman and the intellectual; in then causing intensive contacts with the most distant and alien cultures—above all with China; and in introducing new standards of politics, of law, and above all of art, the Mongols presented a challenge to Islamicate life the response to which long made itself felt even in areas where the Mongols never penetrated. Only at the end of the fifteenth century did new impulses appear, strong enough to outface even in Iran the ghost of Chingiz Khân, the Mongol.

When I started composing this work I assumed, as I had been told, that after the first three centuries of Islam, or certainly at least after the Mongol conquests, there was a time of stagnation, even of decadence, in which there was little cultural innovation and, indeed, even a decline in the level of cultural achievement that was maintained in Islamdom, until its modern 'awakening'. I have come to doubt that this thesis can be substantiated in any general or absolute form; perhaps not even for the 'darkest' period, say 1300–1450. I would suggest that, to the degree that one can speak of general cultural decline in Islamdom at all, one must distinguish two different phenomena at two different periods, which the conventional image has run together. Accentuating certain trends in the Earlier Middle Period, there was a period of economic contraction in the Later Middle Period, of undetermined intensity and with as yet unclear cultural effects. After this came a period of recovery, at least from about 1500, and of cultural as well as political brilliance; the degree to which the economic contraction of the Later Middle Period was then compensated, or not, is likewise undetermined. Then, starting in the seventeenth century but becoming drastic only in the eighteenth century, there was a second period of deterioration, this time far more serious because the result of a drastic new world-historical situation. It is this latter decline alone that is the proper basis for questions comparing the past grandeur of Islamdom with its present difficulties.

The deterioration in the Later Middle Period is, at best, problematic. Even a decrease in economic prosperity, which is the easiest to attest, was not uniform or universal. The level of aesthetic and intellectual awareness may, by at least some standards, actually have risen in those centuries, in the central lands of Islamdom (even if not in some Mediterranean Muslim lands, which have held the attention of European Arabist scholars). It becomes apparent that it was in this Later Middle Period that the new institutional bases were laid down for the Islamicate society that flowered so markedly in the sixteenth and seventeenth centuries; Toynbee has reason for setting off the Later Middle Period as the creative age of a whole new civilization, which he styles the 'Iranic'. In Iran in the fifteenth century, and especially in its latter part, we find a creative ferment in the arts and in related aspects of life which bears many striking analogies to contemporary life in Renaissance Italy, and which issued in the new life of the sixteenth century. The 'stagnation' or 'decadence' of Islamdom, if there ever was such before the eighteenth century, must surely be placed in the Later Middle Period; yet that very period was one of important new beginnings.

Unfortunately, the Later Middle Period, especially in the central areas, has been the least well studied of all Islamicate periods—historians of modern international affairs have not usually probed so far back for background, and philologians, with their passion for origins, have rarely come so far forward except for the Mediterranean littoral, which directly concerned the Occident. We have so few detail studies in the period that one must suspend judgment on its overall character. All generalizations in this work are subject to the caution that Islamicate history is much less well studied than Occidental. Generalizations in this period cannot expect to be better than educated guesses. This lack of studies must leave another mark on this work. It is in part for want of analyzed material that this Book Four is so disproportionately brief. If the reader does not bear in mind that the period covered here is not so much shorter in time than that covered in Book Three, he will lose perspective.

The world-wide crisis

If one cannot speak of overall decadence even in this limited period, one can yet speak of elements of decadence entering into the total picture. Indeed, this is true not only of Islamdom but of the greater part of the Oikoumene. The Later Mid-Islamic Period was one of relative economic retardation or even deterioration very generally. (This is not the only case where Islamdom turns out to be something of a microcosm of world history, though with its own weighting of the several components of the world situation.)

Everywhere in the Afro-Eurasian zone of citied life, the fourteenth and fifteenth centuries seem to have borne the marks of a slackening of economic expansion. Many European towns, which had been adding rapidly to their numbers, ceased to expand (though the development of the fresh Occidental region kept on despite a slower pace); iron production in China, which had been rising phenomenally, levelled off or even decreased; even in India one finds hints: government income in the prosperous Ganges valley now allowed less magnificence. In the midst of this period came the hemisphere-wide Black Death, the great plague of 1346–48; the drastic reduction in population that it caused was in many places not made up for generations later. For almost two centuries, there was something like a world depression reflected in the degree of urbanization, in the volume of trade, in the social resources available, even in sheer numbers of population.

This may have been due partly to the after-effects of the Mongol devastations. These after-effects were both direct, in the lands that had themselves been devastated, and indirect, affecting the sources of world trade; it would be indirect effects, if any, that would have reached western Europe and India, where the devastation itself was relatively slight. Economic decline seems to have been greatest in the regions directly affected. In any case, there must have been a coincidence among quite diverse causes, whatever role the Mongols may have played, to have produced so extensive a series of phenomena.

It is clear, at least, that many Muslim lands were relatively unprosperous during these centuries. Between Nile and Oxus, in the region central to Islamicate society, some lands probably declined markedly in population and cultural activity. Numerous towns seem to have dwindled, even becoming mere villages. New towns, indeed, sometimes arose; but there are many cases where a resort of trade and learning well known in earlier Islamic times had become petty or even disappeared by the end of the Middle Periods without any corresponding centre arising to replace it; probably these two centuries saw proportionately the greatest increment of such cases. The prosperity of the Tigris-Euphrates basin, in particular, was certainly very much less by 1500 than it had been in High ʿAbbâsî times. A perceptive observer in Egypt during the Later Middle Period saw evidence of great impoverishment then even in that rich valley. It seems likely that the same was true of much of Iran. In the Maghrib a notable decrease in the area of cultivation began at least as early as the Earlier Middle Period. Most of the more newly Islamized (and generally less arid) areas, on the other hand, do not seem to have suffered a like attrition.

The degree to which prosperity was reduced must not be estimated too exactly prematurely. Too often we have spotty evidence: it comes more readily from areas that were prominent in better-studied periods (either earlier or later) and prosperous then: but often data for decline at a given locality indicates rather a change in the location of commercial and investment activity than an overall regional decay. The places then prosperous may be little known and less studied. In economic history, our ignorance of the Later Middle Period is compounded by our ignorance of the other periods as well.

Economic reverses in this period in Islamdom were accompanied by other trends that have been called decadent. But here the notion becomes even more problematic.

On the conservative spirit

Cultural conservatism can seem, from a Modern perspective, to be the dominant feature of all pre-Modern societies. From this perspective, 'civilized' agrarianate society and 'primitive' pre-literate society seem hardly to be distinguished as to their overwhelming conservatism—their 'traditionalism'. When one deals with any introduction of new basic institutions, it becomes obvious that such an interpretation by way of custom-bound cultural patterns will not work; otherwise, some seem ready to suppose that a conservative 'traditionalist' spirit has prevailed among mankind, unchallenged almost except by accident, right up to the eve of Modern times, when that spirit has been replaced by the rational spirit of progress. And this supposed captivity to custom is taken as a set of mind explaining all else. We have noted earlier, in treating of the cosmopolitan tendencies in Islamdom, the misleading results of thus classifying all societies into two categories, 'modern' and 'traditional' (and of the corresponding use of the term 'traditional' by some writers to confound a society's being bound by custom with its having patriarchal institutions; so that they refer to the attitude of mind and to the type of institutions by the same term).

For others, more sophisticated historically, the internal development of the pre-Modern 'West' is sufficiently clear so as to obviate this twofold classification in this one region. But apart from certain undeniably creative periods, they commonly use a like perspective in viewing other civilizations, less intimately studied as yet. Indeed (taking their special image of the West as norm), such writers go further, and not only speak of conservatism or traditionalism, but often of outright decadence in all civilizations but that of the Occident.

As we shall see when we come to consider the impact of technicalistic Modernity on Islamdom, either one of these two perspectives results in a misapprehension of what it is that is crucially distinctive in Modernity. Technicalistic Modernity has been not simply rational emancipation from custom, nor has it been simply the further unfolding of a bent for progress peculiar to the Western tradition; it has been a cultural transformation *sui generis*. For studying the mid-Islamic periods, however, it is more important that, as we have already seen, either one of these perspectives makes for a misapprehension of the processes at work in agrarianate-level culture itself. A cultural tradition, by its nature, must keep changing in order to survive. Not only a steadily changing environment imposes this condition, but the very internal dynamic of the cultural dialogue which unfolds the implications latent in the previous moments of creativity in the tradition. We have seen that Islamicate culture was in process of continuous and far-reaching modification and development, and this not only in the spectacular period of its first advent but in the subsequent period of maturity. Any understanding of conservatism must see it as a part of this process.

But there is a truth in the perception of pre-Modern times as conservative, which is valuable if analyzed with care. That is that, contrary to many modern conceptions of 'progress', the most normal pace of cultural change in any agrarianate-level society was slow and often unwelcome, and only partly cumulative—some tentative footholds would normally be lost even as others were being gained. This pace was only exceptionally speeded up into creative florescence; but also only exceptionally slowed down into something that might be called stagnation, or reversed into what might be called decadence. And it is a failure to distinguish between a normal conservatism and what

The Islamic Later Middle Period, 1250–1500, with Reference to Events in the Oikoumene

	Europe	Central Oikoumene	China
1253		Hülegü sets out on western conquests with army larger than Chingiz Khân's	
1256		Hülegü's forces destroy Ismâ'îlî strongholds	
1258		Hülegü's forces sack Baghdad	
1259		Mamlûks take control in Egypt, Syria; in 1260 turn back a Mongol army	Kublai becomes Grand Khân (to 1294); moves capital to Cambaluc (Yenching/Peking); uses Persian architects, court officials; roads, canals built
1261	Latin empire collapses at Constantinople; Byzantine rule restored		Kublai attempts during his reign to expand to Burma, Champa (S. Vietnam); sends expeditions against Java, Japan
1261		Alliance between Mamlûks and Golden Horde built on co-operation of Byzantium and Italian cities; Golden Horde holds Moscow princes and others tributary; later grants title of Grand Prince to Muscovite rulers	
1270	Saint Louis dies crusading in Tunis		Yünnan province added to Chinese empire, becomes Muslim
1274	Death of Thomas Aquinas, fighter against Latin Averoism	Death of Naṣîruddîn Tûsî	
1283	Teutonic order completes conquest of Prussia, converts inhabitants to Christianity	Italian trade interests grow in strength in E. Mediterranean and Black Sea	
1290	Jews ordered expelled from England		
1291		Last of Crusaders expelled from Syria by Mamlûks	
1292			Polos leave China
1295		Ghazan Khân ruling in Iran converts to Islam; Mongol 'unity' now definitely broken	

1299–1326		‘Uthmân Amîr of ‘Ottoman’ Turks		
c. 1300–1326		Russian Orthodox Metropolitanate moved from Kiev to Moscow		
1306	Jews ordered expelled from France		Muslims push into S. India	Civil service examination system and Hanlin academy restored (14th century)
1313		Golden Horde Khâns all Muslims from now on		
1321	Death of Dante			
1326		Ottomans take Bursa		
1335			Death of Abû-Sa‘îd; Îl-khân empire breaks up into warring states	
1336	Death of Giotto			
1337	Beginning of 100 Years War			
1346–50		BLACK DEATH		
1348–49	Jews expelled from Germany, go to Poland			
1360s		Ottomans take Adrianople in Europe, make it their capital; traditional date for establishment of Devshirmé and Janissaries	Timur rises to power in Transoxania	
1368				Mings expel Mongols from Cambaluc
1370		Lithuanian kingdom takes Kiev, expands against Golden Horde Tatars		
1374–75	Death of Petrarch, Boccaccio			Ming restoration sets tone for re-establishment of older (T’ang and Sung) ideals; conservatism in the arts, philosophy, belles-lettres
1379			Timur expands W. across the Oxus	
1393		Ottomans take Bulgaria		
1395		Timur defeats the Golden Horde		
1396–1403		Chrysolorus teaches Greek in Italy		
1398			Timur sacks Delhi	
1400	Death of Chaucer			
1402	John Hus begins preaching		Timur defeats Ottomans at Ankara	

The Islamic Later Middle Period—*continued*

	Europe	Central Oikoumene	China
1403–24			Yung Lo emperor; Chinese launch series of sea expeditions to Malacca Straits and into Indian Ocean; (?) Ceylon pays tribute to China for a time
1405		Death of Timur; his successors cannot maintain the empire, but they become patrons of arts and letters	
1414		Muslim ruler of Bengal encourages conversion of his subjects there	
1415–29	Lost Latin works collected		
1419	Lithuanians able to interfere in internal politics of Golden Horde		
1420–31	Hussite wars		
1429		Ulugh-beg builds observatory at Samarqand	
1431	Joan of Arc burned		
1434	Portuguese round Cape Bojador		
1453	Ottomans take Constantinople		
1460	Death of Prince Henry the Navigator; Portuguese off W. coast of Africa; expedition ordered to reach India		
1462–1505	Ivan III (the Great), Grand Prince of Moscow		
1460s	Printing introduced into Italy and France		
1475	Last Italians driven from Black Sea power		
1488	Portuguese round Cape of Good Hope		
1492	Columbus sails W. to India; Christians take Granada, last Muslim hold in Spain		
1498		Portuguese enter Indian Ocean and become a power there	

can be called stagnation or decadence that I suggest has been peculiarly pernicious in many scholars' attempts to study Islamicate civilization and particularly its later periods.

The pattern of normal conservatism on the agrarianate level has been obscured particularly by three features of the image of 'Western' history cultivated by Modern Westerners. In the place of a history of the lands of the Occident itself, going directly back to the earliest Gauls and their west European predecessors, has been substituted a tendentious figment: a composite history which combines in a single sequence certain florescent periods of Greek history in the east Mediterranean with later Latin history in northwestern Europe. This composite image yields an impression of repeated great progress partly because of the way in which the east Mediterranean component has been selected and partly because of the way in which the west European component has been interpreted: for want of a true world-historical perspective, Westerners describe in the same manner, as 'progress', both the rapid but largely borrowed advance of the frontier area which was the earlier Occident, and the new internal development that took place in the later Occident. Finally, since the great Modern technicalistic transformation took place in the Occident, this has been regarded as a mere continuation and confirmation of the perennial 'progressiveness' of the 'West'. Hence, in this best studied field, agrarianate, actuality has been disguised, and the role of the conservative spirit which informed it has not been appreciated on a general historical basis.

Such a format of interpretation is unavailable for Islamicate history. On the contrary, something partly comparable to our arbitrary annexation of one phase of Greek history to Occidental history—that is, the arbitrary severing of High Caliphal history from its Sâsânian antecedents by race-minded philologians—enhances, as we have seen, an impression of sudden flowering in early Islamic times; and this paradoxically helps make later periods look decadent by comparison. For this and other adventitious reasons, many of them brought out elsewhere in this work, it has been equally difficult to see the nature of normal conservatism in Islamicate history. Answering to an impression of progress for the West, both scholars and the general public have an impression of general decadence in later Islamicate culture. The reasons for this are summarized in the chart of the occasions for the perception of later Islamdom as decadent. It cannot be said, at least at present, that later Islamdom was not at all decadent. But the case for decadence cannot be taken very seriously until the misperceptions contributing gratuitously to such an impression are eliminated.

In any case, first one must understand normal conservatism and the conservative spirit expressed therein. We must recall that the 'old man's' attitude to time—that the younger generation is going to the dogs—has been the normally received one, even in times of great creative florescence. It is not this attitude, but the exceptions to it, found occasionally in the ancient

Mediterranean, in Islamdom, and in the pre-Modern Occident alike, that call for explanation.[1] And one can expect that only a certain number of traditions will be being markedly developed at any one time, while from time to time other potentially important discoveries are not followed up—a sad event that has occurred in the ancient Mediterranean, in Islamdom, and in the pre-Modern Occident alike; and still other traditions may actually be being eroded. It is the flowering of all or most aspects of a culture at once that is to be explained as a special phenomenon. But however prevalent, conservatism was no blind dead hand, acting simply to stifle rational change. Rather, the conservative spirit has itself been one element in the sober rational calculation which has remarkably often guided the leadership of each generation.

The nature of a living cultural tradition ensures that every generation must make its own decisions. It must decide in terms of the effective interests of those groups in the society that are in a position to have their way. A calculation of what is the interest of such groups will take into account not only the material but the cultural resources on hand; and the cultural resources include the sort of expectations that potential leaders must have of how everyone else is going to respond to this or that. It is in this form that past convention and habit can play their most significant role. But it is a delimited and even a precarious role. Innumerable pre-Modern revolts, such as those of the Ismâʻîlîs, have illustrated the willingness of ordinary people to adopt radically new positions once they are convinced these will be to their advantage and that they can actually get away with them. The conservative spirit, when it has prevailed, has reflected for the most part, very practically and very functionally, such matters as the level of available investment and of tolerable risk in a given society, and the awareness of responsible individuals of what is possible and what is not, what will pay and what will not.

It must be conceded that the conservative spirit is more than the sum of cautious evaluations of particular moves. As an overall mood that makes for a presupposition that old ways had best be repeated, that the burden of proof is on the would-be innovator and that, indeed, change will normally be degeneration rather than improvement, the conservative spirit can enter any

[1] The presence of the 'old man's' sense of time is often cited as attesting to cultural decadence; for instance, in the interesting discussion by Robert Brunschvig in 'Problème de la décadence' in *Classicisme et déclin culturel dans l'histoire de l'Islam*, ed. R. Brunschvig and G. E. von Grunebaum (Paris, 1957). It seems to me that such citations could demonstrate something special only if such ideas were shown to be of more effect than usual. Brunschvig, in his historical review of Western ideas of Islamicate decadence, brings out the fact that Westerners did not speak of such decadence till the end of the seventeenth century; as will be seen, I think this date is more significant for the problem as a whole than has been realized. Incidentally, the whole volume edited by Brunschvig and von Grunebaum is of great value for the question of conservatism, even though it suffers throughout from a range of presuppositions which, it seems to me, vitiate most of the larger conclusions arrived at. Some related problems are dealt with in *Unity and Variety in Muslim Civilization*, ed. G. E. von Grunebaum (University of Chicago Press, 1955).

decision at a decisive level before detailed calculation can begin. Even as an overall mood, however, such a spirit can serve a vital social function. In society on the agrarianate level, almost all social groups, villages, local crafts guilds, even whole towns, had to act in what, from a Modern perspective, looks like stark isolation. If one major misstep were made, they could readily lose all they had, and there was nowhere to turn to start over again. The old man's sense of time, his sense that the younger generation, in its inexperience, is always on the verge of ruining everything, was partly justified. It was hard enough to hold on to what one already had; any improvement was at best speculative. The conservative spirit must be taken for granted as underlying all agrarianate-level history even at its most revolutionary. But to a remarkable extent historical actualities hindered the spirit from taking full effect in most periods. It is almost exceptional, at least from the first millennium BC on, to find a period in which the conservative spirit came into its own, on the high-cultural level, fully enough to entail extensive rigid stagnation and the decadence that will accompany it. Decadence was always taking place in certain sectors of culture. But presumably it is only with a general stagnation (not merely slowness of development), which would inhibit the creativity on which cultural traditions must depend to remain vital and viable, that anything that can be called general decadence would ensue. And it seems to me that overall decadence was actually rather rare.

Cultural decadence and the style cycle

At best, cultural decadence is not easy to ascertain. In any particular tradition, decadence is easily identifiable: a particular style of needlework, for instance, ceases to be done with the same care as before, becoming purely a matter of perfunctory imitation for secondary purposes. (Usually one will find that something else has taken its place as focus of attention and cultivation.) Such single cases of decadence are commonplace, but not really to the point. One can also pinpoint objectively a decadence in certain whole sectors of a culture: and this is more relevant. If one is sufficiently well informed, one may be able to say that the level of scientific knowledge, or of fresh scientific inquiry, has declined; and likewise that of industrial or agricultural technique. Here one can even use statistical methods.

But both of these levels, especially the level of technique, can be evaluated only by taking into account still another realm in which 'decadence' or regress can be ascertained (if we are well enough informed): economic prosperity. If the available resources diminish, or if their exploitation is hindered, certain complex techniques, which before were of use, will bring diminishing returns and no longer repay investment in them; rational calculation will dictate their abandonment. The economic dimension is primary, in fact, wherever decline can be objectively demonstrated. Thus loss of prosperity for the privileged elements, whether as a result of absolute decrease of production or merely of greater dispersal of revenues, could result not only in the patronizing of fewer writers or artists, but in an acceptance of work into which less costly materials and less time had been put; and such things can be measured without dispute if there is sufficient information. They are also fairly readily reversible in principle.

But when people speak of the decadence of Islamdom in the Later Middle Period, they do not mean simply a supposed reduction of economic resources and corresponding curtailment of patronage, though they do include that. The notion of decadence, as applied to a culture as a whole, originates with the history of states and of churches, and notably with the history of the Roman empire, where virtue and high morale and the ready recognition of creative genius have been correlated with its period of growth, and a loss of these intangible traits among the ruling classes has been correlated with its decline in political power. With the Roman empire was associated a whole pattern of civilization, subsequently idealized; and with the political decline of the empire was associated a quite different pattern of civilization, subsequently regarded as 'Gothic' and without merit. Similarly, the power of the High Caliphal state is admired, and with it the creative vigour of its privileged classes; and the political and cultural order that succeeded is regarded as lacking in the intangible virtues it displayed. And this is blamed on the stifling triumph of a traditionalistic conservative spirit.

In this sense, cultural decadence is much more elusive. It cannot be easily shown that even general economic contraction (even supposing that it is established) and the several phenomena that may follow from it actually represent a loss of intangible creative virtues. Even in the economic activity itself, a quantitative loss need not be qualitative: the activity may be highly sophisticated even when on a reduced scale; or a wider sphere of operations may make up for reduced resources in any one place. And an economy restricted by forces beyond the participants' control may support, not only on a smaller scale but even with a reduced technical apparatus, other creativity as significant as ever, if less imposing. We must look directly to the quality of mind being displayed; and here there is room for differing opinions even when we are well informed—as, again, we are not about the Later Middle Period.

Practically every period in every society can be, and most periods have been, called times of decadence.There can always be shown to be elements of decadence in any period: the nature of any cultural tradition, in its continuous change, requires the degeneration or lapse of some standards which have been achieved—if only to allow the establishment of new standards for new conditions. What would seem to be important would be the overall balance between creativity and decadence. But even this requires weighted evaluation. From a point of view that rates high the cultural values especially expressed in the High Caliphal Period, the Later Middle Period will clearly be a time of decadence, for the points where decadence can be shown will seem important and the points of innovation will seem petty. For those who rate high the values best expressed in the Islamicate culture of the sixteenth and seventeenth centuries, the reverse may seem to hold.

Nonetheless, there are certain traits, associated with an excessive predominance of the conservative spirit, to which we may apply the term decadence; their cumulative presence, even if not wholly determinative of the course of an age, may have a significant effect on the whole climate and 'style' of an age. Whereas in an age of general florescence, people are comparatively widely expecting and even encouraging a measure of innovation, so that creative individuals are tolerated and even given honour and resources, in other ages ordinary people's natural suspicion of anything new may not be countered by a general expectation of novelty, and their distrust of those who innovate will be given freer rein. The social structure may be such that those whose interest it is to avoid serious change not only rise to posts of power (this, indeed, is usual), but are in a position to exercise very full control from those posts. Thus far a 'normal conservatism'. When this tendency is carried to an extreme, institutions can become 'rigid' and traditions be relatively unresponsive to the pressure either of new needs or even of the logic of internal dialogue.

Such a situation may arise in more than one way, and notably in two ways that may themselves be inter-dependent. When speaking of the exceptional character of florescence, I pointed out two reasons for resistance to change: the uncouthness of new styles at their inception, and especially the small margin for experiment in an agrarian-based economy. Under some circumstances, each of these can make for severe inhibition of cultural development.

When one style of doing things—in art, but also in other fields, even economic or political organization—has been developed, in the course of cultural dialogue within a given tradition, to a high level of perfection, then any alternative pattern, having to start necessarily at a less differentiated level of development, will have difficulty competing even if, in its own limited way, it has something perfect to offer, and even if potentially it could be developed into a range of patterns of much greater promise. Alternative economic methods will commonly simply not pay so well at a cruder level or on a less widely marketed scale of development; yet without application first at such a level, or on such a scale, a method cannot move on to the level where it will be more effective than its competitor. Alternative artistic ideas will seem unsophisticated and uninviting at their initial stages of development if they must appear alongside perfected patterns based on a different sort of artistic idea. Even if an artist were highly creative, his audience would take time to become accustomed to his new style; and since any tradition depends as much on the response to the creative moment as on the creativity itself, the time-lag of the audience would be decisive. Hence in the presence of highly developed forms, new types of form are unlikely to arise unless some discontinuity—of class or ethnic or religious group, for instance—tempers the comparison long enough to permit the new form to be perfected.

Every achievement, every vision, has its own temptations; and every cultural pattern evokes a loyalty that can lead to its own demeanment, as the particular traits of the pattern come to be valued more than the unformulable human excellence that made the pattern worthwhile. This is most starkly visible in religion, but we all know it is a quite general phenomenon.

In the arts especially, and even in other imaginative fields such as philosophy and positive science and scholarship, people do not readily rest content even with perfection. After five minutes, the most beautiful sunset palls. People demand something new. But if they remain too loyal to the respected patterns they know, the new can come only as an exaggeration of its several traits: the requisite novelty can be had only by deviating from the perfected balance within an established tradition. Hence not only is basic innovation inhibited in the presence of perfection; the perfection already achieved within the given form is itself marred. True style gives way to fashion. Artists or thinkers will retain the norms of the form that has been developed to sophistication, but they will tend to over-elaborate, to refine details to the point of disproportion. Thus we find, as art historians have shown, not only after an archaic period of art a classic period which (though the archaic had its own perfection) brings to fulfillment all the major potentialities latent in the viewpoint expressed in the archaic style; we find, also, after a classic period then one of ornateness and perverse exploration of all the minor channels of elaboration left open in the tradition. And epigonal scholars will do this quite as zealously in science as epigonal artists in art.

Fortunately, this over-elaboration is unlikely to persist in a pure form for long: inherent in any cultural dialogue is an openness to other lines of development in which people are also participating, which one can expect to break open any closed pattern. The example of the Baroque style which followed the classic Renaissance reminds us that when the classic forms have been fulfilled, artists—or poets or philosophers or even scientists—may shift focus; so that what may look like over-elaboration can shade creatively into a radically new way of interpreting what yet remains basically the same tradition. Something like this has happened very often. Yet the degenerative phase of the style cycle which runs from the archaic to the classic to the over-elaborate can yet be influential, especially among workers at less than the very top level. The style cycle, then, is a recurrent invitation to decadence, to be overcome only by ever-renewed creativity.

But it is circumstances outside the style cycle as such that are most likely to encourage a whole generation to yield to a degenerative phase of the style cycle in any imaginative field. In particular, any reduction in the resources available for new investment can hinder experiment by established groups, or hinder the rise of new groups, with variant traditions, to positions where their traditions can receive full elaboration. Until a new level was stabilized, a contraction in prosperity, and specifically in the quantity of resources flowing into the cities, necessarily threatened, in the Agrarian Age, any leeway that might have been built into city life for experimentation and innovation, and encouraged over-elaboration of received traditions at the expense of development in new directions.

To the extent that prosperity was being reduced in the central lands of Islamdom in the Later Middle Period, this must have fostered a heightened atmosphere of 'conservatism', more exactly a stronger expectation that established norms would be maintained and that it would be safest for the individual to hew to them. The cultural innovation that did take place in the period was partly grounded in direct local prosperity; but it seems often to have made its way against an overall regional pattern of expectations uncongenial to frank creativity.

In any case, whatever the effects of economic decline or of style cycles, the conservative spirit prevailed enough to prevent any spectacular florescence. As compared to the High Caliphal Period, when the very existence of the Arab caliphate encouraged new syntheses, in the Later Middle Period the new syntheses that were developed had to encounter—and commonly adapt themselves to—vested interests in preserving old patterns unchanged. This difference in cultural posture surely left its mark on the work of the age. Not in an absence of creativity: even when the conservative spirit came most fully into its own, the dynamic of the cultural tradition continued to act, of course. Creativity there was, but the forms it took tended to be more indirect.

I

After the Mongol Irruption: Politics and Society, 1259–1405

Striking analogies can be drawn between the role of the Mongols between Nile and Oxus and that of the Arabs there six hundred years before. In each case, nomads conquered the greater part of a major agrarian region, nomads who were fortified by a significant measure of contact with urban life (to be sure, the Mongols were led by men who had been herdsmen themselves, not by merchants). Each group of nomads carried with it not only strong ethnic pride and solidarity but at least the elements of a social code developed to hold together the large-scale agglomerations of fighting men: the Mongol law, the Yasa, was revered almost as loyally as had been the sense of a common Muslim Sharî'ah. Moreover, the Mongols were not wanting in men of genius, notably Chingiz Khân himself; and many of them had constructive interests, at least after the first generation (though certainly the Mongols used destructive terror to an extreme degree where the Arabs had used it outstandingly little).

Given such roughly comparable starting points, there might have seemed to be occasion for a new beginning, a new recasting of the Irano-Semitic heritage in a new civilization. But instead the Mongols in the Muslim sphere were absorbed into Islamdom and eventually accepted Persian as their language of culture. The historical setting was different. The economy of the age of Mongol rule was not expansive but, at least in some areas, contracting—though (to what degree is not clear) on an Oikoumenic scale the Mongols themselves may have been partly responsible for this. Then the Irano-Semitic society had already found what seems to have been a satisfactorily cosmopolitan solution to its social and intellectual needs—though again it is not clear that the solution found in the Earlier Middle Period could not have been improved upon; certainly it left points of inner tension and contradiction.

Indeed, the Mongols contributed to the resolution of some of these even without so major a redefinition of the situation as the Arabs had produced. These differences of setting might have been decisive. Yet one cannot overlook one of the most startling differences between the Mongols and the Arabs themselves: the Mongols brought nothing comparable to the Qur'ân and the Islamic spiritual impulse.

Agricultural productivity in arid lands: secular blight comes to a head

The Mongol régimes presided over a change in economic and social patterns in much of the mid-Arid Zone and some nearby areas, which any understanding of Mongol state formations must presuppose. We know very little of what went on, but we can hazard some estimate of what sorts of development were important. Earlier I have spoken of the ways in which aridity can make agrarian production and organization precarious in the Agrarian Age, and of nomadic pastoralism as a form of economic production complementary to agriculture in the Arid Zone. In the Later Middle Period, the precariousness of the agrarian economy and the rivalry of the nomadic pastoral economy reached a peak. Here we must trace the long-term evolution, barely intimated in the earlier discussion, and try to see how it led to this juncture at this time—how it led both to the Mongol conquests themselves and to the general economic dispositions of the period. We will first try to delimit the scope and components of a long-range deterioration of the agricultural economy in the mid-Arid Zone, and show possible reasons why that should come to a head at this time. Then we will trace the long-range rise of the nomadic pastoral economy, and try to distinguish the effects it had in the agrarian society as different stages of its own development intersected with different stages in the agrarian deterioration. Finally, we may guess at the relation between the intersection of agrarian weakness and pastoral strength in the Later Mid-Islamic Period and the tendencies toward a slackening of economic growth generally in the Oikoumene at that time.

The human species has often proved a devastatingly destructive phenomenon. Nowhere has this been more readily demonstrable than in the Agrarian Age in the Arid Zone—unless technicalistic Modernity with its wholesale waste may be proving an even more decisive case in point. Agriculture and the whole agrarianate complex probably arose in the Arid Zone because of special potentialities there; but the fact that it arose there, devastating the region's resources and its ecological balance with so great a technological advance, was like a doom impending against the population. By the time that population was converted to Islam, it was presumably too late to avoid some effects, even had Islam carried some special charm against disaster.

It has been noticed throughout the Arid Zone, especially from Nile to Oxus and in the Maghrib, that many areas now good only for grazing once were rich farmlands. Many thousands of years ago there was far more rainfall in the area than now, and for a time the decrease in agriculture was ascribed to a progressive change in the climate. But within the last two thousand years, a period within which agriculture was both at its peak and also in its greatest decline, rainfall does not seem noticeably to have decreased in the area as a whole. The problem, then, has arisen from more short-range causes than a secular desiccation.

Most 'arid' areas, of course, do not suffer from an absolute want of water; the problem is that the water is concentrated in a few places or in a few seasons of the year; what is not used then is normally wasted as regards the rest of the year. There is, then, potentially a good quantity of water; the problem is to convey it or conserve it for the right place and time, so that it can all be used rather than wasted. There are diverse ways of gathering water in arid areas away from immediate water courses—by artificial canals, above ground or below ground, or by basins for garnering seasonal rainwater; but all are dependent upon constant care and upon initiative, sometimes large-scale initiative, in repairing breaks or other disruption. A more indirect means of retaining year-round moisture in the soil seems to be by the presence of masses of trees; but trees are also important for the sake of another resource than water. When trees are cut or burned or prevented from growing, the soil itself is readily eroded unless effective cover is substituted; and without abundant water, good natural cover does not readily arise, nor is new soil readily built up.

Accordingly, in the arid areas, agricultural productivity, once begun, depends more than elsewhere on a continuity of well-balanced human initiative. Continuous working of the land without proper precautions can gradually ruin it. And interruption of agriculture may be the reverse of a remedy. Agriculture there depends upon clearing of the natural cover and upon irrigation; in both cases great care is required, to avoid wastage, even if agriculture is steady and moderate. In neither case does the land always return to its previous condition after a time of neglect; on resumption of care, there will often be less adequate natural resources to work with. Irrigation, mishandled, can result in swamping and—most permanently—in salting up of the soil and especially the groundwater. This salinization could be reversed at the cost of heavy investment; but erosion was (and still is) harder to reverse. Where growth tends to be occasional and sparse, the loss of natural cover can quickly lead to drastic erosion of the soil. In both respects, a failure of human organization can introduce a vicious circle of decline and then private short-run countermeasures which make the decline worse.

Possibly considerable forests had persisted, with gradually altered constitution, from an earlier moister time, which once destroyed could not be naturally reconstituted. In any case, clearing the land for ever-wider agriculture was an almost automatic long-range cause for eventual reduction in agricultural potential: that is, the greater the agrarian prosperity anywhere at an earlier time, the less prosperity could be regained there at a later time; and the more areas were once tilled, the fewer new areas were left to open up later. But there were more immediate sources of disruption to bring to a head the long-term vulnerability.

Destructive warfare could interrupt sound agriculture, especially when its depredations forced such villagers as survived to move elsewhere. Rules on landholding could equally occasion bad management if they discouraged local initiative on an economic scale (either by splitting up landholdings through multiple inheritance, as the Sharî'ah seemed to require, or by encouraging absentee landlordism, as also often happened in the urban-centred Islamicate society). Legal roadblocks could be and often were removed. Perhaps what discouraged local initiative the most was the persistent tendency, from early citied times, toward total exploitation of the peasants by the privileged classes: if all production above a subsistence level was drained off, neither capital nor incentive was left for local effort except in periods of extensive state power which was turned to such efforts, or in response to sporadic action by relatively enlightened private possessors. There was little continuity in such actions. Meanwhile, as land gave less return, grazing gained on tillage; and within grazing, smaller, closer cropping animals were substituted for larger (sheep for cattle), and finally, when the reluctant herdsman was hardpressed, goats for sheep. Goats proved able to find forage in the most difficult conditions, but they found it by destroying all small plants that might have grown larger, notably the shoots of trees; hence the entry of goats into an area sealed the doom of such woods as remained, and left the land yielding less than ever.

It seems likely that the blight of the land began locally soon after agrarianate society itself, and was especially severe where that society had lasted longest. In some parts of the southern Iraq, where the Sumerians had flourished, it may have begun as early as the later part of the Sumerian period itself. As irrigation increased in range and massiveness, the areas subject to blight increased, though with a lag of centuries. In the Iraq, despite a much earlier blight here and there locally, a maximum of irrigative projects seems to have been achieved following the Axial Age, in Hellenistic, Parthian, and Sâsânian times. It is possible that the same period also saw a maximum of irrigation works in other lands between Nile and Oxus. But it is in the Iraq that agricultural investment was greatest, and subsequent decline was most extreme. As we have noted, political, agronomic, and geological factors made the irrigation of the Sawâd increasingly difficult perhaps already from the end of Sâsânian times: salinization and silting, certainly; deforestation and erosion, as well as shifts in land inclination (resulting in a smaller area of natural irrigation), probably; possibly some marginal changes in rain levels at headwaters even so far east. It seems that by the end of High Caliphal times, despite the well-organized efforts of the Muslim rulers, a degree of general blight was permanently reducing overall productivity in the Iraq and possibly elsewhere. With each interruption of the continuity of high-level cultivation, such as occurred too often after the caliphal power declined, the blight became more irreparable. And once the social and economic structure of the area was committed to a highly centralized urban structure, it became hard to restore irrigation patterns even on a much more modest scale by way of local initiative such as had served in the very beginning; the pattern of militarization, which arose partly as a result of the failure of irrigation, itself added to the difficulties.

All this affected most seriously the single region, the Iraq, which alone had been the seat of really massive irrigation. Blight in the Iraq had one massive special consequence: to undermine the financial basis for any bureaucratic imperial structure of the Sâsânian or caliphal type. To the extent that such a structure helped maintain high investment in irrigation elsewhere, the deterioration of the Iraq had wider repercussions. However, even apart from massive investments and massive blight, some degree of deterioration was probably going on elsewhere between Nile and Oxus. Deforestation, salinization, and a degree of nomadization would doubtless reinforce each other in a great many places in the Arid Zone, making a renewal of agriculture far more difficult than its original initiation had been. The maintenance or collapse of a central government probably would delay or advance the blight by at most a few centuries. And there were few new lands left to open up in compensation.

After the decline of central caliphal power, the lack of strong political authorities and the repeated scourges of warfare did not encourage the most careful use of land resources in what had become, probably in a great many areas between Nile and Oxus, a delicately balanced situation. A process of blighting which had begun almost with civilization itself in the arid lands and which had perhaps already reached the point of no return after the vast exploitative efforts following Axial times, before Islam had come on the scene, made itself felt more potently than did any available line of increase of agriculture, either in extent or in intensity. Without basic new insights and methods, such a situation could probably not have been stayed for long, though it might have been delayed. Any mistakes simply precipitated it. By the Later Middle Period mistakes were frequent. With little understanding of the fundamental forces at work, men in government were at least aware of the importance of maintaining cultivation and assuring the peasants a reasonable return; but their advice bore relatively little fruit. Despite some valiant efforts, notably under the Mongols themselves, the governments throughout the Middle Periods and still later proved essentially impotent to cope with so elusive a long-run challenge. At least here and there, the net area effectively open to agriculture cumulatively declined; and in consequence, save for what was contributed by a growing pastoral sector, the whole economy tended not to expand but to contract.

The agricultural decline was commonly accompanied by an extension of stock herding into previously agricultural areas. Sometimes, when new bands of pastoralists found entry to an area, the herdsmen simply drove out the farmers. In some cases, the herdsmen seem to have been able to take over areas temporarily devastated in warfare, with the grudging or forced approval of military rulers dependent on tribal support. Sometimes it seems likely that an extension of herding range resulted rather from the withdrawal of cultivators as agriculture became uneconomic, despite the efforts of the taxing authorities. Keeping land in cultivation became a major preoccupation of many Muslim rulers in the Middle Periods. But whatever the mechanism of transfer, doubtless the herdsmen remained in possession—and remained herdsmen—by and large only where herding was more economic than agriculture under the conditions of the times. Once the pastoralists took over a marginal area, to be sure, the prospects of future agriculture in it, when other conditions should improve, were probably eventually reduced; for overgrazing by sheep and especially goats may have stripped the soil and caused erosion even more rapidly than did over-tilling even with the secondary grazing farmers used. (We may compare the depopulation of parts of Spain, rather later, in favour of sheep ranching, though in Spain that ranching was commercial and reflected a new age in history rather than a marginal shift in the exploitation of agrarianate-level resources.)

The decline of agriculture took different forms in different places. We must recall that a certain decline in inner Syria had been the result of ending an artificial local expansion; any new decline in our period was an independent effect, and must be attested independently. The decline in the Maghrib probably had had its greatest impulse already in the Earlier Middle Period, with the disastrous introduction of camel nomadism there. Probably in the Jazîrah and certainly in central Anatolia, deterioration began in the Earlier Middle Period with the advent of Turkic tribes as an important occasion for it; but it is certain that nomadization increased during the Later Middle Period. Khurâsân we seem to know far less about, but there does seem to have been loss of agriculture there in our period. In southern Spain, the deterioration coincided, at least in some areas, with the withdrawal or expulsion of the intensively skilled Muslims. In Egypt, there seems less reason for a precipitation of secular agricultural blight; yet even nomadization was taking place there in the shadow of militarized misgovernment. One may suspect that the a'yân-amîr system, and then the increasing pattern of relatively arbitrary government, affected in some degree all parts of Islamdom, even where the economic basis for such a political development was not locally operative. Surely the most important components in the agrarian decline in the mid-Arid Zone were internal to the region; yet one may suppose that the decline could be accentuated, in some places at least, as a result of the overall Oikoumenic recession; which may in turn, of course, have been partly the result of economic developments in Islamdom.

The Turks as universal military élite

While the agrarian economy was paying for its earlier triumphs, the pastoralist economy became steadily more effective. In Book Three we have seen how nomadic pastoralism could form its own autonomous economy with its own direct relations to the cities and their trade; and how there would be a tendency for pastoralism to replace agriculture in marginal areas between Nile

The Ages of Mongol Prestige, 1258–1405, and of the Timurîs, 1405–1500

Maghrib and Spain | Sudan | Egypt and Syria | Arabia and East Africa | Anatolia and the Balkans | Iraq, Caucasus, West Iran | East Iran and Transoxania | Central Urasia | North India | South India and Malaysia

1260–77 Mamlûk sultan Baybars defeats Mongols at ʿAyn Jâlût (1260); breaks most Frankish power on Syrian coast; does not restore Arab seapower as against the Italian

1256–1335 Mongol Îl-khâns rule Iran, etc.; wreck Baghdad, 1258; converted to Islam, 1295; patronage by both pagan (Buddhist, Christian) and Muslim Mongols of science, history, and art, inspired from all parts of the Eurasian continent; miniature painting transformed under Chinese influence

1258 Death of al-Shâdhilî, founder of a Ṣûfî ṭarîqah

1273 Death of Jalâluddîn Rûmî, Persian in Anatolia, founded Mevlevî ṭarîqah (whirling dervishes); wrote a mystical *mas̄navî* (epic-type poem)

1257 Saʿdî composes the *Bûstân*, Persian gnomic poetry (d. 1291)

1274 Death of Naṣîruddîn Ṭûsî, scientist and philosopher, protector of the Twelver Shîʿah as Mongol official

1318 Death of Rashîduddîn, vizier, compiler of world history, theologian; reflects the world outlook of Mongols

1280–90 Qalâʾûn, Mamlûk sultan, completes elimination of Franks from Syria; his dynasty lasts till 1382

1263–1328 Ibn-Taymiyyah, Ḥanbalî ʿâlim, attacks the Ṣûfî orientation of official Islam

1307–32 Gonga Musa, and peak of Mandingo imperial power in W. Sudan

1290–1320 Khaljî and, 1320–51, Tughluq dynasties expand Delhi power over most of India

1324 Death of Niẓâmuddîn Awliyâʾ, a founder of Chistî Ṣûfism, exemplar of humaneness

Maghrib and Spain | Sudan | Egypt and Syria | Arabia and East Africa | Anatolia and the Balkans | Iraq, Caucasus, West Iran | East Iran and Transozania | Central Eurasia | North India | South India and Malaysia

1253–1324 Amîr Khusraw, a founder of Indo-Persian poetry

1325–51 Muḥammad Tughluq, fiscal and political experimenter, overexpanded Delhi power

1288 (–**1922**) Ottoman dynasty in Anatolia and Balkans; expands over Greek and Slav territory

1347–48 *The Black Death everywhere*

1359–89 Murâd I, takes Adrianople (1362) which becomes Ottoman capital; defeats Balkan Christians at Kossovo (1389); state dominates W. Anatolia and most of the Balkan peninsula

1336–1502 *Assimilation of newly Islamized areas and of new cultural elements; excesses of military rule at their most devastating; the fixating of the orthodox tradition in religion and science*

1269–1470 Marînid dynasty supersedes Almohads in Morocco, carries on rivalries with Ziyânids at Tilimsân (in present Algeria, 1235–1393) and with the cultivated Ḥafṣids in Tunisia (1228–1534)

1295–1336 Islamized Mongol Il-khâns continue rule of Iraq and Iran; their last descendants puppets under

1336–1411 Chiefs of Jalâyir Mongol tribe, with military hegemony in Iraq and Azerbaijan; in rivalry with Muẓaffarid family in Fârs and 'Irâq-'Ajamî (to 1393) and with others

1288–1326 'Uthmân, ghâzî on Byzantine frontier, makes his corner of the Anatolian Seljuḳ state a military center, founds Osmanlî (or Ottoman) dynasty

1293–1340 al-Nâṣir Muḥammad, son of Qalâ'ûn, almost replaces Mamlûk régime with a dynasty

1326–59 Orkhan, 'Uthmân's son, establishes independent state (capital Brusa) dominating remains of Byzantine empire

1334–53 Yûsuf of Naṣrid dynasty of Granada builds the Alhambra, completed by his son (1353–91)

The Ages of Mongol Prestige—*continued*

Maghrib and Spain | Sudan | Egypt and Syria | Arabia and East Africa | Anatolia and the Balkans | Iraq, Caucasus, West Iran | East Iran and Transoxania | Central Urasia | North India | South India and Malaysia

1322–89 Sa'duddîn Taftâzânî, polyhistor and grammarian

1337–81 Sarbadârs—a popular Shî'î movement in W. Khurâsân—maintain themselves despite dominance in rest of Khurâsân of the Kurt dynasty of Herat; both powers are overthrown by Timur

1390 Death of Ḥâfiẓ, mystic-sensual lyric poet of Shîrâz

1351–1413 Tughluq dynasty of Delhi restricted to northern India (succeeded by Sayyids, 1414–52; and Lôdîs, 1451–1526); thereupon, a multiplication of Indian dynasties adapting Islam to the various nationalities

1336–1576 Kings of Bengal independent; much of E. Bengal converted

1369–1405 Timur-Lang revives Chaghatay Mongol power at Samarqand, conquers destructively much of the Middle East and central Eurasia (sack of Delhi, 1398)

1389–1402 Bâyezîd I expands Ottoman power over all Anatolia, is overthrown by Timur

1396–1572 Gujarât as independent Muslim sea-trade power

1347–1527 Bahmanids erect a strong Muslim power in the Deccan, at war with Hindus in far south

1378–1502 Ḳara-ḳoyunlu (Black sheep) and Aḳ-ḳoyunlu (White sheep) tribal leaders rival Jalâyirids and each other for control of Mesopotamia, Azerbaijan, etc.

1382–1517 Burjî Mamlûks—an oligarchy of military ex-slaves, maintaining itself in Egypt (and Syria) with new slaves each generation; gradual decline of Egyptian prosperity

Maghrib and Spain
Sudan
Egypt and Syria
Arabia and East Africa
Anatolia and the Balkans
Iraq, Caucasus, West Iran
East Iran and Transozania
Central Eurasia
North India
South India and Malaysia

1406 Death of Ibn-Khaldûn, philosopher of history and society whose work was not developed by successors

1364–1442 al-Maqrîzî, Egyptian historian and encyclopedist

1405–94 Timurids in Khurâsân and Trans-oxania, exploit results of Timur's campaigns; foster science and both Turkic and Persian literature; high development of Persian miniature painting

1404–47 Shâhrukh holds main Timurid domains together in mildness

1393–1449 Ulugh-beg, Timurid ruler at Samarqand, patronizes important astronomical investigations

1365–1428 'Abd-al-Karîm al-Jîlî, systematizer of Ibn-al-'Arabî's monism

1403–21 Meḥmed I gradually reunites shattered Osmanlî empire

1421–51 Murâd II asserts Osmanlî power against Hungarian and Western attempts to curb it

1451–81 Meḥmed II, Ottoman sultan, takes Constantinople, which becomes the capital; encourages assimilation of Byzantine cultural traditions, and of learning generally, an attitude continued by his son, Bâyezîd II

1470–1550 Waṭṭâsid family continues Marînid tradition in some weakness

1481–1512 Bâyezîd II

1414–92 Jâmî, Ṣûfî poet, biographer

1445–1505 Jalâl-al-dîn Suyûṭî, polyhistor and encyclopedist

1468–92 Sonni Ali builds Songhai empire beginning with conquest of Timbuctu

1492 Naṣrid state in Spain overwhelmed by Christians

1502–24 Ismâ'îl, heir of the Ṣafavî shaykhs of Ardabîl, sets about Shî'îzing Iran as shâh, provokes persecution of Shî'îs elsewhere and Oxus, with the result that pastoralist chiefs could come to hold a balance of power when the agrarian order was relatively weak. But it was one sector of the pastoralist economy that loomed largest, that of the Turkic horse nomads, though, in the central areas, only from Seljuḳ times onward. This sector was brought into even greater prominence by the Mongol conquests, for the bulk of the tribes that formed the Mongol armies or that migrated under the stimulus of the conquests were Turkic. The Mongols themselves remained an élite and after some generations mostly disappeared, as such, at least west of the Altai mountains. (The name *Tatar*, originally applied to the Mongols and their followers jointly, in some European languages soon was used simply for Turk; more exactly, for the more northerly Turks.) Who were these Turks and how did they come to their pre-eminence?

We have noted already, in the Arab conquests themselves, the consequences of the development of camel nomadism to a point where those nomads were in a position to interfere militarily in the surrounding agrarian lands. In the long run, however, it was the development of horse nomadism in the central Eurasian steppes that was more crucial in world history generally, affecting India, indeed, relatively little as such, but Europe largely, China still more so, and the region from Nile to Oxus, with its especially precarious agricultural economy, far more than any other major region. For as nomadic pastoralism developed—necessarily only after an agricultural base was laid—it proved to be strategically placed, before the full development of gunpowder warfare, to dominate militarily the whole Arid Zone.

The horse nomadism of the central Eurasian steppes displayed special military advantages associated with its very limitations. Horse nomadism could not endure the aridity of deserts such as those of Arabia and the Sahara. While horses gave the nomads mobility and could also yield milk and other products to live on, the most important market animal was sheep, which required relatively dense forage. Moreover, the horse nomads had a rather complex technical apparatus: baggage wagons, relatively elaborate tents for the bleak climate, and a varied complement of animal species for varying purposes, as well as specialists like iron workers. All this contributed to accentuating the stratified character of nomad society. Nevertheless, the nomads could travel far; for sheep and goats thrive in most parts of the Arid Zone far beyond the limits open to agriculture. And the extensive use of horses gave these nomads a raiding power, within their very wide range, that was even harder for sedentary peoples to resist, it seems, than the camel herders' raids. This was partly because the horse nomads were more numerous, and were also glad to graze their sheep even in cultivated areas; it was also because raiding could be concentrated and controlled more readily in a more highly stratified social order. It was largely in response to their raids that defensive mounted gentry had been developed in the agrarian countryside.

These horse nomads were originally, doubtless, a varied lot. At one time, the chief languages of at least the western steppes had been Indo-European, and early horse nomadism was still carried by Indo-Europeans. But there was a strong tendency for ethnic elements to be mingled there, and for a lingua franca to emerge over a very large area. The more easterly tribes, facing the Gobi desert and also the massive agrarian power of China, seem often to have built more durable political agglomerations (and perhaps to have retained their hardihood less contaminated by an urban presence—but this would be hard to demonstrate); and the leadership of the most westerly tribes seems often to have been dispersed by the fleshpots of relative plenty in the grasslands north of the Black Sea. Certainly, political power—and doubtless also a large measure of migration—usually moved from east to west across the Eurasian steppes. Accordingly, it was originally easterly dialects—the Altaic tongues, and especially Turkic—that came to predominate throughout the steppes and form a lingua franca. By the time, therefore, that horse nomadic patterns were fully developed in material and social technique, and able to achieve more than occasional grand raids, the nomads, at least west of Mongolia, were mostly Turkic-speaking.

The very existence of this mass of Turkic warrior horsemen contributed to the militarization of government, and hence of agrarian tenure, in Islamdom both indirectly and directly. The direct contribution of steppe-formed political expectations we will consider later. The indirect contribution began even before Turkic tribes, as such, entered the central Islamicate areas, with the importation of Turkic slaves as soldiers. The common Turkic cast of the military, which began so early, helped to provide a basis for military separation from the civilian population as well as for Islamdom-wide solidarity among the military themselves. Then when whole Turkic tribes found themselves loose in the central lands, especially before they had been fully integrated with the agrarian routine, the ascendancy begun with the slave soldiery came near to becoming a monopoly of military life in many places. The nomads provided the ideal disengaged carriers of military power—even less dependent on the loyalties of settled society than was a slave corps. This development, well under way in the Earlier Middle Pariod, reached its apex in the Later Middle Period.

This dating marked the intersection of two lines of historical development. The unencumbered herdsman made a better soldier than the peasant, who might be brave enough and even on occasion strong enough, but had more to lose. But the greater mobility and the built-in troop organization of the nomads were not of themselves enough to assure their predominance. Only in certain conditions could the advantages of the nomads outweigh their disabilities, their want of technical resources and of permanent large-scale policies. First, this could happen only in a given historical period, coming after the full development of the technical specialization of the horse nomads, but before the commercial and military domination of them by agrarian powers, which followed especially on the full development of gunpowder weapons. This period began well before the Islamic Middle Periods, but ended with their end. Second, it could happen only if the internal conditions of agrarianate society reduced to a minimum the natural power advantages of settled society, notably its large-scale organization, which allowed it to meet piecemeal attacks with a coordinated overall policy. It has been suggested that it was in part the increased urbanization of the privileged classes in Khurâsân and the Oxus basin in Islamic times that had made the mounted gentry there less able than formerly to resist the advent of the Ḳarluḳ and Seljuḳ Turks; if so, it was not so much, probably, because their youths had degenerated through luxury as because they were less free to act politically independent of the urban classes. But once the tribal Turks were well established, they helped perpetuate an urban primacy and a militarization that encouraged more of the same. The atomistic organization of Islamdom in the Middle Periods, after the collapse of the caliphal state and its bureaucracy, provided just what was necessary for extensive nomad penetration.

The nomads took advantage of the way in which Islamicate society had come to be organized and provided much of the military personnel which it then required. Their character as nomads then set limits to the cultural possibilities and even to the economic resources of the society—at more than one point, a vizier's efforts to foster agriculture were hampered by the soldiers' preference for pastoralism. But the advent of the horse nomads probably had only reinforcing effects on the long-range social tendencies.

We have seen how, with the decline of central bureaucracy, the local urban units might have become politically autonomous; and how, since the cities were, in fact, unable to provide a substitute for the central bureaucracy, all they could do was allow each urban group to settle its own affairs; so that when conflict arose among these groups, some outside authority would be needed to arbitrate. For this purpose, even the most autonomous city would require the amîr's garrison. The garrisons had to make up for the one thing that the towns lacked to make them politically viable: the garrisons must possess the one basic military virtue, solidarity. But this one virtue was quite sufficient to ensure unchallenged power. In an atomized society, there was no political force to gainsay such sheer power: the society was bounden to (and at the mercy of) any group which could muster sufficient solidarity to overcome resistance on the part of the largest local group that could depend upon mutual support.

There were two important groups relatively uncontaminated by commitments within the individualist urban society. Among the peasantry, villagers found themselves subservient financially and culturally to the cities, as well as unfitted by their exigent labour to adventuring. But herdsmen were not only, in the nature of their wandering, independent; in the nature of their nomadic work, they were disciplined as a group, yet without involvement in the ties of settled society. It had been mountaineer herdsmen who—turned mercenaries—founded the Bûyid dynasties. The herdsmen of the steppe brought together in their nomadism even larger bodies than those of the mountain or the desert, with greater military potential. It was only fitting that with the elimination of resistance, it was steppe nomads who established the Seljuḳ empire. The second sort of group that possessed the essential solidarity was corps of military slaves. As we have seen in the High Abbâsî time, where no strata of the population were ready to give effective support to the government, the latter found it safest to rely on a soldiery alienated from the population as a whole and so identified only with the government. In the society of Islamdom, it was, above all, slaves who could play such a role: they were alien (as they must come from beyond the Dâr al-Islâm) and rootless. As they were tied to nothing but each other, they developed an unbreakable *esprit de corps*. Despite all the dangers involved, the Sâmânid rulers continued to use them as had the ʿAbbâsids. The Ghaznavid dynasty was founded by such slave (or, rather, freedmen) officers, with their slave troops. When the Seljuḳs became prosperous and could no longer depend on their original loyalty and training as herdsmen, they likewise took to using slave troops; and many of their freedmen officers likewise founded dynasties.

As it happened, the two types of sources for military personnel were ethnically much the same. Just as the steppe nomads had potential military resources which, when once called in outweighed those of any other type of herdsmen, so the same steppes formed the most outstanding source of young slaves with the elements of boyhood military training as horsemen. The pagan tribes of the back steppes were constantly engaged in raiding and glad to sell their captives. The result of this was that Turks formed the most important military classes of the Muslim regions, wherever the central Eurasian steppe was reasonably accessible; that is, from the Nile valley to the Afghân mountains. A similar development resulted in a Berber military class further west, including Spain. Always other military elements were used so as to counterbalance the prevailing element: Armenians, Georgians, Daylamîs, Kurds, Negroes, etc.; but none of these had the weight to change the primary predominance. (In Fâṭimî Egypt, the soldiery was divided between Berbers and Turks; it included also a Negro contingent, which, however, did not rise so high on the whole, the Negro slaves being recruited under much less favourable conditions.) Throughout the land from Nile to Oxus, then, it was Turks, sometimes in intact tribal formation (then they were called Türkmen), more often (in the Earlier Middle Period) welded together in slave corps, who formed the garrisons and furnished the amîrs. To what extent they paid allegiance to the various sultans that arose was a matter of relative indifference. But the Turkic cultural homogeneity surely did contribute something to the increasing strength of the military rulers over the centuries.

The various Turkic groups from Nile to Oxus were culturally and (to a large degree) politically interchangeable. The majority of the nomadic Turks south or west of the Oxus, including the Seljuḳs themselves, were of the southwestern or Oghuz branch of Turks (those who remained pastoral were often simply called Oghuz); and continued largely true even after the Mongol conquests. But this ethnic solidarity, reflected in dialect, was less important than the general social pattern to which all Turks conformed, of whatever dialect. The Turks, then, fulfilled their essential political role well, except for constant fighting among themselves, and long did little more. Thus Muslim social life could proceed, if necessary, without any more developed state at all; and it often did so. But the Turkic alienness—and its international ties from Nile to Oxus, which only reinforced its Turkicness, so that even some non-Turkic military elements tended to become Turkified—deepened still further the breach between the civil life of the towns and the nuclei of political power. This made it all the more difficult to develop any really integrated states. Thus the Turkicness of the garrisons reinforced the breach between civil and military life by accentuating the tendency of the latter to develop its own fraternity and mobility across Islamdom. The dominance of a single ethnic element in the military forces was the outcome of the special circumstances in which the citied zone of the Eastern Hemisphere found itself at the time vis-à-vis the Eurasian steppes. That is, it reflected a moment in Oikoumenic history when the steppe played an unusually significant role in the life of all around it.

Nomadism and the military patronage state

Under the Mongols, at latest, the Turkic mass contributed in a still more direct way to the form of militarization in Islamdom: by way of political patterns originating in the steppe itself. We have seen that, at least since the development of full-scale direct trade between China and western Eurasia during Han and Roman times, steppe nomadism had been developing its own symbiosis between the mercantile cities and the nomadic tribes much more complex than what had existed in Arabia before Muḥammad. On the nomad side, the herdsmen themselves had access to greater power. The potential wealth of any one tribe could be greater. It was politically at least as significant that the range of the nomadism was almost unlimited. Any one tribe, of course, was limited normally to its particular territory. But there was repeated movement of tribes over wide areas. There were few sharp boundaries separating the territories in the far east, giving on empty deserts north of China, from those in the far west, merging into the rainy forests of western Europe. The sharpest would be at the Tien Shan range, dividing the Tarim basin from the Syr-Oxus basin, together with the mountains north of the Tien Shan; but these mountains seem to have formed no great barrier to the passage of tribal groupings, especially when tribes in the relatively more constricted far east, unabsorbable by the strongly agrarian China south of the desert, pushed westward toward areas where the effective boundary between pastoral steppe and cultivated plain was less sharp. Moreover, the population gradient from remoter areas into the citied agricultural regions operated to bring the nomads, steadily or by spurts, in small groups or by large tribes, into the more settled areas especially south of the Oxus or in eastern Europe. This added to the continuous circulation of the tribes. In these vast shifting populations, it became possible for powerful aggregations of tribes under united leadership, such as sometimes arose in inter-tribal struggles, to snow-ball, gathering the potentially military forces of the nomads of extensive areas for plundering expeditions that could overwhelm whole settled nations.

It is possible that cycles of specially dry seasons might cause pressures of one tribe against another, with political consequences. Many climatic circumstances might be at work: thus a relatively cold period might be hard on herds, but then longer retention of snows in the mountains might make for a more continuous distribution of run-off waters. The disadvantaged tribes might be weakened to the point of creating a political vacuum, or advantaged tribes might find themselves in a position to extend their authority. (But contrary to some impressions, it is not drought and weakness that would enable a marginal tribe to overcome its ever-alert neighbours and seize their lands.) Such factors, at best however, must be reckoned in with the effects of arrival at different stages in the long-term development of horse nomadism and of its symbiosis with the mercantile cities: technical leaps like the use of the stirrup, and more gradual alterations like the multiplication of cities and the commercialization of expectations among the nomadic lords. So, we may eventually be able to account, not so much for the particular years of nomad outbursts (a point of multiple political interactions), but for the changing character of them.[1]

The possibility of large nomad aggregations was greatly enhanced as interregional trade strengthened the central Eurasian cities in wealth and in cultural resources. Except when the most homogeneous and massive of the agrarian blocs, China, was able to exert its control, these cities tended to come under the hegemony of the currently most powerful nomad tribal grouping, which was then able to make use of their cultural facilities—their clerks and their arts and crafts, and their financial arrangements—to its own further aggrandizement. For a time, the caliphal state was able to control the Syr-and-Oxus basin, but after 1000 even this southern (but commercially important) margin of the steppe found itself under Turkic tribal hegemony.

Cultural leadership lay with the mercantile cities. As the cities turned

[1] The popular image of apparently contented tribesmen being suddenly forced off their accustomed pastures by drought and then overwhelming unsuspecting settled peoples seems to derive from a sense of history as a series of isolated events in an otherwise fixed setting. Some nomads may indeed have felt it that way, and one bad year may have provoked an otherwise growing tribe into seeing how far it could jostle its neighbours. But we must recall that even in the remote steppe, history has always been a total process: every given situation has elements of disequilibrium in it, and every new disequilibrium grows out of an old one. The tribes always had reason to be probing one another's position, for no position was really immemorial.

Muslim, the tribal leadership tended to follow suit. But in contrast to the symbiosis between the Quraysh and the nomads in the Ḥijâz, everywhere in central Eurasia power was usually on the side of the nomads and only rarely did city republics emerge quite independent. The tribes, on the other hand, were very often themselves less loosely associated than the camel nomads, being ruled by great chiefs who often took on the traits of kings surrounded by their aristocratic families. Among the horse nomads, with their relative wealth, a mobile approximation to the class stratification of agrarian conditions increasingly emerged.

The central Eurasian nomads accordingly developed not only the means of extensive concerted action but a tradition of rule over mercantile cities which they could extend and develop in more agrarian regions. The basic viewpoint in that tradition was that all economic and cultural resources in the settled regions were collectively at the disposal of the conquering tribesmen, as represented by their leading families, to enjoy not only their revenues but whatever else of interest they might yield. No distinction of public and private within the conquered land was made, in principle. On the other hand, this attitude (not unparalleled among conquerors) could be balanced with its complementary attitude: a sort of *noblesse oblige*—it was the obligation, in honour, of the possessing families to protect and patronize whatever of excellence was to be found in the conquered cities (once they were totally submissive), including all the arts of luxury and even the various spiritual cults.

As we have seen, the Mongol conquests came when nomad power was at its peak of destructive potential. But this was also when precedents and patterns for nomad rule in the central Eurasian mercantile-nomad symbiosis were most fully developed. Interregional trade had been important and (with the extension of the zone of citied life) increasing for over a thousand years; the nomadic tribes had fully developed their traditions of using the city skills to their own ends; but the subsequent process had not yet gone far, whereby the ever-spreading cities were later able to bring the tribal chiefs into their commercial nexus so as to join with them in burdening the bulk of the tribesmen with debt and limiting the range in which they could freely wander. At the first, the Mongols' enormous power was largely used for destruction: their conquests were the greatest the world had seen, and their terror the most horrible. The contrast to the attitude of the Arabs under the leadership of the merchants of Quraysh is striking. Under the appearance of supreme self-confidence in which the Mongols proclaimed their divine mission to rule all peoples of the world, could be found the marks of bitterness, as if already they had tasted too much of the later degradation of the common tribesmen by proud and clever merchants.

But to some extent from the beginning, and very extensively from the second and third generations, the energies of the Mongol leadership were directed into patronizing the arts and sciences of their various subjects. On a scale unmatched by the first Arab conquerors, indeed quite unprecedented, they rebuilt old cities or founded new ones, repaired irrigation works, and encouraged agriculture; they tried to assure free passage for merchants, and opened new paths for commercial and cultural contact; and for scholars they built observatories and libraries. One might get the impression that for the first time since the generation of Muḥammad's immediate followers, the region was ruled by men who took independent achievement—'action' in the sense of leaving a magnificent personal impress, for good or ill—as their express goal, rather than conformity to some prior ideal, either courtly or religious.

This patronage had its limits. The advent of the Mongols confirmed and developed the tendency for Turkic elements to dominate the political and military life of the more central and northern Islamicate lands. For though the Mongols themselves, from the farther east of the steppe regions, used a language which (though, like the Turkic it was of the Altaic family) was markedly different from the Turkic tongues, yet the bulk of the conquering tribesmen were necessarily Turks. There was no sense of identity, needless to say, between the Mongol-led Turks and those Turkic military elements among the Muslims who were of slave origin; and even the nomadic Turks who had come into prominence with the Seljuḳ dynasty were not accepted: for one thing, they spoke an Oghuz form of Turkic, whereas the bulk of the new conquerors spoke dialects of what came to be called Chaghatay Turkish. Nevertheless, from the first the Mongol régimes were forced, so as to maintain the favour of the tribesmen on whom their power was founded, to allow considerable range for pastoralism in lands that were on the margin between cultivation and herding—as so often between Nile and Oxus. Few of the pastoralists were ready to settle down as peasants, and there was a limit to how far agriculture could be fostered. The relative favour shown to nomadism in turn could only encourage the Oghuz Turkic elements already present. In any case, Turkic as never before became the tongue of the military.

This encouragement of pastoralism was not immediately inconsistent with patronage for mercantile elements, whose investments were mobile and who could thrive on the luxurious tastes already present in the new ruling class. But it confirmed the already present tendency toward mobility in the mid-Arid Zone, discouraging agriculture and agrarian aristocratic institutions and, of course, industrial investment, which required both massed markets and secure stability in the cities. In the Later Middle Period, following the Mongol conquests, the wastage of agriculture and of civilian agrarian institutions was at its height, as was the militarization of territorial rule among Muslims.

Such phenomena coincided with the ruin of that burgeoning Chinese industrial economy that may have have accounted in part for the earlier commercial prosperity from Nile to Oxus (and indirectly, therefore, for the vigour of the nomad-mercantile symbiosis of central Eurasia which then by its conquests played so large a part in ruining the Chinese economy). But such depression of urban and agricultural life as is noticeable in this period is clearly largely an internal phenomenon. It resulted from an accentuation, once conditions were unfavourable for a time, of a secular threat to agricultural prosperity always pending in an arid region.

The Mongols attempted to establish in their newly acquired agrarian domains what we may call 'military patronage states', in which the steppe principles of nomad patronage of urban culture were generalized; that the Mongols could not, in fact, fully patronize that basic agrarian concern, agriculture, was incidental. They made the attempt. And in doing so, they subtly remoulded the political and cultural climate of all central Islamdom.

Mongol ideals: the potential for renewal in the military patronage state

The state formations of the Later Middle Periods often possessed brilliant courts with very extensive power; occasionally they might guarantee the old woman's purse of gold left on the highway; more often they could donate handsome sums to poets who handsomely praised the great men of court, or they could collect the manpower to build imposing and marvellously decorated mosques and palaces and tombs for the same great men. Some of the rulers attempted seriously to provide good government, fostering culture and agriculture; many of these afforded the areas closest under their authority a time of relative predictability of social conditions and a certain prosperity.

But almost all the state formations remained essentially military constructions, especially between Nile and Oxus. There, however vast the rule of a given dynasty, no boundary remained pushed for long to its widest extent and a devolution of power to the level of provincial and local amîrs always lurked in readiness. The governments failed to provide sufficient strength to self-perpetuating bureaucracies which would have assured a continuity of authority despite the personality of the amîr, and often failed to go far beyond a purely tribal, essentially irresponsible notion of power, in which the whole land became the proper prey of the prowess of a vigorous tribe, as on a more local level a few villages might pay tribute to the near-ranging nomads. Naturally, they were almost impotent to redress the balance of cultivation and to suppress the wasting effects of recurrent warfare at every level.

Many state formations, chiefly away from the region from Nile to Oxus, were founded on a more or less durable political idea, consistent with military notions and usually involving the primacy of Islam over infidel populations. But between Nile and Oxus, where Islamicate tradition was centred and where the agricultural blight had progressed furthest, formative political ideas were usually of the most tenuous sort. Here, so far as any political idea prevailed, it tended to be that of Mongolism: an appeal to the greatness of Mongol imperial power. This was founded partly on a new consciousness of power on a world scale, such as had been achieved by Alexander in legend but now seemed for the first time to have become tangibly real: Mongol arms had made such regions as the Chinese or that from Nile to Oxus look parochial to the most alert of their inhabitants. (We shall find this consciousness of the Oikoumenic scene as a whole reappearing more than once in this age, with a greater actuality than ever before in Oikoumenic history.) The appeal to Mongol greatness was also founded on the *Schrecklichkeit* of a demonstrated willingness to slaughter whole cities. There are fashions in atrocities, and it became the fashion for a time in the fourteenth and fifteenth centuries to display this willingness graphically by building great towers of severed human heads, cemented in a rough masonry, which gleamed afar at night with the flickering decomposition products of the organic materials. The great prestige the Mongols had among most Muslim populations had pervasive consequences for centuries: human beings are always inclined not merely to fear but also to admire the successful predator.

The Mongol ruling élites prided themselves on being ruled by the Yasa of Chingiz Khan, a law with sufficiently elaborate provisions covering personal status and civil criminal liability, and embodying provisions that ought to have ensured the perpetual moral integrity and superiority of the Mongols to any underlings. The Yasa of the Mongols seems to have had prestige, as a platform of rule, sufficient for other states of a Turkic cast, notably the Mamlûk régime (from 1250) in Egypt and Syria, to be inspired by it to follow their own Yasa. Yet neither in the Mongol states proper nor in other Muslim states dazzled by the Mongols did the Yasa go even so far as the old absolute-monarchic ideal had gone in High Caliphal times in supplementing the Sharîʿah to provide a politically viable system. Yasa and Sharîʿah remained unreconciled, and the Yasa itself remained a narrow military ideal, of which the civilian populations took no cognizance. The effective political order remained that of the international Muslim institutions as worked out in the Earlier Middle Period, capped, with increasingly disastrous results, by the military powers-that-be.

The Mongol states did, nevertheless, introduce the notions characterizing the 'military patronage state', which was to have a great future; and in doing so they modified the context of the Muslim institutions. Already in central Eurasia itself, the nomad-urban symbiosis had been raised above the level of simple plundering exploitation. In the agrarian societies of Islamdom, under the impulse of the tremendous successes of the Mongols and of the Turkic tribes that had shared their victories, the symbiosis was raised to a yet higher level. The Mongols from the first acted in a spirit of monumental achievement: they destroyed in the grand manner, they built in the grand manner too. All this had a relatively enduring institutional residue which we may pinpoint under three heads, recalling, however, that no one state is being described, but only features that frequently did occur under the Mongols and among their heirs, and that show mutual relevance. First, a legitimation of independent dynastic law; second, the conception of the whole state as a single military force; third, the attempt to exploit all economic and high-cultural resources as appanages of the chief military families. However, most of these institutional tendencies merely had their beginnings in Mongol times, which still displayed much continuity with the Earlier Middle Period; some were not developed fully till the sixteenth century, when the use of gunpowder weapons had given the central states (and the patterns they embodied) much more power.

In the realm of law, the Yasa did not indeed succeed in a role which might have corresponded to that of the Sharî'ah as social foundation for a new order. Nevertheless it did give rise, eventually, to a new principle of legitimation which was to become of primary political importance: that, alongside the Sharî'ah of Muslim society as a whole and the regional 'âdah (customary) law independent likewise of any state power, could be a third basic source of law: dynastic law—the law of that ruling family which Mongol tradition exalted so insistently. Dynastic law was more than the decrees of a given ruler, it was the sum of such decrees and was to stay in force as long as the family bore rule; it was binding on succeeding sovereigns, at least till explicitly abrogated by them. Eventually, in gunpowder times, this formed a basis for detailed legitimizing of the institutions of a given state.

This dynastic conception of the role of the ruling family gained plausibility from the world-wide power Chingiz Khan had bequeathed; and it was this same conception that justified the use of terror on so vast a scale to enforce obedience. Old arguments for absolutism, articulated now by Faylasûfs, were still used—that the more extensive the ruler's power, the more peace and security for his subjects; especially since the ruler's interest in maintaining his power assured the justice that alone would produce the prosperity that yielded the taxes that paid the soldiers he needed. But the new conception of the ruling family the traditional expectations of the absolute monarchy, with its limited functions, by justifying whatever would add to the grandeur of the dynasty. Then gradually, in the course of the Later Middle Period, a new interpretation even of Shar'î legitimacy was worked out consistent with such ideas. Any sultan that enforced the Sharî'ah was held to be a legitimate caliph for Shar'î purposes (and there might accordingly be more than one such); hence the established rulers received a privileged Shar'î status. But meanwhile, in the same years and partly in the same circles, the role of the 'ulamâ' in the Sharî'ah that the ruler was to enforce was reduced in scope: for the doctrine of *taqlîd*, of adherence to a given legal madhhab, was elaborated into the doctrine that the 'gates of ijtihâd' investigation had closed in the ninth century—a claim not unprecedented, but given substance by authoritative legal compilations in the fifteenth century in which it was laid down just what was the final form of the law as then closed: the Sharî'ah was to be not a continuing instrument of opposition, but a closed set of rules that could be accommodated and encapsulated in more vital legal traditions. Thus the 'ulamâ' were forestalled from attempting any effective rivalry with dynastic authority and law. The new states were thus ascribed a legitimacy, even from a Sharʿî viewpoint, that the ʿAbbâsî rulers had scarcely achieved.

Secondly, in the realm of administration, the civilian bureaucracy tended to be absorbed, as to rank and form of remuneration, into the military. This had not been entirely unprecedented even in Seljuḳ times; but in the new patronage states it was to become systematic. Again, this development was only begun in the Later Middle Period; but it fitted in with the spirit of the military patronage state, in which an essentially military family partitioned out all privileges and responsibilities in its estates to its members. The whole upper realm of society was to be subject to military discipline—and the rest were mere taxpayers, were the 'herds' whom the real men guarded and milked.

In the Mongol states there were no corps of slave soldiers, and even when such were reintroduced in certain later empires, they no longer gained the almost exclusive and independent position they once had had, but were effectively integrated into the royal military household. This was partly because the steppes, more and more incorporated into the international commercial nexus (and their inhabitants turned Muslims, not subject to enslavement), ceased to yield supplies of slaves. But it was also that in the outlook inherited from the steppe, the tribal military élite, ennobled by its nearness to the nobility of the great dynasty, formed a permanent ruling class; and the whole thrust of the Mongol state form was to keep it that way. Between the Muslim Ummah, with its Sharîʿah, and the absolute monarch, with his bureaucracy (such as it was), stood a jealous and massive new nobility, closely tied to the monarch and his family, but not his creatures. Much later, in the central areas, this conception degenerated into a system of deriving all armed force from miscellaneous tribal levies, called on at need; but under the Mongols and for some time after, the great nomad army was the heart of the nomad society itself.

The royal household itself, of course, and the military specialists were both automatically ranged in the military system as Mongols or Turks. The fiscal administration, the chancellery, was commonly composed of non-Turks, in the central areas called 'Tâjîks', using Persian. They were not men of the sword, but yet they were enrolled as an auxiliary part of the army (in the terminology of one empire, they were *ʿaskerî*, army men, but not *sayfî*, sword men). And sometimes even the Sharʿî officials, qâḍîs and imâms, could be ʿaskerî, honorary members of the army, rather than the 'herds' (*riʿâyah*)—and so be exempt from taxes, as being on the receiving end rather than the paying end. But their status, in this respect, was not too different from that of the poets and the painters that likewise were incorporated by their royal patrons into the military establishment, given honorary grants, and exalted above the subject mass.

Finally, in the realm of government as a whole, both these policies reinforced the tendency for an active central political authority to intervene in and dominate the decentralized and depoliticized international network of Islamicate institutions, at least within the area controlled by the dynasty. One expression of this intervention was the habit of deliberate resettlement of populations according to plans for economic development: both city artisans and peasant households would be moved according to master plans, not always in punishment of rebellion, but out of need to develop unpeopled areas. Such activity was considerable under the Mongols and their imitators; one even hears of building a new city not intended to be a capital but merely a trade centre. Later, on occasion, population management became very systematic. The dynastic patronage of the arts and science was in the same spirit. (It must be added that the 'patronage state' did not necessarily increase the total amount of patronage of high culture by the wealthy, but provided a somewhat different framework in which it was distributed.)

The effect on overall land tenure was not negligible. The system of iqṭâ' land grants was modified in the light of Mongol notions of privileged lordship, centring landholding more explicitly on court service and patronage. The cumulative complex of ancient gentry tenure, Islamic Sharî'ah, and military grants had at first been thrown into disarray by the Mongols; and when landholding was straightened out, some of all these elements persisted, but with the addition of provisions from the Yasa. In many areas, the net thrust of the arrangement probably was to reduce independent peasant responsibility in assigned lands still further, and hence peasant effort; but at this distance we cannot really be sure of that. The Mongol pattern of land assignment eventually established likewise a more courtly control of the waqf endowments from which the 'ulamâ' lived—an approach which seems sometimes to have tied the 'ulamâ' more closely to the ruling powers, and to have reinforced the tendency of Ṣûfîs to voice the popular opposition, even sometimes on points of Shar'î strictness against the complaisant 'ulamâ' themselves.

The form of government was dramatized in the military camp itself. Properly speaking, such a state had no capital city: the 'capital' was the army, wherever it happened to be camped at the moment. The monarch was monarch because he was commander-in-chief, and he was expected not to act by deputy; unlike the first caliphs, who might or might not accompany one of the several expeditions they sent out, the Mongol ruler did not send out others but went himself; in principle, all forces were concentrated in one army and so in one expedition. Indeed, the whole state apparatus was organized as a single massive army—from which, of course, detachments might be sent out, but which was always in principle a single body of men camped around the tent of the monarch. To a considerable degree, the files of the state offices could be carried along, as well as its treasure, on any major campaign—that is, on any campaign where the sovereign commanded in person. In any case, all the responsible chiefs of state bureaus were expected to be along with their sovereign. Mongol experience had developed ways of organizing so massive an affair with such expedition that despite its seeming cumbersomeness, this army-state could move with (for the time) extreme rapidity. Travellers were regularly astonished at the efficiency with which what amounted to a major city (for the 'camp followers' of such an administrative centre amounted to that) could be kept in order and mobilized.

As the state became settled, the government was allowed to establish itself increasingly in a conventional city; but the principle of the army-state was clung to even in the sixteenth century when the whole system came to fruition (and began to evolve still further into something else). For though, at the time, the system brought more splendour than stability into Islamicate government, eventually it led to fundamental political renovation.

It is possible to interpret the sequence of forms of government in Islamdom as expressing a series of 'racial' ways, or, more properly, a series of structural possibilities associated with different ruling elements: at the beginning, when Arabs ruled, government was by an egalitarian privileged people en bloc; then as Persian ways emerged, government was by a neutral absolute monarch, before whom the greatest and least were to be mere subjects; but finally, with Turkic conquest, government was by a privileged military family, along with a privileged people as almost an extension of that family through its patronage. But the nuances of a continuous political development will be better understood if we see the evolution less in terms of differing ruling peoples and more in terms of the total development of society in the mid-Arid Zone; and in this way, also, we will be better prepared to understand the great variety with which the elements that we have just been summarizing abstractly actually appeared in different states and in different periods.

Whatever the role of steppe custom and Mongol grandeur in developing the tradition of the military patronage state, the tendencies that I have summed up under that phrase can also be seen as a natural outcome of the militarization already proceeding within Islamdom. After the failure, in the Earlier Middle Period, to push on to some sort of militia autonomy in the cities, the preference of the a'yân for the amîrs' garrisons might have been expected to lead to steadily greater interference in social and cultural affairs by the military, abetted, to be sure, by their own homogeneity as Turks, once a pattern of garrison control and military landed tenure was fully established. The actual rule or the high prestige of the Mongols, in all those central lands where the decentralization and militarization of power was most pronounced, served to provide a mould in which the military ascendancy could take form and be made relatively stable. It was surely in spite of the ancient connection between nomads and traders, and the result of essentially agrarian pressures expressed in military form, if (as it does often seem) the mercantile classes in these later periods had a decreasing prominence in the high culture, which moved away from the market place and perhaps even from the mosque, to focus more frankly on the court (with its love of preciousness) and, complementarily, on the khâniqâh.[2]

The Mongol states (1258–1370)

Three major Mongol realms were established in Muslim territory. The descendants of Hülegü ruled in the Tigris-Euphrates valley and throughout most of the Iranian mountains and plateaus, being also overlords of the Seljuks of Anatolia and then, for a moment, of such lesser states as that of the Ottomans on the frontier by Constantinople (but leaving Syria to the Mamlûk rulers of Egypt). They were titled the Îl-khâns, as representatives—till they became Muslims—of the supreme Mongol khân in China; their capital was Marâghah in Azerbaijan. A second Mongol formation, hostile both to the supreme khân in China and to the other Mongol dynasties that accepted his overlordship, was the Chaghatay Mongol power in the Syr and Oxus basins, the Yedisu steppes northeast thereof, and the Kâbul mountains, which also came to control the Panjâb. The third Mongol state was what came to be called the Golden Horde (originally the 'Blue Horde'), centred in the Volga basin but extending its sway much further westward; it long held in obedience the Christian princes of the Russias. A fourth durable Mongol state west of Mongolia, the 'White Horde' in the Irtysh basin, eventually, like the other three, was won to Islam; the primary Mongol empire, however, ruling all the east from Mongolia and China, played little direct part in Muslim history.

Everywhere the Mongol rulers could be interested in reviving the economy where it had been ruined, but nowhere more than in the domains of the Îl-khâns. Hülegü chose sound administrators once his territories were subjected, restoring the system in use before. As governor of Baghdad and the whole lower Mesopotamian plain—the point of greatest devastation in his own campaigns, which otherwise had tended to be a triumphal march among eager vassals—he appointed (1259) a Muslim scholar, 'Aṭâ-Malik Juvaynî, of an old administrative family of Khurâsân, whose father had already served under the Mongol governors, and who had himself been trained in the fiscal dîwân. He had a long canal dug along the Euphrates and established a hundred and fifty villages on its banks; and generally devoted his efforts to restoring agriculture in his provinces, hoping to make them more prosperous even than before. He patronized other men of letters, and himself (having twice visited Mongolia) wrote a very effective Persian history of the Mongol conquests. Meanwhile, 'Aṭâ-Malik's brother rose to be chief minister of the whole Îl-khânate (1262) and was able to place his sons in several governor-

[2] In speaking of a 'military patronage state', I have made use of ideas of Martin Dixon (oral communication); in contrast to myself, he knows the material well. But I have freely adapted those ideas to the requirements of a general history of the civilization as I have seen them. I hope I have not fallen into too many errors.

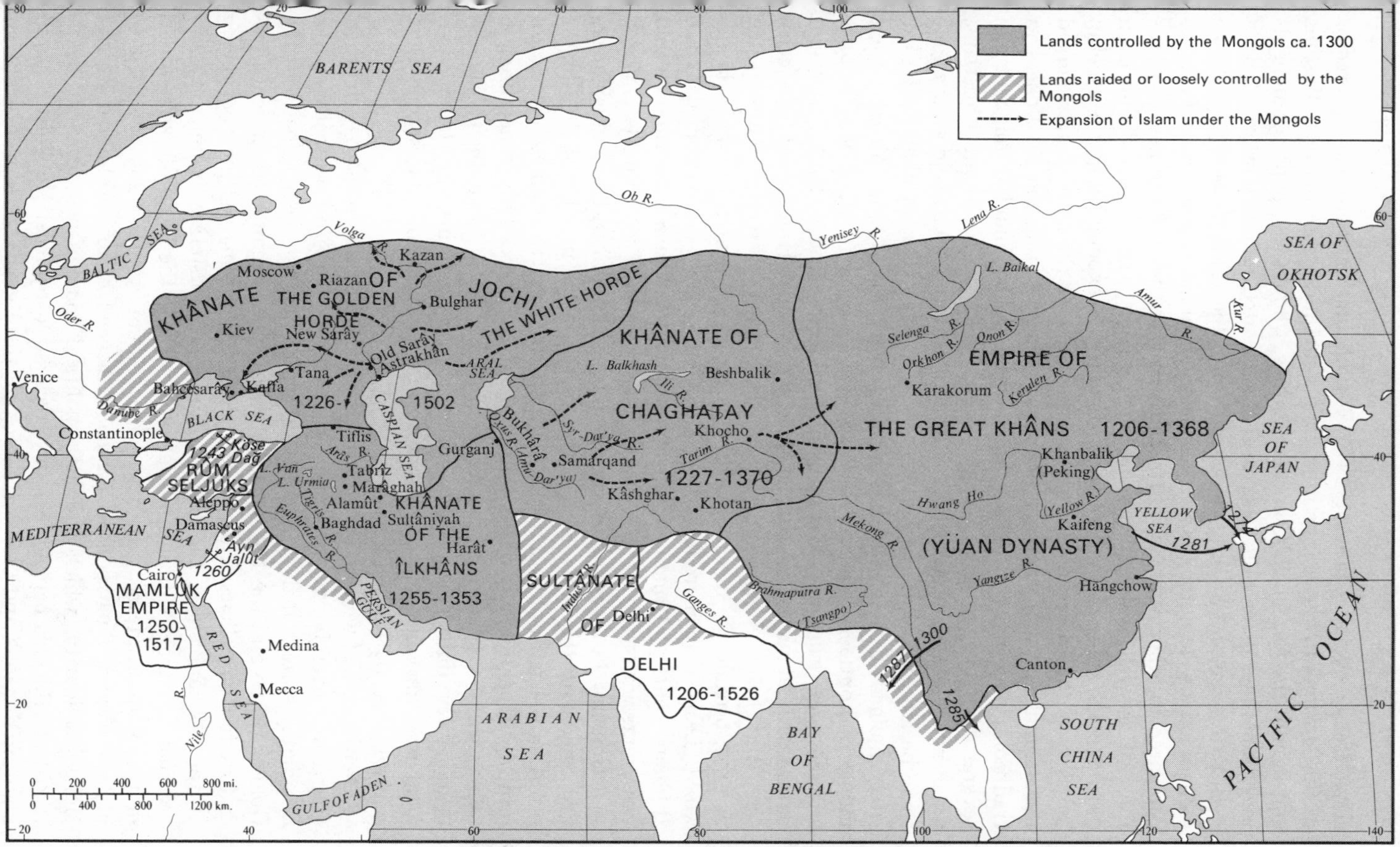

The Mongol Powers in Hülegü's time, 1255–65

ships. He had the same interests as 'Aṭâ-Malik, and was known as a protector of the Muslims in the competition that sometimes arose between Muslims and men of the former dhimmî communities, who under the pagan Mongols were sometimes given preference over the defeated ruling group.

In patronage of letters, likewise, several of the Îl-khâns were active. The Mongol lords were notorious for their heavy drinking and quarrelling even as compared to other military courts, but many of them had serious concerns too. All the religious traditions of their realms were tolerated and even patronized to a degree. Buddhism, particularly as expounded by the Tibetan lamas, was the most popular among the Mongols themselves (they mixed their Buddhism with 'shamanistic' pagan practices from the old Mongolian tradition), and many Buddhist monks were to be found throughout the several Mongol domains. Some Mongols became Nestorian Christians, adopting an allegiance still common then in central Eurasia; and after a time some became Sunnî or Shî'î Muslims also, though without abandoning the rites enjoined in the Yasa that were contrary to the Sharî'ah. But their intellectual outlook could be as broad as the horizons of their vast empire, and (between drinking bouts) many Mongols were curious about history and nature without regard to religious allegiance. Under Hülegü and his successors, Marâghah in Azerbaijan, where a well-equipped observatory was opened in 1259, became the most important astronomical centre, probably, in the world. Learnèd men from all over the hemisphere were welcomed at the Îl-khâns' court and there the Muslim scholars exchanged information and viewpoints with them, with consequences (as we shall see) in fields as varied as astronomy, history, and mysticism. Chinese administrators and engineers had come with the Mongols from the start, and the prestige of the Chinese tradition was naturally especially high; at one point, the Chinese practice of printing paper money, which the Mongols had successfully generalized in China, was introduced in Iran, but proved a total fiasco there. Chinese fashions were imitated especially in the arts, for the Chinese aesthetic refinement was unrivalled. On the other hand, specifically Islamic studies were naturally less patronized for a time.

The three chief western Mongol states rapidly became rivals to each other, quarrelling over border territories in the upper Oxus region (between the Chaghatay state and the Îl-khâns) and in the Caucasus region (between the Golden Horde and the Îl-khâns). Very early they began conducting contradictory foreign policies. Thus while Muslim Egypt remained the chief enemy of the Îl-khânî state, the Golden Horde was fostering commercial and political exchanges with it, and was unfriendly to the Latin Christian forces in the Mediterranean, with whom the Îl-khân Abaḳa (1265–82) tried to make alliances. Such policies hastened the end of any feeling of general Mongol solidarity, which had little political consequence after the death (1294) of Hülegü's nephew Ḳubilay, recognized by most Mongols as grand khân in Mongolia and China. (In 1305 all the Mongol states were still con-

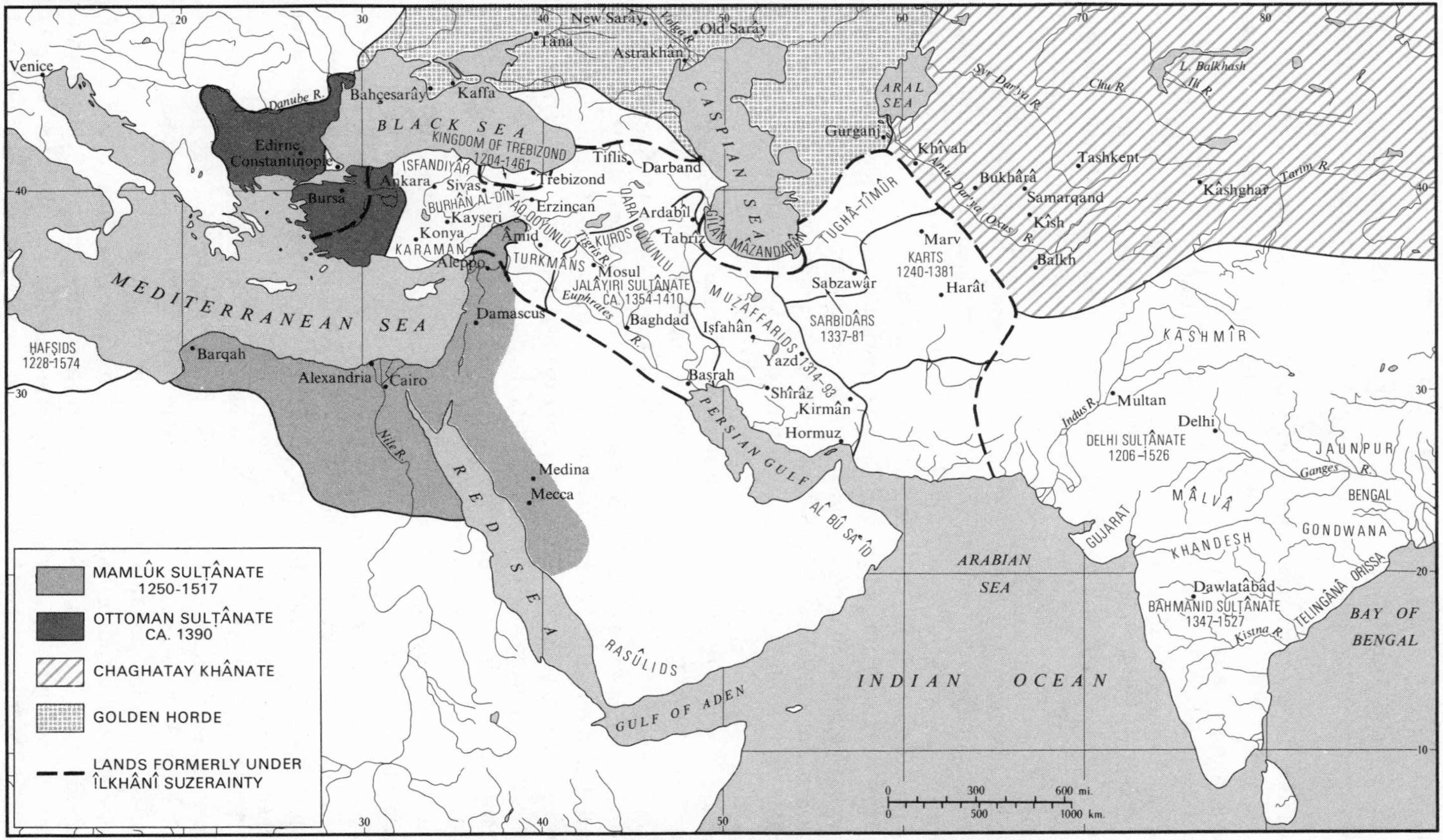

The central Mediterranean through India, fourteenth century

sulting together, but nothing more.) The pressure increased for each state to work out its own political basis, building on the interests and the high culture of its own region.

Since the majority of the more privileged and cultivated classes in each state were Muslim, in each state a growing number among the Mongols turned to Islam as the religion of civilization, and those who had become Muslim tended to form a faction within their respective states. Since the ascendancy of the Muslim faction would mean that the state would be committed to a regionally-oriented policy in solidarity with the local Muslim populations more readily than to any policy that still looked to an all-Mongol sentiment, the point of religious allegiance had potentially major political consequences.

The first state to accept an Islamic orientation was the Golden Horde. The settled population of the Volga valley, in close commercial relations with Khwârazm by the Aral Sea, had become increasingly Muslim in the later years of the High Caliphate. The ruling element of the Khazar state, with its capital at the mouth of the Volga, had become Jewish from the seventh century (perhaps this—as in the Yemen before Muḥammad's time—ensured a neutral independence amidst pressures from the competing religious allegiances in the older centres on either hand). But the people of the capital were largely Muslims and Christians; and after the power of the Khazar state was broken in the 960s under Russian assault, the tribal formations that controlled the area were often favourable to Islam. Meanwhile, farther north up the Volga, the Turkic Bulghârs around what is now Ḳazan had become Muslim in the early 900s—asserting their independence of the Khazars by establishing, direct relation with the caliphal state. By the time of the Mongol conquests, as trade and settlement in the northern areas had increased (typically, in the 900s the Bulghârs could boast a single city, largely of tents; by the 1100s there were several cities built in stone), the Bulghârs were the dominant power throughout the middle and lower Volga basin, though lately they had been on the defensive against the Russians to the west. An active centre of Islamization, the Bulghârs had made some efforts to convert the Russians at Kiev. They had a small literature of their own in Turkic. (Ḳazan was so far north that unanticipated ritual problems arose on the short summer nights, especially as they allowed scant recuperation from the daytime fast of Ramaḍân when it fell in summer.)

The Mongols destroyed the Bulghâr state (and its cities) and, by setting up their main centre nearer the mouth of the Volga, restored the primacy of the lower Volga over the more agrarian north. But the Muslim population persisted and by 1290 the ruler was a Muslim (despite the efforts of Christian missionaries, including some from the Occident). The Muslim population, already Turkic, seems to have identified itself rather soon with the Golden Horde. But the Christian Slavic population farther west, held in tributary relations by the Golden Horde, was further alienated from the main body of the empire by a religious difference, which was to be embittered over the centuries.[3]

The Îl-khânî state next turned to Islam, but only after internal struggles between the Buddhist and Muslim factions. The chief minister, Juvaynî, was executed after he had identified himself with a Muslim Mongol who reigned briefly in 1282–84—though Juvaynî's ruin had been earlier prepared by rival Persian Muslim officials. His successor, a Jewish physician, attempted to eliminate Muslim influence from government; but he too was at last executed, as were the majority of the viziers of the Îl-khâns. (Only Mongols themselves were exempt in their persons from the monarch's suspicious caprice.) On the vizier's death, the Muslims in several cities indulged in a wave of plundering and massacring of Jews. In 1295 a Buddhist, Ghazan, took the throne and forthwith turned Muslim, seeing value in an Islamic policy for the state. He insisted that the Mongol nobles turn Muslim too, and eventually the more old-fashioned Mongols were silenced and the Buddhist monks were largely driven from the realm. At Tabrîz, the capital, not only Buddhist temples but churches and synagogues were torn down. However, the war against Muslim Egypt was continued; by 1300 Damascus was occupied, with much destruction, but in 1303 the Mongols were disastrously defeated in Syria.

Ghazan now patronized specifically Islamic learning, but also retained the old breadth of vision. He had a personal interest in several arts and crafts and in the natural sciences and Mongol history and knew at least something of several languages (besides his own Mongol and presumably Turkic are mentioned Persian, Arabic, Chinese, Tibetan, Kashmiri, and even Latin). The Îl-khânî court received embassies from most parts of the Oikoumene, and itself sent embassies into India and China and as far as England in Europe; lands like Tibet loomed larger in its consciousness, but it was well informed even about the Occident (the pope found it appropriate to send a bishop for the Latins settled at Tabrîz). Ghazan's vizier, whose efforts at sound administration he firmly supported, was a physician and scholar, Rashîduddîn Fażlullâh, whose excellent historical works especially we shall be mentioning later. Rashîduddîn also used his numerous sons as governors of provinces. Along with cutting new water conduits or digging new canals and settling villages along them, providing gifts for men of religion, and arranging military expeditions to Trebizond or Kâbul, he concerned himself especially with providing exotic drugs from India and elsewhere for hospitals. A town for scholars which he built near Tabrîz was provided not only with a great library and arrangements for tradesmen and the like, but with fifty physicians, some of whom were brought from Egypt and India and China (he

[3] Some writers, using the term 'Russia' as a geographical term for all territories eventually settled by Russians, have been misled into writing as if all that they call 'Russia' were somehow naturally Russian, and as if the Muslims were alien intruders throughout, even on the Volga itself, an assumption that can lead to misapprehensions of the implications of the conversion of the Mongol Horde to Islam.

had some of his Persian works translated not only into Arabic but also into Chinese). In the end, Rashîduddîn at seventy was executed (1318), along with a son sixteen years old, on a flimsy charge by a later ruler; his scholarly town, with the many copies of his comprehensive works deposited there, was given over to plunder.

In the Chaghatay state, the Mongols in the more southwestern areas, especially the Oxus basin, tended to become Muslim while those quartered in the more northeastern areas, in the Yedisu steppes (south of Lake Balkhash) and the Tien Shan mountains—where Islam had not yet been well established—resisted Islam jealously as incompatible with being true Mongols. Only in 1326 did a Muslim successfully become khân, and even he was killed within a decade (1334) by rebels from the Yedisu steppes. Soon thereafter, the Chaghatay state broke up; the Syr-Oxus basin remained Muslim, but the khâns of the eastern parts became Muslims only much later.

About this time, all three states began to disintegrate. (The Mongols began to lose their hold now in China also, being expelled by 1368.) Succession to the throne in the Mongol states was by election, from among the ruling family, by the heads of the great families in the presence of a general assembly (the *kuriltay*), which ensured irrevocable publicity. But the basic nomadic principle was always clung to, that a man's domains should be divided equally among his sons (the youngest received the home grounds, but on an equal basis). On this principle, the grand khân, even if recognized by all the others, could not count on their obedience in their independent lands. In the Mongol states that endured, it became clear that the state was not to be divided; but the sense of equal rights among all sons presumably contributed to modifying the election-in-assembly eventually into a pattern of succession by armed contest, in that the ruler was that candidate supported by the strongest faction. When the outcome of the contest was indecisive, a practical division of the realm could result. In any case, authority at the centre became weaker.

Though the Chaghatay khânate was a prey to fighting factions, and so was the Golden Horde especially after 1357, in both steppe states, where the settled population was largely Turkic, Chingizid Mongols retained some sort of authority through the century. In the Îl-khânî state, they disappeared more rapidly. Abû-Sa'îd's reign (1317–35) was troubled by intestine quarrels; like most of the hard-drinking Mongol rulers—indeed, like many of the rulers of those ages—he died young (at about thirty), and after his death a single Îl-khân could no longer be agreed upon and to every claimant another faction proposed a rival. By 1353 the last of these puppet claimants was set aside, and the former Îl-khânî domains had been divided among disparate independent dynasties.

Even at the height of the Îl-khânate, it had proved convenient to allow numerous non-Mongol amîrs to continue to garrison the greater part of the territory, so long as they were submissive in the sense of paying tribute and allowing disputes among them to be settled by the Mongols. Thus the Kurt dynasty, centred in Harât, controlled much of Khurâsân, and the Muẓaffarid dynasty of Shîrâz ruled several provinces of western Iran. Quarrelling members of these families sometimes held out in different towns, fighting one another. The Jalâyirs, a tribe itself linked to the Mongol tradition, attempted longest, after Abû-Sa'îd's reign, to maintain one or another Mongol candidate as Îl-khân; but later in the fourteenth century its chiefs ruled directly in the Iraq and sometimes the Jazîrah and Azerbaijan; they tried to displace the Muẓaffarids, with whom they found themselves on a level. Other minor dynasties played lesser roles. Such powers did not recognize each other's true legitimacy and found their highest calling in recurrent warfare designed to retain old or enforce new submissions.

For the most part, power was held by purely military amîrs. But in some places, the a'yân notables effectively took sides, and in at least one case it was less well-established elements in the town that seized power. At Sabzavâr in western Khurâsân, when Mongol central power became weak, some local Shî'îs of a Ṣûfî cast (called 'Sarbadârs') had formed something like a republic (1337), without benefit of Turkic garrison and dedicated to eliminating oppression. The Sarbadârs—a term meaning 'vowed to the gallows'—were anathema to the Jamâ'î-Sunnî scholars who chronicled the times, and we hear chiefly of the violences they indulged in; for they changed leaders frequently, often by violent coups. (These republican chiefs, mostly not related to each other, have ironically been denominated a dynasty by writers unable to think in other than dynastic terms.) But they enjoyed wide support within their districts, and seem to have become stronger with the years; they captured several towns and around 1370 they were able to persuade Nîshâpûr itself to join them (but soon the Kurts of Herat seized it back). The Kurts failed to defeat them otherwise, however, and Timur, the conqueror from Samarqand, was glad to undertake their extermination (*c.* 1831)—along with that of the other amîrs.

The Mamlûks of Egypt

The one power in the central Muslim area that had resisted the Mongol wave was the government of Egypt. Precisely at the time of Hülegü's advent, the Ayyûbid family of Saladin, which had established a Sunnî Syro-Egyptian state to replace the Fâṭimî one, was excluded from the throne by its military slaves (*mamlûks*), who allowed one of their own number to take the leadership (1250). (The first independent sovereign of the new series was a woman, mother of the last Ayyûbid heir.)

The prestige of the seemingly masterless Mamlûks was established when they managed to defeat the unvanquished Mongols at 'Ayn Jâlût south of Damascus in 1260, expelling them from Syria. The sultan Baybars (1260–77), who came to the throne soon after by way of assassination, organized the state with vigour as a military resource. His defensive arrangements (including rapid message service) at the various garrisons were admired for their efficiency. He quickly eliminated the Ayyûbid principalities that had remained in Syria, centralizing the state of Saladin and his successors, loyal to family ties, had never done. In a campaign of six years, he eliminated most of the Crusader possessions along the coast, and then subjected the Ismâʿîlîs of Syria, who had retained their independence when the other Ismâʿîlîs had been subdued by Hülegü. From his Syro-Egyptian base he sent troops up the Nile into Nubia, down the Red Sea coasts, west to Cyrenaica, into Cilicia against the surviving Armenian state there, and even took the offensive against the Mongols and their Anatolian Seljuḳ vassals to the north. He and most of the other Mamlûk soldiery were Turks, largely from the Ḳîpchaḳ region north of the Black and Caspian seas, that is from the area of the Golden Horde; and he took pains to recruit a large new supply of slaves from the same region for his own personal army. On this force he relied in the first instance; but for a broader legitimation of his rule he set up at Cairo a member of the ʿAbbâsid house, escaped from the destruction of Baghdad, as a latter-day caliph, whose servant he pretended to be. (The fainéant successors of this puppet caliph won occasional titular recognition from a few other Muslim states as well, usually states that were not in close relations with the Mamlûks.)

Baybars did not found a dynasty but rather established an oligarchic régime, in which other sultans followed the pattern he had set. The great amîrs among these freedmen soldiers each proceeded to build his power on the basis of his own corps of imported military slaves. The freeborn sons of Mamlûks were systematically excluded from service in the primary military bodies, though they might do some secondary military service, so that each generation of soldiery was imported afresh from the north and trained in loyalty to his own amîr and his fellow soldier-slaves in that amîr's corps. Except from 1299 to 1382, when hereditary rule, of sorts, was maintained, the state was ruled by a succession of freed slaves; as a general principle, each ruler was succeeded provisionally by his son until the various corps of Mamlûks, jockeying for position, settled (normally by fighting) whose leader should be sultan next (and depose the provisionally titled boy). Even during the period of hereditary sultans, during the latter part of which the sultans were mere boy puppets in the hands of some amîr, and still more under the freedman sultans, the great Mamlûk amîrs formed an exclusive oligarchy. No sultan dared defy them too far, even when he was furthering his concerns for the interests of the state as a whole—interests that were often given consideration by the sultan alone.

Within the limits that their peers would allow them, some of the sultans proved energetic rulers. They carefully fostered trade: among the Occidentals (or 'Franks'), the Venetians were favoured at the expense of the Genoese and Pisans, who had profited from the Crusader position in the Syrian ports; and trade north and south, with the Black Sea and with the Indian Ocean, was protected by political arrangements. Under the sultan Ḳalâwûn (1280–90) and in the year after his death, the remaining Crusader ports were taken—but in fear of Occidental naval superiority, Syrian trade was channelled to only a few strong ports, the rest being razed. The Christian Armenian state in Cilicia was eliminated. The Muslim pressure for dynastic regularity bore fruit in the successful but undistinguished reign of al-Nâṣir Muḥammad (1299–1340), son of Ḳalâwûn, who had to abdicate in 1309 to shake off entrenched control by two amîrs and then return to power in a surprise overturn in 1310, to re-establish his personal rule. But after 1382, when Mamlûks of Circassian rather than Turkic origin came to power (called *Burjî* Mamlûks in contradistinction to the earlier *Baḥrî* Mamlûks), no further hereditary tendencies were tolerated.

In Mamlûk times, Egypt, and Cairo in particular, became the heart of the zone of Islamicate culture that continued to use Arabic with little reference to Persianate culture, and Egyptian men of letters played a greater role in Islamdom than heretofore. Despite a marked decrease in agricultural prosperity in the later Mamlûk period, it was a splendid age for Cairo. Mamlûk power and taste have been eternalized in the mosques of Cairo, most of which date from their rule; instead of the cheaper materials previously more often used, they chose to build in stone, and their architects developed a strong sense of the beauty of well-arranged massive form—at one period, even the beloved arabesques were scarcely allowed to interfere with the monumentality of the lines. They delighted in chivalric forms—in heraldic symbols of personal prowess, in expertise at horsemanship, in the proprieties of their incessant intestine fights. As often with chivalry, this was at the expense of the civilians of Cairo, despised and permanently excluded from power.

In the end it cost the Mamlûks themselves their prized sovereign power: despising the use of firearms (an infantry weapon at the time) as unworthy of a true horseman, they left them to despised Negro slave corps and would not allow the sultans to put many resources into them; at last they were overwhelmed (1517) by the field artillery of the Ottomans from Anatolia. Egypt then passed under Ottoman rule, but the bodies of Mamlûks were long allowed to continue as a sort of subordinate local military aristocracy.

The Delhi sultanate: expansion throughout India

The Delhi sultanate, which the ghâzî warriors from the Afghân mountains had established on beyond the Panjâb in the Ganges valley at the start of the thirteenth century, succeeded in holding off the Mongol assaults and in reward was strengthened in its Islamicate culture with the advent of numerous learnèd men fleeing the pagan Mongols. Like the Mamlûk sultanate at Cairo, the Delhi sultantate grew out of the tradition of slave soldiery; like it, it was tremendously conscious of the Mongol presence, but it had no background of pastoralist institutions and did not share directly in the new government attitudes introduced by the Mongols. As in the first conquest of the Ganges plain, so now too, it was the effective way in which Muslims, in their period of mobile decentralization, complemented an increasingly caste-bound Hindu society that made it possible for them to become, in effect, the ruling caste, very open and cosmopolitan, in the whole region. (We shall discuss further what happened, in Chapter IV, 'The Expansion of Islam'.)

As a field of Muslim adventure as well as a refuge from Mongol rule, it rapidly gained a vigorous corps not only of Muslim military men but of all the kinds of cultural specialists that came with them. Muslim merchants, of course, carrying goods to which people from Iran and the Oxus basin were accustomed, found special favour. Ṣûfîs of a venturesome turn who came to India could receive a revered position as spiritual supports of Islam in a community eager to welcome anyone from more thoroughly Muslim lands; two of them became founders of the two chief Ṣûfî ṭarîqahs of India (Suhravardîs and Chishtîs). Persian poetry was much appreciated, and poets from Iran itself would find an appreciative audience and receive special honours.

By the end of the thirteenth century, Islam was solidly, if thinly, established throughout the Ganges basin; even so far east as Bengal, where an independent Muslim sultanate found no significant Hindu opposition even when it was in direct conflict with the power at Delhi. In the mountains on all sides, the Hindu ruling caste of the previous several centuries, subsequently called Râjpûts, found families able to hold on to local strongholds and to regain a wider independence when Muslim power was at all weak. But the plains, where agricultural production was richest, for the most part acknowledged Muslim supremacy; no local ruling caste was left strong enough to challenge this.

Meanwhile, the original character of the sultanate, as the political expression of a small Turkic military oligarchy, had been changing. A great appeal of the Muslim local communities, on whose growth and support Muslim rule had finally to be based, was the open social opportunities they offered. The Turkic oligarchy, with its narrow favouring of Turks, had limited these opportunities in the sphere of government. This was possibly appropriate to hold the loyalties of newly arrived ghâzî warriors, but not to maintain the Muslim power once it had reached a certain extent and permanence. But the third of the great sultans of Delhi, Balban (ruled *c.* 1249–87, though the reign began officially only in 1266), had insisted effectively on checking the Turkic nobles and on ruling as a monarch. It may have eased his task, that he insisted bigotedly on excluding any but a proper Turk from any position of honour (he himself, like the first two sultans, started life as a Turkic slave). But with the centring of power in the sultan, the exclusiveness of the aristocracy lost, in fact, its basis. Moreover, after the Mongols became established to the north, fresh Turkic slaves were no longer sold in India. Balban's incompetent descendants, who succeeded him, wasted but a few years in discrediting themselves and any pure Turkic policy with them.

The new potentialities of the sultanate were put into relief within a few years of Balban's death. Despite continuing Mongol pressure in the north-west, the sultanate proceeded to expand into the rest of India. It was chiefly under two energetic and eccentric rulers that this was done. 'Alâuddîn Khilijî, himself not a Turk in Balban's sense, began raiding, as provincial amîr, southward into Mâlvâ and even across the Vindhya mountains into the Deccan even before he seized the throne (by treachery). During his reign (1296–1316) much of the more mountainous territory south of the Ganges plain was subjected to Delhi, and his lieutenant carried out a long raid (1307–11) as far south as Madura in Tamilnad at the southern end of the peninsula, exacting spoils and promises of annual tribute from most of the Indic rulers. 'Alâuddîn played well the great monarch: he regulated severely the life of his chief officers, who were scarcely allowed even to drink wine (though otherwise 'Alâuddîn paid little heed to the 'ulamâ'), and who lived in steady fear of the spies which any strong military ruler necessarily placed in his officers' households, but which 'Alâuddîn, an old conspirator, knew the special value of. More important, he also regulated ruthlessly the market at the capital, setting tight limits on the price of food sold to his soldiers.

But the real conquest of the south was carried out by Muḥammad Tughluq (1325–51).[4] Even during a series of brief and licentious or chaotic reigns, the policy of aggression in the south was pursued sporadically. When Muḥammad Tughluq's father, popular with the army, came to the throne, the policy could become more systematic. As deputy for his father already, Muḥammad consolidated Muslim authority in parts of the Deccan (while his father himself subjected eastern Bengal). During Muḥammad's own reign, he concentrated on subduing the whole Deccan and even much of the southern part of the peninsula to direct Muslim rule or at least to severe restraint upon those rulers who were left as tributaries. After a grand triumphal Muslim march through the south about 1330, the greater part of the Indic lands had to acknowledge Muslim authority. Muḥammad Tughluq was as severely monarchic as 'Alâuddîn Khilijî, but he was less successful in his attempts at control at home. He was so devoted to Deccan affairs that he tried, early in his reign, to move his capital south into the Deccan, to Dêogiri in Mahârâsh-trâ. When the chief figures in Delhi were slow to move, despite the elaborate arrangements made to make the move easy, he tried compulsion, ordering all the population of Delhi (presumably all those of any important status—

[4] Historians (taking their cue from the eulogistic Muslim annals) used to write as if the south of India were Muslim domains already under 'Alâuddîn Khiljî and to treat later expeditions as mere repression of rebellions. But (however much agrarianate military rule sometimes may look like the operations of the modern city racketeer who exacts protection money from his 'subjects') we must distinguish between raids in which forced tribute agreements are made—the breaking of which merely risks another raid—and real conquests in which a permanent administration is arranged, some steady legitimation of power arrangements emerges, and hence the term 'rebellion' applies, inasmuch as the act upsets the existing power structure and calls for new arrangements.

dependent persons would have to follow) to move within a set time. Those who stayed behind were so penalized that Delhi was partly ruined, while the new capital was so disliked that he soon had to abandon it. In Muḥammad's later years he was at continuous odds with his officers and faced a series of revolts that he could not suppress; but the work of establishing Muslim power in the south had been done.

Muslim Delhi in the time of these conquests abounded with unusual personalities, who contributed much to the élan of the Muslim community. They were merely the most striking figures among the Muslim cadres that were attracted from abroad or recruited locally. Many Muslims seem to have been willing to try almost anything once: 'Alâuddîn's humane predecessor, perhaps rather whimsically, had rounded up the members of a Hindu hereditary sect that considered it necessary to kill (and rob) travellers as part of their religious cult, and shipped them down the Ganges towards Bengal rather than spilling their blood. The most extraordinary of these unusual personalities was that of Muḥammad Tughluq himself.

As a general, Muḥammad seems always to have been successful (save in an abortive scheme to conquer the Iranian highlands and so establish his fame in the lands of old Islam). It was administrative excesses that finally won him the hostility of many of his officers, of the religious classes, and of other notables. These resulted from a brilliant but not very accommodating mind. Like 'Alâuddîn, he was much concerned with controlling the prices of his soldiers' provisions, and faced, even more than did 'Alâuddîn, a flood of specie plundered from the south, which tended to raise prices. He responded with an imaginative and integrated programme of strict regulations, ranging from rigorous taxation in the Dôâb agricultural districts near Delhi to an attempt, after the Chinese fashion favoured by some Mongol rulers, to institute a token currency. Unfortunately, his taxation rates proved ruinous, the peasants fled, and he was reduced to bringing them back by force and setting up a tardy programme of agricultural aid (loans for seed, digging new wells, relief for new cultivation, etc.); similarly, he failed to provide adequate guarantees against counterfeiting, and had to redeem a proliferating token currency at great loss to the treasury.

Personally well-read in philosophy and even science, Muḥammad Tughluq took great interest in religious questions. It has been suggested that he was acquainted with the radical ideas of his contemporary, the Ḥanbalî Ibn-Taymiyyah of Damascus, who rejected Ṣûfî mysticism and called for a civically-minded reform among the 'ulamâ' scholars. An interest in the tradition of Falsafah might have led to the same general conclusions from a different standpoint. Muḥammad did attack the Ṣûfîs. Then he went to great trouble to assure himself a Shar'î legitimacy by getting himself invested by the 'Abbâsid shadow-caliph whom the Mamlûk rulers maintained at Cairo; but, demanding the support of the 'ulamâ' only on his own terms, he succeeded in alienating them also.

The most prominent of the Ṣûfîs of Delhi in the time of 'Alâuddîn and Muḥammad was Niẓâmuddîn Awliyâ (d. 1324), who ruled the Chishtî ṭarîqah order throughout India. We have already met, in our discussion of ṭarîqah Ṣûfism, his indefatigable care for the spiritual life of individuals of all classes who consulted him, both Hindu and Muslim. Though he would not allow his personal murîd disciples to make their living as dependents of the court—not even as qâḍîs, who were required by strong sultans to decide according to the government interest—he became spiritual adviser to many court figures. His disciple Naṣîruddîn Chirâgh-e Dihlî took over his work and his leadership among the Chishtî Ṣûfîs; a celibate who seems to have spent the nights in prayer and weeping, he was always accessible to anyone's needs.

The most prominent of Niẓâmuddîn's disciples in the court was the great poet, Amîr Khusraw (1253–1324). (Though he was not a military man, his father was a Turkic immigrant and the poet seems to have been given an honorary position in the military hierarchy.) Amîr Khusraw's Persian poetry was respected even in the Iranian highlands, where the majority of Indian poets writing in Persian have always received scant notice. But he loved his Indian homeland and celebrated things Indian in defiance of Iranian conventions. It is said to have been Niẓâmuddîn Awliyâ who suggested that he write poetry in Hindî—in the local language of the Delhi area. It is for his lyric poetry that he is known. But he was expected to be the panegyrist of the court, and among other things wrote a poetic history of a great compaign for 'Alâuddîn in the Deccan, probably a supplement to the official prose history that was also composed. His verses were correctly laudatory at all points, exulting smugly in the deaths either of (pagan) Mongols or of Hindus, and praising *ad nauseam* the slaughter and the booty that the army succeeded in making. But withal an independent spirit, as elsewhere in his poetry, makes itself felt. He pointedly exalts the value of effective rule as compared to mere conquest, and hence touches, though briefly, on 'Alâuddîn's administrative measures before launching on the tale of the expedition; and it has been suggested that some of his exaggeration and conscious artificiality may have had the intention, and not merely the actual result (which it has), of depreciating the accomplishments he describes.[5]

Beginning about 1334, within years of Muḥammad Tughluq's greatest conquests, rebellions among the Muslims (and only secondarily among the Hindus) broke up the unity of the Indian Muslim power, which had covered territories far too vast to be controlled centrally with the administrative methods open to Muslim amîrs at the time. The army's choice as Muḥammad Tughluq's successor, his cousin Fîrôz (1351–88), while maintaining in form the policies of Muḥammad (to whom he was devoted), made a point of reconciling everyone possible. (However, he did behead a man who claimed

[5] Professor Muḥammad Ḥabîb has effectively translated and commented on Amîr Khusraw's *Khazâ'in al-futûḥ*, on the Khiljî campaigns (Madras, 1931).

to be the Mahdî.) He allowed Muslim rulers in the outlying areas to go their own ways, retaining under direct rule from Delhi only the Indus and Ganges plains west of Bengal. He too was sufficiently eccentric; and among other gadgetries, he is credited with inventing a new sort of clockwork. Like some other Muslim rulers in India, he was especially fond of capturing and training wild elephants. After his death, the Delhi sultanate was little more than one Muslim power among many in India, especially after Delhi was sacked (1398) by Timur, the conqueror from Samarqand.

The early Ottoman state in Europe

The Muslim advance into Europe was rather slower than that into India, but by the thirteenth century a solid foothold had been gained in one of the major Hellenic areas, Anatolia: both in the form of Turkic pastoralists and frontier raiders, and in the form of the cultivated Seljuḳ state at Ḳonya. The advent of the Mongols probably added to the available numbers of uprooted tribesmen who became ghâzîs, but did not necessarily speed the process up much. Once the original Muslim-Christian frontier was breached, the social relations among Byzantine peasants, bureaucracy, and army were similar everywhere; there was a second pause in the early fourteenth century while the Muslims who had reached the seacoasts made of the Aegean itself a piratical frontier to replace the inland frontier that had been gradually chewed away. Then when the Aegean was crossed, the movement went faster than ever.

After the Mongol conquests, some efforts were made to restore the Seljuḳ power in Anatolia, but direct Mongol rule was increasingly imposed there as elsewhere. However, Mongol rule in the centre of the peninsula tended to leave the ghâzîs on the frontier toward the western coasts free of interference in their own amîrates, under vague Mongol overlordship. In the last decades of the thirteenth century, the amîrates wrested town after town from the Christians of the remnant Byzantine empire (restored since 1269 to Constantinople). With the breakup of Mongol power in Abû-Sa'îd's time, all Anatolia was divided among small independent amîrates, of which the strongest was that of the Ḳaramanlîs, who inherited Ḳonya.

When most of the frontier ghâzî states had reached the sea, and with it an end to booty save what could be won by piracy, one of the tiniest, in Bithynia, the hill country southeast of the Thracian Straits, was left facing the centre of the restored but greatly reduced Byzantine empire itself (the empire now possessed on the Anatolian side little more than the area nearest Constantinople). This ghâzî state was ruled by the Osmanlî family, a name commonly anglicized as *Ottoman*.

The Byzantine empire which it faced still had substantial holdings on the Balkan side of the straits, however, and vigorously resisted onslaughts so near its capital. Hence any Muslim volunteers who wished for a fight would be sure to find it at the tiny Ottoman amîrate. Attracting resources beyond its size—and also blessed with good leadership—before long the Ottoman amîrate had won the beautiful town of Bursa (1326), which became their first real capital. At the same time, they became strong enough to offer essential support to rival factions at Byzantium. It was as auxiliaries in a factional dispute that they first crossed the straits and occupied Byzantine territory on that side (1353); by 1372 they had seized the greater part of it, reducing the Byzantine emperor to a dependent ally. After 1366, Adrianople (Edirne) on the Balkan side, where the new frontier lay, was as much a capital as the older Bursa.

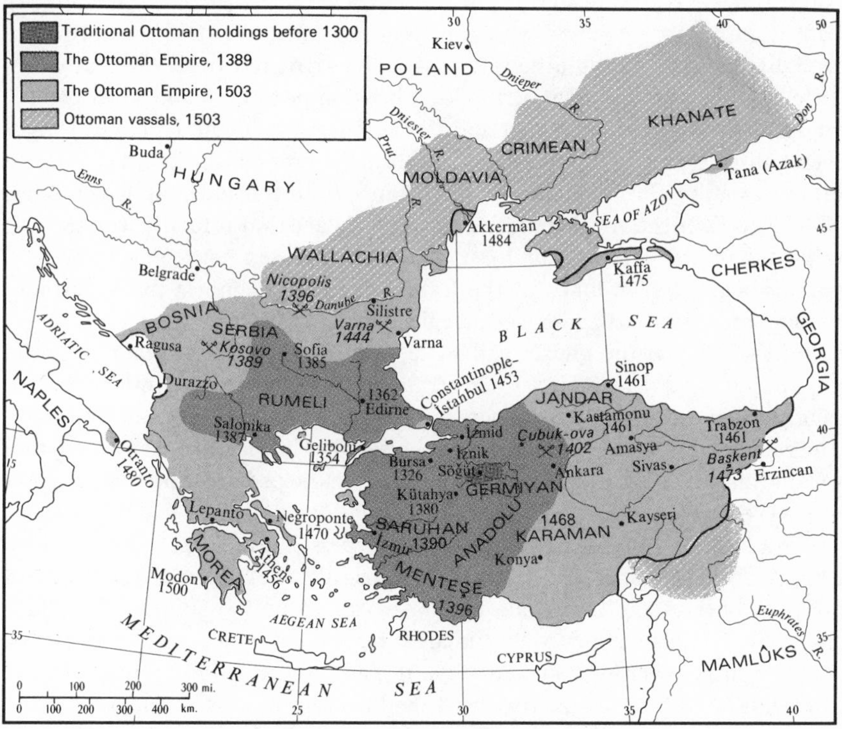

Growth of the Ottoman empire to 1503

The Ottoman state was much under Greek cultural influence—partly by way of Greek converts among its chiefs. At the same time, it was militantly Islamic. The pastoralists tended to be prejudiced against Christian villagers while they were more tolerant of Muslim ones (a point that may have hastened the conversion of some villagers to escape hostile attention); and the wandering darvîshes that pastoralists and ghâzîs alike revered commonly encouraged imposing Islam on the conquered by force (in contrast to the more urbane tradition of many city Ṣûfîs). But the Islamic atmosphere (and a certain commercial activity in lands immediately around Constantinople) attracted a steady influx of cadres of more formal Islamicate culture, bearing the prestige of the lands of old Islam; and notably of 'ulamâ'. These gradually weaned the state away both from Greek ways and also from the converting zeal of the ghâzîs (for the Christians were, after all, dhimmîs, to be protected in their religion); their presence tended, on both counts, to consecrate a gap between established Ottoman classes in the towns and the Greek Christian peasantry.

This gap was maintained specially in the Balkan lands. There, the collapse of Byzantine power had left a large number of petty rulers—Greek and Slavic as well as Latin—uncontrolled even by the larger kingdoms. But despite the end of the central bureaucracy, discontent with the Christian ruling classes had, if anything, increased with time. By now many of the privileged were actually Latins and the others tended to be attracted to Occidental ways, forfeiting the respect of the Orthodox Christian peasantry and townspeople, who resented both the religion and the competition of the favoured Italian merchants. Discontent with the established order was expressed, among other ways, in a Christian monastic resistance to the official church hierarchy, which was so effectively supported by the populace that it finally won the day (and did revitalize the church). Perhaps partly as a consequence of such popular attitudes, in much of the Balkan area the conquest moved rapidly by way of major battles between armies, and there was no time to establish a frontier. Hence the ghâzîs had little occasion to be in contact with the population, and the state administrators could ensure continuity in the village communities; and the aloof policy of the 'ulamâ' proved quite feasible. Thus the weakness of Christian political resistance in the Balkans as compared to Anatolia (as well as a new religious vitality) helped the Christian religion to survive more solidly in the Balkans.

Murâd (1360–89) seems to have been personally gifted and to have attracted good leaders to his cause. Under his rule, the Ottomans relied less on ghâzî volunteers and more on a regular cavalry (*sipâhîs*) supported by land assignments; this cavalry was primarily regularized ghâzî troops, who now turned gentry when not on campaign, it was supplemented by unconverted Christian cavalry taken over without modification from the conquered territory or sent on demand by Christian rulers who had submitted. The Ottomans also recruited a trained infantry force from converted captives and other adventurers, called the 'new troops', *yeñi cheri*—Anglicized 'Janissaries'. The main posts at court were more or less hereditary in old families, the leader- of the original ghâzîs, and policy tended to be formed by consultation among these chiefs. The Ottoman state enjoyed a tradition of firm military discipline, which proved a material help on campaigns: at least in Muslim territory (in Anatolia), the troops were not allowed to pillage but had to pay a fair price for supplies, with the result that the population readily brought an abundance to market. Towns under Ottoman control seem to have been allowed much internal autonomy: Ankara, held from 1354, was ruled by its wealthier merchants, organized in an *akhi* (or futuwwah) form. Clearly, despite the Mongol overlordship of the earliest Ottomans, the structure of the state formed a marked contrast to the tendencies of the military patronage state, being founded in ghâzî traditions rather than steppe traditions. Yet even in this period, the Ottoman rulers undertook occasional transportation of populations, even Muslim populations, when such were required in newly conquered territory to provide Muslim cadres.

By 1372, the Ottomans held northwestern Anatolia and Thrace (except Constantinople itself); they were acknowledged the most powerful of the western Anatolian Muslim states; and Murâd had formed marriage relations with the Byzantine and the Bulgar rulers. From this point on, Constantinople with its scattered Aegean dependencies was increasingly in subjection to the Ottomans, who (from 1390) could freely settle succession disputes there and require contingents of Byzantine troops on their campaigns—even on a campaign to reduce a free Byzantine city. At Rome, some attempt had been made to preach a new Crusade, this time against the Ottomans, but such Occidental knights as had arrived had been repudiated by the Byzantines—though not consistently. In 1386, some of the younger generation of Ottoman and Byzantine nobility alike made common cause, under the joint leadership of a son of Murâd and a son of the emperor in a rebellion supported by the Ottomans' chief Muslim rival state, the Ḳaramanlîs at Ḳonya; on its defeat, Murâd had his own son killed and insisted that the Greek nobles kill thier own rebel sons likewise.

From 1372 on, Murâd had been sending expeditions throughout the main part of the Balkan peninsula, reducing the independent principalities and attacking also the Bulgar and the Serbian kingdoms. The latter had become the most important power in the peninsula (having contributed, along with the Bulgars, to reduce Byzantine power). Now the Ottomans, in effect, replaced the Byzantines as a revived Thracian power, and with their Anatolian hinterland in support were able to turn back the Serbs. This warfare had its vicissitudes, but by 1389 the Ottomans, gathering their full forces, were able to defeat the Serbian army assisted by Albanian, Bulgarian, Bosnian, and even Hungarian allies, at Kossovo Field in central Serbia. In this battle, Murâd was assassinated by a dissimulating Serb, but the Serbian king was captured and executed in revenge; the Ottomans were stimulated, the Serbs disconcerted, by their respective losses; and Serbian independence was effectively ended. Now the Ottomans had effectively occupied the bulk of the peninsula south of the Danube; from this point on began a long struggle with the Hungarians north of the Danube (not conquered till 1526).

Unlike the Orthodox Serbs, the Hungarians were a Latin, an Occidental, power and counted on their solidarity with the rest of western Europe. By 1396 the Crusade was again being preached and large numbers of French and German troops went off to Hungary. The French knights, however, refused a common tactical command under the Hungarian king. The combined army set siege to Nicopolis on the lower Danube. When Murâd's son Bâyezîd marched to its relief, the French were filled with Christian and chivalric zeal. They massacred their Muslim prisoners and claimed the first place in the battle, despite the pleas of the Hungarian king; their indiscipline led them into disastrous disarray, which was reflected back into the rest of the Occidental army; after their victory, the Ottomans sent detachments in pursuit as far as the German highlands. In retaliation for the French murder of Muslim prisoners, Bâyezîd ordered the mass of Christian prisoners to be killed, and thousands were, till in weariness the massacre was stayed.

Meanwhile, the Ottomans had been interested in increasing their power in Anatolia also—from where the Muslim cadres essential to their new empire were mostly recruited. Murâd had found himself in a position to exact (in the form of gifts or of a 'sale') large portions of the amîrates' lands, especially after defeating the Ḳaramanlîs, who alone attempted resistance. Under Bâyezîd Yîldîrîm (1389–1403), expansion in Anatolia was pushed eagerly. Bâyezîd had considerable abilities, though he was perhaps overly headstrong; the group of ghâzî leaders, 'ulamâ', and other chiefs that were attracted to the Ottoman cause continued to work together successfully under him. Soon the Ottomans had absorbed the whole of Anatolia, including the proud Ḳaramanlî principality in the south, deposing the local amîrs. But this process engendered considerable discontent too, and the whole empire was put in question when Timur, the conqueror from Samarqand, overwhelmed it in a single campaign (1402).

The career of Timur

The prestige of the Mongol tradition was renovated, in Islamdom, by two great generals, the greater of whom, Timur, imposed some sort of obedience even on Delhi and Cairo, where the original Mongols had been defied. The lesser of them was Ghiyâs̄uddîn Toḳtamîsh, leader (from 1376) of the White Horde in the Irtysh basin, which (having already adopted Islam) in the decade before his advent had begun interfering in affairs further south, and was presumably benefiting by the steady expansion of the Oikoumenic area of commerce. Toḳtamîsh led the bulk of the White Horde army to the Volga, merging it with the distracted Golden Horde, of which he thus took the leadership (1378; eliminating all rivals by 1380). Then he reasserted the power of the reunited Mongols (by now essentially Turks) over the Russian Christians westward, sacking Moscow, which had been gaining importance, in 1382. At first he had been given support by Timur, but the two quarrelled; Toḳtamîsh invaded Timur's territories north of the Oxus more than once till finally, in 1395, Timur succeeded in launching a full-scale invasion of the Ḳîpchaḳ lands of the Golden Horde, deposing Toḳtamîsh in favour of his own local candidate, but not undoing his work.

Timur (1336–1405—properly the name is *Temür*) was himself no Mongol, but a Turk; though he may have had some Mongol and even Chingizid connections at least in a maternal line. Limping as the result of a wound from an early skirmish, he was called Timur Lang, the Lame (whence the English form 'Tamerlane'); but he seems to have had a tenacious personal prowess;

Early Growth of the Ottoman Empire, 1300–1453

1290	Osman (1290–1326), Ghazi chieftain, raids Byzantine territories and conquers Kara Sie valley south of Nicaea (Iznik)
1299–1308	Osman takes Yenishehir near Bursa, establishing himself as local amîr and serious threat to Byzantium; he captures Ak Hisar and reaches the Bosporus
1326	Osmanlîs capture Bursa and establish their first capital there
1329	Orkhan (1326–59) occupies Iznik and Nicomedia (Izmit) and extends control to Scutari near Constantinople
1354	In return for aid to Byzantine Emperor Cantacuzenos Ottomans cross the Bosporus into Europe and occupy Gallipoli
1358	Thrace occupied
1361	Murâd I (1359–89) captures Angora (Ankara) and Adrianople (Edirne) which becomes the new capital
1366–72	Ottomans enter Bulgaria and Macedonia
1385–89	Sofia and Nish captured; combined Serbian, Bulgarian, Albanian forces defeated at battle of Kossovo
1390–99	Bâyezîd I (1389–1403) seizes amirates of Menteshe and Aydin, advances to the Danube, subdues amirates of Rostomon, Samsun, and Sivas
1402	Timur defeats Bâyezîd at Angora with aid of deserting Turkish vassals; most of Anatolia devastated; amirates re-emerge
1403–13	Civil war among Bâyezîd's sons over succession
1413–21	Meḥmed I defeats rivals and restores empire to its status under Bâyezîd
1416	Turkish fleet defeated by Venetians at Gallipoli
1425–30	Murâd II (1421–51) victorious in war of Venice, enters Morea, captures Salonika
1444	After making peace with crusaders Murâd abdicates but then returns to throne and defeats Christian armies when they break through and attack Ottomans at Varna
1453	Meḥmed 'The Conqueror' (1451–81) captures Constantinople and subdues the Byzantine empire after seven-week siege employing over 100,000 troops, naval units, and artillery

and certainly he aroused an ardent loyalty in his troops. Born a Muslim in the Syr valley, he began as a captain serving the pagan Mongols in the Yedisu steppes, but rapidly attracted his superiors' and even his enemies' attention and rose, amid the contending camps of the time, to be adviser to the Muslim Chaghatayid heir apparent at Samarqand. Allying himself with another amîr, he rebelled against the Chaghatayid and defeated him; then quarrelled with, betrayed, and killed his ally, and emerged at Balkh in 1370 as lone ruler of the greater part of the old Chaghatay dominions. He then confirmed his power in that realm with the subjugation, after years of fighting, of Khwârazm in 1380.

The career of Timur presents in exaggerated form ways of acting and of reacting that were prevailing throughout the period, if usually in less spectacular form. We may use it as a magnifying lens through which to look at one aspect of Islamicate life. Neither his respect for Islam and his communalistic and bigoted way of envisaging it, nor his freedom from inhibitions, either moral or superstitious, that a respect for Islam might seem to have imposed, were unusual; and his thirst for grandiose personal achievement and his desire for bloodshed were atypical only in the scale on which he satisfied them. He has been more amply and repeatedly praised, or invoked in praise of others, than any other Muslim ruler so recent as himself; this is partly because he and his descendants were the wealthiest patrons over so large an area so long, but also because he stirred so many imaginations. His career is revealing not only for his own decisions and initiatives but also because it was a catalyst, releasing impulses and hopes in others of his time.

Though he overthrew the Mongol ruler, Timur was devoted to the Mongol idea. He set up a Mongol of another line as titular ruler, under whom he was supposedly merely a general, an amîr, or (later) sultan; and he claimed Mongol descent for himself by one of those dubious genealogies that panegyrists so readily discover. The idea of universal Mongol supremacy (now that real Mongol tribal solidarity over against the Turks at large had lost its importance) was more than ever a purely military idea; but where no other political ideas existed, then with a general who could ensure military success, such a ground for power could snowball indefinitely—success breeds success. At any rate, as soon as he was thoroughly established in the old Chaghatay realm, he set about a general conquest of the lands formerly ruled by Mongols, chiefly the former Îl-khânî realm. In his campaigns he revived the Mongol tradition of *Schrecklichkeit*, with massive massacres, and the claim that the Mongol power, which he represented, was alone entitled to supreme rule.

However, two other elements were mingled with the more purely Mongol idea. He had an insistent allegiance to Islam. This was sometimes (at least for public purposes) a matter of folk precautions of a petty magical type. On this level, his Islam was not incompatible with various old Turkic and Mongol practices popular among the soldiery, such as mounting a hill to pray; and in the guise of darvîsh Ṣûfism, he respected ways of thinking derived from the shaman tradition. But his Islam was more far-reaching (I think), for it was bound up in his mind with a code of justice on which he prided himself, and which he believed the 'ulamâ' ought to represent—even though he seems sometimes to have felt he understood its principles better than they themselves. He was pleased to suppose that his coming stood for divine vengeance

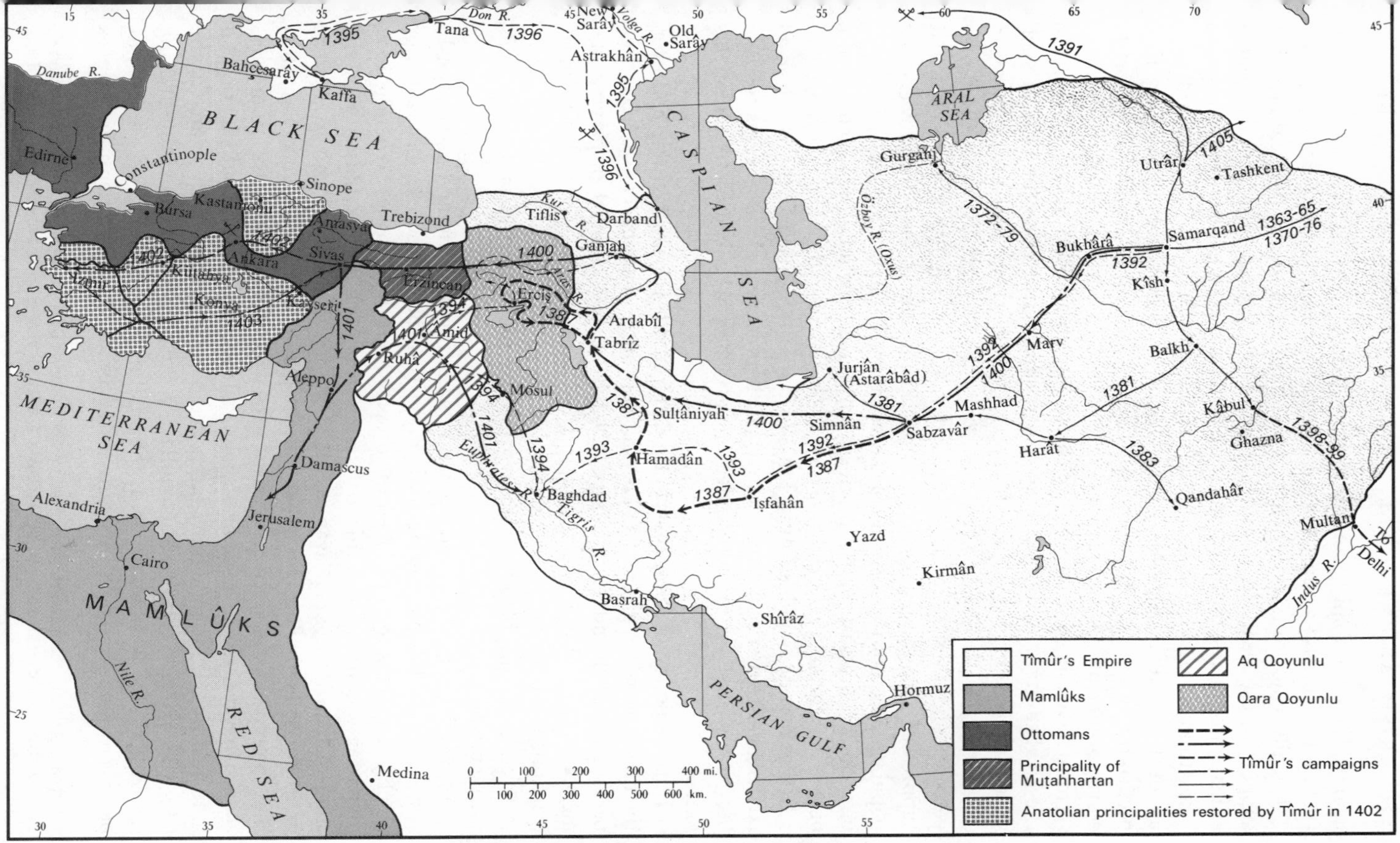

The conquests of Tîmûr, 1370–1405

against the compromises and injustices of the self-styled Muslim amîrs and (in practice chiefly) against the complicity of those who obeyed them.

His allegiance to Islam, then, was one basis for a second political idea: the support of the wealthier bourgeoisie and merchants against local disorder—either that of irresponsible amîrs or that of riotous commons. He took special pains to make trade secure and was quite successful in this by way of drastic use of the usual methods—imposing local responsibility for any banditry that occurred in a given district, and the like. He was pitiless against any sort of corruption or unfair trade practices. The local well-to-do and a'yân notables seem to have longed for a return of the strong Mongol central power to replace the local military despotisms which had supervened since the time of such viziers as Rashîduddîn. Though they were not happy at Timur's policy of savagery, the well-to-do classes were largely spared by it in their own persons; and they evidently preferred it to the popular tumults which it suppressed (sometimes by simply massacring almost the entire lower-class population except the servants of the wealthy). Timur was especially ferocious in opposing any sort of anti-privilege movement, including Shî'î movements of an egalitarian tinge (he included such hostility in a general hatred of religious heresy as judged by a Jamâ'î standard). Consequently, he received fairly consistent support from the upper bourgeoisie. He also seems to have been supported by many wandering darvîshes, who helped to spread his fame.[6]

But the policy of Mongol-style total terror was the most visible and even the most consistent element in his political course. Timur seems to have been personally cruel and bloodthirsty, though he also enjoyed displaying clemency, and could use moderation, in treating the submissive, as a systematic instrument of diplomacy, a foil to his terror. On occasion, the well-to-do suffered from his bloodthirstiness quite as much as the rabble. But his savagery was never random.

As in all his military and economic undertakings, Timur was rigorously systematic in his plundering and massacres—in addition to his taste for cruelty, he seems to have loved the orderly (and the colossal). When he took a city, it was normally subjected to a ransom set by negotiation with the chief men in it; the city was sealed off to prevent escapes and to prevent unauthorized entry of soldiers who might pillage on their own account; then the amount was exacted systematically, with account keepers, from merchants and others, with torture being used regularly to elicit information on hidden stores. If, as sometimes happened, no ransom had been arranged, the city was pillaged yet more completely, the inhabitants sometimes being removed till the work was done. If the inhabitants were not killed, they might be taken prisoner: choice artisans would be distributed among the princes

[6] Jean Aubin, 'Comment Tamerlan prenait les villes', *Studia Islamica*, 19 (1963), 83–122, brings out the sources of Timur's social support, and I have made use of his study also for other aspects of the career.

and the ladies of the royal family for use in their projects. (The conquered were prisoners by old Mongol law, whether Muslim or no.)

If, however, anything went wrong—whether by popular action or the misstep of some amîr—then his response was massacre: the 'general killing', with the avowed object of leaving none, or at least no adult males, alive in the city. But even a 'general killing' had its rigorously enforced rules. He usually excepted those of the wealthy (or the learnèd) who won his approval, and such others as found refuge within their establishments.

Beginning in 1383, the normal emblem of his massacres was the tower of heads. This form of insult had been used in Iran on occasion, especially against defeated pagan tribes, since at least 1340 (and as far back as about 1140 against Ismâ'îlîs). Now Timur used it regularly—in the first instance, to dishonour the enemy slain on the field (this included pastoral tribes that resisted him), but then also to memorialize massacres carried out systematically in cold blood.

But Timur's delight in bloodshed and misery took many forms. All warfare is unscrupulous, and warfare in Islamdom in the Middle Periods tended to be unusually unrestrained and destructive; but his campaigns were noted for wanton brutality even then. Rape was commonplace when soldiers first took a place; then when beautiful young women were led away as slaves, they were forced to leave any suckling babies behind—and many babies are said to have died in consequence. Timur varied more routine methods of executing his enemies by throwing them over precipices or burning them alive. His delight in suffering was not restricted to human beings: he was proud of a hunt where so many animals had been slaughtered that most of the carcasses were not even gathered up for food but were left to rot. (Such a situation was not unparalleled in the royal hunting of the time, for the custom was to make a vast circle around an area where animals ranged, and gradually close in on them till they were crowded together in panic; and no beasts in the area so ringed in were allowed to escape alive.) Some further misery was perhaps unavoidable in the wake of the enormous armies Timur collected: often prisoners starved to death, when the soldiers themselves had difficulty foraging to support their numbers; and of course the peasants in the neighbourhood of his greater campaigns suffered famine. Toward the end of his life, Timur's courtiers tried to moderate his cruelties, but in vain.

When the destruction seemed to be sufficient, Timur sent special task forces to rebuild a city and to restore agriculture; often on new plans oriented to the needs of commerce as he saw it, or to the convenience of nomadic pastoralists in the area, and always with special regard to the fisc. On such occasions he could have new canals dug, with villages established on their banks. To Samarqand especially, which was his capital even though he rarely spent much time there, he gathered artisans and artists from all the provinces that he sacked. and there he caused to be erected magnificent buildings and a resplendent court.

Timur's campaigns had decisive effects politically in the greater part of Islamdom, except for the farther west and the south. So soon as he was solidly established in the Syr-and-Oxus basin, he proceeded to the conquest of Khurâsân. There (1381) he subdued the Kurt amîr of Herat; at first he allowed him the precarious autonomy his ancestors had had under the Îl-khâns, but three years later, when he revolted, the city was sacked and the Kurt dynasty brought to an end there. He subdued a number of independent garrisons in Khurâsân one by one (including the Sarbadârs). Timur was roused to special ferocity on his campaign in Sîstân. The towns of Sîstân, isolated in the middle of Iran by deserts, had a long tradition of independence from outsiders and also (ever since the Ṣaffârid times) of relatively popular government, supported by militia action. These traditions made themselves visible in the form of vigorous resistance to Timur by the ordinary people, which Timur resented both as an affront to himself and probably also as improper in a mere rabble. At one town there, he varied the idea of towers of severed heads by having his towers formed of two thousand live men bound and built up with brick and mortar; presumably, for a time, such a tower would give off sound as well as light. The main city of Sîstân was massacred (with no distinction of sex) and all the country systematically devastated; even the wealthier people, though spared, were led off into exile in Khurâsân. One gets the impression that the present relative desolateness of once-prosperous Sîstân, which must depend on irrigation, dates from that time.

By 1387, almost all the Iranian highlands had submitted, including the old ruling houses of the Caspian coast in Mâzandarân, and the Muẓaffarid rulers in Shîrâz and the western Iranian provinces, as well as Aḥmad Jalâyir, heir to the Jalâyir power in the Mesopotamian plains. He allowed most of these rulers to retain their posts at first, as he had the Kurts; but he had left behind reminders of his wrath; notably a massacre of Iṣfahân, where the common people had spontaneously begun resisting his troops after the ransom had been arranged for: each company of soldiers was required to produce a set number of adult male heads, and when the towers were completed, the head-count was approximately 70,000. A few years later, Timur had to return to these parts and eliminate the main dynasties altogether. (On that occasion, the merchants at Baghdad urged him against the amîr of Takrît, who had interfered with commerce; then, as not infrequently, he was aided by bands of Iranian volunteers.) Meanwhile, he was occupied for a number of years chiefly in campaigns northward, both against the Mongols of the Yedisu steppes, whom he defeated without subduing, and against Toḳtamîsh, much the strongest of his rivals. These compaigns culminated in 1395 with the defeat of Toḳtamîsh and the Golden Horde and the destruction of its chief cities; Timur carried his devastations as far as Moscow. A favourite target of Timur, whenever he was in the vicinity of it, was the Christian kingdom of Georgia in the Caucasus; he and his soldiers loved to plunder and murder there.

In 1398 Timur set out for India, on the grounds that the Muslim rulers there, the successors of Fîrôz Tughluq, were too tolerant of their Hindu subjects and were interfering with trade. Before the decisive battle, the soldiers were ordered to massacre tens of thousands of captives, partly so as to save supplies (refusal to kill one's captives, which formed a major part of one's booty, subjected one to the death penalty); and to the extent that many of the captives were Hindus, the slaughter became an occasion for destroying infidels, which caught up some pious Muslims into a supererogatory murderous zeal as they participated in the work: one revered man of religion, so gentle that he had not even slaughtered the ritual sheep for the 'îd festivals, fervently killed ten (others say fifteen) Hindu captives with his own hand. Delhi itself, when occupied, was to have been spared, but this time the soldiers themselves got out of control and wrecked and massacred the city. The ruin of Delhi, the capital, consummated the collapse of any hope for strong central Muslim rule even in northern India.

To the west, Timur's incursions were politically less disastrous in the end, though not at first. The Anatolian amîrs displaced by the Ottoman Bâyezîd fled to Timur for help. In 1400, he attacked both the Ottoman and the Mamlûk territories on the ground that they were harbouring his enemies (despite murmurs that the Ottomans were, after all, fighting the Frankish infidels). At Sîvas he caused the Christian regiments among the captured Ottoman troops (4,000 of them) to be buried alive, but spared the Muslims. At Damascus the notables did not succeed in raising the agreed ransom, so the city was sacked despite its surrender. After several diversions (including a 'general killing' at Baghdad), Timur was back in 1402; this time he met the main Ottoman army under Bâyezîd at Ankara and smashed it, taking Bâyezîd prisoner. Bâyezîd had to witness the pillage of Bursa, seat of his ancestors, and of Izmir (Smyrna), which Timur now took from the Latin knights who had seized it, a remnant of the Crusader age. The Byzantine emperor, with whom Timur had formed a precautionary alliance before the campaign, sent in his eager submission, and so did the awe-struck Mamlûks; but Timur did not bother actually to go to Egypt. The Anatolian amîrates were given back their independence, and for a time the rest of the Ottoman state seemed destined to be divided up and disappear.

In 1404, after another brief sojourn in Samarqand (beheading shopkeepers who charged too much, overseeing the construction of vast formal gardens, amiably receiving an embassy from Christian Spain), Timur launched a campaign against China with the announced aim of punishing the Chinese for expelling their Mongol rulers (two of his wives were Chinese, and he may actually have intended to push the campaign that far). On the way, he pardoned the exiled Toḳtamîsh. But some days afterward he died (1405). Despite the hopes of the bourgeoisie who had accepted his violences for the sake of a strong central power, he had already begun to parcel out the provinces of his realm to his sons and grandsons. Neither his designee nor any other one successor proved able to maintain the central power intact, though after some years of warfare a relatively peaceful son of his, Shâhrukh, to whom he had assigned Khurâsân, was able to assert control over the greater part of his domains in the Syr-Oxus basin and Iran.

II

Conservation and Courtliness in the Intellectual Traditions, *c.* 1258–1503

In all periods, people have continued to prize originality. The Egyptian scholar al-Suyûṭî (1445–1505) prided himself on how many subjects he had treated which no one before him had dealt with. The Timurid ruler Shâhrukh (1405–47) invited dignitaries to witness the trial run of a newly invented military engine. Yet neither scholar nor inventor had ventured beyond a circumscribed realm of expected types. Al-Suyûṭî dealt with obscurer details of Muslim law or history by methods which had already been applied to more significant questions. I do not know whether Shâhrukh's inventor had produced a more powerful torque machine or an improved gun, but it was for hurling stones. One can readily conclude that fresh excellence was looked for simply in more subtle or more elaborate versions of what had been found excellent before. Even in what passed for inventions, we may perceive (if we look at that side of them) the conservative spirit at work.

Nevertheless, even without full consciousness of the implications of the changes, new forces were at work which were reshaping Islamicate life. Among the military inventions Muslim monarchs were patronizing by the end of Shâhrukh's reign were, in fact, improved guns; and gunpowder carried its own pressures for continuing innovation. The period was largely one of elaboration of the intellectual tradition, often in the spirit of al-Suyûṭî's encyclopedic details; but even in the guise of such elaboration, many scholars were actually doing important new work, even when they were less pretentious about it than al-Suyûṭî and claimed merely to be filling in details. Possibly conscious conservation of past achievements was, in any case, especially characteristic of the madrasahs and of the circles associated with the old decentralized and Sharîʿah-oriented culture. At the increasingly powerful military courts, by the end of the period, scholars and artists, patronized by rulers who, by Mongol tradition, were themselves artists and scholars, were producing a heady new cultural ferment. It was at these courts that the world-wide outlook of the age—visible in receptivity to Chinese art, to Indic piety, even to Occidental gadgetry—had freest play.

Education as conservation

At the core of any cultural tradition, not least in a time of conservatism, is its method of educating the young. The bent of this education will express the culture, of course, but at the same time not merely reinforce it but determine, with some autonomy, the forms in which change in the culture can most readily take place.

The great purpose of all forms of Islamicate education was to pass on the cultural heritage from one generation to the next. In an atmosphere of conservatism, this purpose was taken most seriously. It was expected that the later generations would be on a lower level, morally and intellectually, than the former generations: the old man's view that the younger generation was going to the dogs was accepted along with the general supposition that cultural change could at best be of secondary importance, except change for the worse. Experience had generally confirmed this view. The problem, then, was to delay or mitigate the inevitable decline. The second purpose of education, to prepare individual youths for particular social roles, did not contradict the prime purpose. The only way in which men of learnèd professions were expected to serve, whether as physicians or astrologers or 'ulumâ', was by applying the knowledge handed on by their elders and betters. Most students naturally chose to concentrate on those studies that would be most called for in their actual careers; more studied the legal details of fiqh than the more abstract principles of kalâm. Yet within any given field, at any rate, there was little conflict between a practical orientation to getting a given job done and a more humanistic orientation to fostering broad awareness of truth; at least on the more learnèd levels, the two merged into one. As to a possible third purpose of education, to give youths the tools and the outlook to assimilate for themselves their elders' wisdom and then go beyond their elders, such an expectation, as in all pre-Modern societies, was not entertained even by Faylasûfs and Ṣûfîs.

Two consequences followed that have seemed strange to Modern eyes. First, education was commonly conceived as the teaching of fixed and memorizable statements and formulas which could be adequately learned without any process of thinking as such. A statement was either true or false, and the sum of all true statements was knowledge. One might add to the accessible sum of true statements to be found in one's heritage, but one did not expect to throw new light on old true statements, modifying or outdating them. Hence knowledge that mattered, 'ilm, as against the facts of 'common knowledge' which even illiterates picked up as a matter of course, was implicitly conceived as a static and finite sum of statements, even though not all the potentially valuable statements might be actually known to anyone at a given time. Education meant inculcating as many of these statements in as sound a form as possible. But the soundest form was naturally that in which the most knowledgeable authority for the statements had himself uttered them, though they might be restated more conveniently for popular use. Hence not only was knowledge, in principle, a fixed corpus of statements; its authenticity was made to depend on the word of a limited number of great men, whose authority was not to be questioned, at least not by the student.

Such an approach was congenial to the latter-day 'ulamâ', accustomed to reference to the great imâms of fiqh and even if kalâm, and above all to the great historical revelation of Muḥammad and to the verification of its content by way of authoritative ḥadîth reports. It might have been alien to the spirit of the Faylasûfs and Ṣûfîs, even the more derivative ones, who in different ways still insisted that truth could be discovered anew in every generation. Yet so customary and convenient was the approach that even Faylasûfs and Ṣûfîs, however esoteric their doctrine, tended to teach in this way. The influence of this approach made itself felt on the level of major scholarship, in that it became common to write even quite original treatises in the form of commentaries on authoritative earlier treatises. Sometimes the treatises were not simply explanations or amplifications, but more like modern book review articles—even taking the tenor of refutations and counter-refutations.

The prevalence of this approach to learning even among those who might have been expected to be hostile to it becomes more intelligible in the light of the second consequence of the conservative spirit: that education was, above all, normative in purpose. The high-cultural heritage was, above all, a guide to behaviour: it told the honest man what he was on earth for, and especially the leisured man what the good life was for which he was freed from the necessity of labouring like a peasant. Even in the crafts traditions, apprenticeship taught largely what *ought* to be made and how: it was the established standards of excellence that were to be passed on—even though doubtless pettier tricks of survival were passed on too. But norms were felt to be, almost by definition, something to be received from authority tested over generations, not something that each individual could upset according to his whims.

In the madrasahs the admission that certain Philosophical sciences might be legitimate had not carried with it any wide teaching of observational fact for itself. Neither 'ulamâ' nor Faylasûfs thought of the accumulation of observed natural facts as the purpose of a scholar. Information descriptive of how things work generally and of what had happened at certain moments was indeed collected. But it always had a sharply defined purpose. Either it was to subserve the *technical* aims of a particular craft—say leather tanning or seamanship, for which some chemical or geographical knowledge was worked out—or it was to subserve the establishment of broader *norms* for human life as a whole. It was with the latter that the learnèd man was concerned. All the disciplines normally taught in a madrasah were normative: law, grammar, and theology (how one *ought* to believe to be saved) obviously had this character; the descriptive knowledge of ḥadîth reports or of isnâd-transmitters was ancillary to these primary fields of learning. But even music and astronomy and philosophy were essentially normative in their bent; they were devoted primarily to tracing the ideal rules of natural harmony, the way human beings and the whole universe ought to work. They were mathematical or syllogistic to the highest degree possible, and took little account of the vagaries of observable actuality. The motions of the stars, uncorrupted by sublunar materiality, provided an image of cosmic order; the motions of the clouds did not seem to do so and were ignored. (As we have seen, this was equally true of the hierarchically ordered Occident, though the individual fields of study entered differently into public careers.) In such a scheme, study of ethics and law readily took the central place.

The Modern reader, perusing the scholarly works most prized in that time (not only in Islamdom but everywhere), may come away with the feeling that few of them speak to him: few of them make him better acquainted with the world that all men of all times must live in—rather, they are filled with information or disputes important only if you start as a Muslim (or as a Christian or a Hindu). All the works of fiqh and grammar and apologetic kalâm necessarily have such an air; but even the most philosophic works do also. The reader must often grant them extensive premises before the arguments can come to life; for the intention of the writers is above all to establish what is right and proper, what ought to be, not to describe what is.

It may help the Modern reader to consider an analogy from today's education. There is a strong tendency now to just reverse the pre-Modern pattern. We tend to teach only factual, observational subjects, not normative. In the United States, at least, courses in ethics and logic and even law have disappeared from the secular high school and even from the undergraduate college curriculum. Philosophy courses tend to be histories of philosophical thinking. Religion is very nearly banned as controversial. Even grammar has commonly been turned into a descriptive rather than a prescriptive discipline; our standard dictionaries take care simply to record what is actually spoken or written in cultivated circles and rarely dare suggest that a given usage, though less common, is functionally preferable.

Yet this is not because we regard norms as unimportant. We do not really believe that all ways of structuring a language are equally satisfactory: we know that some grammatical constructions allow more flexibility and encourage more precision than others; we know that some semantic complexes —and hence word usages—are less conducive to confusion than others. And so with logic and ethics and philosophy: we know that these offer significant problems for study which the untutored person risks overlooking no matter how carefully he thinks, and which therefore might be presumed to be worth teaching. But we seem to have despaired of formal schooling having any measurable effect in such lines, if we have not simply been frightened out of taking any position where someone else might disagree. Perhaps, to look to a more serious level, our approach is favoured and almost necessitated by the demands for technical specialization and continuous innovation in the Modern Age. In any case, we leave the teaching of norms, in effect, either to be taken for granted in the case of healthy minds; or to be absorbed from general literature, especially fiction; or to be taught by specialists committed to a given line in advance and not quite respectable intellectually, such as preachers. And some teachers will sneak in norms in the guise of teaching facts.

Correspondingly, the pre-Modern emphasis on norms did not imply lack of awareness of the importance of observable facts. But perhaps, considering how limited was the dependable store of available facts and how contradictory, scholars despaired of teaching nature and history with certainty and without controversy. They largely left the crude natural facts, which anyone could observe, to be picked up on their own by healthy minds; or to be absorbed from general works, like histories, which were not the object of special academic instruction; or to be taught, to those who chanced to be in need of them, by specialists, such as tradesmen or sea captains or artificers, of no intellectual claims. And such observational facts as were still essential to determining law or right or the principles of cosmic harmony were duly marshalled by the better teachers.

Education, conceived broadly, was not limited to the madrasahs. Every craft (and agriculture itself) had its process of apprenticeship. In the simpler or more widespread cases (such as agriculture) this was practically to be identified with a son's growing up under his father's tutelage; in the more complex or more specialized cases (such as certain expensive manufactures) the apprenticeship was often formal and lengthy. The apprenticeship pattern was the norm for most sorts of education: the wrestler and the physician, the bookbinder, the painter, and the chemist, alike studied their specialties by apprenticeship. Most public administration, however, was taught not so much by individual apprenticeship but by way of 'training on the job'; and the military life was taught as nearly as possible in the same way, though it was prepared for by military exercises and games among the youth chosen for such a career, who were likely to have tutors in special arts like using the bow. Private tutors were likewise used by wealthy families for teaching the more humanistic graces, where the chief purpose was to instill good taste: calligraphy, painting, Persian poetry, and the like. It was only in a limited range of bookish and especially Sharîʿah-minded religious studies that a public and relatively impersonal institution like a madrasah seemed appropriate.

For it was in the madrasahs that something like a general social discipline, apart from specialized trades or stations in life, was continued into the level of lettered learning. The core of the madrasah studies were those based on 'transmission', and therefore on the use of the Arabic language; that is, the Sharîʿah-minded studies, which were to maintain basic social order. Other studies, equally normative but less essential to everyday social order, were regarded as supplementary (and called variously 'non-Arabic', in that they did not depend on the Arabic language as such, or 'ancient' or 'rational' in that they did not depend on the Islamic revelation.[1] Everyone, from the humblest to the greatest, was expected to have at least some smattering of the central sort of learning taught in the madrasahs. At the least, they should know enough to perform the ṣalât worship, which needed no special schooling. But schooling of that sort was available to a wide sector of the population. Every village of any pretensions had its *maktab*, its Qur'ân school: there as many boys as could be spared from immediate work in the fields—hopefully at least one boy from every family that was not destitute—learned to recite the Qur'ân, or parts of it, by rote in Arabic (whatever his own tongue—and even for boys who spoke an Arabic dialect, the Qur'ân was practially a foreign work); they were taught to recognize and form the letters it was written in; and sometimes they were taught the meaning of its words. In this way, a bright boy could acquire at the maktab the elements of reading and writing and even some idea of the classical Arabic language. The boy who had memorized the whole of the Qur'ân and won the repute of being a *ḥâfiẓ*, a memorizer of it, was likely to have managed to learn a good deal more as well in the process. Such a boy, then, could go on to the nearest madrasah if his family could afford to dispense with his services. The madrasahs were supported by endowments: a boy received sufficient bread daily to keep himself alive and could, if necessary, sleep in the madrasah or in a mosque.

Only in fortunate families could all the boys go to the maktab school, and only in the most fortunate could girls learn the Qur'ân too, but privately at home. Yet even in the Later Middle Period, when the earlier Muslim tolerance of public roles for women had long since receded, women could be prominent teachers of the religious disciplines. The zealous legist Ibn-Taymiyyah studied under a woman, among others, at Damascus.

Even at the madrasah, the heart of the studies was rote learning of standard textbooks, which then a boy would try to understand once he knew the words. Rote learning was appropriate to a conservative society, in which the best to be hoped was to limit the inevitable decline in the next generation. It was especially appropriate also in the most public sector of education, where social discipline of the most general sort was to be perpetuated. For it continued a type of discipline basic to social order generally.

All training in agrarianate-level society, beginning with the home training of the small child, functioned not only to instill necessary skills but to limit the possible range of individual responsiveness, both moral and intellectual responsiveness: a mind too inquisitive and too ingenious, a personality too

[1] The term *'ulûm al-'ajam*, 'non-Arabic studies', has been mistranslated 'foreign' studies, as if foreign to Islam or even to Islamdom. Needless to say, most Muslims were, properly speaking, themselves 'Ajam, non-Arabs; foreignness or alienness is not in question (save in the mind of the Arabist), but only relation to Arabic linguistic skills.

sensitive and too generous could be a danger to a community in which limited resources were protected by rigorous avoidance of the risks of experimentation, and by narrow in-group loyalties. Very intelligent or very saintly persons might indeed have recast the community life so that it would not need such rigidity, but a majority of geniuses and saints was not to be expected and half-baked experimentation could be disastrous. Accordingly, stultification of personality was not just a result of social ignorance but had its utility. Subordination of children to elders not only flattered the pride of the physically stronger and inculcated conformity to approved practice, but functioned to develop those habitual fears which are the greatest enemy of intellectual or moral openness, though this latter function was not conscious. Sexual taboos functioned not only to maintain essential order and privacy in the most intimate and explosive of personal self-assertions, but also to develop those repressed hostilities on which group and inter-group discipline depended. It has been found that in some modern Egyptian villages, the child is systematically discouraged from giving rein to his imagination; such a pattern must have been quite common in agrarianate villages. Without any conscious intention (except so far as boys were encouraged to be 'tough' and tolerate 'no nonsense'), but with good functional reason, everything was done in training the child to make it impossible that any should grow up to be the sort of person envisaged in either the Socratic dialogues or the Sermon on the Mount.

This sort of discipline was expressed in the maktab school through rote learning, which taught the child to avoid any attempt to think for himself, and through the regular use of the rod to beat any boy who failed to conform in every detail. By the time the boy got to the madrasah, he took rote learning for granted; a gifted lad who did not have a good memory was heavily handicapped and such were probably usually excluded from a career of learning. The rod was no longer needed; the sarcasm of teacher or fellow-students sufficed. The Shar'î tradition was not in itself specially obscurantist; it did not need to be. Thus the protective defences of the everyday culture had their profound influence on the high culture at its very heart.

This sort of preparation reinforced the conservative mood at the very roots of scholarship. Textbooks of all sorts were put into rhyme to facilitate memorization, and the greatest praise was heaped even on mature scholars for the amount of wordage they could reel off by heart. But the human personality is not only malleable but resilient. Alongside rote learning of approved textbooks, even on the exoteric level, were other forms of teaching and learning which, in those who were not completely deadened by their early training, could arouse the sparks of intelligence. The commonest form of teaching was to explain an important book, line by line. All books being in manuscript, and normally full of copyists' mistakes—even apart from the ambiguities of the Arabic script, which as ordinarily written omits certain short vowels and secondary consonant formations—it was necessary for an oral tradition to accompany a book if its very words were to be known exactly. This much the teacher, who had normally heard the book expounded himself, could provide; and he took occasion to comment and interpret also, sometimes discussing the subject at large. It was then the custom for students to question the teacher on hard points and sometimes the questioning could become disputation or even degenerate to heckling. Here quick thinking was called for, though a teacher might simply drive away too troublesome a student.

When a student had read through a book with his teacher and the teacher was satisfied he knew the correct readings and understood the content, the teacher would give him a certificate, an *ijâzah,* stating the fact and authorizing him to teach that book in turn to other students. It was assumed that such ijâzahs would form a chain of links (like an isnâd in ḥadîth reports or a silsilah in a Ṣûfî ṭarîqah) going back to the writer of the book, who would have been its first teacher. Sometimes, however, a teacher might give an ijâzah simply in recognition of the general intelligence and capacity of a student, even though he had not actually read through the book in question with him; in this way, the outstanding mind could be given the trappings of conservative respectability without needing to wear out his efforts with what must often have been minutiae of a text. On occasion, the ijâzah, like any title, depreciated. Some scholars claimed to receive ijâzahs from long-dead authors in dreams, and such a claim might be tolerated; other ijâzahs could be purely honorific, as when a scholar gave them to the tiny son of a friend whom he wished to oblige.

Students and scholars both travelled about very widely, searching for new intellectual milieus to explore or new fields to conquer with their learning. There was no hierarchy of madrasahs, but some centres had special regional importance and attracted students and visitors from afar. At least, rather later, Bukhârâ was a great centre of Shar'î studies with a reputation drawing students from all the Turkic lands of the north as well as other regions; and Cairo, with the Az'har mosque, was a great centre for the eastern Arab lands and for many Muslim lands of the south (Arab-minded scholars have sometimes credited the Az'har with a general primacy it has never had). Among the Twelver Shî'îs, Najaf in the Iraq, with its many small institutions, has had unquestioned prestige in recent centuries, and formerly Ḥillah (not far away) was at least as important. But even such centres never had exclusive priority of repute, and most were subject to eventual displacement by rival centres in the same region. Those who sought learning almost always visited lesser centres as well.

Especially in the central Muslim lands, which benefited not only from circulation among themselves but from the visits of men from more outlying regions, it was hard to avoid the confrontation of several contrasting traditions; students of any alertness made a point of hearing more than one side of a matter. Public disputations would be arranged between prominent scholars; the first one to be unable to reply to a point made by his adversary was acknowledged to have been defeated, even by those who still held to his position and believed that an abler man might have won. The mark of the conservative spirit was on such disputations: the procedure went on the assumption that, of any two given positions, one must be right and the other wrong; as in modern parliamentary procedure, there was in principle no expectation of building, from the different perspectives of the two scholars, an unanticipated new synthesis; modification could come at most by way of amendment of one of the two positions in view of specific objections, or substitution of some third position represented by yet another scholar who would challenge the winner. In any case, impromptu disputation put a premium on a well-stocked and ready memory. Nevertheless, such disputation eliminated those who had nothing but a good memory, otherwise encouraged by the system of rote learning. It focused vividly the process of interchange and dialogue which keep any tradition alive.

Scholars who could speak best in provocative books had a less personally harrowing means of reaching an audience. Booksellers had their shops near the madrasahs and sold whatever would attract a buyer, however heretical the writing. A manuscript, once composed, would be duplicated by several copyists listening to one oral reading of it. The copyists might be the writer's own students or might be employees or slaves of a bookseller. To meet more exacting standards than such oral listening would produce, a wealthy man might hire a scholar to copy a manuscript direct from a good older copy, preferably an autograph of the writer if it could be found; or a scholar might make a copy for his personal use. Such copies were signed and treasured. Rulers and wealthy men, as well as mosques and madrasahs with waqf funds, liked to accumulate well-authenticated copies of important works, and they often did not limit themselves to works approved by the 'ulamâ'. Books might have to be written with care not to arouse the suspicions of the Sharî'ah-minded or the sensibilities of those in power, but with proper care they could become the vehicles of daring innovation, which could gradually make itself very generally accepted; it was thus, for instance, that the ideas of Falsafah gradually achieved high social respectability in ruling circles at the end of the Later Middle Period.

Sunnî and Shî'î images of Islamic history

Education in the madrasahs favoured, and was designed to confirm, the general acceptance of common doctrines about the world at large among all Muslims. In certain spheres, at least, it was able to succeed under the auspices of the conservative spirit.

By the end of the Earlier Middle Period, the diversity of types and schools of piety found among Muslims in the High Caliphal Period had crystallized, in the bulk of the community, into three primary streams, three traditions of

Islamic piety, each of which found its own primary exponents but was present to some degree in the devotional life of an increasing majority of all Muslims, simultaneously with both the others. *Sharî'ah-mindedness,* whether in Shî'î or Jamâ'î-Sunnî form, was generally recognized as the backbone of mass Islam; but it was most commonly combined, in proportions varying with the individual and sometimes the group, with the second stream, *Ṣûfism,* at least in its more or less externalized forms as the masses had adopted them. Finally, an *'Alid loyalism* pervaded not only various explicitly Shî'î sects, but many sectors of Jamâ'î-Sunnism; for with the wide adoption of Sunnism among the city population in the Earlier Middle Period, a Shî'î heritage was retained.

This 'Alid-loyalism was expressed in a special honour paid to all Fâṭimid 'Alids and particularly to the main figures in the Ja'farî line, as well as in other, more subtle ways. Sunnî theorists recognized a 'good Shî'ism', which ought not to be objected to: such Shî'ism was formulated in the thesis that the best of men after Muḥammad was not Abû-Bakr (as with ordinary Jamâ'î-Sunnîs, recognizing the choice of the jamâ'ah) but 'Alî, yet that Abû-Bakr and 'Umar were not to be condemned. But the Shî'î heritage was more pervasive than this. Its most important expressions were a generalized expectation of the coming of a Mahdî, a descendant of Muḥammad, preferably bearing his name and his father's name (Muḥammad b. 'Abd-Allâh), who was to restore justice to the Muslim community and to the world at the end of time; and, more or less associated with this, a special reverence for the person of Muḥammad which (largely through the medium of Ṣûfî thinkers) was given metaphysical status as expression of the cosmic Light of Muḥammad.[2]

Along with these three specifically Islamic traditions of personal orientation went what may be called *Falsafism*: seeing the structure of the world as rational totality and the meaning of human life as its harmonious fulfillment —a tendency not limited to the Faylasûfs proper, but often combined with a quite specifically Islamic piety and especially with either Ṣûfism or 'Alid loyalism or both.

The Sharî'ah-minded stream of piety, as modified by the others, was the only one the formulations of which were universally recognized as authoritative, and with which representatives of the other streams had to come to terms. It represented communal legitimacy and was alone fully and freely exoteric, and the conservative spirit was perhaps at its most triumphant in enforcing the doctrines that embodied it. The 'ulamâ' delighted to suppose that these doctrines had always been held by true Muslims—implicitly at first, and then explicitly as this had become necessary when heresies had appeared. That various revered early figures, such as Ḥasan of Baṣrah and Abû-Ḥanîfah, seemed in fact not to have been 'orthodox' in the latter-day

[2] Tor Andrae has traced the evolution of the conceptions of Muḥammad especially under Ṣûfî auspices in *Die Person Muhammeds in Lehre und Glauben seiner Gemeinde* (Upsala, 1917), especially in the long sixth chapter.

Sharî'ah-minded Jamâ'î-Sunnî sense, was explained away: early 'heresies' were ascribed always to someone else, and the great figures were cleared of what the 'ulamâ' could only suppose were envious calumnies.

There are excellent scholars for whom all cultural phenomena, at least all 'authentic' ones, are expressions of one or another cultural whole; in such a whole it matters little just when a given detail may have been first articulated, for its meaning derives only from its place in the integral whole. All the literature of a given tradition, or complex of traditions, is to be read as a single corpus, every particular writing being understood in the light of all the others. The cultural whole may be conceived as racial or as religious, or as tribal or national; in any case, cultural life is proper to that whole, not to the individuals who are its carriers, or rather its products. All concrete realizations are but variants on traditional, immemorial archetypes—archetypal myths or conceptions or institutions. If one finds any apparent inconsistencies or individual deviations not interpretable as circumstantial variants, these are to be ascribed to degenerate mixed forms, the results of alien influence or of adventitious 'borrowing'; but even 'borrowing' is more normally only a surface appearance, for the alien material is absorbed only as it reinforces or develops the indigenous pattern.

This way of seeing cultural reality raises problems (at what moment, for instance, did these seemingly timeless cultural entities come into being, and in what manner was everything embryonically present in that ever-receding moment?). Yet I suppose it is as valid a perspective, at least on some level, as that (more congenial to myself) which attaches meaning to finding just which human individual did each thing, when, and why. There is no necessary contradiction between seeing a given tradition as an integral nexus, each phase of which is in one or another way conditioned by every other, and seeing a tradition as a development in time, as a cumulation of individual human responses made to ever new situations but always on the basis of what had gone before. At any rate (as noted in volume 1, General Prologue), even Islamicate civilization can be envisaged in its integrality. Cumulatively, all elements of what may be called the Islamicate heritage may be seen at any given moment in retrospect as forming a single intelligible configuration of themes and counter-themes; for, in fact, all the differing sub-traditions had at all times to reckon with each other. Yet one should be aware of the occasion and viewpoint of any retrospective summation undertaken. It is some such summation of certain aspects of the heritage, made however not from a scholarly but from a very partisan viewpoint, that we are about to consider here.

It was only gradually, as the questions that had aroused earlier generations were increasingly settled, that the early diversity of interpretation, accompanied by a keen living historical sense, gave way to standardized Sharî'ah-minded versions of the great events of the Muslim past, and hence of Islamic orthodoxy. By the fourteenth century, the image was established *ne varietur*.

Among Sunnîs, the principle of ijmâʿ was invoked to authenticate it, as the eventually received view of the community as a whole; for later times this was binding, however much individual revered scholars in earlier times may have remained in doubt about particular points. A corresponding principle tended to prevail even among some Shîʿîs.

The latter-day Sharîʿah-mindedness was enforced among Sunnîs by a comprehensive doctrine of taqlîd, acceptance of authority. Taqlîd had originally been the individual acceptance of a learnèd man's authority by one less learnèd. As we have seen, it was naturally held that in matters of religious law the ordinary Muslim should follow the views of such of the ʿulamâʾ as he could trust, without attempting to work out particular points of law for himself on the basis of his own imperfect awareness of all the texts that would bear on the case. This had been early extended to mature scholars also, who were normally expected to follow the decisions of authorities of the legal madhhab in which they had been trained, rather than striking out afresh on their own. By the eleventh century, many held that even the greatest scholars were so bound. Though this notion was combatted by men like Ghazâlî as an unwarranted limitation on the personal responsibility of the qualified, it was generally received in the cause of stability in legal standards. In the Later Middle Period, this extension of taqlîd was confirmed in a more rigorous form with the acceptance of standard compilations even within a madhhab school.

Once it was accepted among Sunnîs that 'the door of ijtihâd inquiry was closed', Sharʿî thought accommodated itself. By the Later Middle Periods the number of established Jamâʿî-Sunnî madhhabs, to one of which every scholar must conform, was reduced to four: besides Shâfiʿîs, Ḥanafîs, and Mâlikîs, Ḥanbalîs, though few in number, were given equal recognition. (Every Muslim must declare his madhhab and abide by his choice; changing from one madhhab to another was frowned on.) Where there was disagreement within a madhhab, scholars should follow the majority in the madhhab (rather than among Muslims generally). In each generation, as it appeared that the majority of the doctors of a given madhhab agreed on a given position, that position was to become binding on subsequent generations. At the same time, scholars in one madhhab were expected to learn something of the other established Sunnî madhhabs; and increasingly, the different madhhabs came, through consciousness of each other's traditions, to have similar positions on most points of fiqh. (The minor points of difference remaining, to be sure, could sometimes cause riots.) As all major points had (in principle) been settled very early, in principle each new generation was left with increasingly minor and secondary points still to settle. We must be reminded that in practice, of course, collections of fatwà judgments kept the law more fluid than might appear.

This process in settling the Sharîʿah itself may be taken as typical of the fixing of lines that took place in that sector of the culture of which the

Sharî'ah is the most striking manifestation. To some degree, comparable principles were extended to all the Sharî'ah-minded religious thought of Islam, and even to some Ṣûfî ideas and practices; such things as rites of initiation, claims to silsilah lines, and the doctrine of sequences of spiritual states were more or less standardized. In Kalâm certain positions which had been upheld by the Ash'arîs and the Mâturîdîs were generally accepted. Mu'tazilism, notably, finally died out among the Sunnîs (and its opponents died out among the Shî'îs). In this way, in the realm of religious studies the conservative spirit was embodied in a religious dogma; and Ṣûfîs readily accepted, as an outward proposition, whatever the Shar'î 'ulamâ' were minded to decree.

The consensus was, of course, not restricted to points of law and theology. It expressed itself in cosmology and, above all, in views of history, though here dogma was not too strictly enforced. The earth was but one realm of being among many: there were hells and heavens and, as among Christians, the present heavens tended to be identified with the paradise that properly would not find its inhabitants till after the Last Judgment. As seen in the common image, at least, the heavens were occupied by angels, God's servants, and (in the highest heaven) by God himself, seated on a Throne that was more massive than all the heavens and the world combined. Angels accompanied every human being, recording his good and bad acts and urging the best on him. The hells were guarded by devils, whose mission was also to tempt human beings into wickedness.

On earth there were two sorts of rational beings: humans and jinn. The jinn were normally invisible but could meddle in human affairs (some writers on fiqh took very seriously such questions as the status of the issue of a union between a human and a jinnî); they were identified with the sprites that fill the folklore of every people, and every sort of superstition could be set forth with reference to their benevolent or (more usually) malevolent activities. (On the other hand, the nature gods of pre-Abrahamic times, which still played an allegorical role in Christian Europe, had disappeared too completely in Irano-Semitic terrain to perpetuate a common corpus of nature myth on a literary level.) The humans lived in the seven climes of the earth, identified by scholars with zones of latitude between the equator and the arctic circle, but in the popular and the literary imagination identified with different human races spaced in a circle around Mecca at the centre. At the circumference of the circle was the great circumambient ocean; beyond the ocean, at the outer rim of the earth, was the great mountain Kâf, where the most magical things could happen.

History had begun with Adam, first man and first prophet, identified also with the First Man of old-Iranian traditions. The sequence of Iranian monarchs (the First Man being the first of them) had ruled down to the time of Islam in the centre of the earth, sharing that central area only with the Bedouin Arabs and their predecessors—identified partly with Biblical genealogies—in Arabia itself. The Biblical and Iranian traditions were merged, and side by side with the Iranian kings were the Biblical patriarchs, interpreted as prophets bringing true Islam each to his generation. Islam was indeed the natural faith of every child born; but parents corrupted children with invented faiths, so that prophets were required to restore the truth. An ordinary prophet, *nabî*, might come at any time, and there had been thousands such scattered in every people on earth; but a great prophet among them, a *rasûl*, 'messenger', came only occasionally, bringing a new Sharî'ah and founding a new community—the greatest having been Adam, Noah, Abraham, Moses, and Jesus.

It was in these earlier ages that both the magical and the legitimate sciences had been taught mankind (by angels, devils, and prophets); those ages had seen much greatness, both among Arabs and Persians and in other peoples, notably the Greeks and Indians, both known for their philosophy (while the Chinese were respected for their handicraft skills and their good government). But as the time of Muḥammad approached, true Islam, carried then chiefly by the followers of Moses and Jesus, had become falsified save among a learnèd or faithful remnant who were looking knowingly forward to the new prophet who would bring the final and fullest revelation and whose Ummah would fill the whole world and never lose the true faith.

The generations before Muḥammad, the 'Jâhiliyyah', were times of dark ignorance and immorality throughout the world and especially in Arabia. Persian government was to be respected and the Sâsânian monarch Nûshîrvân was indeed taken by many as a model of just rule (but on such a point there was no proper ijmâ'); but his immediate successors, the last Sâsânids, had been bad rulers. Though Christianity had been the best of religions to date, its scriptures, like those of the Jews, had been corrupted wilfully, especially in point of deifying Jesus and suppressing references to Muḥammad; and the Christian Roman emperors were proud tyrants. In Arabia, though the Arabs were the noblest of races, idolatry and injustice prevailed despite isolated individuals (ḥanîfs) who stood for truth and foresaw Muḥammad's coming. Then Muḥammad's coming changed everything. At his very birth a light flashed abroad that was seen even in Nûshîrvân's palace.

Muḥammad's chief duty was to bring to mankind the eternal Qur'ân, only fragmentarily anticipated by the other prophets; it was revealed by Gabriel initially all at once, and only later brought again piecemeal for annunciation at appropriate occasions. The Qur'ân contained the whole of the Sharî'ah law, though it must be interpreted by way of the ḥadîth, recording God's continuous direct inspiration to Muḥammad. The Sharî'ah, then, guided mankind back to righteousness.

But Muḥammad was not merely God's instrument of revelation. He was God's favourite, and God's primary channel of favour and blessing to mankind. Not only Shî'îs, but, thanks to Ṣûfî teachings, almost everyone agreed that the holy Light that was the essence of Muḥammad had been the first thing God created, and that all else was created in view of Muḥammad's glory. All the prophets had done him honour and foretold his advent. His life was a sequence of miracles. In his childhood, for instance, his presence brought prosperity to the tribe of his foster mother (when he was given to a Bedouin wet-nurse after the Meccan custom). In his youth he avoided all impropriety, and was so respected that the Meccans chose him for the coveted task of replacing the sacred Black Stone in the wall of the Ka'bah when it was being rebuilt. On a caravan trip to Syria, he was provided supernaturally with shade from the hot sun and a monk recognized him by the mark of prophethood between his shoulders. When he emerged as a prophet his wonders multiplied. His most celebrated miracle was to split the moon in the sky, so that a star could be seen shining between the two halves—a story founded obscurely on a Qur'ânic verse, and which has served as dubious explanation of the later Ottoman Muslim symbol, a crescent moon with a star between its points. On his hijrah, when 'Alî took his place in his bed as the Meccans waited to kill him, Muḥammad passed among his enemies unseen; and when he was hiding with Abû-Bakr in a cave along the way, a spider quickly wove its web across the mouth to put pursuers off the track. A post he had leaned on to preach wept when he left it; mutton he was about to eat spoke to warn him it was poisoned. A small quantity of food became sufficient, in his presence, to feed a large company.

The vision which he had of a night visit to Jerusalem was elaborated magnificently. Led in an instant by Gabriel from Mecca to the rock of Zion where now stands the Dome of the Rock, he there mounted the winged horse Burâq, who carried him through the seven heavens. After conversing with the major prophets on the way, he spoke with God in the heights where even Gabriel dare not approach. At his intercession, God reduced the number of acts of worship to be demanded of Muḥammad's people to an easy five a day. It was generally agreed that, by the permission of God, the ultimate salvation of all true Muslims, even those who sinned greatly, was assured through Muḥammad's intercession at the Last Day.

This exaltation of Muḥammad expressed a hardening communalism which looked less to the eternal islâm that could appear, as the Qur'ân makes clear, in any community, and more to the historical community in which islâm was made most perfect; by the Middle Periods, the other communities were felt to be mere relics of the past, not very relevant to real life anyway. It was only in the thirteenth century, however, that the best Sunnî theologians finally conceded, as Shî'îs had long held, that Muḥammad had been totally sinless, guiltless even of minor errors. Passages in the Qur'ân implying his human weakness were interpreted as purely exemplary, to show Muslims how they should repent for their sins. Insulting Muḥammad had long been made the gravest of misdeeds, for which even dhimmî non-Muslims (not bound to the Sharî'ah as such) were to be killed. At his tomb in Medina he was present and aware; it was popularly told how he had stretched out his hand from the tomb for one of the great saints to kiss. A visit to him at Medina was regarded as almost as important as the ḥajj pilgrimage to Mecca itself, and was commonly combined with it. At the same time, Muḥammad might visit the devout in dreams, and Satan was not permitted to impersonate him in such visits. By this time, the whole area of Mecca and Medina, the scenes of Muḥammad's life, was regarded as sacred territory which, like the Qur'ân itself, should be defiled by the touch of no infidel; whereas, in the early years of Islam, Christians, for instance, had freely visited Mecca, now this was no longer permitted.

The Jamâ'î-Sunnî view of history since Muḥammad was accepted by the great majority, and even Shî'îs paid lip-service to it by way of taqiyyah dissimulation. Even for Jamâ'î-Sunnîs, Muḥammad's family shared to a degree in his sacredness, notably his descendants through Fâṭimah and 'Alî. 'Alî himself was a major hero—in sharp contrast to the attitude of official Islam during Marwânî times, when he was cursed, and even during early 'Abbâsî times, when non-Shî'îs rarely allowed him to be on a level with Abû-Bakr and 'Umar. But—and here came the formal dividing line between Shî'î and Sunnî—most Jamâ'î-Sunnîs insisted that excellence, after the Prophet himself, went by the historical order of the caliphs: Abû-Bakr was the most excellent of all men, 'Umar second, 'Uthmân third, and 'Alî fourth (though a preference for 'Alî above even Abû-Bakr was tolerated as 'good' Shî'ism). The descendants of all these were given a certain honourable recognition; indeed, all who could claim Quraysh or even—in some areas—Arab descent were regarded as specially close to the Prophet. But the descendants of 'Alî by Fâṭimah, as Muḥammad's daughter (not the other 'Alids) were given the special titles of *sayyid* or *sharîf*, with unusual privileges; they were entitled to the alms of the faithful, and their failings were to be overlooked; popularly it was felt that their presence carried a special divine blessing.

While 'Alid-loyalist sentiments about the person and the family of Muḥammad thus received a major place even in Jamâ'î-Sunnî thought, the opposed doctrine of the religious reliability of all the associates of Muḥammad was more integrally enshrined by the Sunnî ijmâ'. In particular, it was held that the first four caliphates—including that of 'Alî, which was assimilated to the other three—were all to be regarded as models of Islamic government. (In concession to Shî'î sentiment, Mu'âwiyah, though an associate of Muḥammad, was not admitted as a fifth.) The warfare among the associates of the Prophet, notably that between 'Alî and Quraysh opponents in the Battle of the Camel, were not to be judged: neither side could be blamed by a good Muslim, since as individuals the protagonists on both sides were divinely approved; all had had good intentions, though at least some had erred. Blame for whatever went wrong was laid at the door of 'trouble-makers' like 'Abd-Allâh b. Saba', whom Sunnî historians treated as the originator of the Shî'ah (and whom Shî'îs commonly regarded as the source of whatever forms of Shî'ism they opposed as too extreme). Not only all the associates of Muḥammad, but all Muslims (for the Shî'îs, only Shî'î Muslims), as Muḥammad's protégés at the Last Day, were to be accorded a prima facie trust.

After the first, each later generation of Muslims was, on the whole, inferior to its predecessors. The Umayyads, however, were blamed even by Sunnîs as especially wicked rulers, who had corrupted Islam irremediably from its original purity. For the Sunnîs, the 'Abbâsids were indeed true caliphs; though in principle any other Quraysh family might be elected to the caliphate, in fact the dignity was reserved to the 'Abbâsids as long as it lasted. But after the fall of Baghdad, Islamic legitimacy declined still further. The very caliphate, in its historical Shar'î sense, disappeared (for the puppet 'Abbâsid line in Cairo was not generally regarded); without authorized claimants, the caliphal title came to be applied (on the initiative of the Faylasûfs) to any regional ruler who was regarded as upholding the Sharî'ah for the time being.

For the first generations the example of Muḥammad had been so close, and they had been so pious, that no learnedly developed fiqh had been necessary. But with the corruption of memory and of morals, more was needed. In addition to the ḥadîth collections of Bukhârî and Muslim, Sunnîs recognized as authoritative, if less well attested, four other collections. Shî'îs recognized four collections made a little later. (In both cases, yet other collections were still studied.) The fiqh had been set forth in explicit form by four great Sunnî imâms; later generations, whose corruption had proceeded yet further, must follow exclusively one or the other of these four—Abû-Ḥanîfah, Mâlik, al-Shâfi'î, or Ibn-Ḥanbal; it was with the creation of their madhhabs that the 'doors of ijtihâd' had been closed. In effect, the opinions of the major disciples of each imâm were assimilated to those of the imâm himself. Twelver Shî'îs correspondingly tended to follow Shaykh Ṭûsî, but evidently did not ascribe the same finality to him.

It was one of the special privileges of Muḥammad that there would be no prophets after him; not only no rasûl, founding a new community, but no ordinary nabî (such as had so abounded especially in the community of Moses). Instead, there were walîs, friends of God: among Shî'îs, these were the imâms (and some of their more honoured descendants, *imâmzâdahs*, were accorded honours almost as great); among Sunnîs, these were the Ṣûfî saints. These walîs had much the same role as the nabîs of ancient times: being inspired by God, keeping alive the faith, and serving as vehicles of divine blessing (*barakah*) to the faithful.

Even heresy was standardized, or rather the majority attitudes to it were. It was agreed that there were just six dozen false Muslim sects, and the number was allotted (differently by different writers) among various movements or schools of thought which had already appeared in Marwânî or classical 'Abbâsî times. Later dissidents were assimilated to one or another of the categories earlier developed: one was a Râfiḍî if he accepted the Shî'ah; one was of the Ghulât if he were 'extreme' Shî'î; a Bâṭinî if he acknowledged priority of an inward secret meaning over the outward revelation; worst of all, a Zindîq, if he combined actual infidelity with a feigned Islam. A man was a heretic if he rejected some point or other of Sunnî ijmâ'; but most agreed he was to be counted a Muslim anyway, for legal purposes, if he conformed in outward essentials, unless he was proved to be a Zindîq. Shî'îs likewise denounced seventy-two sects and likewise allowed heretics such as Sunnîs the title 'Muslim' (though not 'Mu'min', faithful). As for infidels, the dhimmîs within the Dâr al-Islâm had become despised minorities and those beyond the Dâr al-Islâm were regarded as exotic peoples away from the main paths of history. The ordinary world was all Muslim.

Despite the closing of ijtihâd among Sunnîs, it was believed (among both Sunnîs and Shî'îs) that at the beginning of every century God raised up one man (called a mujaddid) to renew the Islamic faith; the mujaddid's teaching dissipated any actual errors that might have crept in among the Muslims. The most notable instance of such a renewer of the faith had been Ghazâlî (admired even by some Shî'îs). Finally, moreover, when mankind was at its lowest ebb, justice nowhere, and the true faith almost forgotten, would come the greatest renewer of them all, the Mahdî, a descendant of Muḥammad. He would conquer the earth, restore Islam, and rule mankind at last in justice. The Dajjâl, or Anti-Christ, would oppose him but Jesus would descend from the heavens, kill the Dajjâl, and perform worship behind the Mahdî. Then, with other 'signs of the Last Hour' (such as the sun's rising in the west), history would close and the Last Judgment come.

The popular image of the after-life was not fully rationalized. Upon a vague picture of sleeping ghosts that might at any time be ominously awakened, the monotheistic traditions had superimposed both the eschatological expectation of the final bodily resurrection, and a moral clarification in the form of anticipatory pleasures and pains for the ghosts meanwhile. All these elements were perpetuated among the Muslims, but the rest were subordinated to the eschatological expectation.

Hell, the permanent reward of the infidels and a place of temporary punishment even for wicked Muslims, was conceived as diversified torments of fire and heat. Paradise, the ultimate reward of all true Muslims and possibly of others if God was merciful to them, would be a garden (not a city paved with glittering stones); with fruit trees and four great rivers of water and honey and milk and a paradisal, non-intoxicating wine. The blessèd would live in luxurious pavillions, served by angelic beings; the more blessèd, the higher and more wondrous the section of Paradise. Man and wife would be together in Paradise, if this were appropriate; but everyone would be in the prime of youth, and the men could enjoy the *ḥûrîs*, bright black-eyed maidens of Paradise. The greatest pleasure of Paradise, however, would be a periodic reception by God himself, to see whom was the height of ecstasy.

Among the sectarian Shî'îs, the same general picture prevailed as among Sunnîs, but with the necessary modifications. The modifications were sometimes serious. To all matters regarding the high status of Muḥammad and of his family, including the Mahdî, they gave even more weight than did the Sunnîs; hence, exalting the exclusive virtues of 'Alî, they rejected the first three caliphs and most of the associates of Muḥammad. The Sunnî Islam that seemed to prevail in the world was therefore not a true Islam, however degenerate; it was renegade, and only the faithful minority of Shî'îs, persecuted and suffering as had been Muḥammad's family, represented the truth. Accordingly, the agreement of those externally Muslim by no means defined truth. Even the ijmâ' among scholars accepted by Shî'îs played a lesser role, in fact, and among Twelvers ijtihâd was still open to learnèd Shî'îs, pending the coming of the imâm himself as Mahdî. Yet in the numerous details the Shî'î image corresponded almost point for point to the Sunnî, and it seems that in the fourteenth and fifteenth centuries most Sharî'ah-minded Shî'î doctrine was almost as conventionally established as the Sharî'ah-minded Sunnî doctrine.

Corruption and localism in Ṣûfism

But despite the zealous conformism of the standard doctrines about the world and its history, people found ways of exploring their individual senses of reality. Sometimes such ways, lacking the discipline that goes with public authorization, were of dubious validity, at least as ways of true growth in a fuller appreciation of reality; sometimes they opened up significant reaches of truth. The harmony of religious outlook that had prevailed among the educated at the end of the Earlier Middle Period was never complete, even in the limited sense that a basic Sharî'ah-mindedness was to be supplemented by general acceptance of ṭarîqah Ṣûfism in some form or other. In the Later Middle Period, such harmony as had existed tended to be dissipated, though usually without yielding to the bitterness of mutual exclusion and persecution and generally without challenging the images of history that we have just traced. The libertarian openness of Ṣûfism already noted, and its accommodation to local folkways, bore fruit most especially in the Later Middle Period.

The most important religious issues were no longer fought out, for the most part, between schools of fiqh or of kalâm but rather within and between differing ṭarîqah orders. In part this represented a shift of interest in an age when Shar'î institutions, whether caliphal or decentralized, no longer offered a point of departure for new political creativity. But often it was the same perennial human issues that were being debated, only cast now in Ṣûfî terms. The Ṣûfî tradition was expanding in range to the point where it could accommodate very diverse temperaments, and with them some of the disparate perspectives that had once been expressed in such contrasts as that between Ṣûfism itself and other sorts of piety.

We have seen how members of the Chishtî ṭarîqah in India forbade government service as corrupting, and were willing to minister personally even to Hindus. Such attitudes were typical of the Chishtiyyah, whereas the other great ṭarîqah in India in this period, the Suhravardiyyah (harking back to Yaḥyà Suhravardî, the friend of the caliph al-Nâṣir), generally was less ascetic and (in particular) encouraged acceptance of government office, at the same time being more Sharîʿah-minded, more shy of grandiose speculation, and less tolerant of Hindus. One can imagine that if the Muʿtazilî friends of al-Ma'mûn had had to choose between the two ṭarîqahs in the new situation, they would have preferred the Suhravardiyyah for its relatively commonsense and 'rational' handling of Ṣûfî ideas, its legal rigour, and its stronger sense of the political community as bearing religious value. Many differences among ṭarîqahs on points of personal discipline had more far-reaching implications as well. When they differed as to whether celibacy should be recommended or whether full-time devotees should be chiefly wandering darvîshes or gathered together in khâniqâh convents, their differences implied contrasting outlooks on the relation of the mystical life to the religious life of the mass of mankind: how much of a 'religious specialist' should a devotee be, and how many of mankind can expect to become such specialists, and how freely should the masses be involved in the devotee's special ways?

We can discern at least three important trends in the Jamâʿî Ṣûfism of the period. The popularization and externalization of the religious structures focused on mystical experience led to such things as cultivating wonders and revering saints, which, from a purely mystical viewpoint at least, must be called corruption; and while all traditions that win power entail a certain amount of corruption, corruption in Ṣûfism could have peculiarly subtle consequences. Then the wide acceptance of speculative cosmology as an integral part of the Ṣûfî life seems to have been associated with emphasis on ecstatic visions, and even the visions of dream-life, as central to spiritual growth. Finally, both popularization and the emphasis on visions encouraged paying attention to relatively quick techniques for achieving ecstatic moments, sometimes including mood drugs. (All these trends may be called decadent, but in different senses. Corruption certainly implies that, among the corrupt, the original creative force of the tradition has been losing vigour; but whatever happened among the popularizers, in other circles, perhaps as numerous as the ancient Ṣûfîs in their time, the tradition may have been as vital as ever. As to visions receiving increased attention, this might offend the moralism of Ḥasan of Baṣrah or even Junayd, but might strike a modern Jungian analyst as a healthy shift in the focus of the tradition once it had fully explored its initial problematic.)

At least as important socially was the rise of Shîʿî versions of Ṣûfism, which challenged much in the complacent Jamâʿî-Sunnî and even Shîʿî ideology of the dominant 'ulamâ', as well as the injustices of the amîrs; I will say more of these later. One can add that the most important developments in the Sharîʿah-minded disciplines themselves were associated with an attack on Ṣûfism.

The corruption of Ṣûfism, obvious in the mass, becomes harder to isolate as one comes to understand each of the several strands that made up the Ṣûfism of the time and also the genuine spiritual concern that commonly went into each strand at some point. Wishful thinking, a component of any religious thinking doubtless from the beginning, becomes an ever-stronger component in a religious tradition as the tradition becomes a function of the total life of a society. Means invented for promising surcease from the miseries that go to make up most of life readily become the largest part of any functioning religion for most human beings. But it is hard to assert unequivocally which points are merely wishful thinking. (And is everything that smacks of wishful thinking to be entitled corruption?) But we may surely see an identifiable process of 'corruption' in one point at least: the depreciation of technical terms. *Fanâ'*, the 'passing away' of consciousness of selfhood, and *baqâ'*, its complement, the 'remaining' of consciousness of God, once terms with ultimate connotations, came sometimes to be thought of as terms for relatively early stages in spiritual growth. Eventually one could speak of many quṭbs, many poles of the cosmos—relatively lesser figures in an extended cosmic hierarchy. However, something of the corruption of Ṣûfism is to be seen in most of the other developments that we will glance at here.

By the Later Middle Period, a striking practical contrast had become prevalent that seems to imply a corruption of the earlier tradition: a fairly sharp distinction between the 'shaykh al-taṣawwuf', the Ṣûfî master, and the wandering mendicant darvîsh. The one maintained a supposedly classical regimen in his khâniqâh, commonly in a town; the other was commonly a free-lance beggar, an adventurer, often enough shading into a trickster or a thief. On both sides can be seen corruption: if many a darvîsh, even when subjectively honest, made religion an excuse for wanderlust and irresponsibility, too often the settled pîr was regurgitating a formula compounded of set moods and stereotyped phrases. But on neither side was the tradition exclusively degenerate: the more serious persons were developing new departures in some ways fully worthy of the tradition at its best.

In particular, the wandering darvîshes often represented an attempt to out-Ṣûfî Ṣûfism itself on the level of religious practice. Spirits adventurous or critical found that Ṣûfî ways had developed their own conventions, their own propriety, the reverse of the ideal of freedom that Rûmî had inculcated through the Ṣûfî forms. Such an attitude was almost as old as organized Ṣûfism, but became more pronounced as Ṣûfism became more established. Thus arose, for instance, a revived Malâmatiyyah, even among the settled pîrs, dedicated to self-mortification through denying themselves the conventional Ṣûfî marks of piety. Some of these men, finding it necessary to pursue sanctity through the very humiliation of not being able to display their unworldliness before the world, joined together in a regular tradition of concealed piety, which people should practice even while appearing worldly and without any Ṣûfism at all. In a more extreme move to free themselves from all outward forms, those that had always insisted that Ṣûfism placed the sincere and accomplished mystic (the *'ârif*, 'knower' or 'gnostic') above the law now founded regular ṭarîqah traditions alongside the more Sharî'ah-minded ones—regular ṭarîqahs but with a tradition of neglecting Shar'î observance. Such men often valued the wandering mendicant life. Nor were these kept greatly distinct from the others; in fact, all new ṭarîqahs, whatever their posture, tended to be independent branches of old ones, rather than founded afresh. Moreover, the disciple of a Sharî'ah-observant pîr might adopt a non-Sharî'ah position, and vice versa. The most famous non-Sharî'ah ṭarîqah was the Qalandariyyah, the wandering darvîshes pre-eminently. This order was marked by a common dress and way of shaving the face, but otherwise was so permissive that it soon seemed rather to form an excuse for fully private (and perhaps irresponsible) styles of piety, rather than an organized movement, however tenuously the members need be interconnected to form such a movement.

A number of ṭarîqahs seem to have arisen in which the chief purpose had become an escape from everyday reality, not necessarily to a keener ultimate awareness, but to various forms of auto-suggestion and ecstatic euphoria taken as goals in themselves. (Not that they did not intend to look to the divine, but distinctions in this sphere have always been hard to see clearly.) In such ṭarîqahs, drugs could quite consciously be used for their direct psychological effects (though probably some of the more serious Ṣûfîs used them as short-cuts to a state of mind that could then be built upon for something more basic). Breathing exercises—uttering the name *Allâh,* for instance, in a prescribed manner, accompanied by deep respiration—and other hypnotic devices could be used for the immediate psychophysical results, which could be delightful enough in their own way. Then the results, often quite astonishing, were displayed (generally sincerely) as evidence of divine blessing. Devotees, self-hypnotized, could endure spectacular pain—the piercing of hot iron or the trampling of horses. Such exploits served to enhance the prestige of the ṭarîqah and to encourage financial contributions in the hope of a borrowed blessing. Certain ṭarîqahs catered especially to the public demand for such display, such as the Sa'diyyah of Egypt. (It must be recalled, however, that at all times the more responsible Ṣûfîs and darvîshes maintained their mission of preaching repentance and godliness to the people.)

In such an atmosphere, responsible pîrs, who could not discuss publicly the more abstruse truths of faith, may themselves have believed and in any case willingly encouraged popularly edifying tales of saints and their wondrous powers, as equally valid with the dry legalism of the 'ulamâ'; a general expectation of magic and miracle was sanctioned by those who could not expect the wider public to rise to the level of Truth in any case. People always expect wonders to issue from what has been authoritatively set forth as holy, whether sacred sites or consecrated images; now the expectation was increasingly focused not only on the dead saints and their tombs, but even on the living adepts themselves, about whose predecessors so many gaudy tales were told even by sober intellectuals. Unfortunately, this had unintended consequences. Charlatans had always found a ready audience; now they seemed to be sanctioned by Islamic piety. Magic was passed as miracle, and magic tricks as the gracious fruits of ascetic continence. Respected orders, even when they did not actually cultivate such show as their primary end, could found their popular appeal on the more glamorous powers of their adepts, expressed in weird psychological or psychophysical feats. The leaders of such ṭarîqahs might recognize the limitations of such feats; the uneducated public commonly distinguished little between them and the footloose darvîsh or faqîr whose chief merit was his supposedly ascetic dirtiness and who wrote charms for women to assure the birth of sons.

The realm of magic received increasing respectability even on the level of academic madrasahs. Already Ghazâlî had made reference to the practical usefulness of various charms, without claiming to know how various items happened to have the powers claimed for them. In divination and in apotropaic magic—the realm of interpretation of dreams and omens and the use of fortune-telling devices and charms (from sand diagrams and palmistry and magic numbers to detached elements of alchemical and astrological lore)—use was made of high symbolism; of psychological perceptivity; of what can only be called parapsychic phenomena (e.g., the use of children on the verge of puberty to induce the discovery of lost or stolen property); and finally of sheer guesswork. A favourite medication (when more specific drugs had failed) was the words of the Qur'ân: the appropriate sûrah would be written on paper, then the ink washed off into water and drunk. The tradition of such things went back to long before Islam, as the Muslims well knew; but as the population became Muslim the lore had been thoroughly assimilated to Islam. It was attached especially to Ṣûfism, but by the Later Middle Period, at latest, it might be studied even by relatively Sharî'ah-minded 'ulamâ' up to a point. A vast literature about this lore was produced which has been little explored in modern times. We have no way of knowing what insights of value might be found in it.

One must not exaggerate the difference between the Earlier and the Later Middle Periods. Magic had been introduced early; and one finds that at any period the two most obvious ways (besides preaching) for a settled pîr to win popularity, at least on a large scale (and to enlarge the area into which he could send his khalîfahs, lieutenants), were an effectively organized distribution of the charity that was entrusted to him, and beautifully, even spectacularly arranged samâ', music listening as spur to more fervent dhikr sessions. Some Ṣûfîs still refused the samâ', but the public at large expected Ṣûfîs to use it; it was the most telling point at which those 'ulamâ' that continued to oppose Ṣûfism levelled their indictment of it. And in some areas inimical 'ulamâ' were still numerous: as late as the early fifteenth century, attacks by the 'ulamâ' kept any of the more prominent Ṣûfîs from settling in Delhi.

As Ṣûfism became popularized, it was assimilated to the local social settings and to their religious traditions in a way that the Shar'ism of the 'ulamâ' could not be. Some ṭarîqahs were primarily rural, their saints being revered at village tomb-shrines and their festivals adapted to village social needs; such ṭarîqahs were likely to be less sophisticated than more urban ṭarîqahs, and to be more concerned with the everyday needs of the villagers. For instance, among the western Turks in Anatolia and the Balkans, the Bektashî ṭarîqah developed a network of khâniqâhs in rustic settings and the poetry that its devotees recited and spread among the people reflected the practical sense (and the scepticism of established authorities) of the more independent-minded of the villagers. At the same time, the Bektashîs catered to local Christian and perhaps even pagan customs that lingered among the converted population—even using a rite that has been compared to the Christian eucharist. In other lands other ṭarîqahs fulfilled a like role. Already in the fifteenth century, the verse of Ṣûfîs writing in Hindi, the language of the Ganges plain, was not very different from that of Hindu mystics; for like literary images were used—though the Muslims did not, of course, acknowledge the Hindu divine figures as such.

One of the most popular Ṣûfî figures in such contexts was Khiḍr (properly, al-Khaḍir), the 'Green man'. This name was given to a mysterious 'servant of God' referred to in the Qur'ân (but without a name) as a teacher of Moses. The story is one of several in the Qur'ân that serve well as points of departure for the mythic imagination. Unlike so many of the stories there, which tell rather repetitiously of the experiences of historical or supposedly historical prophets with their recalcitrant peoples, this one speaks in a more personal and at the same time symbolic mode. Like other Qur'ânic narratives, it is allusive and may seem deceptively simple (sûrah XVIII). 'And when Moses said to his [serving] lad, I'm not stopping till I get to where the two seas meet, though I go on for years. Then when they got to where they meet, they forgot their fish and it took its way in the sea, wriggling.' That is, the fish has come alive; and being told this, Moses knows he has reached his objective. There he meets the mysterious servant of God, Khiḍr, whom he wants to follow in order to learn; but Khiḍr warns Moses he will not understand and will not be able to bear with him. Moses promises to be patient and ask no questions, but when Khiḍr knocks a hole in a ship and then later kills a youth, Moses cannot contain himself and asks why; rebuked, he promises to ask no more, under pain of separation from Khiḍr; and when Khiḍr gratuitously builds up a falling wall, and Moses again protests, he must pay his forfeit. But before leaving, Khiḍr shows, by giving a reasonable explanation of each of his acts, how unreasonable was Moses' impatience.

The immediate point of the story in the Qur'ân is to prefigure the righteousness of God's Judgment by showing even a great prophet convicted of over-confidence in his own judgment. But already in the Qur'ân, the story must have served to evoke a figure and a situation deeply rooted in Semitic lore. Elements of the story go back to the Babylonian Gilgamesh epic and to the legend of Alexander of Macedon: the figure is the hidden saint who will never die but wanders secretly among mankind. The immediate antecedent of most of the story was Jewish; among Jews the figure took the form of Elijah, who had been taken up alive into heaven. The place where the two seas meet—at the end of the world—is the spring of the water of life which will confer immortality, and Moses is in quest of it; the Qur'ân suggests that what is sought is to be found in a wisdom only barely to be glimpsed by human beings. Inevitably, Ṣûfîs were attracted both to the symbolism of the story and to its Qur'ânic moral; Khiḍr became the model Ṣûfî, ever living and likely to be found in out-of-the-way places, ready to help the darvîsh in distress. (Sometimes he was even identified with Elijah.) He was especially likely to help a wanderer in the desert—where the water (and vegetation) with which Khiḍr was always associated was an appropriate symbol of succour. Khiḍr thus had a universal role in Ṣûfism. But he became patron of innumerable local shrines, too, where he took on special features distinctive of a given land. He had many shrines in the Syrian hills where he was invoked for aid in situations of danger; and since in the Qur'ân itself he was assigned a great antiquity, it was not incongruous that his shrines dated back to pre-Islamic times and were sometimes shared with Christians (he had much in common with the popular Saint George, killer of dragons). In northern India, again, he was associated with rivers, especially the Indus, and was invoked in the place, it seems, of former Hindu divinities.

The same sûrah of the Qur'ân, not inappropriately, told the story of the Seven Sleepers of Ephesus, the 'men of the cave', early Christians who took refuge from persecution in a cave and there slept many years, emerging in bewilderment after Christianity had come to prevail in the land, witnesses in their persons to a sort of anticipatory resurrection (and, in the Qur'ânic version, to the psychological immediacy of the Last Judgment). Caves revered as the sites of the story multiplied in Islamdom (as in Christendom); some such shrines seem to have gone back to Megalithic times, retaining in new guise their ancient symbolism of immortality.

Not only particular Ṣûfî figures but the whole character of Ṣûfism could take on a regional colouration. In the Maghrib and the western Sûdânic lands, it was the Shâdhiliyyah ṭarîqah to which most of the local ṭarîqahs traced their affiliation. Al-Shâdhilî (d. 1258) and his immediate followers taught a religious life not readily to be distinguished from much of Ṣûfism anywhere else: strictly observant of the Sharî'ah, and withal mistrustful of government service; and urging an unfailing gentleness of personal life. This Shâdhilî tradition never lost its influence in the Maghrib. Yet there the Ṣûfî tradition was combined with a cult of saintly families—*sharîfs*, descendants of 'Alî and Fâṭimah; and *Murâbiṭs* (*Marabouts* in French), families originating with the devotees in ribâṭs (khâniqâhs), who often played a role of hereditary arbiter among the rural tribes as well as in the cities. Nowhere else was the cult of living saints so vigorous—of hereditary Murâbiṭs, fresh devotees, or madmen sainted by popular repute. And such patterns, whether or not so ancient as sometimes claimed, were integrally woven into the tissue of the distinctive regional social structure. Likewise in India, the Chishtî and Suhravardî ṭarîqahs were not untypical of Ṣûfism at large. Yet increasingly during the centuries, the survival of old caste groupings among Muslims, and of ancient pilgrimage cults (dear to the old Hindu tradition), took place under the patronage of Ṣûfî saints and their revered tombs.

Wujûdism and visional experience

Complementary to the liberty (or licence) allowed in Ṣûfism in the practical sphere of cult and devotional method, as well as in apotropaic ministry to the people, was a liberty (or licence) in speculation allowed increasingly even by highly respected pîrs. Under the guise of Ṣûfism, the most esoteric Shî'î attempts to unravel a natural cosmic symbolism found their legitimacy. More generally, the unitive metaphysics that had been but one intellectual current in the Earlier Middle Period came to be defended among almost all Ṣûfîs. While proprieties were saved in exoteric works, often filled with the grossly miraculous and the didactic, in more private teaching it seems that ever more Ṣûfî pîrs, in espousing the metaphysics, allowed the widest possible latitude in interpreting away the apparent meaning of Qur'ân and ḥadîth. Often Ṣûfîs went yet further: a unitive metaphysic could be regarded as primary, important for itself apart from any way of life; indeed, its full appreciation could be seen as the very goal of the mystical discipline.

Though ṭarîqahs did differ in their hospitality to it, unitive speculation so conceived became a major formative force in Ṣûfî life, and the most universally debated issue among Ṣûfîs took the form of what sort of unitive cosmology was most consistent with the Islamic unitarian doctrine, tawḥîd. Though the works of relatively unmetaphysical earlier men like Qushayrî and 'Abdulqâdir Gîlânî were still authoritative, Ṣûfîs came to look to the thinking of Ibn-al-'Arabî or occasionally Yaḥyà Suhravardî for further speculative clarification. 'Abdulkarîm Jîlî (d. 1428), of Gîlân at the foot of the Caspian, was the most effective popularizer of Ibn-al-'Arabî's solutions. He systematized the great man's visions and concentrated, for a guiding thread, on the notion of the 'perfect man' as ideal microcosm, realizable in mystical experience. But the catchword for Ibn-al-'Arabî's thinking came to be derived from his unitive metaphysic proper: Ibn-al-'Arabî was regarded as master of the *waḥdat al-wujûd*, the 'unity of being', and those who saw this unity in the total way he did were called 'Wujûdîs'.

Even those Ṣûfî thinkers that disavowed the more extreme unitive theories had by now to provide their own metaphysical solutions. Probably the most prominent of such opponents of the Wujûdî position was 'Alâuddawlah Simnânî (1261–1336), who started his career as a courtier under the Mongols; there he came into contact with Buddhist monks as well as Christians and every variety of Muslims. He had reached a high rank with the monarch himself when a vision on the battlefield where he was fighting determined him to abandon his career for a life of religion. He soon retired to his birthplace, Simnân in northern Iran, where he became a respected pîr, called on to reconcile even political disputes, and looked to as a pillar of the Kubrawiyyah ṭarîqah (which was traced back to the speculative-minded Najmuddîn Kubrà of Bukhârâ).

Simnânî's teaching was comprehensively irenic. He was explicitly opposed to the Shî'ah, for instance; but he admitted them freely as good Muslims, only not so balanced in their views as those he called Sunnîs (who held the mid-point not only between Shî'îs and Khârijîs, but between all other extremes of doctrine); and he pointed out (correctly) that when Shî'îs blessed their twelve imâms instead of the four first caliphs, this was no more an innovation than was blessing the four caliphs, which dated only from 'Abbâsî times. His irenic temper went out even to other religious allegiances: he defended ardently the superiority of Islam, but he was willing to undertake to guide non-Muslims in the mystical Way—assuming that when the disciple got to a certain point, he would find it impossible to proceed further without going beyond the prophet he had been clinging to and accepting Muḥammad; and he even referred an inquiring ascetic, who had been halted in his progress by an obscure vision, to a Buddhist monk who was a level high enough to resolve that particular problem.

If the true 'Sunnîs' held to the middle way in point of doctrine, the true Ṣûfîs held the middle ground among the 'Sunnîs'; for they accepted all the four received imâms of fiqh, he said, not preferring one or the other—indeed, with a touch of 'Alid loyalism typical of Ṣûfism by this time, Simnânî seems to have thought of 'Alî as his own master in fiqh, presumably ascribing to him a tutiorist position, taking the most rigorous of the positions found in any of the four madhhabs. Finally within Ṣûfism itself this position was again irenic. He accepted as proper whatever a saint was reported as saying—and then explained it away so far as it appeared to disagree with his own position. (Typically enough, he usually accepted any reported miracle or special vision as being an actuality and then denied that it bore the meaning ascribed to it by those that would defend one or another exclusive position on the basis of it.)

Nevertheless, Simnânî had his own firm positions. He developed a schematic theory of seven 'inferior senses' with which the mystic perceived inward truths, setting each of them under the patronage of one of seven great prophets (Adam, Noah, Abraham, Moses, David—whose Psalms Muslims always regarded as a special scripture—Jesus, and Muḥammad). And he taught—possibly in line with his preference for middle positions, but also, surely, out of a concern for defining the Muslim monotheistic position over against Indic conceptions in which no transcendent divinity seemed needed—his own doctrine about the unity of being: the unity that such mystics as Ibn-al-'Arabî spoke of was not properly an ontological oneness of being as such, but a oneness of witness (*shuhûd*), in that it was a function of how the mystic should perceive himself and all else. This was a way of asserting the central role of monotheistic prophethood. And he carefully interpreted any statement of Ibn-al-'Arabî, on metaphysics or on other controversial points either, such as the superiority of sainthood to prophethood, in such a way as to be consistent with his prophecy-oriented approach (sometimes even by way of obvious, and presumably conscious, quibbles). The position represented by Simnânî was called Shuhûdî, as against the Wujûdî position; it was widely adopted by the relatively Sharî'ah-minded; in the fifteenth century, in India, we find attempts to reconcile the two positions but in a more Wujûdî direction.

Other Ṣûfîs, less concerned with the prophetic side of Islam, worked out practical consequences of the Wujûdî position in a way more drastic than Ibn-al-'Arabî would surely have allowed as following from his ideas. One of the most influential ṭarîqahs in this direction was the Shaṭṭâriyyah (known in some areas as Isḥâqiyyah or Bisṭâmiyyah). They proclaimed that they had discovered a more rapid method of proceeding on the mystical Way than was taught by the cautious masters of more conventional ṭarîqahs. Since (as the Wujûdî principle of the 'unity of being' in God seemed to imply) all those objects of interest other than God, which most Ṣûfîs spent their efforts rejecting, were in fact nothing, it was wasteful to spend time rejecting them. The bold and determined *sâlik*, seeker of mystical truth, should think only of the positive truth of God himself; recognizing that in himself, the seeker, there was in reality nothing but God (here they harked back to figures like Ḥallâj and Bâyazîd Bisṭâmî, taking very seriously the implications of their ecstatic phrases of identity with God). Thus the sâlik, the seeker, could rapidly become an ârif, a knower of God. In contrast to the dominant tradition from Junayd to Simnânî, that mystical 'intoxication' as found in ecstatic moments was less ultimately valid than the mystical 'sobriety' that succeeded and transformed the moral plane of the seeker, the Shaṭṭâriyyah prized 'intoxication' more highly. Though found throughout the Persianate zone of Islamdom from Rûm in Europe through Iran itself, the Shaṭṭâriyyah were eventually especially popular in India, where one of their pîrs brought the teaching in a triumphal march as far as Bengal in the later fifteenth century, and where soon his disciples were taking a great interest in the Yogic discipline and the monist metaphysics of the Hindu tradition (seen as similar to the Wujûdî metaphysics) as well as in Hindi poetry. From India, the ṭarîqah became very prominent also in the Malaysian archipelago.

With the general acceptance of a unitive metaphysic as an integral part (or even as the goal) of the Ṣûfî way, and particularly with the Wujûdî position, can be associated several other points of view that became increasingly tolerated even when not accepted outright by all Ṣûfîs. We have seen that an antinomian position, though strongly opposed by many, was so freely mooted as one legitimate alternative that not only were the non-Sharî'ah ṭarîqahs openly acknowledged, but individual pîrs could feel free to make their choice between the two positions without changing ṭarîqah allegiance.[3] A unitive metaphysic, in which every created thing formed part of a harmonious whole, could not but soften lines drawn between person and person and between act and act, reinforcing any antinomian inclination. The Wujûdî position, in particular, which could seem to imply that all differentiations in actual life were virtually illusory, seems to have been adopted by those who denied the Sharî'ah applied to the 'ârif élite. Again, the Wujûdî position, or indeed any admission of a unitive metaphysic as an integral part of Ṣûfism, was congenial to a related point of view—that which saw the mystical disciplines within all religious communities as essentially at one. When the Ṣûfî life could be seen as almost a logical consequence of a unitive metaphysic, the inevitable similarities to be found in other unitive metaphysics, each with its own divergent supporting disciplines, encouraged an identification across communal lines. Like considerations led to the notion of *ṣulḥ-e kull*, 'universal conciliation' among sects and viewpoints as well as among persons and factions, as a primary Ṣûfî ideal.

Perhaps the most important accompaniment of the general acceptance of unitive metaphysics, in point of actual mystical practice, was a rather less explicit development: an increased reliance on visional experiences, even on dream visions, as guidance in all things pertaining to the Ṣûfî life. I must add that I suggest this even more tentatively than most such generalizations; but a shallow acquaintance with the material seems to suggest that in the Middle Periods and especially in the Later Middle Periods, explicit visions, as readily described as any dream, were given more weight on more varied occasions than in High Caliphal Ṣûfism. It was not an innovation when Sumnânî, like Ibn-al-'Arabî before him, explained that various pieces of historical as well as metaphysical information had come to him from the *ghayb*, the 'unseen', by way of dreams and visions (when the soul, as Avicenna had confirmed, has access to non-sensory levels of awareness). But surely a major function of his analysis of the seven interior senses was to work out a way of disciplining the interpretation of such visions; one can guess that he was more preoccupied with them than was, for instance, Junayd, to whom otherwise he bears some similarity. In the narratives of saints in this period generally, their ecstatic experiences seem to be more prominent than the ascetic experiences that had played so great a role earlier; and this even when there is no question of a short-cut method by way of drugs. Probably

[3] I have tried to indicate some of the dimensions and appeals of antinomianism, and how nearly inescapable it was in at least some sense or other, in the article on *ibâḥa* in the *Encyclopaedia of Islam*, 2nd ed.

even the long retreat in a solitary cell, imposed once a year on each devotee by the Khalwatiyyah ṭarîqah prominent among the western Turks, was less a sheer ascetic discipline than a means of evoking ecstasy and visions.

Reliance on such visions presumably became more important with an emphasis on the ecstatic side of mysticism, as compared to the everyday devotional side of it. But it could also serve the ends of inducing and validating metaphysical insight, as that came to be felt as an integral part of the venture. Both waking and dreaming visions can form a very fruitful resource for personal mythic formation, a process intimately related to the metaphysics of the time (and perhaps to all metaphysics). Such myth formation need not serve merely the delights of a free fantasy. We are learning that there can be dreams of special urgency which can be pointers to areas of crucial importance to the growth of the personality; and this at all levels of that growth, not merely in its correction of elementary neuroses. Dreams readily take on a colouration, in their symbols and format, from the social expectations surrounding the dreamer; but they will give those social expectations a profoundly personal relevance, perhaps more so than can readily be achieved in waking consciousness. If there are, in fact, any interresonant symbolisms tying together validly the elements of human experience both in our personal responses and in the outer natural world, one may suppose that in dreams such symbolisms might be most freely expressed.[4]

Finally, we must refer to another phenomenon related to non-Sharî'ah Ṣûfism. Amid all the experiment, exploration, and controversy enlivening the Ṣûfî tradition of the Later Middle Period, we can glimpse—especially in the Persianate zone—the outlines of a tradition of popular freethinking which we can pinpoint unmistakably only much later, but which surely went back at least to this period even though we probably cannot document a tradition that must have been largely oral. Behind stereotyped accusations hurled at 'Zindîqs' and the like, we can already see the disparate elements of a tradition unambiguously documented for Iran in the nineteenth century: a varying mixture of Falsafah, of Wujûdî Ṣûfism, and of freewheeling intellectual iconoclasm, which was apparently already spiced in the Later Middle Period with a liberal appeal to 'Alid loyalism of a radical sort. Spread among wandering self-educated darvîshes and presumably among marginal elements in the urban population, but taken up (under cover of taqiyyah dissimulation) among the more venturesome of the respectable classes, the mood of this tradition was presumably eclectic and defiant of all received authority, and naturally not always intellectually very consistent or solid. It was in such a mood that could be imagined the tale of the darvîsh who made three clay

[4] In Gustave von Grunebaum and Roger Caillois, ed., *The Dream and Human Societies* (University of California Press, 1966), we can see how some Jungians and non-Jungians alike are coming to take more seriously the role of dreaming in the human organic balance. The volume also contains what is a first beginning in the study of Islamicate dream interpretation; but we still want a study of how dream analysis was actually used by pîrs in analyzing their disciples' progress.

figurines, of 'Alî, of Muḥammad, and of God; he smashed that representing 'Alî for allowing his place as caliph to be usurped and so admitting injustice into the world; then he smashed that of Muḥammad for not having made clear the succession in the first place; and then that of God, for having, in His omnipotence, allowed the wrong to prevail at all. Such a tradition of scepticism, or at least of defiance of any conventional answers, must be borne in mind as ever present in the unspoken background, serving as the complement of the standard image of the world and of history that was taught in the madrasahs; for the freethinking tradition, in its diverse strands, may have been scarcely less influential among that minority of the exceptional who, by their active imaginations, can determine so many decisions in situations of crisis.[5]

When a whole world of deviants from normal social expectations (whether out of high piety or out of neuroticism, even the most discerning need not always be able to tell) displayed itself and won common people's esteem under the name of Ṣûfism, yet another religious tendency of the Later Middle Period was to be expected: the development of new anti-Ṣûfî Sharî'ah-mindedness.

Elaboration of Sharî'ah and Falsafah

The detailed work of elaborating the Sharî'ah-minded disciplines was not all done even by the Later Middle Period. Ṣûfism or no Ṣûfism, studies of ḥadîth, of fiqh, of kalâm, of the Arabic lexicon, and of course of history, notably biographical studies of the 'ulamâ', were still to be completed. Al-Qalqashandî (d. 1418) composed a widely used encyclopedia for kâtib administrators, which included not only a survey of the Egyptian administration in his time but also specimens of elegant chancery letters and an indication of the whole range of religious, historical, and other adab learning which should be indispensable to the refined clerk; in it, of the 213 textbooks he suggested (which include a handful from the Greek), about a hundred were by men who had lived to see the Mongol conquests or were even more recent; of these hundred, the majority seem to have lived into the fourteenth century.[6] That is, the men of the Later Middle Period, much as they revered the old masters, commonly found the most convenient and authoritative works to be those composed more or less in their own time.

Some of the concerns of learning, in this period, can seem petty or far-fetched—as when details were filled in about marriage between jinn and

[5] Edward G. Browne, *A Year amongst the Persians* (London, 1893), has a variant of the anecdote of the darvîsh; it gives many glimpses of this mood, which is also analyzed in a condescending way by Gobineau in his study of 'Central Asian' philosophizing, *Nouvelles Asiatiques* (Paris, 1963).

[6] The statistics from which this emerges are in G. Makdisi's article, 'Ash'arī and the Ash'arites in Islamic Religious History', *Studia Islamica*, 17 (1962), 37–80; 18 (1963), 19–39.

Later Learnèd Men, 1300–1506

1310	Death of Nasafî, mutakallim, commentator on the ideal form of government
1311	Death of Quṭbuddîn Shîrâzî, astronomer associated with Naṣîruddîn Ṭûsî, perfected Ptolemaic planetary theory
1318	Death of Rashîduddîn, vizier, man of letters, sometimes called Persia's greatest historian
1320	Death of Kamâluddîn Fârsî, astronomer associated with Quṭbuddîn Shîrâzî, improved Ibn-al-Haytham's *Optics*, studied reflection and the rainbow
1320	Death of Yunus Emre, Turkish Ṣûfî and folk poet using the common language
1321	Death of Nizârî, Shî'î panegyric poet, traveller
1324	Death of Niẓâmuddîn Awliyâ, Indo-Persian Ṣûfî, principal organizer of the Chistî order
1326	Death of 'Allâma Ḥillî, mutakallim associated with Naṣîruddîn Ṭûsî, codifier of Imâmî Shî'î doctrine
1328	Death of Amîr Khusraw, Indo-Persian Ṣûfî court poet, member of Chistî order, noted for his ghazals and epics
1328	Death of Ibn-Taymiyyah, Ḥanbalî jurisprudent and mutakallim, concerned about orthodoxy and Ṣûfî excesses
1334	Death of Vaṣṣâf, courtier, historian who wrote in ornate prose style
1336	Death of 'Alâuddawlah Simnânî, Ṣûfî opponent of Ibn al-'Arabî and Wujûdism
fl. 1350	Ibn-al-Shâṭir, Damascene astronomer whose lunar model was equivalent to that of Copernicus
1352	Death of Khvâjû, court poet to last of Îl-khâns and to Muẓaffarids and Jalâyirids
1389	Death of al-Taftâzânî, Faylasûf, mutakallim, exegist; wrote in Arabic at the court of Timur
1389	Death of Bahâuddîn Naqshband, Ṣûfî; Naqshbandî order formed around his teaching
1390	Death of Ḥâfiz, poet, master of the ghazal, sometimes called the best of the Persian poets
1406	Death of Ibn-Khaldûn, Faylasûf of Andalusian descent, statesman, qâḍî, writer of universal history
1413	Death of 'Alî al-Jurjânî, mutakallim, contemporary of al-Taftâzânî
1418	Death of al-Qalqashandî, courtier, writer of encyclopedic administrative manual in adab style
1428	Death of 'Abdulkarîm Jîlî, Ṣûfî analyst, commentator on Ibn-'Arabî
1430	Death of Ḥâfiz Âbrû, Timurî historian and well-travelled geographer
1449	Death of Ulugh-beg, ruler, savant, astronomer; built observatory at Samarqand where some important work was carried out

fl. 1480s	Dawlat Shâh, poet, anthologist, biographer of poets
1492	Death of Jâmî, Ṣûfî and court poet; sometimes called last of the greats
1498	Death of Mîrkhvand, court historian
1501	Death of 'Ali-Shêr Neva'i, vizier, sometimes called greatest poet of E. Turkish (Chagatay) language; biographer of poets, critic
1502	Death of Davvânî, Faylasûf, moralist
1504	Death of Kâshifî, preacher, prose moralist
1506	Death of Ḥusayn Bâyqarâ, ruler, poet in Chagatay, patron of Jâmî, Mîrkhvand, Neva'i, and the painter Bihzâd

humans. But such points often prove to be meaningful on investigation. Several scholars continued to stress, on the basis of rare reports, the possibility of long periods of gestation of a human child, even up to four years. Biologically, it may seem unwarranted to base law on such dubious reports. But one practical effect was to protect the rights of a child that might otherwise be declared born out of wedlock, and even to protect the personal safety of the mother who might risk an accusation of adultery.

But some scholars found a special motive for pushing Sharî'ah-minded studies further than they had yet been pushed. As the Islamic tradition had developed, the majority of Shar'î 'ulamâ' were acknowledging the need to supplement the Sharî'ah and its associated disciplines with various aspects of Ṣûfism or even of Falsafah. Those 'ulamâ' who wanted to retain the exclusive position of the Islamic challenge as expressed in its Shar'î form had either to maintain an intransigence that was increasingly unavailing, or else to enlarge the resources of a Sharî'ah-minded approach so as to make it more self-sufficient so that the oppositional character of the Shar'î tradition could be reaffirmed on a more effective level. Some resources for doing this were already present in the logic of the Sharî'ah structure.

Most doctors of fiqh had used systematic principles to guide qiyâs analogy so as to prevent it from becoming a mere arbitrary excuse for drawing any parallel that might be convenient. Ḥanafîs used a principle they called *istiḥsân*, 'judging best', referring to the implicit rationale of the ruling that was being extended. Mâlikîs used a principle they called *istiṣlâḥ*, which was to seek out, in certain cases, the *maṣlaḥah*, the 'human advantage', which could be identified as the occasion of a given Qur'ân or ḥadîth ruling and was to guide any analogy made from that ruling. Some 'ulamâ', while admitting that certain sorts of occasions for ḥadîth rulings could be denominated maṣlaḥah, denied that any special logical process was involved, claiming that reference to the maṣlaḥah was merely a specialized application of the rules of qiyâs as such, which were elaborated in detail. (For instance, priorities, in case of conflicting indications, were to be given to the five primary human interests in order: life, religion, family, reason, property; and perhaps honour.)

Certain Ḥanbalîs, rejecting a simple policy of intransigence, saw in the concept of maṣlaḥah a means of giving the Shar'î tradition a larger social reach than it had had when a limited range of application was accepted for the Sharî'ah in its details, either vis-à-vis the caliphate, legitimized globally, or vis-à-vis the military amîrs, accepted as a substitute. Aḥmad Ibn-Taymiyyah of Damascus (1263–1328), of an old family of Ḥanbalî scholars, took up this idea as part of a many-pronged campaign to counter the prevailing extra-Shar'î tendencies.

He took the offensive against the extra-Shar'î traditions partly through well-informed assault and partly by taking over key points in them for his own. Thus he opposed most aspects of 'Alid loyalism (and fanatically attacked such sectarian Shî'ism as was found in Syria). He attacked most aspects of Ṣûfism (and especially Ibn-al-'Arabî), opposing bitterly such things as revering saints' tombs, which formed a focus for the whole system of popular Ṣûfî piety. He did accept the idea that some men might be singled out as saints; but he insisted that spiritual progress was not toward knowing God but toward serving Him more perfectly; and what the devout must learn to love is not God's essence (unknowable) but His command—in effect, the Sharî'ah. But then that Sharî'ah was not an arbitrary set of rules, but was tied to intelligible human goals. For he accepted the social role that the Faylasûfs ascribed to the prophet as legislator (he built his doctrine of the prophet largely on the doctrine of a Shî'î disciple of Naṣîruddîn Ṭûsî about the imâm, a doctrine in turn based on Falsafah); and he systematically interpreted the Sharî'ah in terms of social utility. However, he took up Ghazâlî's attack on Falsafah and pushed it further (not allowing to the sciences of Falsafah, for instance, any such association with prophecy in their origin as had Ghazâlî).

At the same time, he offered a positive programme: he set about making the Sharî'ah discipline itself more applicable to the manifold conditions of actual life. As a Ḥanbalî, he was basing himself (rather freely) on one of the later traditions of fiqh, kept relatively free of Marwânî-age details and flexible in its own time by its insistence on reference to actual ḥadîth reports and its limitation of the force of ijmâ' to the rare cases of agreement among the first generation of Muslims. In particular, he gave a logically more precise definition to the principle of maṣlaḥah, less extreme than that of an enthusiastic Ḥanbalî predecessor, but still very liberal; so that with close logical dependence on the ḥadîth method, he was able to develop a broad use of the principle. In this way, he could justify not relying, for qiyâs, merely on a literally evident analogy based on reference to the sort of occasion that had produced the original instance from which the analogy was drawn; rather the welfare of the Muslims in their actual circumstances had to be taken into account anew at all times. This doctrine of maṣlaḥah allowed him to claim that the Sharî'ah was absolutely all-inclusive and that there was always a single correct solution to its problems which must be striven for with every logical method available. This was a point which justified at once his interpretation of spiritual life in strictly Sharʿî terms, and his insistence on the duty of the ʿulamâʾ to adapt the Sharîʿah to their own age, for its corollary was that the single correct solution of the given moment must vary according to circumstances. (On this point he invoked the continuity of the one religion taught by the several prophets in different forms for their different ages.)

Such a broad use of the notion of maṣlaḥah allowed a great deal of flexibility to legists, provided they did not feel too much bound by taqlîd and the notion that ijtihâd was closed. Something comparable was used extensively by the later Mâlikî legists of Egypt and especially the Maghrib. But Ibn-Taymiyyah himself made it the basis of an incisive attack on the established order.

Ibn-Taymiyyah was greatly revered by the people of Damascus, most of whom were not Ḥanbalîs—Ḥanbalism was becoming rare anywhere—but who had a tradition of almost fanatical loyalty to a Jamâʿî-Sunnî position as against all Shîʿism, and who tended to join with this a strong Sharîʿah-mindedness. (Many of the revered tombs around Damascus, for which indeed it was famous, were tombs not of Ṣûfîs but of alleged ancient prophets, Syria being known to be the land of prophecy.) But Ibn-Taymiyyah's programme was too radical for the established authorities. He attacked the anti-Sharʿî and extra-Sharʿî practices taken for granted by the Mamlûk government, and his popularity made him dangerous. And he attacked the other ʿulamâʾ for their willingness, as he saw it, to compromise both with non-Sharʿî piety and with the government. He condemned them in particular for their doctrine of taqlîd, which justified their accommodations, and insisted that the right of general ijtihâd still held for any competent legist, such as himself, who was qualified to go back to the sources and puzzle out the law for himself. (Yet he made this demand from within a position which technically satisfied the conservative spirit: as a Ḥanbalî, he was only following the approved position of his own madhhab, which was recognized as one of the legitimate four among Sunnîs.) He was imprisoned more than once; finally when they not only put him in prison but refused to let him have pen, ink, and paper, he died of heartbreak. His funeral procession at Damascus was followed, as was proper, by as many of the faithful as took cognizance of it: in this case, as often among Muslims, it became a demonstration of popular acclaim: it is said (doubtless with the usual chroniclers' exaggeration) that 200,000 men and 15,000 women took part.[7]

Ibn-Taymiyyah had few followers to continue his work. More influential in

[7] Henri Laoust, *Essai sur les doctrines sociales et politiques de Taḳî-d-dîn Aḥmad b. Taimîya (1262–1328)* (Cairo, 1939), the most important of Laoust's works on Ibn-Taymiyyah, contains a rich documentation; though I think Laoust is not so profound as Massignon, one may compare this with Louis Massignon's *La Passion d'al-Ḥallâj* as providing a wide-ranging and perceptive view of a whole range of Muslim religious life; if one reads the two books together, one will get a fairly comprehensive sense of the issues debated in Islam.

the coming centuries was a school of philosopher-theologians whose work was as much Falsafah as kalâm, though in the conservative spirit they called it kalâm. Taftâzânî (1322–89), one of the most respected authorities of this school, was, though himself a Jamâ'î-Sunnî, a defender of the positions of the Shî'î Naṣîruddîn Ṭûsî. Born in a large village in Khurâsân, he travelled (as was typical of scholars) wherever learning was patronized—in Khwârazm and even to the Golden Horde farther northwest. He was highly valued for his reputation by Timur, who insisted that he come to Samarqand. He wrote extensively—often in the form of commentaries on standard works, sometimes in the form of a commentary on a work of his own—on grammar, on rhetoric, on law and jurisprudence, and on logic and metaphysics; his works seem to have come to be more read even in Damascus than Ibn-Taymiyyah's. In a summary of his doctrinal views, he managed to hew closely to the positions laid down by al-Nasafî, author of the most popular Ash'arî catechism from the Earlier Middle Period; yet he seems not to have regarded himself as an Ash'arî, and he commented on more than one work of the great Mu'tazilî, Zamakhsharî, particularly his Qur'ân commentary (Taftâzânî wrote another Qur'ân commentary of his own in Persian). He was also independent enough to write works on both Ḥanafî and Shâfi'î law—and has been claimed by both madhhabs. But it was in his logic and metaphysics that he took up the interesting substantive problem which made him a potent (and controversial) inspirer of the philosophers who followed him.

One of his commentators was Jalâluddîn Davânî of Shîrâz (1427–1502), who reworked Naṣîruddîn's essentially Aristotelian treatise on ethics into a form which long influenced political thought, establishing among other things the point that any de facto ruler who was philosophically righteous (and hence, if a Muslim, applied the Sharî'ah) was true caliph in his realm—as against either the old Shar'î view of the single direct successor to Muḥammad or Ibn-al-'Arabî's view of the invisible Ṣûfî quṭb. But though this position on the caliphate became standard in Muslim governments, scholars most valued Davânî for his logical and metaphysical points: it is said that he solved the liar's paradox ('all statements are lies including this one'—if the statement is true it is false, if it is false it is true) by a device anticipating Russell's theory of logical classes, that statements about statements cannot be included within their own objects.

At the same time, there were enough specialists in positive natural science to be pushing inquiries forward in this field also. It has been suggested that after a certain point inquiry in any complex field of positive studies, such as the natural sciences, depends on so rapidly increasing a pace of investment of human time that only under special conditions can it continue to go forward at a pace comparable to what it can achieve in its earlier periods. As more becomes known, it take more and more time for any individual to assimilate what is already known and move forward to the frontiers of inquiry; this means that scholars in such fields must increasingly become specialists if they are to push inquiry substantially further. It means also that the specialties must become increasingly multiplied, each specialty being subdivided into narrower ones. The erection of new syntheses, in which many disparate facts can be subsumed, can give only a partial respite to such a process. But since serious knowledge is one, such specialties must be interdependent: if they are not all pursued at once, it is hard for any one of them to be far advanced. To the extent that further inquiry did require increasingly narrow specialization, it would have required a steady multiplication of specialists devoted to natural-science inquiry.

This multiplication is unlikely to have occurred in the contracting urban economy of the Later Middle Period. We know that in western Europe, after a promising flowering of natural-science studies in the Earlier Mid-Islamic Period in which the Europeans rivalled the achievements of their Muslim mentors, advance in such studies did slacken off in the Later Mid-Islamic Period; this may not have been due simply to the economic depression of the time, but also to a lack of sufficiently expansive human resources; when scientific studies were finally launched into their modern phase at the end of the sixteenth century, they did acquire new specialties and specialists at a pace measurable by an exponential curve, periodically doubling. However, it is not clear whether scientific studies in our period actually required so much specialization as yet. In any case, we have as yet insufficient knowledge of the state of natural-science studies in Islamdom in the Later Middle Period to know for sure whether in Islamdom also a slackening occurred. Most of the scientific books produced then simply have not been read.

Willy Hartner makes probably as good a case as can now be made for the notion of a decline in natural science in the Later Middle Period.[8] But the reasons he gives for asserting a decline do not hold. He does not so much assert that the level of the best scientific work declined then (he ranks Kâshî, of the fifteenth-century circle of Ulugh-beg, with Archimedes and Bîrûnî, and he grants that a Moroccan astronomer in the sixteenth century may also have been of top rank) but rather that there was less of it; and that one or two subsequent manuals, from after 1500—notably one from the Ottoman empire—show actual qualitative decline.

But the data are susceptible of a different explanation. He bases his quantitative estimates largely on Heinrich Suter; but Suter scarcely offers a good sampling. From Storey's Persian bibliography, we know of a great

[8] Willy Hartner, 'Quand et comment s'est arrêté l'essor de la culture scientifique dans l'Islam?' in *Classicisme et déclin culturel dans l'histoire de l'Islam*, ed. R. Brunschvig and G. E. von Grunebaum (Paris, 1957), pp. 319–38, making use of Heinrich Suter, *Die Mathematiker und Astronomen der Araber und ihre Werke* (Leipzig, 1900). The last portions of Aldo Mieli, *La science arabe* (Leiden, 1938), likewise seem to make out a decline; but he is interested explicitly solely in Arabic works, and in them chiefly just so far as they had, or might have had, a role in the Occident; the decline he speaks of, accordingly, is prima facie a decline in influence in the Occident—which cannot be equated with a decline in science as such.

number of Persian scientific works—to say nothing of Arabic—in the later periods; but Suter knew of very few works after 1400 and almost none after 1500; and what he does list is also biased geographically—being almost all from the Mediterranean region, nothing from later Iran, and practically nothing from India in any period. (Even so, he omits the important Moroccan figure cited by Hartner.) Yet in the later periods, as in the earlier, the most important intellectual activity of other sorts, particularly in Falsafah metaphysics, seems to have been in the neglected areas eastward from the Mediterranean (including, later, India). One would suppose natural science might centre there also.

The explanation of the bias in his data seems to be twofold. He began, of course, with those writers already translated into Latin, that is, the earlier masters. To these, he had to add from Muslim sources. But, first, Suter knew only the Mediterranean tradition, which was always relatively peripheral and where (assuming a real collapse of the traditon in the seventeenth or eighteenth century) more recent works from the central areas would not yet have become well known before the tradition ceased to grow. Second, after the seventeenth- or eighteenth-century collapse of the tradition, the inferior latter-day practitioners of it would be likely to be poor guides to the recent periods (and not only in the Mediterranean area); for they would have to judge this later material independently; whereas those names that had earlier become fully established (and notably those known already in Latin) would continue to be famous also among the epigones. Hence, in the absence of anyone to read all the materials from a modern point of view, there would be no sure way of discovering what was best in the later periods. Then the presumptions about Islamdom and the 'Orient' present in the usual Western image of the world and of its history ensured that that interpretation of the data would be chosen that was least favourable to the vigour of Islamicate culture.

The case of natural science has a special relevance to the question whether there was an Islamicate decadence. Apart from the economy as such, where a reduction of resources might be ascertained (though this might or might not carry with it a reduction in the qualitative level of economic activity), it is only in the sphere of natural science that we might have reasonably objective criteria for judging decline or decadence. The Brunschvig and von Grunebaum volume, in which Hartner's essay appears, tries to trace decline also in Arabic and Persian literature, in the visual arts, and in religious and philosophical thought. Typically, it fails seriously to evaluate the work of the more prominent later figures; in the brief essay on philosophy, for instance, none of them is even mentioned. But, even at best, the judgments passed in favour of the earlier periods are very subjective. Such subjectivity in other fields might seem to matter less if it could be corroborated by data from the field of natural science, where quantitative measures are relatively applicable. However, we must recall that even if such a judgment on Islamicate natural science were available, it would not allow us to pass judgment on the achievement of the whole civilization; for natural science cannot, by itself, be made the criterion of progress or decline in a civilization; and we cannot even assume that it is a good index of creativity in general.

We do know some examples of the scientific work that was being done. The Shî'î Faylasûf Naṣîruddîn Ṭûsî was an active fosterer of the natural sciences as well as of the ethical, metaphysical, and political thinking of Falsafah. He persuaded the Mongols to set up an observatory at Marâghah on the highlands of Azerbaijan. Some of his own experiments—for instance, an experiment with the effects of foreknowledge on soldiers' reactions to sudden noise (perhaps related to an early use of gunpowder for its surprise effect?)—do not seem to have led far; but he encouraged apt students. One of his most prominent students was Quṭbuddîn Shîrâzî (d. 1311), who illustrated grandly the intellectual synthesis of the Middle Periods. Quṭbuddîn loved interesting people—it is said that he sat with the scoffers and drank wine. One of his books bears a title that suggests his sense of humour: 'A Book I've Made, Don't Criticize It, On Astronomy'. He did important work in natural science, developing further in many details a significant synthesis that Ṭûsî had produced. At the same time, he lived the life of a Ṣûfî. He was a disciple of Ḳonyavî, a chief disciple of Ibn-al'Arabî, and he himself wrote one of the most important commentaries on Yaḥyà Suhravardî. Finally his biographer noted that he performed his ṣalât worship along with the ordinary people.

A disciple of Quṭbuddîn Shîrâzî, Kamâluddîn Fârsî (d. *c.* 1320), wrote a commentary on Ibn-al-Haytham's optics which a modern reader has maintained to be equally important with Ibn-al-Haytham's work (which was long prized in the Occident) and perhaps more original.[9] His contributions explicated minutiae, but some of them were of great potential consequence. Thus, he analyzed what refraction of light within a spherical raindrop was required to produce a double rainbow; he studied cloud effects at distances; and he greatly refined the use of Ibn-al-Haytham's camera obscura, showing that with a very small opening, the smaller the opening the more exact the reversed image received, an observation that was decisive in showing how light rays carry total images to every point. Thus painfully slow was progress still from detail to detail.

But sometimes results might be more exciting. One physician came near discovering the circulation of the blood, but the significance of that was not felt. But in astronomy, science was sufficiently developed to make serious innovations immediately recognizable. Naṣîruddîn Ṭûsî had invented a method for eliminating at least some aspects of the planetary eccentricities which the Ptolemaic system presupposed, so that the planets could be conceived as proceeding in a more purely circular manner. He showed that if the

[9] E. Wiedemann, in a series of articles (partly summarized in articles in the first edition of the *Encyclopaedia of Islam*, has patiently set forth just what Kamâluddîn and others did, and compared their work with comparable work in the Occident.

diameter of one of the lesser circles required in tracing orbits be thought of as itself revolving at a fixed rate, then geometrically a scheme of circles could be erected that would account for the eccentricity. This encouraged his successors at the observatory in Marâghah to attempt to find ideally circular motions for all the planets as Aristotle had envisaged them. In particular, the orbits of the moon and of Mercury were resistant to this technique. Ibn-al-Shâṭir of Damascus worked on both these problems and finally came up with a solution at least for the moon's orbit which satisfied him. This turns out to have been essentially the same as that proposed more than a century later by Copernicus.[10] (It is interesting, moreover, that recent scholars regard Copernicus' solution for the lunar orbit to have been the soundest part of his work on planetary orbits and perhaps technically the most crucial element in it; for his heliocentric system as such, with its many perfect circles, was, of course, scientifically quite unsound.)

The isolation of the Maghrib

Most of the exponents of the disciplines of Falsafah (as also, indeed, of the Shar'î disciplines) lived in the zone in which Persian was becoming the great language of culture. In the lands using an Arabic dialect, where (apart from the Iraq) Persian was little known, the ferment of these disciplines had little effect, or came only from the outside with the reputation of such masters as Taftâzânî. Yet the greatest historical thinker of the time, and perhaps the greatest mind in any field, came not only from the Arabic zone but from the Maghrib, where the works of the Persianate tradition penetrated most slowly. This was Ibn-Khaldûn. He did read the new works, but he was heir to the purist Spanish tradition of Falsafah, and his work can be seen more clearly as the climax of the Spanish tradition than as a provincial variant of the Persianate. (However, it found most of its readers, significantly enough, in the Persianate zone.)[11] Probably the new ferments further east formed an essential stimulus to Ibn-Khaldûn's work, but more fundamentally it was a response to what had happened in the Maghrib since the great days of the Spanish tradition of refined culture. In the Maghrib, if nowhere else, we see an unmistakable decline in prosperity and power and cultural taste; and Ibn-Khaldûn was its great analyst, producing from it a major new departure in the scientific study of mankind.

[10] E. S. Kennedy, Victor Roberts, and others have been gradually piecing together, in a series of brief but very illuminating articles scattered here and there, the work of these scientists; in this case, see Victor Roberts, 'The Solar and Lunar Theory of Ibn-al-Shâṭir', *Isis*, 48 (1957), 428–32. I must express my gratitude to David Pingree, who has called my attention to current work in the history of science but is not responsible for my assessment of the potentialities of future inquiries.

[11] Because he was not much commented on in Arabic, Ibn-Khaldûn has been said to have been neglected, which seems not to be true if one traces his fortunes in Islamdom as a whole. Yet persons suffering from the persistent Arabistic bias of so many Islamicists have cited his 'neglect' as evidence of 'decadence' in Islamicate culture.

In the Later Middle Period, the Muwaḥḥid realm had largely broken up into successor-states in the far west, the centre, and the east of the Maghrib, each centred on cities and in uneasy relations with the Berber tribes of the hinterland; and in constant intrigue against each other; while Muslim Spain had been reduced to a small mountain state in the far south, paying tribute to the Christians who had turned the magnificent mosques of the chief Spanish cities into churches and cathedrals. The dynasty at Granada in Spain is still remembered for its high levels of taste and even of luxury, symbolized in the delicate architecture of the Alhambra palace. Muslim industriousness made that tiny mountain district a rich agricultural province, but it could not make up for the loss of the great fertile valleys of Spain. The states on the mainland of the Maghrib, meanwhile, were themselves not recovered from the advent of Bedouin camel nomadism in the Earlier Middle Period. Though the destructiveness of the first raids was no longer repeated, yet some of the then devastated territory was never reclaimed; for with the introduction of a new form of pastoralism, economically effective and highly mobile, alongside the Berber pastoralism that already existed, the balance of political power had shifted; the cities and their agriculture and trade were put persistently on the defensive.

The Muwaḥḥid heritage left its imprint on most of the dynasties that succeeded it on the mainland, though in point of religious allegiance the Mâlikism that the first Muwaḥḥids had attacked ruled without question. (The increased weight of tribalism was not of a sort to move toward the kind of military patronage state we have seen the germs of in the central lands.) The Marînid dynasty had arisen from independent Berber tribal origins, but it had been assimilated into the regional state system when it was still a rising local power in Morocco (1216–69), and when it took over power in Fez it attempted to rebuild the position that the Muwaḥḥids had held throughout the Maghrib and even Spain. But the Marînids never subdued all their rivals; after 1340 the dynasty abandoned hope of intervening further in Spain; and by 1415 the Christian Spaniards (in this case, the state of Portugal) had successfully crossed the waters to the Maghrib mainland at Ceuta. After a collapse of Marînid power in 1420, a related line (the Waṭṭâsids) partly restored the fortunes of the state from 1428 on.

The chief rival of the Marînid dynasty was the Ḥafṣid at Tunis, originally a pillar family of the Muwaḥḥid movement and dynasty; in 1237 a representative of the family, governor at Tunis, threw off the authority of the reigning Muwaḥḥid in the name of Muwaḥḥid religious purity; but he and his son (who had himself named caliph by the sharîf ruling at Mecca after the collapse of the ʻAbbâsids) failed to make good their claim to renew Muwaḥḥid rule in the whole Maghrib. The later Ḥafṣids sometimes ruled all the eastern Maghrib but sometimes had to tolerate independent governors or tribal powers; and sometimes rival members of the dynasty held different areas.

Despite the weakness of many of the Ḥafṣid rulers, Tunis, with the eastern

Maghrib, was probably the most important intellectual centre of the Maghrib. The little court at Granada could not support many scholars. Both in Fez in Morocco, and in Tunis, there were influential communities of Spaniards who had fled the Christian conquest. But it was especially in the western Maghrib that was felt the division of the land into two parts: the relatively limited areas immediately around the cities, in which urban governmental control was effectively felt; and the larger mountainous hinterland in which, whatever the nominal ties with a city dynasty, the tribes ruled themselves in their own ways without even small towns to serve as urban outposts, but making do with shifting market fairs. In a potentially rich region, the cities were almost isolated. Tunis, meanwhile, though its potential agricultural hinterland was narrower than that in the west, was itself becoming prosperous as an entrepôt in a trade between the eastern and western Mediterranean that was increasingly important with the increasing wealth of Christian western Europe; for despite the direct trade of the Italian and Catalan cities with the Levant, Muslim and Jewish merchants also, with convenient relations between Cairo and Tunis, could profit, for the time, from the growing Occidental trade. Trade with the Sûdânic lands, whether from the eastern or from the western Maghrib, must have still been considerably less important.

As compared with India or Rûm (southeastern Europe), the whole Maghrib was relatively isolated from the central Islamicate lands. But it was a time of eager development. It was under the Ḥafṣids that the system of madrasah education was fully established in the Maghrib and that much of the creative work of the Mâlikî jurisprudents was done in the use of the concept maṣlaḥah to open up the resources of fiqh and, by this means, in admitting local custom as an integral and disciplined part of the fiqh. It was in this period that the Maghribî forms of popular Ṣûfism became well established, rooting Islam thoroughly in the further countryside and so tying the land a bit closer to the cities culturally even when not politically. It was also in this period that the distinctive traditions of Maghribî architecture matured. In all this activity, Ibn-Khaldûn saw the processes of civilization at work and studied their dependence on strong government in the cities; at the same time, he was aware of economic and cultural weakness as compared to a remoter past (and to other parts of Islamdom) and related this to the cycles of dynastic rule based on pastoral power, as it had appeared in the Maghrib.[12]

The philosophical historian: Ibn-Khaldûn

Ibn-Khaldûn (1332–1406) was the last great Faylasûf of the cautious Spanish tradition. He was born in Ḥafṣid Tunisia but was of an originally Spanish

[12] Ibn-Khaldûn's Maghribî focus was very fruitful for him. But for a modern scholar to generalize from the Maghrib, as some do, can be very misleading, especially if his notion of the other moiety—'the East'—is almost limited to the Jamâ'î-Sunnî Arabs in a period when the greatest cultural vitality was in the Persianate zone (including Shî'î Arabs).

family. He commentated Ibn-Rushd and ended his life as a Sharî'ah judge, a grand qâḍî. But he began with a certain rebelliousness. Even later he was much impressed with Taftâzânî; he was aware of the work of the Shî'î Faylasûf Naṣîruddîn Ṭûsî; perhaps he took a wider interest in the bolder philosophy of central Islamdom. In any case, as a young man he seems to have hoped that in fact the philosopher did not have to live ever as an isolate in a society which was not his own: that he might expect, if he worked at it, to produce the philosopher king, who could do better things. He became tutor to the heir-apparent of the state of Granada—the remains of Muslim Spain—through the patronage of his Faylasûf friend the famous vizier Ibn-al-Khaṭîb. He seems to have proceeded to teach his ward Falsafah—or, rather, the doctrines of the Faylasûfs; for it soon became clear that the young man was not fit for true philosophy in itself. This the vizier saw sooner than the young idealist; he had his friend expelled, lest the young heir, without becoming wise, become arrogant in his half-knowledge, and unruly. But the friendship of the two Faylasûfs continued.

Ibn-Khaldûn wandered then among the Maghrib courts, serving one faction or another in a political capacity. Ibn-Khaldûn seems to have hoped to have a chance to introduce his own ideas or rule in one or another court, but he himself was valued only for his exceptional political talents—among which was close acquaintance with the nomad tribes and skill in treating with them.

Eventually, he seems to have become disillusioned. He was persuaded that Ibn-Rushd had been right after all: one cannot reform society at will. But he was persuaded also that he had come to a new insight into the reason why: that society has its own rules of development. What can and cannot be done to improve social conditions is limited not simply by that constant, the nature of humanity, but by particular social conditions which characterize particular periods of development; and these conditions, in turn, follow historical rules which may be analyzed.

With difficulty he persuaded his current patron to grant him a leave of absence from politics and retired to the countryside to write the first draft of his magnum opus: a study of history. This took the form of a universal chronicle of pre-Islamic and Islamic times (the latter part chiefly restricted to the Islamicate society and especially concentrating on the Maghrib itself), which was preceded by a lengthy introduction, the *Muqaddimah*, analyzing the nature of historical studies and of the historical process. The history is one of those massive works that fills a whole shelf, and the *Muqaddimah* itself fills a very thick volume. Eventually he retired and put the work in final form in Mamlûk Egypt—where he was appointed Mâlikî grand qâḍî whenever the régime wanted to prove its uprightness.

As a Faylasûf, Ibn-Khaldûn was concerned to work out a 'science' in the sense of a self-consistent body of demonstrable generalizations about historical change, generalizations which would in turn be based on premises taken from the demonstrated results of 'higher', i.e., more abstract, sciences—in this case chiefly biology, psychology, and geography. This was, of course, the proper method, in Falsafah, of ensuring that the observations of the new discipline should not be random and merely 'empirical' but should at each point be comprehensive, covering (in principle) all possible cases. But to introduce a science of history was a radical shift in the usual point of view of the Faylasûfs. They had thought of historical phenomena as the most obvious examples of the transiency of the world of 'becoming'—of what happens to things. Such 'accidental' events were essentially unknowable by way of rational demonstration, that is, in the way the unchanging world of 'being'—of what a thing *is*—was rationally knowable. Historical studies had belonged, at best, to the realm of prudential preparation for the lowly practical art of politics: they were not a subject fit for abstract contemplation. Ibn-Khaldûn pointed out clearly that he was introducing a new science, but he accepted the general Philosophical estimate of the material. He made no claim of high dignity for his new sciences, however important he thought it was.

Yet in a way his science was the final answer of the Spanish school of Faylasûfs to kalâm. History had, in principle, been the ultimate reality for the whole Sharîʿah-minded tendency in Islam, and the men of kalâm had spent much effort in justifying their method by defending the historical validity of ḥadîth reports as dependable foundations for legal and doctrinal decisions. Now the realm of history itself was to be conquered for Falsafah. Even on the level of historical technique, Ibn-Khaldûn carried through his attack. The method of isnâd criticism, the highly elaborated tool of historical verification for the Sharîʿah-minded, was essentially a method of external criticism of historical documents—criticism of their credentials. Ibn-Khaldûn was at pains to point out that external criticism was not enough. To avoid obvious nonsense, it was necessary to have recourse to an internal criticism of the reports, a criticism on the basis of the enduring and universal rules of nature: thus he showed the impossibility that the army of Moses could have numbered 600,000, as reported, on the basis of logistics and biology. (His actual methods of internal criticism remained rudimentary; he was less concerned with establishing particular data than with the naturalistic principle.) Like Ibn-Rushd, he carried his mistrust of the more abstract side of the Sharîʿah-minded disciplines to a virtual rejection of kalâm, though it was too deeply rooted by his time to forbid outright. Ibn-Khaldûn was willing to grant that kalâm might, in Ghazâlî's time, have had the valid purpose Ghazâlî reserved for it. But in the Maghrib and Cairo in the fourteenth century (when—let us add—Ṣûfism provided a legitimizing cloak for almost every point of view) doctrinal heresy as such was no longer a problem and kalâm, however popular, was irrelevant.

Instead, Ibn-Khaldûn developed a new, historically oriented kind of political science. He rejected the classification of 'cities' in the older philosophers as irrelevant: their several types, with their best and worst forms, were abstract and unreal. Rather, the condition of a state was to be gauged according to its situation in a natural sequence of historical processes. All this was rooted in what we would call hominid ecology.

The natural and necessary human social unit was rural and lacked the refinements of culture. It was the group solidarity or party spirit (*'aṣabiyyah*) of such units that was the very condition of rural group survival; under favourable circumstances the same solidarity allowed one strong group to achieve dominance over many—or, where urban life was already developed, over an urban society. This dominance meant that the resources of the many could be concentrated by the dominant groups, with resultant economic specialization and all the other traits of city life. The strength of the central power freshly erected allowed the settled arts to develop or—where already developed—to flourish. But the state depended on the solidarity of the ruling group, and as that group tasted of luxury, its solidarity changed. It learned to command by force of money more than by force of personal vigour, and in prosperity its members could become more jealous of each other than mutually bound in alertness against their disarmed subjects. Its single leader became a king and eventually found it necessary to rely on mercenaries more than on the now luxurious group members. At this point, fiscal difficulties set in; and as increased taxes sapped the settled arts, the base for taxation itself declined. With the decline of the original group solidarity, there converged, accordingly, a restriction of the economic base of the society; henceforth reform was essentially impossible from within and the state became easy prey to the next fresh rural, especially pastoral, group with strong solidarity. Meanwhile, the arts of culture might languish. (He noted, however, that the effects of such a cycle were far more severe in lands like the Maghrib than in a long and deeply cultural land like Egypt.)

In the course of this analysis, greatly simplified in my summary, Ibn-Khaldûn had occasion to develop the essentials of economics and money theory. He showed effectively how it can be that in some social conditions an ample government revenue in no way handicaps the economy as a whole, while in other conditions that economy is ruined by the expenses of a government that yet seems to take in less revenue. (These ideas were not wholly unprecedented, but went far beyond the usual Muslim treatments of economics—fiscal manuals for rulers stressing the need to protect agriculture, and handbooks for merchants, weighing various sorts of investment, or even guides to market supervisors.) More generally, Ibn-Khaldûn studied the role of the various arts of necessity and of luxury in the political and social order. Indeed, so detailed and so comprehensive was his presentation of the various arts that his book forms a magnificent introduction to Islamicate culture generally.[13]

[13] Unfortunately, the English translation by Franz Rosenthal, *The Muqaddimah: An Introduction to History*, 3 vols. (New York, 1958), while not so bad on the arts and crafts, is quite unusable for the more general viewpoint of Ibn-Khaldûn, which it misrepresents radically time and again. Technical terms are almost regularly misren-

As had earlier political science among the Faylasûfs, his presentation takes special pains to analyze the place of the prophetically founded state in this system. Here, of course, he is careful not to offend Shar'î principles overtly; but it becomes clear to the thoughtful reader that the prophetic imagination, which as in Ibn-Sînâ is granted great practical wisdom, while it can produce excellent political results, can do so only within the framework of the cycle of group solidarity: the prophetic impulse is an adjunct to natural state formation, adding to the imaginative appeal of one group's strength, and it can be only in the first period of vigour that the prophetic rules can operate without corruption. Not only the Philosophical but even the would-be Shar'î reformer must await the right times and seasons and depend on ecological and historical conditions to favour him. Revelation becomes a historical phenomenon indeed, as the Sharî'ah-minded had insisted, but in a context where history itself is the product of natural law.

Ibn-Khaldûn has been acclaimed as the 'father of sociology' and his ideas have been assimilated to modern Western sociological thought. Unfortunately, this side of Ibn-Khaldûn was followed up but little among Muslims and he was not even known in the Occident before late in the nineteenth century, so that his place in the modern history of social studies is actually very marginal. But he was widely read, for instance, in the Persianate milieu of Ottoman society, and was translated into Turkish. His greatest achievement was not to anticipate various later Occidental social theories but to annex history to Falsafah in his own Islamicate context.[14] This becomes especially clear in the body of his work, the actual history.

Ibn-Khaldûn's work can be contrasted both as to its principles and as to its practice with Ṭabarî's: they represented opposite poles, the Faylasûf and the Ḥadîth man, the exalter of universal truths and the collector of particular facts. Just as the killing of 'Uthmân and the launching of party divisions among Muslims was a crucial moment to Ṭabarî, so for Ibn-Khaldûn's

dered—thus *ghayb*, the 'unseen' (e.g., the sex of the foetus in the womb), is rendered 'supernatural', contrary to Ibn-Khaldûn's most basic position; and *'arab*, an ecological term for camel nomad, is rendered 'Arab' as if it were a linguistic, ethnic term in the modern sense (causing Ibn-Khaldûn paradoxically to denigrate 'the Arabs'). But far worse than this, because less easily remediable, is the steady distortion of sentence after sentence through incomprehension. Cf. the review by H. A. R. Gibb in *Speculum*, 35 (1960), 139–42. A sample of a better English translation is given by Duncan MacDonald in *The Religious Attitude and Life in Islam* (University of California Press, 1909). Unfortunately, the excerpts by Charles Issawi, another partial translation, are so strung together (out of order and out of context) as to make Ibn-Khaldûn look like an anticipation of nineteenth-century European sociology (and not a very good one). The old French translation by de Slane, which also fails to recognize his Philosophical exactitude, is only better than the English by Rosenthal in that it does not mislead so systematically.

[14] Muḥsin Mahdi, in his epochal *Ibn Khaldûn's Philosophy of History: A Study in the Philosophic Foundation of the Science of Culture* (London, 1957), has made all earlier studies of Ibn-Khaldûn out of date. To be added is Mahdi's article, 'Die Kritik der islamischen politischen Philosophie bei Ibn Khaldûn', in *Wissenschaftliche Politik, eine Einführung in Grundfragen ihrer Tradition und Theorie*, ed. D. Oberndörfer (Frieburg im Breisgau, 1962).

historical environment the founding of the Muwaḥḥid state was almost as central. When Ibn-Khaldûn deals with the origin and development of Muwaḥḥid power, every step reveals his concern with the universals that were manifesting themselves.[15]

In the personality of Ibn-Tûmart and the development of his career are brought out deftly those elements that mattered for the foundation of so momentous a political movement. The first point we get—after his identification with one of the strongest of Berber tribes—is his ambitious personality, pointed up quickly in two details. The second of these details leads also to the second point: the ripeness of the times. 'He promised himself that the state would belong to his people under his rule, according to the diviners' and augurers' prediction that a state would appear at that time in the Maghrib. As they claim, he encountered Abû-Ḥâmid al-Ghazâlî and revealed to him what was in his heart on this matter. He encouraged him in it on account of the condition of Islam at that time in the regions of the Maghrib, to wit: the weakening of the state and the shaking of the pillars of authority that united the Lamtûnah [the tribe that supported the then ruling Murabiṭ power] . . .' That is, what the diviners sensed through the imaginative faculty, the sage reasoned out with the rational faculty. Ibn-Tûmart went on to acquire a core of enthusiasts because of his wide religious and intellectual horizons (as a result of bringing back Ghazâlî's teaching) and a reputation among the people of the towns for opposing the luxuries of the Murâbiṭ dynasty. All this was necessary, but the movement became politically significant and the religious reform effective only when the followers he had gained for his ideas became the nucleus of a power organization founded on the tribe with which he was identified. Then the ideas sustained the tribesmen in their independent course in spite of defeats; but it was the tribal solidarity that was able to carry them to victory. This becomes all the clearer from the story immediately following in Ibn-Khaldûn's narrative: a city-based counter-reformer arouses great enthusiasm but is easily crushed for want of solid tribal support.

All this takes the form of a smooth narrative without isnâds or repetitions, a form that had become common among the chroniclers. But a subtler but perhaps more telling contrast to Ṭabarî lies in the use each made of dubious reports. Whereas Ṭabarî could use them (but with documentation such as will alert the wary reader) as contrast to highlight the problems emerging in sounder materials, Ibn-Khaldûn sometimes seems rather casual about matters of factual accuracy. Ibn-Tûmart's political interview with Ghazâlî is probably apocryphal, as Ibn-Khaldûn's own verb, 'as they claim', suggests;

[15] Unfortunately, the French translator, Wm. MacGulkin de Slane, of the *Histoire des Berbères* (Algiers, 1849–51, 1852–66) seems to have had difficulty with passages of Arabic above the level of 'who killed whom'. Perhaps he felt that only the chronology was important, anyway. At any rate, he simply omitted some more complex passages in which Ibn-Khaldûn's social analysis became explicit. This may have contributed to a misimpression sometimes found, that Ibn-Khaldûn's actual history is not seriously informed by his principles.

what Ibn-Khaldûn is interested in is the philosophical illumination its use can give. Again, Ibn-Tûmart—as a close reading of Ibn-Khaldûn's own reports will also suggest—was almost surely of an old Berber family; yet Ibn-Khaldûn brings to the fore the flattering claims made for him of 'Alid ancestry, as if simply to make a point about tribal solidarity: that while it is cast in genealogical forms, it is really based on no inexplicable feeling in the blood but on quite intelligible facts of common social interests. Hence, even if Ibn-Tûmart's ancestry was 'Alid, his solidarity was with the Berber tribe because 'his stock became involved with theirs and . . . assumed their ties of kinship. Having adopted their genealogy, he became one of their number'.

Rhetoricism and subtlety in the Persianate literary tradition

For most cultured persons—courtiers, such persons as still staffed the bureaucracy, and wealthier merchants or landholders—the most interesting aspects of intellectual life (as for the adîbs of the High Caliphal Period) were those expressed in the various forms of humane literature. Whereas even in the Persianate zone, the most respected works embodying the standard Islamic doctrines about the world and human duties therein were primarily in Arabic, as were even most of the works on Falsafah and natural science, in the literary field the favoured language was Persian, a more widely used tongue which the ordinary educated person more readily understood without becoming a scholar. Here a cultivated audience imposed a public discipline other than that of the 'ulamâ'; and though the predominant spirit was likewise conservative, yet much of the work done was highly creative.

Ibn-Khaldûn was not the only serious thinker to see historical studies as the most effective form for expressing his insights. Islam carried with it a relative freedom from an overall dramatic framework based on some cosmic cyclicism; this freedom combined with the strong sense of historicity in the prophetic tradition, of each event counting once and for all, encouraged a factualistic historiography. The Later Middle Period saw a great variety of historical interests. In Arabic—and perhaps especially in Arabic-using areas—the old tradition of religious historical scholarship was maintained: generation by new generation were recorded the important carriers of the learning and mission of the prophetically founded community. This tradition went wherever Islam spread, so that in numerous areas where history had been on the level of legend or even of myth the coming of Islam meant the introduction of an awareness of the relevance of objective historical data. Not only the 'ulamâ', of course, but the rulers and also the saints were increasingly kept account of. In the Sûdânic lands, in much of India, and yet elsewhere, it is from this period, with its often carefully dated chronicles, that we can begin to trace detailed continuity of public events. But in the more central Arabic-using lands, notably in Egypt, arose a school of historians that went beyond such interests, and took pains to record or document much local detail. The most prominent of them was al-Maqrîzî, who collected all the information he could find about the significant sites and local traditions in Egypt: a type of endeavour not new to Islamdom but rarely so minutely worked through.

But at least as suggestive developments in historical writing came in the Persianate realm, where history was accepted as an important part of belles-lettres, as part of the glory of the Turkic amîrs and sultans. With Mongol rule had come a broadening in the world perspective that already was relatively broad among Muslims. The vizier of the Il-khâns, Rashîduddîn Fażlullâh, whom we have met as a vigorous administrator supplying hospitals and establishing villages, had broad intellectual interests; by profession originally a physician, he wrote on diverse subjects, including theology and most notably history. He was a patron of many historians, but himself compiled the most substantial historical work of the time. His 'Collection of Histories' may be reckoned as the first of the works having some claim to be called 'world histories' that could justify such a claim in the sense of being reasonably comprehensive. Taking advantage of the extensive official contacts of the Mongol court, as well as of the distant trade that converged on Marâghah and Tabrîz the capitals, Rashîduddîn enlisted the services of learnèd men from all regions, even from such relatively out-of-the-way lands as the Occident or Kashmîr and Tibet (whose missionaries were wide-ranging at the time, however). He evidently chose his informants for their reliability and had such records as they could produce or recall rendered—and doubtless normally abridged—into Persian, and edited them in an accurate and matter-of-fact way. The result was a systematic set of accounts of the peoples of the greater part of the citied societies of the Oikoumene. The whole was more balanced in its coverage, having substantial amounts of material not only on Muslim but on non-Muslim peoples, than any Islamicate history written before—or, indeed, than any other history written up to that time; and, though his example was followed to some degree in the subsequent Persian historical tradition, Rashîduddîn's work was more comprehensive and balanced than any later history claiming to be a world history until the twentieth century. His work was integrated at most, however, only by the old Iranian and Muslim sequence of great dynasties, thought of as central to mankind and as more or less dominating their respective ages; though no other sequence of dynasties would have had any better claim to such a role, this was no more satisfactory as a basis for understanding world history as a whole than the corresponding parochialism of modern Western historians.

The work of Rashîduddîn was not only comprehensive; it was painstakingly fair. His account of the Nizârî Ismâ'îlîs, execrated by the Jamâ'î-Sunnî Muslim world, runs closely parallel to that of an earlier historian who was also a major official for the Mongols, 'Aṭâ-Malik Juvaynî; he used much of the same material that Juvaynî had used, and sometimes in the form Juvaynî had given it. The contrast is illuminating; it is not merely that where Juvaynî took the trouble to curse and abuse the heretics he was chronicling, Rashîduddîn avoided comment. He went further: on points of detail that might be discreditable to his Mongol patrons and reflect credit on the Ismâ'îlîs, he was careful to rectify the official Mongol story where his evidence favoured the Ismâ'îlî version.

Rashîduddîn, through his patronage, inspired a school of historians dedicated to exact work and generally holding a broad viewpoint. But the extremely simple and straightforward prose in which he chose to enshrine his matter-of-fact work was not generally imitated. History was felt to be fine literature and was expected to be artfully constructed and adorned, after the increasingly elaborate style that had already made an appearance in the Earlier Middle Period. Already Juvaynî, Rashîduddîn's senior, who had written with a relatively simple clarity, was fond of rounding his periods with balanced adjectives or phrases. Among Rashîduddîn's disciples, ornateness was carried to extremes. One historian whom he patronized, Vaṣṣâf, is known among modern scholars for his great accuracy—and also for the extraordinary difficulty of getting at the facts which he accurately portrays, because he swathes them in masses of beauteous verbiage quite irrelevant to his account. An army does not set out at dawn but rather at the moment when the sun (but it is not the sun, it is an elaborately developed figure of speech which familiarity can make penetrable) is drying up the dew (which again is not simply dew but an intricate complex of metaphors). Among Persian littérateurs, who might be concerned about historical fact but were more concerned for eloquent amusement, Vaṣṣâf was known as a model historian, whom others tried in vain to equal not in his accuracy but in the freshness and delight of his floridness.

The Persian literary model became the basis for a growing literature in certain other languages. A violent enemy of Timur (Ibn-'Arabshâh) chronicled and condemned his bloody expeditions in Arabic rather after the manner that might be expected in the Persian historical school—except for its not being aimed to the glory of its protagonist. But the most important literary language so moulded in the Persianate tradition was Turkish. The Turkic dialects were given standard literary form in three areas, yielding three literary dialects and to some degree three literary traditions, though the dialects did not become mutually unintelligible and throughout this period writers in any form might be read elsewhere. In the Syr and Oxus basins, poets and even prose writers used a form of Turkish known as Chaghatay; in Azerbaijan (and nearby lands) and in the Ottoman domains they used two differing forms of Oghuz Turkish. If the ornateness of the later Persian style was in part the effect of a style cycle in which novelty could be achieved only by exaggeration, the impasse found little relief on being transferred into Turkish: the Turkish littérateurs were so imbued with a contemporary Persian taste that their work moved very rapidly from the simplicity of Turkic folk literature to ornateness in full flower.

It was not merely the style cycle that made for ornateness in the Persianate tradition. Once Persian literature became well established as a social vehicle, it was subject to a series of social pressures. Though Persian was the actual folk tongue in wide areas, in a much wider area—even in parts of Iran—as a 'lingua franca' it was a second language, not the mother tongue of those who wrote or read it. The Turkic patrons, of course, knew it only as a courtly language; but even people who used one or another different Iranian tongue—people of Khwârazm or Mâzandarân or Gîlân or Kurdistân—were not natively at home in it. Hence many Persian writers were conscious of using a more or less artificial instrument for delimited social purposes. The language was expected to conform to the canons of courtly civility. Like the older Arabic literary criticism, Persian literary criticism (apart from vague aesthetic evaluations, conveyed in various sorts of praise words) looked to the propriety of the work: how proper it was morally, socially, and even doctrinally (the greatest Persian poet, Ḥâfiẓ, was criticized for improprieties of all three sorts); it rejected obscurity, because (for one thing) in recitation before a group, everything must be clear; but once the work was proper and clear, it delighted in virtuosity. However, unlike the Arabic criticism, it was less preoccupied with linguistic purism, for some of the social reasons for maintaining strict cultural homogeneity among the early Arabs did not apply to any Persian ruling class. One must add that among the pressures for an unnatural ornateness was the pervasive attraction of Ṣûfî language with its inherent ambiguity and subtlety of implications, which could lend a multiple resonance to some sorts of complex phrasings.

Poetry was the most respected literary medium, in Persian as in Arabic; virtuosity could be most spectacularly displayed within its tight formal requirements. Among many great poets of the period, one stands out. The poet Ḥâfiẓ of Shîrâz (d. 1389) set himself up to rival Sa'dî, also of Shîrâz, already acknowledged as the inimitable master of Persian letters; Ḥâfiẓ did not indeed attempt the broad range of Sa'dî's work; yet in his one chosen medium, the ghazal, the short lyric, he equalled and surpassed Sa'dî, becoming one of the four best loved of all Persian writers. He is regarded as having perfected the form of the ghazal, and was perhaps partly responsible for its enormous popularity. Ḥâfiẓ is famous above all for his honesty. The expression of his verses is pure and sincere, and in this purity is much of its charm. His life, moreover, was sincere also. He wrote no hijâ', insulting any opponents; and relatively few qaṣîdahs of sheer praise—their rarity presumably added to their monetary value. He was almost unique in his failure to travel: though he was tempted by rich offers to leave Shîrâz for wealthier courts, he could never bring himself to do so; the one time when he actually started on such a journey (to India), he gave up before embarking and gave away the money he had been sent. He loved the Shîrâz he celebrated in his verse and stayed there to share its often unhappy vicissitudes under the amîrs.

Such a poet does not seem like a poet of a time of decadence nor of a time of stagnant overelaboration of traditional materials. He was greatly creative, and has some of the essential traits of simplicity. Yet Ḥâfiẓ was very much a man of his time: no rare bird left over from the Earlier Middle Period, but singularly expressive of the age that followed the Mongol conquests.

It is perhaps the very richness of what he could presuppose in sophisticated traditional expectations that made possible Ḥâfiẓ' excellence. His simplicity is not necessarily evident as simplicity at first sight. He is full of allusive images, often very far-fetched ones or at least images in themselves bizarre. A first reader may think to enjoy Ḥâfiẓ for those images. Yet by and large they turn out to be the same images as have already been met with—over and over—in the Persian literature of the Earlier Middle Period. The rose and the nightingale and his love were not new with Ḥâfiẓ, and he repeated them endlessly. Ḥâfiẓ' creativity, his very simplicity, must be found in something that transcends the similes he utilizes. We may take an example.

Ḥâfiẓ expresses his unappeasable passion, contrasted to conventional religiosity, in a concentrated poem with the rhyme pattern *-âb' kujâ* (the word *kujâ*, repeated not only in every line at the rhyme, but often elsewhere in the verse, means 'where?'). It begins *Salâḥ'-kâr' kujâ? û-man kharâb' kujâ?*

He of pious works, where [is he]? and I, ruined, where? See, what a distant way from where he is to where [I am]!
My heart is sick of the [Ṣûfî] cloister and of the deceptive khirqah; where is the Mazdean temple, and the unmixed wine, where?
What has a drink to do with piety and devotion? Listening to sermons is where—the melody of a rebeck is where?
Of the face of the heart's friend, what do enemies discern? The extinguished lamp is where, the sun's candle is where?
(Like eye-lotion on our sight is the dust of your threshold; where shall we go, be pleased to say, from this refuge where?)
Do not look at the rounding of his chin, for a dimple is in the way; where are you going, heart, in this haste, where?
He has gone—may his memory be sweet on the Day of Union; even that kind glance, where has it gone, and that reproach where?
Repose and sleep do not expect of Ḥâfiẓ, friend: what is repose? what is patience? sleep is where?'

We have here a series of contrasts between Ḥâfiẓ' situation, as a music-loving wine-bibber, and that of the properly devout men of a conservative Ṣûfî khâniqâh. In the course of it, Ḥâfiẓ' disreputable state turns out to be due to his distraction with longing for the divine Friend and His beauty—concentrated in the dimple on His chin, which can of course also stand for His point of Unity; a desperate longing which the proper Ṣûfî, virtually hypocritical in his propriety, cannot begin to understand. But the spiritual message, even in this relatively unambiguous poem, is put in very human terms. Everywhere there are double meanings: the Mazdean temple is not only a place of infidel, and hence improper, worship, a figure for the unconventional ways of coming to God that Ḥâfiẓ feels are less hypocritical than the standardized Ṣûfî ways; it also points to the actual wine which Mazdeans, like Jews and Christians, were not forbidden to make—and sell. And the beloved youth who captivates him and disappears is described in phrases entirely appropriate to a mortal, though also unexceptionable as applying to the fleeting delight in God's presence, which hopefully may foreshadow divine forgiveness in the end. (Incidentally, much of the poem can also be interpreted as if dedicated to Ḥâfiẓ' patron—any amîr being commonly cast as the generous friend and refuge from every sort of distress; and as possessing, moreover, at least an echo of the attributes of the divine King.)

This is all done with simple directness. Once the allusions are understood—and they are never very recondite if the poetic tradition is known—there are few problems of obscure language or involved construction. And the human mood is immediately clear.

A ghazal is not necessarily to be read as developing a line of thought from beginning to end (as often happens in our sonnets), though in our example there is clearly a certain development. (Hence it is unfortunate, but not always disastrous, that different manuscripts tend to shift lines to different places within a poem, or even to different poems.) Rather, at least in Ḥâfiẓ, such unity as the ghazal has will result chiefly from the interresonance of the various overtones of the images used. To appreciate this, one must not only know the ways in which ordinary Persian words were idiomatically used, but also the ways in which the images of the Persian poetic tradition had been used.

The translation of Ḥâfiẓ by Peter Avery and John Heath-Stubbs offers a convenient example of how the resonances of these images are developed.[16] Their last selection presents the theme of the nightingale and the rose in almost classic directness: the nightingale was 'stricken in anguish for the love of the rose, and sprinkled the meadows round with his sobs' . . . 'the [rose] will grant no favours, yet the [nightingale] still remains constant' . . . 'no one has plucked the rose without the stab of a thorn'. Elsewhere, these qualities of rose and nightingale are presupposed, and variants in the use of those figures stand out in contrast. Thus in their fourth selection, Ḥâfiẓ starts by addressing a gazelle—another image of the beloved, going back to Bedouin Arabic imagery—who has left him wandering in the desert; addresses next a sugar-seller, to whom the parrot has not come for the sweet sugar that parrots (lovers) like; and in the third verse addresses a rose, whose identity with the

[16] *Hafiz of Shiraz: Thirty Poems* (London, 1952). Their translations are as close to real study translations as an attempt to produce an English poem out of Ḥâfiẓ' materials is likely to get; for though they do sometimes fail to render this or that detail, and forgo the accuracy that brackets and footnotes make possible, yet they take advantage of the freedom of free verse to remain astonishingly faithful.

preceding figures is taken for granted, with a slight variant on the theme of its immobile inaccessibility: 'Perhaps, O rose, your beauty makes you too proud to be asking after the love-stricken nightingale'; a speciously reproachful tone which is also a variant on the theme of hopeless distance developed in the first two verses; and behind which, we know, lies an acceptance of the rose's unresponsiveness. It will be seen that to be used in this way, the images must be stock ones already well known to the listener.

In other poets than Ḥâfiẓ, it seems, other things may be more stressed than these subtle shades of what the Persian critics called 'meaning': some poets have been known for their verbal charm or for their virtuosity, and much poetry was essentially decorative—decorating some polite occasion. It was such poetry that became over-ornate. Ḥâfiẓ used, rather, everyday language, but caught so many shades of human feeling that he has been used, like the Qur'ân, for drawing auguries: one opened the book at random and put his finger on a verse, whose implications were taken as defining one's fate.[17]

The ferment of Persianate culture: the Timurids and their neighbours

In the fifteenth century, the central lands of Persianate culture saw a vigorous flowering of Persian literature and of all the more imaginative arts, especially, but not exclusively, under the rule of Timur's descendants. The descendants of Timur, the bigoted, murderous conqueror, stand out in Islamicate history for their high personal cultivation and their patronage of arts and letters. Timur had patronized scholars and artists, it would appear, largely for the prestige they would give him; brilliant as he was as a general, he did not necessarily recognize a great man of letters (like Taftâzânî) till someone else pointed him out. A remarkable number of his descendants showed a high order of creative genius themselves and a personal talent for recognizing genius in others: probably Ulugh-beg the scientist, Bâbur the memoirist, and Akbar the maecenas would have shone out even if born to a somewhat humbler station. Accordingly, in the field of the arts the Timurids illustrate the patronage state at its best, though the pattern was more widespread than their dynasty, and they were not the only princely family in their time to produce highly cultivated rulers.

On Timur's death, his sons and grandsons, in accordance with Mongol principles governors of the several provinces of his empire, became in effect independent at first; but his fourth son, Shâhrukh, governor of Khurâsân, was soon acknowledged the primacy and then, in the course of a series of warrings among the sons (in which a revived Jalâyirid power in the Iraq

[17] Eric Schroeder, 'Verse Translation and Hafiz', *Journal of Near Eastern Studies*, 71, (1948), 209–22, and 'The Wild Deer Mathnavi', *Journal of Aesthetics and Art Criticism*, 11 (1952–53), 118–34, presents a fascinating study of Ḥâfiẓ' poetic and religious references (and suggests that he had an express theory of poetry as transmuting sorrow to insight by way of revelation); and, incidentally, beautifully states the case against attempting versified translations.

briefly intervened), Shâhrukh gained effective control over the greater part of Timur's empire, though not of any territories beyond Caucasus and in the Volga regions. Shâhrukh himself remained at Herat and ruled much of Iran directly; his son Ulugh-beg was set over Samarqand and the Zarafshân valley. Shâhrukh appeared as a pious Muslim in happy relations with the several sorts of religious. He himself had pretensions as a painter and a poet. Another of his sons, Bâysunqur, achieved some repute as a painter, but was especially known as a patron of the bookbinding art at his own court. Shâhrukh himself patronized the arts and letters, and especially encouraged historians, commissioning the universal history of Ḥâfiẓ Âbrû which was to bring up to date the tradition of comprehensive histories going back to Rashîduddîn, and also his geographical work. In the latter part of his reign, revolts were few and he was able to beautify Herat, though his fortifications there could not prevent the great plague, as it travelled round the world, from carrying off (it is dubiously reported) hundred of thousands in 1435.

Ulugh-beg at Samarqand was less interested in Shar'î piety than his father; he met opposition among the Ṣûfî pîrs, who, with a popular following, protested his courtly culture from a puritanical viewpoint; but he retained the support of the great courtly 'ulamâ'. He fostered architecture in Samarqand and Bukhârâ as lavishly as did his father at Herat (and as had his grandfather, Timur, himself); but he was less interested in history, more interested in Falsafah. He gathered the ablest astronomers of the time to Samarqand, where he built a large observatory and took part himself in the labour of astronomical observation and calculation. New astronomical tables were drawn up of a greater accuracy than any theretofore. On his death, his team of astronomers dispersed and became the leading authorities in the field in several parts of Islamdom.

After Shâhrukh's death, in 1447, the Timurî empire was not reunited. Ulugh-beg, nominally his successor, did not long survive the intrigues set up against him at Samarqand. His own son rebelled and had him executed and then was murdered after reigning six months. The more westerly areas were mostly dominated by 'Türkmen' (pastoral Turkic) tribal leaders, who tried to serve as grand patrons but with less success than the Timurids. (One or two also tried to enforce the relatively mild Shar'î criminal law, with consequences disconcerting at least for men of property.) In the Tigris-Euphrates basin and Azerbaijan, where local power was usually fragmented among the amîrs, the Turkic (and largely Shî'î) tribal federation of the Ḳara-ḳoyunlu, the 'Black-sheep', had replaced the Jalâyirids as major superior power after Timur's death. Their chief had been supported as his subordinate by Shâhrukh; now they built a considerable empire in southwest Iran and the Persian Gulf area, even seizing Fârs for a time from the Timurîs. In the greater part of Iran and the Oxus basin, however, the Timurid Abû-Sa'îd (1452–69) succeeded in restoring and maintaining a state in which the arts, and notably painting, continued to flourish. He had to undertake repeated expeditions, however, until he finally fell into the hands of the chief of another Turkic tribal federation which had replaced their rivals the Black-sheep. By 1466 the White-sheep (Aḳ-ḳoyunlu), who under mutually feuding leaders had maintained a semi-independent rule in part of the Jazîrah for some time, had found a strong chief in Uzun Ḥasan, who not only replaced the Black-sheep in the Tigris-Euphrates basin and the surrounding lands but on defeating Abû-Sa'îd extended his rule over all western Iran; on his death in 1478, his successors maintained much of his power for twenty years.

In the generation after Abû-Sa'îd's death, the chronicle of the Timurid reigns is even fuller of fratricide and power lust and low intrigue than is most Muslim history in the Middle Periods. Every Timurid prince, in his father's life ruling his own province, could expect to become independent or else paramount lord on his father's death. Especially in the Syr and Oxus basins there were several independent courts, some of which were important centres of the arts. The most prominent of these was the court of Ḥusayn Bâyqarâ at Herat (1469–1506). In the earlier part of his reign he was successful militarily, like Shâhrukh, in pacifying a large part of the Timurî heritage, though on a smaller scale: he acquired all Khurâsân plus neighbouring lands from Mâzandarân to Qandahâr. But like Shâhrukh, his great strength was in the arts, though he was himself only a minor painter and poet. His vizier, Mîr 'Alî-Shêr Neva'i, counts as the greatest master of Chaghatay Turkish poetry and his tradition influenced deeply Ottoman Turkish poetry as well. Between them the two lords gathered together the most brilliant cultural assemblage the Iranians could recall.

Poets of fame abounded, and historians and prose moralists. The most prominent writer was Jâmî (d. 1492), who counts as one of the great poets of Persian literature, but whose simple, lucid prose was perhaps almost as important as his poetry: in particular, he wrote a model biographical history of Ṣûfism and a concise (but not especially orginal) compendium of Ṣûfî theosophy which are gems in their kind. Philosophers, mathematicians, and physicians, like every sort of learnèd specialists, were attracted to the circle of intellectuals as much as to the material bounty of the court. But the greatest glory of the Herat of Ḥusayn Bâyqarâ was its painting. Throughout the fifteenth century, the Chinese influence on the art of the Iranian and Turkic lands, which had been so strong under the Mongol dynasties, was being assimilated; the 'Timurî miniatures' which embodied the maturing Persianate style count for many as the high point of all Islamicate art. At Herat this Timurî style was brought to its own high point in the work of Bihzâd, who combined, with all ease, a high level of stylization which the Timurî painting had been establishing with a naturalistic grace which seemed to be all his own, though its elements were in the tradition. Marking the culmination of the Timurî tradition, he became the starting point for the sophisticated Ṣafavî art of the following century. (We will see more of him.)

It was perhaps largely in Timurî times that was consolidated the triumph of Falsafized kalâm, with official support, over what remained of Ḥadîthî textualism. But more distinctive of the cultural life of the Timurî period was an increasing interest—on the part of biographers, of patrons, and perhaps of the artists themselves—in the individuality of the creative artist, now included among the military élite as protégé. Though not only poets but calligraphers and singers had long been singled out, it is only during this time that painters and architects come to be known to us by name. Courtiers prized and collected specimens of individual artists' works, and fashions could shift rapidly—for instance, the style of carpets favoured. The whole Mongol tradition of the patronage state had perhaps always had a strong sense of human distinction: of the high possibilities of personal achievement. This was to find its most acute expression in the autobiographies of the sixteenth and seventeenth centuries, but the careful education of the Timurid princes and their sense that greatness depended as much on aesthetic splendour as on extensive conquest reflected the standards that had been established and were steadily being raised as each prince outdid the others.[18]

Movements of social protest

The vigour of urban public activity, partisan or patriotic, which still displayed itself in the midst even of Timur's repressions, had long been a source of protest movements; especially in the series of Ismâ'îlî revolts, and perhaps most promisingly in the manifestations of lower-class militia strength at the time of the last and most massive of them. Some urban protest continued in this time of increasing courtly power, even after Timur; but a new source of protest had come to join with it. It is not clear how much the new pastoralist use of marginal land may have restored healthy balance at least to the popular economy. Certainly, the new pastoralists did contribute another element of resistance against agrarian lordship. And this likewise tended to take a Shî'î form.

One can say that Ibn-Taymiyyah represents a reaffirmation of the oppositional character of the Sharî'ah-minded tradition, even in its Jamâ'î-Sunnî form. But most opposition was 'Alid-loyalist and even bâṭinî in tone. Protest by the relatively dispossessed against the amîrs and the upper social classes was also directed against the official Jamâ'î-Sunnî 'ulamâ' who had made their peace with the amîrs and received appointments from them. Hence it had long been often Shî'î. With the collapse of the Ismâ'îlî movement, however, Shî'ism of the older form, looking to an imâm of the house of 'Alî to

[18] Some day someone will make a study of Islamicate autobiography, in all phases and periods and also across confessional lines, and so throw light on the human image in that civilization. I can cite two important strands in the autobiographical genre: the Ismâ'îlî accounts of one's own spiritual search and discovery, with which Ghazâlî's has something in common; and the later Persianate autobiographies, of which the most prominent examples are those of the Timurids, especially in India. But diaries and memories of various sorts have survived from many periods and areas.

lead the faithful in a head-on assault on the old caliphate, no longer had attractions outside of the Yemen, where Zaydism also had struck permanent root. A new Shî'ism now arose which was expressed largely in Ṣûfî forms, in special ṭarîqahs whose esoteric wisdom was less a general Ṣûfî doctrine than a special revelation supposed to be derived from the secret teachings of 'Alî. This new Shî'ism may be called 'ṭarîqah Shî'ism'.

In a sense, it accepted the Ṣûfî political notion of a universal mystical hierarchy over against and above the military powers; but it rejected the political outcome of the Sunnî synthesis of the Earlier Middle Period, as not, in practice, satisfying the demand for populistic egalitarian justice, which the Muslim conscience demanded. Instead, it looked for the quṭb saint to come down out of the skies and be installed as universal monarch on earth; if not in full effective glory, then at least as guide for the faithful, with as much autonomy as possible. This ṭarîqah Shî'ism, commonly devoted to a bâṭinî 'inward' and esoteric doctrine, often carried elements of a Gnostic-type approach to understanding the cosmos and human beings in it: in a cosmos where truth and good were veiled, the élite soul could escape from misery and falsehood by esoteric knowledge of the secret ultimate reality. Such an approach has sometimes been associated with 'world-weariness' (whatever that means); but certainly these bâṭinîs were expressing a very positive and highly expectant attitude to life (as always, what matters is not the sort of implications that might logically be deduced from the formulation of a doctrine, but its actual meaning on the level of direct experiencing). These new Shî'îs, then, often had a vigorously chiliastic vision (what I would call a kerygmatic outlook) even while pursuing a course of mystical inner purification which ought to prepare them for the chiliastic advent.

As a general rule, one may differentiate, somewhat arbitrarily, two sorts of movements of social dissent: anti-privilege, demanding equal justice and naturally tending to stress disciplined responsibility; and anti-conventional, demanding free expression and tending to stress open responsiveness. Anti-privilege movements often become ruthless, so committedly do they seek social change, whereas anti-conventional movements often become reckless, disregarding social consequences as one phase of their very emancipation.

I think one will find in these latter-day Shî'î movements as much as anti-conventional defiance of established social norms as an anti-privilege militancy. In west European chiliastic movements, a 'pre-Adamite' emancipation from received norms (harking back, in an antinomian appeal, to the innocence of uncorrupted paradise) was wont to crystallize into regimented campaigns for overturning the oppressive government and higher society (and in such campaigns, adherents of the embattled cause lost again their new-found personal licence). Probably something like this had happened in sections of each of the several Ismâ'îlî revolutions. In any case, a genuinely antinomian defiance rarely seems to last long without some new conventionality coming to prevail, whatever the seeming fate of the cause. However, in Ṣûfî forms had been found a way to institutionalize a certain defiance of conventionality (and even, in extreme cases, real licence). It seems possible that in these ṭarîqah Shî'î movements, the dissent expressed was always at least as much defiance of conventionality as moralistic anti-privilege militancy; indeed, occasionally at least, a movement appealed especially to privileged persons (whose dissent, unlike that of lower-class movements, is more likely to be anti-conventional than anti-privilege; if only because it may take a fair amount of personal resources safely to flout established ways).

The Sarbadâr republic of the mid-fourteenth century in western Khurâsân, which Timur had destroyed, had been largely led by disciples of Shaykh Ḥusayn Jûrî, who combined Ṣûfî and Shî'î ideas and looked to revolutionary justice. This was perhaps the most consistent expression of the new mood, as well as one of the earliest.

By the fifteenth century, we find widespread evidence of a general increase in the Shî'î allegiance. The old contrasts between Shî'î Qum and its neighbour Sunnî Qazvîn, between half-Shî'î Aleppo and all-Sunnî Damascus, and so on persisted. But now the two great factions in Iṣfahân were no longer Ḥanafî and Shâfi'î but Sunnî and Shî'î. In Indian Ṣûfism, increasing numbers of pîrs in Jamâ'î-Sunnî ṭarîqahs were individually adopting a Shî'î position (and the antinomian non-Sharî'ah position was likewise becoming more frequent), especially in the Deccan. In Iran, 'Alid-loyalism was being accentuated in some ṭarîqahs. We have a careful study of the Kubrawiyyah ṭarîqah.[19] In that ṭarîqah, already Simnânî (d. 1336), despite his opposition to the Shî'î allegiance as such, espoused the 'good Shî'îsm' that allowed 'Alî primacy among the first caliphs. He granted that the Twelvers' Hidden Imâm had indeed been the quṭb of his time (but he denied that their other imâms, at least after 'Alî, had been quṭbs, despite his reverence for Ḥasan and Ḥusayn; and also that the Hidden Imâm had lived longer than a normal lifespan; the final Mahdî was yet to come). His successors in the ṭarîqah emphasized 'Alid loyalism increasingly, as well as the teachings of Ibn-al-'Arabî (even while not formally denying Simnânî's contrary *waḥdat-e shuhûd* position); by the end of the fourteenth century, one of them preached the key Shî'î doctrine of dissociating oneself from 'Ali's enemies—though unlike most Shî'îs, he exempted the first three caliphs from that category. And his 'Alid loyalism still carried no implication of actual rebellion.

Finally, early in the fifteenth century, the chief leader in the Naqshbandî ṭarîqah declared (on the basis of a dream) that a young Shî'î disciple of his, whom he called Nûrbakhsh (1393–1465), was to be the Mahdî; and at the same time abandoned the Shâfi'î madhhab in law, which had been preferred by

[19] J. Molé, 'Les Kubrawiya entre Sunnisme et Shiisme aux huitième et neuvième siècles de l'hégire', *Revue des Etudes Islamiques*, 29 (1961), 61–142, a very perceptive study. I have not had access to Petrushevski, *Zemledelie u agrarniye otnosheniya v Irane XIII–XIV vekov*, 1960, which has a chapter relevant to this section—and which is said to be very important for this whole period.

Naqshbandîs as by a great many other Ṣûfîs, in favour of a Shî'î fiqh. A substantial number of the ṭarîqah in Iran—probably the majority—accepted Nûrbakhsh. Nûrbakhsh moderated his Shî'ism in an irenic direction, as Simnânî had modified his Jamâ'î-Sunnism. But he did emphasize his own role as the Mahdî; he taught that, like 'Alî and unlike the other Twelver imâms, the Mahdî must be qualified to be a full imâm—that is, to carry out the greater jihâd as well as the lesser: the public war with the sword against injustice as well as the private struggle with individuals' vices. (As often with the reformers, and especially in this period, jihâd warfare was envisaged as being waged as much against unjust Muslim rulers as against non-Muslim 'tyrants'.) Accordingly, he made attempts to assert his power. He had coins struck in his own name in Kurdistân and was arrested several times as a rebel against the Timurid Shâhrukh. But he was not executed; and on the ground that he had renounced his claim, he was released after Shâhrukh's death. The section of the Naqshbandiyyah that had accepted him (called now 'Nûrbakhshiyyah') continued to be actively Shî'î: one of his khalîfahs, after building a khâniqâh in Shîrâz, is said to have won over many Ḥanafîs to Shî'ism in Kashmîr. But they glossed over Nûrbakhsh's special claims and passed as ordinary Twelver Shî'îs.

In other Ṣûfî circles, also, 'Alid-loyalist chiliastic hopes flared up. Sometimes their exponents could be popular with the established classes. Shâh Ni'matullâh (1330–1431; the term Shâh came to be prefixed to the name of many Ṣûfî saints), born in Aleppo, brought up in the Iraq, and residing variously from Mecca to Samarqand, was favoured by Shâhrukh, and the ruler of the Deccan in India was pleased to persuade his grandsons to come live there. He is known especially for his apocalyptic prophecies. But such persons could also arouse suspicion and ire which were not to be lulled by the usual immunities of the Ṣûfî. Nûrbakhsh was treated relatively gently, but an earlier Ṣûfî claimant to the Mahdîship, Fażlullâh Astarâbâdî (d. 1394), had been killed on the orders of Timur, and his followers (called 'Ḥurûfîs') were persecuted most ferociously in the course of the fifteenth century. One of their most outspoken adherents was the greatest of the early west Turkish poets, Nesimi; he was flayed alive in 1404 at Aleppo as a rebel.

The Ḥurûfîs did reject the legitimacy of current rulers. They taught that in human history there was a rising curve of revelation: first had come the prophets, whose greatest was the last of them, Muḥammad; then the saints, that is, the twelve Shî'î imâms; and finally, beginning with Fażlullâh, men who were in their own persons direct loci of divine revelation. With them, a more perfect age was soon to dawn, in which the unjust rulers of this world were to be swept away. On a transcendent level, at least, one may say they expressed a 'young man's sense of time' with reference to the sequence of history at large, as well as in their immediate chiliastic visions. But their dissent was largely anti-conventional rather than anti-privilege; they were more concerned with emancipation than with equality. It was the degree to which they expressed this mood frankly, perhaps, that gained them such intense persecution.

During the fifteenth century, Ḥurûfî leaders continued to write books that were regarded as sacred equally with the chief book of Fażlullâh himself. In these works they used means of expression differing little from those current in the Ṣûfî tradition at large—in this sense they conformed to the conservative spirit of the age—but to the practiced eye, their radical dissent was visible. They saw in the Arabic (more particularly, the Persian) alphabet—building on an old philosophic tradition and also, perhaps, on some Ismâʿîlî interpretations—the essential components of verbal roots and hence the ultimate units of all possible meanings; in their analysis of the letters, numerical and phonemic symbolism were joined in an elaborate system in which all reality was contained as in a microcosm. It was their preoccupation with the letters of the alphabet that earned them the name *Ḥurûfî*, letter-men; and here they pushed the principles of a bâṭinî interpretation of both text and nature to a symbolic extreme. But what probably most frightened the conventional was more substantive. Not only the letters of the alphabet, but the human figure and especially the human face was a microcosm in which the beauty of the cosmic order and of divinity itself was palpably revealed. Appreciation of human beauty was not merely a parable of appreciation of divine beauty, or perhaps a first approximation and a stimulus to it, as with many Ṣûfîs; it was itself already the appreciation of divine beauty, though this appreciation of human beauty ought to be elevated to higher and higher levels.

In experiential actuality, the difference might be slight between seeing in a human face a symbol of the divine beauty that was to be found on higher levels, and seeing the divine beauty itself in a human face but at ever higher levels. But the new reality assigned to the palpable symbolism served to elicit a heady response from those who felt that now the beauty of life and love was at last being given its due in the face of all the repressive conformists of an old order about to be swept away. Not only Nesimi but other poets were attracted to this faith and produced ecstatic verse in its spirit (in Persian and especially Turkish), which was sometimes quite fine. At the same time, defenders of social responsibility felt a special zeal in wiping out so overt a defiance, found ample occasion of scandal in the divinity assigned to Fażlullâh in particular, and ferociously tormented any Ḥurûfî whom they could denounce. Even though the Ḥurûfîs won some favour with Meḥmed II, the Ottoman sultan who took Constantinople, yet the Ottoman muftî, a scholar trained in the Falsafah tradition, had some of them burned alive.[20]

[20] On these movements, information can often be found in works dealing principally with other periods. Thus Saiyid Athar Abbas Rizvi, *Muslim Revivalist Movements in Northern India in the 16th and 17th Centuries* (Agra University, 1965), has much information on the fifteenth-century origins of the Mahdavî movement, which was important in India through Akbar's time (and also in eastern Iran); and at the same time mentions such groups as the Nuqtawiyyah in Gîlân, who followed another of the many Mahdîs

What we are calling ṭarîqah Shî'ism was to be found only, I think, in the Persianate zone; and it took root especially among the western Turks of Azerbaijan and Anatolia. Perhaps, among the Turks, the populistic and anti-privilege side of ṭarîqah Shî'ism was more consistently emphasized. Old Turkic shamanic traditions for meeting the divinatory and apotropaic needs of people very naturally coalesced, locally, with Ṣûfî traditions for meeting the same sort of needs. It seems that now it was largely for an 'Alid-loyalist type of Ṣûfism that the shamanic traditions were captured. As early as 1240, an 'Alid-loyalist Ṣûfî revolt (that of the Bâbâ'îs) in Anatolia, supported by many pastoral tribesmen, had opposed at once the Seljuḳ aristocracy and the urban Mevlevî Ṣûfî order. But 'Alid-loyalist ideas had been popular among even the settled Turks ever since the days when the futuwwah men's clubs (their members were called, in Turkish, *akhis*) played a major role in developing town life in Anatolia. We have seen how as early as 'Umar Suhravardî and the caliph al-Nâṣir, an 'Alid-loyalist tendency and an association with the futuwwah went hand in hand. In Simnânî, whom we have already discussed, this connection occurred again; this time it was explicitly with Turkic akhis. And it is not surprising to learn that, in at least one of his successors, both the 'Alid-loyalist and the akhi connections were yet stronger.

In 1416 occurred a great popular revolt in Anatolia and the Balkans against the Ottoman power, to which the tradition of the Bâbâ'î rebels almost certainly contributed. The rebels of 1416, composed of bands of darvîshes as well as recruits from both Muslim and Christian populations of the lower classes, proclaimed the equality of all in property rights and decreed simplicity of garb and universal brotherhood; in particular, they forbade Muslims to deny that Christians too were genuine worshippers of God. They were assured that their leader was divinely sent to bring justice, and would soon succeed despite any initial setbacks.

Their ideological guide (it is not clear whether he was an actual leader or not, but he was hanged for complicity) was Bedreddîn of Samâvnâ (1358–1416), a famous and widely travelled scholar. Brought up in Edirne (Adrianople), he won renown in the disciplines both of fiqh law and of Falsafah and, like many such Faylasûfs, was opposed to Ṣûfism; but while tutor to the son of the Mamlûk sultan at Cairo, he was converted to Ṣûfism by an Âzerî Turk. After heading a khâniqâh for a time, he went home to the Ottoman empire, where he preached an extreme Wujûdî Ṣûfism on which he based demands for egalitarian social justice—frightening the possessing classes with the specter of community of property. (This is one of the several cases where Ibn-al-'Arabî's expansive ideas about human nature contributed to an optimistic outlook on possibilities of social change.) For a time he seems to have attracted much attention among the populace; but then he retired for

of the Later Middle Period (and flourished into the time of Shâh 'Abbâs). Here also the unpublished study of Sayyid Nurul-Ḥasan of Aligarh on the Ṣûfîs of the period offers information.

study in Edirne—from which, against his will, he was brought forth, about 1410, to be made a chief judge by one of the claimants to the Ottoman throne, presumably in a bid for popular support. When the revolt of 1416 failed, his ideas were yet kept alive. Some of the rebels turned to the Bektashî movement, others probably to the Ṣafavî ṭarîqah, with which Bedreddîn himself had been in touch; it was these two groups that had the most enduring success of all the ṭarîqah Shî'î movements of the time.

Some movements were restricted to particular tribal groups. A Shî'î movement popular earlier among certain Kurds, the Ahl-e Ḥaqq, who had associated with their Shî'ism certain Ṣûfî pîrs and shrines, was spread in the fifteenth century very widely among the Turkic tribes, especially in the area of Ḳara-ḳoyunlu (Black-sheep) rule; many of the dynasty itself seem to have been patrons of Shî'î ideas. The Ahl-e Ḥaqq professed an elaborate system of spiritual cycles, each with its own revelatory hierarchy, in which the cycle of Muḥammad and 'Alî was merely one episode, and perhaps not even so important a one as some other more recent epiphanies of divine grace. This movement remained politically relatively passive, though it surely served to support a sense of their own righteousness on the part of tribesmen threatened by encroachment from city-based rulers. (Ahl-e Ḥaqq sects have persisted to the present on a tribal basis.) Another Shî'î movement, launched by a man who claimed the Mahdîship, was more active politically: the Musha'sha'. In this case, a Turkic tribal bloc fought its way south as far as Khûzistân, where it finally imposed its rule as a pastoralist aristocracy.

The Bektashî ṭarîqah, on the contrary, seems to have appealed generally to the Turkic countryside as well as to lower classes in the towns of Anatolia. This ṭarîqah professed a Twelver Shî'î position; but it was not particularly centralized, and many other points of view were welcome among its ranks. In particular, it became the chief milieu for the perpetuation of Ḥurûfî teachings and reverence for Fażlullâh Astarâbâdî after the public extirpation of the movement. In the guise of Ṣûfism it was accepted (if grudgingly) by the most ardently Jamâ'î-Summî Ottoman rulers. The Bektashî darvîshes had a broad popular following in the Anatolian countryside. The populace associated with the Bektashiyyah every sort of irreverent tale about anything official, including all religious dogmas. Later it became the official ṭarîqah of the prime infantry force of the Ottomans, the Janissaries, backing their frequent obstreperousness against the government.

Among the Bektashîs there seems to have been much sympathy for yet another ṭarîqah Shî'î movement, the Ṣafaviyyah centred on Ardabîl in Azerbaijan. This order was politically inclined like the Musha'sha', but had a far wider tribal following as well as connections in the cities, and finally enjoyed a much larger political success. At Ardabîl the hereditary Ṣafavi pîrs, originally Jamâ'î-Sunnî, became ardently Shî'î in the fifteenth century. Gathering loyal support from diverse tribes all the way west into Anatolia, the pîrs led expeditions of jihâd against the infidel Christians of independent

Georgia, and eventually found themselves at militant loggerheads with the chief amîrs of Azerbaijan. We shall see how after 1500 they founded one of the great Muslim empires. They effected the lasting conversion of the majority of Persians to Shîʿism at that time, and much of the popular Shîʿî 'Alevi' allegiance found among the modern western Turks can be traced to their activity.

III

The Visual Arts in an Islamic Setting, *c.* 1258–1503

Doubtless the first attempts to create something which would arouse, overawe, or appeal to a person by its very visual qualities were as much attempts to evoke magical powers as to delight the senses. The great visual arts of the agrarianate civilizations remained, if not magical, at least insistently symbolical for the most part. The appeal was not merely through the movement of line and the play of colour, answering to human emotions and moods; the art often represented graphically various objects and beings and appealed as much through people's conceptions of the things represented as through what actually struck the eye. That is, it had an objective symbolical content, appealing to human imaginations, as does poetry, through people's awareness of the symbolic correspondences among things and of their overtones by association. The figure of a beautiful woman might represent love, and fertility, and motherhood, and finally the intimate, ultimate source-springs of life altogether. The figure of a strong man might represent prowess, and generative potency, and lordly authority, and finally the creative and destructive ultimate power of nature itself. All that was woman might be seen emblematically in the moon, or in the sea; all that was man might be seen in the sun, or in the sky. In such ways the power of artistic vision was for long, though not exactly magical, yet through its symbolism in some sense moral, even religious: it echoed and set forth in cosmic terms the sense people had of the ultimate meaning of themselves and what was around them.

An artist's inclination to make use of such overtones was reinforced by the agrarianate citied economy. The wealthy, whether by royal or by priestly privilege, in whose service the most highly trained artisans worked, had always required monumental objects: objects that would not only display the expensive splendour of their luxury, but would also set forth graphically, emblematically, the meaning of their social position and of all they stood for; and would inspire devotion and loyalty thereto. Such requirements called for just that symbolizing manner of art we have been speaking of. The art of the temple was directly devotional and sacramental: it was founded on explicit myths of nature. Even the very shape of the temple building was likely to be symbolically representational. Dynastic or seignorial art was just as evocatively emblematic to its own ends. Heraldic art proper was but one example of this. The art of the palace presented the majesty of the king in a manner to evoke awe and loyal fervour, even apart from any religious overtones. In Sâsânian painting or sculpture, the king was represented in heroic scenes, surrounded by resonant emblems of his power, or he was depicted centred and elevated amidst his teeming courtiers. The interests of luxury and authority of both kinds and the imaginative inspirations of an artist tended thus to coincide in a symbolically representational art.

But in the Irano-Semitic lands a tendency had been developing which depreciated this explicitly emblematic representational art in religious contexts—whether the art was naturalistic in the old pagan manner or stylized in newer ways. Among the circles influenced by religion of the prophetic type, with its rejection of nature cults and of the attendant myths, visual symbolism taken from nature was not greatly favoured. In the art of the temple it was gradually being suppressed. The prophetic Deity was an invisible moral force above the visible order of nature, and stories of men and beasts might illustrate His moral will but could not symbolize Him Himself. Though statues were still used by the Mazdeans, they felt the intangible fire to be a better symbol of divinity. Jews rejected cult-images altogether, even though not every sort of graphic symbolism, and Christians were for long chary of using them. When in the last generations before Islam, with the Christianizing of much of the population, pressure arose to restore the use of cult-images in a Christianized form, the more prophetic-minded Christians responded with an insistence on eliminating even such images as had formerly been tolerated in the cult: a response called 'iconoclasm', image-breaking.[1] Among the Jews, beginning perhaps even earlier, hostility to the image went still further; all figural imagery—that in human or animal form—was ruled out in places of worship, even when there was no question of directing the cult to the images; and the pious went on to rule out all such imagery even in ordinary places, that the whole of life might be dedicated only to God. (Such a generalized mistrust of figural images, going beyond merely the elimination of them from cult use, can better be designated 'iconophobia'.)

This iconophobia inevitably had ramifying effects on art. Even when representational art was forbidden only in the cult itself, this affected indirectly other sorts of art; for however potent was the heraldic or dynastic inspiration, the devotional inspiration had a more fundamental appeal and was more formative of artistic vision. The whole artistic tradition of the Irano-Semitic lands was being challenged at a crucial point: in its right to

[1] Gustave E. von Grunebaum, 'Byzantine Iconoclasm and the Influence of the Islamic Environment', *History of Religions*, 2 (1962), 1–10, which indicates this sequence, also suggests some of the spiritual correlations that may be drawn between iconoclasm and an emphasis on divine transcendence.

express symbolically the highest truths the artist could look to—those of his faith. The full response to this challenge came only under Islam.[2]

The impact of Islam on the Irano-Semitic visual arts

Primitive Muslims accepted the arts of the lands into which they came, as they accepted other aspects of culture, patronizing the same artists that the great before them had patronized. The Qur'ân condemned several frivolities, including poetry; but it did not condemn figural art as such. But inevitably Islam was soon involved in the quarrel. All the conditions that had made for iconophobia before held in Islam also.[3]

From the first, the Qur'ân, with the whole of Muḥammad's message, was in the line of the Irano-Semitic prophetic tradition; its natural bent was against the nature cults with which the peoples from Nile to Oxus had associated cult figures. Then the Sharî'ah-minded—holding a specially potent vantage point

[2] There is no satisfactory general treatment of Islamicate art, nor even any satisfactory separate treatment of architecture or of painting. Georges Marçais, *L'art de l'Islam* (Paris, 1946) is probably still as good an attempt as any, and has the virtue of being reasonably interesting; but it is practically restricted to the Arab lands, especially the Maghrib. Since it focuses on architecture, it can be complemented by Maurice S. Dimand, *A Handbook of Muhammadan Art* (3rd ed., New York, 1958), which deals with most visual arts except architecture and gardening, and which is much more representative geographically; this is a glorified museum catalogue (Metropolitan Museum of Art), however, and is chiefly useful for reference (profuse illustrations). Ernst Kühnel, who produced a suggestive but slight general study of Islamicate painting in *Miniaturmalerei im islamischen Orient* (Berlin, 1923), has given us *Die Kunst des Islam* (Stuttgart, 1962), translated by Katherine Watson as *Islamic Art and Architecture* (London, 1966), which is a quick survey of all kinds of art, particularly in the Mediterranean lands, with technical analysis (and little sense of aesthetic meaning); his historical data are almost invariably incorrect. David Talbott Rice, *Islamic Art* (New York, 1965), concentrates somewhat less than Kühnel on the Mediterranean lands, but has nothing, for instance, on India; it is superficial and misinformed; and petty in its concern for dating of individual museum pieces in a brief general text. Arthur U. Pope, *A Survey of Persian Art* (London and New York, 1938–39), is the richest collection of plates. His rather weak *Introduction to Persian Art since the 7th Century A.D.* (London, 1930) is to be replaced by his *Persian Architecture, the Triumph of Form and Colour* (New York, 1965), very good. Heinrich Glück and Ernst Diez, *Die Kunst des Islam* (Berlin, 1925), has solid technical analysis (and the usual ignorance of general culture and history) but, especially, excellent plates and diagrams. Ernst J. Grube, *Landmarks of the World's Art: The World of Islam* (New York, [1966?]), also has magnificent reproductions. Unfortunately, these works do represent the state of studies in Islamicate art; despite the many reasonably competent surveys of the architectural monuments in the various countries, and also of other art objects, interpretations of the art generally show little acquaintance with the rest of Islamicate culture, and a stereotyped response to aesthetic problems.

[3] For the development of early Muslim hostility to images, see most recently K. A. C. Cresswell, 'The Lawfulness of Painting in Early Islam', *Islamic Culture*, 24 (1950), 218–25, which mentions briefly the main evidence that images were not forbidden in early pious circles, but remains superficial (its incidental ascription of iconophobia in part to 'inherent temperamental dislike of Semitic races for representational art', a silly piece of Western racialism, does not usually come so near the surface in other respectable writers). Rudi Paret, 'Textbelege sum islamischen Bilderverbot', *Das Werk des Künstlers: Hubert Schrade sum 60. Geburtstag* (Stuttgart, 1960), pp. 36–48, starts with useful bibliographical notes, then shows just what the fiqh writers did and did not prohibit.

within Islam—reinforced with moral considerations the inherited prejudices against nature images, condemning figural visual art both within the cult and outside it. Already among the Hebrew prophets there had been contempt for the aesthetic luxuries of the wealthy—for women's jewellery, for instance, as well as for magnificent cult monuments: such luxuries were seen as wrung from the sweat of the poor and as inconsistent with the simplicity of the morally pure. The egalitarian populistic social consciousness of the Sharîʿah-minded echoed such sentiments—condemning golden dishes and silken clothing and music (for men, that is—they scarcely tried to control women in all these respects) along with the rich decoration provided by figural imagery. Perhaps as important, the Sharîʿah-minded were intensely mistrustful of anything that smacked of magic, which by definition escaped the limits on human ambition imposed by a matter-of-fact, egalitarian propriety.

Finally, these moralistic reasons for rejecting aesthetic culture were given support among the more sensitive by immediate devotional considerations, which we have noticed in Book Two. The pure monotheistic devotional experience was intensely exclusivist: the moral challenge of the divine Transcendent demanded total and unified attention. A unitarian theology was the expression of unity in the act of worship. The Qur'ân, through which the divine challenge was presented, was the sole acceptable symbol; the worshipper must focus on the Qur'ân itself all the imaginative and visional powers of his being.[4] Any other symbolism, particularly in such seductive forms as music and visual imagery, must appear as a rival to the Qur'ânic presence, dissipating the soul's attention. This was for the same reasons as ruled out ordained priests and their specialized sacraments: the worshipper must be wholly and unmediatedly confronted with God's commands and monitions. And in a tradition in which, therefore, worship was not confined to a special consecrated temple, imaged symbolism could appear dangerous wherever it might be found. This support for the iconophobic moralists was probably decisive, for it assured enduring respect for what otherwise might have remained a mere puritanical complaint.

A pure unitarian cult, hostile to whatever might grip the human imagination short of itself; a moralistic egalitarianism with little respect for the expensive arts of luxury—so, in Sharîʿah-minded Islam, the piety of the devout combined with the illiberality of the bourgeoisie to disparage all that seemed morally superfluous. The Sharîʿah spirit was hostile, at least in principle, to all the more cultivated arts. It was unable to eliminate all luxury and all art. But it did throw the full weight of its authority against whatever art

[4] On the Qur'ân as symbol, cf. pp. 222 and 241 in my 'Islam and Image' in *History of Religions*, 3 (1964), 220–60. In that whole article I developed more fully some of the ideas here presented on art, and indeed on Islamicate society generally, but with less attention to the historical development, and hence with an unsatisfactory analysis of the dynamics of iconophobia. I have been persuaded also that its references to Modern art are unduly one-sided. Here I must thank Harold Rosenberg for making me take a slightly more cautious and hence less misleading approach in this chapter.

it could accuse with some show of pretext. Along with the singing of slave-girls, linked to wine and sexual licence, and the aesthetic use of gold or of silk, it banned all figural imagery (at least if prominently displayed), on the ground that it might tempt the weak to idolatry. Ḥanafî and Uṣûlî Shîʻî law books banned images apropos of avoiding what might distract from the ṣalât worship; Shâfiʻîs and Mâlikîs implicitly linked art to luxury by discussing the question apropos of accepting an invitation to a wedding feast; but they all came to like conclusions. The painter of animate figures was doomed (he must try to breathe life into his figures at the Judgment, and would fail); and once made, the figures must not be used save in ways that clearly degraded them, as to step on on the floor.

The artistic effect of this was confirmed by Islamicate political development. From this denial of transcendent reference in devotional art, there was not even a partial refuge in the emblematic symbolism of dynastic or heraldic art. There was no well-established ruling gentry, which might cultivate an imaginative sense of its own status and a high taste over generations. Even the ʻAbbâsid caliphate developed no independent basis for its own legitimation that the imagination might have seized hold on and art glorified. Still less could the short-lived military dynasties that followed lay claim to such legitimacy. The monied rulers, as military men, were often enough newly risen from the ranks, and turned chiefly to the Sharîʻah itself for what proper legitimation they could find. The new men that were the amîrs offered no alternative to the severity of the ʻulamâʼ scholars; even the Mongol and Timurid dynasties, though they were effective patrons, proved unable to establish autonomously a full emblematic legitimation of their power. A symbolic representational art, then, was not to be expected from either normal source. Accordingly, as in politics, so in turn also in the arts, there was no ready source of public legitimation for myths and symbols except the Sharîʻah, which refused to accord legitimacy.

Inside the mosque, of course, the Sharʻî ban was effective. (And the iconoclastic tendencies in church and synagogue too were encouraged.) Even in secular buildings, the ban generally eliminated sculpture (though not always). Finally (in conjunction with the want of a solid political basis for an art of a heraldic type, as we shall see) though the ban did not prevent widespread use of two-dimensional figural imagery, the attitude from which the ban sprang did leave its impress on such imagery and on all the varied arts of the Muslim peoples. This is not only because such a ban reinforced popular superstitious fears of the magic implicit in symbolic art. Marks of such fears have been common in Islamdom, where if a peasant came upon ancient paintings or statues he was likely to destroy them at once, and even a scholar (with the sanction of fiqh law) might ritually draw a line across the throat of a painted figure to show that it was not alive. But iconophobia was still more significant, I think, through its indirect effects on the imaginative range open to the artist.

We have noted how art between Nile and Oxus under Muslim patronage carried forward the insistence on stylization and on simple narrative forms that had arisen to challenge the classical monumentalism and naturalism; and how art styles that were visibly Islamicate gradually arose, being fully established by the Earlier Middle Period, styles distinguished by such traits as the recurrent use of patterned calligraphy and also of intricate and symmetrical abstract design, both of which carried further the bent toward stylization. In this intensified stylization, the iconophobic tendency seems to have played a role already. For though a limited stylizing might enhance the devotional or heraldic power of a figure, to push such rendition too far could emasculate the living effect of the figure instead, merging it into its aesthetic background. However, this was not the only effect of the iconophobic pressure. By ruling out the art of myth, of objective symbolism at its highest, it set the artists a problem at the heart of their inspiration. The problem was solved in several positive ways. The solutions the artists developed not only set the tone of monumental art of all kinds, but even seem to have influenced creatively those branches of art where the iconophobic impulse had no direct effect at all. From the intricate geometry that set shimmering a massive dome, to the fanciful play of colour in the crowded scenes of a carpet, the artists finally were able to create a new world of the imagination, a world no longer that of the nature myths and yet rich in its own expression of wonder and delight.

Several writers have attempted a general interpretation of Islamicate art or of sectors of it in terms of the taboo on figural images. Some suppose the taboo caused artists to reduce the vitality even of those representational figures which were in fact made.[5] I think there is little evidence of any

[5] Thomas Arnold's *Painting in Islam* (Oxford, 1928), an interesting set of studies which should form the starting point for any inquiries into the effects of iconophobia, notes among other points the expressionlessness usual on the human faces in paintings. This would come, for Richard Ettinghausen (whose works must be read by any student of Islamicate art), under a larger category of deliberate unrealism which took a great many forms ('The Character of Islamic Art' in *The Arab Heritage*, ed. Nabih A. Faris, [Princeton University Press, 1944]); but Ettinghausen's psychological thesis is dubious and some of his explanations do not hold: his introduction on the lack of art in old Mecca is irrelevant and his association of many non-naturalistic tendencies with notions of the 'ulamâ' and even with kalâm is quite unconvincing, especially since the same tendencies occur in arts untroubled by any iconophobia. Subtler is Gustav von Grunebaum's analysis, restricted to art in the Arab lands, 'Idéologie musulmane et esthétique arabe', *Studia Islamica*, 3 (1955), 5–23. He notes in Sharî'ah-minded Islam the lack of a sense of the dramatic on the one hand and a depreciation of the status of the human personality as such, as compared with certain archaic heroic traditions; suggesting that accordingly Sharî'ah-minded Islam gave no impetus to representational art either in painting or in literature. But since Sharî'ah-minded Islam was not the only cultural force at work, this does not carry us very far; for instance, though he notes the effect of the Pahlavî background in the Iranian plateau, he makes no corresponding reference to the Semitic (Syriac) background in the Fertile Crescent, which area he is chiefly discussing. (In most of these discussions, I fear, there is a tendency to philologian's myopia —to overlook the main stream of cultural continuity in favour of such continuity as is represented by the Arabic language itself.)

deliberate dehumanizing of their figures by artists; by and large, painters seem to have been proud of the degree to which their paintings might visibly simulate nature. Nor was art thought of as 'creative' in pre-Modern times (anywhere) in such a sense that artists need take too much to heart the accusation of some 'ulamâ' (as some scholars have suggested) that they were trying to 'create' living beings and so to rival God. If there was an influence, it was surely more indirect. Unfortunately, we have no really concrete documentary appreciations of what was expected from art either by artists or by the public, and our analysis of aesthetic motivations and ideas must be based, by way of conjecture, upon the works themselves. But it does seem probable that certain traits of much Islamicate representational art reflect the devaluation of the type of awareness that could give the figures a naturally symbolical, even a philosophical dimension; so that figural images at best must mean less.

What was essentially distinctive in Islamicate art (I believe) is that, as compared with other arts of the Agrarian Age, it was to a much greater degree independent of emblematically symbolic functions, either religious or political, apart from the intention of immediate visual appeal. This was true even of that art that happened to be lavished on mosques or devoted to royal palaces. It was all, in this special sense, a 'secular' art.

In the twentieth century (after a century and a half of 'art for art's sake') we are perhaps in a better position to appreciate such art than even a century ago. We can see in Islamicate art an anticipation of certain strains in the Modern secular autonomy of art, which can be interpreted as insisting on pure visual effect—though not an anticipation of Modern art as a whole, which presupposes the world of technicalized Modernity. It is perhaps no accident that such anticipations should be especially noticeable in the art of a society in which urban, mercantile cosmopolitanism, relatively divorced from nature, effectively derogated from the legitimacy of any sacramental or seignorial institutions. An elaborate dependence on non-representational art, and an abstract dissolution even of representational art into purely visual elements, both occurred more extensively among the Muslims than perhaps in any other agrarianate-level culture. And both among Muslims and among Moderns, it is possible to associate these effects in part with an alienation from the old nature myths. The differences are more numerous than the likenesses. For instance, among Muslims the re-evaluation of figural imagery did not build upon nor revolt against a tradition of illusionist 'imitation'; nor did it lead to personal expressionism nor to pressure for regular innovation in style, for Islamicate art remained an art of the Agrarian Age. But the points of analogy can be suggestive.

What happened in Islamdom is especially demonstrable in figural art, though I think it happened more generally. The great objective symbols of nature and of social order, which play so central a role in agrarian religion and polity, call for a figural art that stresses the vital, even the biological aspects of its figures. The figures in themselves must command awe or devotion, must excite contemplation of what they embody. But when they could no longer serve a devotional or a heraldic function, figural symbols became mere private resources, to be used as occasion seemed to require. Symbols of this sort were developed not in an established liturgy, but in private poetry; and visual art in turn took its symbols from the poetry rather than from the cult. Such figures served not for devotional contemplation but to arouse immediate admiration. The focus of live interest could hardly continue for long to be in the figure for itself.[6] Other sources of inspiration for a figural art than a publicly legitimized objective symbolism had to be found; and they were. In a way, the history of Islamicate art is a history of the several answers to this search.

In the intellectual and religious sphere, the imaginative life that could not be legitimized by populist institutions became esoteric, vesting itself with an initiatory tradition which could evolve, in its private dialogue, its own richness. It is possible to imagine an esoteric art, in which Ṣûfî symbolism might have become the basis for a representational symbolism. There may indeed have been some tendencies in this direction in the bourgeois art of the Earlier Middle Period.[7] But such an art had a relatively thin practical basis: except perhaps in music, it had to be divorced from the actual Ṣûfî worship, which the esoteric principle prevented from becoming highly elaborated materially. Then when a high courtly art (though not yet an art of heraldic symbolism) was more highly developed under the Mongols, that courtly art probably proved overwhelmingly attractive in other circles also, and left any other tendencies without social sustenance. An esoteric devotional alternative, then, did not prove viable.

The secularizing of art did not result, however, in a single 'secular' style, even in a single sort of style. Rather, it was a condition that underlay several sorts of artistic development and many contrasting styles. (It would also be more significant in some media than in others. To restrict representational symbolism in sacred buildings could, indeed, be consequential, but the restriction was not nearly so decisive there as in the dance or in the graphic arts.) Secularization could have very different effects in different social milieux. In particular, among merchants, and so in Sharîʿah-minded circles, it could result in a certain literalism—in a secular narrative art lightened by humour, such as that which we have taken note of in the Earlier Middle Period. In aristocratic circles, especially when after the Mongol invasion a tradition of aristocratic patronage of taste was accentuated, it resulted

[6] Here I must refer again, for a fuller development, to 'Islam and Image', pp. 249–52, with due warnings as in note 4 above.

[7] G. D. Guest and R. Ettinghausen, 'The Iconography of a Kāshān Luster Plate', *Ars Orientalis*, 4 (1961), 25–64, have shown that the handling of imagery on a ceramic bowl, superficially referring to sailors' tales, probably has Ṣûfî overtones. I must thank Oleg Grabar for drawing this article to my attention and for much other help; but he is not responsible for my errors of fact or viewpoint.

instead in a tendency toward non-representational or at least clearly abstractive art rendered with less reference to symbolically evocative content than to its immediate visual impact; to its pure visuality. (This could be combined with a persistence of the narrative interest.)

The secularizing of art was not carried to the point of the radical individualization of the artist's cultural world, as we sometimes see it in Modern art, where each work of art may seem to presuppose its own world of cultural assumptions and meanings, and the viewer must extrapolate from it after his own private manner. The most important element of social continuity lay in the craftsmanly standards of the artisans themselves. These generally sufficed to assure a precision and often a painstaking finish in the non-objective art, which in these respects contrasted to most twentieth-century non-objective art.

In the art of pure visuality, especially in forms favoured in more aristocratic circles, this sense of craftsmanship contributed to a tendency for the art to become an expression of virtuosity in achieving desired artistic effects. One of the commonest effects sought was that of sheer richness: in which was displayed the status of the man who could command the rich resources a piece of art required, as well as the high craftsmanship of the artist who could effectively use them. This effect was especially accessible in producing the rich textural quality that results from an intricate design on a surface. The philosophic content of such visual art could be limited in routine pieces: not only was the symbolic evocation of the imagination restricted, but even the extent to which the eye was being taught to see a wider range of effects in nature. Yet the very singleness of purpose of such an art of pure visuality could also be grandly creative in its own way.

Certain crests of such achievement seem to stand out in the Later Middle Period. One was the art of the arabesque and related arts of composition by line-patterning. This type of art had been largely perfected in the Earlier Middle Period, but continued in full quality in the Mongol-Timurî period; it is only from the latter period (and later) that we have a large number of surviving examples (as is the case with Islamicate art generally).

The arabesque was a development from vegetal design patterns which had been used as marginal decorations in pre-Islamic Coptic and Sâsânian art. The stylized interlacing of leaves and stems then used was developed intricately so that a wonderfully varied yet completely balanced and satisfying network of abstract forms could be used over a complete surface without seeming either boring or obtrusive. Complete compositions of line-patterning of this sort were sometimes made with other means, notably through pure geometric inventions. Circles, triangles, squares, and other polygons were inter-woven in extraordinarily complex combinations, of which the overall effect cannot avoid being impressive, but which gain in power, like musical compositions, as one sorts out visually the various geometrical elements and observes how they are being fitted together. But most favoured were various combinations of the arabesque with other motifs: with the pure geometric figures; with other sorts of vegetal motif (such as 'palmette' trees, stylized twofold trees—see the diagram); with animal and human figures—which sometimes were simply variations of the 'leaves' growing out of the 'stems' of the arabesques; and perhaps most especially with the highly cultivated lines of the Arabic writing.

Such line-pattern compositions doubtless arose under the influence of pious circles, and particularly in the mosques, as substitutes for figural compositions. They often stand sufficient to themselves, not merely as decorative adjuncts to something else, despite their freedom from any myth-based symbolism. When combined with the tall parallels and curved knots and tails of the rounded calligraphy that came into monumental style in the Earlier Middle Period, the arabesque composition takes on a certain meaning-content as a glorification of sacred phrases from Qur'ân or ḥadîth. Especially suggestive is the use of the Word of God, which took the place, devotionally, of the images of the old nature divinities. For the devout reader of Arabic, such compositions can have a unique splendour. But the form was so effective even without the enshrinement of texts that it came to be used in every context and in every material: not only on the walls of buildings but as the carving on wooden doors or chests, as frontispieces or covers of books, as monumental carpets.[8] (We should doubtless no longer refer to this as 'total surface decoration', as if it merely expressed intolerance of empty space, but as complete exploitation of the surface in its potentialities of colour and line: what could be a surfeit if it were mere decoration may be a wonder as a total independent work of art.)

It has been claimed that these compositions figure forth eternity, presenting the infinite complexity and movement of existence and at the same time resolving it in total harmony of detail with detail and of part with whole so that all that movement is seen in overall repose. Certainly, the effect of such a composition can be one of unparalleled richness; the innumerable details are each felt as precious, yet no one item stands out to dominate the whole: the eye is fed with an infinitude of beauty. Whether there was any explicit intention of metaphysical symbolism here is dubious (we have no evidence that anyone saw it that way). However, when in such a composition little human figures are lost, as it were, in the corners of the vast growth of interweaving lines, one may suppose that something of the resultant feeling was in fact intended.[9]

[8] A. C. Edwards has been the standard authority on carpets; his approach is quickly available in the chapter 'Persian Carpets' in *Legacy of Persia*, ed. A. J. Arberry (Oxford, 1953), pp. 230–58.

[9] Carl J. Lamm, 'The Spirit of Moslem Art', *Bulletin of the Faculty of Arts of Cairo University*, 3 (1935), 1–7, is an early example of the several writers who see the arabesque as expressive of monotheism and as at the core of Islamicate art.

The Timurî miniatures: abstract visuality with figures

Less universal in Islamdom but equally striking, another crest in the achievement of a visual art independent of the representational symbolism of nature myth appears in manuscript illustration in Mongol-Timurî times. The painting of Iran, and to a degree that of the other lands of the Persianate zone, passed through a period of unsurpassed flowering in the Later Middle Period—or, better, roughly between 1300 and 1600. This flowering inevitably calls for comparison with the Italian Renaissance art. The earlier Islamicate figural painting, like earlier Italian work, had bespoken a general Irano-Mediterranean tradition which is generally felt to be best represented in Byzantine art; it had had important virtues, qualities that were sometimes lost in the later period. But just as in the case of Italian art, the splendour of the Later Middle Period can blind us to the substantial vitality of the earlier. Moreover, as in the case of Italian art, this is not entirely unjustified. Such painting passed wherever did Persian poetry, to form one of the most characteristic expressions of that Persianate imaginative spirit which pervaded the greater part of Islamdom from Mongol times onward; the sophisticated spirit that was also expressed in the subtlety and vigour with which Ṣûfism entered into Persian poetry.[10]

Despite the 'ulamâ', figural depiction continued to be almost universal, at least in the central Muslim lands, in murals and manuscript illustration and ceramics, always apart from specifically religious buildings. The tradition was most commonly much the same in all these media, subject to variations imposed by technique, though perhaps it was at its best in manuscripts, which in any case have been better preserved for us than murals. We use the term 'miniatures' to contrast manuscript illustrations, or even paintings on independent sheets, such as were sometimes made, to the compositions on walls or floors, which were generally on a larger scale. But of course the term 'miniature' does not imply that the art was a lesser one. A 'miniature' was not painted overnight. (Indeed, as art historians point out, the ways of classifying art works that prove useful within one culture are likely to prove misleading in another—and notably the Western division between major and minor arts, which would relegate painting on ceramic ware to a completely different realm from painting on either paper or canvas.)

A primary source of inspiration drawn on by the Timurî figural painters (in any medium) was a close alliance with the Persian poetic tradition, in which the poets, serving successive ruling elements with sovereign impartiality, had developed their own world of the imagination. Persian poetry had learned to

[10] Lawrence Binyon, 'Art in Persia', in *The Spirit of Man in Asian Art* (Harvard University Press, 1932), pp. 116–42, is a sensitive interpretation of miniature painting which brings out some of the possibilities in the Timurî approach. (It is a pleasant contrast to such a work as E. Blochet, *Musulman Painting, XII–XVIIIth Centuries*, transl. by C. M. Binyon, 2 [London, 1929], which is chiefly a misinformed and racialist tirade against Islam.)

stress the immediate impact of the many-faceted, scintillating word, as more crucial than the presentation of new human insights. The more this tendency developed in the poetry, the less it may have been able, especially after Ḥâfiẓ, to generate fresh work of high quality. But translated into painting, this immediacy of the formal components inspired a new art, which had some of the abstract qualities of the arabesque but which made crucial use precisely of the emotive implications of human figures in narrative scenes.

The emotive quality of the painting was founded on the human situation which was the theme at once of the illustrated lines of verse and of the painting; but it did not depend on any obvious appeal to the sympathetic emotions. Let me try to put it more generally. The emotive quality was portrayed without the aid of any indirect, conceptual mediation through the human figures. Such mediation can happen in two ways: through objective symbols such as moon or stars or seashell; or through the much less conceptual, yet still not purely visual, use of biological tokens—the line of the lip, the tension of the fingers, the stance of the legs, suggesting the mood or passion of the figure by imitating the bodily signs of emotions. Rather, in this painting (as in some twentieth-century abstract art, though without the intense personal involvement of some of that) the impact came directly through the visuality of colour and line. The mood might be one of agitation or clarity or splendour; in some periods, perhaps the presentation was most often heroic, in others most often lyric; but always the most important means of evoking response was the use of tones and shapes, rather than enlisting the viewer's emotional participation in the scene. (That the more intensely personal moods were not accessible by this means was not felt as a loss.) The figures themselves, then, were but the starting point for evoking all the overtones possible in the sheerly visual elements (as, in the verse, the figures were the starting point for the use of sheerly verbal elements).[11] The great potency of these visual qualities has made the resultant painting an art of singularly universal appeal.

Comment on Islamicate art has so often stressed what it did *not* have, I want to suggest what it did have. To this end, I must try to clarify what I suppose pure visuality can mean in representational art: I shall call it *graphic autonomy*, fidelity to the graphic surface. In the Timurî miniatures the eye is called into play alone: all other senses are rigorously excluded. One is not tempted to touch the figures, for there is no sense of substantiality in them. One is not even allowed to take a physical posture with relation to them—there is no positioning of the viewer with relation to the objects in the pictures; they are all equally present—or equally remote. There is not even a single focus of interest in the way that happens in some other arts: the field tends to be broken up into many little vignettes handled with equal care, and every detail is presented with equal clarity.

[11] Here again I must refer for greater detail to 'Islam and Image', pp. 245–47.

A particular scene is eternalized in these pictures; but the manner of eternalizing must be contrasted to the illusionism of the Renaissance or of impressionism, which captures the way the scene looked in a total organic sense; or to the subjective mood painting of some Chinese schools. The Timurî spectator was detached both physically and emotionally. The style served readily as a narrative art—and here it maintained continuity with the painting of the Earlier Middle Period—for the detached position of the spectator preserved his freedom to survey the action depicted from every viewpoint: an impersonal attitude prized also in the literature of the time. (Hence, perhaps, the style was especially appropriate to book illustration.)

The qualities I refer to collectively as forming graphic autonomy are often called 'decorative', but I think this is a mistake. Properly, decorative art is that which is subordinate in design to a larger whole of which it forms part of the décor. In the Occident, at least until recently, it has been only in decorative panels or details that the autonomy of the graphic surface has been retained. But when this isolation of colour and line for themselves becomes the centre of attention, it takes on qualities that cannot be exhausted in the notion of decorativeness. Fidelity to the graphic surface has the advantage of establishing complete freedom of colour and line, which can then be developed in their own inherent terms—rather as freedom from polyphony in music permits a luxuriance of modes and shaded tones which must be sacrificed if harmony is introduced.

The temptation that beset such an art—that beset, in fact, much of Islamicate art—was indeed that of becoming a merely decorative art: an art of detail, valued simply as part of a wider décor, as ornament to something more important, but not able to hold its own as an independent composition, expressing an independent vision. As we have seen, when objective symbolism ceased to be the focus, what naturally remained was virtuosity in sheer visual richness; this was all that the critical public expected. The accepted ideal of the painter was to adorn beautifully either a precious manuscript or the walls of a wealthy home. For a long while his craft was reckoned as less honourable and perhaps even less skilled than that of the calligrapher who produced the elegant text of the same manuscripts. He was not expected to express the inner meaning of any scene that he might chance to be representing, but to clothe it in the beauty of line and colour, to transform it—whether it were a scene of love-making or of slaughter—into a delight for the eye.

A subsidiary role was almost demanded by the conventional social status of the artist. The calligrapher could be felt to be almost learnèd: he did deal, somehow, with words. The painter was a hired workman. The Islamicate artist—like the artist everywhere in the Agrarian Age—was a craftsman, trained in the use of a particular set of techniques (commonly from childhood) and hired by his patron for express purposes. Sometimes several hands worked on a single painting, each handling a specialized aspect of it:

e.g., the gold work, or the faces. The artist was not normally a man who segregated himself from his fellows to devote himself to art, and starved in a garret—such persons were likely to become darvîshes and live by the artistry of the imagination. Already in the Earlier Middle Period, the artists did cease to be entirely anonymous: individual works could be signed and, more important, a man could become well-known and his work sought after, even if no individual creation of his was famous as such. But, like the ancient Greek artists, they left no records of what their art meant to them, nor did anyone care to record their thoughts about it. (We do have a book by a member of a famous tile-making family of Kâshân in 'Irâq 'Ajamî, which records techniques equally of chemistry and of design.) In such conditions, it was a special credit to the artist and to patrons of taste that in fact the limits of decorativeness were broken through and great works were produced. The military patronage state encouraged virtuosity within a specialized style; probably this helped give the painters the increasingly high positions they gained during the Later Middle Period and helped in the escape from decorativeness (even if not from the threat of over-elaboration in a late phase of the style cycle).

Assimilating the Chinese examples

A new form of art, of course, does not normally grow spontaneously simply because the social occasion for it exists. As in political life—or in devotional or intellectual life too, for that matter—at the heart of any new aesthetic tradition is what may be called an aesthetic idea, a special combination of materials to be used with a viewpoint in using them. But new aesthetic ideas arise out of old. That is, given certain techniques and certain purposes, artistic possibilities of a particular sort will be developed as far as possible; as they are explored, dilemmas will arise when the idea of what might be done next outruns the technique given, or finally when even perfection palls on those who have been brought up on it and they become aware of how much is not being expressed that ought to be and cannot be, in the the given terms. Out of these dilemmas may arise new artistic ideas and new styles, as creative individuals discover new techniques and express new interests. But new techniques and new ideas can seem very crude when first invented; when occasion for them arises, the presence of an alien art on alien foundations can show such possibilities in a refined and developed form. Contact with an alien art, then, can provide an effective short-cut to new artistic ideas; contact extensive enough may even so speed up the process of innovation as to revolutionize an artistic tradition that seems to need revolutionizing. Normally, however, any such effect will be merely a facilitating of changes in some sense already called for within the tradition.

It was the graphic arts of China that provided the example and the stimulus for transforming the painting of the Islamicate lands into the special form it took in the Timurî miniatures. Chinese silks and other decorated products had long been imported, but under the Mongols there was a more active interchange not only of goods but of people: cultured Chinese came to the Nile-to-Oxus region as engineers, for instance, and men from the Nile-to-Oxus region went to China as administrators. Muslims in high position under Mongol rulers rubbed shoulders with foreigners of all kinds and had little reason to be afraid of exploring things alien if their temperament was so inclined. Rashîduddîn the vizier, for instance, was interested not only in the history and the scientific knowledge of alien peoples but also in their art. He had his manuscripts illustrated by painters with an equal open-mindedness, who produced pictures unexampled anywhere: for instance, in some, elongated, flowing individuals were formed by lines recalling Chinese painting but set in contexts typical of the Islamicate tradition.

In the late thirteenth and fourteenth centuries we still find the older narrative painting (especially in the Fertile Crescent), sometimes touched with elements of Chinese landscape; and side by side with it, elegant importations from China (especially in the Oxus basin), whether Chinese originals or local imitations; and various experimental forms such as those painted for Rashîduddîn in Azerbaijan. On the Iranian side, this marked as great a breach in the earlier Irano-Mediterranean continuity as did the Renaissance art on the Occidental side. Then gradually the Chinese impulses were assimilated, especially in west Iran and in Khurâsân. The most obvious Chinese influences are to be seen in details of handling the landscape backgrounds of figures. Even here, the importation was very selective. The Muslims imitated Chinese birds and flowers and clouds as found in the more colourful daylight scenes. The mighty Sung Buddhist or Taoist landscape, in which (seen as from some high, unworldly vantage point) towering rock-mountains overwhelm infinitesimal human figures straggling or contemplating along a Way which is at once material and mystical, was not reproduced. In general, it was a less mystical but more exuberant side of Chinese painting that caught the Islamicate painter's eye: for instance, the delicate embodiment of imaginative figures like dragons and racing clouds, combining to form a thoroughly unsymmetrical yet nevertheless harmonious whole. Here the Chinese had developed a form of expression somewhat comparable to the endlessly proliferated detail which Islamicate artists combined into a living unity; but the Chinese handled this in a way just the reverse of the arabesque, with its exact design and perfect symmetry.

Confrontation of such alternatives seems to have set off a chain of experimentation in which (most notably) the old paintings with their self-contained, clumsy, but often remarkably valid and vital figures were replaced by an art where graceful figures enlivened a whole in which they formed mere elements. But the replacement was fully in an Islamicate spirit. Thus the Chinese device of presenting a scene in depth by marking off several planes was adapted in a form that produced a very different effect—the depth depicted did not yield a sense of distance or of movement but rather an enhancement of the sense of structure in the compositional design. In the end, the most important resultant of the Chinese example was the sense of free flow in the composition as a whole.[12]

It was especially at Herat, capital of Khurâsân under the Timurids, that the new style found its most perfect embodiment. Under the patronage of the dynasties of Mongol origin, gradually individual painters and architects won the high personal recognition that calligraphers and singers had long had; their names came to be written up by biographers and their works individually prized. While some earlier paintings had been signed by the draftsman responsible, it is with fifteenth-century art that forgeries and the question of correct ascriptions become an issue. The greatest name of the century was Bihzâd, a painter trained at Herat and sought after by the great rulers. Bihzâd brought the Timurî painting to its peak. He was noted for the liveliness of his compositions, for the sense of movement and reality in his figures (always within the Timurî conventions), and especially perhaps for his individualization of faces; as well as for the subtlety of his colouring, often in blues and greens. The wonder of him was that he could make the art of graphic autonomy naturalistic without sacrificing its pure visuality.

At the start of the sixteenth century, when the Timurid dynasty fell, he worked first under the patronage of the Özbeg Shaybânî, who had occupied Khurâsân, and then under that of Shâh Ismâ'îl, founder of the Ṣafavid dynasty in west Iran, when he defeated Shaybânî and took Herat. For Ismâ'îl he moved to Tabrîz (Ismâ'îl allegedly hid him in a cave before the battle of Chaldirân, lest the battle be lost, as it was, and the victorious Ottoman claim the painter in the booty); he immediately became the master of painting at Tabrîz. Later, his signature was so often inserted illegitimately that we can be sure of only a few ascriptions. In any case, in both Tabrîz and Harât, and thence in Bukhârâ, where his students were taken by the Shaybânids, his manners dominated or formed the point of departure for many subsequent painters during the sixteenth century. It was the high point of Timurî art, but by pushing beyond the Timurî conventions it opened the way to new moods which broke up the Timurî synthesis.

How to view the miniatures

The school of painting at Herat was not, of course, the only school even in Iran. At Shîrâz, for instance, a rather different resolution of the same problems arose; there painters exploited especially the subtle shades of monochrome (also found in the Chinese tradition). It must be noted, also,

[12] The most detailed study of Timurî miniatures is Ivan V. Stchoukine, *Les peintures des manuscrits timurides* (Paris, 1954), with many plates. He sorts out the historical evidence on painting and analyzes techniques of depicting various subjects, and filiations of schools; often he is perceptive. Unfortunately, he has little to say of what the artists may be trying to do, and judges them chiefly by Western illusionist standards.

that the fact that it is especially manuscript illustrations that have survived probably causes us to underestimate the less narrative sides of painting—landscapes, still-lifes, even portraits—some of which will have been more prominent, for instance, in mural painting. Portraiture was prized for police purposes in a day before photography. (We can refer only hastily to the remarkable achievements in still other media—ceramic and crystal and wood and leather and fabric, and to the famous carpets of Iran.) However, to some degree what we have to say now about the Timurî manuscript illustrations will apply to any other figural depiction of the period—and, in lesser degree, of other periods.

It may sometimes be wise to look at Islamicate paintings, to begin with, from the point of view of decoration, till the eye becomes accustomed to their conventions. When one has learned to see the art generally as ornamental, sensuous beauty, one can then go on to feel the power of individual compositions. For once one appreciates the conventions, one ought not to rest there, enjoying merely the style of the age. The common conventions are but the scaffolding on which the individual masters built their interpretations. Each great artist struggled with the limitations of the style and remoulded it with every struggle: for the individual artist, the style of an age is not so much what he expresses as what he must overcome and transform (hence its alteration from one generation to the next). Eventually one can find the greater artists opening our eyes, with their lines and colours, to new possibilities of perceiving the realities around us; or committing our spirits more fully to what we do see. But (as with most other non-religious art) such ulterior fruits are not necessarily the first aim of the artist and need not be the first preoccupation of the viewer.

As we know, all art that represents the visual world distorts that world in pursuit of its particular aesthetic purposes, if only through subtle omissions. (The prime aesthetic purpose of the Timurî artist was, of course, visual delight.) Art is intended to be not a 'photographic' reproduction of nature, but a heightening of it. But artistic distortion, to be intelligible to a wide audience, must remain within or near the bounds of what that audience has learned to appreciate. If the distortion is too extreme, or of too unfamiliar a sort, the eye cannot readily follow what the artist is doing. Hence, of course, have arisen the characteristic and highly cultivated styles of art which (at least until recently) persisted among whole nations for periods of centuries with only relatively subtle variations over time. Each style had not only its own craft techniques but also its characteristic manners of distorting reality to heighten its effects.

The Islamicate artists, like other artists of the Agrarian Age, had their own patterns of artistic distortion, which we must become accustomed to, as the eye becomes accustomed to a dark room, before we can appreciate what they are doing. For our purposes these may usefully be described from the standpoint of their contrast to the conventions imposed by the art of the

Italian Renaissance, for Occidental art tended to follow in its train until quite recently, and it still predisposes the eye of many Occidental viewers and even of some other Moderns.

The first point to recognize is the degree to which every sort of visual element was accommodated at almost any cost to the demands of formal design. Nothing was spared. Observe first how writing could be transformed into intricate design, so that one is scarcely aware that any other principles than those of a purely formal intricacy could have determined the choice of shapes—which are, however, recognizably the letters of actual words. Such decorative writing was used lavishly in almost every form of Islamicate art. Geometrical forms, in their subtly interwoven perfection, formed a whole genre of art all their own, of which it takes a skilled eye to perceive the full harmonious movement. But the same skill in design was readily applied to plant forms, stalk and leaf being etherealized not only in the arabesque but in countless detailed ways. Further, since there was rarely much religious intention in the art, nor any primary concern with symbolical or evocative elucidation of deeper psychological meaning, there was nothing to prevent animal and human figures being used in precisely the same way. When the prejudice (common amongst at least an older generation of us) against the use of the human figure as an element of pure design is overcome, much that seems 'doll-like' or even 'dehumanized' about the figures in Islamicate miniatures ceases to affront and can be appreciated for its consummate skill in its own terms. The arms and legs seem to be articulated by no sinews and muscles, the stance is braced against no solid earth—nor should it be, for the purpose was to abstract from the lines of the body only those that serve the beauty of a graceful design.

The same principle helps to account for the expressionless faces which (especially in the Timurî art) Islamicate painters clung to with only occasional deviation—apart from actual portraiture. (The success of some of the deviations—old men were often painted with quite life-like features—reminds us that these faces do not simply result from want of skill to do something else.) Two points are involved here. The first is the overriding aim of presenting sensuous beauty. In poetry, the face of the belovèd must always be round and shining like the moon; so likewise in painting, every face—at least every face representing persons young and elegant—must answer the same description. This was ideal facial beauty, and the purpose of art (whether in poetry or painting) was to present this. If emotional tokens were wanted for the sake of the story, they could be indicated sufficiently by conventional gestures without interrupting the perfection of the typical moonlike face. (One such gesture, for instance, is that of putting the fingers to the lips in indication of astonishment—a gesture correspondingly referred to in poetry, often enough, as 'biting the finger of astonishment'.) But the point was not merely to present a handsome moon-face. The moon-faces, so disturbing to many modern Western viewers, were, above all, elements of design—thus several such smiling circles in a row formed a favourite backdrop for almost any scene of action. When seen as an element in the total design, the moon-face adds to the charm of the whole.

The design of the miniatures commonly involves another characteristic that throws off some modern Westerners: the tendency to block out the whole picture into more or less self-contained subsections. Typically, this appears in its extreme form in scenes involving buildings and interiors. Each wall, each floor-area, each section of the garden forms a sharply delimited block with its own self-contained design of line and colour. The result is, of course, anything but naturalistic. This it was not intended to be. Originally, it was in part a narrative device to indicate more than one plane of distance. But it was then used for direct compositional purposes (often superfluous figures were brought in simply to provide the excuse for an extra plane). The visual purpose was to draw maximum advantage from the possibilities of line and colour. When the block patterning was done well, it added to the formal balance and brilliance of the larger design. Sometimes, for instance, the angular geometry of marginal blocks was contrasted effectively to the organic curves of the central figures. Always the contrast of colours was a main purpose. The pervasiveness of this approach to design can be seen in the frequency with which in scenes with natural settings, where the rectangular blocks afforded by buildings are out of the question, rocks and trees were used to form similar subsections, with similar results.

One incidental result of this approach to design was a sometimes daring rejection of natural shading and perspective. Distance perspective in the sense of the Italian Renaissance was of course not considered—at least until well after the Middle Periods, when various foreign themes were sometimes toyed with. The blurring of the dwindling image with distance, like the dulling of its colour and form by shadow, was one of the most obvious failings of natural vision that must be overcome through art. It was readily sacrificed to the clarity and precision of formal design. The experience of recent art is helping modern Western viewers to shed their ancestors' prejudices on this point; it is less hard for us to see the distant figure presented merely a little higher on the page, but hardly or not at all any smaller, and never any fuzzier.

What can be harder for some to become reconciled to is a complete change of viewpoint from one element in a picture to another, especially where detail is handled realistically. Muslim artists might tolerate perspectival drawing: using oblique angles to represent right angles on a receding surface, for instance, if the effect was to enhance the overall design. But artists felt free to dispense with use of such perspective altogether if they wished to retain the rectangular shape for its own sake. Thus rugs and canopies sometimes appear spread out four-square as if they were hanging on the line to dry rather than lying under the hero's feet or shading his head. Or a fountain or a duck may be seen in side elevation while the ornamentally shaped pond it is on is seen as if perpendicularly from above. Often we find what is called reverse perspective—that is, the nearer side of a thing is presented not larger but actually smaller than the farther side. This can have several functions. It may allow three sides of a building, say, to be depicted without the front obscuring the rest. Very commonly it serves to fit foreground objects unobtrusively into the lines of a design in which the focus of interest is something at the rear centre. Natural perspective, on the contrary, is often awkward in design, and calls for extraneous kinetic effects; it was avoided except where it was inescapable—as in doors opening inward. Despite his often impeccable and seemingly naturalistic precision of detail, the artist was not trying to substitute for a camera, but was trying to create, out of the sometimes rather miscellaneous elements of a given scene, a design that would crystallize a moment of the narrative till it shone with sensuous beauty. This the Islamicate artists did uncommonly well.

Graphic autonomy provided a remarkable freedom on occasion. The cliché of dotting brilliantly clear and precise spring flowers over every landscape could take on a rather startling overtone when, precisely as cliché, and hence with seeming innocuousness, it appeared as setting for a battle scene in which a severed neck is wildly spouting blood. Especially for narrative purposes, it is convenient to show at once the inside and the outside of a house; or to show the hero larger than the other actors (as he does appear also in poetry), even when farther away. Such unrealisms, as well as the conventional gestures or symbols to indicate mood or status which inevitably go along with them, seem in no way incongruous when they are handled on this basis.

Finally, the viewer should remember (in contrast to art where at least the tradition has been oriented to heraldic or religious contemplative uses) that each bit of painting, however complete in itself, was commissioned to fit into a wider whole. Mural painting was a part of architecture. Nor were the manuscript miniatures meant to be seen simply as isolated units, but as peculiarly rich pages in a book all the pages of which might be works of art, both in their fine calligraphy and in the poetry or prose they contained. Not only painting but any work of art, even when in itself it was not just decorative, was yet expected to form part of an elegant larger décor which expressed the same spirit in whatever medium was used. Vases and wall tiles in a man's rooms, book covers and miniatures in his hands, metal cups and fine robes for his use, along with the more transient arts that he would enjoy—song and music and the dance—all were expected to form a harmonious whole. Hence not only as a point of inspiration but also for the sake of a basic aesthetic ideal, the spirit of the verses in the books and of the painting that illustrated them needed to be, and commonly was, one. The sense of beautiful design, therefore, which pervaded the miniature itself was largely an extension of a sense of beauty in the ensemble, of which the miniature and the book it was in formed a part.

Architecture: the symmetry of arches and domes

The art that most dominated any aesthetic setting was architecture: indeed, the master visual art of the Islamicate society. All other arts, and nowhere more so than in Islamdom, can be seen as adjuncts to architecture: large furniture was in relatively little use and the distinction between outdoors and indoors was blurred by the inner court areas which were half one and half the other; hence the structure of the building might overshadow any particular items among its contents. Such furnishings as there were, vases and bowls, handsome wooden chests and carpets, all were displayed directly against the walls and floors and vistaways of the buildings. Free objects, like vases, were set in niches in the walls or stood in corners unobscured by armchairs and couches. In mosques, there were no pews to distract from the sense of extended floor space or to conceal the carpets which set it off. Large-scale painting was not put on canvases which could be transported from wall to wall regardless of original intention; it was done directly on the wall in the form of murals, and the alternative to it was decorated tile or perhaps marble slabs. Such sculpture as there was (mostly of animals such as lions) always formed an integral part of entryways or columns or of fountains in a court. Even the art of the book, displayed on the carved wooden stands that could hold a large book open at a special page, was not entirely abstracted from the setting of the building where the book was used.

The comprehensiveness of architecture can be illustrated especially in the highly developed art of gardening, from which architecture can almost never be entirely distinguished. The commonest pattern of Islamicate gardens (at least those in Iran) can be traced back to Sâsânian times: a rectangle divided evenly into four parts by streams of water crossing it in both directions and joining in a pool in the middle. This touch of formal symmetry might be varied, but was rarely entirely lost. Within the four parts, beds of flowering plants might make patterns of colour; but more important than flowers were trees for raising the eyes and for giving shade. Indeed, a garden could dispense with flowers far more readily than with trees or flowing water; these, set into a formal pattern, were the essence of a garden. Flowers were an embellishment of a garden much as was the presence of birds—sometimes thick foliage was cultivated so as to encourage singing nightingales, the bulbuls that love roses in Persian poetry. Sometimes a pavilion was set into such a garden, intensifying the formality of a key spot in it, and forming a focus for the walks and streams of the rest. Almost equally well, the essential elements of a garden—a pool and trees—could be set in the midst of a building. The spirit of a garden and of a building was much the same, and the one was generally not conceived without at least something of the other being present.[13]

[13] Donald N. Wilber, *Persian Gardens and Garden Pavilions* (Rutland, Vt., 1962) is neither very systematic nor very scholarly, but has interesting accounts of numerous gardens and seems to be the best study available in English.

While private homes might be built with artistic skill, especially as regards the interior (in the Arab and Persian lands, the exterior was often only an unassuming wall along a narrow street), the greatest art was naturally lavished on public buildings: above all, on religious buildings, mosques, memorial tombs, hospitals, khâniqâhs, madrasahs, but also on buildings less closely associated with religion, caravanserais, covered markets, public baths, and citadels and palaces. To the extent that such buildings were erected as a pious act by rulers or rich men wanting to use their wealth to a godly end, Shar'î norms tended to prevail in the structure of the building itself. Accordingly, except in palaces and public baths, mural painting was usually replaced by non-representational art; the central role of architecture thus played a part in keeping figural art in its relatively subordinate position in Islamicate art as a whole.

It is from the Later Middle Period that we begin to have substantial numbers of monuments surviving that the traveller can visit. In architecture, as in most other arts, there is no single Islamicate style. Once one gets to know the monuments, differences come to loom greater than any similarities from country to country and from period to period. In some periods, wall decoration was not allowed to interfere with an often austere stress on the architectonic form; more often, the surface patterns on the walls predominated, even relegating such form to second place. There were fashions in shapes of domes, in types of minaret, in the treatment of vaults and arches, which can leave the quick visitor bewildered to find any consistency of style at all. But we may point to the profuse use together of arches and domes, of one sort or another, as decisive features, conceived in a spirit of ordered symmetry of detail. This way of using arches and domes, with this spirit of order, was persistent throughout most Islamicate architecture from the end of the High Caliphal Period, and sets it off sharply from contemporary Occidental, Hindu Indian, or Chinese forms in architecture. The styles so developed (especially from Nile to Oxus) were widely felt by Muslims to be associated expressly with Islam. On this basis it is possible, I suppose (for some purposes), to speak of architectural forms used by Muslims in various more outlying areas as being more or less Islamicate in tone.[14]

The architecture of Iran and the Syr-Oxus basin seems to have moved toward using colour as decisive architectural medium; and this use of colour came to be very closely related to the use of colour in the Timurî paintings of the same period. Already in the Earlier Middle Period, Iranians had made use of the colour effects of faience glaze work. Now they learned to govern a building's decorative scheme, and to some degree even the architectonic form, in consideration of these colour effects. Under Mongol rulers, the splendour of this sort of work was heightened; the domes were raised higher

[14] On the problem of finding any unity in Islamicate art, see Richard Ettinghausen, 'Interaction and Integration in Islamic Art' in *Unity and Variety in Muslim Civilization*, ed. G. E. von Grunebaum (University of Chicago Press, 1955), pp. 107–31.

and the (usually) dominant blue of the patterned wall tiles and of the ceramic coating of the domes was shown off more brilliantly. The most remarkable buildings in much of this area were great free-standing memorial tombs outside the towns, mausoleums to glorify the mighty even after death (later, at least, these were set in gardens where even the living could take their pleasure). Such tombs, with their brilliant hues, dominated a landscape.

Some modern critics complain that the vigorous sense of structural form present in the Earlier Middle Period was obscured with the emphasis on colour; thus even the details of 'corner work' in domes, which originally served to bring a polygonal base and a round dome into harmony, often appear to be developed in a purely ornamental way. But this does not seem to me to be all that is to be said about the use of colour. Once one gets accustomed to the glitter of tiles and can discount it with a selective eye, the architectonic form comes through clearly enough. What we have, I think, is an architecture of which a major foundation is the total exploitation of the possibilities, for line and colour, of surface: not merely of flat surface but of three-dimensional surface. Thus we may analyze the 'corner work' in domes more positively. The exploitation of the inner wall surfaces of a mosque is tied in directly with that of the domes by way of what originally was merely corner work: the transition from one two-dimensional flat surface to another two-dimensional, but curved, surface is made with perfect smoothness by way of a three-dimensional complex of lines and colour at the juncture, which allows the whole to become a seamless adventure in colour and line. Looked at this way, the corner work is not an overelaboration of what should have been a direct structural theme, but is rather triumph in its own right of an art of pure visuality, from which the viewer should be materially detached except for the luxury that fills his eyes: to stress the lines of material force would contaminate the visual purity.

The whole realm of Islamicate architecture is as yet very inadequately studied. But I suggest that here, as in figural art, we have in part a consequence of the divorce from—or liberation from—objective symbolism. The mosque also, like any other object of art, was not allowed to serve as representational symbol except in one limited respect: the main hall must be oriented toward Mecca, implying to that extent a focusing of devotion. Unlike a Christian church, which was not only oriented eastward but came to be so fully built round the sacrifice of the mass and the altar at which that occurred that finally some churches were built in the shape of crosses; and unlike a Hindu temple, which imaged forth the living cosmos; the shape of a mosque had no ulterior significance. It was as unsacramental as the worship it housed. There was every reason, therefore, for mosque architecture —and with it other building, influenced by that building that was most in view—to move, like figural art, in the direction of pure visuality and the autonomy of the visual surface.

Modern Westerners suffer from a number of prejudices that may prevent them from appreciating such a development. On a most obvious point, we find it hard to see colour as an integral element, let alone a basic formative element, in architecture; partly because in the Occidental tradition such conscious use of colour as there was tended to be subordinated to the didactic symbolism of depictive art, as in windows. More generally, we are prejudiced against what we call 'decoration' and see as ancillary to the structural form—which originally carried the all-important symbolism, directly or through its semi-conscious evocation of such spiritual qualities as protective quiet and strength. Some persons will acknowledge certain Islamicate buildings as beautiful, but almost guiltily; depreciating them as if that beauty came from some illegitimate source. It is as if Islamicate art were emancipated from extraneous symbolic demands by which we feel still bound.

The high point in building in the Iranian manner, in the Later Middle Period, was reached at Samarqand as a by-product of the devastations of Timur. Under Mongol rule, the cities of the Zarafshân river had been ruined and the Chaghatay dynasty had only inadequately restored the country. However, the area was still on the great overland trade routes, and Samarqand in particular was famous for the beauty of its fertile surroundings. In the mid-fourteenth century it struck a visitor as a mass of ruins amidst which the standing houses seemed very few. Then Timur chose to make it his capital for a revived Chaghatay state, and as he systematically destroyed other cities he as systematically rounded up artisans and builders from them to people and reconstruct Samarqand. Timur and his successors, notably the scholarly Ulugh-beg, caused so many great works to be built there (and also at Bukhârâ) that the Zarafshân cities and especially Samarqand were from that time forth an architectural showplace. The glories of Samarqand illustrate an extreme case of forced aesthetic incubation: as much as ever in history, it was the will of one man who gathered the artisans of all Iran to one spot and built a major city within decades. The style, naturally enough, was not new but it was expressed to perfection.

Suitably enough, the most striking monument of the whole period in Iran and the Syr-Oxus basin together is the Gûr-e Mîr, the mausoleum of Timur himself at Samarqand. Its most notable feature is its tall dome, bulging slightly from its base and curving inward only toward the top, more like a tower than a cupola; the upward thrust is emphasized by heavily incised lines vertically all around; and it is completed by blue faience over the whole.[15]

[15] Donald N. Wilber has done the decisive material analysis of Iranian building in the Later Middle Period, corresponding to the work of Cresswell in other periods. In a review article of Wilber's *Architecture of Islamic Iran: The Il-Khanid Period* (Princeton University Press, 1955), called 'Scientific Description of Art', *Journal of Near Eastern Studies*, 15 (1956), 93–102, Eric Schroeder has shown how *surface* can become the prime concern of this architecture. (I must doubt, however, his attempt to associate this with a possible feeling by Iranians that they—representing mind—were being pushed to the periphery by the Mongols—representing force, so that the Iranians rejected structural force and glorified a free subtle surface!) Schroeder's article is important in a wider way also: it presents incisively and persuasively the importance of studying what a painter or architect

It is in India that the identification of a given sort of architecture with Muslim life in general can be felt most vividly. The great centre of Muslim resistance to the Mongols (besides Mamlûk Egypt) was the sultanate of Delhi; thither not only scholars and merchants but also craftsmen fled from the central Muslim lands. In northern India they helped launch a major Islamicate art in the midst of what had been, till decades before, a quite alien cultural region.[16]

For a short time, in fact, the Muslim conquerors seem to have had to work with Hindu craftsmen in large part. The Quwwat al-Islâm mosque at Delhi illustrates the pressure the Muslims felt to maintain Islamicate cultural patterns nonetheless. Begun immediately upon the conquest, in its oldest parts it makes use of old Hindu pillars, taken as spoil from temples, and even makes do with the flat lintel roofs that Hindu architects used where Muslims would use the arch. In the great 'screen' or façade of arches, which was an indispensable feature in Iranian mosques of the Earlier Middle Period, pointed arches were felt to be so important that the Hindu masons were made to build them anyway—but for want of the relevant skills, they were edged together without keystones and could not have borne any serious weight. The carving flowed organically in the Hindu manner even though it was limited to vegetal forms and enclosed Arabic script. A generation later, however, under Iltutmish, Muslim craftsmen from Iran were present; when the mosque was enlarged, it was made as severely Islamicate as possible. Not only were keystones used to produce true arches. The carving on the façades was as rigorously geometric as Islamicate example could offer; even some of the more flowing types of arabesque were avoided here. (Only rather later, however, was the full dome introduced, a feature that required numerous skilled men.)

The architectural contrast between Hindu and Muslim answers to a more general contrast in the sense of public order. The disciplined simplicity and directness of the ṣalât worship contrasts startlingly, in the Indian scene, to the dispersed and variegated casualness of Hindu public worship. Likewise in the architecture of the mosques: in the rectangular plan of the whole as in every detail, the Muslim buildings were made to represent the order, the openness and symmetry dear to Muslim hearts, which stood out here in special contrast to the dense vital confusion of the temples of the Hindu hinterland.

---

was doing *as artist*, the impressions he hoped to make, and not merely what he was doing as craftsman, the tools he used. This more serious work has been too little done for Islamicate materials.

[16] James Fergusson, *History of Indian and Eastern Architecture*, vol. 2, (New York, 1899; first published 1876), is antiquated and has mistakes, which can be rectified by consulting more recent works, of which Percy Brown, *Indian Architecture* (Bombay, 1943 or 1952) seems to be at least as respectable as any; but Fergusson was a philosophic pioneer who brought to his work both enthusiasm and insight which make it still worth reading.

In the same reigns was built the Quṭb Minâr, said to be the highest single tower in the world. It was not a minaret; the mosques of the Delhi sultanate did not have minarets (the call to worship was given from the roof). Rather it was evidently an emblem of victory—such towers had been built in eastern Iran—and it was a triumph of the architectural solidity and strength of the Earlier Middle Period. It too was made severely Islamicate. The patterning of the red stone as it rises tier by tier is lovely in its detail but combines inexorably to concert and intensify the effect of towering force which makes the Quṭb Minâr one of those few very great buildings that seize and hold the viewer and stay with him even when he has gone away.

In the city of Delhi was reflected the pride of Muslim power and also the concern for a strong urban life that went with that. During the Delhi sultanate, a number of monarchs chose to build a new nucleus for city life in a new part of the plain—new palace, new *jâmi'* mosque, new walls, and often enough other new institutional buildings. Delhi formed a series of monumental cities, the older ones doubtless decaying but still splendid with royal remains, the newest one grand and busy within the framework of the massive buildings which determined the main lines of its layout.

The style set in those first reigns was maintained through the great period of the sultanate. Starting from a similar background to that of the Iranian, the Indian architecture stressed structural form and geometrical ornamentation in stone (or, for a time, in plaster) rather than the ceramic-based colour that came to dominate Iran. Variations of colour were made possible by the use of contrasting stones, often from distant quarries; but such colour, limited in detail and relatively subdued in hue, could be at best only a subordinate element. Gradually old Hindu elements were reintroduced on a more voluntary basis—for instance, the use of linteled doorways rather than arched ones in some contexts. In the other Indic countries, as their Muslim rulers became independent of Delhi, new and markedly varied 'provincial' styles arose which often softened still more their resistance to Hinduism and gradually introduced tendencies from the Hindu artistic tradition into their respective styles. Yet the strongly Islamicate feeling was never lost. Thus after its initial intense self-consciousness there, Islamicate art in India proved its assimilative power as well as its varied resources for creativity.

Mamlûk Cairo: city in flux

In Syria and Egypt in the later Middle Period we find an architecture that contrasts most strikingly to that of Iran and the Oxus basin. Among the Arabs, as in India, the concern for architectonic form was often given satisfying prominence and the extensive use of coloured tiles was most rare. But there also one can find creative effects, I think, of the Islamicate freedom from objective symbolism beyond the avoidance of figural art in most buildings.

The wealth of the period tended to flow into Egypt, and the surviving monuments of Egypt under the Mamlûks are concentrated chiefly in Cairo. There each transient ruler hoped to perpetuate his fame though he could hardly hope to perpetuate his family. It is these monuments that give Islamicate Cairo its distinctive architectural tone: the Mamlûk mosques are what the tourist sees, almost to the exclusion of anything earlier (or later). There is a reason. In classical 'Abbâsî times, the typical Islamicate architecture had been dominated by the brick and plaster tradition of the stoneless Iraq, which had made for ready flexibility and innovation. Nowhere was this more inappropriate than in Egypt, with its inexhaustible stone quarries and the example of Pharaonic construction; yet the practice continued there right through the Earlier Middle Period, when Egypt's culture continued to be rather an extension of the international Islamicate patterns. The Ismâ'îlî movement, quite as much as the Jamâ'î-Sunnî, was inspired and led by men from the central Muslim lands.

After the Mongol conquests and with the decline of Jamâ'î-Sunnî culture in the Iraq, Egypt became more of a centre for independent Muslim culture in the Sunnî Arab lands. As in Delhi facing the Mongols and as in Timur's Samarqand, in Cairo also a mixing of craftsmen was creative. The influx of numerous craftsmen from the Fertile Crescent fleeing from the Mongols helped, somewhat paradoxically, to launch a new national style by the very co-presence of so many novel manners to open artists' eyes to new possibilities. But it was the convergent efforts of many experimenters over generations, encouraged by a ruling class no one member of which was strong enough to impress his will on the whole city, that created the monuments of Cairo. The new Egyptian cultural independence was marked artistically by the restoration of stone to its natural position, and the new stone monuments have endured as the old brick ones could not.[17]

It was in mosques that the new methods were initiated, and the most important innovation in plan was the introduction in the thirteenth century (eventually from Iran) of a way of building mosques especially adapted to their use for madrasahs. For a large public assembly all saying the ṣalât together, as in a jâmi' Friday mosque, the vast open court with columned porticoes on each side and a specially deep one on the Mecca side was useful enough. For the more private purposes of scholarship, all those columns were less appropriate. Instead, the architect surrounded a relatively small court with four *lîwân* halls—halls open at one end on the court—roofed by a barrel-vault rising from solid stone walls. The lîwâns served well for holding

[17] R. H. C. Davis, *The Mosques of Cairo* (Cairo, 1947), is not so respectable technically as the many other discussions of Mamlûk architecture, but it has the advantage of being alive. It is uncritically romantic and its history is bad, and I think it is unfair to Fâṭimî art, but its chapters on the Mamlûk period are very illuminating. I must add that here as elsewhere I have been helped by Myron Smith, expert both in art criticism and in photography.

classes out of the strong sun.[18] Round about could be compactly built, often to considerable height, chambers for various purposes; notably a memorial tomb room for the donor, which could be surmounted by a high dome. The compactness and height of the whole complex made possible a very visible arrangement of walls and dome and minarets, and the use of stone even for the dome made possible a smoother construction. The result was not only convenient for faculty and students but architectonically solid and well-shaped, beautiful even in its sheer shape.

In the later fourteenth century, when in Egypt the new style was perfected, very little ornament was allowed except for the contrast of red and white stone, which was commonly used to set off the lines of the construction. Carved plaster was quite eliminated and the stone itself was carved only to a minimal degree. Doubtless this was because the technique of stone carving was not yet fully learned; but it also presumably reflected an awareness that too much decoration of any sort could obscure the lines of the form. Even marble panelling was relatively muted in the best building. So effective was the new 'madrasah' form that it was adapted for other than madrasah uses. The most outstanding example of the madrasah-type building in Cairo is the mosque of Sultan Ḥasan, a strong, sombre edifice on a hill, which the visitor gradually learns to love.

The 'madrasah' style spread elsewhere, notably to the Maghrib, where it developed its own variations before being abandoned. In Cairo itself, the style became less stern in the fifteenth century. The stone carving became more decorative and some critics have considered this period one of a 'late' manner—that is, where the inherent excellence of a style is being obscured in the hopeless yet inevitable effort to improve on the past. Yet one of the most impressive triumphs of Cairo dates largely from this fifteenth-century effort: the myriad delicacy of its minarets, whose original square-tower form yielded now to octagonal turrets, stepped in as they rise till they give the effect of wonderful slenderness, decorated in a manner to match the nearby dome and set them off against it. It is in this period that was built the mosque of Qâ'it-bey, most popular of them all with the tourists, partly because of the quietly colourful effect of the sunlight through its stained glass windows (the effectiveness of windows was a specialty of the time); though experts regard it as a bit too showy.

In the last generation before the occupation of Egypt by the Ottomans, the architects were experimenting restlessly once more—for instance, in one case with striking paired minarets; sometimes their inspiration came precisely from the Ottoman dominions. But after the Ottoman conquest, Egypt was

[18] For a time, Western observers imagined that the four lïwâns were used for the teaching of the four received Jamâ'î-Sunnî madhhabs, an error more amusing than serious. It is true that where all sat on the ground, simple arrangements were sufficient for holding class and presumably the choice of space might often be governed by the time of day, according to the availability of shade.

swept into the Ottoman imperial style and subsequent building there ceased to be of special interest.

The buildings of Cairo are not, for the most part, to be viewed as wholes from a distance, still less as grand façades; their unity appears, above all, in the relationship of part to part as one moves through them. Indeed, Islamicate architecture in general often stressed less the static unity of the plan of a monument than what may be called its unity of passage, its unity as one passes through it. Except for tombs, buildings tended to be situated within an established town, with limited access along the streets; if any exterior part was to be viewed it was the dome, seen at a certain distance. This was especially true of Cairo, where the same built-up area was used for centuries, in contrast, say, to Delhi. What was indeed to be seen head-on was generally the great portal, where various decorative methods were carefully used to proportion the overall half-vault (often used there) to the actual doorways. Even here, the best view is sometimes what one gets if one looks upward as one passes through, rather than, say, the view from across the street. One must, then, observe a monument of this period while in motion: from a distance one sees the domes and the minarets above the surrounding buildings; as one comes closer one sees the portal against the uniform street walls; then one enters out of the hot sun into the relative shelter of the compound, where one may pass through halls and colonnades and courts, sometimes past fountains, till one faces (in the case of any building that includes a place for worship) the focal niche indicating the direction of Mecca. At every point, the varying relation of walls and columns sets off differently the overall wall-patterning of monumental calligraphy and arabesque.

It may be said that architecture in general tends to be an art of motion, in that even the most isolated building is designed to be viewed not just from one direction but from all round. An architectural monument can almost never be captured with a few exposures of a still camera; it requires motion picture film or at least, perhaps, a series of overlapping shots which give something of that effect. But this quality takes on special importance in some Islamicate architecture. Even though in Cairo the quest for pure visuality did not take the form of building through colour as it finally did in Iran, it was the same fact, that the building as such symbolized nothing, that freed the architect to give primacy to the unity of passage over the unity imposed in a structural plan—though the latter unity was not, of course, entirely absent. (In the showy mosque of Qâ'it-bey, for instance, we find a unity of static form which is less prominent in the grander mosque of Sultân Ḥasan.) When the needs of the city as a whole required a more mobile perspective, no symbolic considerations stood in its way.

If architecture was the master art, with which all other arts formed an aesthetic ensemble, the architecture of individual buildings, in turn, was completed in the living ensemble which was a city. It was in this perspective that the arts meant most to the population at large. In the high art which was offered by the city as a whole, the ordinary man, however economically deprived, could participate. The beggar who slept in a mosque courtyard was heir to the greatest art of the high tradition; as he went about the city streets he could enjoy, if he were so inclined, a varied aesthetic scene in almost any direction; and if he travelled, as a poor Ṣûfî commonly did, he could savour the special aesthetic flavour that a combination of local situation with the interest of great patrons had given to each of many different cities. Some cities, such as Damascus or Shîrâz, were especially famed for their beauty, natural and artificial, but every city of mark had its own claims.

What was charming about Aleppo was the strength of the place. The great walled citadel on its steep hill set in the midst was never out of sight; it was matched by the thick stone walls of the citizens' homes, designed to outface fire or earthquake till Judgment day. The Aleppines were loyal to their town, and though goods from the most distant points eastward passed through it on their way to the Mediterranean seaways, Aleppo seems to have retained an air of being above all the Aleppines' home town. What was most charming about Aleppo's perennial rival, Damascus, was the whole oasis in which it was set. As one came in from the desert, the sight was lush and cool. But Damascus was at least as much the city par excellence of Jamâ'î-Sunnî piety. In conscious contrast to Aleppo, which long was largely Shî'î, the Damascenes were proud of their Sunnism, and this was expressed in the innumerable little shrines of ancient aspect, in the city and its environs, supposed to be the tombs of ancient pre-Islamic prophets and Islamic saints. The greatest shrine of them all (and the heart of Damascene opposition to 'Alid claims) was the great Umayyad mosque, which had itself an ancient, almost pre-Islamic air; it could recall both in its form, modified from a basilica, and in its mosaic murals, depicting buildings and landscapes, the old Byzantine heritage.

Cairo was decidedly larger than Aleppo or even Damascus, and in the form it had under the Mamlûks it dated only from Islamic times. It breathed the cosmopolitanism and mobility of Islamicate society. Not only its Mamlûk rulers were foreigners; often enough its great merchants and its scholars, even its judges, like Ibn-Khaldûn, were foreigners too. Whereas in Aleppo and Damascus, local factions and other local interests built up the effective structures of local organization that we have described as typical of the Islamicate Middle Periods, in Cairo such organization was much less strong: it was as if, in the big city with its distant trade in every direction, everyone were on his way through and no one were sure of staying.

Cairo had no true centre of attraction like Aleppo's citadel or Damascus' Umayyad mosque. It was built between the river and the cliffs at the desert's edge, but it did not use the river to make vistas, and the cliffs formed a fairly unobtrusive backdrop. Rather, Cairo must have absorbed the visitor gradually into its varied life, and just in this variety and movement would be its charm. There would be (one must imagine) numerous points of concentration, where life was heightened and might be beautified. The river front must have been bustling, where goods from all the Southern Seas were transshipped and sent out to the Mediterranean and northward; from here one would come to the tall commodious caravanserais, which in ruins still give one a sense of ordered dependability. Other concentrations of life would be at the several mosques, likely to be set by busy bazaars, and notably at the Az'har mosque. Students came thither from far beyond Egypt and were welcomed to the special spots reserved for their ethnic group. The citadel, seat of authority, and the exercise grounds where the Mamlûks practiced their war games, would be but another point of concentration.

All was crowded between the cliffs and the river, and what was once built up continued to accumulate its human habitations; all traces of the broad avenues of the Fâṭimî foundation were long since lost. Hence, presumably, there was little space for vistas: more than elsewhere, the very weight of the city ensured that the static unity of a building's plan be outweighed by the unity it yielded as one moved into and through it. Cairo produced few manuscript illustrations; it was not, even architecturally, a city for painting. Its architecture exulted in the light and shade of movement. When there was coloured glass in the windows, it was set in a pattern of plaster grille thick enough to have its own shadows—not made into a flat picture broken by dead lead. Within the single constructions, the angles and play of the light on the shifting yet not unrelated patterns of wall that one passed as one advanced must have absorbed one gladly into the relative cool and quiet of a mosque; and must have done so with an effect not unlike that of the city at large as it absorbed one into its activities.

In the city as a whole, also, the beauty was to be found in particular spots almost unexpectedly as they turned up. Delicate minarets would appear at a distance over the house tops, almost detached from their mosques; or grand entrance-ways to mosques would be signalled by a slight widening of the bazaar street; much as the intense ornament of a miḥrâb turned up almost unheralded on a facing wall within the madrasah or the mosque. The walls of Cairo, massive and imposing, broken by subtly decorated gates which could, indeed, sometimes be seen in their strength for a certain distance within the city, must have reappeared from time to time to remind one of the great size of the city; and the style of building still possessed a certain consistency which let one know one was still in Cairo. Otherwise, little tied the various concentrations of life to one another except the pervasive movement and repeated interchange of the metropolis, in which every man was received equally as one of God's servants, and might try his fortune.

IV

The Expansion of Islam, *c.* 1258–1503

As we have noted, after about 1000 CE Islamic faith spread gradually throughout most of the more densely inhabited parts of the hemisphere, and with the faith very often went Muslim rule. It was during the Later Middle Period that the Islamicate society, still relatively homogeneous despite its wide dispersal, achieved a predominant position among the Afro-Eurasian societies from which it was not dislodged even by the west European conquest of the oceans in the early sixteenth century. We may almost speak of a Muslim hegemony in the greater part of the Oikoumene.

By the thirteenth century, Islamdom had extended its sway over all the old core area of the Sanskritic culture which prevailed in India, Indochina, and Malaysia; by the end of the fourteenth century it had extended it over two of the three peninsulas which formed the old core area of the Hellenic culture which prevailed throughout Europe; and it was soon to threaten Italy too. Islam held sway in Banaras and in Athens. In the fifteenth century, its position was further extended in all directions. It had come to prevail in parts of the Eurasian steppe where Chinese influence had once been strong, and latterly was rolling back Occidental influence in eastern Europe. At the same time, it was far more active on the Oikoumenic frontiers than even the Chinese or the Occidentals. It had become the most important cultural tradition in the Indian Ocean basin and the central Eurasian steppe, as well as in the vast Sûdânic savannas and the Volga-Irtysh plains in the far north. The eastern Christian peoples who were not subject to Muslim rule or at least Muslim overlordship (like most of the Russians) formed enclaves within largely Muslim surroundings, like Georgia or Abyssinia; the Hindu and Theravada Buddhist peoples likewise, those which were not actually under Muslim rule, found increasingly the sea-lanes on which most of them depended for contact with the outside world to be in the hands of Muslims; so that they looked more and more out upon the world through an Islamicate filter, and were increasingly affected by it in their own cultural life, though a Chinese influence also affected the Theravadin societies. (To a lesser degree, Lamaist Tibet and Mongolia likewise fronted on Muslim-controlled trade routes.) The reviving Hindu kingdom of Vijayanagar in the south of India not only employed Muslim troops but used Islamicate fashions in its court.

If we may look upon the Indic and the European cultural traditions as organic wholes (which they have been in a restricted sense), we may remark that the effect of the Muslim expansion was more drastically fateful for the Indic tradition than for the European. While the main older centres of Greek civilization (except southern Italy) were subjected to Muslims, its tradition was maintained in relative independence in the wide areas of the Russian north and especially the Latin west. In the case of Sanskrit civilization, on the contrary, not only were the old centres in northern India largely Islamized, but southern India also came under Muslim domination, as did even a great part of the overseas footholds of Indic civilization in the Indochinese and Malaysian countries; though both there and in the Lamaist lands northward an Indic high culture maintained its autonomy in the face of Muslim surroundings. Nevertheless, the Islamicate impact was enormous, not only in the Indic zone but even in the remoter parts of Europe, where the inescapable presence of Islamdom had a deeply formative effect on the sense of Christian cultural and social identity. And everywhere, of course, the Muslims coloured the social and cultural sides of international trade, with incalculable results throughout the hemisphere.

The world impact of Islamdom, then, was greatly out of proportion to the number of Muslims. Geographical advantages of the position of the lands from Nile to Oxus in the trade routes of the hemisphere helped account for this; at least as important were the social and political flexibility of the international Islamicate institutions; and the relative accessibility of the essentials of the Islamicate culture to new converts, so that they could add immediately to its strength. But at the base of the whole structure were those converts themselves: great numbers in vast and diverse areas were gladly turning Muslim.

Pressures for conversion to Islam

How did such widespread conversion take place? When Islam had been a badge of privilege among the Arab rulers of a conquered empire, there had been little wish to convert others and share the privileges more widely than necessary. Such pressure as there was (apart from isolated incidents) resulted from a desire to distinguish the ruling Arabs from ordinary mankind, partly so as to enhance their dignity and partly, no doubt, to prevent their corruption. Arabs, it was felt, as Muḥammad's own people, should all be Muslims, submitting to the discipline and sharing in the privileges of Islam. Pagan Arabs were simply not tolerated, but these disappeared very early. Those Christian Bedouin tribes that, as Arabs, were allowed a share in the status of conquering class (they were not classified as dhimmîs), were under intense pressure, informally, to turn Muslim; they had explicitly to defend their rights more than once; and finally they all succumbed. The land of the Arabs —which was early defined to include not merely Bedouin Arabia but the whole peninsula south of the Fertile Crescent (i.e., including the early

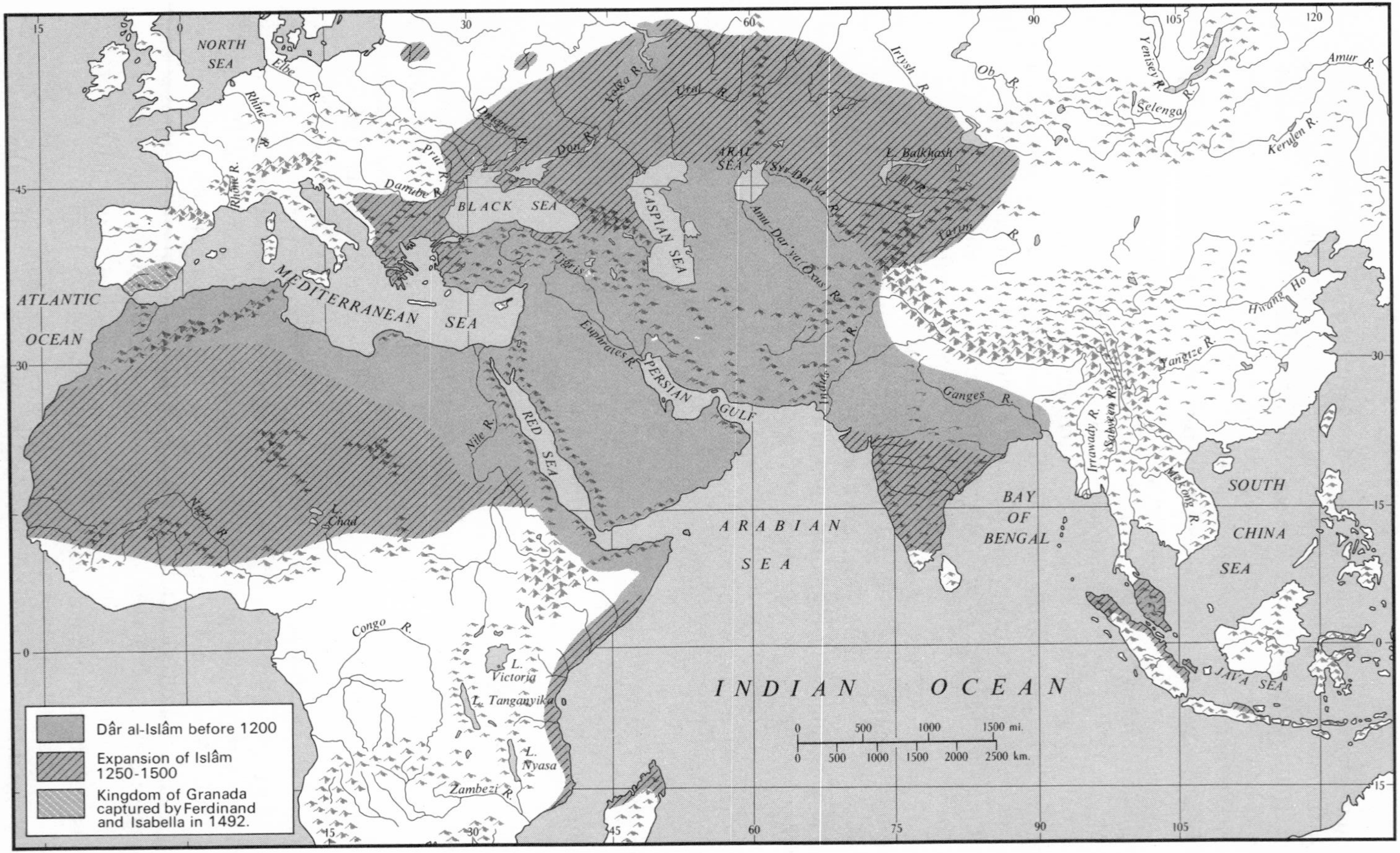

The expansion of Islam, 1250–1500

Arabized Yemen)—also should be protected from contamination by infidels. Various settled Jewish and Christian groups—despite the fact of their being under protection as dhimmîs—were moved from their Arabian homes to lands in the Fertile Crescent that were supposed to compensate them for their losses in the Peninsula. The idea that all Arabia should be free of infidels was never carried out entirely, but eventually it was agreed that infidels should anyway not be allowed (even as visitors) into the immediate vicinity of Mecca and Medina. But otherwise, the numerous eager non-Arab converts to Islam were often welcomed only lukewarmly or even rebuffed.

But, as we have seen, before the end of Marwânî times some of the pious were becoming eager to see conversions take place as widely as possible; this was an attitude in obvious harmony with Muḥammad's own. After a time, it became standard for the biographer of a great preacher—Ṣûfî or not—to boast of the number of infidels he converted by his preaching. Few Muslims seem to have set out to make a career of converting infidels: conversion was normally a by-product of public preaching among Muslims, to which non-Muslims came by invitation or out of curiosity. (And, of course, there was no organized mission work in which funds were set aside for the purpose by a home organization, such as has been the basis of Christian missions under Modern technical conditions; there was not even a sufficiently centralized organization to delegate the responsibility officially, as even pre-Modern Christians sometimes did through the church hierarchy.) But a certain number of Muslims, especially Ṣûfîs, seem to have made a special point of attracting infidels; and some deliberately wandered in infidel lands—wherever sufficient nuclei of Muslims existed to receive them here and there (and this included most of the citied part of the hemisphere outside the confines of persecuting Christendom)—converting as they could.

Muslims seem to have made converts in two ways. First, they made a personal appeal to people's religious consciousness. On the level of straight argument, they often put forward the populistic intelligibility of Islam. Muslims commonly ridiculed, in the name of intellectual good sense, the more mythically convoluted teachings of older rival traditions, in favour of a basic monotheistic and unitarian position; this could seem attractively straightforward to people dissatisfied with taking things on faith from a learnèd priest whose mysteries they could not comprehend. On this level, Islam must have appealed to persons who, in a socially mobile situation, were having to make up their own minds on points of world view, without being able to fall back on automatic conformity to established authority. A single Creator-god, to be worshipped by each person for himself on the basis of revelation that had been given to a famous prophet whom millions already acknowledged—this was at once intelligible and plausible.

This was only one level of the religious appeal, of course. Conviction on such points, however attractive, does not normally proceed merely from an abstract conversation. Adherence to a living tradition requires at least some preliminary participation in it to enlist a person's whole mind. But the formal scriptures and cult of Islam did not invite such participation. It was not exposure to the Qur'ân that converted infidels, nor even tentative sharing in the Muslim ritual at the mosque. Muslims commonly felt that the Qur'ân and even books of ḥadîth reports were much too sacred to be defiled by the touch of infidels (who were not, after all, in a state of ritual purity, as defined for purposes of performing the ṣalât worship) until they had already committed themselves to Islam. In any case, these documents were rarely translated from the original Arabic; for every Muslim ought to learn at least enough Arabic to perform ṣalât in the original—so that God could be honoured publicly in his own universal forms, whatever the local dialect (and perhaps so that the cosmopolitan universality of the Ummah should not be breached). Nor were Muslims willing to let infidels casually profane the mosques with their curious or scoffing irreverence; at least during the Middle Periods, though less often earlier, infidels were sometimes even forbidden entry. Reciting the Qur'ân and performing ṣalât were public duties, a part of maintaining God's good order on earth, a consequence of the act of islâm; before he was either obligated or entitled to perform those duties, a person must first decide to obey God.

Hence it was only in more informal preaching sessions, and especially at Ṣûfî khâniqâhs, where the concern was not the public order and dignity of Islam but the welfare of the individual soul, that the inquiring infidel could begin to participate enough in Islam to be moved to commit himself to it. Or such participation, in an indirect but generally effective way, could take the form of witnessing or at least being impressed, by hearsay, with some wonder—a healing or a trick of endurance such as Ṣûfîs performed or were credited with. Non-Muslims (and Muslims too) could have recourse to any person, whatever his affiliation, whose reputation promised that he might help them in a difficulty; and contact on such an occasion could then lead non-Muslims to an appreciation of the message of Islam.

But a second way of conversion may have been at least as important, though it was probably usually at least supported by the first way (the way of intellectual and emotional conviction). That is, many came to Islam for essentially social reasons. They had models among the early Muslims—those Quraysh of Mecca who accepted Muḥammad when they found no alternative but helpless isolation, and whom Muḥammad was inordinately generous to as new converts. Relevant social pressures were manifold and usually interrelated. Men might become Muslim to marry Muslim girls, who were not allowed by the Sharî'ah to marry out of their own group; or women might become Muslim upon marriage to a Muslim man—who could legally have a Christian or Jewish woman as wife, but none from a more dubious religious background. But marriage was rarely sought except as part of a wider social involvement. Once Muslim cadres in a place had been able to become economically or politically powerful, there would always be advantages to joining them. Non-Muslims might, indeed, make commercial partnerships with Muslims or even rise high in Muslim administration, but a Muslim always had the advantage in bidding for such arrangements. As a rule, Muslims could more certainly count on arrangements made with other Muslims, who were subject to the same rules and social pressures as themselves.

These social pressures were supported by a psychological pressure: Muslims were normally prejudiced against non-Muslims as such. Though technically submission to God, true islâm, might be a personal matter, to be seen in the moral quality of a person's living rather than in external tokens and affiliations, in fact most Muslims (themselves not necessarily above the spiritual average of mankind) judged by affiliation rather than by life. They drew a sharp line at the point of explicit religious allegiance: the most righteous non-Muslim, though he might win grudging respect, was normally regarded as inferior in status to any Muslim, however dubious his claims to probity. The feeling was almost as strong as ethnic feeling and did, indeed, have something of an ethnic tone to it: a new convert, though he was accepted as a Muslim, was not always accorded the full respect reserved for those who were Muslim by birth. Nevertheless, the convert to Islam did normally escape the obloquy and contempt that non-Muslims received at Muslim hands. In an environment where Muslims predominated numerically or even in key roles, non-Muslims were under constant temptation to conform. Comparable counterpressures from within their own groups would counteract this temptation for those whose lives were sufficiently restricted within their own cricles; but not for those who found themselves socially isolated or sufficiently active to be much in contact with Muslims.

The social pressures were reinforced in Muslim lands by the several discriminatory provisions of the Sharî'ah law. A non-Muslim's word was not accepted against a Muslim in the qâḍî's court (though it might be in an amîr's court); nor was murder of a non-Muslim quite so heinous a crime as was murder of a Muslim (though again an amîr's court might make no distinction). Non-Muslims were frequently subjected to sumptuary laws that forbade them to wear clothes fashionable among Muslims, or even forced them to wear a special token of their status. They might not be permitted that public proof of manly affluence, riding a horse. If non-Muslims could not inherit from Muslims, then neither could Muslims from non-Muslims (which might discourage conversion among young non-Muslims of wealthy family); but non-Muslims commonly paid higher taxes at various points than Muslims, notably sometimes—but not always—at customs stations. The most important special tax paid by non-Muslims, of course, was the jizyah poll tax; paupers and other dependents were exempt, and it was graduated according to wealth, but not enough to avoid substantial hardship in some cases.

These provisions were supplemented on occasion, contrary to the Sharî'ah, by outright persecution. Captives in the jihâd war, of course, might be offered their lives in return for conversion; but their more usual fate was enslavement. Within the Dâr al-Islâm, a non-Muslim was usually free to hold to his own tradition. But prejudice and passion could interfere even there. Once in a while a ruler insisted on the conversion of a prominent non-Muslim figure, perhaps on the pretext of some infringement that would otherwise cost him his life. We hear of a Suhravardî pîr in the Panjâb whose bigotry was murderous. A Hindu of high position had praised the pîr—either genuinely or out of politeness—as being the best of (Muslim) saints as Muḥammad had been the best of (non-Hindu) prophets; and to add to the grace of his tribute, he had used a standard Muslim formula in referring to Muḥammad. The pîr maintained that the latter statement implied the shahâdah declaration, uttering which made a man a Muslim, and demanded that the Hindu acknowledge Islam on pain of death as an apostate. The local ruler dared not defy the pîr in favour of an infidel, and the Hindu had to flee to Delhi. But the pîr pursued him even to Delhi and had him executed.

Occasionally there were large-scale persecutions in a whole city, or even a larger area, such as those of al-Ḥâkim of Egypt, when non-Muslims had to convert or go into exile. On such occasions, popular Muslim feeling might supplement official persecution with rioting; more often, a street riot directed against non-Muslims, set off by a chance dispute or by current popular suspicions, had to be suppressed by the authorities. Sometimes, after the crisis was over, those who had been subjected to forced conversion were allowed to return to their former status. Sometimes they formed a distinctive group of their own, outwardly Muslim but privately retaining their own allegiance and not inter-marrying with the other Muslims. A group of Jews who were forced into conversion in Egypt in 1301 remained distinct and secretly Jewish as late as the sixteenth century. (Corresponding phenomena occurred in Christian Spain.) But such violence was infrequent—at least by the standards set by contemporary Christendom; and the wholesale massacres that Christians so often perpetrated against the Jews in their midst were not paralleled in Islamdom. Some persecution occurred occasionally even as early as the time of al-Mutawakkil in the High Caliphate, but it usually took place only in later periods, and then only where the bulk of the population was already Muslim, so that non-Muslims formed minorities, always suspect to any majority. Rarely can any substantial amount of conversion to Islam in a broad area be ascribed to direct persecution.

As a result of all these pressures, both religious and social, once Muslims came to power or even pre-eminence in a land, there was a steady tendency for the land to become solidly Muslim. The like might be expected of any confessional religious community in some measure; and especially of the monotheistic ones, with their stress on the single saved community. In fact, the Christian churches, much more tightly organized, violently intolerant of any rival community (unless possibly the Jewish), and almost always ready to suppress in blood any expression even of unorthodoxy, were able to impose total conversion, where they came to power, much more rapidly than

Muslims ever did. But their relative tolerance doubtless made it easier for Muslims to come to power as a minority. And in a quieter and more gradual way the Muslims were almost as efficient in conversion, though few Muslim lands did not retain at least a few dhimmî groups right down to Modern times. The Muslim communal spirit was expressed in the fierce rule against apostasy: he who publicly abjures Islam must die—and if a government were not at hand to carry out the sentence, the person's own family was likely to do it. But this rule had rarely to be invoked (save occasionally in cases of religious dispute, where the victim claimed he was still a Muslim); for very few Muslims have ever wanted to abandon Islam.

The attractiveness of Islamicate culture

What we must investigate, then, in tracing the geographical expansion of Islamdom and of its religious allegiance, is how Islam came to predominate on key social levels in so many places, so that further conversions became advantageous. What we have described of the processes of personal conversion tells us something of what happened, but cannot account for the particular distribution of conversion in time and space, or even for its success at all: for other allegiances were attractive in their own ways. Sometimes appeal is made, therefore, simply to the effects of military conquest: to the intervention of the sword on a different level. But where conquest occurred, what is to be explained is why the conquest happened; for Muslims were not the only ones that had recourse to the sword. Why were Muslim victories so often not reversed? And in most areas, a certain Muslim pre-eminence preceded actual Muslim power. Or else appeal is made to the effects of intermarriage by Muslims (those for whom Islam is an Arab phenomenon speak of marriage by Arabs). But others married, and married more than one wife at a time if they could afford it; why should the religious effects be all in one direction? We are forced to look to the general attractiveness of the Islamicate culture, which seems to have been decisive; not so much its highest cultural qualities, not usually very visible on the frontier, as the overall social role it filled.

At this point, as so often, I must invoke some general considerations about society in the Agrarian Age. Corresponding to, and just the reverse of, the population gradient from the remoter rural areas into the cities, was what may be called a 'culture gradient'. Elements of culture tended to move from the most cosmopolitan centres to the most isolated. In this connection, 'cosmopolitan' centres will be those that had the most active relations, commercial or cultural, with areas the most distant; and where simultaneously wealth and power are most concentrated. The combination is not a chance one. Commonly, centres of long-distance contact were also centres of concentration of wealth and power: whether it is because wealth attracted distant trade or because distant trade developed wealth, they went together; and since wealth is a prime foundation of power, centres of trade, of power, and of wealth have tended to coincide more often than not. There, the conflict and interaction of contrasting cultural traditions became most active, sometimes eroding the specific content of the individual traditions, but in any case occasioning a maximum rapidity of dialogue within and among them, a maximum rapidity of development of their potentialities.

The innovations that resulted were clothed with maximum prestige. Because the cultural patterns were inherently attractive, or because they possessed compelling efficiency in competition (military, commercial, or intellectual), or, more generally, because they had prestige on the widest horizons open to those who came in contact with them, the culture of the more cosmopolitan centres tended to be adopted in those slightly less cosmopolitan centres in most immediate and active contact with them, if they were possessed of sufficient wealth to allow such innovation. From these centres, in turn, the cultural elements radiated into the smaller towns about, and finally into the countryside and even into the remotest regions, ever carried by the prestige of wealth and power generally, as well as by any inherent qualities. (This seems to be the mechanism underlying, for instance, Toynbee's notion of 'mimesis' by outlying peoples—and lower classes—of the attractive styles of life developed by creative élites.)

But how much this meant diffusion of isolated cultural elements merely, assimilated into a continuing indigenous culture, how far it meant diffusion of major individual cultural traditions in one or another field of life, how far it might mean diffusion of a civilization as a whole, is a matter of how steep the gradient was. In some areas of the Oikoumene, the contrast between local people and Muslims in degree of cosmopolitanism was great; there Islamicate patterns spread with little competition. In other areas, however, the contrast was much less great and the spread of Islam must be accounted for in more differentiated detail, by showing just how the 'culture gradient', though slight, could be effective.

The actual mechanism of Islamicate expansion was the development of relatively self-contained local cadres. Except in the Confucian Far East, in all the areas where the religion was allowed to penetrate—whether centres of high civilization or areas, as in much of Africa, which had lacked even literacy before Islam—Muslim faith and Muslim rule tended to go together. In some places Islam was introduced by merchants or by local warrior-missionaries; often the religion spread by ever-increasing conversions long before there was question of Muslim rule. Always wherever there were numerous Muslims, there arose a demand for various sorts of Muslim specialists—not only 'ulamâ' and qâḍîs, but representatives of the material and intellectual norms that gained their prestige from association with the lands of old Islam. And there were always merchants and scholars ready to come. Then, however, the multiplying body of the faithful were glad to see political power be in the hands of fellow-Muslims; that is, apart from more mundane considerations, in the hands of men who would see to it, however imperfectly, that the decencies of God's order among men were maintained. And Muslim communal solidarity often made possible a bid for power. Hence Muslim rule tended to follow the faith.

Where it was Muslim rule that came first—by conversion of rulers or, notably in Europe and India, by direct conquest, the process was similar; for conquest, of course, could not be lasting unless the faith also spread into the conquered area at the same time or soon after; and this it usually did, for a community of soldiers would have drawing power similar to that of a community of merchants.

Whichever way Muslim faith and rule came, once it had endured any length of time there tended to follow the whole Islamicate civilization as found in the area from which the Islamization had come. Even more than before, after an area came under Muslim rule Muslim cadres quickly formed. Traders, administrators, architects, poets, wandering Ṣûfîs, soldiers, ʿAlids (revered as descendants of Muḥammad and hence indefinitely multiplied by this time), all tended to drift into the newly opened territories to take advantage of fresh opportunities; and converts multiplied in response to the same opportunities. The few Muslims, having the upper hand, welcomed as a support the strength that came of sheer numbers, as well as the cultural skills brought by the newcomers. Adventurers were attracted by a freshly unsettled situation in which anyone with quick wits and a Muslim name might hope to make his fortune. Very soon mosques were built and towns took on an Islamicate veneer; eventually many towns became genuine centres of Islamicate culture. Gradually, as merchants or soldiers became landlords, and as minor Ṣûfîs carried a missionary zeal to the villages, the countryside also was in a measure integrated into the Islamicate society. Perso-Arabic Islamicate culture, to be sure, was more or less modified by local conditions and traditions; but the recognized norm remained a universal, cosmopolitan one, largely common to Islamdom as a whole.

Writers have often associated Islam with a particular sort of geographic terrain. Once it was associated with heat; now, more often, with the Arid Zone.[1] The lines of the expansion of Islam can probably be analyzed most

[1] The association of Islamic expansion with the Arid Zone has been much clarified by Xavier de Planhol, *Le Monde islamique: essai de géographie religieuse* (Paris, 1957); he notes that there is no psychological affinity of Islam for aridity, but says it came to be spread especially by steppe nomads and by city merchants, both of which had greater success where the peasant population was relatively thin and subject to domination from long-range trade routes or herding areas, citing certain secondary factors also. But his analysis remains unsatisfactory. It underestimates the variety of political forms Islamicate societies have taken and exaggerates the transient, ephemeral tendencies in Islamicate culture; analogously, he lays too much stress on the trade between India and western Europe, not recognizing, for instance, the degree to which the Nile-to-Oxus region itself consisted of termini. His stress on the bias in Islam against the *land* has much validity, but it is too simple. In some points it is pushed too far: the suppression of the pig (in favour of the goat) need not always have the anti-cultivator, pro-herdsman effects that under some circumstances it does seem to have; and his lament over the loss of the vine would be cryingly disproportionate in any but a Frenchman. In any case, it is too direct, as if a general rule could be formulated about what sorts of peoples were accessible to conversion.

flexibly in terms of multiple historical interactions. It arose in the mid-Arid Zone; it took an unusually cosmopolitan form, which seems to have allowed it unusual strength especially along trade routes and in areas being newly integrated into the inter-regional agrarianate complex. Hence it expanded into central Eurasia and Africa as the most accessible such areas, and into the relatively frontier areas of Bengal and Yünnan when it became neighbour to these places (perhaps Albania was a like case); but also into Keralam (southwest India) and Malaysia because of the dependence of these commercially dominated areas on cosmopolitan forces. But in the Panjâb and Anatolia and other old culture centres, it won out through the weight of centuries of overall Islamicate political or social superiority over the great neighbouring societies. That many of these various areas were also arid reflects the fact that more of the world's land surface is in some degree arid than is well watered. Such details as growth in Albania more than in Bulgaria call for an explanation by local historical interactions which will teach us to beware of undemonstrable generalizations in more ambiguous cases. What we can say is that wherever the Muslim cadres had an opportunity to become socially autonomous and flourish, there the Islamicate society took root and, often, power.

The Islamicizing of the Southern Seas

Linking the most distant parts of the Afro-Eurasian citied zone was a chain of great seas through which passed the bulk of the more long-distance trade of the Oikoumene. It is these that can best be called 'the Seven Seas' (if they are counted judiciously), for no other group of seas has more right to the phrase: the *East China Sea* from Japan southward, the *South China Sea* to the Malacca straits, the *Gulf of Bengal*, the *Arabian Sea*, the *Red Sea*, then across the Egyptian isthmus the *Mediterranean Sea*, and the *Northeast Atlantic* northward to Britain. The farther citied culture spread, the greater was the trade upon these seas—not only on the remote terminal ones, but on the seas between. The richest part of this chain of seas was naturally the Southern Seas, those from the South China Sea to the Red Sea, which carried the goods of the lands from Nile to Indus, and of China, and of the Indic lands between; and of East Africa and of Malaysia. During the first millennium CE, as we have noted, all of this area had seen an overall increase of commercial activity and of urban settlement. Earlier, the Southern Seas, for the most part, had carried trade only of restricted kinds and between relatively distant points; by the end of that millennium, when the Muslim expansion began, their shores had come to teem with ports which not only introduced a greater variety of local products into the trade, but themselves formed markets and termini as well as way stations. To citied expansion in the far east, north, and west, that is, had also been added expansion around the Southern Seas themselves, and the commercial importance and cosmopolitan character of this central part of the chain of 'the Seven Seas' was accordingly accentuated.

With the increased cosmopolitanism of the Southern Seas regions, the prestige of the Irano-Semitic culture spread there. Even before Islam, as we have noted, Christianity, the earlier major allegiance of the Fertile Crescent, had found a solid foothold both in Abyssinia and in southwest India (Keralam) at the other end of the Arabian Sea; in Islamic times, Islam in turn spread around the 'Horn' of Africa, and the Christians of Keralam had to make room for an equally numerous Muslim community there. But Islam spread to points where Christianity had not reached. By the Later Middle Period it was entrenched in East African islands like Zanzibar and the Comoros and at trading points all along the coast. Here it had no major urban religion as rival. But from Gujarât east, the urban societies were committed to Hindu and Hindu-Buddhist traditions. In all the ports of these lands Islam became important; by the fourteenth century it was even making headway (largely via south Indian commercial groups) along the Malay peninsula and the north Sumatra coast, where commerce passed between the Bay of Bengal and the South China Sea. Higher culture in the Far Southeast had always looked to the Indian mercantile groups for inspiration, and for centuries this had meant Hinduism; now it came more often to mean Islam, and with it the Perso-Arabic culture. By about 1500, Islam was a major force in all of the Malaysian archipelago and along the Indo-Chinese coasts; in the following century, much of inland Sumatra and Java accepted Islam also.

With its role in the Southern Seas, Islamdom moved toward a hegemony in the Oikoumene perhaps even more decisively than in its expansion in more continental parts. How is this to be accounted for concretely?

We must point to the special role of the commercial community. Such a community can live more smoothly if it has common cultural standards, including both legal norms and overall social expectations. A group of commercial centres in relations with each other will gain a like advantage from sharing a common culture. Hence if one form of culture is able to become dominant in a substantial portion of a commercial network, it stands a good chance of becoming dominant universally within that network. Even if the 'culture gradient' is not steep, there is a good possibility for a band-wagon effect. This chance is enhanced by the fact that of all groups, the mercantile are likely to be least attached to old norms and traditions—far less attached than the agrarian; conversion to a new cultural standard is relatively easy if only because the personnel of any merchant community is likely to change fairly rapidly and be drawn from widely scattered sources.

At least in the ports of the western coasts of the Southern Seas—along East Africa, southern Arabia, if not even the western Indian coast, it was likely that a single one of the major citied cultures might become widely dominant: for in much of the area, the 'culture gradient' between cities of high culture and remote unlettered communities was steep. The alternative to the Irano-Semitic high culture would have been the Indic: the 'Umân coast is nearer to the mouth of the Indus than to the mouth of the Euphrates, and the eastern Horn of Africa is as accessible from there as from the Yemen (which might retain special links to the north by way of the Ḥijâz and then through the pressure of Bedouin Arabia). And even climate might indicate links to a more tropical India. But an Indic high-cultural dominance seems to have been ruled out for at least two reasons (apart from the possible role of a relatively well-populated Yemen). The centres between Nile and Oxus were perhaps more important directly as channels of trade to a very wide range of distant regions. But this might not have weighed against the almost equally important role of Indian ports themselves and the points east with which they were in contact. Surely, at least by Islamic times it was also important that—partly because of the very extent and diversity of trade contacts in the region between Nile and Oxus—the Irano-Semitic culture proved to be so remarkably adaptable for commercial life. Above all, the Islamicate system provided a superbly rapid means for mobilizing to the utmost the human resources available, because of its minimal dependence on political or military or even priestly establishments already set up, and because of the relative social openness for the rise of men of talent once they had entered Islam. In any case, even along the west coast of India before the Muslim conquest, and in areas where there never was any Muslim conquest, the prestige of the Muslim merchant communities was very high; they were accorded special privileges by the local Hindu rulers and tended to take the lead in commercial ventures.

Islamdom in the westerly coasts of the Indian Ocean formed a political and intellectual world of its own. Politically, the only large-scale powers were in the anciently Muslim Yemen, where the Rasûlid dynasty (1229–1454), replacing the Ayyûbid and contending with the Mamlûk power, was strongly influenced from Syria and Egypt. Occasionally the captains of slave troops ruled—not so much Turkic here as Negro. But the focus of power lay in the Muslim communities of the many coastal towns—though along the west Indian coasts, these communities, however important, never seized power. The Shâfi'î tradition was developed in relative independence of centres further north.

Once the westerly coasts were predominantly Muslim, it is perhaps not too surprising that, by the bandwagon principle, the commercial centres of the more easterly coasts should eventually be brought into the Islamicate system. But this was at most a possibility—other pressures will have worked against Islamicization. In fact, Islamicization there proceeded by slow stages under special circumstances. Its greatest successes were in the Malaysian archipelago (this term includes Malaya and the Philippines but no part of New Guinea).

The population of the archipelago, accustomed to passing from island to island, had long since developed a high level of enterprise in shipping, which had carried its cultural traditions as far as Madagascar. But it was tied into the interregional citied commercial nexus first in contacts with India at the beginning of the first millennium. Soon after, direct Chinese trade also became important, and the region began to be integrated into the Oikoumene. This was the time of the great expansion of Indic culture, and Indic culture took the lead in commercial circles. Buddhist monks and Brahman priests served as effective missionaries throughout the Indochinese and Malaysian regions. From the ports, they penetrated even into the hinterlands. The increasing trade contacts of the agrarian rice kingdoms of the interior led them to look for a lettered high culture of broader horizons than their own parochial pre-lettered traditions. They were led to adopt the Buddhist and Shaivite religious and cultural systems which had won such prestige already in the commercial ports. Accordingly, by the end of the first millennium the whole region was largely Indic in high-cultural orientation.

As the trade of the Southern Seas became more extensive, more complex, and more important in the various local economies, however, the advantages and prestige of a common maritime culture presumably became that much greater. After the turn of the millennium the Muslim position on the coasts of India itself became steadily stronger, partly because of the conquests in the interior by Islamicate powers. After 1200, both Bengal and then Gujarât—whose ports were important in the Southern Seas trade—came under Muslim rule. Gradually it came to be that those Indian merchants who had most prestige were Muslims.

The crucial event was the Islamizing of the Malay Straits. Sea trade between the Chinese far east and the Indic lands, since the early centuries of the first millennium, had passed through those straits; the settlements along their coasts were in at least as direct a relation with ports in India and China as with any of the areas more nearby. The Straits, then, were among the most cosmopolitan spots on the globe. The first great urban power in the region was centred on the Straits—the Buddhist mercantile state of Shrivijaya, which flourished by controlling the trade through the Straits and providing a compulsory exchange point for it. When it broke up at the end of the twelfth century, numerous independent trader cities took its place, none strong enough to prevent other exactions, or piracy, than its own.

In the late 1200s, at least two ports on the Sumatran side of the Straits adopted Islam. Before long, other ports, including the strongest of them, Malacca (on the Malay peninsula side of the Straits), followed suit, sealing the decision sometimes with a marriage of the dominant local figure with a Muslim woman. Not only Muslims from India and points west helped establish these Muslim centres, but local converts to Islam and even, on occasion, adventurous Chinese. This cannot be understood entirely in the same terms as the Muslim prevalence further west in the Southern Seas. As the interregional trade became more substantial and better organized, the trade of any one group seems to have become, in one way, more limited. With the development of regular long-distance trading patterns, major depots grew up, points of interchange, of relay, dividing the ocean voyages into stages. From points farther west, merchants rarely came farther east than Cambay, the main port of Gujarât, or at most than other west Indian ports. (To go farther, indeed, would have required a second monsoon season—that is, a second year.) From Cambay, in turn, merchants rarely went farther than Malacca in the Straits. The Chinese merchants, then, largely ceased coming westward from Malacca. Under such circumstances, one might have envisaged at least three quite separate merchant cultures in the three areas. But once Muslims had taken the lead even in the Indic ports, they had an opportunity to present a rival to the Indic traditions wherever these had prevailed.

As compared with the Indic tradition, the Islamicate had the same overall advantages, as a context for maximal social mobility, that it had farther west. But by this period, with the collapse of the relatively merchant-oriented Buddhism within India and with the diminishing venturesomeness of the Brahmans, Islam was far more strongly missionary-minded than was any old-Indic tradition. Every merchant was a missionary, and even sayyids, sometimes from the older centres from Nile to Oxus and in this case from Arabia itself, were wont to tour the remoter outposts to gather honours and perhaps also souls. But, above all, the development of Ṣûfism as matrix of a faith of the masses brought forth a host of itinerant preachers, whose moral, revivalistic, and relatively non-communal preaching was accessible to people of any background. Islam in the archipelago was, almost from the beginning, as strongly Ṣûfî-minded as it was anywhere else in that period. The prestige of Muslim rule in India, the propagative vigour of the Ṣûfîs in the full flush of their popular development, and the example of more westerly seas combined to recommend Islam in the Straits.

The alternative possibility in the Malaysian archipelago was the adoption of a Chinese type of culture, as did happen in Vietnam, on the east coast of the Indochinese peninsula. The Chinese were, at least for an item like pepper, the best customers of the archipelago as a whole; they were the most advanced and the strongest at sea—their vessels were more massive and stronger than those used in the Indian Ocean; and they seem to have passed for the wealthiest merchants in the whole region. They were perhaps limited by the fact that in later times they no longer went far past the stage of Malacca. But perhaps more important was the very effectiveness of their political organization at home. One can say that the Muslims won out over the Buddhists and Hindus because of their political flexibility—which indicated a complex of traits which made for extreme political instability in the Islamicate cultural centres. That is, they won out, in a sense, because they built politically less solidly than the Hindus. But both Hindus and Muslims built, politically, far less solidly than the Chinese. Chinese institutions could be exported only with difficulty apart from the home imperial establishment with its bureaucracy; but wherever a handful of Muslims was gathered, there was the Sharîʿah in the midst of them, and they could readily add to their numbers and resources both from home and by conversion. At the end of the thirteenth and again at the beginning of the fifteenth century, fleets were sent, representing the Chinese government, to exercise a certain oversight in the region; the latter fleets went throughout the Southern Seas, even to East African coasts, and were victorious everywhere. Chinese settlers were many. But there were no general adoptions of the Chinese cultural system as a whole.

Once the Malay Straits had turned Muslim, the rest of the archipelago readily followed in due time. The Far Southeast (the region east of India and south of China) was articulated into several contrasting parts, though all were in mutual interaction commercially and politically. The first contrast is between the great mainland river valleys and the island archipelago. Along the Irawaddy, Ping, and Mekong valleys grew the great kingdoms of the Burmese, Thais, and Cambodians. Each river reached the sea in a great delta; but between the river and other coastlands were mountains or hills which often limited direct contact; the kingdoms were essentially inland ones. Though Cambodia, least isolated from the sea of the three, saw its king converted to Islam at one point, and though there were many Muslims along some of the coasts (and a relatively small people on the east Indochinese coast, the Chiams, became predominantly Muslim), yet these large kingdoms remained Buddhist once the original wave of Indic expansion had established its high culture there.

In the archipelago, including the Malay peninsula, the reverse was the case. The archipelago can be divided into three parts. The Straits themselves were repeatedly the seat of a commercial empire, in direct relations with major Oikoumenic core areas, but also the focus of much of the internal commercial life of the archipelago, so far as it was stimulated by the long-distance trade. The development of both Malaya and Sumatra (so far as the interior of the latter did not simply remain pre-literate) was largely tied to the life of the Straits; and the language of the Straits, Malay, became the lingua franca of the whole archipelago. Java and Bali formed a second separate unit. There agrarian rice-growing kingdoms had arisen in the interior, to which the trader ports along the northern shores were subordinate. The Javanese language, after 1000, developed a rich literature in the Indic tradition. When the power at the Straits was weak, and one Javanese kingdom gained hegemony over most of Java, that Javanese kingdom might attempt to dominate the Straits themselves—as did, on occasion, also the Thais from the mainland. Finally, there were the lesser, 'outer' islands and littorals (notably the coastlands of Borneo, or Kalimantan). Especially the Moluccas, which formed the eastern extreme of the archipelago, became, with the increase of trade, a major source of spices. They and the relay points along the way became increasingly dependent on commerce. The Banda islands, in the southern Moluccas, formed commercial republics which largely imported their food from elsewhere, in return for their nutmeg exports. In contrast to Java, the interior of those islands where there were only relay stations was hardly touched by the international high culture or even locally by agrarianate-level social forms.

On the 'bandwagon' principle, the ports not only of Malaya and Sumatra but of many of the 'outer islands' became predominantly Muslim in the fourteenth and fifteenth centuries. Once Muslims had gained a stronghold here or there, the solidarity that they maintained among themselves allowed them sometimes to seize power elsewhere as well, and once in power, they encouraged further conversion. It was only long after 1500, however, that the Javanese interior became Muslim. In contrast to the great river kingdoms of the mainland to the north, Java (about the size of the Italian peninsula) was everywhere near to the sea, and each sector of it had its own immediate port along the northern coast, directly involved in the trade. The prestige of Islam as the vehicle of cosmopolitan culture was tremendous, and when finally the chief inland kingdom became weak, the commercial cities were in a position to league together and impose on their hinterland not only their power but their religious allegiance in permanence.

The naturalization of Islam in Malaysia and Indochina

The Muslims in all these southeastern areas brought their traditional culture from the lands from Nile to Oxus, as it had developed by the Earlier Middle Period. In particular, the forms Islam had taken in southern Arabia and the west coast of India were propagated. Jamâ'î-Sunnî Islam of the Southern Seas generally became Shâfi'î; with the weakening of Shâfi'ism further north under the great Ḥanafî and Shî'î empires of the sixteenth century, Ḥaḍramawt along the south Arabian coast became a major Shâfi'î centre, influential throughout the Southern Seas and helping to give southern Islamdom a distinctive tone. (The various other sects of southern Arabia also flourished on occasion. Ismâ'îlism proved strong in Gujarât as well as Sind, and from there eventually came across to East Africa; even sooner the Khârijism of 'Umân was to become a major force in East Africa.) Throughout these lands, Arabs and Persians had a certain prestige as bearers of true Islam; but the various regions developed the all-Muslim cultural heritage in terms of their regional tongues. Swahili was a somewhat Arabicized Bantu in East Africa which carried a refined poetic culture by the fifteenth century; Gujarati and Tamil were used as Islamicate cultural vehicles in India perhaps rather later; but by the sixteenth century, Malay, which had seen a fine literature under Hindu influence, was developing an Islamicate literature in which universal Muslim themes, especially those of a Ṣufî cast, were found side by side with poetry of a more indigenous turn.

Of all the Muslim expansion in the Southern Seas, that in the Malaysian archipelago was the most extensive and the most successful in penetrating large hinterland populations. Hindu and Hindu-Buddhist culture in these lands had been adopted by the ruling classes in the rich rice farmlands and had produced impressive monuments in conjunction with local genius. Not only in the long inland river valleys of the Indochinese mainland, but in the islands, also, the inland states long stayed aloof from the cosmopolitan and therefore at least partly Islamicized port cities. There are indications that Islam penetrated inland first among the lower classes, at least in the small towns, presumably (as in Bengal) giving these humbler folk a more egalitarian equivalent to the proud Hinduism of the gentry. But the royal courts were eventually won over. With the establishment of inland Muslim sultanates, the remaining population adopted an Islamic allegiance. Only one island, Bali, away from the main commercial course, continued solidly Hindu; but that area of the Islamized islands where the inland rice civilization had been strongest, inner (that is, central and eastern) Java, retained a strong old-Indic tradition in its aristocratic arts and literature.

Coming by way of coastal India, Islamicate culture in Malaysia was of a mixed Arabic and Persian heritage; Arabic, Persian, and Malay were all languages of high culture. All three languages, moreover, were vehicles, from the first, of the Ṣûfî-oriented Islam of the Later Middle Periods, a form of Islam fully adapted to popular needs in an age of proliferating cultural contacts. Throughout Malaysia, Ṣûfism was more fully accepted as containing the whole of Islam than anywhere else. All phases of the Islamic tradition were presented within the framework of ṭarîqah Ṣufî institutions. At least in inner Java, the ṭarîqah orders developed a special pattern of transmission of Muslim lore (not only Ṣûfism but fiqh jurisprudence, kalâm, and all the associated disciplines): in rural centres which dotted the countryside, relatively retired masters taught pupils who came from nearby to live there; this allowed the whole peasantry a reasonably intimate access to the spiritual life. It was therefore under Ṣûfî auspices, in large part, that the Sharîʿah was transmitted, and before Modern times the more rigorous Sharʿî ʿulamâʾ scholars had little opportunity to have their way. Sharîʿah-mindedness was relatively weak, at least in inner Java. The Sharîʿah did, indeed, play a basic role; but, at least as much as anywhere else, considerable leeway was given to modifications in favour of popular customary law, and the less essentially Muslim customs of the more central Muslim lands, such as the veiling of women, were never adopted.

The popular Islam of the countryside schools was partly nourished from old Malaysian cultural roots. The open category of *jinn* was filled (as it had been in every Muslim land) by the local sprites. Beneficently or mischievously, these filled every corner of nature and became (more than almost anywhere else in Islamdom) the foundation for the whole structure of daily etiquette and of inter-personal relations, all with the blessing of the representatives and rites of Islam. Among the gentry, the scene was naturally more complex. Alongside these old-Malaysian elements, especially in inner Java, the richest country in the region, the aristocratic elements maintained

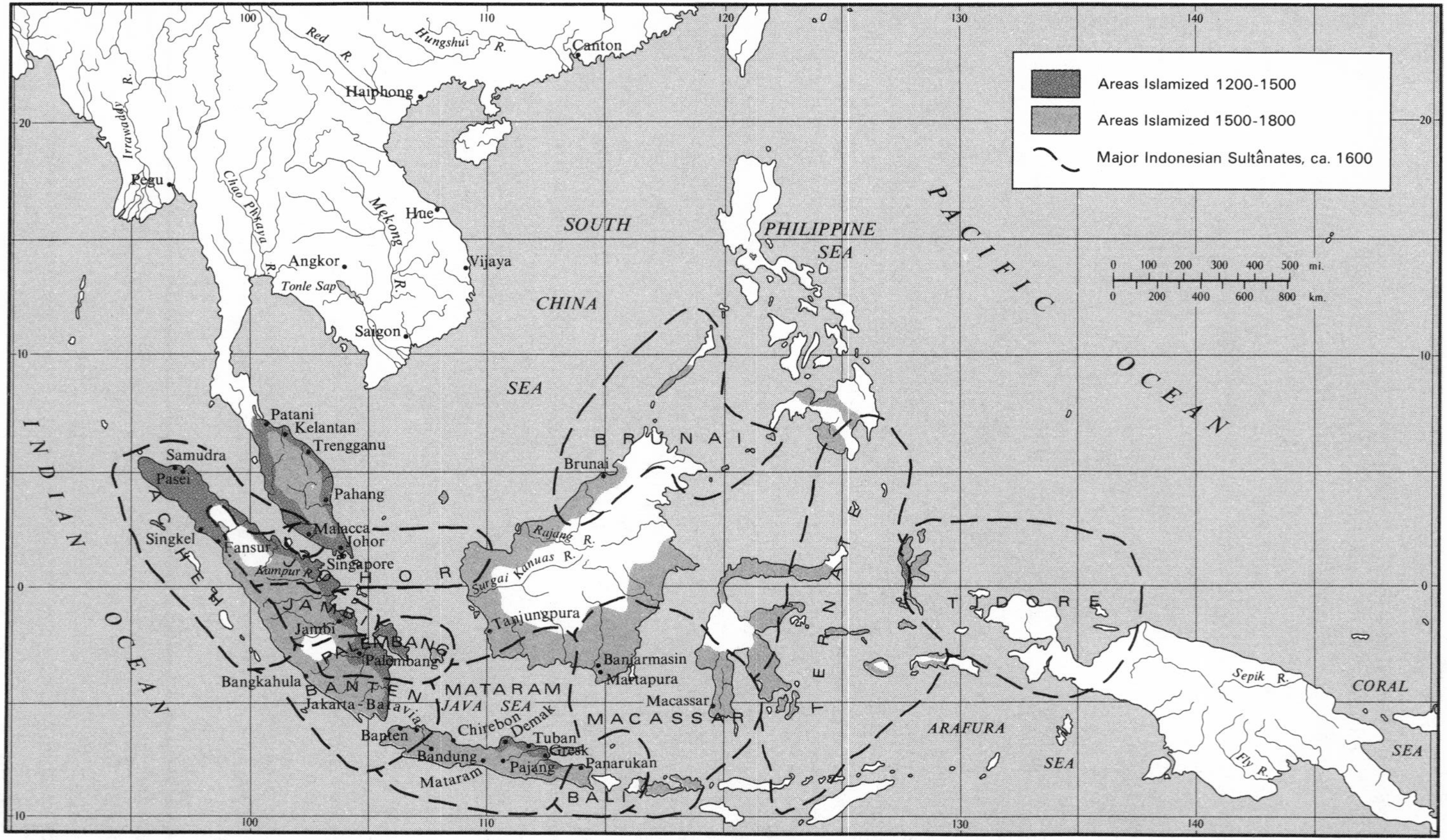

Malaysia and Indochina

their older Indic-derived traditions in an Islamicized form. Their poetry, retaining the older Javanese tradition, was filled with references to the heroes of the Sanskrit Mahâbhârata, who took the place of the pre-Islamic Arab horsemen or the ancient Persian kings, so much written of in the more central lands, in offering an extra-Islamic background for winning a sense of human reality. This heritage also affected the Ṣûfî ṭarîqahs, at least on the aristocratic level, leaving its mark in the language and perhaps in some of the ideas of the Ṣûfîs. On the whole, Ṣûfism differed little even in inner Java from elsewhere in Islamdom; if Islam was first adopted among the lower classes, then Ṣûfism, here as elsewhere, was implicitly opposed to the aristocratic Hinduism. (The common evaluation of Ṣûfism in Malaysia as 'Hindu-Buddhist'—following its rejection by a Modern Shar'î puritanism—is seriously misleading.) But perhaps nowhere else in Islamdom did the earlier heroic legendry retain so active a religious valuation as in eastern Javanese aristocratic circles. When the gentry adopted Islam, these traditions were woven into Ṣûfism, which they enriched and endowed with a distinctively Javanese beauty.[2]

Islamdom across the Sahara

From the time when camel transport was introduced into the Sahara, in the early centuries of our era, trade between the Sûdânic lands and the Mediterranean was greatly increased. The Sûdânic lands, that vast belt of savanna between the Sahara deserts and the Guinea forests, had yet earlier been opened up to a flourishing agriculture; but for long, save for a minimal trade

[2] The most important study of Islam in Malaysia is Clifford Geertz' *The Religion of Java* (Glencoe, 1960); it deals with the twentieth century, and with inner Java in particular, but much in it throws light on what happened earlier and is relevant to other parts of the archipelago. Unfortunately, its general high excellence is marred by a major systematic error: influenced by the polemics of a certain school of modern Sharî'ah-minded Muslims, Geertz identifies 'Islam' only with what that school of modernists happens to approve, and ascribes everything else to an aboriginal or a Hindu-Buddhist background, gratuitously labelling much of the Muslim religious life in Java 'Hindu'. He identifies a long series of phenomena, virtually universal to Islam and sometimes found even in the Qur'ân itself, as un-Islamic; and hence his interpretation of the Islamic past as well as of some recent anti-Islamic reactions is highly misleading. His error has at least three roots. When he refers to the archipelago having long been cut off from 'the centres of orthodoxy at Mecca and Cairo', the irrelevant inclusion of Cairo betrays a modern source of Geertz' bias. We must suspect also the urge of many colonialists to minimize their subjects' ties with a disturbingly world-wide Islam (a tendency found also among French colonialists in the Maghrib); and finally his anthropological techniques of investigation, looking to a functional analysis of a culture in momentary cross-section without serious regard to the historical dimension. Other writers have recognized better the Islamic character even or inner-Javanese religion: C. A. O. van Nieuwenhuijze, *Aspects of Islam in Post-Colonial Indonesia* (The Hague, 1958); W. F. Wertheim, *Indonesian Society in Transition* (2nd ed., The Hague, 1959), but Geertz stands out in the field. For one who knows Islam, his comprehensive data—despite his intention—show how very little has survived from the Hindu past even in inner Java and raise the question why the triumph of Islam was so complete.

across the Sahara, they had been in touch with the citied Oikoumene only at long distance through the eastern Sûdân and up the Nile. Now the Chad and especially the Niger Sudan had more flourishing direct contacts. They traded gold and slaves and the tropical products of the Guinea coast for handicraft articles. By the time that commercial towns and large-scale kingdoms had arisen there, the prevailing culture north of the Sahara was the Islamicate. At first the Sûdânic kingdoms remained pagan even while patronizing Muslim traders and scholars (and physicians); eventually dynasties were converted to Islam, or (later) newly Muslim tribes built up substantial political structures. Gradually the Islamic allegiance spread from the mercantile towns out among the peasantry; normally the new allegiance did not much displace the inherited agricultural lore, of course, whether practical or cultic. (Despite some modern zealots, a people need not be the less Muslim for that, even though the lore was different from that of the mid-Arid Zone.) Tribe after tribe took up the cause, especially when a tribe became the base for an expansive empire.

Except for the Murâbiṭ power on the Senegal at the very beginning of Islamization in the Sudan, a power based on ghâzî activity from the north, all these states were of local origin. Commonly, relatively local kingdoms endured for considerable times under tribally based dynasties, in support of which Islamic sanctions were commonly intermingled with older tribal sanctions. But (as can be seen from the chart) superimposed on this decentralized political life was a series of empires, commonly rising out of one of the tribally based dynasties which found itself in a position to subdue most of the others; sometimes (as ghâzîs) imposing Islam on courts that submitted, or wiping them away and introducing major social disruption. With each new state, its capital city became a centre not only of wealth but increasingly of Islamization and of Islamic learning; Sûdânic scholars fairly soon took to writing chronicles of the kings' exploits and built up their own high-cultural tradition, which, however, long used Arabic as sole literary vehicle.

After the Hilâl Arab tribes had effectively introduced camel nomadism to the Maghrib in the eleventh century, and thence to the Sahara (well after the use of camels for transport there), the local evolution of the Sûdânic lands became increasingly complicated by pastoralist interference. More important, in the end, than any Arab tribal grouping (though such were important especially in the more easterly Sahara and its fringes) was a Berber people, the Touareg, who developed into specialists in camel transport along the Sahara routes but also built up a systematic domination over the settled populations, especially at the southern termini of their routes. Their men prided themselves both on their hardiness as warriors and on their skills in finding the way across the greatest wastes in the world. The society was organized matrilineally and matrilocally, children belonging to their uncles' families rather than their visiting fathers; and the women at home, while the men were off hundreds of miles distant, developed their own home culture, with its own (non-Arabic) scheme of writing and its own literature of fiction and poetry. The Touareg thought of themselves less as a people than as an aristocracy; the peoples among whom they moved were dependent classes to them. In the oases along their routes they settled Negro slaves to cultivate the ground for them as serfs (and here the aridity was much too great to allow the relatively free mobility which often prevented such serfdom between Nile and Oxus); they also had slaves to exploit the rich salt mines of the desert. The Sûdânic peoples increasingly had to pay tribute as protection money to the dominant group of Touareg, and many villages came under their lordship.

Islamic Expansion in Africa and Southeast Asia

Before 600	Introduction of camel into Sahara
758	Muslims raid Canton; Muslims regularly resident in Chinese ports
Eleventh century	Islam begins to be felt in Sûdânic lands through trading contacts; Muslims already resident in Champa (area of S. Vietnam)
1040s	Murâbiṭûn (Almoravids), a Lamtûna Berber group, establish a center in Mauritania for propagation of Islam in the western Sudan; begin militant action there against Soninke kings of Ghana
1060s	Murâbiṭûn subjugate the Maghrib and al-Andalus—first Berber group to form an Islamic empire; Ghana empire, center of western Sûdânic trade, weakened
Eleventh–thirteenth centuries	Only some rulers of Sûdânic kingdoms as well as the resident merchant traders are Muslims; rulers occasionally go on pilgrimage; trading contacts grow
Thirteenth century	Ghana empire already collapsed; Mali rises; trade encouraged; rulers of Kanam (Lake Chad area) are Muslim; *c.* 1250 a student hostel established in Cairo
End thirteen century	Muslims already resident in northern Sumatra ports, maintain close contacts with Gujarât
1324–25	Mansa Musa, king of Mali, goes on pilgrimage in grand style with consequent economic effects and visual impressions on peoples in Cairo and along his route; trading caravans are large and regular with the Maghrib and Egypt
Fourteenth century	Mali, Gao, Timbuctu become important Muslim centers
Fifteenth century	Ruler of Malacca converts to Islam beginning fifteenth century; city soon becomes important entrepôt of China-Indian Ocean trade; by end of fifteenth century, city is influential in spreading Islam in southern Malay peninsula and neighboring islands; contacts with city of Cambay in Gujarât remain strong
End fifteenth century	Mali empire falls; Songhai-Askiya empire in central Sudan rises

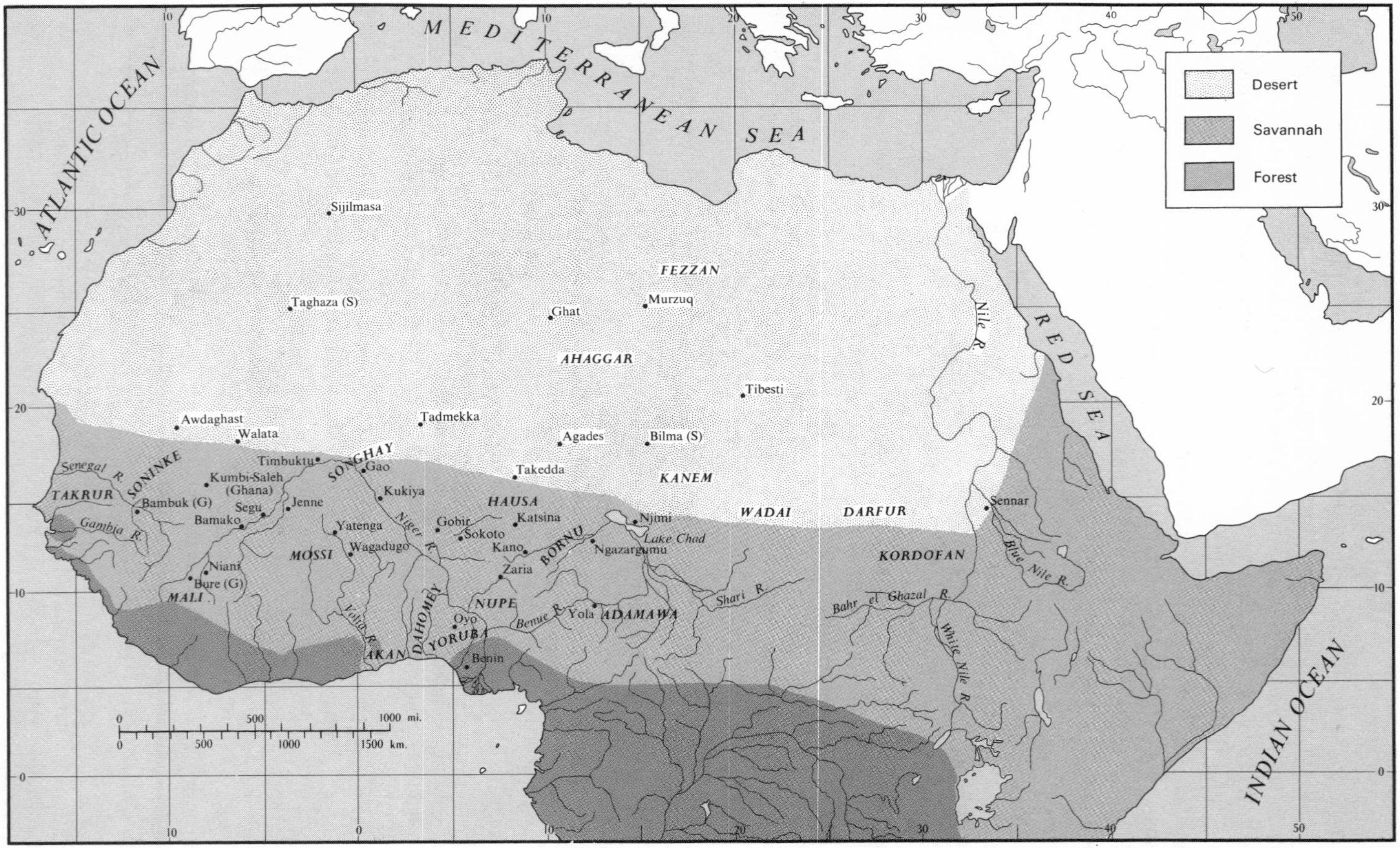

The Sûdânic lands

Only the Ibâḍî Khârijîs, who had withdrawn at last into a group of oases in some central and relatively fertile highlands of the northern Sahara, were able to withstand Touareg control. The Ibâḍîs established a federation of city republics in the Mzab area and built up a rich agriculture and eventually a commerce with the Mediterranean. Nonetheless, they remained carefully aloof from other Muslims, except so far as they could maintain ties with other Ibâḍîs in 'Umân; their republican solidarity defended them.

The Touareg could be drastically destructive on occasion, but they did, on the whole, allow the Sûdânic cities to develop. Perhaps the most splendid Sûdânic cultural centre was Timbuctu in the sixteenth century, to whose madrasah students came from afar. Even then, the local architecture seemed unambitious to visiting Muslims, who found that mud huts prevailed; yet the scholarship won their praise. Sûdânic Islamdom still welcomed visiting scholars from the lands of 'old Islam', but they could maintain the Islamic tradition at its highest intellectual levels on their own, training their own new generations of specialists.

But by the sixteenth century, new forces were at work. With the advent in the Oikoumene of the full use of gunpowder weapons, the Sûdânic lands were to lose their isolation a degree further than they had even with the advent of camel nomadism in the Sahara. A sultan of Morocco in mid-century, having defeated the Portuguese at home, looked for new fields for exploits—and for a surer source of Negro slave-soldiery and of gold to bolster his attempted absolutism. Making use of the new arms, he daringly transported an army across the desert routes and, with good luck, arrived at Timbuctu, where the new weapons were yet unknown; he sacked the town and reduced that large part of the Niger Sudan which it had been ruling to dependence on his agents—and eventually on his soldiery, who then turned independent of him, but remained rapacious. Meanwhile, the products of the Guinea coast were going to the Mediterranean increasingly by sea in Portuguese vessels, and Timbuctu and indeed the whole Niger Sudan never fully recovered.

Islam in India and in Europe: the fifteenth century

The expansion of Islam and of Muslim power in the two great civilized regions flanking the Nile-to-Oxus region had some distinctive features, as compared to the expansion in more peripheral areas; but the fundamental pressures were similar. In these ancient citied lands, Muslim conquest came first and Muslim cadres afterward; moreover, the social bodies that maintained the indigenous religious allegiance played a far more persistent and complex role within the Muslim-ruled states. But here, too, the social effectiveness of the Muslim cadres was surely decisive. At the particular juncture reached by each of them in its own development, by the mid-Islamic periods the Muslim and the Hindu social orders proved complementary.

As post-Axial times had progressed, the Hindu Indian society had passed through its own evolution, carrying it as far from its classical forms as had Islamicate evolution carried the lands from Nile to Oxus. Indian society had articulated itself with increasing severity into innumerable castes, hereditary endogamous and autonomous groups; each had its typical economic function in the wider society, its formalized ties to other castes; each ruled itself by its own legal and ritual norms so far as its internal relations were concerned. These castes defined an individual's social possibilities far more rigidly than any craft-guild group or even religious sect between Nile and Oxus; mobility among them was restricted to a minimum by fierce rules of exclusion from all society of any member who violated caste practice. Actually there was some individual leeway, and certain castes could develop new functions and new status as groups. But the function of ruler was left (in principle) to a few hereditary families; when these were eliminated, there were no natural claimants; almost anyone could take their place without meeting entrenched rivals, if only he could find support not inhibited by caste restrictions.

This is just what the Muslims could increasingly do as the post-caliphal international institutions made Muslims of all sorts more freely mobile. The two processes, then, within Hindu society and within Islamicate society, crossed at a point in time where each fitted perfectly into the other's possibilities: the Muslims were just then ideally suited to form a ruling caste for the Hindu system. But, in contrast to numerous other ruling groups that had found a high place in Hindu society and had become just so many more Hindu castes in the end, the Muslims did not become Hindus. Precisely part of the Muslim strength was that Muslims could draw on the resources of a large and sophisticated cultural tradition beyond the borders of the Hindu sphere. For without this strong international consciousness, the Muslims would have lost their cultural as well as political sense of distinctness from the local population; this it was that prevented them from losing their cohesion, from drifting into permanent alliances with Hindu groups that might have meant more to them than any Muslim solidarity. Whatever temporary Hindu alliances they might make, they retained a sense of cultural superiority which caused them to long to return, when threatened, to the supremacy of Islam as such. In this way, Muslim rule could perpetuate itself even though most of the population remained Hindus; for whom their Muslim rulers were, in point of ritual, not too different from the 'untouchables', the lowest castes, who were by birth excluded from the Hindu system and were ritually unclean for high castes.

Muslim rule, therefore, did not depend on the policies or fortunes of sultans at Delhi. The depredations of Timur disturbed but little most of the Indian provincial states. The solidarity of a minority group, very conscious of its moral and cultural ties with the wider Muslim international community as against the local Hindus, made possible extensive and relatively stable Muslim states. The whole Deccan, or at least the main centres of it, was controlled for generations by the Bahmanid sultans. Gujarât, an extensive country in the west centre, acknowledged a strong Muslim dynasty which pursued a constructive commercial policy, oriented to the Indian Ocean trade, till well into the sixteenth century. The rich nation Bengal maintained its own tradition under Muslim rulers, who were able eventually to convert large numbers of the lower-class population to the east of the Ganges mouths, where the ruling classes had lately become Hindu but where it seems Hinduism had not yet been spread among the peasants, newly integrated into agrarianate-level society. From the time of Fîrôz, a territory in itself quite vast was reserved, in the upper Ganges valley and the neighbouring valleys to the south, for the Delhi sultanate to try to control when it was strong, and to share with independent Muslim rulers otherwise. (Timur's invasion affected chiefly this particular state.) In the fifteenth century, Afghans from the east Iranian highlands, the Muslim highlander area most accessible, served increasingly as military men in northern India; by the end of the century, they formed an important basis for the power of the Lôdî sultans, who were restoring Delhi's authority within its zone.

Though Hindu (and in some areas pre-Hindu tribal) rulers persisted locally in India here and there, after Muḥammad Tughluq's great march almost every part of the subcontinent owned Muslim supremacy in at least a general way. It was only in the peninsula, south of the Bahmanid dominions, that a reviving Hindu tradition put a vigorous family on the throne at Vijayanagar and erected an empire which resisted further Muslim encroachments till the end of the Later Middle Period.

Islam had a twofold religious impact on India. It surely had a far-reaching effect, though a rather hidden one, by way of selective conversion. Certain castes and trades were converted to Islam en bloc, abandoning allegiance to the Brahmans, who merely despised them, to try their fortunes in a community where they might—in principle—attain equality. Moreover, certain religious traditions apparently were more susceptible to erosion by Islam than others; the most likely case is Buddhism—we have seen that many areas where Buddhism had been strong became strongly Muslim. Probably Buddhism did not yield to Islam so much by direct conversion as by a more insidious route: the sources of recruitment to the relatively unaristocratic Buddhism—for instance, villagers coming into the cities and adopting a new allegiance to accord with their new status—turned now rather to Islam than to an outdated Buddhism. The record of the massacre of one monastery in Bengal, combined with the inherited Christian conception of Muslims as devotees of the sword, has yielded the widely repeated statement that the Muslims violently 'destroyed' Buddhism in India. Muslims were not friendly to it, but there is no evidence that they simply killed off all the Buddhists, or even all the Buddhist monks. It will take much active revision before such assessments of the role of Islam, based largely on unexamined preconceptions, are eliminated even from educated mentalities.

Whoever the converts were, the most influential preachers may have been pîrs of the lesser ṭarîqahs, humbly working out among the people, more often than those of the great ṭarîqahs—though these latter had to claim conversions also. Such lesser preachers, free of the tacit supervision of the upper classes, could be especially open to encouraging those elements that were looking to a rise in their social status. At any rate, Hinduism was presumably left, in many areas, with the less readily mobile sectors of the population. Such a tendency may well have reinforced the already existent tendency among Hindus toward an increasing caste rigidity.

Islam had also a direct impact on the Hindu traditions themselves. This probably rarely meant modification of explicit doctrinal formulations—for instance, an espousal of monotheism. Rather it meant a changed attitude toward those formulations and toward the whole tradition—presumably sometimes by way of reaction against Islam as well as by way of assimilation to it. The tendency among Hindus toward an increasing caste rigidity was accompanied fairly early by movements toward transcending caste—doubtless such movements were in part a compensation for or a reaction to the rigidity. Such movements were prominent among the Vaishnavas in the form of what is called Bhakti mysticism: a love mysticism growing roughly parallel to the love mysticism of eastern Christianity and of Islam in those same ages. This Bhakti mysticism stressed a simple, direct faith in a single deity, without much reliance on ritual forms. It was matched by tendencies within Ṣûfism which pointed in the same way—not only toward a mystically interpreted monotheism, essential to the Bhakti movements, but also toward a certain resistance to established authority which made any external law secondary, whether the law of the 'ulamâ' or that of the Brahmans. Doubtless these tendencies represented an egalitarian resistance to the elaborate forms beloved of social privilege, and probably the Islamic presence helped to give them form. Apart from the usual mingling of cults on the folk level, the most striking effects of an interpenetration of Islamic and Hindu religious life are to be seen in a series of popular monotheistic movements, opposed to both the Muslim and the Hindu religious leaders, but intentionally using the language of both traditions. We shall see more of these in Book Five.[3]

India, separated from the lands of old Islam by wild mountains and wide deserts, proved (when Islamdom had evolved to the point of ready expansion) very quickly vulnerable to Muslim conquest; Europe on the other hand, from which any dividing line had always been arbitrary at best, held out much more solidly. To be sure, an outlying province had in each case been taken very early—Sindh from India, and Spain (perhaps we should include also the Maghrib) from Europe; but in each case these were marginal to the Sanskrit

[3] Relations between Islam and Hinduism on the religious level are as yet only fragmentarily studied. Tara Chand, *Influence of Islam on Indian Culture* (Allahabad, 1954), suggesting an improbably great direct influence, has (I think) not been replaced (for instance, not by Yusuf Husain, *L'Inde mystique au moyen âge* [Paris, 1929]) but is long outdated by incidental studies and references here and there. An adequate theoretical basis for such studies is still wanting.

and Hellenic culture areas. At the outset of the Muslim expansion of the Earlier Middle Period, a more important province had been occupied in each case: the Panjâb in India, a land where the Vedas had largely grown up, and Anatolia in Europe, the land of the ancient Ionians and Lydians, source of so much that we associate with Hellas, and mainstay of the Byzantine empire; both were occupied, at least in part, in the eleventh century. The thirteenth-century expansion throughout the Ganges valley was not paralleled in Europe till the fourteenth century: then came a corresponding Muslim thrust across the Balkans, but this was stopped short at the Adriatic; Italy (almost equally a home of classical Hellas) was never subjugated. For the most part, it was the east Europeans, Greeks and Slavs, that came under Muslim rule (Ottoman and Mongol); the Latin west of Europe resisted painfully but, apart from Hungary, for the most part with success. Perhaps partly because of this successful resistance, the Ottoman state, which carried out the most important of the conquests in Europe, became a much more solid structure than the Delhi sultanate.

It was in the fifteenth century that the Ottoman state, from a frontier ghâzî state, became an absolutism assimilable to the military patronage type, and one of the cultural foci of Islamdom. The solidity of the state structure was demonstrated when Timur broke it up after thoroughly defeating its forces (1402); for though it was effectively partitioned among aspiring princes, affording a separate realm for each prince and his entourage, it yet regained its previous condition almost intact. After Bâyezîd Yïldïrïm's death (1403), four of his sons contested his succession. This was normal enough—the Ottomans regarded the succession as up to God, whose will was shown in the outcome of an armed contest. But these succession wars, beginning under Timur's shadow, lasted for eleven years, and most of the time the portion of the realm in the Balkan peninsula (called 'Rumelia') was ruled by one heir, and what was left of the realm in Anatolia by another; meanwhile the several Anatolian amîrates maintained independence under their own dynasties. Yet by 1413, one son, Meḥmed, had reunited the main Ottoman territories, and before his death in 1421 he had begun to subject anew the Anatolian amîrates and to restore the eroded Ottoman strength in Rumelia (the Balkan peninsula). His attempt to subdue the Latins of the Aegean isles (chiefly Venetians) failed for want of sea power. But he effectively suppressed the rebellion of 1416 associated with Bedreddîn, led by darvîshes and monks, and such an event may have knit the Shar'î 'ulamâ' and the dynasty yet closer together. In any case, he renewed the firm rule, based on balanced interests, that had made for Ottoman strength before Timur's advent.

By 1428, under Murâd II (1421–51), most of the Anatolian amîrates had been resubjugated (except the Ḳaramanlï at Ḳonya), if in a milder form than before. Under Murâd II, the Ottomans had to confront vigorous efforts among some of the Christian populations to resist Muslim rule—Albanians revolted under their hero Skanderbeg, who had been brought up as a hostage at the Ottoman court, while the Hungarian general, Hunyadi, supported Serbian resistance; each received occasional support from Occidental powers. But at crucial moments, the Ottomans were able to win sufficient support among the Christians—Serbs and Wallachians (Rumanians)—to maintain and improve their position. Skanderbeg, who had returned to Christianity, was a rare exception; most men who had once become a part of the Ottoman Muslim society remained a part of it, for better or for worse. Even the populations that remained Christian commonly preferred the Ottoman power to any alternative.

The Ottomans had more than once threatened to occupy Constantinople, the imperial city in the heart of their dominions, but had been restrained by accident or by policy, and remained content to keep it in tributary dependency. But when the Ottomans were in difficulties, the Byzantine emperor had proved a nuisance—he had negotiated even with Timur—and a new intrigue on the emperor's part, at the accession of Meḥmed II in 1451, precipitated the conquest. In 1453, Meḥmed II (1451–81) took the impregnable city by storm, using new gunpowder siege artillery. (A few years later, such siege artillery was to prove decisive for the new central authorities in western Europe likewise.) Occidental naval support came too late. The Ottomans proceeded to make Constantinople their capital, calling it by the vernacular name, *Istanbul.* They fostered its existing commercial and cultural life as much as possible, but they also settled many new families—Slavs, Greeks, and Turks—in the city which had been half-empty after years of imperial decline. Soon, as the city resumed its natural role as economic and administrative centre of the whole region, Istanbul became once again the most populous and prosperous city in Europe.

As Wittek has taught us, with the adoption of its natural capital the Ottoman state became a durable empire, supported by much the same constellation of political interests on the geographic and economic level as had supported the Byzantine empire, and by cultural and religious interests analogous to those of the Byzantines. The Ottoman state had already been stronger and more durable than most of those in the more central Muslim lands in the Middle Periods. The settled ghâzî troops, who had turned regular cavalry and local landholders; the Christian auxiliary troops based on the ancient Balkan gentry; and the new Janissary infantry, more and more levied on the countryside, converted to Islam, and trained in loyalty to the centre—together all formed a balanced military force, in which local concerns and dynastic loyalty both made themselves felt. Likewise, the remnants of independent ghâzî organization, and of futuwwah men's clubs among the townsmen, together with the newer cadres of Shar'î 'ulamâ' and the coherent Greek Orthodox religious and social structure among the dhimmî Christians—all proved complementary to one another as sources of stability, under the leadership of the small group of old Ottoman families surrounding the ruling house itself. The dynasty was the supreme symbol and instrument of the common interests rather than the champion of any one party, and hence was in a position to look to the interests of the state as such. The Ottoman state had thus proved able to make a singularly happy use of the social and military resources available to Muslims in the fifteenth century on the expanding frontier: old independent cavalry and new gunpowder infantry, new Muslim cadres and old dhimmî continuity. But on the addition of Istanbul as capital, all this was given a new dimension which allowed the state to persist even when some of the elements that formed the original balance were displaced.[4]

The Ottoman state had begun with a conscious mission on one of the most historic fronts of militant Islamdom. Taking Constantinople had long been regarded as so high a Muslim goal, after the many costly failures under the caliphs, that the coveted event had been painted in apocalyptic colours (possibly this fact, as well as the impregnable site, had helped discourage earlier Ottoman attempts). Hence the dynasty that could make Istanbul its capital could not only concentrate in one spot the far-flung trade between Black Sea and eastern Mediterranean, and the ample resources of Anatolia and of Rumelia; it could provide a focus for the imagination of Islam: the greatest church of Christendom, Hagia Sophia, was made over into a great mosque, and the name of the quondam capital of Christendom, Istanbul, was transmuted by many a pen to *Islambul*, city of Islam. At the same time, the taking of the imperial city, seat of the ecumenical patriarchate, assured control over the Christian hierarchy in the whole region, and reinforced the growing ties between the Ottoman state and the Orthodox church. (These ties apparently served to confirm the gap between Christian and Muslim. Although Muslims, as they did everywhere, inherited Christian—and pre-Christian—elements in local cults and even in some phases of darvîsh practice, the main body of Christians, given a tight official organization under their church, remained firmly aloof from Islam.)

Meḥmed II and his ministers took advantage of both worlds, the Christian and the Muslim, to strengthen the sultan's absolutism. They integrated the Balkan Christian tributaries more closely into the Ottoman structure, organizing their holdings on much the same basis as the Muslim cavalry, and encouraging them to come to an understanding with the Muslim infantry and the central administrative corps. Meḥmed and some of his courtiers were personally interested in the Greek culture, reading Byzantine and Roman history with a new sense of actuality not found among Muslims hitherto. But at the same time, under Meḥmed II the Ottoman state came more fully into the main currents of Islamicate culture (that is, in this period, for the most part a Persianate culture). The Ottoman court now was able to attract Muslim scholars of the highest quality from the lands of old Islam.[5]

[4] Paul Wittek, 'De la défaite d'Ankara à la prise de Constantinople', *Revue des Etudes Islamiques*, 12 (1938), 1–34, supplements importantly his *Rise of the Ottoman Empire*.

[5] Abd-ul-Hak Adnan, 'La science chez les turcs ottomans du commencement jusqu'à la fin du moyen-âge', *Archeion, Archivio di storia della scienza*, 19 (1937), 347–65—see also

Not only Persian literature but even a Persianate form of Turkish was in high esteem at the court (soon to be influenced by the Turkish poetry of 'Alî-Shêr Neva'i of Herat), displacing the old Turkish poetry that had been based on a count of syllables rather than on patterns of syllable length; that more indigenous form of Turkish poetry was left to popular balladry. However, Persian did not actually become the language of state (except for international correspondence). A highly Persianate Turkish (called *Osmanlî*, 'Ottoman') was perfected and every state servant was expected to be accomplished in its use. This official use of Turkish stands in contrast to India, where likewise the military element and its dynasties had Turkic origins and where likewise the Persian was the model literature though the ordinary population did not speak Persian. Doubtless the special role of Turkish in southeastern Europe resulted from the relatively heavy migration of Turkic tribes because of the relative accessibility of the region. But this did not take effect so much simply on account of the number of Turks present (probably always the immigrants were a minority at any given time) as on account of the resultant relative solidarity of Turkic ghâzî institutions apart from any central government. Thus it seems to have been the Ḳaramanlî ghâzî state at Ḳonya (rather than the Seljuḳ state there) that first used Turkish for high-cultural administration. Nevertheless, the Persian tradition became the norm even for Turkish letters.

The Ottomans had legitimized their rule, hitherto, first as leaders of ghâzî troops against the infidels; then, when their little state became independent, as delegates of the expiring Seljuḳ sultans, who in turn could claim ancestral authority as appointees of the caliphs of old; and, more recently, as alleged descendants of the senior tribe among the Oghuz Turks, thought of as natural rulers among all sedentary mankind. But after Meḥmed II, especially, the idea was also stressed that an amîr was a natural necessity in human society, that he who was strongest had the obligation to extend his sway as far as possible in order to increase the area of social order and peace, and even that the amîr who ruled justly (that is, in principle, according to the Sharî'ah) was himself the true caliph, the lieutenant of God on earth. These were Faylasûf ideas and were already being used to justify what I have called the 'military patronage state'. In fact, the dynastic laws (*qânûns*) laid down by Meḥmed II were virtually independent of the Shar'î tradition in its detail; in their overall tendency they marked an assimilation of the Ottoman state to that institutional pattern traceable, in other Muslim states of the period: an absolutism in which the whole government—even the imâms of the mosques, as governmental appointees—were regarded as military

pp. 411–14, 433–34, 468); 21 (1938), 35–61, traces the naturalization of natural science in the Ottoman lands, especially by way of Turkish translations—though the most important work was still done in Arabic and Persian; and incidentally brings out the strong tradition of academic freedom defended there. (He also discusses sixteenth-century scientific life up to the point where an awareness of contemporary Occidental advances was accompanied by exhaustion of the indigenous tradition.)

(*'askerî*) even though not as 'men of the sword' (*sayfî*); and all that was valuable in society at large was regarded as in the dispensation of the royal family and its servants.

The empire did not much expand in the half-century following the taking of Constantinople. But its character as a stable regional empire was consolidated. Under Meḥmed II, the remnants of rebellion among Serbs and Albanians were eliminated—sometimes with great cruelty, for which the highly cultured Meḥmed became noted, alongside his control of several languages and his interest in the fine arts even of the Christians. At least as important was the building of a major navy, which the Ottomans had lacked (despite the early ventures of ghâzîs in the Aegean). By means of the new navy, Venice was forced (by 1479) to cede most of its territory in the Aegean and Balkan areas. The Ottomans did not depend only on their navy, however; they hastened their victory by land incursions into Venetian territory in north Italy itself (and the Venetians tried, without much success, to co-ordinate their efforts with those of the Aḳ-ḳoyunlu 'White-sheep' rulers, attacking the unwontedly powerful Ottoman state by land from the Jazîrah). Venice's rival Genoa also was forced to give up the independent posts it had won on the northern Black Sea coast (and the Crimean Mongol dynasty was made tributary to Ottoman Istanbul). The long impotence of Constantinople against the power of the Italian traders was reversed. However, Ottoman naval power remained largely military; the Italian cities retained the dominant position of their merchant marines that they had won in the time of the Crusades. This fact occasioned a number of points of potential weakness in the Ottoman navy; yet it remained fully effective into the seventeenth century.

Meḥmed's son, Bâyezîd II (1481–1512), undertook few wars (and few were ventured against him). He was known as a builder. Like his father, he beautified Istanbul. Under him was also built a network of roads through the empire; for roads were becoming more important with the new prominence of footmen armed with gunpowder weapons. The importance of these troops—among the Ottomans, it was the Janissary corps—had been brought home to him when at his accession he was forced to yield a pay increase to prevent their unruly interference (a pay increase which had to be repeated at each succeeding new reign—and not unreasonably so, once the steady monetary inflation of the sixteenth century set in all over the world). It was again these troops, and the demand of the Ottomans generally for more active leadership, that forced him to resign in favour of a son he had hoped to exclude from the succession. Thus was asserted the effectiveness of the collective Ottoman will—expressed through succession by contest; and the result, as we shall see, was to extend Ottoman rule far beyond its European homelands.

For long, Ottoman high culture had been an imported matter, subject to the intellectual imposture which frontier peoples eager to gain status sometimes succumb to. By the beginning of the sixteenth century the Ottoman state, with its stable dynasty, had attracted sufficiently large numbers of scholars and artists of all kinds to boast a high level of Islamicate culture, though perhaps it never did become quite so important a centre as some others. Its area was relatively compact and homogeneous, rich in agriculture and commerce, largely free of the worst problems of the Arid Zone; its ruling classes were devoted to its institutions. Though not necessarily the largest, it was one of the strongest states in Islamdom, one of the few to escape reasonably well the political dilemmas posed by the military régimes of the Later Middle Period.

Northern Islamdom: from the Crimea to Yünnan

The central Eurasian steppes and deserts formed, from an urban viewpoint, a waste something like the Indian Ocean; across it stretched (by the Middle Periods) more than one trade route—not only the more southerly ones leading from China into Iran but the more northerly one leading to the southern Don and Volga plains. However, the vast area had more unity than the Indian Ocean; as we have seen, not only among the horse nomads themselves but in all the lands round about, even among the agricultural populations, the older local languages were losing out and the Turkic language and traditions were prevailing—or else the related Mongol, in some of the more easterly areas.

The lands of the Syr and Oxus basins had been included in the original caliphal state already; the Turkic tribes around them had been gradually Islamized thereafter from that base, which represented the most active centre of cosmopolitan culture in the central parts of the steppe. Already before the end of the High Caliphate, the settled Turkic speakers of the Volga basin had largely adopted Islam. Then among most settled Turks around the margin of the steppes, both north and south, the Islamic allegiance was well established in the course of the Middle Periods. Accordingly, west of the point where Buddhism made its way, the conquering Mongols had been converted to Islam.

This led gradually to acceptance of the Islamic allegiance among most even of the pastoral tribes throughout the Turkic areas. At the same time, though the Mongol rulers there long resisted Islam, the Tarim basin eastwards from the Syr basin was being Islamized; Islamdom reached out a long arm along the main trade routes through the middle of the zone of central Eurasian Buddhism, between Tibet and Mongolia. Under Mongol rule, which deliberately favoured aliens, originated the important body of Muslims living throughout China. They have been numerous especially in Kansu (the Chinese province of the northwest, leading out to the Tarim basin) but also elsewhere, notably in the frontier province of Yünnan in the southwest; but in no part of China did the Muslims come to form a majority or even establish a Muslim government.

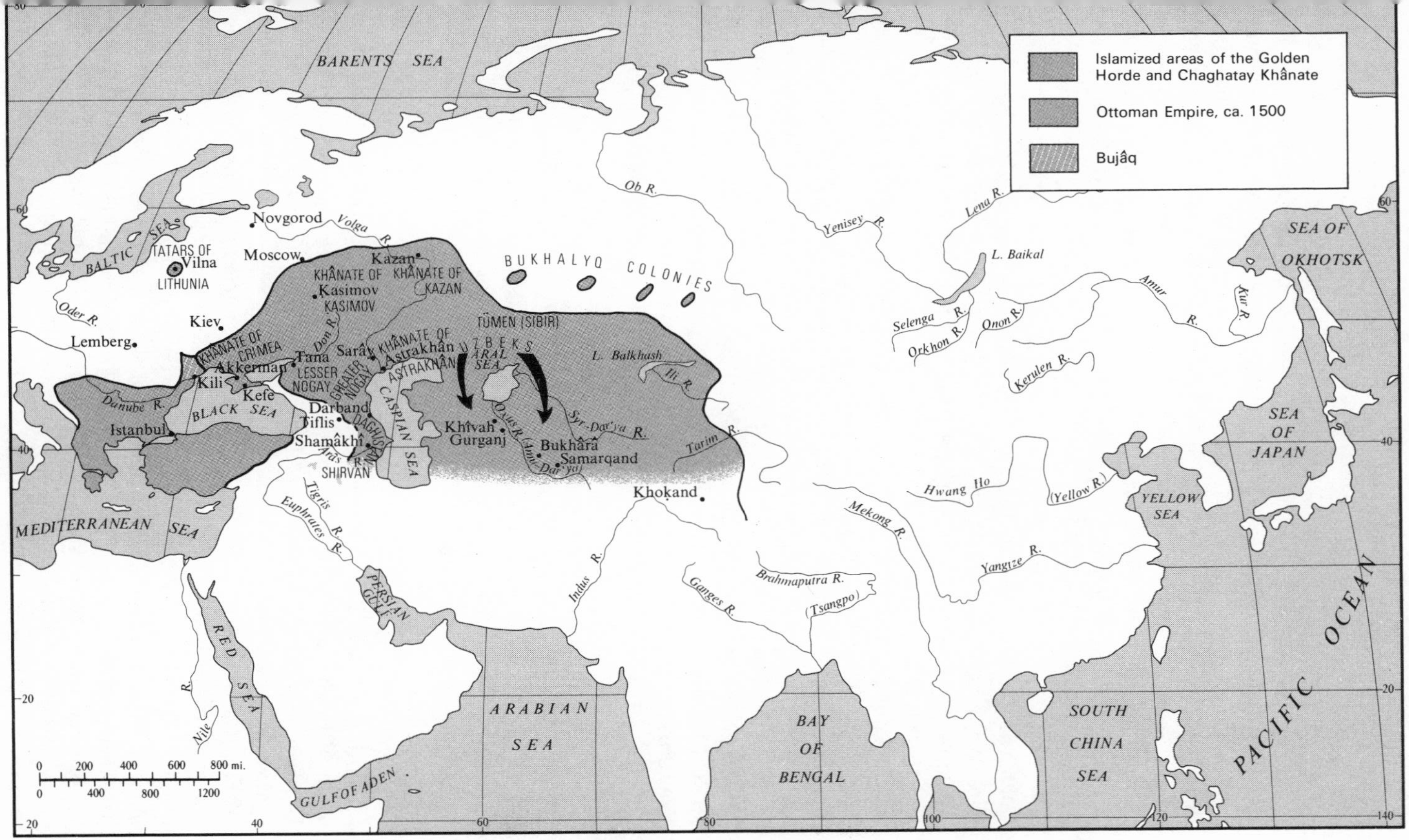

The northern regions

The Turkic Muslims of the farther north accepted avidly the norms of Islamicate culture. In writing they used Chaghatay (eastern) Turkish, whatever their own dialect, and indeed continued (unlike the Ottomans) to give the Persian language unchallenged priority for serious work, and not only diplomatic correspondence. But they maintained their own sense of independence and dignity. They declined to veil their women as if they could not be trusted; and continued to honour their Turkic heroic traditions, meagre as these sometimes were as compared, say, with the ancient Iranian.

Toḳtamîsh and Timur had restored Mongol-Turkic power at the end of the fourteenth century, but not for long. In the fifteenth century, several steppe states broke up into independent khânates. In the west, succeeding to the Golden Horde, were most notable the khânate of Crimea, controlling a large part of the agricultural and pasture lands of the Ukraine; the khânate of Kazan at the bend of the Volga, independent of the Golden Horde in 1438; and the khânate of Astrakhân, at the mouth of the Volga (maintaining the remnants of the political tradition of the Golden Horde). At this time, the weight of political power in the Volga basin shifted again northward to Kazan, marking perhaps a resurgence of agrarian interests even within the Muslim sphere. In the north was the khânate of Tyumen (Tura) or Sibir (Esker), from which Siberia gets its name. In the Syr and Oxus basins Timurî power was fragmented and then challenged by a dynamic dynasty of Mongol origin, the Özbeg (an offshoot of the White Horde), which occupied Khwârazm with pastoral troops. In the Yedisu districts northeast of the upper Syr basin, and in the Tarim basin at Kâshghar, were other Muslim rulers.

There was little cooperation among these rulers. An important state among the Russians, that of Moscow, was allowed to become independent of Muslim overlordship and very soon was entering powerfully into the disputes among them. This Christian state was coming to represent the most active agrarian interests in the region. The khânate of Ḳâsimov, founded soon after that of Kazan in the more westerly territories of Kazan toward Moscow, from the beginning was in alliance with the Muscovites and in the course of the fifteenth century fell frankly under their protection and control. The khâns of the Crimea consistently supported the Muscovites against the Golden Horde at Astrakhân—and the latter supported the Christian Lithuanians against Muscovites and Crimeans.

With the sixteenth century, as elsewhere in Islamdom, new conditions intervened which put in question the Muslim expansion in the remoter regions. The Özbegs almost alone reasserted the traditional power of the Muslim Mongol houses; at the beginning of the sixteenth century, from their base in Khwârazm, they occupied the rest of the Syr and Oxus basins under the brilliant leader Shaybânî Khân (1500–10), who routed the Timurids both north and south of the Oxus, but was then expelled from Khurâsân. For a century the Özbeg Shaybânids maintained a resplendent court at Bukhârâ, a centre of the arts and philosophy as well as of commerical prosperity. (They have given their name to the Turkic population of the area.) For much of that century, considerable overland trade across the steppe was still maintained. It has been theorized that the Oxus then flowed direct to the Caspian (and that for a time, perhaps, a main branch of the Syr flowed into the Oxus), making possible considerable direct water traffic between the eastern mountains and the Caspian and the Volga—and a special commercial strength in Khwârazm. But in any case by the end of the sixteenth century the river did not flow so; and more generally, all the trade was becoming much less, rivalled by ocean routes. Firearms, which required continual technical improvement, were shifting the weight of military power to those who were in closest contact with centres of industrial investment. In the sixteenth century, all the khânates of the steppe region seem to have suffered some loss of power; especially those in the Volga basin were subjected to the increasing power of Moscow and by the end of the century they were conquered outright.

World horizons and the lands of old Islam

Very few studies have been made of the consequences of the expansion of Islam for the life and culture of the lands of old Islam. Certainly, representatives of Islamicate high culture mingled as equals with travellers—pilgrims, darvîshes, visiting scholars, as well as soldiers and merchants—from an increasingly wide range of distant lands of diverse cultural backgrounds. Not only at the season of the ḥajj pilgrimage but throughout the year, men from all over Islamdom met and studied at Mecca and Medina; and to a lesser degree, the same thing happened in all the cities that were way stations on pilgrim routes from farther on, Cairo and Damascus, Baghdad and Iṣfahân. Poets and 'ulamâ' and Ṣûfîs and soldiers were themselves lured out to the distant lands and sometimes returned to their homelands later; in any case, they kept in touch. How much this all proved a stimulus to the imagination or an encouragement of hidden talents can only be surmised. The wide horizons invoked by the *Thousand and One Nights* are suggestive. We can touch on a few types of activity where the lively distant contacts seem to have been relevant.

With the centuries, new inventions and new discoveries made throughout the hemisphere changed not only the level of artistic or military technique, but the popular life of the towns and even of the countryside. Perhaps especially in the Middle Periods, a number of these combined to alter the tone of life. We cannot yet trace the history of cookery, but it is clear that condiments of distant provenance gradually became more varied and more popular; and with sugar refining a relatively recent innovation, one can suppose that it was only gradually that the recipes for the various later sweets were popularized; they were not all introduced along with the refining process. Some other forms of popular entertainment, found widely in the hemisphere, were probably also fairly late. Conjuring tricks, sometimes quite spectacular, seem to have been perfected—psychologically and technically—over the ages and probably reached their peak as a market-place art in mid-Islamic times. They were associated especially with India. Taking the place, no doubt, of the ancient Mediterranean mimes, in later times shadow-puppet shows became popular with all classes: shows in which certain stock puppet figures ranted or loved or fought behind a curtain, so that only their silhouettes were seen by the proper public. The art was developed to a certain refinement, and supplemented the story-tellers' narration of pious or heroic tales with visible satires on town or village life, raised from the level of gossip to a certain dignity in abstractness. (In the sixteenth century, new crops introduced from the Americas, notably maize, were to have extensive effects in some Muslim lands.)

Possibly of special import for the growth of a human personality, new sorts of mood-moulding consumables, introduced from many local origins, were increasingly displacing the wine and other alcoholic drinks traditionally used for moulding moods between Nile and Oxus. Again there are no studies to go by, but I can indicate a few highlights. Ḥashîsh (one of the hemp products), a depressant known for a long time, became popular among some urban circles in the Earlier and especially in the Later Middle Period. (Opium and other narcotics were also being introduced and used by the more daring.) In the fifteenth century a new stimulant, coffee, was introduced from the Indian Ocean coasts into the Nile-to-Oxus region generally. In the sixteenth century, tobacco was introduced from the Americas. Betel, widely used among eastern Muslims, did not spread between Nile and Oxus. But even without it, there was sufficient variety in mood drugs available to suit contrasting personal temperaments or social situations.

Wine, which set the mood chiefly by reducing the sense of responsibility, was the most convivial of mood drugs; its use was associated with singing slave-girls, with games of passion such as gambling, and finally, of course, with drunken madness. With time, of course, it undermined the constitution, bringing many princes to an early death; but no number of sad examples prevented indulgence in it. The other mood drugs were also used socially, but with different tendencies. Ḥashîsh took away men's cares by numbing sensibility and eventually substituting a dreamy play of the imagination; it called for no women, and in the immediate situation was less obstreperous and dangerous, but the habit of it led in the long run to debilitation. Coffee and tobacco were milder both in their immediate results and in their long-run degenerative effects; both were more adaptable to peaceable all-male gatherings than wine, bringing a certain mental excitement or relief without loss of responsibility. In some urban circles, at the end of the Later Middle Period, they may have contributed to reducing the tumultuousness of life and increasing its respectability. While the peasantry continued to use their relatively harsh alcoholic beverages made from dates or other plants, the alcoholic drink of the cultivated classes, wine, was undeniably reduced in use, and with it the once-famed vineyards of the east Mediterranean tended to disappear.

Could it be that the pettiness and bourgeois respectability of such things as the shadow plays and coffee houses were appropriate to a broadly contracting economy in which potential leaders might become merely marginal instead of dynamic, and proper society turned in upon itself?[6] Perhaps, at any rate, the diversity of culinary, entertainment, and mood-moulding resources, as well as ethnic variety and a certain transiency of population, may have enhanced the satisfactions of household and neighbourhood life at the expense of grand civic displays, whether royal or religious or popular.

The 'ulamâ' received the newer mood drugs with distrust; they inclined to assimilate them to alcohol and ban them all. All of them could be seen as at best frivolous luxuries, and (more seriously) as interfering with the sober, responsible mood that a moralistic faith required. Eventually the 'ulamâ' came to terms with coffee and tobacco. The narcotics, on the other hand, were not to be tolerated. Some Ṣûfîs, on the contrary, welcomed these new physical props to the imagination. It is said to have been a Ṣûfî ṭarîqah of the Yemen that discovered the delights of coffee (brewed very strong) and popularized it elsewhere.

The religious development of Islam itself must have been modified at least in matters of proportion and balance by the spread of Islam beyond the old Irano-Semitic territory. Ṣûfism, being called on in the newly opened lands to form a bridge between local customs and international Islam, may well have been further confirmed in its course of popular externalization and in blessing local practices with Islamic credentials. It varied according to region: carrying the whole of Islam in the Malaysian archipelago, or attenuated into limited and perhaps hereditary functions in the western Sûdânic lands; and assimilating elements from the older confessional traditions in the more ancient citied areas. Then, from whatever region they came, Ṣûfî darvîshes were constantly circulating abroad; and new branches of ṭarîqahs were regularly founded to represent new syntheses that emerged.

But whatever the Ṣûfî role, the defence of Shar'î norms was stimulated by a steady struggle with local customs, especially as those customs deviated from Irano-Semitic custom long since accommodated. Conscientious Muslims were readily reminded how much the integrity of the Ummah community depended on the Shar'î law alone. The form of Shar'î régime that became general was naturally the Jamâ'î-Sunnî rather than the Shî'î. The expansion

[6] One may compare the suggestion by Carleton Coon in his *Caravan: The Story of the Middle East* (New York, 1951), as part of his concluding chapter, 'A Lesson in Austerity', that many rules and customs in the Islamicate Arid Zone helped to level rich and poor so as to minimize discontent and conserve resources in an increasingly impoverished environment.

of Islamdom had been well launched under the auspices of the Sunnî synthesis of the Earlier Middle Period (well tempered with 'Alid loyalism), and ween Shî'ism subsequently revived in the older areas, its chiliastic concern with established Muslim institutions was of little relevance to relatively isolated communities struggling for dominance in the Southern Seas or even around the central Eurasian steppe. Hence Sunnism became dominant in Islamdom at large by weight of numbers; and even when Shî'ism later came to power in much of the core of the lands of old Islam, it retained something of a sense of minoritarian status; for at least educated Muslims could not but be conscious of its minority position in the Ummah at large. (Perhaps the situation made for a certain gap between the high-cultural life at the centre and the culture of the outlying regions.)

Finally, along with Shar'ism, doubtless Muslim communalism was reinforced: that great temptation of the prophetic monotheisms, to set loyalty to the community of revelation ahead of all other moral demands, even of recognizing moral values maintained by infidels. For communal strength was a first requirement where the community was an embattled minority on the rise. Communal and Shar'î sentiment readily became the prime channels for expressing a social conscience.

The Muslim pre-eminence and the Occidental Renaissance

The Muslims, by 1500, when they cooperated (as they often did) could control the political fates of most of the more centrally placed regions of the hemisphere and many of the more outlying regions; in the sixteenth century, on the whole, the Muslim expansion continued and, though in some places Muslim dominance was being shaken Islamdom continued to form the most potent social bloc in the world. By their own acts, Muslims had placed themselves in a situation in which the story of Islamdom henceforth can, even less than before, be clearly separated out from the story of the world at large.

This rise of Muslim pre-eminence had coincided first with the tremendous thrust of Chinese culture and economic development in the time of the Sung dynasty, whereby the Chinese raised themselves in almost all respects to a much higher level of social complexity and power than the Muslims; then at the end of the Later Middle Period it coincided with an equally remarkable cultural thrust in the Occident, the Renaissance, which likewise pushed the Occidentals, in some respects at least, to higher cultural levels than the Muslims. Muslim Oikoumenic leadership held despite these cultural flowerings; even largely in disregard of them. This raises a problem.

The Muslims had been moved in secondary ways to admire and even emulate the Chinese; most of Islamdom was scarcely moved at all by the Occidental Renaissance, which yet was closer home historically and even geographically for most Muslims. The Renaissance was partly inspired from ultimately Muslim sources and, in any case, built in its more imaginative side on that same Greek heritage that still played so large a role in Islamicate culture. Moreover, Modern Westerners are inclined to see in the Renaissance, and especially in the voyages of discovery during that period, the beginning of the Modern Western world domination. They see it as developing further the sort of social strength that had already resulted in Occidental preponderance in Mediterranean trade, a preponderance based on the locally increased economic weight of northwestern Europe and with it of the northwest Mediterranean ports, but which they see as the first steps toward Modern world power. They suggest that the Muslims were proving unpardonably obtuse in their neglect of the Renaissance achievements and imply that some radical cultural defect must have been at work among the Muslims to cause them to ignore them. The actual degree of continuing Muslim pre-eminence in the hemisphere at large—and even in the Mediterranean itself—then becomes a paradox. We must briefly consider the historical nature of the Renaissance from the viewpoint of that world history in the context of which its relevance to Muslims of the time must be assessed.

The Occidental Renaissance was one of the great florescences of world history and indeed carries a special interest in that it formed the immediate background out of which grew the Modern technicalistic transformations, which we shall have to discuss from a world-historical viewpoint subsequently. But in itself the Renaissance did not exceed, in its creativity or in its basic institutional novelty, a number of other great florescences that had occurred in the Agrarian Age of Oikoumenic history; in particular it was no more remarkable than the flowering of Sung China or even than the startling cultural renovations and initiatives of the High Caliphal Period in Islamdom. Only slightly did the excitement of Renaissance times, even in the north, still reside in their contrast to the earlier regional backwardness as an Oikoumenic frontier area; such backwardness had been largely overcome already in the High Middle Ages. Yet it is hard for us to evaluate the Renaissance period without some overtones of such an essentially parochial contrast: we compare it not to contemporary Oikoumenic levels of civilization but to the earlier Occidental level. But what is decisive just here is not so much its positive achievement—either its advance over the Occidental past or even its brilliance among its contemporaries—but the more tenuous and negative but crucial point that the Renaissance, as such, did not escape the range of the basic historical presuppositions of agrarianate-level society.

Something world-historically significant for the long run was indeed happening in the later post-Axial centuries, of which the Renaissance was an expression. It was after the steady expansion and interregional interaction in the Afro-Eurasian Oikoumene had carried very far and the accumulated inventions and products had travelled widely, that one finds for the first time, in relatively northerly lands, notably in northwestern Europe and in northern China, a more prominent role for industrial investment as compared with mercantile investment. Possibly, once a high level of industrial investment became determinative of the nature of urban life anywhere, the relative strength of a society geared more to mercantile than to industrial investment was implicitly threatened. Doubtless we may already trace the increasing prominence of the Occident and of China in their neighbours' affairs—notably in the Mediterranean and in the Far Southeast—partly to the increasing prominence of industrial investment within those two societies. In both the Mediterranean and the Far Southeast, Islamicate influence was being limited by its two rivals, if in different ways. But no large-scale consequences ensued from any concentration of industrial power, Chinese or Occidental, till much later.

That is, the later fifteenth and the early sixteenth centuries in the Occident did not mark a change in the basic social structure in which agrarian production and distribution remained the backbone of the economy of the region as a whole, while the cities were islands of privilege depending on the surplus from the land. Nor did the industrial and commercial life of the cities escape from the consequences of this fact: indeed, the industrial development of Renaissance Europe went much less far than had that of Sung China. It was only at the end of the sixteenth century that appeared, in northwestern Europe, that crucial trait which was to liberate the economy from an agrarian dependence: the self-perpetuating social accumulation of investment capital at a much more rapid rate than the increase in agricultural productivity, and on a sustained basis—and on a scale such that it could have more than merely local effects such as had occurred here and there before.

Accordingly, the political structures feasible remained within the range which agrarianate-level society had long offered everywhere: the territorial state might be more monarchic and bureaucratic or more oligarchic, controlled by a more or less militarized body of landholders, while only favourably situated cities (or occasional isolated peasant bodies) could assert a republican (but normally oligarchic) autonomy or even, for a time, govern areas of dependent territory. Fundamentally, military methods and methods of craft production and even intellectual methods, whatever advances occurred, remained on a level that would be directly intelligible in its social presuppositions to any other society on the agrarianate level. To speak a bit more abstractly, the pace of historical change remained within the same order of speed: in any agrarianate-level cultural florescence, there was a relative encouragement of freedom for innovation within the context of a predominating continuity from generation to generation; it may seem as if all cultural elements were rethought anew, but this was done within very serious limits. In the Renaissance, as the men of the Renaissance themselves realized, there was not nearly so great a change as had already occurred in all parts of the Oikoumene in the florescences of the Axial Age; no serious break was made in the pattern of post-Axial agrarianate-level culture.

At least a bit later in the first part of the sixteenth century—as the

Occident was moving toward the actual technicalistic transformations of Modernity—some notable scientific developments took place. Vesalius and Copernicus were moving medicine and astronomy substantially beyond what the Latins had inherited from Greek and Arabic. But in such figures, the advance was as yet no greater in degree than what the Muslims had achieved in their own greatest period of florescence; and the scientific work was still done on the same sort of human bases as among the classical Greeks and the Muslims. As we have noted, the scientifically most valid part of Copernicus' work had been anticipated two centuries before in Azerbaijan. The mood of the time—even in the midst of a great cultural florescence—remained hostile to the specialized and collaborative labours that marked the later Western technical transformations; for instance, solutions to difficult algebraic equations were still deliberately kept secret as private treasures.

There was no decisive break even on a level crucial for world history, that of contacts among societies. Though a new trade route was found around Africa—as earlier, new passages had been opened up across the Sahara, or north of the central Eurasian steppe—and though new areas on the margin of citied society were opened up (as also had been happening steadily already, if at less distance than across the Atlantic), yet most of the older trade routes retained their importance at least through the greater part of the sixteenth century. For on the level of contacts among societies, no marked contrasts developed between one society and another. The social power that could be worked up in an Islamicate society was as great as in an Occidental society; as the Ottoman empire showed, in carrying its conquests into the Occident itself. Some Occidental societies showed special vigour, but not enough to shift permanently the overall balance of power.

Thus the most important of the technological changes of the time, which was transforming the historical situation throughout Islamdom at the start of the sixteenth century (as we shall see shortly), that is the development of a dominant military role for gunpowder weapons, proceeded at practically the same pace in Islamdom and in the Occident. It may be (we cannot tell; the documentation for the Occident is as yet much fuller than for elsewhere and suggests a slight margin of priority, but on the basis largely of the uncertain evidence of silence) that the Occident, in its florescence, was a specially important centre of gunpowder innovations. But it is clear that these innovations were going on at roughly the same pace, and at least sometimes, we know, independently, throughout most of Islamdom; it was the internal developments in Islamdom that forced the changes there which gunpowder weapons produced.

Finally, as we shall see shortly, the most important Occidental intervention in Islamdom in the time of the Renaissance was the Portuguese invasion of the Indian Ocean. The coming of the Portuguese at the start of the sixteenth century was a major commercial and political blow to the Muslim dominance in the Southern Seas, but the Portuguese were able to hold only certain crucial ports; in many ports and in some of the hinterland, the Muslims continued to be the most powerful single element wherever a non-Islamicate culture had not been sufficiently deeply entrenched. Chinese merchants and Japanese adventurers were, in places, almost as important as the Portuguese as rivals to the Muslims. In the latter part of the sixteenth century, the Muslims were able to contain the Portuguese threat. The Muslims seem to have matched the technological advantages which the Portuguese had developed in a different clime and under Renaissance stimulation; and since the Portuguese advantages were largely tactical, they proved transitory. The Portuguese superiority was even more transient than that of the Arabs in the seventh century. Only with the coming of a later wave of Europeans, this time from northwestern Europe (especially the Dutch) in the seventeenth century, did the Muslim commercial control of the Southern Seas definitely cease. Even then, of course, not only a considerable short-range Muslim commerce but a general Islamicate colouring remained, to a greater or lesser degree, almost everywhere.

Despite the increasing importance of Occidental control of Mediterranean trade, then, and even European oceanic ventures, the west European Renaissance with what accompanied it, did not in itself seriously threaten the long-term chances for a Muslim Oikoumenic hegemony. If its advances did not prove readily accessible to the neighbouring Muslims, this was partly because the main centres of Islamicate culture, which were still the core areas between Nile and Oxus, were relatively distant from the Occidental centres. But it was more because of the same principle which, for instance, prevented the Occidentals, somewhat earlier when they were translating from the Arabic, from translating the most recent works of importance, which had not yet gained the respect due to age; and prevented them from entering into most phases of Islamicate culture at all. In Agrarian times, the development within the several civilizational traditions proceeded on the basis chiefly of its own internal dialogue, and took cognizance of alien dialogues only at a leisurely pace which could allow several centuries for catching up. Even in the sixteenth century, this time-pace was still sufficient. Islamdom had as yet no need to attend to most west European advances in order to retain its advantaged position in the world at large.

A Selective Bibliography for Further Reading

NOTE: General works are listed in the bibliography of volume 1.

On the state formations of the Middle Periods:

Angel Gonzalez-Palencia, *Historia de la España musulmana,* 4th ed. (Editorial Labor, Barcelona, 1945). A concise account for the period of the eleventh and later centuries.

Ch.-André Julien, *Histoire de l'Afrique du Nord,* Vol. II, 2nd ed. (Payot, Paris, 1964). Among the best one-volume summaries.

Georges Marçais, *La Berbérie musulmane et l'orient au moyen âge* (Montaigne, Paris, 1946), up to the decline of the Muwaḥḥid state.

Henri Terrasse, *Histoire du Maroc des origines à l'établissement du protectorat français,* 2 vols. (Éditions Atlantides, Casablanca, 1949–50); translated into English by Hilary Tee (Éditions Atlantides, Casablanca, 1952). Especially for the period since the Muwaḥḥids.

Gaston Wiet, *L'Egypte arabe de la conquête arabe à la conquête ottomane,* 642–1517; Vol. IV of *Histoire de la nation égyptienne,* ed. Gabriel Hanotaux (Pion, Paris, 1937) is to be preferred to

Stanley Lane-Poole, *A History of Egypt in the Middle Ages* (600–1500) (Methuen, London, 1901), which is readable.

Steven Runciman, *A History of the Crusades,* 3 vols. (Cambridge University Press, 1951–54). Readable and brings out the Byzantine viewpoint.

Kenneth M. Setton, *A History of the Crusades,* 5 vols. of which 2 are so far published (University of Pennsylvania Press, 1955–). A definitive collection of monographs. Includes important treatments of the Islamic states involved.

Claude Cahen, *La Syrie du nord à l'époque des croisades et la principauté franque d'Antioche* (P. Geuthner, Paris, 1940). Intensive and illuminating study.

Claude Cahen, *Pre-Ottoman Turkey; a general survey . . . c.* 1071–1330, translated by J. Jones-Williams (Sidgwick and Jackson, London, 1968). A masterful study considering the present state of our knowledge. Two older studies remain useful, however:

Mehmed F. Köprülü, *Les Origines de l'empire ottoman* (Boccard, Paris, 1935), and

Paul Wittek, *The Rise of the Ottoman Empire* (Royal Asiatic Society, London, 1938).

The Cambridge History of Iran, Vol. V: 'The Saljuq and Mongol Periods', ed. by J. A. Boyle (Cambridge University Press, 1968). Excellent on the subjects it covers. A few studies emphasizing certain developments may usefully be read in addition:

Muhammad Habib, *Sultan Mahmud of Ghaznin* [1st ed. 1924], 2nd ed. (Cosmopolitan Publishers, Aligarh, 1951). Old but still useful appreciation of the conqueror, with an attempt to set his actions in the context of Islamdom in the period. Should only be read in conjunction with

Clifford E. Bosworth, *The Ghaznavids: Their Empire in Afghanistan and Eastern Iran* 994–1040 (Edinburgh University Press, 1963). A careful study of administration and society.

Marshall G. S. Hodgson, *The Order of Assassins: The Struggle of the Early Nizârî Ismâ'îlîs against the Islamic World* (Mouton, The Hague, 1955). Story of the Ismâ'ili state and religion, suggesting some of the Islamic attitudes important at the time.

Vasilii V. Barthold has done a number of studies of Central Eurasia, which have been translated from Russian into a number of European languages, and collectively form the foundation for subsequent studies of the area. See especially *Turkestan down to the Mongol Invasion* [1900], 2nd ed. translated by the author (E. J. W. Gibb Memorial, London, 1928, repr. 1958); *Zwölf Vorlesungen über die Geschichte der Türken Mittelasiens* [1926], translated by M. Donskis as *Histoire des Turcs d'Asie Centrale* (Adrien-Maisonneuve, Paris, 1945); and his studies collected as *Four Studies on the History of Central Asia*, 3 vols. (E. J. Brill, Leiden, 1956–62).

Niẓâm al-Mulk, *Siyâsat-Nâmah*, translated by Hubert Darke as *The Book of Government or Rules for Kings* (Routledge and Kegan Paul, London, 1960). The celebrated Seljûq vizier's advice to his sovereign.

Abul Barkat M. Habibullah, *Foundation of Muslim Rule in India* (Muhammad Ashraf, Lahore, 1945). A study of the political development and administrative patterns of the Delhi Sultanate in the thirteenth century.

Ishwari Prasad, *History of Medieval India from 647* AD *to the Mughal Conquest* (Indian Press, Allahabad, 1925). Chiefly a political history, useful where other works are not available.

Khaliq A. Nizami, *Some Aspects of Religion and Politics in India during the Thirteenth Century* (Muslim University, Aligarh, 1961). A recent example of studies on the period.

Ziyâ al-Dîn Baranî, *Fatâwa-e jahândarî*, translated and studied by Mohammed Habib and Afsar Umar Salim Khan as *The Political Theory of the Delhi Sultanate* (Kitab Mahal, Allahabad, 19—). A fourteenth century CE political treatise which may be compared to Niẓâm al-Mulk's (see above).

On ṭarîqah Ṣûfism:

Octave Depont and Xavier Coppolani, *Les confréries religieuses musulmanes* (Jourdan, Algiers, 1897). A massive study of the orders of the Maghrib, with a far wider bearing.

John K. Birge, *The Bektashi Order of Dervishes* (Hartford Seminary Press, 1937). On a popular Turkish order, sufficiently well done to be illuminating about all popular life.

John P. Brown, *The Dervishes; or Oriental Spiritualism* [1868] (Oxford University Press, 1927). Uncritical but full on Turkey.

John A. Subhan, *Sufism, Its Saints and Shrines* [1938], revised ed. (Lucknow Publishing House, Lucknow, 1960). Uncritical but full on India.

Jalâl-al-dîn Rûmî, *The Mathnawî of Jalâlu'ddîn Rûmî*, translated and ed. by R. A. Nicholson, 8 vols. (Gibb Memorial Series, London, 1925–40), a sound but not very readable translation of the most monumental Ṣûfî popular work.

On classical Persian literature:

Edward G. Browne, *A Literary History of Persia*, 4 vols. [1902–24] (Cambridge University Press, 1964 repr.). A magnificent pioneering survey by a sensitive reader of Persian, concentrating on the literature of Iran itself; contains many useful notes on the history of the period.

Muhammad 'Abdal-Ghani, *A History of Persian Language and Literature at the Moghul Court*, 3 vols. (The Indian Press, Allahabad, 1929–30). Supplements Browne on India.

Arthur J. Arberry, *Classical Persian Literature* (George Allen and Unwin, London, 1958). Provides brief descriptions and samplings in translation, supplementing Browne on some authors.

Alessandro Bausani and Antonio Pagliaro, *Storia della Letteratura Persiana* (Nuova Accademia Editrice, Milan, 1960). An up-to-date, authoritative, and sensitive survey by genre.

Hellmut Ritter, *Das Meer der Seele; Mensch, Welt, und Gott in den Geschichten des Farîduddîn 'Aṭṭâr* (E. J. Brill, Leiden, 1955). Rich analysis of attitudes to life and love expressed in 'Aṭṭâr's Ṣûfî work and in others; full quotations and thick index.

Firdawsî, *Shâh-Nâmah*, translated by Arthur G. Warner and Edmond Warner, 8 vols. (Kegan Paul, London, 1908–23). A Victorian rendering of the great epic, but fairly complete.

On social and economic life in later centuries:

Solomon D. Goitein, *A Mediterranean Society: the Jewish Communities of the Arab World . . .*, Vol. I 'Economic Foundations' (University of California

Press, 1967). A study based on the Cairo Geniza documents, the wider implications of which must be carefully assessed.

Ira Lapidus, *Muslim Cities in the Later Middle Ages* (Harvard University Press, 1967). A study of the relations of the Mamlûk ruling group to townspeople, principally in Syria.

Roger LeTourneau, *Les Villes musulmanes de l'Afrique du Nord* (Maison des livres, Algiers, 1957). A suggestive survey based in part on observations of recent periods.

George F. Hourani, *Arab Seafaring in the Indian Ocean* (Princeton University Press, 1951). A sketch on long-distance trade.

Ann K. S. Lambton, *Landlord and Peasant in Persia* (Oxford University Press, 1953). A massive, masterly, though not always lucid study of agrarian conditions from the beginning of Islamic times.

ibn-Khaldûn, *The Muqaddimah,* translated by Franz Rosenthal, 3 vols. (Pantheon, New York, 1958). The selections on crafts, etc., provide a comprehensive survey of institutions, especially in the Maghrib.

ibn-Baṭṭûṭah, *Riḥlah,* translated by Hamilton A. R. Gibb as *The Travels of Ibn Battuta,* 2 vols. so far (Cambridge University Press, 1956–). A lively narrative by the celebrated fourteenth century traveller; the work contains important remarks on the social conditions of the period.

Carleton S. Coon, *Caravan: The Story of the Middle East* [1951], 2nd ed. (Henry Holt, New York, 1958). A popular study by a physical anthropologist of the pre-Modern life patterns of 'the arid zone'; its descriptive portions are most usable.

Edward W. Lane, *Manners and Customs of the Modern Egyptians* [1836], revised ed. 1860 (reprinted Everyman's Library). Magnificent description of Egyptian life before the impact of Modernity had yet much changed it.

On the visual arts in Islamdom:

Katharina Otto-Dorn, *Die Kunst des Islam* (Holle Verlag, Baden-Baden, 1964). A usable introduction.

Ernst J. Grube, *The World of Islam* (McGraw-Hill, New York, 1966). A brief survey in English with good colour plates.

Derek Hill and Oleg Grabar, *Islamic Architecture and Its Decoration* [1964] 2nd ed. (Faber and Faber, London, 1967). Good survey of Seljûq and later developments.

Arthur U. Pope, *A Survey of Persian Art,* 6 vols. (Oxford University Press, 1938–39). A massive compendium.

K. A. C. Creswell, *A Short Account of Early Muslim Architecture* (Penguin Books, 1958). A brief study of the first centuries by a master of meticulous description of monuments, whose many works are all important for the specialist.

Ernst Kühnel, *Miniaturmalerei im Islamischen Orient* (Bruno Cassirer, Berlin, 1923). A well illustrated study of 'Irâqî, Iranian and Indo-Muslim painting.

The studies of Ivan Stchoukine are solid and important though not always imaginative; they cover Indo-Muslim and Iranian miniatures up through early Ṣafavî times, distinguishing the several schools.

Important are the works of Richard Ettinghausen and Oleg Grabar, many of which are journal articles, traceable in the *Index Islamicus*.

On Muslims in Africa and Southeast Asia in the pre-Modern periods:

E. W. Bovill, *The Golden Trade of the Moors* (Oxford University Press, 1958). An improvement over the same author's earlier version, *Caravans of the Old Sahara*, presenting fascinatingly the story of the Islamic Niger and Chad Sudan and its relation to the Maghrib; somewhat lacking in scholarly detail.

J. Spencer Trimingham, *Islam in Ethiopia* (Oxford University Press, 1952), on the whole 'horn' of East Africa, and *A History of Islam in West Africa* (Oxford University Press, 1962). Two studies in a series of very thorough inquiries, with considerable historical background as well as social analysis.

Alphonse Gouilly, *L'Islam dans l'Afrique occidentale française* (Larose, Paris, 1952). Comprehensively detailed yet readable on the form Islam has taken and the effects it has had in the western Sudan.

Jacob C. van Leur, *Indonesian Trade and Society* (van Hoeve, The Hague, 1955). Collected studies by an iconoclastic young scholar, not always reliable in his generalizations, but the starting point for further studies. One may compare Marie A. P. Meilink-Roelofsz, *Asian Trade and European Influence in the Indonesian Archipelago between 1500 and about 1630* (Nijhoff, The Hague, 1962). Less perceptive than van Leur.

Bernard H. M. Vlekke, *Nusantara; A History of Indonesia* [1943], 2nd ed. (Van Hoeve, The Hague, 1960). An ordinary narrative, chiefly useful on the periods since the Portuguese.

Christiaan Snouck-Hurgronje, *The Achehnese* [1893–94], translated by A. W. S. O'Sullivan, 2 vols. (E. J. Brill, Leiden, 1906).

Glossary of Selected Terms and Names

Listings in the Glossary are technical terms frequently appearing in the text. Definitions and explanations given in the text of other terms, including geographical designations, may be located by consulting the Index.

akhî: a young man, member of a community of young men found in Anatolia in the fourteenth century who held to the ideals of *futuwwah* (q.v.); they were generally of the urban artisan classes.

'Alid: a descendant of 'Alî, cousin and son-in-law of the Prophet; the Shî'îs believed certain 'Alids should be *imâms* (q.v.). 'Alî's first wife was Fâṭimah, the Prophet's daughter, 'Alî's descendants by her (the only descendants of the Prophet) are in particular called Fâṭimids. Descendants of her son Ḥasan are often called *sharîf*s: those of her son Ḥusayn are often called *sayyid*s.

'âlim (pl. *'ulamâ'*): a learnèd man, in particular one learnèd in the Islamic legal and religious studies.

Allâh: an Arabic (both Muslim and Christian) name for the One God.

amîr (also *emir*): a general or other military commander; after classical 'Abbâsî times, many independent rulers held this title; sometimes assigned to members of the ruler's family. *Amîr al-mu'minîn*, commander of the faithful, was the proper title of the caliph; *amîr al-umarâ'* meant supreme commander, generalissimo: used especially of the military ruler in the decline of the High Caliphate.

'ârif: one who knows, a 'gnostic', used by Ṣûfîs (q.v.) to designate themselves, contrasting their mystical knowledge (*ma'rifah*) to that of the *'âlim*'s *'ilm* (qq.v.).

'asabiyyah: as used by Ibn-Khaldûn, the spirit of tribal solidarity that enables a relatively small number of hardened pastoralists to conquer a larger number of city dwellers who have grown effete.

'askerî: in the Ottoman empire a member of the military ruling class, including wives and children of that class.

atabeg (also *lâlâ*): a Turkish title applied to guardians of minor rulers, especially young sons sent out as governors; some of them founded independent dynasties with this title.

awliyâ': see *walî*.

awqâf: see *waqf*.

a'yân (sing. *'ayn*): notable persons; in the Middle and Late Periods, town notables with prestige and influence; in the later Ottoman times, holders of a recognized political power.

baqâ': remaining with the world, survival; for Ṣûfîs (q.v.) the complement of *fanâ'* (q.v.), each term referring to an individual's state of consciousness as he proceeds along the Ṣûfî pathway.

bâṭin: the inner, hidden, or esoteric meaning of a text; hence Bâṭinîs, Bâṭiniyyah, the groups associated with such ideas. Most of these groups were Shî'îs, particularly Ismâ'îlîs.

dâ'î: a propagandist, especially for Shî'î movements; a high Ismâ'îlî official in religion.

Dâr al-Islâm: lands under Muslim rule; later, any lands in which Muslim institutions are maintained, whether or not under Muslim rule. It is converse of *Dâr al-Ḥarb* the 'land of war'.

dervish: *see* Ṣûfî.

dhikr (also *ẕikr*): Ṣûfî (q.v.) practices designed to foster the remembering of God; usually phrases to repeat, often more elaborate devotional services.

dhimmî (also *ẕimmî*): a 'protected subject', follower of a religion tolerated by Islam, within Muslim ruled territory. The protection is called *dhimmah.*

dihqân: one of the old Iranian landed gentry in High Caliphal times.

dîwân (also *dîvân*): a public financial register; or a government bureau, or council; or its chief officer; also the collected works of a poet.

emir: see *amîr*.

fakir: *see* Ṣûfî.

Falsafah: philosophy, including natural and moral science, as expounded, on the basis of the Greek tradition, in the Islamicate society.

fanâ': among Ṣûfîs (q.v.), the passing away of personal consciousness.

faqîh: see *fiqh*.

faqîr: *see* Ṣûfî.

fidâ'î: one who devotes his life to a cause; particularly those Nizârî Ismâ'îlîs who took the risk of assassinating the sect's enemies.

fiqh: jurisprudence; the discipline of elucidating the *Sharî'ah* (q.v.); also the resultant body of rules. A *faqîh* (pl. *fuqahâ'*) is an exponent of *fiqh*.

futuwwah: as developed over the centuries, a corporate-type group of young men of the urban classes that after the twelfth century held to certain ideals and actions, having formal ceremonies of initiation, rituals, sworn support to a leader, etc.

ghâzî: a warrior for the faith carrying out *jihâd* (q.v.); sometimes applied to organized bands of frontier raiders.

ḥabûs: see *waqf*.

ḥadîth (also *ḥadîs*; pl. *aḥâdîth*): a report of saying or action of the Prophet, or such reports collectively. Sometimes this is translated 'tradition', as having been transmitted from reporter to reporter; it has nothing to do with traditions in the ordinary sense of anonymously inherited group lore.

ḥajj: the annual pilgrimage to Mecca in the month of Dhû-l-Ḥijjah, the last month of the Muslim calendar; required of every Muslim once in his life if possible.

Ḥanafî: referring to the Sunnî legal *madhhab* (q.v.) ascribed to Abû-Ḥanîfah (699–767 CE).

Ḥanbalî: referring to the Sunnî legal *madhhab* (q.v.) ascribed to Aḥmad ibn-Ḥanbal (780–855 CE).

harem: Turkish name (from Arabic *ḥaram*; also *ḥarîm*) for the portion of a house which the male guest cannot enter; extended to the women who live there; called *zanânah* in India; equal to Italian term *seraglio*.

ijâzah: a certificate of permission to teach a given book, as thoroughly understanding it; given in principle, by the author of it or by one who has himself received the *ijâzah*.

ijtihâd: individual inquiry to establish the ruling of the *Sharî'ah* (q.v.) upon a given point, by a *mujtahid*, a person qualified for the inquiry. The Jamâ'î-Sunnîs long considered *ijtihâd* permissible only on points not already decided by recognized authorities; on points already so decided they required *taqlîd*, adherence to the usual view of one's *madhhab* (q.v.). The Shî'îs have mostly permitted full *ijtihâd* to their great scholars.

'ilm: learnèd lore; particularly, religious knowledge, of *ḥadîth* (q.v.) reports, of *fiqh* (q.v.), etc. In modern Arabic the word is used to render 'science'. Among many Shî'îs it was supposed the *imâm* (q.v.) had a special secret knowledge, *'ilm*.

imâm: leader of the *ṣalât* worship; or leader of the Muslim community. Among Shî'îs 'Alî and his descendants as proper leaders of the Islamic community, even when rejected by it, are held to have a spiritual function as successors to Muḥammad. Among Jamâ'î-Sunnîs, any great *'âlim* (q.v.), especially the founder of a legal *madhhab* (q.v.), was called an *imâm*.

iqṭâ': an assignment or grant of land or of its revenues by a government to an individual; sometimes granted as payment for military service. Sometimes misleadingly translated 'fief'.

Jamâ'î-Sunnîs: *see* Sunnîs.

jâmi': *see* mosque.

Janissary (*yeñi-cheri*): member of an Ottoman infantry corps formed at one time from captured or conscripted young Christians converted to Islam.

jihâd: war in accordance with the *Sharî'ah* (q.v.) against unbelievers; there are different opinions as to the circumstances under which such war becomes necessary. Also applied to a person's own struggle against his baser impulses.

kalâm: discussion, on the basis of Muslim assumptions, of questions of theology and cosmology; sometimes called 'scholastic theology'.

kazi: see *qâḍî*.

khân: a Turkish title, originally the ruler of a state; also, a hostel for travelling merchants (caravansary).

khâniqâh (also *khângâh*): a building for Ṣûfî (q.v.) activities, where *dhikr* (q.v.) was observed and where one or more *shaykhs* (q.v.) lived, entertained travelling Ṣûfîs, and taught their disciples. This form is originally Persian; synonyms are *tekke* (from *takyah*), largely Turkish in use; *zâwiyah* (Arabic); and *ribâṭ* (Arabic), also used for a frontier fortress.

kuttâb (or *maktab*): an elementary school for learning, recitation of the Qur'ân, and sometimes also reading and writing.

lâlâ: see *atabeg*.

madhhab (pl. *madhâhib*): a system of *fiqh* (q.v.), or generally the system followed by any given religious group; particularly, four *madhâhib* were ultimately accepted as legitimate by the Jamâ'î-Sunnîs while Shî'îs and Khârijîs had other *madhâhib*. Sometimes rendered 'sect', 'school', or 'rite'.

madrasah: a school for *'ulamâ'*, especially for *fiqh* (q.v.), generally built in the form of a specially endowed mosque, often with dormitories.

maktab: see *kuttâb*.

Mâlikî: referring to the Sunnî legal *madhhab* (q.v.) ascribed to Mâlik b. Anas (715–95 CE).

masjid: *see* mosque.

mas̄navî (Arabic, *mathnawî*): a long poem in Persian and related literatures, on almost any subject, with rhyme *aa bb cc dd ee*, etc.; sometimes called 'epic'.

mosque (Arabic, *masjid*): any place of worship for the Muslims where the *ṣalât* worship is performed in a group; a major one, where official Friday services are held, is called *jâmi'*.

mujtahid: see *ijtihâd*.

murîd: disciple of a Ṣûfî *pîr* (qq.v.).

naṣṣ: explicit designation (of a successor by his predecessor), particularly relating to the Shî'î view of succession to the imâmate; it thus comes to confer upon the successor a power of knowledge and understanding that no one else has.

pîr: a Ṣûfî (q.v.) master, able to lead disciples on the mystical way.

qâḍî (also *kazi*): a judge administering *Sharî'ah* (q.v.) law.

qânûn: laws apart from the *Sharî'ah* (q.v.), sometimes as promulgated by the government.

sayyid: *see* ‘Alid.

sepoy: see *sipâhî.*

Shâfi‘î: referring to the Sunnî legal *madhhab* (q.v.) ascribed to al-Shâfi‘î (767–820 CE).

shaikh: see *shaykh.*

Sharî‘ah (or *Shar‘*): the whole body of rules guiding the life of a Muslim, in law, ethics, and etiquette; sometimes called *Sacred Law* (or *Canon Law*). The provisions of the *Sharî‘ah* are worked out through the discipline of *fiqh* (q.v.) on the basis of the *uṣûl al-fiqh* (basic sources of legal authority), which Sunnîs commonly list as Qur’ân, *ḥadith* (q.v.), *ijmâ‘* (consensus of the community), and *qiyâs* (legal analogical reasoning). Shî‘îs commonly substitute *‘aql* (reasoning) for *qiyâs* and interpret *ijmâ‘* as consensus of the *imâms* (q.v.).

sharîf: *see* ‘Alid.

shaykh: literally ‘old man’; the chief of a tribe (and, by extension, head of certain petty states); any religious leader; in particular, an independent Ṣûfî (q.v.), in a position to lead aspirants on the Ṣûfî way; in this sense called in Persian, *pîr* (q.v.); his disciple is a *murîd* (q.v.).

Shî‘ah (‘party [of ‘Alî]’): general name for that part of the Muslims that held to the rights of ‘Alî and his descendants to leadership in the community whether recognized by the majority or not; or any particular sect holding this position. Shî‘î is the adjective, or refers as a noun to an adherent of the Shî‘ah. Shî‘ism (*tashayyu‘*) denotes the attitude or doctrines of the Shî‘ah. The most well known Shî‘î groups are the Zaydîs, the Ismâ‘îlîs or Seveners, and the Twelvers.

silsilah: the sequence of (actual or alleged) Ṣûfî *shaykh*s (qq.v.), reaching back usually to Muḥammad, through whom the teachings of a particular Ṣûfî ‘brotherhood’ have come.

sipâhî: a soldier; used of various troops, especially cavalry in the Ottoman empire; in India often spelled *sepoy.*

Ṣûfî: an exponent of Ṣûfism (*taṣawwuf*), the commonest term for that aspect of Islam which is based on the mystical way. The Arabic *faqîr* (*fakir*) and the Persian *darvîsh* (dervish), both meaning ‘poor’, are applied to Ṣûfîs in reference to their poor or wandering life.

sulṭân: the reigning source of authority; in the Earlier Middle Period, applied to the actual, often military holder of power in contrast to the caliph; later became the normal Muslim term for sovereign.

sunnah: received custom, particularly that associated with Muhammad; it is embodied in *ḥadîth* (q.v.).

Sunnîs: properly *Ahl al-sunnah wa-l-jamâ‘ah* (‘people of the custom and the community’), in this work often Jamâ‘î-Sunnîs: that majority of Muslims which accept the authority of the whole first generation of Muslims and the validity of the historical community, in contrast to the Khârijîs and the Shî'ìs; Sunnî as adjective refers to the doctrinal position, as noun it refers to an adherent of the position. Sunnism is sometimes referred to as 'Orthodoxy'. The term 'Sunnî' is often restricted to particular positions within the Jamâ'ah-î-Sunnî camp; e.g., often it excludes Mu'tazilîs, Karrâmîs, and other groups which did not survive to command recognition. In older Muslim works it sometimes included only the particular faction of the writer.

taqlîd: see *ijtihâd*.

ṭarîqah: the mystical way; specifically, any one of the Ṣûfî (q.v.) 'brotherhoods' or 'orders'; groupings of Ṣûfîs with a common *silsilah* and a common *dhikr* (qq.v.).

tekke: see *khâniqâh*.

'ulamâ': see *'âlim*.

Ummah: any people as followers of a particular prophet, in particular Muslims as forming a community following Muḥammad.

uṣûl al-fiqh: see *Sharî'ah*.

vizier: anglicized form of *wazîr* (q.v.).

walî (pl. *awliyâ'*): a friend of God, a saint, commonly a Ṣûfî (q.v.) or an alleged Ṣûfî, whose tomb is visited for blessing. Also, the legal guardian of a minor, a woman, or of one incapacitated.

waqf (pl. *awqâf*): a pious endowment (or 'foundation') of certain incomes, commonly rents or land revenues, for the upkeep of a mosque, a hospital, etc.; in the Maghrib called *ḥabûs*. Sometimes the main purpose of such an endowment was to provide entailed and unconfiscatable income for one's descendants.

wazîr (Anglicized vizier): an officer to whom a ruler delegated (as 'minister') the administration of his realm; often there were several who divided the job among them.

zanânah: see *harem*.

zâwiyah: see *khâniqâh*.

z̄ikr: see *dhikr*.

z̄immî: see *dhimmî*.

Index

Note: Names and terms beginning with the Arabic definite article (al-) are indexed under the letter following the article.